Th [illegible]

OF

Personal Prayer

THE ONE YEAR®

book of

Personal Prayer

TYNDALE HOUSE PUBLISHERS, INC.
WHEATON, ILLINOIS

Visit Tyndale's exciting Web site at www.tyndale.com

The prayers and quotes in *The One Year Book of Personal Prayer* were collected and edited by Daniel Partner. The idea for this book originated with, and was introduced by, Bruce Barton. Mark R. Norton served as the Tyndale House coordinating and advisory editor. The interior and cover of this book were designed by Andrea Gjeldum.

ISBN 0-8423-7745-X
Printed in China

06 05 04 03
5 4 3 2

Copyright Acknowledgments

One of the prayers of Anselm of Canterbury (Mar. 24) is from *The Prayers and Meditations of St. Anselm,* translated by Sister Benedicta Ward, S L G (Penguin Classics, 1973), copyright © by Benedicta Ward, 1973.

The prayers of George Appleton (Mar. 15, 21) are reprinted from *The Oxford Book of Prayer,* edited by George Appleton (1985), by commission of Oxford University Press on behalf of the author.

The prayers of John Baillie (Jan. 10; Mar. 3; Apr. 30; May 13; June 13; July 15; Aug. 23; Sept. 5; Oct. 18; Nov. 3) are reprinted with permission of Charles Scribner's Sons, an imprint of MacMillan Publishing Company, and Oxford University Press from *A Diary of Private Prayer* by John Baillie. Copyright © 1949 by Charles Scribner's Sons; copyright renewed © 1977 by Ian Fowler Baillie.

The prayers of Dietrich Bonhoeffer (Mar. 26; Apr. 10; Oct. 17) are reprinted with permission of MacMillan Publishing Company and SCM Press, Ltd. from *Letters and Papers from Prison* by Dietrich Bonhoeffer. Copyright © 1953, 1967, 1971 by SCM Press Ltd.

The prayers of Avery Brooke (July 30; Aug. 19; Oct. 14; Nov. 5; Dec. 11) are from *Plain Prayers for a Complicated World,* published by Vineyard Books, Inc., 129 Nearwater Lane, Noroton, CT 06820. Copyright © 1975 by Avery Brooke. Used by permission of Vineyard Books, Inc.

The prayers of Ruth Harms Calkin are from *Lord, You Love to Say Yes* (Feb. 26; Aug. 6), published by Tyndale House Publishers, Inc., copyright © 1988 by Ruth Harms Calkin; *Marriage Is So Much More, Lord* (Mar. 18) published by Tyndale House Publishers, Inc., copyright © 1979 by Ruth Harms Calkin; and *Lord, I Keep Running Back to You* (Apr. 15; May 5; June 19; July 26; Sept. 7) published by Tyndale House Publishers, Inc., copyright © 1979 by Ruth Harms Calkin. Used by permission of Tyndale House Publishers, Inc.

The prayers of John B. Coburn (Sept. 28; Oct. 11; Dec. 12) are from *A Diary of Prayer: Personal and Public* by John B. Coburn. Copyright © 1975 by The Westminster Press. Used by permission of Westminster/John Knox Press.

The prayer of David M. Currie (Feb. 23) is from *Come, Let Us Worship God: A Handbook of Prayer for Leaders of Worship* by David M. Currie. Copyright © 1977 by The Westminster Press. Used by permission of Westminster/John Knox Press.

The prayers of Ralph S. Cushman (Aug. 5; Sept. 4; Oct. 1; Nov. 11) are from *Hilltop Verses and Prayers,* published by Abingdon Press, copyright © 1945 by Ralph S. Cushman. Reprinted by permission of Robert E. Luckman.

The prayers of Dag Hammarskjöld (Feb. 16; Mar. 31) are from *Markings,* by Dag Hammarskjöld, translated by Leif Sjoberg and W. H. Auden. Translation copyright © 1964 by Alfred A. Knopf, Inc. and Faber & Faber Ltd. Reprinted by permission of Alfred A. Knopf, Inc. and Faber & Faber Ltd.

The prayer of Jack W. Hayford (Apr. 28) is from *Prayer Is Invading the Impossible,* copyright © 1977 by Logos International, Plainfield, New Jersey. Reprinted by permission of Logos International.

The prayers of Michael Hollings and Etta Gullick (Aug. 3; Sept. 3; Oct. 2; Nov. 10; Dec. 20) are from *It's Me, O Lord!* copyright © 1973 by Michael Hollings and Etta Gullick. Used by permission of Doubleday, a division of Bantam Doubleday Dell Publishing Group, Inc., and McCrimmon Publishing Co. Ltd., Great Wakening, Essex, England. All rights reserved.

The prayer of Søren Kierkegaard (Mar. 26) is from *The Prayers of Kierkegaard,* edited by Perry F. LeFevre, copyright © 1978 by the University of Chicago Press. Used by permission.

The prayers of Martin Luther (Feb. 28; Apr. 6) are from *Devotions and Prayers of Martin Luther,* translated by Andrew Kosten, copyright © by Baker Book House, 1956. Used by permission of Baker Book House.

The prayer of Paul Simpson McElroy (Feb. 4) is from *Table Graces, Prayers of Thanks,* copyright © 1986 by Peter Pauper Press, White Plains, New York. Used by permission.

The prayer of Catherine Marshall (May 28) is from *Adventures in Prayer* by Catherine Marshall. Copyright © 1975 by Catherine Marshall LeSourd. Published by Chosen Books, Fleming H. Revell Company. Used by permission.

The prayers of Peter Marshall (Jan. 29; Apr. 1; May 9) are from *Mr. Jones, Meet the Master,* edited by Catherine Marshall. Copyright © 1949, 1950 by Fleming H. Revell Company. Renewed © 1976, 1977 by Catherine Marshall LeSourd. Used by permission of Chosen Books, Fleming H. Revell Company.

The prayers of Peter Marshall (Feb. 5; June 18; July 16; Aug. 14; Sept. 20; Dec. 25) are from *The Prayers of Peter Marshall,* compiled and edited by

Table of Contents

Publisher's Note

The One Year Book of Personal Prayer has been prepared to help you in the discipline of daily prayer. It is an ideal starting point for both private and family devotions. The selections for each day include a portion from the Psalms, a selected prayer, and a short inspirational quote emphasizing an important aspect of prayer. Author and Scripture indexes are provided to help you locate and review prayers and quotes that especially speak to you.

The outdated pronouns of some older prayers have been changed from *thee, thou,* and *thy* to the more contemporary *you* and *your,* making the prayers easier for most contemporary readers to read and understand. Plural pronouns in some corporate prayers have been changed to the singular forms, creating a more personal quality. Prayers altered in these ways are identified as having been "adapted" from the original. Some portions of Scripture have been modified just enough to fit the form of a personal prayer and are also shown to be "adapted."

Over the ages, innumerable prayers have been spoken from the lips of humanity to the listening ears of God. The prayers gathered in this book are among the relatively few that have been recorded and passed along to the present day. They are the words of a wide variety of authors. Some are well known, like the apostle Paul and Pat Boone. Others will never be known, like a fallen Confederate soldier and an unknown Chinese woman. Some of the prayers are as ancient as the Old Testament, and others are so new they were written especially for this volume.

It is important to remember that these prayers are not replacements for the expression of your own heart's desire toward God. Rather, they are inspirational guides to lead you into the practice of personal daily prayer. Their words should serve as fuel to fire your own prayers, praises, and thanksgivings. They should cheer you and encourage you to lighten your lives every day by drawing near to God. We pray that your lives will be enriched, this year and every year, by a growing intimacy with God through regular personal prayer.

*J*anuary 1

Blessed is the man who does not walk in the counsel of the wicked or stand in the way of sinners or sit in the seat of mockers. PSALM 1:1

Eternal God, you make all things new, and abide for ever the same: grant me to begin this year in your faith, and to continue it in your favor, that, being guided in all my doings, and guarded all my days, I may spend my life in your service, and finally, by your grace, attain the glory of everlasting life, through Jesus Christ my Lord.

W. E. ORCHARD (adapted)

When you pray, rather let your heart be without words than your words without heart.

JOHN BUNYAN

January 2

Therefore, you kings, be wise; be warned, you rulers of the earth. Serve the LORD with fear and rejoice with trembling.
PSALM 2:10-11

O Lord God, Holy Father, . . . I am no longer my own, but Thine. Put me to what Thou wilt, rank me with whom Thou wilt; put me to doing, put me to suffering; let me be employed for Thee or laid aside for Thee, exalted for Thee or brought low for Thee; let me be full, let me be empty; let me have all things, let me have nothing; I freely and heartily yield all things to Thy pleasure and disposal.

And now, O glorious and blessed God, Father, Son, and Holy Spirit, Thou art mine, and I am Thine. So be it. And the Covenant which I have made on earth, let it be ratified in heaven.

Methodist Shorter Book of Offices

In prayer the lips ne'er act the winning part,
Without the sweet concurrence of the heart.

ROBERT HERRICK

January 3

Many are saying of me, "God will not deliver him." But you are a shield around me, O LORD; you bestow glory on me and lift up my head. PSALM 3:2-3

Blessing and honor, thanksgiving and praise
more than we can utter be unto you,
O most adorable Trinity, Father, Son, and Holy Ghost,
by all angels, all men, all creatures
for ever and ever. Amen and amen.
To God the Father, who first loved us,
and made us accepted in the beloved;
to God the Son who loved us,
and washed us from our sins in his own blood;
to God the Holy Ghost,
who sheds the love of God abroad in our hearts
be all love and all glory for time and for eternity.
Amen.

THOMAS KEN

I have lived to thank God that all my prayers have not been answered.

JEAN INGELOW

January 4

Know that the LORD has set apart the godly for himself; the LORD will hear when I call to him. PSALM 4:3

I bind unto myself today
The power of God to hold and lead,
His eye to watch, his might to stay,
His ear to hearken to my need.
The wisdom of my God to teach,
His hand to guide, his shield to ward;
The word of God to give me speech,
His heavenly host to be my guard.

I bind unto myself the name,
The strong name of the Trinity;
By invocation of the same,
The Three in One, the One in Three,
Of whom all nature hath creation;
Eternal Father, Spirit, Word,
Praise to the Lord of my salvation,
Salvation is of Christ the Lord.

PATRICK OF IRELAND

If Christians spent as much time praying as they do grumbling, they would soon have nothing to grumble about.

ANONYMOUS

January 5

Listen to my cry for help, my King and my God, for to you I pray. In the morning, O LORD, you hear my voice; in the morning I lay my requests before you and wait in expectation.
PSALM 5:2-3

Give me, O Lord, a steadfast heart, which no unworthy affection may drag downwards; give me an unconquered heart, which no tribulation can wear out; give me an upright heart, which no unworthy purpose may tempt aside. Bestow on me also, O Lord my God, understanding to know you, diligence to seek you, wisdom to find you, and a faithfulness that may finally embrace you, through Jesus Christ our Lord. Amen.

THOMAS AQUINAS

He who aims at inward and spiritual things must, with Jesus, turn aside from the crowd.

THOMAS À KEMPIS

January 6

Be merciful to me, LORD, for I am faint; O LORD, heal me, for my bones are in agony. . . . Turn, O LORD, and deliver me; save me because of your unfailing love. PSALM 6:2, 4

Almighty God, Lord of the storm and of the calm, the vexed sea and the quiet haven, of day and of night, of life and of death, grant unto us so to have our hearts stayed upon your faithfulness, your unchangingness and love, that, whatsoever betide us, however black the cloud or dark the night, with quiet faith trusting in you we may look upon you with untroubled eye, and walking in lowliness toward you, and in lovingness toward another, abide all storms and troubles of this mortal life, begging you that they may turn to the soul's true good. We ask it for your mercy's sake, shown in Jesus Christ our Lord.

GEORGE DAWSON

The prayer of faith is the only power in the universe to which the great Jehovah yields.

ROBERT HALL

January 7

Let the assembled peoples gather around you. Rule over them from on high; let the LORD judge the peoples. Judge me, O LORD, according to my righteousness, according to my integrity, O Most High. PSALM 7:7-8

Glorious God, give me grace to amend my life, and to have an eye to my end without begrudging death, which to those who die in you, good Lord, is the gate of a wealthy life.

Give me, good Lord, a full faith, a firm hope, and a fervent charity, a love of you incomparably above the love of myself.

Give me, good Lord, a longing to be with you, not to avoid the calamities of this world, not so much to attain the joys of heaven, as simply for love of you.

And give me, good Lord, your love and favor, which my love of you, however great it might be, could not deserve were it not for your great goodness.

These things, good Lord, that I pray for, give me your grace to labor for.

THOMAS MORE

O Lord, let me not live to be useless!

BISHOP JOHN DE STRATFORD

January 8

LORD, our Lord, how majestic is your name in all the earth! You have set your glory above the heavens. From the lips of children and infants you have ordained praise. PSALM 8:1-2

Behold, Lord, an empty vessel that needs to be filled. My Lord, fill it. I am weak in the faith; strengthen me. I am cold in love; warm me and make me fervent, that my love may go out to my neighbor. I do not have a strong and firm faith; at times I doubt and am unable to trust you altogether. O Lord, help me. Strengthen my faith and trust in you. In you I have sealed the treasure of all I have. I am poor; you are rich and came to be merciful to the poor. I am a sinner; you are upright. With me, there is an abundance of sin; in you is the fullness of righteousness. Therefore I will remain with you, of whom I can receive, but to whom I may not give.

MARTIN LUTHER

It is good for us to keep some account of our prayers, that we may not unsay them in our practice.

MATTHEW HENRY

January 9

I will praise you, O LORD, with all my heart; I will tell of all your wonders. I will be glad and rejoice in you; I will sing praise to your name, O Most High. PSALM 9:1-2

Use me then, my Savior, for whatever purpose, and in whatever way, you may require. Here is my poor heart, an empty vessel; fill it with your grace. Here is my sinful and troubled soul; quicken it and refresh it with your love. Take my heart for your abode; my mouth to spread abroad the glory of your name; my love and all my powers, for the advancement of your believing people; and never suffer the steadfastness and confidence of my faith to abate; so that at all times I may be enabled from the heart to say, "Jesus needs me, and I am his."

DWIGHT L. MOODY

When you go to your knees,
God will help you stand up to anything.

ANONYMOUS

January 10

Arise, O LORD, let not man triumph; let the nations be judged in your presence. Strike them with terror, O LORD; let the nations know they are but men. PSALM 9:19-20

O God, ever blessed, who hast given me the night for rest and the day for labor and service, grant that the refreshing sleep of the night now past may be turned to Thy greater glory in the life of the day now before me. Let it breed no slothfulness within me, but rather send me to more diligent action and more willing obedience. Teach me, O God, so to use all the circumstances of my life today that they may bring forth in me the fruits of holiness rather than the fruits of sin.

JOHN BAILLIE

For each new morning with its light,
For rest and shelter of the night,
For health and food, for love and friends,
For everything Thy goodness sends.

RALPH WALDO EMERSON

January 11

Arise, LORD! Lift up your hand, O God. Do not forget the helpless. PSALM 10:12

Give us courage, O Lord, to stand up and be counted,
to stand up for those who cannot stand up for themselves,
to stand up for ourselves when it is needful for us to do so.
Let us fear nothing more than we fear you.
Let us love nothing more than we love you,
for thus we shall fear nothing also.
Let us have no other God before you,
whether nation or party or state or church.
Let us seek no other peace but the peace which is yours,
and make us its instruments,
opening our eyes and our ears and our hearts,
so that we should know always what work of peace we
may do for you.

ALAN PATON

Keep us, Lord, so awake in the duties of our calling that we may sleep in thy peace and wake in thy glory.

JOHN DONNE

January 12

The LORD is King for ever and ever; the nations will perish from his land. You hear, O LORD, the desire of the afflicted; you encourage them, and you listen to their cry. PSALM 10:16-17

Dear God, you are the heavenly Father. I am a father too, but I am earthly. One small family has come out from me and bears my name, yet, in truth, every family in heaven and earth takes its name from you. So I pray that you would care for this family because of your holy name. Give them what only a heavenly Father can give. That is, just as I gave them their first birth on earth, you would give them a second birth from heaven. I ask you this because I know that it is only in this way that they can have the eternal life you promised in your beloved Son, Jesus Christ our Lord. Amen.

DANIEL PARTNER

Prayer, in its simplest definition, is merely a wish turned God-ward.

PHILLIPS BROOKS

January 13

The LORD is in his holy temple; the LORD is on his heavenly throne. He observes the sons of men; his eyes examine them.
PSALM 11:4

O Lord God, whose will it is that, next to yourself, we should hold our parents in highest honor; it is not the least of our duties to beseech your goodness towards them. Preserve, I pray, my parents and home, in the love of your religion and in health of body and mind. Grant that through me no sorrow may befall them; and finally, as they are kind to me, so may you be to them, O supreme Father of all.

DESIDERIUS ERASMUS

Religion is no more possible without prayer than poetry without language or music without atmosphere.

JAMES MARTINEAU

January 14

Help, LORD, for the godly are no more; the faithful have vanished from among men. Everyone lies to his neighbor; their flattering lips speak with deception. . . . "Because of the oppression of the weak and the groaning of the needy, I will now arise," says the LORD. PSALM 12:1-2, 5

Our Father, You come seeking fruit. Teach me, I pray You, to realize how truly this is the one object of my existence, and of my union to Christ. Make it the one desire of my heart to be a branch, so filled with the Spirit of the Vine, as to bring forth fruit abundantly.

ANDREW MURRAY (adapted)

Take my will, and make it Thine,
It shall be no longer mine;
Take my heart, it is Thine own;
It shall be Thy royal throne.

FRANCES R. HAVERGAL

January 15

Look on me and answer, O LORD my God. Give light to my eyes, or I will sleep in death. PSALM 13:3

I bow my knees before you Father, from whom every family in heaven and on earth takes its name. I pray that, according to the riches of your glory, you may grant that I may be strengthened in my inner being with power through your Spirit, and that Christ may dwell in my heart through faith, as I am being rooted and grounded in love. I pray that I may have the power to comprehend, with all the saints, what is the breadth and length and height and depth, and to know the love of Christ that surpasses knowledge, so that I may be filled with all the fullness of God.

EPHESIANS 3:14-19 (adapted)

We ought to act with God in the greatest simplicity, speaking to Him frankly and plainly, and imploring His assistance in our affairs, just as they happen.

BROTHER LAWRENCE

January 16

Oh, that salvation for Israel would come out of Zion! When the LORD restores the fortunes of his people, let Jacob rejoice and Israel be glad! PSALM 14:7

We thank you, O Lord our God, for all Your goodness. You have shielded, rescued, helped and guided us all the days of our lives, and brought us unto this hour. Grant in Your goodness that we may spend this day without sin, in joy and reverence of You. Drive away from us all envy, all fear. Bestow upon us what is good and meet. And lead us not into temptation, but deliver us from evil.

ANONYMOUS

In seasons of distress and grief,
My soul has often found relief,
And oft escaped the tempter's snare,
By thy return, sweet hour of prayer.

W. W. WALFORD

January 17

LORD, who may dwell in your sanctuary? Who may live on your holy hill? He whose walk is blameless and who does what is righteous, who speaks the truth from his heart. PSALM 15:1-2

We thank thee, Lord, that however hopeless our work may seem, however dark the night around us, however meager the response to Thy Spirit, still Thou hast ordained for us a hope.

We thank Thee that we can never despair because we know, past all doubting, that here and there in this world Thy kingdom has already come, Thy will has already begun to rule.

We thank Thee that here and there are homes made beautiful by Thy presence, lives lived purely and faithfully for Thee, children and child-like souls whose clear and simple trust brings Thee Thyself down amongst men.

J. S. HOWLAND

Prayer opens our eyes that we may see ourselves and others as God sees us.

CLARA PALMER

January 18

Keep me safe, O God, for in you I take refuge. I said to the LORD, "You are my Lord; apart from you I have no good thing."
PSALM 16:1-2

O Lord, Jesus Christ,
who is as the shadow of a great rock
in a weary land,
who beholds your weak creatures
weary of labor, weary of pleasure,
weary of hope deferred, weary of self;
in your abundant compassion,
and fellow feeling with us,
and unutterable tenderness,
bring us, we pray you,
into your rest.

CHRISTINA ROSSETTI

There is no life that is not in community,
And no community not lived in praise of God.

T. S. ELIOT

January 19

Show the wonder of your great love, you who save by your right hand those who take refuge in you from their foes. Keep me as the apple of your eye; hide me in the shadow of your wings.
PSALM 17:7-8

Thanks be to you, Lord Jesus Christ, for all the benefits which you have won for us, for all the pains and insults which you have borne for us. O most merciful Redeemer, Friend and Brother, may we know you more clearly, love you more dearly, and follow you more nearly, day by day.

RICHARD OF CHICHESTER

More things are wrought by prayer than this world dreams of.

ALFRED, LORD TENNYSON

January 20

I love you, O LORD, my strength. The LORD is my rock, my fortress and my deliverer; my God is my rock, in whom I take refuge. He is my shield and the horn of my salvation, my stronghold. PSALM 18:1-2

Morning and evening I commit my soul to Jesus Christ, the Savior of the world. Enable me, O God, to observe what He says to me: resolutely to obey His precepts and endeavor to follow His example in those things wherein He is exhibited to us as a pattern for our imitation. Make plain to me that no circumstance nor time of life can occur but I may find something either spoken by our Lord Himself or by His Spirit in the prophets or apostles that will direct my conduct, if I am but faithful to You and my own soul. Amen.

SUSANNA WESLEY

Ask, and it shall be given you; seek, and ye shall find; knock, and it shall be opened unto you.

MATTHEW 7:7, *KJV*

January 21

He reached down from on high and took hold of me; he drew me out of deep waters. He rescued me from my powerful enemy, from my foes, who were too strong for me. PSALM 18:16-17

Come, Therefore, O Lord Jesus, divest yourself of your garments which you have put on for my sake. Be naked, that you may clothe us with your mercy. Gird yourself with a towel for our sakes, that you may gird us with your gift of immortality. Pour water into the basin; wash not only our feet but also the head, and not only the footprints of the body, but also of the mind. I wish to put off all the filth of my frailty, so that I, too, may say: "I have put off my garment, how shall I put it on? I have washed my feet, how shall I defile them?"

AMBROSE

Rejoice always, pray constantly,
and in all circumstances give thanks.

THE DESERT FATHERS

January 22

The LORD lives! Praise be to my Rock! Exalted be God my Savior. PSALM 18:46

O Lord:
Keep me from vain strife or
words:
Grant to me a constant
Profession of the truth!
Preserve me in the faith,
True faith and undefiled,
That ever I may hold fast
That which I professed when I
was baptized
Unto, and in the name of,
Father,
The Son,
The Holy Ghost—
That I may have you for my
Father,
That in your Son I may abide,
And in the fellowship of the
Holy Ghost:
Through the same Jesus
Christ,
Our Lord. Amen.

HILARY OF POITIERS (adapted)

Deep down in me I knowed it was a lie, and He knowed it. You can't pray a lie—I found that out.

MARK TWAIN, *Huck Finn*

January 23

The heavens declare the glory of God; the skies proclaim the work of his hands. Day after day they pour forth speech; night after night they display knowledge. PSALM 19:1-2

O Lord and Saviour Christ, who comes not to strive nor cry, but to let your words fall as the drops that water the earth; grant all who contend for the faith once delivered, never to injure it by clamour and impatience; but speaking your precious truth in love so to present it that it may be loved, and that men may see in it your goodness and your beauty.

WILLIAM BRIGHT

Let me depend on God alone:
who never changes,
who knows what is best for me so much better than I;
and gives in a thousand ways, at all times
all that the perfect Father can for the son's good growth,
things needful, things salutary,
things wise, beneficent and happy.

ERIC MILNER-WHITE

January 24

May the LORD answer you when you are in distress; may the name of the God of Jacob protect you. May he send you help from the sanctuary and grant you support from Zion. PSALM 20:1-2

Be off, Satan, from this door and from these four walls. This is no place for you; there is nothing for you to do here. This is the place for Peter and Paul and the holy gospel; and this is where I mean to sleep, now that my worship is done, in the name of the Father and of the Holy Spirit.

In the name of our Lord Jesus Christ, send me your Spirit; instill the wisdom of your Holy Spirit into my heart; protect my soul and body, every limb in my body, every fiber of my being, from all possible harm and all traps the Devil may set for me and every temptation to sin.

EUCHOLOGIUM SINAITICUM

O what peace we often forfeit,
O what needless pain we bear,
All because we do not carry
Everything to God in prayer!

JOSEPH SCRIVEN

January 25

O LORD, the king rejoices in your strength. How great is his joy in the victories you give! You have granted him the desire of his heart and have not withheld the request of his lips. PSALM 21:1-2

I call upon you, O LORD; come quickly to me;
give ear to my voice when I call to you.
Let my prayer be counted as incense before you,
and the lifting up of my hands as an evening sacrifice.
Set a guard over my mouth, O LORD;
keep watch over the door of my lips.
Do not turn my heart to any evil,
to busy myself with wicked deeds
in company with those who work iniquity;
do not let me eat of their delicacies.

PSALM 141:1-4, *NRSV*

God eagerly awaits the chance to bless the person whose heart is turned toward Him.

ANONYMOUS

January 26

Yet you are enthroned as the Holy One; you are the praise of Israel. In you our fathers put their trust; they trusted and you delivered them. PSALM 22:3-4

O Lord God, when you give to your servants to endeavor any great matter, grant us also to know that it is not the beginning, but the continuing of the same to the end, until it be thoroughly finished, which yields the true glory; through him who for the finishing of your work laid down his life, our Redeemer, Jesus Christ.

FRANCIS DRAKE

Pray, always pray; though weary, faint,
and lone,
Prayer nestles by the Father's
sheltering throne.

A. B. SIMPSON

January 27

You who fear the LORD, praise him! All you descendants of Jacob, honor him! Revere him, all you descendants of Israel!
PSALM 22:23

Who can tell what a day may bring forth? Cause me therefore, gracious God, to live every day as if it were to be my last, for I know not but that it may be such. Cause me to live now as I shall wish I had done when I come to die. O grant that I may not die with any guilt on my conscience, or any known sin unrepented of, but that I may be found in Christ, who is my only Saviour and Redeemer.

THOMAS À KEMPIS

Prayer should be the key of the day and the lock of the night.

THOMAS FULLER

January 28

The LORD is my shepherd, I shall lack nothing. He makes me lie down in green pastures, he leads me beside quiet waters, he restores my soul. PSALM 23:1-3

Lord, behold our family here assembled. We thank you for this place in which we dwell, for the love that unites us, for the peace accorded us this day, for the hope with which we expect the morrow; for the health, the work, the food, and the bright skies that make our lives delightful; for our friends in all parts of the earth.

Bless us, if it may be, in all our innocent endeavors; if it may not, give us the strength to endure that which is to come that we may be brave in peril, constant in tribulation, temperate in wrath, and in all changes of fortune, and down to the gates of death, loyal and loving to one another.

As the clay to the potter, as the windmill to the wind, as children of their sire, we beseech of you this help and mercy for Christ's sake.

ROBERT LOUIS STEVENSON

Our thanks to God should always precede our requests.

ANONYMOUS

January 29

Who may ascend the hill of the LORD? Who may stand in his holy place? He who has clean hands and a pure heart, who does not lift up his soul to an idol or swear by what is false.
PSALM 24:3-4

O Lord our God, even at this moment as we come blundering into Thy presence in prayer, we are haunted by memories of duties unperformed, promptings disobeyed, and beckonings ignored. Opportunities to be kind knocked on the door of our hearts and went weeping away. We are ashamed, O Lord, and tired of failure.

If Thou art drawing close to us now, come nearer still, till selfishness is burned out within us and our wills lose their weakness in union with Thine own. Amen.

PETER MARSHALL

They tell about a fifteen-year-old boy in an orphans' home who had an incurable stutter. One Sunday the minister was detained and the boy volunteered to say the prayer in his stead. He did it perfectly, too, without a single stutter. Later he explained, "I don't stutter when I talk to God. He loves me."

BENNETT CERF

January 30

Show me your ways, O LORD, teach me your paths; guide me in your truth and teach me, for you are God my Savior, and my hope is in you all day long. PSALM 25:4-5

O thou, who art the Light of the minds that know Thee, and the Life of the souls that love Thee, and the Strength of the thoughts that seek Thee; help us so to know Thee that we may truly love Thee; so to love Thee that we may truly serve Thee, whose service is perfect freedom; through Jesus Christ our Lord. Amen.

GELASIAN SACRAMENTARY

There is nothing that makes us love a man so much as praying for him.

WILLIAM LAW

January 31

Turn to me and be gracious to me, for I am lonely and afflicted. The troubles of my heart have multiplied; free me from my anguish. PSALM 25:16-17

Lord, you know better than I know myself that I am growing older, and will someday be old. Keep me from getting talkative, and particularly from the fatal habit of thinking that I must say something on every subject and on every occasion.

I ask for grace enough to listen to the tales of others' pains. But seal my lips on my own aches and pains; help me to endure them with patience.

Give me the ability to see good things in unexpected places, and talents in unexpected people. And give me, O Lord, the grace to tell them so.

ANONYMOUS

We must lay before him what is in us, not what ought to be in us.

C. S. LEWIS

February 1

Test me, O LORD, and try me, examine my heart and my mind; for your love is ever before me, and I walk continually in your truth. PSALM 26:2-3

O Lord, you are my redemption, also be my protector; direct my mind by your gracious presence, and watch over my path with guiding love; that, among the snares which lie hidden in this path in which I walk, I may so pass onwards with my heart fixed on you, that by the track of faith I may come to be where you would have me.

MOZARABIC SACRAMENTARY

God showed Abraham that asking for anything is allowed with the understanding that God's answers come from God's perspective. They are not always in harmony with our expectations, for only he knows the whole story.

LIFE APPLICATION BIBLE on Genesis 18:33

February 2

The LORD is my light and my salvation—whom shall I fear? The LORD is the stronghold of my life—of whom shall I be afraid? PSALM 27:1

Father Almighty, who are not served by men's hands as though you need anything, but who delights in the worship of a contrite heart, grant us grace in this hour of worship to forswear the pride to which our hearts are prone, to remember that you have made us and not we ourselves, that you are the beginning and the end of our life. Grant us to know the limit of our knowledge that we may seek your wisdom, and to know the limit of our power so that we may glory in your strength which is made perfect in weakness. So may we worship you in humility, and arise to newness of life by fellowship with you. Amen.

REINHOLD NIEBUHR

Help me to work and pray,
Help me to live each day,
That all I do may say,
Thy kingdom come.

A. B. SIMPSON

February 3

Hear my voice when I call, O LORD; be merciful to me and answer me. My heart says of you, "Seek his face!" Your face, LORD, I will seek. PSALM 27:7-8

O Lord Jesus Christ, you have said that you are the way, the truth, and the life. Suffer us not to stray from you, who are the way, nor to distrust you who are the truth, nor to rest in anything other than you, who are the life.

DESIDERIUS ERASMUS

There are two main pitfalls on the road to mastery of the art of prayer. If a person gets what he asks for, his humility is in danger. If he fails to get what he asks for, he is apt to lose confidence. Indeed, no matter whether prayer seems to be succeeding or failing, humility and confidence are two virtues which are absolutely essential.

A TRAPPIST MONK

February 4

Praise be to the LORD, for he has heard my cry for mercy. The LORD is my strength and my shield; my heart trusts in him, and I am helped. PSALM 28:6-7

So much of the world goes to bed hungry every night, but we are blessed with abundance. The bellies of Third World children swell through malnutrition, but the only way our bellies swell is through overeating. We wonder what God's plan on this earth must be. Help us, O Lord, to an awareness of our spiritual and physical needs, and of the needs of people in all countries of this world—as we give thanks for the food that is set before us. Amen.

PAUL SIMPSON MCELROY

Our Father, let the spirit of gratitude so prevail in our hearts that we may manifest thy Spirit in our lives.

W. B. SLACK

February 5

Ascribe to the LORD, O mighty ones, ascribe to the LORD glory and strength. Ascribe to the LORD the glory due his name; worship the LORD in the splendor of his holiness. PSALM 29:1-2

Father, I am beginning to know how much I miss when I fail to talk to thee in prayer, and through prayer to receive into my life the strength and the guidance which only thou canst give. Forgive me for the pride and the presumption that make me continue to struggle to manage my own affairs to the exhaustion of my body, the weariness of my mind, the trial of my faith.

Let not, I pray, any future forgetfulness of mine, or a false sense of self-sufficiency, any spiritual laziness, or doubt of thy faithfulness keep me from taking everything to thee in prayer.

And now, I thank thee that the fresh breath of heaven is even now blowing away the close, damp air of all my failure, of every doubt and fear. I ask thee for that soul tonic of prayer that shall reburnish my faith, brighten my hope, revive and rekindle my love. In thy name, I pray. Amen.

PETER MARSHALL

Lord, you know how busy I must be this day. If I forget you, do not you forget me.

JACOB ASTLEY

February 6

Sing to the LORD, you saints of his; praise his holy name. For his anger lasts only a moment, but his favor lasts a lifetime; weeping may remain for a night, but rejoicing comes in the morning. PSALM 30:4-5

Lord Jesus Christ, who stretched out your hands on the cross, and redeemed us by your blood: forgive me, a sinner, for none of my thoughts are hid from you. Pardon I ask, pardon I hope for, pardon I trust to have. You who are full of pity and mercy: spare me, and forgive.

AMBROSE

Have we trials and temptations?
Is there trouble anywhere?
We should never be discouraged,
Take it to the Lord in prayer.

JOSEPH SCRIVEN

February 7

In you, O LORD, I have taken refuge; let me never be put to shame; deliver me in your righteousness. Turn your ear to me, come quickly to my rescue; be my rock of refuge, a strong fortress to save me. PSALM 31:1-2

Jesus, my feet are dirty. Come and slave for me; pour your water into your basin and come and wash my feet. I am over bold, I know, in asking this, but I dread what you threatened when you said: "If I do not wash your feet, it means you have no companionship with me." Wash my feet, then, because I do want to have companionship with you. And yet, why am I saying: "Wash my feet"? It was all very well for Peter to say that, for in his case all that needed washing was his feet: he was clean through and through. My position is quite different: you may wash me now, but I shall still need that other washing you were thinking of, Lord, when you said: "There is a baptism I must needs be baptized with."

ORIGEN OF ALEXANDRIA

For food, for raiment, for life
and opportunity, for sun and rain,
for water and the portage trails,
we give you thanks, O Lord.

A PRAYER FROM THE NORTH WOODS

February 8

Be merciful to me, O LORD, for I am in distress; my eyes grow weak with sorrow, my soul and my body with grief. PSALM 31:9

Helper of men who turn to you,
Light of men in the dark,
Creator of all that grows from seed,
Promoter of all spiritual growth,
have mercy, Lord, on me
and make me a temple fit for yourself.
Do not scan my transgressions too closely,
for if you are quick to notice my offenses,
I shall not dare to appear before you.
In your great mercy,
in your boundless compassion,
wash away my sins, through Jesus Christ,
your only Child, the truly holy,
the chief of our souls' healers.
Through him may all glory be given you,
all power and honor and praise,
throughout the ending succession of ages.
Amen.

BERLIN PAPYRUS

Who rises from prayer a better man, his prayer is answered.

GEORGE MEREDITH

February 9

How great is your goodness, which you have stored up for those who fear you, which you bestow in the sight of men on those who take refuge in you. PSALM 31:19

Let us not seek out of you what we can only find in you,
O Lord.
Peace and rest and joy and bliss,
which abide only in your abiding joy.
Lift up our souls above the weary fount of harassing
thoughts to your eternal presence.
Lift up our minds to the pure, bright serene atmosphere of
your presence,
that we may breathe freely,
there repose in your love,
there be at rest from ourselves
and from all things that weary us:
and then return, arrayed in thy peace,
to do and to bear
whatsoever shall best please you, O blessed Lord.

E. B. PUSEY

We do pray for mercy, and that same prayer doth teach us all to render the deeds of mercy.

WILLIAM SHAKESPEARE, *Merchant of Venice*

*F*ebruary 10

Blessed is he whose transgressions are forgiven, whose sins are covered. Blessed is the man whose sin the LORD does not count against him and in whose spirit is no deceit. PSALM 32:1-2

O God, make the door of this house wide enough to receive all who need human love and fellowship; narrow enough to shut out all envy, pride, and strife.

Make its threshold smooth enough to be no stumbling block to children nor to straying feet, but rugged and strong enough to turn back the tempter's power. God, make the door of this house the gateway to thine eternal kingdom.

ON ST. STEPHEN'S WALLBROOK, LONDON

And now unto him who is able to keep us from falling and lift us from the dark valley of despair to the bright mountain of hope, from the midnight of desperation to the daybreak of joy; to him be power and authority, for ever and ever.

MARTIN LUTHER KING JR.

February 11

Sing joyfully to the LORD, you righteous; it is fitting for the upright to praise him. Praise the LORD with the harp; make music to him on the ten-stringed lyre. PSALM 33:1-2

O Lord God, I am learning that I can do nothing apart from your Holy Spirit. Your Spirit lifts me up in prayer. Your Spirit prepares my heart for prayer. Your Spirit aids me in resting my heart and mind in you in prayer. Your Spirit prompts me to pray for the things of your heart, and he leads me beyond selfish desires. May I be continually inspired by your Spirit to say and do and pray consistently, that my life might be a witness to others regarding the blessed power of prayer and your work through your Spirit. Amen.

LOUIS GIFFORD PARKHURST JR.

Prayer is an end to isolation. It is living our daily life with someone; with him who alone can deliver us from solitude.

GEORGES LEFEVRE

February 12

From heaven the LORD looks down and sees all mankind; from his dwelling place he watches all who live on earth—he who forms the hearts of all, who considers everything they do. PSALM 33:13-15

Father, when your Son Jesus Christ prayed, he looked up to heaven and spoke to you, so now I follow his example. I will confidently speak with you as a man on earth to his God in heaven.

Your kingdom is in heaven, O God, but my feet stand on earth and my eyes look up in prayer. Father, I ask you, bring your kingdom to earth. Just as John looked up and saw the holy city, the New Jerusalem, coming down out of heaven, I pray that my eyes would see the coming of your kingdom. Just as he heard the voice from the throne, so may I hear the voices at the seventh trumpet proclaim, "The kingdom of the world has become the kingdom of our Lord and of his Christ, and he will reign forever and ever." Amen.

DANIEL PARTNER

O Christ my Lord and King,
This is the prayer I bring,
This is the song I sing,
Thy kingdom come.

A. B. SIMPSON

February 13

The angel of the LORD encamps around those who fear him, and he delivers them. Taste and see that the LORD is good; blessed is the man who takes refuge in him. PSALM 34:7-8

We beg you, Lord, to help and defend us. Deliver the oppressed, pity the insignificant, raise the fallen, show yourself to the needy, heal the sick, bring back those of your people who have gone astray, feed the hungry, lift up the weak, take off the prisoner's chains. May every nation come to know that you alone are God, that Jesus Christ is your Child, that we are your people, the sheep that you pasture.

CLEMENT OF ROME

Restraining prayer, we cease to fight;
Prayer keeps the Christian's armor bright;
And Satan trembles when he sees
The weakest saint upon his knees.

WILLIAM COWPER

February 14

The righteous cry out, and the LORD hears them; he delivers them from all their troubles. The LORD is close to the brokenhearted and saves those who are crushed in spirit.
PSALM 34:17-18

O Lord, you are never weary of doing me good. Let me never be weary of doing you service. But as you have pleasure in the prosperity of your servants, so let me take pleasure in the service of my Lord, and abound in your work, and in your love and praise evermore. O fill up all that is wanting, reform whatever is amiss in me, perfect the thing that concerns me. Let the witness of your pardoning love ever abide in my heart.

JOHN WESLEY (adapted)

The right way to pray, then, is any way that allows us to communicate with God. For prayer is not a ritual; it is the soul's inherent response to a relationship with a loving Father.

COLLEEN TOWNSEND EVANS

February 15

My soul will rejoice in the LORD and delight in his salvation. My whole being will exclaim, "Who is like you, O LORD? You rescue the poor from those too strong for them, the poor and needy from those who rob them." PSALM 35:9-10

May none of God's wonderful works keep silence, night or morning. Bright stars, high mountains, the depths of the seas, sources of rushing rivers: may all these break into song as I sing to Father, Son, and Holy Spirit. May all the angels in the heavens reply: Amen, Amen, Amen. Power, praise, honor, eternal glory to God, the only giver of grace, Amen, Amen, Amen.

ANONYMOUS

O Lord, heavenly Father, in whom is the fullness of light and wisdom, enlighten our minds by your Holy Spirit, and give us grace to receive your Word with reverence and humility, without which no one can understand your truth. For Christ's sake, amen.

JOHN CALVIN

February 16

O LORD, how long will you look on? Rescue my life from their ravages, my precious life from these lions. I will give you thanks in the great assembly; among throngs of people I will praise you.
PSALM 35:17-18

Almighty,

forgive my doubt,

my anger,

my pride.

By your mercy abase me,

in your strictness

raise me up.

DAG HAMMARSKJÖLD, *Mercy and Justice*

Joshua poured out his real thoughts to God. Hiding your needs from God is ignoring the only one who can really help. Any believer can become more honest in prayer by remembering that God is all-knowing and all-powerful.

LIFE APPLICATION BIBLE on Joshua *7:7-9*

February 17

Your love, O LORD, reaches to the heavens, your faithfulness to the skies. Your righteousness is like the mighty mountains, your justice like the great deep. PSALM 36:5-6

God of all grace, give me your peace that passes understanding, the quietness that comes from friendliness with human beings, and may true divine friendship with you possess my soul; that I, withdrawn awhile from the turmoil of the world, may gather the strength that I have lost, and established and strengthened by your grace, pass on through all the troubles of this my earthly life, safe into the haven of eternal rest; through Jesus Christ my Lord. Amen.

GEORGE DAWSON

The first purpose of prayer is to know God.

CHARLES L. ALLEN

February 18

Trust in the LORD and do good; dwell in the land and enjoy safe pasture. Delight yourself in the LORD and he will give you the desires of your heart. PSALM 37:3-4

O my Lord, you have said, "Ask for whatever you wish and it will be done for you." Why is it that my heart is so little able to accept these words in their divine simplicity? Oh, help me to see that what I need is nothing less than this promise to overcome the powers of the world and Satan! Teach me to pray in the faith of this Thy promise.

ANDREW MURRAY (adapted)

If ye abide in me, and my words abide in you, ye shall ask what ye will, and it shall be done unto you.

JOHN 15:7, *KJV*

February 19

If the LORD delights in a man's way, he makes his steps firm; though he stumble, he will not fall, for the LORD upholds him with his hand. PSALM 37:23-24

Gracious and holy Father, give me wisdom to perceive you, intelligence to fathom you, patience to wait for you, eyes to behold you, a heart to meditate upon you, and a life to proclaim you, through the power of the Spirit of Jesus Christ our Lord.

BENEDICT

Prayer covers the whole of a man's life. There is no thought, feeling, yearning, or desire, however low, trifling, or vulgar we may deem it, which, if it affects our real interest or happiness, we may not lay before God and be sure of sympathy. His nature is such that our often coming does not tire him. The whole burden of the whole life of every man may be rolled on to God and not weary him, though it has wearied the man.

HENRY WARD BEECHER

February 20

The mouth of the righteous man utters wisdom, and his tongue speaks what is just. The law of his God is in his heart; his feet do not slip. PSALM 37:30-31

Almighty God, our heavenly Father, without whose help labour is useless, without whose light search is vain, invigorate my studies and establish myself and others in your holy Faith. Take not, O Lord, your Holy Spirit from me, let not evil thoughts have dominion in my mind. Let me not linger in ignorance and doubt, but enlighten and support me for the sake of Jesus Christ our Lord. Amen.

SAMUEL JOHNSON

The cry of a young raven is nothing but the natural cry of a creature, but your cry, if it be sincere, is the result of a work of grace in your heart.

CHARLES H. SPURGEON

February 21

O LORD, do not forsake me; be not far from me, O my God. Come quickly to help me, O Lord my Savior. PSALM 38:21-22

Write Thy blessed name, O Lord, upon my heart, there to remain so indelibly engraven that no prosperity, no adversity shall ever move me from Thy love. Be Thou to me a strong Tower of defense, a Comforter in tribulation, a Deliverer in distress, a very present Help in trouble, and a Guide to heaven through the many temptations and dangers of this life. Amen.

THOMAS À KEMPIS

He went up into a mountain apart to pray: and when the evening was come, he was there alone.

MATTHEW 14:23, *KJV*

February 22

But now, Lord, what do I look for? My hope is in you. Save me from all my transgressions; do not make me the scorn of fools.
PSALM 39:7-8

If my soul has turned perversely to the dark;
If I have left some brother wounded by the way;
If I have preferred my aims to yours;
If I have been impatient and would not wait;
If I have marred the pattern drawn out for my life;
If I have cost tears to those I loved;
If my heart has murmured against your will,
O Lord, forgive.

F. B. Meyer

I firmly believe a great many prayers are not answered because we are not willing to forgive someone.

DWIGHT L. MOODY

February 23

I waited patiently for the LORD; he turned to me and heard my cry. He lifted me out of the slimy pit, out of the mud and mire; he set my feet on a rock and gave me a firm place to stand. PSALM 40:1-2

O God,

In the crush of traffic, the push and shove of shopping, the surge in corridors of school, we often wonder if we are known by you, or by anyone else.

In the isolation of apartments, the solitude of speeding automobiles, the seclusion of a nursing-home bed, we often wonder if we are remembered by you, or by anyone else.

Remind us anew, this day, O God, that you have the whole wide world in your hands.

Assure us, once more, that you know us, each one by name and by need.

Let us never feel forsaken, nor believe that multitudes are outside your providence.

Here and now, with fresh courage and full assurance, we call you Father, and together pray to you.

DAVID M. CURRIE

Prayer is exhaling the spirit of man and inhaling the spirit of God.

EDWIN KEITH

February 24

Do not withhold your mercy from me, O LORD; may your love and your truth always protect me. PSALM 40:11

O God, fill me with the knowledge of your will through all spiritual wisdom and understanding. I pray this in order that I may live a life worthy of the Lord and may please him in every way: bearing fruit in every good work, growing in the knowledge of God, being strengthened with all power according to his glorious might. Then I may have great endurance and patience, and joyfully give thanks to the Father, who has qualified me to share in the inheritance of the saints in the kingdom of light. He has rescued me from the dominion of darkness and brought me into the kingdom of the Son he loves, in whom I have redemption, the forgiveness of sins.

COLOSSIANS 1:9-12 (adapted)

God bless all those that I love; God bless all those that love me; God bless all those that love those that I love and all those that love those that love me.

A NEW ENGLAND SAMPLER

February 25

Blessed is he who has regard for the weak; the LORD delivers him in times of trouble. The LORD will protect him and preserve his life. PSALM 41:1-2

O Lord, who wills that all your children should be one in you, I pray to you for the unity of your church. Pardon all our pride, and our lack of faith, of understanding and of charity, which are the cause of our divisions. Deliver us from our narrow-mindedness, from our bitterness, from our prejudices. Preserve us from considering as normal that which is a scandal to the world and an offense to your love. Teach us to recognize the gifts of thy grace among all those who call upon you.

THE LITURGY OF THE REFORMED CHURCH OF FRANCE (adapted)

At church, with meek and unaffected grace,
His looks adorn'd the venerable place;
Truth from his lips prevail'd with double sway,
And fools, who came to scoff, remain'd to pray.

OLIVER GOLDSMITH

February 26

As the deer pants for streams of water, so my soul pants for you, O God. My soul thirsts for God, for the living God. PSALM 42:1-2

O Lord
Here I am again
Just plain old me
Coming to You
As I've come a thousand times—
And this is what always happens:
Your response is immediate
You open Your arms unhesitatingly
You draw me to Yourself
You clasp me to Your Father-heart.
Then You reaffirm my position:
I am a child of the King
And all that is Yours is mine.
When I begin my stammering account
Of gross unworthiness
Your gentle smile hushes me.
With endless patience
You remind me once more
That my value never determines Your love.
Rather, Your love determines my value.

RUTH HARMS CALKIN

One of his disciples said to him, "Lord, teach us to pray."

LUKE 11:1, *NRSV*

February 27

Why are you downcast, O my soul? Why so disturbed within me? Put your hope in God, for I will yet praise him, my Savior and my God. PSALM 43:5

Almighty God, I thank you because day after day has verified the truth of our Saviour's words: "Sufficient to the day is the evil thereof." Through the weakness and corruption of human nature and the unavoidable business of my station in life: in many unforeseen accidents and unexpected company: in cross occurrences, with abundance of other things incident to human life, I find occasion given to me daily to exercise virtues of one kind or another.

One day calls me to use justice and patience, and another prudence, temperance, and charity in forgiving injuries. I draw near unto you, the supreme fountain of virtue, for grace in the perplexed affairs of life, and thank you for every occasion on which I have found your strength to be made perfect in weakness; and I thank you that you are truth itself and that all your promises are yea and amen, through Jesus Christ, your mediator. Amen.

SUSANNA WESLEY

Pray, always pray; beneath sin's heaviest load,
Prayer claims the blood from Jesus' side that flowed.

A. B. SIMPSON

February 28

I do not trust in my bow, my sword does not bring me victory; but you give us victory over our enemies, you put our adversaries to shame. PSALM 44:6-7

Almighty God, grant us grace to hear Jesus Christ, the heavenly bread, preached throughout the world and truly to understand him. May all evil, heretical and human doctrines be cut off, while your Word as the living bread be distributed. Amen.

MARTIN LUTHER

But you, dear friends, must build up your lives ever more strongly upon the foundation of our holy faith, learning to pray in the power and strength of the Holy Spirit.

JUDE 1:20, *TLB*

March 1

If we had forgotten the name of our God or spread out our hands to a foreign god, would not God have discovered it, since he knows the secrets of the heart? PSALM 44:20-21

Our Father, remove from us the sophistication of our age and the skepticism that has come, like frost, to blight our faith and to make it weak. We pray for a return of that simple faith, that old-fashioned trust in God, that made strong and great the homes of our ancestors who built this good land and who in building left us our heritage. In the strong name of Jesus, our Lord, we make this prayer. Amen.

PETER MARSHALL

Prayer has marked the trees across
the wilderness of a skeptical world
to direct the traveler in distress,
and all paths lead to a single light.

DOUGLAS MEADOR

March 2

Your throne, O God, will last for ever and ever; a scepter of justice will be the scepter of your kingdom. PSALM 45:6

O God, the God of all goodness and of all grace, who art worthy of a greater love than we can either give or understand: Fill our hearts, we beseech you, with such love toward you that nothing may seem too hard for us to do or to suffer in obedience to your will; and grant that thus loving you, we may become daily more like unto you, and finally obtain the crown of life which thou hast promised to those that love you; through Jesus Christ our Lord.

BROOKE FOSS WESTCOTT

To be a branch means not only bearing fruit on earth, but power in prayer to bring down blessing from heaven. Abiding fully means praying much.

ANDREW MURRAY

March 3

God is our refuge and strength, an ever-present help in trouble. Therefore we will not fear, though the earth give way and the mountains fall into the heart of the sea. PSALM 46:1-2

Give me open hands, O God, hands ready to share with all who are in want the blessings with which Thou hast enriched my life. Deliver me from all meanness and miserliness. Let me hold my money in stewardship and all my worldly goods in trust for Thee; to whom now be all honour and glory. Amen.

JOHN BAILLIE

He prayeth well, who loveth well
Both man and bird and beast.
He prayeth best, who loveth best
All things both great and small;
For the dear God who loveth us,
He made and loveth all.

SAMUEL TAYLOR COLERIDGE

March 4

Clap your hands, all you nations; shout to God with cries of joy. How awesome is the LORD Most High, the great King over all the earth! PSALM 47:1-2

O Lord Jesus, Let not your word become a judgment upon us, that we hear it and do it not, that we know it and love it not, that we believe it and obey it not. We ask this of you who lives eternally with the Father and the Holy Spirit, world without end. Amen.

THOMAS À KEMPIS

Prayer is the incense of a holy heart
Rising to God from bruised and broken things,
When kindled by the Spirit's burning breath
And upward borne by faith's ascending wings.

A. B. SIMPSON

March 5

Great is the LORD, and most worthy of praise, in the city of our God, his holy mountain. PSALM 48:1

O Lord Jesus Christ, word and revelation of the eternal Father, come, we pray you, take possession of our hearts and reign where you have right to reign. So fill our minds with the thought and our imaginations with the picture of your love, that there may be in us no room for any desire that is discordant with your holy will. Cleanse us, we pray you, from all that may make us deaf to your call or slow to obey it, Who, with the Father and the Holy Spirit, art one God, blessed for ever.

WILLIAM TEMPLE

True prayer brings a person's will into accordance with God's will, not the other way around.

ANONYMOUS

March 6

But God will redeem my life from the grave; he will surely take me to himself. PSALM 49:15

O sovereign and almighty Lord, bless all your people and all your flock. Give peace, your help, your love unto us, your servants, the sheep of your fold, that we may be united in the bond of peace and love, one body and one spirit, in one hope of our calling, in your divine and boundless love; for the sake of Jesus Christ, the great Shepherd of the sheep.

LITURGY OF SAINT MARK

I always love to begin a journey on Sundays, because I shall have the prayers of the church, to preserve all that travel by land, or by water.

JONATHAN SWIFT

March 7

Consider this, you who forget God, or I will tear you to pieces, with none to rescue: He who sacrifices thank offerings honors me, and he prepares the way so that I may show him the salvation of God. PSALM 50:22-23

Make me to know your ways, O LORD;
teach me your paths.
Lead me in your truth, and teach me,
for you are the God of my salvation;
for you I wait all day long.

Be mindful of your mercy, O LORD, and of your
steadfast love,
for they have been from old.

Do not remember the sins of my youth or my
transgressions;
according to your steadfast love remember me,
for your goodness' sake, O LORD!

PSALM 25:4-7, *NRSV*

Trouble and perplexity drive me to prayer and prayer drives away perplexity and trouble.

PHILIP MELANCHTHON

March 8

Have mercy on me, O God, according to your unfailing love;
according to your great compassion blot out my transgressions.
Wash away all my iniquity and cleanse me from my sin.
PSALM 51:1-2

In confidence of Thy goodness and great mercy, O Lord, I draw near unto Thee, as a sick person to the Healer, as one hungry and thirsty to the Fountain of Life, a creature to the Creator, a desolate soul to my own tender Comforter. Behold, in Thee is all whatsoever I can or ought to desire. Rejoice therefore this day the soul of Thy servant; for unto Thee, O Lord, have I lifted up my soul. Amen.

THOMAS À KEMPIS

Plenteous grace with Thee is found,
Grace to cover all my sin;
Let the healing streams abound,
Make and keep me pure within.

CHARLES WESLEY

March 9

I trust in God's unfailing love for ever and ever. I will praise you forever for what you have done; in your name I will hope, for your name is good. PSALM 52:8-9

Come, my Light, and illumine my darkness.
Come, my Life and revive me from death.
Come, my Physician, and heal my wounds.
Come, Flame of divine love, and burn up the thorns of my
sins, kindling my heart with the flame of your love.
Come, my King, sit upon the throne of my heart and
reign there.
For thou alone art my King and my Lord.

DIMITRI OF ROSTOV

God answers sharp and sudden
on some prayers,
And thrusts the thing we have
prayed for in our face,
A gauntlet with a gift in't.

ELIZABETH BARRETT BROWNING

March 10

The fool says in his heart, "There is no God." They are corrupt, and their ways are vile; there is no one who does good. PSALM 53:1

Lord, why should I doubt any more, when you have given me such assured pledges of your love? First, you are my Creator, I your creature, you my Master, I your servant. But hence arises not my comfort: you are my Father, I your child. "You shall be my sons and daughters," says the Lord Almighty. Christ is my brother: "I ascend to my Father and your Father, to my God and your God"; but, lest this should not be enough, "your maker is your husband." Nay, more, I am a member of his body, he my head. Such privileges—had not the Word of truth made them known, who or where is the man that dared in his heart to have presumed to have thought it? So wonderful are these thoughts that my spirit fails in me at their consideration.

ANNE BRADSTREET

Spread out your petition before God, and then say, "Thy will, not mine, be done." The sweetest lesson I have learned in God's school is to let the Lord choose for me.

DWIGHT L. MOODY

March 11

Save me, O God, by your name; vindicate me by your might.
Hear my prayer, O God; listen to the words of my mouth.
PSALM 54:1-2

O God almighty, who made Heaven and earth and sea and all that is therein, help me, have mercy upon me, wash away my sins, save me in this world and in the world to come, through our Lord and Savior Jesus Christ, through whom is the glory and the power for ever and ever. Amen.

OXYRHYNCHUS PAPYRUS

Just when I need Him, He is my all,
Answering when upon Him I call;
Tenderly watching lest I should fall.

WILLIAM POOLE

March 12

But I call to God, and the LORD saves me. Evening, morning and noon I cry out in distress, and he hears my voice. PSALM 55:16-17

O my God, how does it happen in this poor old world that you are so great and yet nobody finds you, that you call so loudly and yet nobody hears you, that you are so near and yet nobody feels you, that you give yourself to everybody and yet nobody knows your name? Men flee from you and say they cannot find you; they turn their backs and say they cannot see you; they stop their ears and say they cannot hear you.

HANS DENCK

How those holy men of old could storm the battlements above! When there was no way to look but up, they lifted up their eyes to God who made the hills, with unshakeable confidence.

HERBERT LOCKYER

March 13

When I am afraid, I will trust in you. In God, whose word I praise, in God I trust; I will not be afraid. What can mortal man do to me? PSALM 56:3-4

O Lord, who has mercy upon all, take away from me my sins, and mercifully kindle in me the fire of your Holy Spirit. Take away from me the heart of stone, and give me a heart of flesh, a heart to love and adore you, a heart to delight in you, to follow and to enjoy you, for Christ's sake.

AMBROSE

The fewer words, the better prayer.

MARTIN LUTHER

March 14

I will praise you, O Lord, among the nations; I will sing of you among the peoples. For great is your love, reaching to the heavens; your faithfulness reaches to the skies. PSALM 57:9-10

O you who through the light of nature has aroused in us a longing for the light of grace, so that we may be raised in the light of your majesty, to you, I give thanks, Creator and Lord, that you allow me to rejoice in your works. Praise the Lord you heavenly harmonies, and you who know the revealed harmonies. For from him, through him and in him, all is, which is perceptible as well as spiritual; that which we know and that which we do not know, for there is still much to learn.

JOHANN KEPLER

Or what man is there among you who, if his son asks for bread, will give him a stone? Or if he asks for a fish, will he give him a serpent? If you then, being evil, know how to give good gifts to your children, how much more will your Father who is in heaven give good things to those who ask Him!

MATTHEW 7:9-11, *NKJV*

March 15

The righteous will be glad when they are avenged. . . . Then men will say, "Surely the righteous still are rewarded; surely there is a God who judges the earth." PSALM 58:10-11

Lord, my heart is not large enough,
my memory is not good enough,
my will is not strong enough:
Take my heart and enlarge it,
Take my memory and give it quicker recall,
Take my will and make it strong
and make me conscious of thee
ever present,
ever accompanying.

GEORGE APPLETON

If your prayer is selfish, the answer will be something that will rebuke your selfishness. You may not recognize it as having come at all, but it is sure to be there.

WILLIAM TEMPLE

*M*arch 16

O my strength, I watch for you; you, O God, are my fortress, my loving God. PSALM 59:9-10

I arise today
Through a mighty strength:
  Christ to protect me today
  Against every poison,
  Against burning,
  Against drowning,
  Against deathly wounds,
  That I may receive abundant reward.

Christ with me, Christ before me,
Christ with me, Christ above,
Christ at my right, Christ at my left,
Christ in the fort, Christ in the chariot seat,
Christ on the poop deck,
Christ to every eye that sees me,
Christ in every ear that hears me,
That I may receive abundant reward.

I arise today through a mighty strength:
The strength of invocation of the Trinity.

Amen.

PATRICK OF IRELAND

Prayer is conversation with God.

CLEMENT OF ALEXANDRIA

March 17

You have shown your people desperate times; you have given us wine that makes us stagger. But for those who fear you, you have raised a banner to be unfurled against the bow. PSALM 60:3-4

O God! I bless you for the wondrous revelation of yourself in Christ crucified, the wisdom of God, and the power of God. I bless you, that while man's wisdom leaves him helpless in presence of the power of sin and death, Christ crucified proves that he is the wisdom of God by the mighty redemption he works as the power of God. And I bless you, that what he wrought and bestows as an almighty Saviour is revealed within us by the divine light of your own Holy Spirit.

ANDREW MURRAY

For we know not what we should pray for as we ought: but the Spirit itself maketh intercession for us with groanings which cannot be uttered.

ROMANS 8:26, *KJV*

*M*arch 18

Hear my cry, O God; listen to my prayer. From the ends of the earth I call to you, I call as my heart grows faint; lead me to the rock that is higher than I. PSALM 61:1-2

O God
Help me to face myself honestly
In the revealing mirror of Your Word.
The longer I am a wife
The more utterly convinced I am
That there is only one solution
To personal discontent:
The complete surrender of myself
To Your method, Your schedule
Your purpose, Your will.
If I am honestly willing to obey You
If I submit to Your Word
As my high standard
You will undertake the necessary surgery
To make me spiritually whole.
Surgery hurts, dear Lord—
No doubt about that.
But after the cutting comes healing
And You always send flowers!

RUTH HARMS CALKIN

Prayer is invading the impossible.

JACK W. HAYFORD

March 19

My soul finds rest in God alone; my salvation comes from him. He alone is my rock and my salvation; he is my fortress, I will never be shaken. PSALM 62:1-2

I pray to you, the God of my Lord Jesus Christ, the Father of glory. Give to me a spirit of wisdom and revelation in the knowledge of him. Enlighten the eyes of my understanding that I may know what is the hope of his calling, what are the riches of his glorious inheritance in the saints, and what is the exceeding greatness of his power for me because I believe. You put this power to work in Christ when you raised him from the dead and seated him at your right hand in the heavenly places.

EPHESIANS 1:16-20 (adapted)

Prayer is communion with God, usually comprising petition, adoration, praise, confession, and thanksgiving.

INTERNATIONAL STANDARD BIBLE ENCYCLOPEDIA

March 20

O God, you are my God, earnestly I seek you; my soul thirsts for you, my body longs for you, in a dry and weary land where there is no water. PSALM 63:1

Lord,
make me an instrument of your peace!
Where there is hatred,
let me show love;
where there is injury, pardon;
where there is doubt, faith;
where there is despair, hope;
where there is darkness, light;
and where there is sadness, joy.

FRANCIS OF ASSISI

The prime need of the church is not
men of money nor men of brains,
but men of prayer.

E. M. BOUNDS

March 21

Let the righteous rejoice in the LORD and take refuge in him;
let all the upright in heart praise him! PSALM 64:10

O God, I thank thee for all the creatures thou hast made,
so perfect in their kind—
great animals like the elephant and the rhinoceros,
humorous animals like the camel and the monkey,
friendly ones like the dog and the cat,
working ones like the horse and the ox,
timid ones like the squirrel and the rabbit,
majestic ones like the lion and the tiger,
for birds with their songs.
O Lord, give us such love for thy creation,
that love may cast out fear,
and all thy creatures see in man
their priest and friend,
through Jesus Christ our Lord.

GEORGE APPLETON

*He offered a prayer so deeply
devout that he seemed kneeling
and praying at the bottom of the sea.*

HERMAN MELVILLE, *Moby Dick*

March 22

Blessed are those you choose and bring near to live in your courts! We are filled with the good things of your house, of your holy temple. PSALM 65:4

Grant to us, O Lord, not to mind earthly things, but rather to love heavenly things, that whilst all things around us pass away, we even now may hold fast to those things which abide forever.

LEO THE GREAT

Away in foreign fields they wondered how
Their simple words had power—
At home the Christians, two or three, had met
To pray an hour.
Yes, we are always wondering, wondering how—
Because we do not see
Someone—perhaps unknown and far away—
On bended knee.

ANONYMOUS

March 23

Shout with joy to God, all the earth! Sing the glory of his name; make his praise glorious! PSALM 66:1-2

Almighty God, you have given us grace at this time with one accord to make our common supplication to you; and you have promised through your well beloved Son that when two or three are gathered together in his name you will be in the midst of them: Fulfill now, O Lord, our desires and petitions as may be best for us; granting us in this world knowledge of your truth and in the age to come life everlasting. Amen.

JOHN CHRYSOSTOM

O Lord, help me not to despise or oppose what I do not understand.

WILLIAM PENN

March 24

May God be gracious to us and bless us and make his face shine upon us, that your ways may be known on earth, your salvation among all nations. PSALM 67:1-2

I confess, Lord, with thanksgiving, that you have made me in your image, so that I can remember you, think of you, and love you.

But that image is so worn and blotted out by faults, and darkened by the smoke of sin, that it cannot do that for which it was made, unless you renew and refashion it.

Lord, I am not trying to make my way to your height, for my understanding is in no way equal to that, but I do desire to understand a little of your truth which my heart already believes and loves.

I do not seek to understand so that I can believe, but I believe so that I may understand; and what is more, I believe that unless I do believe, I shall not understand.

ANSELM OF CANTERBURY

Prayer requires more of the heart than of the tongue.

ADAM CLARKE

*M*arch 25

A father to the fatherless, a defender of widows, is God in his holy dwelling. God sets the lonely in families, he leads forth the prisoners with singing. PSALM 68:5-6

Father, you are not only mine,
but the Father of everyone who believes.
By this I grasp, finally, why
your Son taught us to say,
"Our Father who is in heaven," not
"My Father who is in heaven."

With freedom today I pray "our Father."
These two words loose my loneliness
and invade my isolation.
They unlock the door of time
and banish the barrier of space.

From the mountainside in Galilee
where he was asked, "Teach us to pray,"
through countless lives until mine today
a slender cord is stretching;
braided and spliced with the faith
of those who call you Father.

DANIEL PARTNER

Prayer is the spiritual gymnasium in
which we exercise and practice godliness.

V. L. CRAWFORD

March 26

Praise be to the Lord, to God our Savior, who daily bears our burdens. Our God is a God who saves; from the Sovereign LORD comes escape from death. PSALM 68:19-20

In me there is darkness,

But with you there is light;

I am lonely, but you do not leave me;

I am feeble in heart, but with you there is help;

I am restless, but with you there is peace.

In me there is bitterness, but with you there is patience;

I do not understand your ways,

But you know the way for me.

DIETRICH BONHOEFFER

Teach me, O God, not to torture myself,
not to make a martyr out of myself
through stifling reflection, but rather
teach me to breathe deeply in faith.

SØREN KIERKEGAARD

March 27

But I pray to you, O LORD, in the time of your favor; in your great love, O God, answer me with your sure salvation. Rescue me from the mire, do not let me sink; deliver me from those who hate me, from the deep waters. PSALM 69:13-14

God, of your goodness, give me yourself for you are sufficient for me. I cannot properly ask anything less, to be worthy of you. If I were to ask less, I should always be in want. In you alone do I have all.

JULIAN OF NORWICH

Sincerity is the prime requisite in every approach to the God who requires "truth in the inward parts" and who hates all hypocrisy, falsehood, and deceit.

GEOFFREY B. WILSON

March 28

The poor will see and be glad—you who seek God, may your hearts live! The LORD hears the needy and does not despise his captive people. PSALM 69:32-33

We thank you, Lord,
That of your tender grace,
In our distress
Thou hast not left us wholly comfortless.

We thank you, Lord,
That of your wondrous might,
Into our night
Thou hast sent down the glory of the Light.

We thank you, Lord,
That all your wondrous ways,
Through all your days,
Are wisdom, right, and ceaseless tenderness.

JOHN OXENHAM

Productive prayer requires earnestness, not eloquence.

ANONYMOUS

March 29

Yet I am poor and needy; come quickly to me, O God. You are my help and my deliverer; O LORD, do not delay. PSALM 70:5

Almighty, ever-gracious Father, since all my salvation depends upon my having truly understood your holy Word, therefore grant that my heart be set free from worldly things so that I may with all diligence and faith hear and apprehend your holy Word. Do this that I may thereby understand your gracious will and in all sincerity live according to the same, to your praise and glory, through our Lord Jesus Christ. Amen.

JOHN CALVIN

Rejoice evermore. Pray without ceasing. In every thing give thanks: for this is the will of God in Christ Jesus concerning you.

1 THESSALONIANS 5:16-18, *KJV*

March 30

In you, O LORD, I have taken refuge; let me never be put to shame. Rescue me and deliver me in your righteousness; turn your ear to me and save me. PSALM 71:1-2

Gracious God, giving our neighbors to us,
and us to them, and bidding us love
our neighbors as ourselves;
help us by loving to understand,
and by understanding to help,
and to have the grace to accept their help,
along the way to your Kingdom;
through Jesus Christ our Lord. Amen.

WILLIAM BOOTH

Not what we wish, but what we need,
Oh! let your grace supply,
The good unasked, in mercy grant;
The ill, though asked, deny.

JAMES MERRIK

March 31

Praise be to the LORD God, the God of Israel, who alone does marvelous deeds. Praise be to his glorious name forever; may the whole earth be filled with his glory. Amen and Amen. PSALM 72:18-19

You take the pen
  and the lines dance.
You take the flute,
  and the notes shimmer.
You take the brush, and the colors sing.
So all things have meaning and beauty in that space
    beyond time where you are.
How, then, can I hold back anything from you?

DAG HAMMARSKJÖLD, *God the Artist*

To you, O Son of God, Lord Jesus Christ, as you pray to the eternal Father, we pray, make us one in him. Lighten our personal distress and that of our society. Receive us into the fellowship of those who believe. Turn our hearts, O Christ, to everlasting truth and healing harmony.

PHILIP MELANCHTHON

April 1

Those who are far from you will perish; you destroy all who are unfaithful to you. But as for me, it is good to be near God. I have made the Sovereign LORD my refuge. PSALM 73:27-28

We pray to Thee, O Christ, to keep us under the spell of immortality. May we never again think and act as if Thou wert dead. Let us more and more come to know Thee as a living Lord who hath promised to them that believe: "Because I live, ye shall live also."

Help us to remember that we are praying to the Conqueror of Death, that we may no longer be afraid nor be dismayed by the world's problems and threats, since Thou hast overcome the world. In Thy strong name, we ask for Thy living presence and Thy victorious power. Amen.

PETER MARSHALL

I have been driven many times to my knees by the overwhelming conviction that I had nowhere else to go.

ABRAHAM LINCOLN

April 2

But you, O God, are my king from of old; you bring salvation upon the earth. It was you who split open the sea by your power; you broke the heads of the monster in the waters. PSALM 74:12-13

Who is a God like you, pardoning iniquity
and passing over the transgression
of the remnant of your possession?
You do not retain your anger forever because you delight
in steadfast love.
You will again have compassion upon me; you will tread
my iniquities under foot.
You will cast all my sins into the depths of the sea.

MICAH 7:18-19 (adapted)

Lord, if any have to die this day,
let it be me, for I am ready.

BILLY BRAY

April 3

No one from the east or the west or from the desert can exalt a man. But it is God who judges: He brings one down, he exalts another. PSALM 75:6-7

O Lord, the house of my soul is narrow; enlarge it that you may enter in. It is ruined, O repair it! It displeases your sight; I confess it, I know. But who shall cleanse it, or to whom shall I cry but unto you? Cleanse me from my secret faults, O Lord, and spare your servant from strange sins.

AUGUSTINE

Do I want to pray or only to think about my human problems? Do I want to pray or simply kneel there contemplating my sorrow? Do I want to direct my prayer towards God or let it direct itself towards me?

HUBERT VAN ZELLER

April 4

In Judah God is known; his name is great in Israel. . . . There he broke the flashing arrows, the shields and the swords, the weapons of war. PSALM 76:1, 3

Blessed Lord, through whose gift of the Holy Scriptures we learn of your mighty saving acts for mankind, help us so to hear, remember, and understand your Holy Word, that strengthened and sustained thereby, we may know in this temporal life the hope of eternity which you have given us in our Savior Jesus Christ, who lives and rules with you and the Holy Spirit now and ever. Amen.

DONALD J. SELBY

You art coming to a King,
Large petitions with you bring
For his grace and power are such
None can ever ask too much.

JOHN NEWTON

April 5

I cried out to God for help; I cried out to God to hear me. When I was in distress, I sought the Lord. PSALM 77:1-2

We understand, Father, that our temptations are common to man, and that You are faithful and will not suffer us to be tempted above what we are able to bear, but will with the temptation make a way to escape, so that we may be able to bear it. Help us to see the way of escape and take it. We pray for Your strength. Give us daily strength for daily needs.

JO PETTY

It is quite useless knocking at the door of heaven for earthly comfort. It's not the sort of comfort they supply there.

C. S. LEWIS

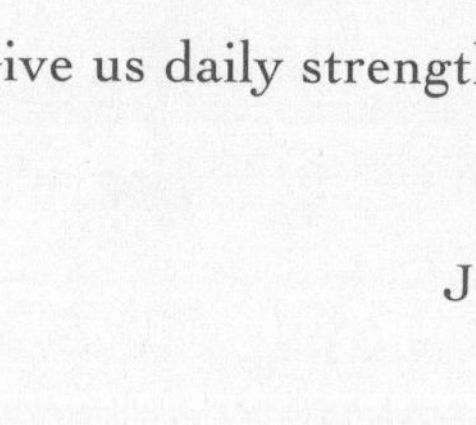

April 6

We will tell the next generation the praiseworthy deeds of the LORD, his power, and the wonders he has done. PSALM 78:4

Lord God, you have placed me in your church. You know how unsuitable I am. Were it not for your guidance I would long since have brought everything to destruction. I wish to give my heart and mouth to your service. I desire to teach your people, and long to be taught your work. Use me as your workman, dear Lord. Do not forsake me; for if I am alone I shall bring all to nought. Amen.

MARTIN LUTHER

We ought not to tolerate for a minute the ghastly and grievous thought that God will not answer prayer. History, as manifested in Christ Jesus, demands it.

CHARLES H. SPURGEON

April 7

Their hearts were not loyal to him, they were not faithful to his covenant. Yet he was merciful; he forgave their iniquities and did not destroy them. PSALM 78:37-38

O Lord, prepare my heart, I beseech you, to reverence you, to adore you, to love you; to hate, for love of you, all my sins and imperfections, short-comings, whatever in me displeases you; and to love all which you love, and whom you love. Give me, Lord, fervour of love, shame for my unthankfulness, sorrow for my sins, longing for your grace, and to be wholly united with you. Let my very coldness call for the glow of your love; let my emptiness and dryness, like a barren and thirsty land, thirst for you, call on you to come into my soul, who refreshes those who are weary. Let my heart ache to you and for you, who stills the aching of the heart. Let my mute longings praise you, crave you, who satisfies the empty soul that waits on you.

E. B. PUSEY

Our ordinary views of prayer are not found in the New Testament. We look upon prayer as a means of getting things for ourselves; The Bible idea of prayer is that we may get to know God Himself.

OSWALD CHAMBERS

April 8

But they put God to the test and rebelled against the Most High; they did not keep his statutes. . . . When God heard them, he was very angry; he rejected Israel completely. PSALM 78:56, 59

Dear Master, in whose life I see
All that I would, but fail, to be,
Let your clear light forever shine,
To shame and guide this life of mine.

Though what I dream and what I do
In all my days are often two,
Help me, oppressed by things undone,
O you whose deeds and dreams were one.

JOHN HUNTER

Prayer serves as an edge and border to preserve the web of life from unraveling.

ROBERT HALL

April 9

He chose David his servant . . . to be the shepherd of his people Jacob, of Israel his inheritance. And David shepherded them with integrity of heart; with skillful hands he led them. PSALM 78:70-72

O Lord, you have examined my heart and know everything about me. . . . You chart the path ahead of me, and tell me where to stop and rest. Every moment, you know where I am. You know what I am going to say before I even say it. . . .

This is too glorious, too wonderful to believe! I can never be lost to your Spirit! I can never get away from my God! If I go up to heaven, you are there; if I go down to the place of the dead, you are there. If I ride the morning winds to the farthest oceans, even there your hand will guide me, your strength will support me. . . .

Search me, O God, and know my heart; test my thoughts. Point out anything you find in me that makes you sad, and lead me along the path of everlasting life.

PSALM 139:1-10, 23-24, *TLB*

The deepest wishes of the heart find expression in secret prayer.

GEORGE E. REES

April 10

Help us, O God our Savior, for the glory of your name; deliver us and forgive our sins for your name's sake. PSALM 79:9

Lord Jesus Christ,

You were poor and in distress,

a captive and forsaken as I am.

You know all man's troubles;

You abide with me

when all men fail me;

You remember and seek me;

It is your will that I should know you and turn to you.

Lord I hear your call and follow;

Help me.

DIETRICH BONHOEFFER

Trouble and prayer are closely related to each other. Prayer is of great value to trouble. Trouble often drives men to God in prayer, while prayer is but the voice of men in trouble.

E. M. BOUNDS

April 11

Restore us, O LORD God Almighty; make your face shine upon us, that we may be saved. PSALM 80:19

Lord my God, teach me, I beseech you, to ask you aright for the right blessings. Steer you the vessel of my life toward yourself, you tranquil haven of all storm-tossed souls. Show me the course wherein I should go. Renew a willing spirit within me. Let your Spirit curb my wayward senses, and guide and enable me unto that which is my true good, to keep your laws, and in all my works evermore to rejoice in your glorious and gladdening presence. For yours is the glory and praise from all your saints for ever and ever. Amen.

BASIL THE GREAT

Teach us to pray that we may cause
The enemy to flee,
That we his evil power may bind,
His prisoners to free.

WATCHMAN NEE

April 12

Sing for joy to God our strength; shout aloud to the God of Jacob! Begin the music, strike the tambourine, play the melodious harp and lyre. PSALM 81:1-2

I thank you for the house in which I live,
For the gray roof on which the raindrops slant;
I thank you for a garden and the slim young shoots
  That mark the old-fashioned things I plant.

I thank you for a daily task to do,
  For books that are my ships with golden wings.
For mighty gifts let others offer praise
  Lord, I am thanking you for little things.

ANONYMOUS

Fear of trouble, present and future, often blinds us to the numerous small blessings we enjoy, silencing our prayers of praise and thanksgiving.

ANONYMOUS

April 13

God presides in the great assembly; he gives judgment among the "gods." PSALM 82:1

Almighty God, I cannot possibly aspire vigorously toward you or have any clear perception of spiritual things without the assistance of your grace. Only the same almighty power that raised Jesus Christ from the dead can raise this soul of mine from the death of sin to a life of holiness. I do not question that power and I believe that these desires proceed from you. Give me faith and patience. Help me to wait for your enabling grace without discouragement, remembering the words of our Saviour, that men ought always to pray and not to faint. Amen.

SUSANNA WESLEY

Sometimes . . . God answers our prayers in the way our parents do, who reply to the pleas of their children with "Not just now" or "I'll have to think about that for a little while."

ROY M. PEARSON

April 14

Let them [your enemies] know that you, whose name is the LORD—that you alone are the Most High over all the earth.
PSALM 83:18

O God almighty, who cleansed the lips of the prophet Isaiah with a burning coal: Cleanse my heart and my lips: so grant to cleanse me, of your mercy, that I may be able to proclaim worthily your holy gospel: through Jesus Christ our Lord. Amen.

AMBROSE

O thou, by whom we come to God,
The Life, the Truth, the Way,
The path of prayer Thyself hast trod—
Lord teach us how to pray.

JAMES MONTGOMERY

April 15

How lovely is your dwelling place, O LORD Almighty! My soul yearns, even faints, for the courts of the LORD; my heart and my flesh cry out for the living God. PSALM 84:1-2

God, why am I so often defeated?
Why am I so full of dread and anxiety?
Why am I so lamentably weak—
So perilously susceptible to temptation?
Why am I often inhospitable
So intolerant of the needs of others?
Why am I so undisciplined
So restless and dissatisfied?
Why do I protest so violently?
Above all, God
Why do I so frequently lose
The sense of Your shining Presence?
God, why?
Why?
Because you pray so little.

RUTH HARMS CALKIN

And this is the boldness we have in him, that if we ask anything according to his will, he hears us.

1 JOHN 5:14, *NRSV*

April 16

Will you not revive us again, that your people may rejoice in you? Show us your unfailing love, O LORD, and grant us your salvation. PSALM 85:6-7

O God, sometimes I am tempted because cheating seems to be the easiest and quickest way to get what I want.
Forgive me for the times
I have told lies, kept miscounted change,
or misled my friends. Grant that I shall come to
love truth and hate lies—especially my own.
May all my words and deeds be free of sham and make-believe.

In the classroom, in games
with my friends, as I trade at the store, help me
to be completely trustworthy.

Day by day may I live
in such close friendship with you that there will be
nothing in my life
which is counterfeit or insincere. Amen.

WALTER L. COOK

You do not have because you do not ask.

JAMES 4:2, *NRSV*

April 17

Hear, O LORD, and answer me, for I am poor and needy. Guard my life, for I am devoted to you. You are my God; save your servant who trusts in you. PSALM 86:1-2

O Lord God, ruler of the heaven and of the earth, creator of things visible and invisible, giver of eternal life, and consoler of the sorrowful, make me to stand firm in confession of your name that as with your aid I have begun the good fight, so with your aid I may be deemed worthy to gain the victory, lest the adversary spitefully mock at me saying: "Where is now her God in whom she trusted?"

But let the angel of your light come and restore to me the light which the darkness of my cell has taken from me; and let the right hand of your majesty scatter the phantom hosts of the ancient enemy. For we know, O Lord, that your mercy will aid us in all temptations.

MARGARET OF ANTIOCH

Ask and you will receive,
so that your joy may be complete.

JOHN 16:24, *NRSV*

April 18

Indeed, of Zion it will be said, "This one and that one were born in her, and the Most High himself will establish her." The LORD will write in the register of the peoples: "This one was born in Zion." PSALM 87:5-6

Divine and gracious Savior, I ask You to take full possession of my heart and life. Let me know that each moment of today You are with me, protecting me with Your grace and preserving me through Your love. Help me to overcome the discouragements that are coming to me and ease my pain. Remove from my heart all self-pity, take all resentment from my mind, and let me live trustingly one day at a time as I lean on You. Give me a hopeful outlook for today, and remove all irritation from the coming night. Let my patience increase as I consider Your mercies, precious Savior. Amen.

MY PRAYER BOOK

In the war upon the powers of darkness, prayer is the primary and mightiest weapon, both in aggressive war upon them and their works; in the deliverance of men from their power; and against them as an hierarchy of powers opposed to Christ and His Church.

JESSIE PENN-LEWIS

April 19

O LORD, the God who saves me, day and night I cry out before you. May my prayer come before you; turn your ear to my cry.
PSALM 88:1-2

O Lord, our Heavenly Father, who orderest all things for our eternal good, mercifully enlighten our minds, and give us a firm and abiding trust in Thy love and care. Silence our murmurings, quiet our fears, and dispel our doubts, that rising above our afflictions and our anxieties, we may rest on Thee, the Rock of everlasting strength.

NEW CHURCH BOOK OF WORSHIP

Pray in the Spirit at all times in every prayer and supplication. To that end keep alert and always persevere.

EPHESIANS 6:18, *NRSV*

April 20

I will sing of the LORD's great love forever; with my mouth I will make your faithfulness known through all generations. PSALM 89:1

Lord, you have taken the fear of death away from us. The end of our life here you have made the beginning of the true life. For a little while you will let our bodies rest in sleep, and then with the last trumpet you will wake them from their sleep.

You gave this earth of ours to keep for you, which you shaped with your own hands; and you will take it back again, and from a mortal, formless lump transform it into a thing of immortal beauty.

To free us from sin and from the curse laid upon us, you took both sin and the curse upon yourself.

If out of the weakness of human nature I have fallen and sinned in word or deed or thought, forgive it me; for you have power to forgive sins on earth. When I am divested of my body, may I stand before you with my soul unspotted: receive it, blameless and faultless, with your own hands.

MACRINA

Men ought always to pray, and not to faint.

LUKE 18:1, *KJV*

April 21

Righteousness and justice are the foundation of your throne; love and faithfulness go before you. Blessed are those who have learned to acclaim you, who walk in the light of your presence, O LORD. PSALM 89:14-15

God, your name is Father.
The Son of your love
  made known this name.
Please, keep me in its meaning.

Father, your name is Holy.
The people of today
  don't know this name.
Please, show them its holiness.

Father, your children are holy.
The offspring of your life
  who bear your name.
Please, hold them in its love.

DANIEL PARTNER

Prayer is the language of a man burdened with a sense of need.

E. M. BOUNDS

April 22

How long, O LORD? Will you hide yourself forever? How long will your wrath burn like fire? Remember how fleeting is my life. For what futility you have created all men! PSALM 89:46-47

I am still not sure, God, what I want to do with my life. You see, I think there ought to be more to life than working. I'd like to have a family and spend some time with them. I want to be part of my children's lives while they're growing up. But I'm no slouch God. I work hard. I want to be good at what I do. But I want to be good at being a person first of all.

BILLINGS HODGETT

Work as if you were to live one hundred years; pray as if you were to die tomorrow.

BENJAMIN FRANKLIN

April 23

He who dwells in the shelter of the Most High will rest in the shadow of the Almighty. I will say of the LORD, "He is my refuge and my fortress, my God, in whom I trust." PSALM 91:1-2

I arise today
Through a mighty strength,
Strong virtue of invocation of the Trinity:
  Through belief in the Threeness,
  Through the confession of the Oneness
  Of the Creator of creation.
I arise today
Through a mighty strength:
  The strength of the Incarnation of Christ,
  The strength of Christ in his Baptisms,
  The strength of his Crucifixion and his Burial,
  The strength of his Resurrection and his Ascension,
  The strength of his Coming on Judgment Day.

PATRICK OF IRELAND

He who prays as he ought, will endeavor to live as he prays.

JOHN OWEN

April 24

It is good to praise the LORD and make music to your name, O Most High, to proclaim your love in the morning and your faithfulness at night. PSALM 92:1-2

O Lord, you are my God;
I will exalt you, I will praise your name;
for you have done wonderful things,
  plans formed of old, faithful and sure. . . .
For you have been a refuge to the poor,
  a refuge to the needy in their distress,
  a shelter from the rainstorm and a shade from the heat.
When the blast of the ruthless was like a winter rainstorm,
  the noise of aliens like heat in a dry place,
you subdued the heat with the shade of clouds;
  the song of the ruthless was stilled.

ISAIAH 25:1, 4-5, *NRSV*

Your Father knows what you need before you ask him.

MATTHEW 6:8, *NRSV*

April 25

Blessed is the man you discipline, O LORD, the man you teach from your law; you grant him relief from days of trouble, till a pit is dug for the wicked. PSALM 94:12-13

Holy Lord Jesus! Look upon your church, look upon our hearts. And wherever you see that there is not love like yours, oh, make haste and deliver your saints from all that is still selfish and unloving! Teach them to yield that self, which cannot love, to the accursed cross, to await the fate it deserves. Teach us to believe that we can love, because the Holy Spirit has been given us. Teach us to begin to love and serve, to sacrifice self and live for others, that love in action may learn its power, may be increased and perfected. Oh, teach us to believe that because you live in us, your love is in us too, and we can love as you do. Lord Jesus, you Love of God! your own Spirit is within us; oh, let him break through, and fill our whole life with love! Amen.

ANDREW MURRAY

Call to me and I will answer you, and will tell you great and hidden things that you have not known.

JEREMIAH 33:3, *NRSV*

April 26

Come, let us bow down in worship, let us kneel before the LORD our Maker; for he is our God and we are the people of his pasture, the flock under his care. PSALM 95:6-7

O Lord: Give to your people, we pray you, the spirit of truth and peace, that they may know you with all their minds; and that, following with all their hearts after those things which are pleasing to you, they ever may possess the gifts of your bountiful goodness.

LEO THE GREAT

Each of us is a person, with individual masks, scars, celebrations, moments of rejecting God, and experiences of conversion. Our prayers must spring from the indigenous soil of our own personal confrontation with the Spirit of God in our lives.

MALCOLM BOYD

April 27

Sing to the LORD a new song, for he has done marvelous things; his right hand and his holy arm have worked salvation for him.
PSALM 98:1

Teach us, good Lord, to serve You as You deserve; to give and not to count the cost; to fight and not to heed the wounds; to toil and not to ask for rest; to labour and not to ask for any reward save knowing that we do Your will. Through Jesus Christ our Lord.

IGNATIUS OF LOYOLA

Heaven is never deaf but when man's heart is dumb.

FRANCIS QUARLES

April 28

Exalt the LORD our God and worship at his holy mountain, for the LORD our God is holy. PSALM 99:9

Loving Father God, my heart is filled upon rethinking the greatness of your love and the completeness of your plan. I want to please you, but how often my flesh folds under the pressure of temptation.

I thank you that you know my frame, and you remember I am dust. And I thank you for the abundance of grace and the gift of your righteousness which you have made available to me through the cross of your Son.

Thank you for receiving me, gracious Lord. Amen.

JACK W. HAYFORD

When my children do wrong, I ache to hear their stumbling requests for forgiveness. I'm sure our heavenly Father aches even more deeply to hear from us.

AN UNKNOWN FATHER

April 29

For the LORD is good and his love endures forever; his faithfulness continues through all generations. PSALM 100:5

Help me, O God, to be a good and a true friend,
To be always loyal, and never to let my friends down;
Never to talk about them behind their backs in a way in which I would not do before their faces;
Never to betray a confidence or talk about the things about which I ought to be silent;
Always to be ready to share everything I have;
To be as true to my friends as I would wish them to be to me.
This I ask for the sake of him who is the greatest and truest of all friends. For Jesus' sake, amen.

WILLIAM BARCLAY

To pray together, in whatever tongue or ritual, is the most tender brotherhood of hope and sympathy that man can contract in this life.

ANNE GERMAINE DE STAËL

April 30

I will sing of your love and justice; to you, O LORD, I will sing praise. I will be careful to lead a blameless life—when will you come to me? PSALM 101:1-2

Almighty God, in this hour of quiet I seek communion with Thee. From the fret and fever of the day's business, from the world's discordant noises, from the praise and blame of men, from the confused thoughts and vain imaginations of my own heart, I would now turn aside and seek the quietness of Thy presence. All day long have I toiled and striven; but now, in stillness of heart and in the clear light of Thine eternity, I would ponder the pattern my life has been weaving.

JOHN BAILLIE

O Lord, forgive what I have been,
sanctify what I am,
and order what I shall be.

ANONYMOUS

M a y 1

Hear my prayer, O LORD; let my cry for help come to you. Do not hide your face from me when I am in distress. Turn your ear to me; when I call, answer me quickly. PSALM 102:1-2

Grant us, O Lord, the blessing of those whose minds are stayed on you, so that we may be kept in perfect peace: a peace which cannot be broken. Let not our minds rest upon any creature, but only in the Creator; not upon goods, things, houses, lands, inventions of vanities or foolish fashions, lest, our peace being broken, we become cross and brittle and given over to envy. From all such deliver us, O God, and grant us your peace.

GEORGE FOX

No matter what may be the test,
God will take care of you;
Lean weary one, upon His breast,
God will take care of you.

C. D. MARTIN

May 2

Praise the LORD, O my soul; all my inmost being, praise his holy name. Praise the LORD, O my soul, and forget not all his benefits. PSALM 103:1-2

You are as faultless as the heaven is high, Almighty God.
How can I comprehend you?
Your mind is fathomless.
How can I try to understand it?
I have this dilemma: Love inflames my heart and
constrains me to speak.
Yet if I try to tell of your greatness, what shall I say?
How can I fathom your mysteries and your purposes?
How can I probe the limits of the Almighty?
You are far beyond comprehension for this finite mind of mine.
So it is with childlike simplicity that I try to worship and
adore you,
and I merely whisper, *Father, with all my heart I love you.*

ROBERT C. SAVAGE

Prayer moves the hand that moves the world.

JOHN AIKMAN WALLACE

May 3

Praise the LORD, O my soul. O LORD my God, you are very great; you are clothed with splendor and majesty. PSALM 104:1

Come and help us, Lord Jesus. A vision of your face will brighten us; but to feel your Spirit touching us will make us vigorous. Oh! for the leaping and walking of the man born lame. May we today dance with holy joy like David before the ark of God. May a holy exhilaration take possession of every part of us; may we be glad in the Lord; may our mouth be filled with laughter, and our tongue with singing, "for the Lord hath done great things for us whereof we are glad."

CHARLES H. SPURGEON

I don't know of a single foreign product that enters this country untaxed except the answer to prayer.

MARK TWAIN

May 4

How many are your works, O LORD! In wisdom you made them all; the earth is full of your creatures. PSALM 104:24

Lord God, heavenly Father, we know that we are dear children of yours and that you are our beloved Father, not because we deserve it, nor ever could merit it, but because our dear Lord, your only-begotten Son, Jesus Christ, wills to be our brother, and of his own accord offers and makes this blessing known to us. Since we may consider ourselves his brothers and sisters and he regards us as such, you will permit us to become and remain your children for ever. Amen.

MARTIN LUTHER

Prayer is a rising up and a drawing near to God in mind and in heart, and in spirit.

ALEXANDER WHYTE

M a y 5

Look to the LORD and his strength; seek his face always. Remember the wonders he has done, his miracles, and the judgments he pronounced. PSALM 105:4-5

Lord, make me aware of . . .
Sunlight filtering through the trees
The song of the March wind
Crickets at twilight
Water splashing in soapsuds
Yellow daffodils in a crystal vase
Delicate china on pink mats
The aroma of fresh coffee
The first day of spring
Green peas and red beets
A dewdrop on a rose
Freckles on a grinning face
The longing in my husband's eyes.

RUTH HARMS CALKIN

Prayer is the golden key that opens heaven.

THOMAS WATSON

May 6

He sent a man before them—Joseph, sold as a slave. They bruised his feet with shackles, his neck was put in irons, till what he foretold came to pass, till the word of the LORD proved him true. PSALM 105:17-19

O Lord our God, refresh me with quiet sleep, when I am wearied with the day's labor; that being assisted with the help which my weakness needs, I may be devoted to you both in body and mind; through Jesus Christ our Lord.

Be present, O Lord, to my prayers, and protect me by day and night that in all successive changes of times I may ever be strengthened by your unchangeableness; through Jesus Christ our Lord.

THE LEONINE SACRAMENTARY (adapted)

Every chain that spirits wear
Crumbles in the breath of prayer.

JOHN GREENLEAF WHITTIER

May 7

He [the LORD] brought out Israel, laden with silver and gold, and from among their tribes no one faltered. PSALM 105:37

O God, whose eternal providence has embarked our soul in our bodies, not to expect any port of anchorage on the sea of this world, to steer directly through it to your glorious kingdom, preserve us from the dangers that on all sides assault us, and keep our affections still fitly disposed to receive your holy inspirations, that being carried strongly forward by your Holy Spirit we may happily arrive at last in the haven of eternal salvation, through our Lord Jesus Christ.

JOHN WESLEY

Now I am past all comforts here,
but prayers.

WILLIAM SHAKESPEARE, *Henry VIII*

May 8

Praise the LORD. Give thanks to the LORD, for he is good; his love endures forever. PSALM 106:1

O Lord Jesus Christ, who embraces children with the arms of your mercy, and makes them living members of your Church; give them grace, we pray, to stand fast in your faith, to obey your word, and to abide in your love; that, being made strong by your Holy Spirit, they may resist temptation and overcome evil, and may rejoice in the life that now is, and dwell with you in the life that is to come; through your merits, O merciful Saviour, who with the Father and Holy Ghost lives and reigns one God, world without end. Amen.

THE BOOK OF COMMON PRAYER

In the midst of Peter's arrest and Herod's plot to execute him, Luke injects the very important word, "but." Herod's plan was to execute him, but the believers were praying for Peter's safety.

LIFE APPLICATION BIBLE on Acts 12:5

May 9

They [the Israelites] forgot the God who saved them, who had done great things in Egypt . . . . So he said he would destroy them. PSALM 106:21, 23

Lord Jesus, we come to Thee now as little children. Dress us again in clean pinafores; make us tidy once more with the tidiness of true remorse and confession. O, wash our hearts, that they may be clean again.

Make us to know the strengthening joys of the Spirit, and the newness of life which only Thou canst give. Amen.

PETER MARSHALL

Pray, always pray; when sickness
wastes thy frame,
Prayer brings the healing power of
Jesus' name.

A. B. SIMPSON

May 10

Save us, O LORD our God, and gather us from the nations, that we may give thanks to your holy name and glory in your praise.
PSALM 106:47

Help me, O Lord, to make a true use of all disappointments and calamities in this life, in such a way that they may unite my heart more closely with you. Cause them to separate my affections from worldly things and inspire my soul with more vigor in the pursuit of true happiness.

SUSANNA WESLEY

Whenever you pray, go into your room and shut the door and pray to your Father who is in secret; and your Father who sees in secret will reward you.

MATTHEW 6:6, *NRSV*

May 11

Give thanks to the LORD, for he is good; his love endures forever. PSALM 107:1

From all eternity, O Jesus Christ, you have been our Lord and our God: so did the Father will it. Yet in this, the last of all periods of time, you also had your birth; you were born of a virgin, of one that had no knowledge of any man. To redeem us from the Law, you submitted to the Law. Your purpose was to free us from the slavery to which our corruption had reduced us and to confer upon us the rank of sons.

Deliver us, now, Lord, from all that is vain; fulfill your promise and free us from sin and shame; fill our hearts with your Holy Spirit and enable us to say: "Abba, Father."

A SYRIAC LITURGY (adapted)

They who have steeped their soul in prayer
Can every anguish calmly bear.

RICHARD M. MILNES

May 12

Be exalted, O God, above the heavens, and let your glory be over all the earth. Save us and help us with your right hand, that those you love may be delivered. PSALM 108:5-6

O God, we have known and believed the love which Thou hast for us. May we, by dwelling in love, dwell in Thee and Thou in us. May we learn to love Thee Whom we have not seen, by loving our brethren whom we have seen. Teach us, O heavenly Father, the love wherewith Thou hast loved us; fashion us, O blessed Lord, after Thine own example of love; shed abroad, O Thou Holy Spirit of Love, the love of God and man in our hearts. Amen.

HENRY ALFORD

Pray till you pray.

D.M. MCINTYRE

May 13

But you, O Sovereign LORD, deal well with me for your name's sake; out of the goodness of your love, deliver me. For I am poor and needy, and my heart is wounded within me. PSALM 109:21-22

O Christ, who camest not to be ministered unto but to minister, have mercy upon all who labour faithfully to serve the common good. O Christ, who didst feed the hungry multitude with loaves and fishes, have mercy upon all who labour to earn their daily bread. O Christ, who didst call unto Thyself all them that labour and are heavy laden, have mercy upon all whose work is beyond their strength. And to Thee, with the Father and the Holy Spirit, be all the glory and the praise. Amen.

JOHN BAILLIE

For everything God made is good,
and we may eat it gladly if we are
thankful for it, and if we ask
God to bless it, for it is made good
by the Word of God and prayer.

1 TIMOTHY 4:4-5, *TLB*

May 14

The LORD says to my Lord: "Sit at my right hand until I make your enemies a footstool for your feet." PSALM 110:1

Gracious God, Heavenly Father, I must confess that I am sometimes upset by the many changes that come in life. I find it difficult to make the necessary adjustments. I do not ask to understand, but help me, I pray You, always to realize that no matter what happens to me, and what changes must be made, You still love me and will make every experience work together for my good.

Give me the faith to trust Your promise, "My grace is sufficient for you." In mercy forgive all grumbling and complaining of which I have been guilty in the past. Teach me to follow the example of Jesus, my Savior and Lord, who in trial and tribulation said, "Not My will, but Thine, be done." In that spirit I shall be able to meet whatever life has in store for me. For Jesus' sake, amen.

MY PRAYER BOOK

By prayer, the ability is secured to feel the law of love, to speak according to the law of love, and to do everything in harmony with the law of love.

E. M. BOUNDS

*M*ay 15

Praise the LORD. I will extol the LORD with all my heart in the council of the upright and in the assembly. PSALM 111:1

Fill thou my life, O Lord my God,
In ev'ry part with praise,
That my whole being may proclaim
Thy being and Thy ways.
Not for the lip of praise alone,
Nor e'en the praising heart,
I ask, but for a life made up
Of praise in every part:
Praise in the common things of life,
Its goings out and in;
Praise in each duty and each deed,
However small and mean.
Fill every part of me with praise;
Let all my being speak
Of Thee and of Thy love,
O Lord, Poor though I be
and weak.
So shall no part of day nor night
From sacredness be free,
But all my life, in every step,
Be fellowship with Thee.

HORATIUS BONAR

God receives little thanks,
even for his greatest gifts.

ANONYMOUS

*M*ay 16

Praise the LORD. Blessed is the man who fears the LORD, who finds great delight in his commands. PSALM 112:1

There is one thing I ask of the LORD, the thing I seek most of all: to live in the house of the LORD all the days of my life, to behold the beauty of the LORD, and to inquire in his temple.

For he will hide me in his shelter in the day of trouble; he will conceal me under the cover of his tent; he will set me high on a rock.

Now my head is lifted up above my enemies, and I will offer in his tent sacrifices with shouts of joy; I will sing and make melody to the LORD.

PSALM 27:4-6 (adapted)

Without the incense of heartfelt prayer,
even the greatest of cathedrals is dead.

ANONYMOUS

*M*ay 17

Who is like the LORD our God, the One who sits enthroned on high, who stoops down to look on the heavens and the earth? He raises the poor from the dust and lifts the needy from the ash heap. PSALM 113:5-7

Lord, who has mercy upon all, take away from me my sins, and mercifully kindle in me the fire of your Holy Spirit. Take away from me the heart of stone, and give me a heart of flesh, a heart to love and adore you, a heart to delight in you, to follow and to enjoy you. For Christ's sake, amen.

AMBROSE

And whenever you pray, do not be like the hypocrites; for they love to stand and pray in the synagogues and at the street corners, so that they may be seen by others.

MATTHEW 6:5, *NRSV*

May 18

Not to us, O LORD, not to us but to your name be the glory, because of your love and faithfulness. PSALM 115:1

Blessed Lord! I see why my prayer has not been more believing and prevailing. I was more occupied with my speaking to you than your speaking to me. I did not understand that the secret of faith is this: there can be only so much faith as there is of the Living Word dwelling in the soul.

And your Word had taught me so clearly: Let every man be swift to hear, slow to speak; let not your heart be hasty to utter anything before God.

Lord, teach me that it is only with your Word taken up into my life that my words can be taken into your heart; that your work, if it is a living power within me, will be a living power with you; what your mouth has spoken your hand will perform.

ANDREW MURRAY

Do not have as your motive the desire to be known as a praying man. Get an inner chamber in which to pray where no one knows you are praying, shut the door, and talk to God in secret.

OSWALD CHAMBERS

May 19

I love the LORD, for he heard my voice; he heard my cry for mercy. Because he turned his ear to me, I will call on him as long as I live. PSALM 116:1-2

O eternal and most glorious God . . . You who assure us that precious in your sight is the death of your saints, enable us in life and death, seriously to consider the value, the price of a soul. It is precious, O Lord, because your image is stamped and imprinted upon it; precious, because the blood of your Son was paid for it; precious, because your blessed Spirit, the Holy Ghost works upon it, and tests it, by his various fires; and precious, because it is entered into your revenue and made a part of your treasure.

JOHN DONNE

The wings of prayer carry high and far.

ANONYMOUS

May 20

Praise the LORD, all you nations; extol him, all you peoples. For great is his love toward us. PSALM 117:1-2

Jesus, my own kind of love is flawed and conditional. I think I'd like to love the way you do—but I know you'll have to give it to me because I can't manufacture it. Please fill me with your Spirit, and soften my heart toward others. When someone treats me badly, whisper to me again, "Father forgive them, for they know not what they do."

PAT BOONE

Our prayers must mean something to us if they are to mean anything to God.

MALTBIE D. BABCOCK

May 21

Give thanks to the LORD, for he is good; his love endures forever. PSALM 118:1

I arise today
Through a mighty strength:
    God's power to guide me,
    God's might to uphold me,
    God's wisdom to teach me,
    God's eyes to watch over me,
    God's ear to hear me,
    God's Word to give me speech,
    God's hand to guard me,
    God's way to lie before me,
    God's shield to shelter me,
    God's host to secure me:
        Against the snares of devils,
        Against the seductions of vices,
        Against the lusts of nature,
        Against everyone who shall wish me ill,
        Whether far or near, many or few.

PATRICK OF IRELAND

A person must recognize his need for God before he can request divine aid and give God due thanks.

ANONYMOUS

May 22

You are my God, and I will give you thanks; you are my God, and I will exalt you. Give thanks to the LORD, for he is good; his love endures forever. PSALM 118:28-29

O Jesus Christ, the mirror of all gentleness of mind, the example of highest obedience and patience, grant me your servant true devotion to consider how you, innocent and undefiled Lamb, were bound, taken, and hauled away to death for my sins; how well content you were to suffer such things, not opening your mouth in impatience, but willingly offering yourself unto death. O gracious God, how vilely were you mishandled for my sake! O Lord, let this never come out of my heart. Expel through its coldness and sloth, stir up love and fervency towards you; provoke me to earnest prayer and make me cheerful and diligent in your will. Amen.

MILES COVERDALE (adapted)

He went forward a little, and fell face downward on the ground, and prayed.

MATTHEW 26:39, *TLB*

May 23

Blessed are they whose ways are blameless, who walk according to the law of the LORD. PSALM 119:1

Your throne, O God, is forever and ever, and the righteous scepter is the scepter of your kingdom. You have loved righteousness and hated wickedness; therefore God, even your God, has anointed you with the oil of gladness beyond your companions.

In the beginning, Lord, you founded the earth, and the heavens are the work of your hands; they will perish, but you remain; they will all wear out like clothing; like a cloak you will roll them up, and like clothing they will be changed. But you are the same, and your years will never end.

HEBREWS 1:8-12 (adapted)

The efficacy of prayer is founded on the dependability of God.

ANONYMOUS

May 24

Do good to your servant, and I will live; I will obey your word. Open my eyes that I may see wonderful things in your law.
PSALM 119:17-18

O Lord God, in whom we live, and move, and have our being, open our eyes that we may behold your fatherly presence ever about us. Draw our hearts to you with the power of your love. Teach us to be careful for nothing, and when we have done what you have given us to do, help us, O God, our Saviour, to leave the issue to your wisdom. Take from us all doubt and distrust. Lift our thoughts up to thee in heaven, and make us to know that all things are possible to us through thy Son, our Redeemer.

BROOKE FOSS WESTCOTT

Lord, take my lips and speak through them; take my mind and think through it; take my heart and set it on fire.

W. H. H. AITKEN

May 25

Teach me, O LORD, to follow your decrees; then I will keep them to the end. Give me understanding, and I will keep your law and obey it with all my heart. PSALM 119:33-34

Lord Jesus, I know you have clearly shown us the pattern for prayer. But it seems you put the hard part first: The Father's name, his kingdom, and his will. I am eloquent when praying for daily bread, forgiveness, or deliverance. Yet, I have few holy words when I consider the holiness of my Father's name. Also, how can I truthfully pray for the kingdom's coming? I am so little ruled by the King. And, can a rebel pray for another's will?

O Lord! I want what the Father can daily provide but often don't live as a child of a heavenly Father. I seek his forgiveness but don't live in the love that forgives. I tend toward temptation and don't cry for rescue.

Oh, my life prevents my prayer! So I gather with your disciples again and with them ask once more, "Lord, teach us to pray."

DANIEL PARTNER

Do not pray by heart but with the heart.

ANONYMOUS

May 26

You are my portion, O LORD; I have promised to obey your words. I have sought your face with all my heart; be gracious to me according to your promise. PSALM 119:57-58

Grant me, O most merciful Jesus, your grace, that it may be with me, and labour with me, and abide with me even to the end.

Give me grace ever to desire and to will what is most acceptable to you and most pleasing in your sight.

Let your will be mine, and let my will ever follow yours, and fully accord with it.

Let there be between you and me but one will, so that I may love what you love, and abhor what you hate; and let me not be able to will any thing which you do not will, nor to dislike any thing which you do will.

THOMAS À KEMPIS

Prayer is the spirit speaking truth to Truth.

PHILIP JAMES BAILEY

May 27

I know, O LORD, that your laws are righteous, and in faithfulness you have afflicted me. May your unfailing love be my comfort, according to your promise to your servant. PSALM 119:75-76

O heavenly Father, your hand replenishes all living creatures with blessing and gives meat to the hungry in due season; I acknowledge my meat and drink to be your gifts, prepared by your fatherly providence to be received by me for the comfort of my body with thanksgiving: I most humbly beg you to bless me and my food and to give me grace so to use these your benefits that I may be thankful to you and liberal to my poor neighbors, through Jesus Christ our Lord. Amen.

THOMAS BECON (adapted)

Do I want to pray or only to think about my human problems? Do I want to pray or simply kneel there contemplating my sorrow? Do I want to direct my prayer towards God or let it direct itself towards me?

HUBERT VAN ZELLER

May 28

My soul faints with longing for your salvation, but I have put my hope in your word. PSALM 119:81

I want to be teachable, Lord. Is there something You want to show me, some block You want removed, some change You want in me or my attitudes before You can answer my prayer? Give me the gift of eyes that see, of ears that hear what You are saying to me.

Come Lord Jesus, and abide in my heart. How grateful I am to realize that the answer to my prayer does not depend on me at all. As I quietly abide in You and let Your life flow into me, what freedom it is to know that the Father does not see my threadbare patience or insufficient trust, rather only Your patience, Lord, and Your confidence that the Father has everything in hand.

In Your faith I thank You right now for a more glorious answer to my prayer than I can imagine. Amen.

CATHERINE MARSHALL

Father, forgive us our trash baskets,
as we forgive those who put their trash in our baskets.

A YOUNG CHILD

May 29

Oh, how I love your law! I meditate on it all day long. Your commands make me wiser than my enemies, for they are ever with me. PSALM 119:97-98

Grant, Almighty God, that as you have, in various ways, testified and daily also prove how dear and precious to you is humanity as we enjoy daily so many and so remarkable proofs of your goodness and favor—O grant that we learn to rely wholly on your goodness. You have brought endless examples of your goodness before us, which you would have us continually to experience, that we may not only pass through our earthly course, but also confidently aspire to the hope of that blessed and celestial life which is laid up for us in heaven; through Christ alone, our Lord. Amen.

JOHN CALVIN

Prayer is essentially man standing before his God in wonder, awe, and humility; man, made in the image of God, responding to his maker.

GEORGE APPLETON

May 30

Sustain me according to your promise, and I will live; do not let my hopes be dashed. Uphold me, and I will be delivered; I will always have regard for your decrees. PSALM 119:116-117

Give us grace, O Lord, to work while it is day, fulfilling diligently and patiently whatever duty Thou appointest us; doing small things in the day of small things, and great labors if Thou summon us to any. . . . Go with me, and I will go; but if Thou go not with me, send me not; let me hear Thy voice when I follow. Amen.

CHRISTINA ROSSETTI

You need not cry very loud;
he is nearer to us than we think.

BROTHER LAWRENCE

May 31

Your statutes are wonderful; therefore I obey them. The unfolding of your words gives light; it gives understanding to the simple. PSALM 119:129-130

O Lord, I give myself to Thee, I trust Thee wholly. Thou art wiser than I—more loving to me than I myself. Deign to fulfill Thy high purposes in me whatever they be—work in and through me. I am born to serve Thee, to be Thine, to be Thy instrument. Let me be Thy blind instrument. I ask not to see—I ask not to know—I ask simply to be used.

JOHN HENRY NEWMAN

Prayer does not change God,
but it changes him who prays.

SØREN KIERKEGAARD

June 1

Your compassion is great, O LORD; preserve my life according to your laws. Many are the foes who persecute me, but I have not turned from your statutes. PSALM 119:156-157

Lord Jesus, I ask with Peter of old: How often must I forgive those who sin against me and offend me? O Lord, if I am to forgive seventy times seven, then You must give me the grace and the will to do so. My sinful heart is resentful and often filled with bitterness against others. So often I have been hurt and sinned against. I must confess to You, Lord Jesus, that I do not find it easy to forgive and forget. Help me, O Lord.

I know You have forgiven me times without number. That is why I am coming to You, asking for help. Enable me in all sincerity of heart to say as You did on the cross: Father, forgive them; and then help me to forgive as You have forgiven me more than seventy times seven.

Hear my plea, gracious Lord. Amen.

MY PRAYER BOOK

Pray not for lighter burdens
but for stronger backs.

THEODORE ROOSEVELT

June 2

I call on the LORD in my distress, and he answers me. Save me, O LORD, from lying lips and from deceitful tongues. PSALM 120:1-2

Save me, O God! For the waters have come up to my neck. I sink in deep mire, where there is no foothold; I have come into deep waters, and the flood sweeps over me. I am weary with my crying; my throat is parched. My eyes grow dim with waiting for my God.

O God, You know my folly; the wrongs I have done are not hidden from You. But as for me, my prayer is to You, O Lord. At an acceptable time, O God, in the abundance of Your steadfast love, answer me.

Answer me, O Lord, for Your steadfast love is good; according to Your abundant mercy, turn to me. Hide not Your face from Your servant; for I am in distress—hurry to answer me. Draw near to me, redeem me. Amen.

PSALM 69 (adapted)

I would have no desire other
than to accomplish thy will.
Teach me to pray; pray thyself in me.

FRANÇOIS FÉNELON

June 3

I lift up my eyes to the hills—where does my help come from? My help comes from the LORD, the Maker of heaven and earth.
PSALM 121:1-2

I thank you, O God, for the relief and satisfaction of mind that come with the firm assurance that you govern the world; for the patience and resignation to your providence that are afforded as I reflect that even the tumultuous and irregular actions of the sinful are, nevertheless, under your direction, who are wise, good, and omnipotent, and have promised to make all things work together for good to those who love you.

SUSANNA WESLEY

Ask, and it will be given you;
search, and you will find;
knock, and the door will be opened.

MATTHEW 7:7, *NRSV*

June 4

I rejoiced with those who said to me, "Let us go to the house of the LORD." Our feet are standing in your gates, O Jerusalem.
PSALM 122:1-2

Oh, I long to be filled more with God! Lord, stir me up more in earnest. I want to be more like Jesus. I see that nothing will do but being continually filled with the divine presence and glory. I know all that you have is mine, but I want to feel a close union. Lord, increase my faith.

WILLIAM CARVOSSO

Oh, what a cause of thankfulness it is that we have a gracious God to go to on all occasions! Use and enjoy this privilege and you can never be miserable. Oh, what an unspeakable privilege is prayer!

LADY MAXWELL

June 5

As the eyes of slaves look to the hand of their master, as the eyes of a maid look to the hand of her mistress, so our eyes look to the LORD our God, till he shows us his mercy. PSALM 123:2

For our absent loved ones we implore your loving-kindness. Keep them in life, keep them in glowing honor; and for us, grant that we remain worthy of their love. For Christ's sake, let not our beloved blush for us, nor we for them. Grant us but that, and grant us courage to endure lesser ills unshaken, and to accept death, loss, and disappointment as it were straws upon the tide of life.

ROBERT LOUIS STEVENSON

Epaphras . . . greets you. He is always wrestling in his prayers on your behalf.

COLOSSIANS 4:12, *NRSV*

June 6

Praise be to the LORD, who has not let us be torn by their teeth. We have escaped like a bird out of the fowler's snare; the snare has been broken, and we have escaped. PSALM 124:6-7

When the signs of age begin to mark my body (and still more when they touch my mind); when the ill that is to diminish me or carry me off strikes from without or is born within me; when the painful moment comes in which I suddenly awaken to the fact that I am ill or growing old; and above all at that last moment when I feel I am losing hold of myself and am absolutely passive within the hands of the great unknown forces that have formed me; in all those dark moments, O God, grant that I may understand that it is you (provided only my faith is strong enough) who are painfully parting the fibers of my being in order to penetrate to the very marrow of my substance and bear me away within yourself.

TEILHARD DE CHARDIN

Devote yourselves to prayer, keeping alert in it with thanksgiving.

COLOSSIANS 4:2, *NRSV*

June 7

Those who trust in the LORD are like Mount Zion, which cannot be shaken but endures forever. PSALM 125:1

Oh, the depths of the riches both of your wisdom and
knowledge, O God!
How unsearchable are your judgments and your ways are
past finding out.
Your greatness cannot be imagined.
You are greater than all language, and no words can
express your majesty.
You are above all, outside of all, and beyond all I can even
imagine.
You are without limit.
When I speak of you I cannot refer to amount or size or
weight, for you are beyond measure.
You are not less or more, large or small.
You are simply God, the infinite One.
A human mind has no capacity to comprehend you.
What I can do is praise, adore, and worship you.

ROBERT C. SAVAGE

God deserves far more praise
than any of us could ever give Him.

ANONYMOUS

June 8

The LORD has done great things for us, and we are filled with joy. Restore our fortunes, O LORD, like streams in the Negev.
PSALM 126:3-4

Almighty God, give me a measure of true religion and thereby set me free from vain and disappointing hopes, from lawless and exorbitant appetites, from frothy and empty joys, from anxious, self-devouring cares, from a dull and black melancholy, from an eating envy and swelling pride, and from rigid sourness and severity of spirit, so that I may possess that peace which passes all understanding, through Jesus Christ our Lord.

BENJAMIN WHICHCOTE (adapted)

God give me work
Till my life shall end
And life
Till my work is done.

EPITAPH, WINIFRED HOLTBY

June 9

Unless the LORD builds the house, its builders labor in vain. Unless the LORD watches over the city, the watchmen stand guard in vain. PSALM 127:1

O God our Father, Good beyond all that is good, Fair beyond all that is fair, in whom is calmness and peace: do thou make up the dissensions which divide us from each other, and bring us back into an unity of love, which may bear some likeness to Thine divine nature. Grant us that we may be spiritually one, as well in ourselves as in each other, through that peace of Thine which maketh all things peaceful, and through the grace, mercy, and tenderness of Thine only Son. Amen.

JACOBITE LITURGY OF SAINT DIONYSIUS

Seven days without prayer makes one weak.

ALLEN E. BARTLETT

June 10

Blessed are all who fear the LORD, who walk in his ways. You will eat the fruit of your labor; blessings and prosperity will be yours. PSALM 128:1-2

O God Almighty, Father of our Lord Jesus Christ, grant us, we pray you, to be grounded and settled in your truth by the coming down of the Holy Spirit into our hearts. That which we know not, do reveal; that which is wanting in us, do fill up; that which we know, do confirm, and keep us blameless in your service, through the same Jesus Christ our Lord.

CLEMENT OF ROME

O Jesus, Son of God, who was silent before Pilate, do not let us wag our tongues without thinking of what we are to say and how to say it.

GAELIC PRAYER

June 11

Plowmen have plowed my back and made their furrows long. But the LORD is righteous; he has cut me free from the cords of the wicked. PSALM 129:3-4

I asked for strength that I might achieve;
I was made weak that I might learn humbly to obey.
I asked for health that I might do greater things;
I was given infirmity that I might do better things.
I asked for riches that I might be happy;
I was given poverty that I might be wise.
I asked for power that I might have the praise of men;
I was given weakness that I might feel the need of God.
I asked for all things that I might enjoy life;
I was given life that I might enjoy all things.
I got nothing that I had asked for,
but everything that I had hoped for.
Almost despite myself my unspoken prayers were answered;
I am, among all men, most richly blessed.

AN UNKNOWN CONFEDERATE SOLDIER

Our prayers are often filled with selfish "wants"; God always answers with what we need.

ANONYMOUS

June 12

I wait for the LORD, my soul waits, and in his word I put my hope. My soul waits for the Lord more than watchmen wait for the morning. PSALM 130:5-6

O Lord,
let nothing divert my advance towards you,
but in this dangerous labyrinth of the world and the whole
course of my pilgrimage here,
May your heavenly dictates be my map and your holy life
be my guide.

JOHN WESLEY (adapted)

Prayer covers the whole of a man's life. There is no thought, feeling, yearning, or desire, however low, trifling, or vulgar we may deem it, which, if it affects our real interest or happiness, we may not lay before God and be sure of sympathy. His nature is such that our often coming does not tire him. The whole burden of the whole life of every man may be rolled on to God and not weary him, though it has wearied the man.

HENRY WARD BEECHER

June 13

My heart is not proud, O LORD. . . . But I have stilled and quieted my soul; like a weaned child with its mother. PSALM 131:1-2

I confess, O God—
that often I let my mind wander down unclean and forbidden ways:
that often I deceive myself as to where my plain duty lies:
that often, by concealing my real motives, I pretend to be better than I am:
that often my honesty is only a matter of policy:
that often my affection for my friends is only a refined form of caring for myself:
that often my sparing of my enemy is due to nothing more than cowardice:
that often I do good deeds only that they be seen of men, and shun evil
ones only because I fear they may be found out.
O holy One, let the fire of Thy love enter my heart, and burn up all this coil of meanness and hypocrisy, and make my heart as the heart of a little child.

JOHN BAILLIE

He who ceases to pray ceases to prosper.

WILLIAM GURNEY BENHAM

June 14

Let us go to his dwelling place; let us worship at his footstool—arise, O LORD, and come to your resting place, you and the ark of your might. PSALM 132:7-8

O Thou beloved: Love eternal, my whole good, happiness which has no bounds, I desire to appropriate you with the most vehement desire and the most worthy reverence. I desire to reserve nothing unto myself.

O everlasting light, surpassing all created luminaries, flash forth thy lightning from above, piercing all the most inward parts of my heart.

Make clean, make glad, make bright, and make alive my spirit, with all the powers thereof, that I may cleave to you in ecstasies of joy.

THOMAS À KEMPIS

I pray on the principle that wine knocks the cork out of a bottle. There is an inward fermentation, and there must be a vent.

HENRY WARD BEECHER

June 15

How good and pleasant it is when brothers live together in unity! It is like precious oil poured on the head, running down on the beard. PSALM 133:1-2

Be pleased to visit your Church with the Holy Spirit. Renew the day of Pentecost in our midst, and in the midst of all gatherings of your people, may there come the downfall of the holy fire, the uprising of the heavenly wind. May matters that are now slow and dead become quick and full of life, and may the Lord Jesus Christ be exalted in the midst of his Church which is his fullness—"the fullness of him that filleth all in all." May multitudes be converted; may they come flocking to Christ with holy eagerness to find in him a refuge as the doves fly to their dovecotes.

CHARLES H. SPURGEON

In the morning, prayer is the key that opens to us the treasures of God's mercies and blessings; in the evening, it is the key that shuts us up under His protection and safeguard.

ANONYMOUS

June 16

Praise the LORD, all you servants of the LORD. . . . Lift up your hands in the sanctuary and praise the LORD. PSALM 134:1-2

Lord Jesus, today my son came to the breakfast table displaying the laces in his shoes. He had tied them by himself for the first time. He learned to do this so quickly, Lord; he's growing too fast for me.

For fun I sometimes ask him to stop growing because I love him just as he is. He protests that he can't stop growing.

So Lord, this is my prayer for him—that he would not stop growing; that throughout his life, long past the day of my death, he would continue to grow in grace; that the curtains of his tents would be stretched out, his cords lengthened, and his stakes strengthened.

Like you as a youth may he grow in favor with God and man; may he increase in wisdom and in years and become a man enlarged in his spirit and his heart.

Do this, O Lord, and give me the wisdom and the way to redeem the brief time he and I are together. Amen.

DANIEL PARTNER

Keep alert and always persevere in supplication for all the saints.

EPHESIANS 6:18, *NRSV*

June 17

Praise the LORD, for the LORD is good; sing praise to his name, for that is pleasant. PSALM 135:3

Father! It is your will that your child should enjoy your presence and blessing. It is your will that everything in the life of your child should be in accordance with your will, and that the Holy Spirit should work this in him. It is your will that your child should live in the daily experience of distinct answers to prayer, so as to enjoy living and direct fellowship with yourself. It is your will that your name should be glorified in and through your children, and that it will be in those who trust you. O my Father! Let this your will be my confidence is all I ask.

ANDREW MURRAY

If you are swept off your feet,
it's time to get on your knees.

FRED BECK

June 18

Give thanks to the LORD, for he is good. *His love endures forever.* PSALM 136:1

Give us open eyes, our Father, to see the beauty all around us and to see it in Thy handiwork. Let all lovely things fill us with gladness and let them lift up our hearts in true worship.

Give us this day, O Lord, a strong and vivid sense that Thou art by our side. By Thy grace, let us go nowhere this day where Thou canst not come nor court any companionship that would rob us of Thine. Through Jesus Christ our Lord. Amen.

PETER MARSHALL

Give us Lord, a bit o' sun,
A bit o' work and a bit o' fun;
Give us all in the struggle and sputter
Our daily bread and a bit o' butter.

ON AN OLD INN, LANCASTER, ENGLAND

June 19

By the rivers of Babylon we sat and wept when we remembered Zion. . . . for there our captors asked us for songs, our tormentors demanded songs of joy. PSALM 137:1, 3

Lord, You told the impotent man
To take up his bed and walk.
Today, when mountainous problems
Seem to loom sky-high
 And the business of living
Demands so much rigid attention
Empower me, I pray
To take up my task and work.

RUTH HARMS CALKIN

Faith, and hope, and patience and all the strong, beautiful, vital forces of piety are withered and dead in a prayerless life. The life of the individual believer, his personal salvation, and personal Christian graces have their being, bloom, and fruitage in prayer.

E. M. BOUNDS

June 20

May all the kings of the earth praise you, O LORD, when they hear the words of your mouth. May they sing of the ways of the LORD, for the glory of the LORD is great. PSALM 138:4-5

Dear God and Father of my Lord Jesus Christ, you are blessed. You are the Father of mercies and God of all comfort who comforts me in all my troubles. You do this so that I may be able to comfort those who are in any trouble with the comfort with which I myself am comforted by you. Just as I share abundantly in the sufferings of Christ, thank you that my comfort is also abundant through Christ.

2 CORINTHIANS 1:3-5 (adapted)

All earth born hopes with time must
pass away;
Prayer grasps eternal things; pray,
always pray.

A. B. SIMPSON

June 21

O LORD, you have searched me and you know me. You know when I sit and when I rise; you perceive my thoughts from afar.
PSALM 139:1-2

Eternal and most glorious God, you have stamped the soul of humanity with your image, received it into your revenue, and made it part of your treasure; do not allow us to undervalue ourselves, so to impoverish you as to give away these souls for nothing, and all the world is nothing if the soul must be given for it. Do this, O God, for his sake who knows our natural infirmities, for he had them, and knows the weight of our sins, for he paid a dear price for them; your Son, our Savior Jesus Christ.

JOHN DONNE

Do you know what is wrong with the world today? There's too much theologian and not enough kneeologian.

DALLAS F. BILLINGTON

June 22

O LORD, I say to you, "You are my God." Hear, O LORD, my cry for mercy. PSALM 140:6

Blessed are all your saints, O God and King, who have travelled over the tempestuous sea of this mortal life, and have made the harbor of peace and happiness. Watch over us who are still in our dangerous voyage; and remember such as lie exposed to the rough storms of trouble and temptations. Frail is our vessel, and the ocean is wide; but as in your mercy you have set our course, so steer the vessel of our life toward the everlasting shore of peace. Bring us at length to the quiet haven of our heart's desire, where you, O our God, are blessed, and live and reign for ever and ever.

AUGUSTINE

O, do not pray for easy lives. Pray to be stronger men. Do not pray for tasks equal to your powers. Pray for powers equal to your tasks.

PHILLIPS BROOKS

June 23

O LORD, I call to you; come quickly to me. Hear my voice when I call to you. PSALM 141:1

I need Thee, precious Jesus!
A friend to soothe and comfort,
  A friend to care for me:
I need the heart of Jesus,
  To feel each anxious care,
To bear my every burden,
  And all my sorrow share.

I need thee, precious Jesus!
  I need thee day by day,
To fill me with thy fullness,
  To lead me on my way;
I need thy Holy Spirit
  To teach me what I am;
To show me more of Jesus,
  To point me to the Lamb.

F. WHITFIELD

It is impossible to conduct your life as a disciple without definite times of secret prayer.

OSWALD CHAMBERS

June 24

I cry aloud to the LORD; I lift up my voice to the LORD for mercy. I pour out my complaint before him; before him I tell my trouble. PSALM 142:1-2

O God, renew our spirits by your Holy Spirit, and draw our hearts unto yourself, that our work may not be a burden, but a delight. Let us not serve as slaves with the spirit of bondage, but with freedom and gladness as your sons, rejoicing in your will; for Jesus Christ's sake.

BENJAMIN JENKS

Prayer is the soul's sincere desire,
Uttered, or unexpressed;
The motion of a hidden fire
That trembles in the breast.

JAMES MONTGOMERY

June 25

O LORD, hear my prayer, listen to my cry for mercy; in your faithfulness and righteousness come to my relief. PSALM 143:1

Almighty Father, teach me to do everything with the utmost sincerity. Save me from posing even to myself. Make my life unaffected, simple, and sincere. Cleanse me from selfishness; let my gaze be outward rather than inward. Teach me to think more of others than of myself. Forbid that my own interests should be paramount. Pardon, I beseech you, all that is and has been wrong in my life and character. Had I always sought your will I should now have been strong in the Lord. But it is never too late. Help me to remedy the evil and henceforth to build with honesty and prayer.

WALTER JAMES

When you cannot pray as you would, pray as you can.

EDWARD M. GOULBURN

June 26

O LORD, what is man that you care for him, the son of man that you think of him? Man is like a breath; his days are like a fleeting shadow. PSALM 144:3-4

As the hand is made for holding and the eye for seeing, you have fashioned me for joy. Share with me the vision that shall find it everywhere: in the wild violet's beauty; in the lark's melody; in the face of a steadfast man; in a child's smile; in a mother's love; in the purity of Jesus.

A GAELIC PRAYER

To get nations back on their feet, we must get down on our knees first.

A LETTER TO THE EDITOR, the *Des Moines Register*

June 27

Great is the LORD and most worthy of praise; his greatness no one can fathom. PSALM 145:3

Nothing has been capable, dear Lord, to hinder you from being all mine, neither heaven, nor your divinity, nor the gibbet of the cross: grant me the grace, that nothing may hinder me from being all yours, to whom I owe myself both for creation and redemption.

'Twas never heard that in your mortal life, you lodg'd with any, which you did not liberally reward with your gifts: I beg you will do the same to your present habitation, which is my heart: let the touch of yours, which consecrates all things, sanctify my heart that it may be grateful to you.

LUCY HERBERT

Ah, dearest Jesus, holy Child,
Make thee a bed, soft, undefiled,
Within my heart, that it may be
A quiet chamber kept for thee.

MARTIN LUTHER

June 28

Praise the LORD. Praise the LORD, O my soul. I will praise the LORD all my life; I will sing praise to my God as long as I live. PSALM 146:1-2

O Lord Jesus Christ, you are the sun of the world, evermore arising, and never going down, which by your most wholesome appearing and sight, brings forth, preserves, nourishes, and refreshes all things, as well that are in heaven as also that are on earth; we beg you mercifully and faithfully to shine in our hearts, so that the night and darkness of sins, and the mists of errors on every side may be driven away; with you brightly shining in our hearts we may all our life space go without stumbling or offense, and may decently and seemly walk (as in the day time), being pure and clean from the works of darkness, and abounding in all good works which God has prepared us to walk in; you who with the Father and with the Holy Ghost live and reign for ever and ever.

THOMAS CRANMER

Teach us to pray often;
that we may pray oftener.

JEREMY TAYLOR

*J*une 29

Praise the LORD. How good it is to sing praises to our God, how pleasant and fitting to praise him! PSALM 147:1

O You, from whom to be turned is to fall,
to whom to be turned is to rise,
and in whom to stand is to abide for ever:
Grant us in all our duties your help
in all our perplexities your guidance,
in all our dangers your protection,
and in all our sorrows your peace;
through Jesus Christ our Lord.

AUGUSTINE

To One alone my thoughts arise,
The Eternal Truth, the Good and Wise,
To Him I cry,
Who shared on earth our common lot,
But the world comprehended not
His deity.

HENRY WADSWORTH LONGFELLOW

June 30

Praise the LORD. Praise the LORD from the heavens, praise him in the heights above. PSALM 148:1

O Lord, by all your dealings with us, whether of joy or pain, of light or darkness, let us be brought to you. Let us value no treatment of your grace simply because it gives us or denies us what we want; but may all that you send us bring us to you; that knowing your perfectness, we may be sure in every disappointment you are still loving us, in every darkness you are still enlightening us, and in every enforced idleness you are giving us life, as in his death you gave life to your Son, our Savior, Jesus Christ. Amen.

PHILLIPS BROOKS

Especially we pray you to make Christianity more Christian.

HARRY EMERSON FOSDICK

July 1

For the LORD takes delight in his people; he crowns the humble with salvation. Let the saints rejoice in this honor and sing for joy on their beds. PSALM 149:4-5

Lord, bless us, if it may be, in all our innocent endeavors. If it may not, give us the strength to encounter what is to come, that we be brave in peril, constant in tribulation, temperate in wrath and in all changes of fortune, and, down to the gates of death, loyal and loving one to another. As the clay to the potter, as the windmill to the wind, as children of their sire, we beg of you this help and mercy for Christ's sake.

ROBERT LOUIS STEVENSON

The answer of our prayers is secured by the fact that in rejecting them God would in a certain sense deny his own nature.

JOHN CALVIN

July 2

Praise the LORD. Praise God in his sanctuary; praise him in his mighty heavens. PSALM 150:1

O Lord God, praise your name for ever and ever! Yours is the mighty power and glory and victory and majesty. Everything in the heavens and earth is yours, O Lord, and this is your kingdom. I adore you as being in control of everything. Riches and honor come from you alone, and you are the Ruler of all mankind; your hand controls power and might and it is at your discretion that men are made great and given strength. O my God, I thank you and praise your glorious name, but who am I that I should be permitted to give anything to you? Everything I have has come from you, and I only give you what is yours already!

1 CHRONICLES 29:10-14 (adapted)

And take . . . the sword of the Spirit, which is the word of God; praying always with all prayer and supplication in the Spirit.

EPHESIANS 6:17-18, *NKJV*

July 3

He [the righteous man] is like a tree planted by streams of water, which yields its fruit in season and whose leaf does not wither. Whatever he does prospers. PSALM 1:3

You have said that in virtue of your going to the Father, whatever we ask, you will do. . . . Blessed Lord! Forgive me that I have so little believed you and your promise, and so little proved your faithfulness in fulfilling it. O forgive me that I have so little honored your all-prevailing name in heaven or upon earth.

Lord! Teach me to pray so that I may prove that your name is indeed all-prevailing with God and men and devils. Yea, teach me so to work and so to pray that you can glorify yourself in me as the Omnipotent One, and do your great works through me too. Amen.

ANDREW MURRAY

We must hear Jesus speak if we expect him to hear us speak.

CHARLES H. SPURGEON

July 4

Therefore, you kings, be wise; be warned, you rulers of the earth. Serve the LORD with fear and rejoice with trembling. PSALM 2:10-11

Almighty God, we make our earnest prayer that you will keep the United States in your holy protection; that you will incline the hearts of the citizens to cultivate a spirit of subordination and obedience to government, and entertain a brotherly affection and love for one another and for their fellow-citizens of the United States at large. And, finally, that you will most graciously be pleased to dispose us all to do justice, to love mercy, and to demean ourselves with that charity, humility, and pacific temper of mind which were the characteristics of the Divine Author of our blessed religion and without which we can never be a happy nation. Grant our supplications, we beseech you, through Jesus Christ our Lord. Amen.

GEORGE WASHINGTON

Indeed, I tremble for my country when I reflect that God is just.

THOMAS JEFFERSON

July 5

I lie down and sleep; I wake again, because the LORD sustains me. I will not fear the tens of thousands drawn up against me on every side. PSALM 3:5-6

O Most Loving Father, you who will us to give thanks for all things, to dread nothing but the loss of yourself, and to cast all our care on you, who care for us; preserve us from faithless fears and worldly anxieties, and grant that no clouds of this mortal life may hide from us the light of that love which is immortal, and which you have manifested unto us in your Son, Jesus Christ our Lord.

WILLIAM BRIGHT

Prayer reaches out in love to a dying world and says, "I care."

DICK EASTMAN

July 6

Answer me when I call to you, O my righteous God. Give me relief from my distress; be merciful to me and hear my prayer.
PSALM 4:1

Dear Father, I've become your child,
  and your Son's Spirit
  is in my heart crying,
"Abba! Father!"
I'm no longer enslaved to any law
  because I'm your child!
  And if I'm a child,
  I'm an heir through God.
Mine is not a spirit of slavery.
  I've received the Spirit of sonship.
  He cries within me, "Abba! Father!"
This Spirit speaks in mine, saying,
  "You're a child and heir;
    an heir of God,
    a joint heir with Christ!"
Abba, Father, if as an heir
I must suffer with your Son,
  these sufferings can't compare
    to the glory soon to be revealed in me.

DANIEL PARTNER

Prayer changes things.

ANONYMOUS

July 7

But let all who take refuge in you be glad; let them ever sing for joy. Spread your protection over them, that those who love your name may rejoice in you. PSALM 5:11

We beseech you, O God, the God of truth,
That what we know not of things we ought to know
You will teach us.
That what we know of truth
You will keep us therein.
That what we are mistaken in, as men must be,
You will correct.
That at whatever things we stumble
You will yet establish us.

And from all things that are false
And from all knowledge that would be hurtful,
You will evermore defend us,
Through Jesus Christ, our Lord.

BROOKE FOSS WESTCOTT

Praying is learned by praying.

L. A. T. VAN DOOREN

July 8

My soul is in anguish. How long, O LORD, how long? Turn, O LORD, and deliver me; save me because of your unfailing love.
PSALM 6:3-4

And now, O God, give me a quiet mind, as I lie down to rest. Dwell in my thoughts until sleep overtake me. Let me rejoice in the knowledge that, whether awake or asleep, I am still with Thee. Let me not be fretted by any anxiety over the lesser interests of life. Let no troubled dreams disturb me, so that I may awake refreshed and ready for the tasks of another day. And to Thy Name be all the glory. Amen.

JOHN BAILLIE

The man who says his prayers in the evening is a captain posting his sentries. After that, he can sleep.

CHARLES BAUDELAIRE

July 9

O LORD my God, I take refuge in you; save and deliver me from all who pursue me, or they will tear me like a lion and rip me to pieces with no one to rescue me. PSALM 7:1-2

O God in heaven, have mercy on us! Lord Jesus Christ, intercede for your people, deliver us at the opportune time, preserve in us the true genuine Christian faith, collect your scattered sheep with your voice, your divine Word as Holy Writ calls it. Help us to recognize your voice, help us not to be allured by the madness of the world, so that we may never fall away from you, O Lord Jesus Christ.

ALBRECHT DÜRER

Other duties become pressing and absorbing and crowd out prayer. "Choked to death" would be the coroner's verdict in many cases of dead praying if an inquest could be secured on this dire, spiritual calamity.

E. M. BOUNDS

July 10

When I consider your heavens, the work of your fingers, the moon and the stars, which you have set in place, what is man that you are mindful of him, the son of man that you care for him? PSALM 8:3-4

O Gracious Father, keep me through your Holy Spirit; keep my heart soft and tender now in health and amidst the bustle of the world; keep the thought of yourself present to me as my Father in Jesus Christ; and keep alive in me a spirit of love and meekness to all, that I may be at once gentle and active and firm. O strengthen me to bear pain or sickness, or danger, or whatever you shall be pleased to lay upon me, as Christ's soldier and servant: and let my faith overcome the world daily. Perfect and bless the works of your Spirit in the hearts of all your people, and may your kingdom come and your will be done in earth as it is in heaven.

THOMAS ARNOLD

Do not work so hard for Christ that you have no strength to pray, for prayer requires strength.

J. HUDSON TAYLOR

July 11

The LORD reigns forever; he has established his throne for judgment. He will judge the world in righteousness; he will govern the peoples with justice. PSALM 9:7-8

Lord God, let us keep your Scriptures in mind and meditate on them day and night, persevering in prayer, always on the watch. We beg you, Lord, to give us real knowledge of what we read and to show us not only how to understand it, but how to put it into practice, so that we may deserve to obtain spiritual grace, enlightened by the law of the Holy Spirit, through Jesus Christ our Lord, whose power and glory will endure throughout all ages. Amen.

ORIGEN OF ALEXANDRIA

Of all things, guard against neglecting God in the secret place of prayer.

WILLIAM WILBERFORCE

July 12

O LORD, see how my enemies persecute me! Have mercy and lift me up from the gates of death, that I may declare your praises. PSALM 9:13-14

O My God, let me, with thanksgiving, remember, and confess unto you your mercies on me. Let my bones be bedewed with your love, and let them say unto you, who is like unto you, O Lord? You have broken my bonds in pieces. I will offer to you the sacrifice of thanksgiving. And how you have broken them, I will declare; and all who worship you, when they hear this, will say, "Blessed is the Lord, in Heaven and in earth, great and wonderful is his name."

AUGUSTINE

And since He bids me seek His face,
Believe His word and trust His grace,
I'll cast on Him my every care,
And wait for thee, sweet hour of prayer.

W. W. WALFORD

July 13

But you, O God, do see trouble and grief; you consider it to take it in hand. The victim commits himself to you; you are the helper of the fatherless. PSALM 10:14

Grant us grace, O Father, not to pass by suffering or joy without eyes to see; give us understanding and sympathy; and guard us from selfishness that we may enter into the joys and sufferings of others; use us to gladden and strengthen those who are weak and suffering; that by our lives we may help others who believe and serve you, and project your light which is the light of life.

H. R. L. SHEPPARD

God's promises are to be our pleas in prayer.

MATTHEW HENRY

July 14

You hear, O LORD, the desire of the afflicted; you encourage them, and you listen to their cry. PSALM 10:17

O God, take all my sorrows and use them to show me the nature of your joy. Take all my sins and, forgiving them, use them to show me the ways of true pleasantness and the path of true peace. Take all my broken purposes and disappointed hopes and use them to make your perfect rainbow arch. Take all my clouds of sadness and calamity and from them make your sunset glories. Take my night and make it bright with stars. Take my ill-health and pain until they accomplish in your purpose as much as health could achieve. Take us as we are with impulses, strivings, longings so often frustrated and thwarted. And even with what is broken and imperfect, make your dreams come true, through him who made of human life a sacrament, of thorns a crown, of a cross a throne, even through Jesus Christ our Lord.

LESLIE D. WEATHERHEAD (adapted)

I have to hurry
all day to get time to pray.

MARTIN LUTHER

July 15

For the LORD is righteous, he loves justice; upright men will see his face. PSALM 11:7

O Infinite God, the brightness of whose face is often shrouded from my mortal gaze, I thank Thee that Thou didst send Thy Son Jesus Christ to be a light in a dark world. O Christ, Thou Light of Light, I thank Thee that in Thy most holy life Thou didst pierce the eternal mystery as with a great shaft of heavenly light, so that in seeing Thee we see Him whom no man hath seen at any time.

And if still I cannot find Thee, O God, then let me search my heart and know whether it is not rather I who am blind than Thou who art obscure, and I who am fleeing from Thee rather than Thou from me: and let me confess these my sins before Thee and seek Thy pardon in Jesus Christ my Lord. Amen.

JOHN BAILLIE

God's chief gift to those who seek him is himself.

E. B. PUSEY

July 16

"Because of the oppression of the weak and the groaning of the needy, I will now arise," says the LORD. "I will protect them from those who malign them." PSALM 12:5

Lord Jesus, bless all who serve us, who have dedicated their lives to the ministry of others—all the teachers of our schools who labor so patiently with so little appreciation; all who wait upon the public, the clerks in the stores who have to accept criticism, complaints, bad manners, selfishness at the hands of a thoughtless public. Bless the mailmen, the drivers of streetcars and buses who must listen to people who lose their tempers.

Bless every humble soul who, in these days of stress and strain, preaches sermons without words. In the name of Him who called us to be the servants of all. Amen.

PETER MARSHALL

What is the life of a Christian but a life of prayer?

DAVID BROWN

July 17

But I trust in your unfailing love; my heart rejoices in your salvation. I will sing to the LORD, for he has been good to me.
PSALM 13:5-6

As this day closes, dear heavenly Father, I come to You to thank You for Your unfailing love, which even during the darkness of night continues to shine upon me and those I love. The wrongs and mistakes that have marred my life again today show me plainly how much I need You in my everyday life. Pardon me for Jesus' sake, and take away every impure thought and wish. Make my heart right, and make my actions reflect Your love. I want to become more like Jesus, Your dear Son, who went about doing good. Heal the sick, relieve the suffering, strengthen the weak, recall the erring, curb the wicked, help the troubled, comfort the sorrowing, and give peace to the dying. O Lord, who does not sleep, keep me safe until morning comes again. In Jesus' name, amen.

My Prayer Book

Prayer requires more of the heart than of the tongue.

ADAM CLARKE

July 18

The LORD looks down from heaven on the sons of men to see if there are any who understand, any who seek God. All have turned aside, they have together become corrupt; there is no one who does good, not even one. PSALM 14:2-3

Deliver us, good Lord, from the excessive demands of business and social life that limit family relationship; from the insensitivity and harshness of judgment that prevent understanding; from domineering ways and selfish imposition of our will; from softness and indulgence mistaken for love. Bless us with wise and understanding hearts that we may demand neither too much nor too little, and grant us such a measure of love that we may nurture our children to that fullness of manhood and womanhood, which you purposed for them, through Jesus Christ our Lord.

CHARLES S. MARTIN

I seldom made an errand to God for another but I got something for myself.

SAMUEL RUTHERFORD

July 19

LORD, who may dwell in your sanctuary? Who may live on your holy hill? He whose walk is blameless and who does what is righteous, who speaks the truth from his heart. PSALM 15:1-2

Grant me, O most sweet and loving Jesus, to rest in you above every creature, above all health and beauty, above all glory and honor, above all power and dignity, above all knowledge and subtility, above all riches and arts, above all joy and exultation, above all fame and praise, above all sweetness and consolation, above all hope and promise, above all desert and desire, above all gifts and presents which you are able to bestow or infuse, above all joy and gladness which the mind is capable of receiving and feeling; finally, above angels and archangels, and above all the host of heaven, above all things visible and invisible, and above all that falls short of yourself, O you, my God!

THOMAS À KEMPIS

Prayer is the most difficult and costly activity of the Christian.

ALAN WALKER

July 20

I will praise the LORD, who counsels me; even at night my heart instructs me. I have set the LORD always before me. Because he is at my right hand, I will not be shaken. PSALM 16:7-8

Heavenly Father, from whom all fatherhood in heaven and earth is named, bless, we beg you, all children, and give to their parents and to all in whose charge they may be, your Spirit of wisdom and love; so that the home in which they grow up may be to them an image of your kingdom, and the care of their parents a likeness of your love; through Jesus Christ our Lord.

LESLIE HUNTER

Prayer is a sincere, sensible, affectionate pouring out of the soul to God, through Christ, in the strength and assistance of the Spirit, for such things as God has promised.

JOHN BUNYAN

July 21

I call on you, O God, for you will answer me; give ear to me and hear my prayer. Show the wonder of your great love, you who save by your right hand those who take refuge in you from their foes. PSALM 17:6-7

Lord, educate us for a higher life, and let that life be begun here. May we be always in the school, always disciples, and when we are out in the world may we be trying to put into practice what we have learned at Jesus' feet. What he tells us in darkness may we proclaim in the light, and what he whispers in our ear in the closets may we sound forth upon the housetops.

CHARLES H. SPURGEON

Don't forget to pray for us too, that God will give us many chances to preach the Good News of Christ for which I am here in jail.

COLOSSIANS 4:3, *TLB*

July 22

I love you, O LORD, my strength. The LORD is my rock, my fortress and my deliverer; my God is my rock, in whom I take refuge. He is my shield and the horn of my salvation, my stronghold. PSALM 18:1-2

Sovereign Lord, you are so good to me.

You are a stronghold in the day of trouble.

When trials come, where can I go but to you?

I have no other refuge.

O Christ, you are all I want.

Just and holy is your name.

Plenteous grace I find in you—grace that covers all my sin.

You are the fountain of life.

You satisfy all my longings.

I praise and exalt you from the depths of my heart.

ROBERT C. SAVAGE

Real prayer seeks an audience and an answer.

WILLIAM S. PLUMER

July 23

As for God, his way is perfect; the word of the LORD is flawless. He is a shield for all who take refuge in him. PSALM 18:30

I have much need of humbling myself before You, the great and holy God, because of the sins that I am daily guilty of in thought, word, and deed against Your divine majesty. Help me to overcome habitual levity in my thoughts and to shun vain and impure thoughts which, though they do not make their abode in my mind for any long period of time, yet in their passing through, often leave a tincture of impurity.

Enable me to keep my heart with all diligence, my thoughts and affections, for out of them are the issues of life. How often have I offended in this kind! Cleanse me from secret faults, for out of the abundance of the heart the mouth speaks. Help me to guard against vain and unnecessary words, and to speak of You, my God, with that reverence, that humility, that gravity that I ought. Amen.

SUSANNA WESLEY

Cold prayers shall never have any warm answers.

THOMAS BROOKS

July 24

You exalted me above my foes; from violent men you rescued me. Therefore I will praise you among the nations, O LORD; I will sing praises to your name. PSALM 18:48-49

Dear God and Father of my Lord Jesus Christ, you are blessed! By your great mercy I have been given a new birth into a living hope through the resurrection of Jesus Christ from the dead. There is now an inheritance which is imperishable, undefiled, and unfading, kept in heaven for me. By God's power I am protected through faith for a salvation that is ready to be revealed in the last time. Now I rejoice in thanksgiving for your mercy, this hope, and my inheritance and salvation.

1 PETER 1:3-6 (adapted)

God's ear lies close to the believer's lip.

ANONYMOUS

July 25

May the words of my mouth and the meditation of my heart be pleasing in your sight, O LORD, my Rock and my Redeemer.
PSALM 19:14

O Divine Master,

Grant that I may not so much seek to be consoled as to
console;
to be understood as to understand;
to be loved as to love.

For it is in giving that we receive;
it is in pardoning that we are pardoned;
and it is in dying that we are born to eternal life.

FRANCIS OF ASSISI

Prayer is the acid test of devotion.
SAMUEL CHADWICK

July 26

Some trust in chariots and some in horses, but we trust in the name of the LORD our God. PSALM 20:7

Lord
You want me to trust You so totally
That I am unmoved by any circumstance:
Then work in me that steadfast trust.
You want me to choose to do right:
Then turn me from wanting any plan but Yours.
You want me to revere and honor You:
Then refresh and revive me.
You want me to obey You uninterruptedly:
Then reassure me that Your promises are mine.
You want Your will to be my will:
Then help me to love Your every wish.

I expect Your help, dear Lord
For You've never broken a single promise
And You're not going to start with me.

RUTH HARMS CALKIN

*God can pick sense
out of a confused prayer.*

RICHARD SIBBES

July 27

Be exalted, O LORD, in your strength; we will sing and praise your might. PSALM 21:13

O God, Creator of all things, you are perpetually renewing the face of the world and have created us new in Jesus Christ; grant that in our worship of you and in communion with you, your created energy may more and more flood our lives, so that we may play our part in the fulfillment of your purpose, which transcends all that we can think or understand. Amen.

WILLEM VISSER 'T HOOFT

I would rather stand against the cannons of the wicked than against the prayers of the righteous.

THOMAS LYE

*J*uly 28

In you our fathers put their trust; they trusted and you delivered them. They cried to you and were saved; in you they trusted and were not disappointed. PSALM 22:4-5

O Lord God, grant us always, whatever the world may say, to content ourselves with what you will say, and to care only for your approval, which will outweigh all words.

CHARLES GORDON

I said, "Let me walk in the fields."
He said, "Nay, walk in the town."
I said, "There are no flowers there."
He said, "No flowers, but a crown."
I said, "But the sky is black,
There is nothing but noise and din."
But he wept as he sent me back—
"There is more," he said, "there is sin."

GEORGE MACDONALD

July 29

All the ends of the earth will remember and turn to the LORD, and all the families of the nations will bow down before him, for dominion belongs to the LORD and he rules over the nations.
PSALM 22:27-28

O Lord of changeless power and endless life, be favorable to your Church throughout the world. Gather, enlighten, sanctify and sustain it by your Holy Spirit. Give us more and more to trust the silent working of your perpetual grace, which brings forth in Christ the salvation of humanity. And let the whole world know that the things which were cast down are being raised up, and the things which had grown old are being made new, and all the things are returning to the perfection of him from whom they came. Amen.

PETER TAYLOR FORSYTH

No answer to prayer is an indication of our merit; every answer to prayer is an indication of God's mercy.

JOHN BLANCHARD

July 30

Even though I walk through the valley of the shadow of death, I will fear no evil, for you are with me; your rod and your staff, they comfort me. PSALM 23:4

Take my hand, Lord, and lead me through this day, step by step. Remind me that I cannot do everything I wish, nor do any of it perfectly. Only you are perfect, and only with your help can I do my best. Help me to remember to ask for that help.

AVERY BROOKE

Never was a faithful prayer lost. Some prayers have a longer voyage than others, but then they return with their richer lading at last, so that the praying soul is a gainer by waiting for an answer.

WILLIAM GURNALL

July 31

Lift up your heads, O you gates; lift them up, you ancient doors, that the King of glory may come in. Who is he, this King of glory? The LORD Almighty—he is the King of glory. PSALM 24:9-10

Christ, whose glory fills the skies,
  Christ, the true and only light,
Sun of Righteousness, arise,
  Triumph o'er the shades of night;
Dayspring from on high, be near;
Daystar, in my heart appear!

Visit, then, this soul of mine,
  Pierce the gloom of sin and grief;
Fill me, Radiancy Divine,
Shining to the perfect day!

CHARLES WESLEY

Jesus, remember me when you come into your kingdom.

LUKE 23:42, *NRSV*

August 1

Remember, O LORD, your great mercy and love, for they are from of old. Remember not the sins of my youth and my rebellious ways; according to your love remember me, for you are good, O LORD. PSALM 25:6-7

O Lord, reassure me with your quickening Spirit; without you I can do nothing. Mortify in me all ambition, vanity, vainglory, worldliness, pride, selfishness, and resistance from God, and fill me with love, peace, and all the fruits of the Spirit. O Lord, I know not what I am, but to you I flee for refuge. I would surrender myself to you, trusting your precious promises and against hope believing in hope. You are the same yesterday, today, and for ever; and therefore, waiting on the Lord, I trust I shall at length renew my strength.

WILLIAM WILBERFORCE

When we make self the end of prayer, it is not worship but self-seeking.

THOMAS MANTON

August 2

Guard my life and rescue me; let me not be put to shame, for I take refuge in you. May integrity and uprightness protect me, because my hope is in you. PSALM 25:20-21

Almighty God, my heavenly Father, who declares your glory and shows your handiwork in the heavens and in the earth; please deliver me from the service of mammon, that I may do the work which you give me to do, in truth, in beauty, and in righteousness, with singleness of heart as your servant, and to the benefit of my fellowmen; for the sake of him who came as one that serves, your Son Jesus Christ my Lord.

The Book of Common Prayer (adapted)

Hide me, O my Savior, hide,
Till the storm of life is past;
Safe into the haven guide,
O receive my soul at last!

CHARLES WESLEY

August 3

Test me, O LORD, and try me, examine my heart and my mind; for your love is ever before me, and I walk continually in your truth. PSALM 26:2-3

Lord, teach me to ask in faith. I pray for wars to cease, but I am halfhearted because I don't believe man could stop being greedy so I think there will always be war. I pray that people may become more loving and tolerant to each other, but I don't really think that they will change. I pray for people to recover from their illnesses, or if they don't that they will grow more like you and will learn from their pain, but I ask halfheartedly, not believing.

Lord, increase my faith in you, in your goodness and love, and help me really to believe in your power to work in others and in myself. Save me from being cynical and give me faith as a grain of mustard seed which will grow and flourish. Jesus, I ask this in your name.

MICHAEL HOLLINGS and ETTA GULLICK

Unless I had the spirit of prayer, I could do nothing.

CHARLES G. FINNEY

*A*ugust 4

One thing I ask of the LORD, this is what I seek: that I may dwell in the house of the LORD all the days of my life, to gaze upon the beauty of the LORD and to seek him in his temple.
PSALM 27:4

O God, who made of one blood all nations to dwell on the face of the whole earth and who sent your blessed Son to preach peace to those who are far off and to those that are near; grant that all everywhere may seek after you and find you. Bring the nations into your fold, pour out your Spirit upon all flesh, and hasten your kingdom; through the same, your Son, Jesus Christ our Lord.

GEORGE E. L. COTTON

The greatest need of foreign missions today is prayer.

R. A. TORREY

August 5

I am still confident of this: I will see the goodness of the LORD in the land of the living. Wait for the LORD; be strong and take heart and wait for the LORD. PSALM 27:13-14

O blessed Spirit, have right of way in me this day. Help me to grow by the way of surrender. Let me lose my life that I may find it—in Thee. Give me power over the world, the flesh, and over all the devils of word or thought or deed. Teach me Thy strength; and when the night shall come, may I lie down in peace with Thee. Amen.

RALPH S. CUSHMAN

The one concern of the devil is to keep Christians from praying. He fears nothing from prayerless studies, prayerless work, and prayerless religion. He laughs at our toil, mocks at our wisdom, but trembles when we pray.

SAMUEL CHADWICK

August 6

To you I call, O LORD my Rock; do not turn a deaf ear to me. For if you remain silent, I will be like those who have gone down to the pit. PSALM 28:1

Oh, what a terrible
Predicament I'm in!
Who will free me from my slavery
To this deadly lower nature?"

Lord, Paul's question
Is my question
But I'm sick of forever repeating
the question.

Push me on
To the glorious answer:
"Thank God!
It has been done
By Jesus Christ our Lord.
He has set me free."

RUTH HARMS CALKIN,
Romans 7:25

Prayer means that we have come boldly into the throne room and we are standing in His presence.

E. W. KENYON

August 7

The LORD sits enthroned over the flood; the LORD is enthroned as King forever. The LORD gives strength to his people; the LORD blesses his people with peace. PSALM 29:10-11

O my Father! I desire this day to walk before you with a good conscience, to do nothing that might grieve you or my blessed Lord Jesus. I ask you, may, in the power of the Holy Spirit, the cleansing in the blood be a living, continual, and most effectual deliverance from the power of sin, binding and strengthening me to your perfect service. And may my whole walk with you be in the joy of the united witness of conscience and your Spirit that I am well-pleasing to you. Amen.

ANDREW MURRAY

Whatever you do in revenge against your brother will appear all at once in your heart at the time of prayer.

THE DESERT FATHERS

August 8

You turned my wailing into dancing; you removed my sackcloth and clothed me with joy, that my heart may sing to you and not be silent. PSALM 30:11

Lord Jesus, remind me that you were born in the presence of farm animals, and that unlike the foxes and birds you had nowhere to lay your head. You prayed in the desert places, and when you sanctified the people with your blood you suffered outside the city gate. Lord, recall to my memory that Abraham lived in tents, as did Isaac and Jacob, while looking forward to the city which has foundations.

O Lord! I am too often seeking a continuing city today rather than looking for the city that is to come. Establish my heart among the heirs of the promise; those of whom the world was not worthy; those with a continual sacrifice of praise, the sweet fruit of lips that confess your name; the permanent residents of New Jerusalem, the city whose architect and builder is God.

DANIEL PARTNER

God shapes the world by prayer.
Prayers are deathless. They outlive
the lives of those who uttered them.

E. M. BOUNDS

August 9

Free me from the trap that is set for me, for you are my refuge. Into your hands I commit my spirit; redeem me, O LORD, the God of truth. PSALM 31:4-5

My faith looks up to Thee,
Thou Lamb of Calvary,
Savior divine;
Now hear me while I pray;
Take all my guilt away;
O, let me from this day
Be wholly Thine!

May Thy rich grace impart
Strength to my fainting heart,
My zeal inspire;
As Thou hast died for me,
O may my love to Thee
Pure, warm, and changeless be,
A living fire!

RAY PALMER

Dealing in generalities is the death of prayer.

J. H. EVANS

August 10

Let your face shine on your servant; save me in your unfailing love. Let me not be put to shame, O LORD, for I have cried out to you. PSALM 31:16-17

Lord Jesus Christ, Sun of Righteousness, shine into my heart and life today. Help me to reflect Your light that someone who does not yet know You as Lord and Savior may be directed to You.

I thank You that You have carried the guilt of my sins. Let the sin and evil that may threaten today have no power over me. Grant me the grace to recognize Your will and the faith to do it. In all my dealings with others today, let me be guided by Your precept: "Whatever you wish that men would do to you, do so to them."

Keep me united with You as a branch of the true Vine, that I may draw from You the strength to abound in good works. May You be glorified today in all that I do; for Your name's sake, amen.

MY PRAYER BOOK

All who have walked with God have viewed prayer as the main business of their lives.

DELMA JACKSON

August 11

Love the LORD, all his saints! The LORD preserves the faithful, but the proud he pays back in full. Be strong and take heart, all you who hope in the LORD. PSALM 31:23-24

Grant us, our Father, your grace, that, seeing ourselves in the light of your holiness, we may be cleansed of the pride and vainglory which obscures your truth; and knowing that from you no secrets are hid, we may perceive and confront those deceits and disguises by which we deceive ourselves and our fellowmen. So may we worship you in spirit and in truth and in your light. Amen.

REINHOLD NIEBUHR

When the knees are not often bent, the feet soon slide.

ANONYMOUS

August 12

You are my hiding place; you will protect me from trouble and surround me with songs of deliverance. Rejoice in the LORD and be glad, you righteous; sing, all you who are upright in heart!
PSALM 32:7, 11

We bring before you, O Lord, the troubles and perils of people and nations, the sighing of prisoners and captives, the sorrows of the bereaved, the necessities of strangers, the helplessness of the weak, the despondency of the weary, the failing powers of the aged. O Lord, draw near to each; for the sake of Jesus Christ our Lord. Amen.

ANSELM OF CANTERBURY

We are never more like Christ than in prayers of intercession.

AUSTIN PHELPS

August 13

Sing to him a new song; play skillfully, and shout for joy. For the word of the LORD is right and true; he is faithful in all he does.
PSALM 33:3-4

We must praise your goodness that you have left nothing undone to draw us to yourself. But one thing we ask of you, our God, not to cease to work in our improvement. Let us tend towards you, no matter by what means, and be fruitful in good works, for the sake of Jesus Christ our Lord.

LUDWIG VAN BEETHOVEN

From silly devotions
and from sour-faced saints,
good Lord, deliver us.

TERESA OF AVILA

August 14

May your unfailing love rest upon us, O LORD, even as we put our hope in you. PSALM 33:22

Father I know now, if I never knew it before, that only in Thee can my restless human heart find any peace.

For I began life without knowledge, but full of needs. And the turmoil of my mind, the dissatisfaction of my life all stem from trying to meet those needs with the wrong things and in the wrong places.

Help me so to live that my conscience shall not have to accuse, so that I may be saved the necessity of trying to mend that which need never be broken. I know that only then will the civil war within me cease.

May I be willing to have Thee with me in play as well as in work, knowing that with Thee I shall have peace and joy and no regrets. Through Jesus Christ, my Lord. Amen.

PETER MARSHALL

None can pray well but he that lives well.

THOMAS FULLER

August 15

Fear the LORD, you his saints, for those who fear him lack nothing. The lions may grow weak and hungry, but those who seek the LORD lack no good thing. PSALM 34:9-10

O God, in whose one Gospel all are made one, let not your saving work fail in the broken order of Christendom because we have failed to understand your message. Prosper the labors of all churches bearing the name of Christ and striving to further righteousness and faith in him. Help us to place the truth above our conception of it, and joyfully to recognize the presence of the Holy Spirit wherever he may choose to dwell in human beings; through Jesus Christ our Lord.

CHARLES HENRY BRENT

So I tell you, whatever you ask for in prayer, believe that you have received it, and it will be yours.

MARK 11:24, *NRSV*

August 16

A righteous man may have many troubles, but the LORD delivers him from them all; he protects all his bones, not one of them will be broken. PSALM 34:19-20

O God, my Father, who sent your Son to be my Savior; renew in me day by day the power of your Holy Spirit; that with knowledge and zeal, with courage and love, with gratitude and hope, I may strive powerfully in your service: may he keep my vision clear, my aspiration high, my purpose firm and my sympathy wide; that I may live as a faithful soldier and servant of my Lord Jesus Christ.

WILLIAM TEMPLE (adapted)

Prayer is the great engine to overthrow
and rout my spiritual enemies,
the great means to procure the graces
of which I stand in hourly need.

JOHN NEWTON

August 17

My soul will rejoice in the LORD and delight in his salvation. My whole being will exclaim, "Who is like you, O LORD? You rescue the poor from those too strong for them, the poor and needy from those who rob them." PSALM 35:9-10

Help us this day, we pray, to see the Christ
Who died for the world,
Who came not to bring the righteous but sinners to repentance
Who came to love the lost, and save the sinful, and bring all men home to You.
And make us love with His Love until we too are burdened—
To preach the Gospel to the poor, to heal the brokenhearted,
To preach deliverance to the captives, and recovering of sight to the blind,
And to set all men at liberty until the kingdom comes.

ARTHUR A. ROUNER JR.

The prayer that is faithless is fruitless.

THOMAS WATSON

August 18

My tongue will speak of your righteousness and of your praises all day long. PSALM 35:28

I am inflamed, I am kindled by your gift; and am carried upwards; I glow inwardly, and go forwards. I ascend your ways that are in my heart, and sing a song of degrees; I glow inwardly with your fire, with your good fire, and I go; because I go upwards to the peace of Jerusalem: for I was gladdened in those who said unto me, "We will go up to the house of the Lord." Your good pleasure has placed us there, that we may desire nothing else, but to abide there forever.

AUGUSTINE (adapted)

A sensible thanksgiving for mercies received is a mighty prayer in the Spirit of God. It prevails with Him unspeakably.

JOHN BUNYAN

August 19

How priceless is your unfailing love! Both high and low among men find refuge in the shadow of your wings. They feast on the abundance of your house; you give them drink from your river of delights. PSALM 36:7-8

God, when I am in need, or those I know and love are in need, it is easy to ask for your help. But it is more difficult to pray for strangers. Even when I know they are in great trouble, their needs seem very distant. Help me to imagine how they feel so that I may pray for them, not just with words but with my heart.

AVERY BROOKE

Selfishness is never so exquisitely selfish as when it is on its knees. . . . Self turns what would otherwise be a pure and powerful prayer into a weak and ineffective one.

A. W. TOZER

August 20

Commit your way to the LORD; trust in him and he will do this: He will make your righteousness shine like the dawn, the justice of your cause like the noonday sun. PSALM 37:5-6

You are the God of peace who brought my Lord Jesus back from the dead. You are the great shepherd of the sheep. Because of the blood of the eternal covenant, equip me with everything good so that I may do your will. Work in me that which is pleasing in your sight, through Jesus Christ, to whom be the glory forever. Amen.

HEBREWS 13:20-21 (adapted)

*When they had prayed,
the place in which they were gathered
together was shaken; and they were
all filled with the Holy Spirit and
spoke the word of God with boldness.*

ACTS 4:31, *NRSV*

August 21

Turn from evil and do good; then you will dwell in the land forever. For the LORD loves the just and will not forsake his faithful ones. PSALM 37:27-28

I thank you for the peace and rest you give, blessed Lord.

How amazing that even though you are totally omnipotent
you are also meek and lowly in heart.

I exalt and worship you today because you make my yoke
easy and my burden light.

Then you whisper, *Come unto me, all you who are weary and*
heavy-laden, and I will give you rest.

You are so good to me.

Amen and amen!

ROBERT C. SAVAGE,
Matthew 11:28-30

The Christian will find his parentheses for prayer even in the busiest hours of life.

RICHARD CECIL

August 22

The salvation of the righteous comes from the LORD; he is their stronghold in time of trouble. PSALM 37:39

Make me a captive, Lord, and then I shall be free;
Force me to render up my sword, and I shall conq'ror be.
I sink in life's alarms when by myself I stand,
Imprison me within your arms, and strong shall be my hand.
My heart is weak and poor until it master find:
It has no spring of action sure, it varies with the wind;
It cannot freely move till you have wrought its chain;
Enslave it with your matchless love, and deathless it
shall reign.
My power is faint and low till I have learned to serve:
It wants the needed fire to glow, it wants the breeze to nerve;
It cannot drive the world until itself be driven;
Its flag can only be unfurled when you shall breathe
from heaven.

GEORGE MATHESON

Work as if everything depended upon work and pray as if everything depended upon prayer.

WILLIAM BOOTH

August 23

O LORD, do not forsake me; be not far from me, O my God. Come quickly to help me, O Lord my Savior. PSALM 38:21-22

I pray, O God, for all human hearts that today are lifted up to Thee in earnest desire, and for every group of men and women who are met together to praise and magnify Thy name. Whatever their mode of worship, be graciously pleased to accept their humble offices of prayer and praise, and lead them unto life eternal, through Jesus Christ our Lord. Amen.

JOHN BAILLIE

Elijah was as completely human as we are, and yet when he prayed earnestly that no rain would fall, none fell for the next three and one half years! Then he prayed again, this time that it would rain, and down it poured and the grass turned green and the gardens began to grow again.

JAMES 5:17-18, *TLB*

August 24

But now, Lord, what do I look for? My hope is in you. Save me from all my transgressions; do not make me the scorn of fools.
PSALM 39:7-8

Almighty and Holy Spirit, the comforter, pure, living, true—illumine, govern, sanctify me, and confirm my heart and mind in the faith, and in all genuine consolation; preserve and rule over me so that, dwelling in the house of the Lord, all the days of my life, I may behold the Lord and praise him with a joyful spirit, and in union with all the heavenly church. Amen.

PHILIP MELANCHTHON

Prayer is the ascending vapor which supplies
The showers of blessing, and the stream that flows
Through earth's dry places, till on every side
"The wilderness shall blossom as the rose."

A. B. SIMPSON

August 25

Many, O LORD my God, are the wonders you have done. The things you planned for us no one can recount to you; were I to speak and tell of them, they would be too many to declare.
PSALM 40:5

O Source of Life and Strength, many of Thy mercies do we plainly see, and we believe in a boundless store behind. No morning stars that sing together can have greater call than we for grateful joy. Thou hast given us a life of high vocation and Thine own breathing in our hearts interprets for us its sacred opportunities. Not a cloud of sorrow but Thou hast touched with glory; not a dusty atmosphere of care but that Thy light shines through. Let the time past suffice to have done our own will, and now make us consecrate to Thine. Amen.

JAMES MARTINEAU

It is in recognizing the actual presence of God that we find prayer no longer a chore, but a supreme delight.

GORDON LINDSAY

August 26

Yet I am poor and needy; may the Lord think of me. You are my help and my deliverer; O my God, do not delay. PSALM 40:17

God, help me to remember that being alone is not the same as being lonely. Being alone, I'm in good company—I have many guests: You, first of all, then my good friends and the love they have for me, and then there's me. These times alone with just You and I together can be very wonderful, if I take advantage of them. I can get to know You and myself so much better. I can have rich conversations with You. I can learn from You how to live my life in a way that is pleasing to You. And I'd like to live that way, God. So, please sit down and visit awhile.

EMILY RICHTER

Because God is the living God, he can hear; because he is a loving God, he will hear; because he is our covenant God, he has bound himself to hear.

CHARLES H. SPURGEON

August 27

Blessed is he who has regard for the weak; the LORD delivers him in times of trouble. PSALM 41:1

O God—when I have food,
Help me to remember the hungry;
When I have work,
Help me to remember the jobless;
When I have a warm home,
Help me to remember the homeless;
When I am without pain,
Help me to remember those who suffer;
And remembering,
Help me to destroy my complacency,
And bestir my compassion.
Make me concerned enough to help,
By word and deed, those who cry out—
For what we take for granted.

ANONYMOUS

Prayers not felt by us
are seldom heard by God.

PHILIP HENRY

August 28

Why are you downcast, O my soul? Why so disturbed within me? Put your hope in God, for I will yet praise him, my Savior and my God. PSALM 42:11

I will sing to the LORD, for he has triumphed gloriously;
horse and rider he has thrown into the sea.
The LORD is my strength and my might,
  and he has become my salvation;
this is my God, and I will praise him,
  my father's God, and I will exalt him.
In your steadfast love you led the people whom you redeemed;
  you guided them by your strength to your holy abode.
You brought them in and planted them on the mountain of
    your own possession,
  the place, O LORD, that you made your abode,
  the sanctuary, O LORD, that your hands have established.
The LORD will reign forever and ever.

EXODUS 15:1-2, 13, 17-18, *NRSV*

Let prayer be the key of the day and the bolt of the night.

JEAN PAUL RICHTER

August 29

Send forth your light and your truth, let them guide me; let them bring me to your holy mountain, to the place where you dwell. Then I will go to the altar of God, to God, my joy and my delight. I will praise you with the harp, O God, my God. PSALM 43:3-4

It's hard to be a man, today, God.
I don't know which way to go—tough guy or softie?
I can't act on instinct anymore,
  because it really isn't instinct after all, I'm told,
  but rather the way our fathers taught us to be.
But You must have had something in mind when You made
    a man, God.
Am I getting at all close to it?
  That's where I'd like to be.
  Maybe—even—something like Your Son—
  Who was quite a man.

MICHAEL BARROWS

Time spent in prayer is never wasted.

FRANÇOIS FÉNELON

August 30

I do not trust in my bow, my sword does not bring me victory; but you give us victory over our enemies, you put our adversaries to shame. PSALM 44:6-7

Almighty and everliving God, who for the confirmation of the faith, allowed your holy apostle Thomas to be doubtful of your Son's resurrection: grant us so perfectly, and without all doubt, to believe in your Son, Jesus Christ, that our faith in your sight may never be reproved. Hear us, O Lord, through the same Jesus Christ, to whom with you and the Holy Spirit, be all honor and glory, now and forever more. Amen.

THOMAS CRANMER

No one is a firmer believer in the power of prayer than the devil; not that he practices it, but he suffers from it.

GUY H. KING

August 31

We are brought down to the dust; our bodies cling to the ground. Rise up and help us; redeem us because of your unfailing love.
PSALM 44:25-26

Show unto me, O Lord, your mercy, and delight my heart with it. Let me find you, whom so longingly I seek.

See: here is the man whom the robbers seized, and mishandled, and left half dead on the road to Jericho. O you who can do what the kindhearted Samaritan cannot: come to my aid!

I am the sheep who wandered into the wilderness: seek after me, and bring me home again to your fold. Do with me what you will, that all the days of my life I may abide by you, and praise you, with all those who are in heaven with you for all of eternity. Amen.

JEROME

He who has learned to pray has learned the greatest secret of a holy and a happy life.
WILLIAM LAW

September 1

Your throne, O God, will last for ever and ever; a scepter of justice will be the scepter of your kingdom. PSALM 45:6

O Lord, come quickly and reign on your throne, for now often something rises up within me, and tries to take possession of your throne; pride, covetousness, uncleanness, and sloth want to be my kings; and then evil-speaking, anger, hatred, and the whole train of vices join with me in warring against myself, and try to reign over me. I resist them, I cry out against them and say, "I have no other king than Christ." O King of Peace, come and reign in me, for I will have no king but you! Amen.

BERNARD OF CLAIRVAUX

The devil enjoys hearing a prayer that is addressed to an audience.

ANONYMOUS

September 2

"Be still, and know that I am God; I will be exalted among the nations, I will be exalted in the earth." The LORD Almighty is with us; the God of Jacob is our fortress. PSALM 46:10-11

Guide me, O Lord, in all the changes and varieties of the world, that in all things that shall happen, I may have an evenness and tranquility of spirit, that my soul may be wholly resigned to your divine will and pleasure, never murmuring at your gentle chastisements and fatherly correction. Amen.

JEREMY TAYLOR

Many words do not a good prayer make; what counts is the heartfelt desire to commune with God, and the faith to back it up.

ANONYMOUS

September 3

For God is King of all the earth; sing to him a psalm of praise. God reigns over the nations; God is seated on his holy throne.
PSALM 47:7-8

Lord, open my eyes so that I may see you; open my heart so I may experience your love. My eyes will be blinded by the vision of you, and my heart will be overwhelmed by the fire of your love. Let me not be afraid of dying to myself so that you may become my vision and the be-all and end-all of my life.

MICHAEL HOLLINGS and ETTA GULLICK

Time spent on the knees in prayer will do more to remedy heart strain and nerve worry than anything else.

GEORGE DAVID STEWART

September 4

Within your temple, O God, we meditate on your unfailing love. Like your name, O God, your praise reaches to the ends of the earth; your right hand is filled with righteousness. PSALM 48:9-10

O Thou who changest not though all else changeth, abide with me. The years pass, the springtime changes into autumn, the shadows lengthen; help me to find the victory of each day and hour. And if, afar or near, I sometimes glimpse the valley of the shadow, deliver me, in Christ's dear Name, from all bondage of the fear of death. Help me to thrill forever with Eternal Spring.

RALPH S. CUSHMAN

But they that wait upon the LORD
shall renew their strength; they shall
mount up with wings as eagles;
they shall run, and not be weary;
and they shall walk, and not faint.

ISAIAH 40:31, *KJV*

September 5

Do not be overawed when a man grows rich, when the splendor of his house increases; for he will take nothing with him when he dies, his splendor will not descend with him. PSALM 49:16-17

O light that never fades, as the light of day now streams through these windows and floods this room, so let me open to Thee the windows of my heart, that all my life may be filled by the radiance of Thy presence. Let no corner of my being be unillumined by the light of Thy countenance. Let there be nothing within me to darken the brightness of the day. Let the Spirit of Him whose life was the light of men rule within my heart till eventide. Amen.

JOHN BAILLIE

Is any among you afflicted?
let him pray. Is any merry?
let him sing psalms.

JAMES 5:13, *KJV*

September 6

He who sacrifices thank offerings honors me, and he prepares the way so that I may show him the salvation of God. PSALM 50:23

Gracious Lord, I thank You for Your Word of salvation, for it is a lamp unto my feet and a light unto my path. Grant that I may love it, understand it, believe it, and live according to it.

Make the Bible my comfort and guide. Open my heart and mind when I read Your Word that its sacred message may take root and grow. Help me to regard all faithful pastors and teachers as Your representatives, and strengthen my faith through their preaching and teaching.

Teach me to regard Sunday not only as a day of rest from my labors, but also as a day on which I may gladly hear and lean on Your holy Word.

Help me today, and at all times, to seek and find You as You have revealed Yourself in the Scriptures. Grant that I may daily worship and glorify You as my Creator, my Redeemer, and my Comforter; through Jesus Christ. Amen.

My Prayer Book

A wicked man in prayer may lift up his hands, but he cannot lift up his face.

THOMAS WATSON

September 7

Create in me a pure heart, O God, and renew a steadfast spirit within me. Do not cast me from your presence or take your Holy Spirit from me. Restore to me the joy of your salvation and grant me a willing spirit, to sustain me. PSALM 51:10-12

Change me,
God please change me.
Though I cringe
Kick
Resist and resent
Pay no attention to me whatever.
When I run to hide
Drag me out of my safe little shelter.
Change me totally
Whatever it takes
However long You must work at the job.
Change me—and save me
From spiritual self-destruction.

RUTH HARMS CALKIN

Prayer is not simply getting things from God, that is a most initial form of prayer; prayer is getting into perfect communion with God.

OSWALD CHAMBERS

September 8

I will praise you forever for what you have done; in your name I will hope, for your name is good. I will praise you in the presence of your saints. PSALM 52:9

O LORD, I do groan and sigh when I think of the immense tasks and responsibilities you have laid on my shoulders because I know too well my failings and inadequacies. I groan and sigh, but I take hope in the promise that in my groans and confessions I am strengthened and forgiven and I am empowered and prayed for by your Spirit. I groan and I sigh, but I know full well that your yoke is easy and your burden is light compared to my trying to live and work without you. I praise you that I have experienced the difference between slavery in fear and service in friendship with you. May I never forget my need of your Spirit each moment of my life, and when I am groaning and sighing, may I be encouraged with the knowledge that you are there praying with me and for me through Jesus Christ my Savior. Amen.

LOUIS GIFFORD PARKHURST JR.

The best prayers have often more groans than words.

JOHN BUNYAN

September 9

Oh, that salvation for Israel would come out of Zion! When God restores the fortunes of his people, let Jacob rejoice and Israel be glad! PSALM 53:6

O God, who has made of one blood all nations of men to dwell on the face of the whole earth, and did send your blessed Son to preach peace to them that are far off and to them that are near; grant that all men everywhere may seek after you and find you. Bring the nations into your fold, pour out your Spirit upon all flesh, and hasten your kingdom; through your Son, Jesus Christ our Lord. Amen.

The Book of Common Prayer

Prayer puts God's work in his hands—and keeps it there.

E. M. BOUNDS

September 10

I will sacrifice a freewill offering to you; I will praise your name, O LORD, for it is good. PSALM 54:6

I give you praise, O God, for a well-spent day. But I am yet unsatisfied, because I do not enjoy enough of you. I would have my soul more closely united to you by faith and love. I would love you above all things. You, who has made me, knows my desires, my expectations. My joys all center in you and it is you yourself that I desire; it is your favor, your acceptance, the communications of your grace that I earnestly wish for, more than anything in the world.

I rejoice in my relation to you, who are my Father, my Lord, and my God. I rejoice that you have power over me and that I desire to live in subjection to you. I thank you that you have brought me so far. I will beware of despairing of your mercy for the time which is to come, and will give you the glory of your free grace. Amen.

SUSANNA WESLEY

There must be fired affections before our prayers will go up.

WILLIAM JENKYN

September 11

Cast your cares on the LORD and he will sustain you; he will never let the righteous fall. PSALM 55:22

The Lord is my shepherd; I shall not want. He maketh me to lie down in green pastures: he leadeth me beside the still waters. He restoreth my soul: he leadeth me in the paths of righteousness for his name's sake. Yea, though I walk through the valley of the shadow of death, I will fear no evil: for thou art with me; thy rod and thy staff they comfort me.

Thou preparest a table before me in the presence of mine enemies: thou anointest my head with oil; my cup runneth over. Surely goodness and mercy shall follow me all the days of my life: and I will dwell in the house of the LORD for ever.

PSALM 23, *KJV*

It is impossible to lose your footing while on your knees.

ANONYMOUS

September 12

In God, whose word I praise, in the LORD, whose word I praise—in God I trust; I will not be afraid. What can man do to me?
PSALM 56:10-11

Blessed Father! I thank you that the Holy Spirit is to me the bearer of the fullness of Jesus, and that in being filled with the Spirit I am made full with the fullness. I thank you that there have been people on earth since Pentecost, not a few, of whom you have said that they were full of the Holy Spirit. O my God! Make me full. Let the Holy Spirit take and keep possession of my deepest, inmost life. Let your Spirit fill my spirit. Let then the fountain flow through all the soul's affections and powers. Let it flow over and flow through my lips, speaking your praise and love. Let the very body, by the quickening and sanctifying energy of the Spirit, be your temple, full of the divine life. Lord my God! I believe you hear me. You have given it to me; I accept it as mine.

ANDREW MURRAY (adapted)

'Answered prayers cover the field of providential history as flowers cover western prairies.

T. L. CUYLER

September 13

My heart is steadfast, O God, my heart is steadfast; I will sing and make music. Awake, my soul! Awake, harp and lyre! I will awaken the dawn. PSALM 57:7-8

Eternal Light, shine into my heart;
Eternal Goodness, deliver me from evil;
Eternal Power, be my support;
Eternal Wisdom, scatter the darkness of my ignorance;
Eternal Pity, have mercy upon me;
that with all my heart and mind and soul and strength I may seek your face and be brought by your infinite mercy to your holy presence, through Jesus Christ our Lord.

ALCUIN OF YORK (adapted)

Be not hot in prayer and cold in praise.

ANONYMOUS

September 14

The righteous will be glad when they are avenged. . . . Then men will say, "Surely the righteous still are rewarded; surely there is a God who judges the earth." PSALM 58:10-11

Fill Thou my life, O Lord my God,
In every part with praise
That my whole being may proclaim
Thy being and Thy ways.

Not for the lip of praise alone,
Nor even the praising heart,
I ask but for a life made up
Of praise in every part.

So shall no part of day or night
From sacredness be free;
But all my life, in every step,
Be fellowship with Thee.

HORATIUS BONAR

Do not want things to turn out as they seem best to you, but as God pleases. Then you will be free from confusion and thankful in prayer.

THE DESERT FATHERS

September 15

But I will sing of your strength, in the morning I will sing of your love; for you are my fortress, my refuge in times of trouble. O my Strength, I sing praise to you; you, O God, are my fortress, my loving God. PSALM 59:16-17

O God! You are able to keep me from falling and to make me stand without a defect in the presence of your glory with rejoicing. You are the only God, my Savior. To you be glory, majesty, power, and authority, before all time and now and forever through Jesus Christ our Lord. Amen.

JUDE 1:24-25 (adapted)

I rise before the dawning of the morning and cry for help; I hope in your word.

PSALM 119:147, *NKJV*

September 16

Give us aid against the enemy, for the help of man is worthless. With God we will gain the victory, and he will trample down our enemies. PSALM 60:11-12

What a choir this is, Lord, singing celestial harmonies in
your praise.
Millions of angels blend their
voices in an exuberant tribute to you.
"Worthy is the Lamb that was slain!
Worthy is the Lamb that was slain!
Worthy to receive power and riches and wisdom and
strength!
Worthy to receive honor and glory and blessing!"
My voice is lost in such a multitude, but I worship you
with heartfelt praise.
Thank you, thank you, blessed Jesus!

ROBERT C. SAVAGE,
Revelation 5:11-12

Those who trade with heaven by prayer grow rich by quick returns.

WILLIAM S. PLUMER

September 17

For you have been my refuge, a strong tower against the foe. I long to dwell in your tent forever and take refuge in the shelter of your wings. PSALM 61:3-4

Almighty God, you who have made all things for me, and me for your glory, sanctify my body and soul, my thoughts and my intentions, my words and actions, that whatsoever I shall think, or speak, or do, may by me be designed to the glorification of your name. And let no pride or self-seeking, no impure motive or unworthy purpose, no little ends or low imagination stain my spirit, or profane any of my words and actions. But let my body be a servant to my spirit, and both body and spirit servants of Jesus Christ.

THOMAS À KEMPIS (adapted)

Prayer, to the patriarchs and prophets, was more than the recital of well-known and well-worn phrases—it was the outpouring of the heart.

HERBERT LOCKYER

September 18

Find rest, O my soul, in God alone; my hope comes from him. He alone is my rock and my salvation; he is my fortress, I will not be shaken. PSALM 62:5-6

Father, I will not ask for wealth or fame,
Though once they would have joyed my carnal sense;
I shudder not to bear a hated name,
Wanting all wealth, myself my sole defense,
But give me, Lord, eyes to behold the truth,
A seeing sense that knows the eternal right;
A heart with pity filled and gentlest ruth;
A valiant faith that makes all darkness light;
Give me the power to labor for mankind;
Make me the mouth of such as cannot speak;
Eyes let me be to groping folk, and blind;
A conscience to the base; and to the weak
Let me be hands and feet; and to the foolish, mind;
And lead still further on such as your kingdom seek.

THEODORE PARKER

God never denied that soul anything that went as far as heaven to ask it.

JOHN TRAPP

September 19

Because your love is better than life, my lips will glorify you. I will praise you as long as I live, and in your name I will lift up my hands. PSALM 63:3-4

Use me, my Savior, for whatever purpose and in whatever way you may require. Here is my poor heart, an empty vessel: fill it with your grace. Here is my sinful and troubled soul; quicken it and refresh it with your love. Take my heart for your abode; my mouth to spread abroad the glory of your name; my love and all my powers for the advancement of your believing people; and never allow the steadfastness and confidence of my faith to abate.

DWIGHT L. MOODY

Let me burn out for God.
After all, whatever God may appoint,
prayer is the great thing.
Oh, that I may be a man of prayer!

HENRY MARTYN

September 20

Let the righteous rejoice in the LORD and take refuge in him; let all the upright in heart praise him! PSALM 64:10

Our Father, I think of all the pain and heartache, the tears and sorrow, the greed and cruelty unloosed around the world.

Help me to be an instrument of Thine to alleviate the pain, by this day:

returning good for evil,
returning soft answers for sharp criticisms,
being polite when I receive rudeness,
being understanding when I am confronted by
ignorance and stupidity.

So may I, in gentleness and love, check the hasty answer, choke back the unkind retort, and thus short-circuit some of the bitterness and unkindness that has overflowed Thy world. I ask this in the name of Jesus, who alone can give me the grace so to act. Amen.

PETER MARSHALL

Whether we like it or not,
asking is the rule of the Kingdom.

CHARLES H. SPURGEON

September 21

You answer us with awesome deeds of righteousness, O God our Savior, the hope of all the ends of the earth and of the farthest seas, who formed the mountains by your power, having armed yourself with strength. PSALM 65:5-6

I am not worthy, Master and Lord, that you should come beneath the roof of my soul: yet since you in your love toward all wish to dwell in me, in boldness I come. You command, open the gates—which you alone have forged; and you will come in with love toward all as is your nature; you will come in and enlighten my darkened reason. I believe that you will do this: for you did not send away the harlot that came to you with tears; nor cast out the repentant publican; nor reject the thief who acknowledged your kingdom; nor forsake the repentant persecutor, a yet greater act; but all of those who came to you in repentance, were counted in the band of your friends, who alone abide blessed forever, now, and unto the endless ages.

JOHN CHRYSOSTOM

The great thing in prayer is to feel that we are putting our supplications into the bosom of omnipotent love.

ANDREW MURRAY

September 22

Say to God, "How awesome are your deeds! So great is your power that your enemies cringe before you. All the earth bows down to you; they sing praise to you, they sing praise to your name." PSALM 66:3-4

We pray, O Lord, for deliverance from all that weakens
faith in you:
from pompous solemnity;
from mistaking earnestness for trust in you;
from seeking easy answers to large questions;
from being overawed by the self-confident;
from dependence upon mood and feelings;
from despondency and the loss of self-respect;
from timidity and hesitation in making decisions.
In Christ, we pray. Amen.

WILLARD SPERRY

Beyond our utmost wants
His love and power can bless;
To praying souls he always grants
More than they can express.

JOHN NEWTON

September 23

May the peoples praise you, O God; may all the peoples praise you. May the nations be glad and sing for joy, for you rule the peoples justly and guide the nations of the earth. PSALM 67:3-4

Almighty God and heavenly Father, whose Son Jesus Christ was subject to Mary and Joseph at Nazareth, and shared there the life of an earthly home; send down your blessing, we beg you, upon all Christian families. Grant to parents the spirit of obedience and true reverence; and so bind each to each with the bond of mutual love, that to all its members of whatever age, every Christian family may be an image of the Holy Family of Nazareth.

EDWARD C. RATCLIFFE

The firmament of the Bible is ablaze with answers to prayer.

T. L. CUYLER

September 24

Sing to God, sing praise to his name, extol him who rides on the clouds—his name is the LORD—and rejoice before him. PSALM 68:4

O God, who made us once a Christian people who strode to live by heaven's law, who loved Your Word in Scripture and in Psalm, who felt themselves privileged to worship every Sabbath day in the house of the Lord:

We have not loved You as our fathers loved. We have grown careless in our faith, and we have made worship in Your house a matter of convenience and not of conscience; a matter of comfort instead of sacrifice; a matter of fancy instead of faith.

Forgive us, Lord, that we think more of ourselves than we do of You. And forgive the Church in this land that before the world has seemed really to care so little. Give us a new heart, Lord, and a new spirit, we pray.

ARTHUR A. ROUNER JR.

Prayer is a serious thing.
We may be taken at our words.

DWIGHT L. MOODY

September 25

Sing to God, O kingdoms of the earth, sing praise to the Lord, to him who rides the ancient skies above, who thunders with mighty voice. PSALM 68:32-33

O God of interstellar space, in whose sight a thousand years are as an evening gone; enlarge our horizons, we beg you, that we may behold your majesty in all your works and know your lordship in all your ways.

ROBERT N. RODENMAYER

Our prayers run along one road and God's answers by another, and by and by they meet.

ADONIRAM JUDSON

September 26

Answer me, O LORD, out of the goodness of your love; in your great mercy turn to me. Do not hide your face from your servant; answer me quickly, for I am in trouble. PSALM 69:16-17

I desire, O Lord, that you will, to all your other mercies, add that gift by which I shall trust in you—faith that works by love; faith that abides with me; faith that transforms material things, and gives them to me in spiritual meanings; faith that illumines the world by a light that never sets, that shines brighter than the day, and that clears the night quite out of my experience. I beg you to grant me this faith, that shall give me victory over the world and over myself; that shall make me valiant in all temptation and bring me off a conqueror and more than a conqueror through him that loved me. Amen.

HENRY WARD BEECHER

In our prayer time, there ought to be on our part a deep desire to have a conscience void of offense toward God and toward men.

PARIS REIDHEAD

September 27

I will praise God's name in song and glorify him with thanksgiving. This will please the LORD more than an ox, more than a bull with its horns and hoofs. PSALM 69:30-31

Holy Spirit of God, who prefers before all temples the upright heart and pure, instruct us in all truth; what is dark, illumine; what is low, raise and support; what is shallow, deepen; that every chapter in our lives may witness to your power and justify the ways of God to men. In the name of Jesus, giver of all grace. Amen.

JOHN MILTON

We must wrestle earnestly in prayer, like men contending with a deadly enemy for life.

J. C. RYLE

September 28

Yet I am poor and needy; come quickly to me, O God. You are my help and my deliverer; O LORD, do not delay. PSALM 70:5

Our Father, you made us. You made us so that we are restless until we rest in you. Accept, we beseech you, those pressure points in life where we know we need you. And help us. For you are our Father and we know who we are because you sent your Son, our brother, Jesus Christ. Amen.

JOHN B. COBURN

What a Friend we have in Jesus,
All our sins and griefs to bear!
What a privilege to carry
Everything to God in prayer!

JOSEPH SCRIVEN

September 29

Your righteousness reaches to the skies, O God, you who have done great things. Who, O God, is like you? PSALM 71:19

How lovely is your dwelling place
O LORD of hosts!
My soul longs, indeed it faints
for the courts of the LORD;
my heart and my flesh sing for joy to the living God. . . .

For a day in your courts is better than a thousand elsewhere.
I would rather be a doorkeeper in the house of my God
than live in the tents of wickedness.
For the LORD God is a sun and shield; he bestows favor
and honor.
No good thing does the LORD withhold from those who
walk uprightly.
O LORD of hosts, happy is everyone who trusts in you.

PSALM 84:1-2, 10-12, *NRSV*

I find in the Psalms much the same range of mood and expression as I perceive within my own life of prayer.

MALCOLM BOYD

September 30

Praise be to the LORD God, the God of Israel, who alone does marvelous deeds. Praise be to his glorious name forever; may the whole earth be filled with his glory. Amen and Amen. PSALM 72:18-19

O God, grant that looking upon the face of the Lord, as into a glass, I may be changed into his likeness, from glory to glory. Take out of me all pride and vanity, boasting and forwardness, and give me the true courage which shows itself by gentleness, the true wisdom which shows itself by simplicity, and the true power which shows itself by modesty.

CHARLES KINGSLEY (adapted)

A saint is to put forth his faith in prayer, and afterwards follow his prayer with faith.

VAVASOR POWELL

October 1

Whom have I in heaven but you? And earth has nothing I desire besides you. My flesh and my heart may fail, but God is the strength of my heart and my portion forever. PSALM 73:25-26

Almighty God, it seems that the great people of earth are people who pray—not those who talk about prayer, nor those who say they believe in prayer, but those who take time to pray. Help me to be such a one, dear God, for my soul's sake and Thy Kingdom's sake. Amen.

RALPH S. CUSHMAN

The more praying there is in the world, the better the world will be; the mightier the forces against evil everywhere.

E. M. BOUNDS

October 2

Rise up, O God, and defend your cause; remember how fools mock you all day long. Do not ignore the clamor of your adversaries, the uproar of your enemies, which rises continually. PSALM 74:22-23

Lord Jesus, we are constantly shown on TV, in the newspapers, and in the movies the horrors of the world, the evil and perverted behavior of mankind, so that we come close to despair. You, Lord, in your life knew failure, saw men betray and torture each other. You knew hell on earth as we do, but you did not despair, for you loved men and trusted your Father.

Keep alight in our hearts the flame of hope, make us to see the beautiful and good things in the world, not just the drab, the squalid and sordid. Help us to see the goodness of men, and by our love increase this and make it grow and spread among the people, for we are your instruments in the world. Make your hope and love shine through us so that the hells of others may be lightened and they may glimpse something of your glory.

MICHAEL HOLLINGS and ETTA GULLICK

Revival fires flame where hearts are praying.

DICK EASTMAN

October 3

We give thanks to you, O God, we give thanks, for your Name is near; men tell of your wonderful deeds. PSALM 75:1

I most humbly beg you to give me grace not only to be a hearer of the Word, but a doer also of the same; not only to love, but also to live your gospel; not only to favor, but also to follow your godly doctrine; not only to profess, but also to practice your blessed commandments, to the honor of your Holy Name, and the health of my soul.

THOMAS BECON (adapted)

*If we do not love one another,
we certainly shall not have much
power with God in prayer.*

DWIGHT L. MOODY

October 4

Make vows to the LORD your God and fulfill them; let all the neighboring lands bring gifts to the One to be feared. He breaks the spirit of rulers; he is feared by the kings of the earth.
PSALM 76:11-12

Grant, Almighty God, since I have already entered in hope upon the threshold of my eternal inheritance, and know that there is a mansion for me in heaven since Christ, my head and the firstfruits of my salvation, has been received there; grant that I may proceed more and more in the way of your holy calling until at length I reach the goal and so enjoy the eternal glory of which you have given me a taste in this world, by the same Christ my Lord.

JOHN CALVIN

Saints of the early church reaped great harvests in the field of prayer and found the mercy seat to be a mine of untold treasures.

CHARLES H. SPURGEON

October 5

Your ways, O God, are holy. What god is so great as our God? You are the God who performs miracles; you display your power among the peoples. PSALM 77:13-14

O Lord God, in whom we live and move and have our being, open our eyes that we may behold your fatherly presence ever about us. Teach us to be anxious for nothing, and when we have done what you have given us to do, help us, O God our Savior, to leave the issue to your wisdom, knowing that all things are possible to us through your Son our Savior, Jesus Christ.

RICHARD MEUX BENSON

Prayer is a shield to the soul,
a sacrifice to God, and a scourge for Satan.

JOHN BUNYAN

October 6

We will tell the next generation the praiseworthy deeds of the LORD, his power, and the wonders he has done. PSALM 78:4

Bless my children with healthful bodies, with good understandings, with the graces and gifts of your Spirit, with sweet dispositions and holy habits, and sanctify them throughout in their bodies and souls and spirits, and keep them unblamable to the coming of the Lord Jesus.

JEREMY TAYLOR

Beware of the barrenness of a busy life.

CORRIE TEN BOOM

October 7

Their hearts were not loyal to him, they were not faithful to his covenant. Yet he was merciful; he forgave their iniquities and did not destroy them. PSALM 78:37-38

Give me, O God,
A steadfast heart, which no unworthy affection may drag
downwards;
An unconquered heart, which no tribulation can wear out;
An upright heart, which no unworthy purpose may
tempt aside.

THOMAS AQUINAS

The great thing in prayer is to feel
that we are putting our supplications
into the bosom of omnipotent love.

ANDREW MURRAY

October 8

He chose David his servant and took him from the sheep pens. . . . And David shepherded them with integrity of heart; with skillful hands he led them. PSALM 78:70, 72

May the strength of God pilot me. May the power of God preserve me. May the wisdom of God instruct me. May the hand of God protect me. May the way of God direct me. May the shield of God defend me.

PATRICK OF IRELAND (adapted)

Bear up the hands that hang down, by faith and prayer; support the tottering knees. Storm the throne of grace and persevere therein, and mercy will come down.

JOHN WESLEY

October 9

Help us, O God our Savior, for the glory of your name; deliver us and forgive our sins for your name's sake. PSALM 79:9

O God, as the day returns and brings us the petty round of irritating duties, help us to perform them with laughter and kind faces; let cheerfulness abound with industry; give us to go blithely on our business all this day; bring us to our resting beds weary and content and undishonored; and grant us in the end the gift of sleep.

ROBERT LOUIS STEVENSON

Prayer is the soul's breathing itself into the bosom of its heavenly Father.

THOMAS WATSON

October 14

Better is one day in your courts than a thousand elsewhere; I would rather be a doorkeeper in the house of my God than dwell in the tents of the wicked. PSALM 84:10

Jesus, you know what it is to be human and that it is not easy to love our neighbor as ourselves.

When we do not understand our neighbors, nor they us, help us to think more about how we could understand them and less about how they could understand us. May we never let fear keep us from speaking or acting in love, nor thoughtlessness spoil the impulse of the heart.

May we do all that we do in gratitude to you, rather than in desire for praise, and when our time, energy or talent are at an end, may we quietly ask your help and remember that you love and care for them much more than we do.

AVERY BROOKE

The beginning of anxiety is the end of faith, and the beginning of true faith is the end of anxiety.

GEORGE MUELLER

October 15

Will you not revive us again, that your people may rejoice in you? Show us your unfailing love, O LORD, and grant us your salvation. PSALM 85:6-7

Give us, O Lord God, a deep sense of your holiness; how you are of purer eyes than to behold iniquity, and cannot overlook or pass by that which is evil.

Give us no less, O Lord, a deep sense of your wonderful love towards us; how you would not let us alone in our ruin, but did come after us, in the person of your Son, Jesus Christ, to bring us back to our true home with you.

Quicken in us, O Lord, the Spirit of gratitude, of loyalty and of sacrifice, that we may seek in all things to please him who humbled himself for us, even to the death of the cross, by dying unto sin and living unto righteousness; through the same Jesus Christ our Lord.

DEAN VAUGHAN

God tells us to burden him with whatever burdens us.

ANONYMOUS

October 16

Teach me your way, O LORD, and I will walk in your truth; give me an undivided heart, that I may fear your name. PSALM 86:11

O God, You have glorified our victorious Savior with a visible, triumphant resurrection from the dead, and ascension into heaven, where he sits at your right hand; grant, we beg you, that his triumphs and glories may ever shine in our eyes, to make us endure our own; being assured by his example, that if we endeavor to live and die like him, for the advancement of your love in ourselves and others, you will raise our dead bodies again, and conforming them to his glorious body, call us above the clouds, and give us possession of your everlasting kingdom.

JOHN WESLEY

Prayer time must be kept up as duly as meal-time.

MATTHEW HENRY

October 17

Indeed, of Zion it will be said, "This one and that one were born in her, and the Most High himself will establish her." The LORD will write in the register of the peoples: "This one was born in Zion." PSALM 87:5-6

O heavenly Father,

I praise and thank you

For the peace of the night.

I praise and thank you for this new day.

I praise and thank you for all your goodness

and faithfulness throughout my life.

You have granted me many blessings;

Now let me also accept what is hard from your hand.

You will lay on me no more than I can bear.

You make all things work together for good for your
children.

DIETRICH BONHOEFFER

I will pray morning, noon, and night.

PSALM 55:17, *TLB*

October 18

But I cry to you for help, O LORD; in the morning my prayer comes before you. PSALM 88:13

Grant, O heavenly Father, that the spiritual refreshment I have this day enjoyed may not be left behind and forgotten as tomorrow I return to the cycle of common tasks. Here is a fountain of inward strength. Here is a purifying wind that must blow through all my business and all my pleasures. Here is light to enlighten all my road. Therefore, O God, do Thou enable me so to discipline my will that in hours of stress I may honestly seek after those things for which I have prayed in hours of peace.

JOHN BAILLIE

O Lord, you know what is best for me.
Let this or that be done, as you please.
Give what you will, how much you
will, and when you will.

THOMAS À KEMPIS

*O*ctober 19

The heavens praise your wonders, O LORD, your faithfulness too, in the assembly of the holy ones. For who in the skies above can compare with the LORD? Who is like the LORD among the heavenly beings? PSALM 89:5-6

Show me, O God, that the one great hindrance is my own wisdom, my imagination that I can understand the Word and Truth of God. Oh teach me to become a fool that I may be wise. May my whole life become one continued act of faith, that the Holy Spirit will surely do his work of teaching, guiding, and leading into the truth. Father, you gave him that he might reveal Jesus in his glory within me; I wait for this. Amen.

ANDREW MURRAY

We are going home to many who cannot read. So, Lord, make us to be Bibles so that those who cannot read the Book can read it in us.

AN UNKNOWN CHINESE WOMAN

October 20

Righteousness and justice are the foundation of your throne; love and faithfulness go before you. Blessed are those who have learned to acclaim you, who walk in the light of your presence, O LORD. PSALM 89:14-15

Eternal Father, you alone can control the days that are gone and the deeds that are done; remove from my burdened memory the weight of past years, that being set free both from the glamour of complacency and from the palsy of remorse, I may reach forth unto those things which are before, and press towards the mark for the prize of the high calling of God in Christ Jesus.

CHARLES HENRY BRENT

Prayer is a strong wall
and fortress of the church;
it is a goodly Christian's weapon.

MARTIN LUTHER

October 21

How long, O LORD? Will you hide yourself forever? How long will your wrath burn like fire? Remember how fleeting is my life. For what futility you have created all men! PSALM 89:46-47

We bring before you, O Lord, the troubles and perils of people and nations, the sighing of prisoners and captives, the sorrows of the bereaved, the necessities of strangers, the helplessness of the weak, the despondency of the weary, the failing powers of the aged. O Lord, draw near to each; for the sake of Jesus Christ our Lord. Amen.

ANSELM OF CANTERBURY

A man's state before God may always be measured by his prayers.

J. C. RYLE

*O*ctober 22

If you make the Most High your dwelling—even the LORD, who is my refuge—then no harm will befall you, no disaster will come near your tent. PSALM 91:9-10

Give, I pray you, to all children grace reverently to love their parents, and lovingly to obey them. Teach us all that filial duty never ends or lessens; and bless all parents in their children, and all children in their parents.

CHRISTINA ROSSETTI

All the prayers in the Scripture you will find to be reasoning with God, not a multitude of words heaped together.

STEPHEN CHARNOCK

October 23

The LORD reigns, he is robed in majesty; the LORD is robed in majesty and is armed with strength. The world is firmly established; it cannot be moved. PSALM 93:1

Though the fig tree does not blossom,
    and no fruit is on the vines;
    though the produce of the olive fails
    and the fields yield no food;
though the flock is cut off from the fold and there is no
        herd in the stalls,
yet I will rejoice in the Lord; I will exult in the God of my
        salvation.
Lord, you are my strength; you make my feet like the feet
        of a deer,
and make me tread upon the heights.

HABAKKUK 3:17-19 (adapted)

The LORD is far from the wicked,
but he hears the prayer of therighteous.

PROVERBS 15:29, *NRSV*

October 24

Blessed is the man you discipline, O LORD, the man you teach from your law; you grant him relief from days of trouble, till a pit is dug for the wicked. PSALM 94:12-13

O God, we do not desire new contentions and discord. We pray only that the Son of God, our Lord Jesus Christ, who for us died and rose from the grave, will guide us, that all of us who are in many churches and many communions may be one Church, one Communion, and one in him. As he himself earnestly prayed for us in his hour of death, saying, "I pray also for those who through your Word will believe in me, that they may be one as you, Father, are in union with me and I with you, and that they may be one in us," so also we pray. Amen.

PHILIP MELANCHTHON

In Gethsemane the holiest of all petitioners prayed three times that a certain cup might pass from Him. It did not. After that the idea that prayer is recommended to us as a sort of infallible gimmick may be dismissed.

C. S. LEWIS

October 25

Declare his glory among the nations, his marvelous deeds among all peoples. For great is the LORD and most worthy of praise; he is to be feared above all gods. PSALM 96:3-4

Our Father which art in heaven, Hallowed be thy name. Thy Kingdom come. Thy will be done in earth, as it is in heaven. Give us this day our daily bread. And forgive us our debts, as we forgive our debtors. And lead us not into temptation, but deliver us from evil: For thine is the kingdom, and the power, and the glory, for ever. Amen.

MATTHEW 6:9-13, *KJV*

The Lord's Prayer may be committed to memory quickly, but it is slowly learnt by heart.

FREDERICK DENISON MAURICE

October 26

Light is shed upon the righteous and joy on the upright in heart. Rejoice in the LORD, you who are righteous, and praise his holy name. PSALM 97:11-12

Grant, O my God, that I may know you, love you and rejoice in you; and if in this life I cannot do these things fully, grant that I may at the least progress in them from day to day, for Christ's sake. Amen.

ANSELM OF CANTERBURY (adapted)

In the calm of sweet communion
Let thy daily work be done;
In the peace of soul-outpouring
Care be banished, patience won;
And if earth with its enchantments
Seek thy spirit to enthrall,
Ere thou listen, ere thou answer,
Turn to Jesus, tell Him all.

G. M. TAYLOR

October 27

The LORD reigns, let the nations tremble; he sits enthroned between the cherubim, let the earth shake. Great is the LORD in Zion; he is exalted over all the nations. PSALM 99:1-2

Eternal Father, source of life and light, whose love extends to all people, all creatures, all things: Grant us that reverence for life which becomes those who believe in you; lest we despise it, degrade it, or come callously to destroy it. Rather let us save it, secure it, and sanctify it, after the example of your Son, Jesus Christ our Lord.

ROBERT RUNCIE

God is not a cosmic bellboy for whom we can press a button to get things.

HARRY EMERSON FOSDICK

October 28

Know that the LORD is God. It is he who made us, and we are his; we are his people, the sheep of his pasture. PSALM 100:3

O Lord, keep us sensitive to the grace that is around us. May the familiar not become neglected. May we see your goodness in our daily bread, and may the comforts of our home take our thoughts to the mercifulness of God. Through Jesus Christ. Amen.

J. H. JOWETT

Even if no command to pray had existed,
our very weakness would have suggested it.

FRANÇOIS FÉNELON

October 29

I will sing of your love and justice; to you, O LORD, I will sing praise. I will be careful to lead a blameless life—when will you come to me? PSALM 101:1-2

O Prince of Life, teach me to stand more boldly on your side, to face the world and all my adversaries more courageously, and not to let myself be dismayed by any storm of temptation; may my eyes be steadfastly fixed on you in fearless faith; may I trust you with perfect confidence that you will keep me, save me, and bring me through by the power of your grace and the riches of your mercy.

GERHARD TERSTEEGEN (adapted)

The prayers of the Christian are secret, but their effect cannot be hidden.

HOWARD CHANDLER ROBBINS

October 30

In the beginning you laid the foundations of the earth, and the heavens are the work of your hands. They will perish, but you remain . . . the same, and your years will never end. PSALM 102:25-27

Almighty and most merciful God, you have given the Bible to be the revelation of your great love to us, and of your power and will to save us: grant that our study of it may not be made in vain by the callousness or carelessness of our heart, but that by it we may be confirmed in penitence, lifted to hope, made strong for service, and, above all, filled with the true knowledge of yourself and of your Son, Jesus Christ.

GEORGE ADAM SMITH

If you can't pray as you want to, pray as you can. God knows what you mean.

VANCE HAVNER

October 31

The LORD is compassionate and gracious, slow to anger, abounding in love. He will not always accuse, nor will he harbor his anger forever; he does not treat us as our sins deserve or repay us according to our iniquities. PSALM 103:8-10

Help me, O God, to look back on the long way you have brought me, on the long days in which I have been served, not according to my deserts, but my desires; on the pit and the miry clay, the blackness of despair, the horror of misconduct, from which my feet have been plucked out. For my sins forgiven or prevented, for my shame unpublished, I bless and thank you, O God.

Help me yet again and ever. So order events, so strengthen my frailty, as that day by day I shall come before you with this song of gratitude, and in the end be dismissed with honor. In my weakness and in my fear, this vessel of your handiwork so prays to you, so praise to you. Amen.

ROBERT LOUIS STEVENSON (adapted)

Men of God are always men of prayer.

HENRY T. MAHAN

*N*ovember 1

Praise the LORD, O my soul. O LORD my God, you are very great; you are clothed with splendor and majesty. PSALM 104:1

We thank you, Lord God, heavenly Father, for Your faithful providence which we have enjoyed and for Your gracious provision of fellowship with one another and with You. Teach us to receive Your gifts with thanksgiving, that with grateful hearts we may enjoy the gifts that have come from You, who together with the Son and the Holy Ghost are one God and one Lord. Amen.

MY PRAYER BOOK

We may as well not pray at all
as offer our prayers in a lifeless manner.

WILLIAM S. PLUMER

November 2

I will sing to the LORD all my life; I will sing praise to my God as long as I live. May my meditation be pleasing to him, as I rejoice in the LORD. PSALM 104:33-34

Lord, I pray not for tranquility, nor that my tribulations may cease; I pray for your spirit and your love, that you grant me strength and grace to overcome adversity; through Jesus Christ. Amen.

GIROLAMO SAVONAROLA (adapted)

God likes to see his people shut up to this, that there is no hope but in prayer. Herein lies the church's power against the world.

ANDREW BONAR

November 3

Give thanks to the LORD, call on his name; make known among the nations what he has done. Sing to him, sing praise to him; tell of all his wonderful acts. PSALM 105:1-2

I, a pilgrim of eternity, stand before Thee, O eternal One. Let me not seek to deaden or destroy the desire for Thee that disturbs my heart. Let me rather yield myself to its constraint and go where it leads me. Make me wise to see all things today under the form of eternity, and make me brave to face all the changes in my life which such a vision may entail: through the grace of Christ my Saviour. Amen.

JOHN BAILLIE

Look, as a painted man is no man,
and as painted fire is no fire,
so a cold prayer is no prayer.

THOMAS BROOKS

November 4

He sent a man before them—Joseph, sold as a slave. They bruised his feet with shackles, his neck was put in irons, till what he foretold came to pass, till the word of the LORD proved him true. PSALM 105:17-19

I beseech Thee, my most gracious God, preserve me from the cares of this life, lest I should be too much entangled therein; also from the many necessities of the body, lest I should be ensnared by pleasure; and from whatsoever is an obstacle to the soul, lest, being broken with troubles, I should be overthrown. Give me the strength to resist, patience to endure, and constancy to persevere. Amen.

THOMAS À KEMPIS

Are we weak and heavy laden,
Cumbered with a load of care?
Precious Saviour, still our refuge,
Take it to the Lord in prayer.

JOSEPH SCRIVEN

November 5

[The Israelites] asked, and [the LORD] brought them quail and satisfied them with the bread of heaven. He opened the rock, and water gushed out; like a river it flowed in the desert. PSALM 105:40-41

Father, I have much to be grateful for tonight, and I thank you. I have much to regret and I ask your forgiveness. But even as I ask your forgiveness I know that I receive it, and a deep peace fills my heart.

Help me to sleep well tonight and to wake ready for that daily yet greatest of gifts, a fresh start.

AVERY BROOKE

Though we cannot by our prayers give God any information, yet we must by our prayers give him honor.

MATTHEW HENRY

November 6

Who can proclaim the mighty acts of the LORD or fully declare his praise? Blessed are they who maintain justice, who constantly do what is right. PSALM 106:2-3

Since it is of your mercy, O gracious Father, that another day is added to my life; I here dedicate both my soul and my body to you and your service, in a sober, righteous, and godly life: in which resolution do you, O merciful God, confirm and strengthen me; that, as I grow in age, I may grow in grace, and in the knowledge of my Lord and Savior Jesus Christ. Amen.

The Book of Common Prayer (adapted)

Prayer at its best is the expression of the total life, for all things else being equal, our prayers are only as powerful as our lives.

A. W. TOZER

November 7

[The Israelites] forgot the God who saved them, who had done great things in Egypt. . . . So he said he would destroy them.
PSALM 106:21, 23

O God, you are the light of the world, the desire of all nations, and the shepherd of our souls: let your light shine in the darkness, that all the ends of the earth may see the salvation of our God. By the lifting up of your Cross gather the peoples to your obedience; let your sheep hear your voice and be brought home to your fold so that there may be one flock, one shepherd, one holy kingdom of righteousness and peace, one God and Father of all, above all, and in all, and through all.

W. E. Orchard

In Fellowship; alone
To God with Faith draw near,
Approach His Courts, besiege His Throne
With all the power of Prayer.

CHARLES WESLEY

November 8

Praise be to the LORD, the God of Israel, from everlasting to everlasting. Let all the people say, "Amen." Praise the LORD.
PSALM 106:48

O my God! Your fullness of love and of glory is like a boundless ocean infinite and inconceivable. I bless You that, in revealing Your Son, it pleased You that all the fullness of the Godhead should dwell in Him bodily, that in Him we might see that fullness in human life and weakness. I bless You that His Church on earth is even now, in all its weakness, His body, the fullness of Him that fills all in all; that in Him we are made full; that by the mighty working of Your Spirit, and the indwelling of Your Son, and the knowledge of Your love, we may be filled to all the fullness of God.

ANDREW MURRAY

God may turn his ears from prattling prayers, or preaching prayers, but never from penitent, believing prayers.

WILLIAM S. PLUMER

November 9

Give thanks to the LORD, for he is good; his love endures forever. PSALM 107:1

O great companion of my soul, do go with me today and comfort me by the sense of Your presence in the hours of spiritual isolation. Give me a single eye for duty. Guide me by the voice within. May I take heed of all the judgments of men and gather patiently whatever truth they hold, but teach me still to test them by the words and the spirit of the One who alone is my Master. Amen.

WALTER RAUSCHENBUSCH (adapted)

Most Christians expect little from God, ask little, and therefore receive little and are content with little.

A. W. PINK

November 10

I will praise you, O LORD, among the nations; I will sing of you among the peoples. For great is your love, higher than the heavens; your faithfulness reaches to the skies. PSALM 108:3-4

Lord Jesus, you are all I want and I find in you more than I could possibly need. Lord, though I know this now and swear that I will never leave you, yet I realize I will go searching after other things in order to fulfill my never-ending wants and desires. Fountain of everlasting life, spring up in my heart and satisfy all my needs so that I will never wish to leave you again.

MICHAEL HOLLINGS and ETTA GULLICK

Sincerity is the prime requisite in every approach to the God who requires "Truth in the inward parts" and who hates all hypocrisy, falsehood, and deceit.

GEOFFREY B. WILSON

N o v e m b e r 1 1

With my mouth I will greatly extol the LORD; in the great throng I will praise him. For he stands at the right hand of the needy one, to save his life from those who condemn him. PSALM 109:30-31

O thou eternal God, who hast promised that the kingdoms of this world shall become the Kingdom of our Lord and Saviour Jesus Christ, increase our faith. We believe, but help our unbelief. Thou dost speak to us with the still small voice, but speak also with the voices of the years. Help us to see Thee walking triumphantly across the pages of the past. And hasten the time, we pray, when swords shall be beaten into plowshares, when every knee shall bow and every tongue confess Thee Lord. Amen.

RALPH S. CUSHMAN

If we be empty and poor, it is not because God's hand is straitened, but ours is not opened.

THOMAS MANTON

November 12

The Lord is at your right hand; he will crush kings on the day of his wrath. PSALM 110:5

Heavenly Father, in your word you have given us a vision of that holy city to which the nations of the world bring their glory: Behold and visit, we pray, the cities of the earth. Renew the ties of mutual regard which form our civic life. Send us honest and able leaders. Enable us to eliminate poverty, prejudice, and oppression, that peace may prevail with righteousness, and justice with order, and that men and women from different cultures and with differing talents may find with one another the fulfillment of their humanity; through Jesus Christ our Lord. Amen

THE BOOK OF COMMON PRAYER

Prayer is the sovereign remedy.

ROBERT HALL

November 13

The fear of the LORD is the beginning of wisdom; all who follow his precepts have good understanding. To him belongs eternal praise. PSALM 111:10

Father, the very last thing that happened to me yesterday was that I got offended. Today that offense is still painfully present in my heart. I am afraid of it and of what it may cause me to say to the one I love. I know that you forgive me in the same way that I forgive others. So, oh please, flood me with forgiveness! I want to put away all bitterness and wrath and anger and wrangling. I open to you, dear God! Today, in this, I pray that I could be kind, tenderhearted, and loving; forgiving just as you in Christ have forgiven me.

By faith in your word and in your Son, I thank you.

DANIEL PARTNER

No prayers can be heard which do not come from a forgiving heart.

J. C. RYLE

November 14

Praise the LORD. Blessed is the man who fears the LORD, who finds great delight in his commands. PSALM 112:1

Grant unto me your servant:

To my God—a heart of flame

To my fellow men—a heart of love

To myself—a heart of steel.

AUGUSTINE (adapted)

There is no effort comparable with prayer to God. When you undertake any other good work, and persevere in it, you gain rest. But prayer is a battle all the way to the last breath.

THE DESERT FATHERS

November 15

Let the name of the LORD be praised, both now and forevermore. From the rising of the sun to the place where it sets, the name of the LORD is to be praised. PSALM 113:2-3

I resign into your hands my sleeping body, my cold hearth and open door. Give me to awaken with smiles; give me to labor smiling. As the sun returns in the east, so let my patience be renewed with dawn; as the sun lightens the world, so let my loving-kindness make bright this house of my habitation.

ROBERT LOUIS STEVENSON (adapted)

We lie to God in prayer if we do not rely on him afterwards.

ROBERT LEIGHTON

November 16

Not to us, O LORD, not to us but to your name be the glory, because of your love and faithfulness. PSALM 115:1

I give you thanks, O God, for those who mean so much to me—
Those to whom I can go at any time.
Those with whom I can talk and keep nothing back,
knowing that they will not laugh at my dreams or my failures.
Those in whose presence it is easier to be good.
Those who by their warning have held me back from
mistakes I might have made.
Above all, I thank you for Jesus Christ, Lord of my heart
and Savior of my soul, in whose Name I offer this
thanksgiving.

WILLIAM BARCLAY (adapted)

You have given so much to me,
Give one thing more, a grateful heart.

GEORGE HERBERT

*N*ovember 17

I love the LORD, for he heard my voice; he heard my cry for mercy. Because he turned his ear to me, I will call on him as long as I live. PSALM 116:1-2

Since your departure from Olivet's Mountain,
Why is your coming again so delayed?
Thru the long years we have longed for your coming
Have you not heard all the prayers that we've prayed?

Beloved Lord, since the year you ascended
Everything here has been tasteless and dry;
Often in praying and often in watching,
In every movement, for you, Lord, we sigh.

O Lord, remember the days have been lengthened
Since you have promised ere going away;
We hope and hope and are endlessly hoping,
That you will come. Can you come e'en today?

WATCHMAN NEE

Prayer is the heavenly telephone
that brings
The distant near, till heaven to earth
comes down.

A. B. SIMPSON

November 18

Praise the LORD, all you nations; extol him, all you peoples. For great is his love toward us, and the faithfulness of the LORD endures forever. Praise the LORD. PSALM 117:1-2

Almighty God, who sent the Spirit of truth to me to guide me into all truth: so rule my life by your power that I may be truthful in thought and word and deed. May no fear or hope ever make me false in act or speech; cast out from me whatsoever loves or makes a lie, and bring me into the perfect freedom of your truth, through Jesus Christ our Lord.

BROOKE FOSS WESTCOTT (adapted)

The granting of prayer, when offered in the name of Jesus, reveals the Father's love to him, and the honor which he has put upon him.

CHARLES H. SPURGEON

November 19

I was pushed back and about to fall, but the LORD helped me. The LORD is my strength and my song; he has become my salvation. PSALM 118:13-14

O Lord, prepare my heart, I beseech you, to reverence you, to adore you, to love you; to hate, for love of you, all my sins and imperfections, short-comings, whatever in me displeases you; and to love all which you love. Give me, Lord, fervor of love, shame for my unthankfulness, sorrow for my sins, longing for your grace, and to be wholly united with you. Let my very coldness call for the glow of your love; let my emptiness and dryness, like a barren and thirsty land, thirst for you, call on you to come into my soul, who refreshes those who are weary. Let my heart ache to you and for you, who stills the aching of the heart. Let my mute longings praise you, crave you, who satisfies the empty soul that waits on you.

E. B. PUSEY

Nothing is discussed more and practiced less than prayer.

ANONYMOUS

November 20

The stone the builders rejected has become the capstone; the LORD has done this, and it is marvelous in our eyes. This is the day the LORD has made; let us rejoice and be glad in it. PSALM 118:22-24

Lord Jesus, I confess I am not able to comprehend what it meant for you to lay aside your glory and condescend to spend thirty-three years here on earth, a period of hardship, rejection, malice, and finally the most agonizing form of death.

Your incarnation means uttermost love for unlovely sinners like me.

It means pardon for me.

It means peace for me.

It means hope of glory.

It is the most wonderful message the world has ever heard and I am a beneficiary of what you did!

Amen! Hallelujah!

ROBERT C. SAVAGE

Straight praying is never born of crooked conduct.

E. M. BOUNDS

November 21

I seek you with all my heart; do not let me stray from your commands. I have hidden your word in my heart that I might not sin against you. PSALM 119:10-11

Give me, O Lord
   unlimited patience
unlimited understanding
   unlimited love
Then I will be able to forgive
   as I have been forgiven
to bless
   as I have been blessed. Amen.

DENIS DUNCAN

The great thing in prayer is to feel that we are putting our supplications into the bosom of omnipotent love.

ANDREW MURRAY

November 22

I hold fast to your statutes, O LORD; do not let me be put to shame. I run in the path of your commands, for you have set my heart free. PSALM 119:31-32

Almighty God, Father of all mercies, we your unworthy servants give you most humble and hearty thanks for all your goodness and loving-kindness to us, and to all. We bless you for your creation, preservation, and all the blessings of this life; but above all, for your inestimable love in the redemption of the world by our Lord Jesus Christ; for the means of grace, and for the hope of glory. And, we beg you, give us that due sense of all your mercies, that our hearts may be unfeignedly thankful, and that we show forth your praise, not only with our lips, but in our lives: by giving up ourselves to your service and by walking before you in holiness and righteousness all our days; through Jesus Christ our Lord, to whom with you and the Holy Spirit be all honor and glory, world without end.

The Book of Common Prayer

Thanks be unto God for his unspeakable gift.

2 CORINTHIANS 9:15, *KJV*

November 23

Turn my heart toward your statutes and not toward selfish gain. Turn my eyes away from worthless things; preserve my life according to your word. PSALM 119:36-37

Almighty and Holy Spirit, the Comforter, pure, living, true—illumine, govern, sanctify me, and confirm my heart and mind in the faith, and in all genuine consolation; preserve and rule over me so that, dwelling in the house of the Lord, all the days of my life, I may behold the Lord and praise him with a joyful spirit, and in union with all the heavenly church. Amen.

PHILIP MELANCHTHON

No heart thrives without much secret converse with God and nothing will make amends for the want of it.

JOHN BERRIDGE

November 24

In the night I remember your name, O LORD, and I will keep your law. This has been my practice: I obey your precepts.
PSALM 119:55-56

O God of peace, entirely sanctify me; keep my spirit and soul and body sound and blameless at the coming of our Lord Jesus Christ. You are the one who calls me, you are faithful, and you will do this.

1 THESSALONIANS 5:23-24 (adapted)

We read of preaching the Word out of season, but we do not read of praying out of season, for that is never out of season.

MATTHEW HENRY

November 25

May your unfailing love be my comfort, according to your promise to your servant. Let your compassion come to me that I may live, for your law is my delight. PSALM 119:76-77

O Thou who camest from above,
The pure celestial fire to impart,
Kindle a flame of sacred love
On the mean altar of my heart.

There let it for thy glory burn
With inextinguishable blaze,
And trembling to its source return
In humble prayer, and fervent praise.

CHARLES WESLEY

The spirit of prayer is the fruit and token of the Spirit of adoption.

JOHN NEWTON

November 26

Your word, O LORD, is eternal; it stands firm in the heavens. Your faithfulness continues through all generations; you established the earth, and it endures. PSALM 119:89-90

My Father, do with me as you will, only help me against myself and for you; I am your child, the inheritor of your spirit, your being, a part of yourself, glorious in you, but grown poor in me: let me be your dog, your horse, your anything, anything you will; let me be yours in any shape the love that is my Father may please to have me; let me be yours in any way, and my own or another's in no way but yours.

GEORGE MACDONALD

Prayers are the leeches of care.

ANONYMOUS

November 27

Your word is a lamp to my feet and a light for my path. I have taken an oath and confirmed it, that I will follow your righteous laws. PSALM 119:105-106

Your words were found, and I ate them, and your words
became to me a joy and the delight of my heart;
for I am called by your name,
O LORD, God of hosts.

JEREMIAH 15:16, *NRSV*

The mightier any is in the Word,
the more mighty he will be in prayer.

WILLIAM GURNALL

November 28

I hate double-minded men, but I love your law. You are my refuge and my shield; I have put my hope in your word.
PSALM 119:113-114

O Jesus

Be the canoe that holds me in the sea of life.

Be the steer that keeps me straight.

Be the outrigger that supports me in times of great temptation.

Let thy Spirit be my sail that carries me through each day.

Keep my body strong,

so that I can paddle steadfastly on,

in the long voyage of life.

A NEW HEBRIDEAN PRAYER

Prayer is not conquering God's reluctance, but taking hold of God's willingness.

PHILLIPS BROOKS

November 29

Righteous are you, O LORD, and your laws are right. The statutes you have laid down are righteous; they are fully trustworthy. PSALM 119:137-138

Grant to me, O Lord, to know what I ought to know, to love what I ought to love, to praise what delights you most, to value what is precious in your sight, to hate what is offensive to you. Do not suffer me to judge according to the sight of my eyes, nor to pass sentence according to the hearing of the ears of ignorant men; but to discern with true judgment between things visible and spiritual, and above all things to enquire what is the good pleasure of your will.

THOMAS À KEMPIS

Prayer is and remains always a native and deepest impulse of the soul of man.

THOMAS CARLYLE

November 30

I long for your salvation, O LORD, and your law is my delight. Let me live that I may praise you, and may your laws sustain me. PSALM 119:174-175

From the cowardice that dare not face new truth
From the laziness that is contented with half truth
From the arrogance that thinks it knows all truth,
Good Lord, deliver me.

A PRAYER FROM KENYA

Two went to pray? Oh, rather say
One went to brag, the other to pray;
One stands up close and treads on high
Where the other dares not send his eye;
One nearer to God's altar trod,
the other to the altar's God.

RICHARD CRANSHAW, *Luke 18:9-14*

December 1

I call on the LORD in my distress, and he answers me. Save me, O LORD, from lying lips and from deceitful tongues. PSALM 120:1-2

Grant, O God, that we may wait patiently, as servants standing before their Lord, to know your will; that we may welcome all truth, under whatever outward form it may be uttered; that we may bless every good deed, by whomsoever it may be done; that we may rise above all strife to the contemplation of your eternal truth and goodness; through Jesus Christ our Savior.

CHARLES KINGSLEY

Faith is the fountain of prayer, and prayer should be nothing else but faith exercised.

THOMAS MANTON

December 2

The LORD will keep you from all harm—he will watch over your life; the LORD will watch over your coming and going both now and forevermore. PSALM 121:7-8

Our Father in heaven, I thank you that you have led me into the light. I thank you for sending the Savior to call me from death to life. I confess that I was dead in sin before I heard his call, but when I heard him, like Lazarus, I arose. But, O my Father, the grave clothes bind me still. Old habits that I cannot throw off, old customs that are so much a part of my life that I am helpless to live the new life that Christ calls me to live. Give me strength, O Father, to break the bonds; give me courage to live a new life in you, give me faith, to believe that with your help I cannot fail. And this I ask in the Savior's name who has taught me to come to you.

A PRAYER FROM TAIWAN

No time is so well spent in every day as that which we spend upon our knees.

J. C. RYLE

December 3

I rejoiced with those who said to me, "Let us go to the house of the LORD." Our feet are standing in your gates, O Jerusalem.
PSALM 122:1-2

Give me
The girdle, the helmet,
The breastplate, the shield,
The shoes, the sword,
    over all, prayer.
Grant me the power and the opportunity of welldoing
  that before the day of my decease
  I may at all adventure effect some good thing
    whereof the fruit may remain:
that I may be able to appear with righteousness
    and be satisfied with glory.
And grant me a good end—
  What is above every gift—a good a holy end of life,
  a glorious and joyful resurrection.

LANCELOT ANDREWES (adapted)

Amazing things start
happening when we start praying!

ANONYMOUS

December 4

As the eyes of slaves look to the hand of their master, as the eyes of a maid look to the hand of her mistress, so our eyes look to the LORD our God, till he shows us his mercy. PSALM 123:2

Let no riches make me ever forget myself, no poverty make me to forget you: let no hope or fear, no pleasure or pain, no accident without, no weakness within, hinder or discompose my duty, or turn me from the ways of your commandments. O let your Spirit dwell with me forever, and make my soul just and charitable, full of honesty, full of religion, resolute and constant in holy purposes, but inflexible to evil. Make me humble and obedient, peaceable and pious: let me never envy any man's good, nor deserve to be despised myself: and if I be, teach me to bear it with meekness and charity.

JEREMY TAYLOR

Sometimes we think we are too busy to pray. That is a great mistake, for praying is a saving of time.

CHARLES H. SPURGEON

December 5

We have escaped like a bird out of the fowler's snare; the snare has been broken, and we have escaped. Our help is in the name of the LORD, the Maker of heaven and earth. PSALM 124:7-8

Help each one of us, gracious Father, to live in such magnanimity and restraint that the Head of the church may never have cause to say to any one of us, This is my body, broken by you.

A PRAYER FROM CHINA

Every time you pray, if your prayer is sincere, there will be new feeling and new meaning in it which will give you fresh courage, and you will understand that prayer is an education.

FEODOR DOSTOEVSKI, *The Brothers Karamazov*

December 6

Those who trust in the LORD are like Mount Zion, which cannot be shaken but endures forever. PSALM 125:1

O God, Make the door of this house wide enough to receive all who need human love and fellowship, and a heavenly Father's care; and narrow enough to shut out all envy, pride and hate.

Make its threshold smooth enough to be no stumbling-block to children, nor to straying feet, but rugged enough to turn back the tempter's power:

Make it a gateway to thine eternal kingdom.

THOMAS KEN

Those who always pray are necessary to those who never pray.

VICTOR HUGO

December 7

When the LORD brought back the captives to Zion, we were like men who dreamed. Our mouths were filled with laughter, our tongues with songs of joy. Then it was said among the nations, "The LORD has done great things for them." PSALM 126:1-2

Inspire rulers and peoples with counsels of meekness. Heal the discords that tear nations asunder. You who did shed your precious blood that they might live as brothers, bring men together once more in loving harmony. To the cry of the Apostle Peter: "Save us, Lord, we perish," you did answer words of mercy and did still the raging waves. Stoop now to hear our trustful prayers and give back to the world order and peace.

POPE BENEDICT XV

The spectacle of a nation praying is more awe-inspiring than the explosion of an atomic bomb. The force of prayer is greater than any possible combination of man-controlled power, because prayer is man's greatest means of trapping the infinite resources of God.

J. EDGAR HOOVER

December 8

Sons are a heritage from the LORD, children a reward from him. Like arrows in the hands of a warrior are sons born in one's youth. Blessed is the man whose quiver is full of them. PSALM 127:3-5

Father, I really thank you for my family. Sometimes I take them for granted, in the hustle and bustle and challenges of my daily life. Help me to take a long look at them today, and see what I can do—with your help—to demonstrate my love. In Jesus' name.

PAT BOONE

I know not by what methods rare,
But this I know: God answers prayer.
I know not if the blessing sought
Will come in just the guise I thought.
I leave my prayer to Him alone
Whose will is wiser than my own.

ELIZA M. HICKOK

December 9

Blessed are all who fear the LORD, who walk in his ways. You will eat the fruit of your labor; blessings and prosperity will be yours. PSALM 128:1-2

O God, I thank you because, when I have been for some time interrupted in my work and my thoughts of you have been diverted, I have found how pleasing it is to my mind to feel the motions of your Spirit quickening me and exciting me to return.

SUSANNA WESLEY

To God your every Want
In instant Prayer display,
Pray always; pray, and never faint;
Pray, without ceasing Pray.

CHARLES WESLEY

December 10

Plowmen have plowed my back and made their furrows long. But the LORD is righteous; he has cut me free from the cords of the wicked. PSALM 129:3-4

Blessed Lord, who was tempted in all things like as we are, have mercy upon my frailty. Out of weakness give me strength. Grant to me your fear that I may fear only you. Support me in time of temptation. Embolden me in the time of danger. Help me to do your work with good courage, and to continue your faithful soldier and servant unto my life's end; through Jesus Christ our Lord.

BROOKE FOSS WESTCOTT (adapted)

Prayers are heard in heaven very much in proportion to your faith. Little faith will get very great mercies, but great faith still greater.

CHARLES H. SPURGEON

December 11

Out of the depths I cry to you, O LORD; O Lord, hear my voice. Let your ears be attentive to my cry for mercy. PSALM 130:1-2

O Lord, when I am bewildered and the world is all noise and confusion around me and I don't know which way to go and am frightened, then be with me. Put your hand on my shoulder and let your strength invade my weakness and your light burn the mist from my mind. Help me to step forward with faith in the way I should go.

AVERY BROOKE

We, on our side, are praying to Him to give us victory, because we believe we are right; but those on the other side pray to Him, too, for victory, believing they are right. What must He think of us?

ABRAHAM LINCOLN

December 12

My heart is not proud, O LORD, my eyes are not haughty. . . . But I have stilled and quieted my soul; like a weaned child with its mother. PSALM 131:1-2

Don't make me good, Lord.
  Make me yours.
If all I am is good
  And I give it,
    Then I give myself only.
But if I'm yours
  when I give myself,
    I give you.
And those I love
  don't need me, good or bad.
    They need you.
So, make me yours.

JOHN B. COBURN

Don't be timid when you pray; rather, batter the very gates of heaven with storms of prayer.

ANONYMOUS

December 13

Let us go to his dwelling place; let us worship at his footstool—arise, O LORD, and come to your resting place, you and the ark of your might. PSALM 132:7-8

Holy Spirit, truth divine,
Dawn upon this soul of mine;
Word of God and inward light,
Wake my spirit, clear my sight.

Holy Spirit, love divine,
Glow within this heart of mine,
Kindle every high desire,
Purge me now in thy pure fire.

Holy Spirit, peace divine,
Still this restless heart of mine,
Speak to calm this tossing sea,
Stayed in thy tranquility.

Holy Spirit, joy divine,
Gladden thou this heart of mine;
In the desert ways I'll sing,
Spring, O well, forever spring.

SAMUEL LONGFELLOW

It is not well for man to pray cream, and live skim milk.

HENRY WARD BEECHER

December 14

How good and pleasant it is when brothers live together in unity! It is like precious oil poured on the head, running down on the beard. PSALM 133:1-2

Almighty God, our heavenly Father, who sets the solitary in families; we commend to your continual care the homes in which your people dwell. Put far from them, we beseech you, every root of bitterness, the desire of vain-glory, and the pride of life. Fill them with faith, virtue, knowledge, temperance, patience, godliness. Knit together in constant affection those who, in holy wedlock, have been made one flesh; turn the heart of the fathers to the children, and the heart of the children to the fathers; and so enkindle fervent charity among us all, that we be evermore kindly affectioned with brotherly love; through Jesus Christ our Lord. Amen.

The Book of Common Prayer

For You, O LORD of hosts, God of Israel, have revealed this to Your servant, saying, "I will build you a house." Therefore Your servant found it in his heart to pray this prayer to You.

2 SAMUEL 7:27, *NKJV*

December 15

Lift up your hands in the sanctuary and praise the LORD. May the LORD, the Maker of heaven and earth, bless you from Zion.
PSALM 134:2-3

Grant, Almighty God, that as you shine on me by your Word, I may not be blind at midday, nor willfully seek darkness, and thus lull my mind asleep: but, may I be roused daily by your words, and may I stir up myself more and more to fear your name and thus present myself and all my pursuits, as a sacrifice to you, that you may peaceably rule and perpetually dwell in me, until you gather me to your celestial habitation, where there is reserved for me eternal rest and glory, through Jesus Christ our Lord. Amen.

JOHN CALVIN (adapted)

Prayer is a strong wall and fortress of the church: it is a goodly Christian weapon.
MARTIN LUTHER

December 16

I know that the LORD is great, that our Lord is greater than all gods. The LORD does whatever pleases him, in the heavens and on the earth, in the seas and all their depths. PSALM 135:5-6

O God, light of the minds that see you, life of the souls that love you, and strength of the souls that seek you, enlarge my mind and raise the vision of my heart, that, with swift wings of thought, my spirit may reach you, the eternal wisdom, you who live from everlasting to everlasting; through Jesus Christ our Lord. Amen.

AUGUSTINE (adapted)

The man who prays grows,
and the muscles of the soul swell
from this whipcord to iron bands.

F. B. MEYER

December 17

Give thanks to the LORD, for he is good. *His love endures forever.* PSALM 136:1

I love you, O my God; and I desire to love you more and more. Grant to me that I may love you as much as I desire, and as much as I ought. O dearest Friend, who has so loved and saved me, the thought of whom is so sweet and always growing sweeter, watch over my lips, my steps, my deeds, and I shall not need to be anxious either for my soul or my body. Give me love, sweetest of all gifts, which knows no enemy. Give me in my heart pure love, born of your love to me, that I may love others as you love me. O most loving Father of Jesus Christ, from whom flows all love, let my heart, frozen in sin, cold to you and cold to others, be warmed by this divine fire. So help and bless me in your Son. Amen.

ANSELM OF CANTERBURY (adapted)

Prayer is not eloquence, but earnestness;
not the definition of helplessness,
but the feeling of it; not figures
of speech, but earnestness of soul.

HANNAH MORE

December 18

By the rivers of Babylon we sat and wept when we remembered Zion. . . . for there our captors asked us for songs, our tormentors demanded songs of joy. PSALM 137:1, 3

O God, you gave us the grace to carry the sword of your kingdom of peace; and you made us messengers of peace in a world of strife, and messengers of strife in a world of false peace: make strong our hand, make clear our voice, give us humility with firmness and insight with passion, that we may fight, not to conquer, but to redeem.

GREGORY VLASTOS

Prayer is not artful monologue
Of voice uplifted from the son;
It is Love's tender dialogue
Between the soul and God.

JOHN RICHARD MORELAND

December 19

I will praise you, O LORD, with all my heart; before the "gods" I will sing your praise. I will bow down toward your holy temple and will praise your name for your love and your faithfulness.
PSALM 138:1-2

O Lord Christ, who, when your hour was come, went without fear amongst those who sought your life: grant us grace to confess you before all, without arrogance and without fear, that your Holy Name may be glorified.

J. H. OLDHAM

Prayer is not merely an occasional impulse to which we respond when we are in trouble: prayer is a life attitude.

WALTER A. MUELLER

December 20

Where can I go from your Spirit? Where can I flee from your presence? If I go up to the heavens, you are there; if I make my bed in the depths, you are there. PSALM 139:7-8

Though it has not happened to me, I know and love some to whom it has happened, Lord. They are yours and they are my fellows, but they have drifted on to drugs. There are so many reasons, Lord. You know them, I can only try to sense them. They are shy, they are weak, they can't communicate, they're misfits, their homes don't work, they want to belong, they want to be loved, Lord. Give them your understanding when we don't understand them; give them your strength when they feel the craving; above all, let them feel your love in you and through us. Help them, Lord.

MICHAEL HOLLINGS and ETTA GULLICK

The effectual fervent prayer of a righteous man availeth much.

JAMES 5:16, *KJV*

December 21

I know that the LORD secures justice for the poor and upholds the cause of the needy. Surely the righteous will praise your name and the upright will live before you. PSALM 140:12-13

When days are cold and grey and
short,
and nights grow long,
Cause me God to sing this song:
The Word became flesh.

When friends and loves and lives
can't know
my pain, my fear,
Open up my ears to hear:
The Word became flesh.

When heart and will and thought
presume
you're far away,
Let me touch the truth and say:
The Word became flesh.

Since Word and flesh and life
were one
to show your love,
Lift human eyes to see above:
The Word became flesh.

DANIEL PARTNER

Constant prayer quickly straightens out our thoughts.

THE DESERT FATHERS

December 22

But my eyes are fixed on you, O Sovereign LORD; in you I take refuge—do not give me over to death. PSALM 141:8

Out of my bondage, sorrow, and night,
Jesus, I come! Jesus I come!
Into Thy freedom, gladness, and light,
Jesus, I come to Thee!
Out of my sickness into Thy health,
Out of my want and into Thy wealth,
Out of my sin and into Thyself,
Jesus, I come to Thee!

Out of my shameful failure and loss,
Jesus, I come! Jesus I come!
Into the glorious gain of Thy cross,
Jesus, I come to Thee!
Out of earth's sorrows into Thy balm,
Out of life's storm and into Thy calm,
Out of distress to jubilant psalm,
Jesus, I come to Thee!

WILLIAM T. SLEEPER

My house shall be called the house of prayer.

MATTHEW 21:13, *KJV*

December 23

Set me free from my prison, that I may praise your name. Then the righteous will gather about me because of your goodness to me. PSALM 142:7

O Christ, you were called the man of sorrows, and yet you prayed for your disciples that they might have your joy; grant me such sympathy as takes upon itself the burden for the sorrowing; and with it such glad courage as shall turn the way of sadness into the way of joy, because we follow in your footsteps, O blessed Master, Jesus Christ. Amen.

WALTER RUSSELL BOWIE (adapted)

Prayer crowns God with the honor and glory due to His name, and God crowns prayer with assurance and comfort. The most praying souls are the most assured souls.

THOMAS BROOKS

December 24

Let the morning bring me word of your unfailing love, for I have put my trust in you. Show me the way I should go, for to you I lift up my soul. PSALM 143:8

O Holy Child of Bethlehem,

Descend on us, we pray;

Cast out our sin, and enter in,

Be born in us today.

We hear the Christmas angels

The great glad tidings tell;

O come to us, abide in us,

Our Lord Emmanuel! Amen.

PHILLIPS BROOKS

Jesus Christ is a God whom we approach without pride, and before whom we humble ourselves without despair.

BLAISE PASCAL

December 25

O LORD, what is man that you care for him, the son of man that you think of him? PSALM 144:3

We yearn, our Father, for the simple beauty of Christmas—for all the old familiar melodies and words that remind us of that great miracle when He who had made all things was one night to come as a babe, to lie in the crook of a woman's arm.

Before such mystery we kneel, as we follow the shepherds and Wise Men to bring Thee the gift of our love—a love we confess has not always been as warm or sincere or real as it should have been. But now, on this Christmas Day, that love would find its Beloved, and from Thee receive the grace to make it pure again, warm and real.

May the loving-kindness of Christmas not only creep into our hearts, but there abide, so that not even the return to earthly cares and responsibilities, not all the festivities of our own devising may cause it to creep away weeping. May the joy and spirit of Christmas stay with us now and forever.

PETER MARSHALL

The simple heart that freely asks in love, obtains.

JOHN GREENLEAF WHITTIER

December 26

The LORD is gracious and compassionate, slow to anger and rich in love. The LORD is good to all; he has compassion on all he has made. PSALM 145:8-9

What miracles of the human spirit are Yours, O God.
There is so much that seems so often without hope to us;
so much that hangs heavy on our minds;
so much that is a burden and a heartache to us, Lord.
And then You come on wings of love and say:
"Let not your heart be troubled . . . peace be unto you.
In the world ye shall have tribulation, but be of good cheer,
I have overcome the world!"
O Jesus Christ, You are indeed the light of the world, and in You is no darkness at all!

ARTHUR A. ROUNER JR.

Always look for ways to act upon the faith you display in your prayers.

ANONYMOUS

December 27

Blessed is he whose help is the God of Jacob, whose hope is in the LORD his God, the Maker of heaven and earth, the sea, and everything in them—the LORD, who remains faithful forever.
PSALM 146:5-6

I acknowledged my sin to you,
and I did not hide my iniquity;
I said, "I will confess my transgressions to the LORD."
and you forgave the guilt of my sin.

Therefore let all who are faithful
offer prayer to you;
at a time of distress, the rush of mighty waters
shall not reach them.
You are a hiding place for me;
you preserve me from trouble;
you surround me with glad cries of deliverance.

PSALM 32:5-7, *NRSV*

We must pray for more prayer, for it is the world's mightiest healing force.

FRANK C. LAUBACH

December 28

Sing to the LORD with thanksgiving; make music to our God on the harp. He covers the sky with clouds; he supplies the earth with rain and makes grass grow on the hills. PSALM 147:7-8

Let me not seek outside of you what I can only find in you,
O Lord.
Peace and rest, and joy and bliss,
which abide only in your abiding joy.
Lift up my soul above the weary round of harassing
thoughts to your eternal presence.
Lift up my mind to the pure, bright, serene atmosphere of
your presence,
that I may breathe freely,
there repose in your love,
there be at rest from myself
and from all things that weary me:
and thence return, arrayed in your peace, to do and to bear
whatsoever shall best please you, O blessed Lord.

E. B. PUSEY

Watch and pray, lest you enter into temptation.

MATTHEW 26:41, *NKJV*

December 29

Praise him, you highest heavens and you waters above the skies. Let them praise the name of the LORD, for he commanded and they were created. PSALM 148:4-5

O God of steadfastness and encouragement, grant all Christians to live in harmony with one another in accordance with Christ Jesus, so that together we may with one voice glorify the God and Father of our Lord Jesus Christ.

You are the God of hope. May you fill us with all joy and peace in believing, so that we may abound in hope by the power of the Holy Spirit.

O God of all peace, be with all of us. Amen.

ROMANS 15:5-6, 13, 33 (adapted)

Though I am weak, yet God, when prayed,
Cannot withhold his conquering aid.

RALPH WALDO EMERSON

December 30

Praise the LORD. Sing to the LORD a new song, his praise in the assembly of the saints. PSALM 149:1

Break Thou the Bread of Life,
Dear Lord, to me,
As Thou didst break the loaves
Beside the sea;
Beyond the sacred page
I seek Thee, Lord;
My spirit pants for Thee,
O Living Word.

Bless Thou the truth, dear Lord,
To me, to me,
As Thou didst bless the bread
By Galilee;
Then shall all bondage cease,
All fetters fall;
And I shall find my peace,
My All in all.

MARY A. LATHBURY

Non-praying is lawlessness, discord, anarchy.

E. M. BOUNDS

December 31

Praise him with the clash of cymbals, praise him with resounding cymbals. Let everything that has breath praise the LORD. Praise the LORD. PSALM 150:5-6

And I offer also for all those whom I have in any way grieved, vexed, oppressed, and scandalized, by word or deed, knowingly or unknowingly; that you may equally forgive us all our sins, and all our offenses against each other.

Take away, O Lord, from our hearts all suspiciousness, indignation, anger, and contention, and whatever is calculated to wound charity, and to lessen brotherly love.

Have mercy, O Lord, have mercy on those who seek your mercy; give grace to the needy; make us so to live, that we may be found worthy to enjoy the fruition of your grace, and that we may attain to eternal life.

THOMAS À KEMPIS

Whenever you stand praying, forgive, if you have anything against anyone; so that your Father in heaven may also forgive you your trespasses.

MARK 11:25, *NRSV*

Author Index

SCRIPTURE INDEX

OLD TESTAMENT

NEW TESTAMENT

The One Year® book of Bible Promises

with poems from Ruth Harms Calkin

TYNDALE HOUSE PUBLISHERS, INC.
WHEATON, ILLINOIS

Visit Tyndale's exciting Web site at www.tyndale.com

ISBN 0-8423-7744-1

Printed in China

05 04 03
5 4 3 2

Introduction

God keeps his promises. You've heard it; in fact, you've probably even said it a few times. But how well do you know it? God's intention is for this great truth to be so foundational in your heart that you confidently live life resting in his faithfulness.

God can be trusted. Discover his promises in new ways this year and deepen your understanding of his faithfulness.

> Deep in your hearts you know that every promise of the Lord your God has come true. Not a single one has failed! *Joshua 23:14, NLT*

January

The Promise of New Beginnings

Great is his faithfulness!

Morning by morning he wakens me and opens my understanding to his will. Isaiah 50:4, NLT

January 1

Happy New Year

This very first day
Of the fresh new year
I sing a new song—
A joyful, exalted song!
With Israel's sweet singer I exclaim:
"How good it is to sing God's praise
How delightful and how right."
The volume increases
The tempo accelerates.
With glorious anticipation
I shout a rousing welcome
To the up-and-coming days.
The future cannot daunt me
Every inscrutable mystery
Becomes a consolation of joy
For with You in control, dear God
The worst may happen
But the best is yet to come.

Praise the Lord! Praise the Lord, I tell myself. I will praise the Lord as long as I live. I will sing praises to my God even with my dying breath.

Psalm 146:1-2, NLT

January 2

His Part—My Part

Lord

You want me to trust You so totally

That I am unmoved by any circumstance:

Then work in me that steadfast trust.

You want me to choose to do right:

Then turn me from wanting any plan but Yours.

You want me to revere and honor You:

Then refresh and revive me.

You want me to obey You uninterruptedly:

Then make Your Word my guide.

You want me to depend upon You increasingly:

Then reassure me that Your promises are mine.

You want Your will to be my will:

Then help me to love Your every wish.

I expect Your help, dear Lord

For You've never broken a single promise

And You're not going to start with me.

Direct my footsteps according to your word; let no sin rule over me.

Psalm 119:133, NIV

January 3

To the New Year

Mysterious New Year
So wrapped in reserve and surprise
You have no reason to feel smug
Or even condescending.
After all, the majestic God
Has full knowledge of you
Just as He has of me.
There is not an issue that you can evade.
Furthermore, you are powerless
To do anything to me
That God does not permit.
All He allows in His infinite wisdom
Is for my ultimate good
And His greatest glory.
Consequently, New Year
You cannot trick or disillusion me
By your baffling unexplainables
Or your feverish activity.
My times are in the hands
Of my sovereign God
Whose power is limitless
And whose love for me is everlasting.

I pray that your hearts will be flooded with light so that you can understand the wonderful future he has promised to those he called. I want you to realize what a rich and glorious inheritance he has given to his people. Ephesians 1:18, NLT

January 4

The Promise

God, on a long, lonely Saturday
Just before New Year's Day
You spoke so clearly through Your Word:
"Your days of mourning all will end.
You will live in joy and peace."
O God, what a glorious promise
As we begin a brand new year!
Again You said:
"Always be expecting much
From Him, your God."
I trust You implicitly, my Lord
For Your "much" exceeds by far
My greatest comprehension of much.
Surely You have planned a beautiful surprise!
I open my heart wide to receive it.

"For I know the plans I have for you," declares the Lord, "plans to prosper you and not to harm you, plans to give you hope and a future."
Jeremiah 29:11, NIV

January 5

January

It's January, Lord—
The drab, dreary middle—
And my thoughts are as drab
As the miserable month.
Does everybody hit a January slump
Or am I the only one?
The first week wasn't too bad:
There were Christmas thank-yous to write
A few resolutions to store away
The huddle of year-end sales.
But thank-you notes bring no returns
And resolutions are quickly broken
And marked-down trinkets fast lose appeal.
When You said
Behold, I make all things new
Did You forget January, Lord?
Or in January do *I* sometimes forget You?

Therefore, since we are surrounded by such a great cloud of witnesses, let us throw off everything that hinders and the sin that so easily entangles, and let us run with perseverance the race marked out for us.

Hebrews 12:1, NIV

January 6

Insight

While I was "praying," Lord
Demanding this
Insisting on that
You pierced me
With lightning-swift insight.

My bitter complaints
My self-centered whims
Do not constitute prayer
Just because they begin
"Dear God."

Your kingdom come, your will be done. — Matthew 6:10, NIV

January 7

Another Year

Another new year! How did it steal in so silently? How did it arrive so quickly? So many things I determined to do in January of last year are still completely undone. So many notes and letters still unwritten. Friends I planned to entertain were never invited. The books I planned to read haven't been opened.

The cupboards and drawers I hoped to clean are still cluttered with things I don't need or use. Clothes I no longer wear still crowd my closet. I planned to have coffee with our neighbors, but often I managed no more than a quick wave between errands.

If only I could have held on to the old year a little longer! But the old year is gone. I must put it away with all its failures and broken resolves. There is no way I can reclaim even one week of last year.

I see that the road to good intentions is wide and circular. I've walked around it until I am utterly exhausted. I confess my failures, my procrastination. I know God, in his graciousness, will forgive me. I have one more request. I pray for God's power to keep my forgiveness up-to-date.

Let me hear of your unfailing love to me in the morning, for I am trusting you. Show me where to walk, for I have come to you in prayer. Psalm 143:8, NLT

January 8

Missing Chapter

Often, Lord
I feel achingly incomplete
Like the missing chapter
in a book.
But then I remember
You have not yet finished
The manuscript.
Forgive me
If I seem presumptuous
But have You set
A publication date?

And I am sure that God, who began the good work within you, will continue his work until it is finally finished on that day when Christ Jesus comes back again.
Philippians 1:6, NLT

January 9

The Choice

Lord, You are indeed relentless:

You insist that my love be unrivaled

That my loyalty be uncompromising

That my surrender be irrevocable.

What do You want, Lord

Everything?

It's frightening.

Yet not as frightening

As staying as I am.

And you must love the Lord your God with all your heart, all your soul, and all your strength. Deuteronomy 6:5, NLT

January 10

Now You Have Me, God

Now You have me, God!
You have me irrevocably.
No reserve
No retreat
No turning back.

Now You have me, God!
All I feel
Dream
Aspire
All I long withheld.
My resistance
Triumphs
Defeats
My stalwart resolves
My crumbling dreams
My glittering awards
My blind alleys.

Now You have me, God!
All which is past
All which is now
All that may yet unfold.
The barriers are broken
The turmoil has stilled
Your Word is my Yes
Your notes are my song.

Now You have me, God!
You knocked
And still knocked
And I opened the door.
Now at last—
At long last
I know:

Joy!
As the rushing sea.
Peace!
As a meadow at twilight.
Strength!
As a towering mountain.
Trust!
As a wide-eyed child
Who walks
In the gentle rain
Holding
A father's hand.

Whom have I in heaven but you? I desire you more than anything on earth. My health may fail, and my spirit may grow weak, but God remains the strength of my heart; he is mine forever.

Psalm 73:25-26, NLT

January 11

Make Yourself at Home

With extreme joy, Lord
I offer my heart as Your home.
I have purposely left it unfurnished
Without lavish decor:
No plush carpeting
No velvet drapes
Not even an original oil
Or an engraved silver service.
Examine it first for cleanliness—
Every room
Every closet
Then furnish it according
To Your own magnificent taste.
The door is wide open—
Don't even bother to ring the bell.

Here I am! I stand at the door and knock. If anyone hears my voice and opens the door, I will come in and eat with him, and he with me.
Revelation 3:20, NIV

January 12

Today, Lord

Yesterday, Lord
When You asked what I wanted
Above all else
I said I wanted to be
Exclusively Yours.
Today, as You startle me
With opportunities
Keep me from begging off
Until tomorrow.

What is more pleasing to the Lord: your burnt offerings and sacrifices or your obedience to his voice? Obedience is far better than sacrifice. Listening to him is much better than offering the fat of rams.

1 Samuel 15:22, NLT

January 13

Unpredictable

Sometimes, Lord
You come up with such
Unpredictable answers—
Today
I related my predicament
I explained my desperation
I begged You
To get me out of this mess.
Your only answer:
"I beg you to let Me in on this mess."

Each time he said, "My gracious favor is all you need. My power works best in your weakness." So now I am glad to boast about my weaknesses, so that the power of Christ may work through me.

2 Corinthians 12:9, NLT

January 14

God's Promises Are for Keeping

Losses, depression, disappointments, frustrated desires—how debilitating they can be. This is indeed a fact. But so often we must distinguish between the facts and the promises of God. I am always helped by the Bible story of Abraham and Sarah. Sarah was too old for childbearing, but God had promised that they would have a child. So they gave preference to the promise of God, as impossible as it seemed.

In the midst of all that troubles you, all that seems impossible at times,

- God's PROMISE is: Give all your worries and cares to God, for he cares about what happens to you. (1 Peter 5:7, NLT)
- The PROMISE is: I will answer them before they even call to me. (Isaiah 65:24, NLT)
- The PROMISE is: If you look for me in earnest, you will find me when you seek me. (Jeremiah 29:13, NLT)

Underline God's promises. Memorize them. Know with assurance that God has never broken a single promise, and he's not going to start with you. He wants our commitment, our obedience, and our trust. If you have surrendered to him completely, he will not fail you! Take his word for it!

All of God's promises have been fulfilled in him. That is why we say "Amen" when we give glory to God through Christ.

2 Corinthians 1:20, NLT

January 15

Suddenly Mine

O Lord

May I believe in the darkness

When all hope has vanished

When waves beat with fury

And no star lights my sky.

May I believe without

Feeling or knowing or proving

Till one shining moment when

You shatter the darkness

And all I believed for

Is suddenly mine.

Weeping may remain for a night, but rejoicing comes in the morning.

Psalm 30:5, NIV

January 16

Marvelous Moments

What a beautiful relief, dear God
To sit quietly in my own living room
Soaking up the luxury of aloneness.
No demanding voices
No radio or television
No shouts from the bathroom
Just these few marvelous moments
To kick off my shoes
Shed my confusion
And reclaim myself . . .
These few marvelous moments
To respond to Your persistent plea
"Be still and know that I am God."

You will keep in perfect peace all who trust in you, whose thoughts are fixed on you!
Isaiah 26:3, NLT

January 17

Empower Me, I Pray

Lord, You told the impotent man
To take up his bed and walk.
Today, when mountainous problems
Seem to loom sky-high
And the business of living
Demands so much rigid attention
Empower me, I pray
To take up my task and work.

And whatever you do, whether in word or deed, do it all in the name of the Lord Jesus, giving thanks to God the Father through him.

Colossians 3:17, NIV

January 18

You Dreamed Me Up

O dear God
It was You, You alone
Who dreamed me up.
Nobody else
Would ever have thought of me
Or planned for me
Or looked right through me
With future contemplation.
Right from the beginning of Time
I was all Your idea.
You had big things in mind for me
Good things, glorious things
And now, with magnificent dexterity
You are making them come to pass.
And I?
Well, I stand amazed on the sideline
And praise Your infinite patience.

You saw me before I was born. Every day of my life was recorded in your book. Every moment was laid out before a single day had passed.

Psalm 139:16, NLT

January 19

Too Often

Dear, dear Lord

Too often in my life

I've messed around

In my tiny dirt plots

When through Your glorious power

I could have moved mountains.

Please change me!

Turn my eyes from worthless things, and give me life through your word.

Psalm 119:37, NLT

January 20

It's for Keeps

Lord
Even when I came to You
As a little child
Not quite nine years old
You knew the worst, the very worst
About each future sin and failure.
Still You accepted me
With Your arms wide open.
You held me close to Your loving heart
And whispered, "It's for keeps!"
Had I been an adult
You might have captured my attention
With Your cry from the Cross:
"It is finished."
But You whispered to a little girl
Who understood perfectly, "It's for keeps."

O Lord
I praise You for the liberating fact
That through all the passing years
I have never had to produce or perform
To guarantee my position in You.
It is You, not I, who maintains my status.
Nobody, NOBODY can produce an ounce of evidence
To cause You to change Your mind.
Year after year, day by day
Your words still ring in my heart:
"It's for keeps!"

The Lord himself goes before you and will be with you; he will never leave you nor forsake you. Do not be afraid; do not be discouraged.

Deuteronomy 31:8, NIV

January 21

God's Promises

With increasing joy I am discovering that God's promises do not suddenly disappear when our courage fails and our fears become overwhelming. Feeling or no feeling, when God gives a promise that speaks directly to our need, it stands firm regardless of negative circumstances. There may be times of questioning, and we may not understand God's timing, but his promise remains certain through our deepest trial. If we consistently rely on his immutable Word, we can disregard the darkness.

Oswald Chambers says, "Are you in the dark right now regarding your circumstances? Then listen, and God will give you a very precious message for someone else when you are in the light."

God waits for us to trust him when trusting seems the most difficult thing of all.

Do not throw away this confident trust in the Lord, no matter what happens. Remember the great reward it brings you! Patient endurance is what you need now, so you will continue to do God's will. Then you will receive all that he has promised. Hebrews 10:35-36, NLT

January 22

To Know God

O God
There is an aching longing within
me
To know more and more
Of Your kindness and peace.
You have promised to give me
(As I learn to know You better)
Everything I could possibly need
For walking in newness of life.
By Your mighty power
You have promised to implant
Your own character within me.
But Your Word makes it clear,
Lord
That to obtain these gifts
I need more than faith.
I must discover what You want
me to do.
I must put aside my own desires
And strive to become patient and
godly.
I must gladly let You have your way
with me.
I must learn to enjoy and love
others deeply.

You make it very clear, dear Lord
That the process is a build-up—
Addition upon addition.
But as I willingly yield to You
The reward will be the fulfillment
Of my deepest longing:
I will be spiritually strong
I will be fruitful and useful.
Above all, I will fulfill
Your divine purpose for my life.
For to know You, the eternal God
Is exactly what I was made for.

Draw close to God, and God will draw close to you. James 4:8, NLT

January 23

Fruitless Hours

My Lord

Forgive me for spending

So many fruitless hours

Debating, analyzing, mulling over

What I think I should do

In future years—

When again and again

You have proven

That the hours of each *today*

Lived in explicit obedience

Reveal sufficient spiritual insight

To make *tomorrow* surprisingly clear!

But seek first his kingdom and his righteousness, and all these things will be given to you as well. Therefore do not worry about tomorrow, for tomorrow will worry about itself. Each day has enough trouble of its own.

Matthew 6:33-34, NIV

January 24

Something Beautiful

Here I am, dear God

Your child

A member of Your Family

Asking You

To make something beautiful

Of my life.

Yet, even as I ask

I am convinced

That the one beautiful thing

About a child of God

Is You, Jesus Christ.

So, dear Lord

As You saturate me with Yourself

My life will be beautiful.

For we are God's masterpiece. He has created us anew in Christ Jesus, so that we can do the good things he planned for us long ago.

Ephesians 2:10, NLT

January 25

For This New Year

O Lord God
You are able.

Able to make me clean
Without self-righteousness and
sham.
Able to make me real
Without hypocrisy.

You are able
To give me wisdom
In all my priorities
My decisions, my goals.

You are able
To transform my fears
Into vibrant faith
And quiet trust.

You are able
To make this present year
The most challenging
The most productive
Of all my life.

So for this new year
I covenant with You, dear God.
Please work in me
To the very depth of my being.

Renovate me
Transform me
For You are able—miraculously
able
To make all things new.

As the Spirit of the Lord works within us, we become more and more like him and reflect his glory even more. 2 Corinthians 3:18, NLT

January 26

I Trust

O God, thank You
That Your promises are valid
As long as the world lasts.
They do not suddenly dissolve
When my faith is feeble
And my courage fails.
When You have given a promise
You will perform it—
Sight or no sight
Feeling or no feeling.

You may take me
Through the darkest night
The deepest waters.
The very worst may happen
But out of it
You will bring the very best
For Your Word remains secure.

Lord, keep me faithful in my trust.
When I can articulate no other prayer
May my waiting heart
Continually avow:
I trust!
I trust!

Trust in the Lord with all your heart; do not depend on your own understanding. Seek his will in all you do, and he will direct your paths.
Proverbs 3:5-6, NLT

January 27

You Promised Me

Lord, just today I read again
The words of the prophet, Ezra.
Long years ago he prayed
"You have done what You promised
For You are always true to Your word."
My dear Lord, look into my heart.
Listen to my repeated plea.
You promised me, Lord
You promised me.
You promised deliverance
From crushing defeat.
You promised Your peace
In my aching despair.
You promised release
From agonizing pain.
I've waited so long . . . so long.
Still I cling tenaciously
To this solemn truth:
You are always true to Your word.
I trust You, dear God.
I expect to pray as Ezra prayed:
"You have done what You promised
For You are always true to Your word."

And you have done what you promised, for you are always true to your word. Nehemiah 9:8, NLT

January 28

God Gives the Very Best

She stood alone at the card counter reading sentimental valentines. A thousand painful memories crowded her heart. She longed to buy one special card. It seemed so right for him—as though she had written it herself.

Four weeks ago they had said a final good-bye. The break was heart-wrenching. He was so alive, so much fun, so intelligent. But day after day he stubbornly insisted he had no need or desire for God. "Let's take our moments of pleasure now," he begged.

When he proposed to her, the conflict was overwhelming. She longed to say yes, but above all else she wanted a Christian home. The wrong decision would negate all she believed about marriage.

Did she buy the card that lonely day? No, for she was convinced it would only prolong the pain. What is she doing now? She is living in daily contact with God, grateful for the gift of his peace. Since the day of her total commitment she is learning, sharing, giving—and she is trusting. She is confident that God gives the very best to those who leave the choice with him. She waits with an open heart!

The peace of God, which transcends all understanding, will guard your hearts and your minds in Christ Jesus. Philippians 4:7, NIV

January 29

Accept—Expect

My Father

Empower me to *accept*

All You have promised

And to *expect*

Every promise fulfilled.

May I never forget

How completely I am in Your hands.

Let us hold unswervingly to the hope we profess, for he who promised is faithful.

Hebrews 10:23, NIV

January 30

Be Thou Exalted

"Be thou exalted, Lord
In thine own strength;
So will we sing
And praise thy power."

Yes, Lord, Yes!
David's prayer is my prayer.

Be exalted in my day-by-day agenda
In my motives and dreams
My priorities and goals.
Even in my failures, Lord
As You turn them into stepping-stones
Toward spiritual growth.
Be exalted in my worship and praise
In my sobbing and singing.
Be exalted in my secret thoughts
My emotional responses.
Be exalted in my daily routine
The delays, the unexpected emergencies
The disappointments that often come.
Lord God, as You are exalted
In heaven and on earth
Be exalted in Your home—my heart.

Be exalted, O God, above the highest heavens. May your glory shine over all the earth.
Psalm 57:11, NLT

January 31

Count It All Joy

Dear Lord
It is a comparatively simple thing
To face a group of hurting women
At a retreat or seminar
And share with them
The triumph that comes through suffering.
Over and over I proclaim from Your Word:
"Count it all joy."
I say it emphatically
And with genuine conviction.
But last month, dear God
When physical pain seemed unendurable
And my guarded emotions collapsed
All my carefully planned outlines
Crumbled like sand castles on a windy beach.
O God, forgive me! Forgive me!
Help me to recall often
The piercing words of Oswald Chambers:
"Our worth to God in public
Will always be determined
By our lives in private."
Teach me, dear Lord—teach ME
To count it all joy.
I have so much to learn.

Dear brothers and sisters, whenever trouble comes your way, let it be an opportunity for joy. For when your faith is tested, your endurance has a chance to grow. James 1:2-3, NLT

February

The Promise of Answered Prayer

Following God is something far more thrilling than anyone has dared to dream.

Listen to my voice in the morning, Lord. Each morning
I bring my requests to you and wait expectantly.

Psalm 5:3, NLT

February 1

Another Word for Trusting

Lord, I used to think

I could prove my trust in You

By refusing to fear.

Now I see that fear

Does not dissolve

With any timid command.

Far better to cling to You

While You rebuke the fear.

Clinging is another word

For trusting.

He will cover you with his feathers, and under his wings you will find refuge; his faithfulness will be your shield and rampart. Psalm 91:4, NIV

February 2

Longing to Please You

With all my heart, Lord

I long to please You.

But too often I lack wisdom

Or am shackled by indecision

Or deterred by incalculables.

Enable me, Lord

To relax in Your love

Released and radiantly confident

That my longing to please You

Pleases You most.

No, O people, the Lord has already told you what is good, and this is what he requires: to do what is right, to love mercy, and to walk humbly with your God.

Micah 6:8, NLT

February 3

Heartstrings

Lord, with no sense of direction
I'm forever losing my way.
Please tie a string
From Your heart to mine
So that even in the darkness
I'll feel the tug of Your heart
And find my way home.

He will feed his flock like a shepherd. He will carry the lambs in his arms, holding them close to his heart. He will gently lead the mother sheep with their young.

Isaiah 40:11, NLT

February 4

It's Your Move

All through the long dreary hours
Of this rough toilsome day
I have struggled to believe
That Your plan is good
That the blows and bruises
Will stablish me
That the staggering changes
Will settle me.
I have struggled to believe
That Your way is perfect.

But waiting here alone
Shrouded in thick loneliness
I confess I don't see it.
Frankly I just don't see
That Your way is perfect.
And now I hear You say
I didn't say you would see it—
I only said—it is.
So, Lord, it's Your move.
Good-night.

Oh, the depth of the riches of the wisdom and knowledge of God!
How unsearchable his judgments, and his paths beyond tracing out!
Romans 11:33, NIV

February 5

Thank You for Waiting

Had You given in to me, Lord
On the thing I wanted so much
My life today
Would be a sorry mess.

I tell You nothing new—
I simply repeat
What You told me
Long, long ago.
Finally today I see it—
From Your point of view.
Thank You for not giving in to me.
Thank You most of all
For patiently waiting
For me to give in to You.

Instantly Jesus reached out his hand and grabbed him. "You don't have much faith," Jesus said. "Why did you doubt me?" And when they climbed back into the boat, the wind stopped.

Matthew 14:31-32, NLT

February 6

Discovery

Lord, I have discovered

That when I try

In simple ways

To be something to others

I utterly fail

Unless You are everything

To me.

Yes, I am the vine; you are the branches. Those who remain in me, and I in them, will produce much fruit. For apart from me you can do nothing.

John 15:5, NLT

February 7

Forgiveness

Forgiveness. What does it do for us? In an amazing way it creates a fresh beginning. It lifts us out of the tangled seaweed of resentment. A miracle is performed!

It may not happen in a moment or a day. We may have to forgive at six o'clock on Monday and start over again at two o'clock on Tuesday. There is no magic wand to simplify forgiveness. Forgiveness is a deliberate setting of our will, often with no emotional high whatsoever. But once having genuinely forgiven, our soul is washed clean. We walk in dignity again. We sense a new vitality. We're no longer concentrating on hurts; we're concentrating on God.

If we would only forgive, our lives would undergo transformations beyond our highest expectations. Above all, Jesus Christ would be exalted, for it is his forgiveness that makes the difference.

Forgiveness is a beautiful word. It is God's word passed to us to use freely, joyfully. When we ask for the gift of forgiveness, God always says yes. He gave his Son to make us free, and forgiveness is the secret key to freedom.

You must make allowance for each other's faults and forgive the person who offends you. Remember, the Lord forgave you, so you must forgive others.

Colossians 3:13, NLT

February 8

Thank You for Saying No

Lord, day after day I've thanked You
For saying yes.
But when have I genuinely thanked You
For saying no?

Yet I shudder to think
Of the possible smears
The cumulative blots on my life
Had You not been sufficiently wise
To say an *unalterable* no.

So thank You for saying no
When my wantlist for things
Far exceeded my longing for You.
When I asked for a stone
Foolishly certain I asked for bread.
Thank You for saying no
To my petulant "Just this time, Lord?"
Thank You for saying no
To senseless excuses
Selfish motives
Dangerous diversions.

Thank You for saying no
When the temptation that enticed me
Would have bound me beyond escape.

Thank You for saying no
When I asked You to leave me alone.

Above all
Thank You for saying no
When in anguish I asked
"If I give You all else
May I keep *this?*"
Lord, my awe increases
When I see the wisdom
Of Your divine no.

There is more hope for fools than for people who think they are wise.
Proverbs 26:12, NLT

February 9

I Promise You Spring

O God . . . God
On this sullen winter day
When the sky is threatening
And the driving wind
Pushes against our small house
I walk from room to room
Tortured, twisted, torn.
Without a whispered warning
Without a turn or a touch
You have taken my dearest
love—
And I am left utterly defenseless
In the cruel, crushing arms
Of intolerable grief.
I am lost and listless
Waves of despair crash over me
I am bereft of love, of joy.

Do You understand, God?
There is no splendor anymore.
There is no magic, no laughter.
There is no one who speaks my
language
Or reads my thoughts
Or gentles my turbulent heart.
O God—there are two winters now
And the winter within me
Is by far the more dismal.
Do You understand?

Child of My love
In My infinite Plan
There are four seasons.
Trust Me . . . Trust Me . . .
I promise you—Spring.

I will never forget this awful time, as I grieve over my loss. Yet I still dare to hope when I remember this: The unfailing love of the Lord never ends! By his mercies we have been kept from complete destruction. Great is his faithfulness; his mercies begin afresh each day.

Lamentations 3:20-23, NLT

February 10

Nothing Can Separate Me

God, who or what in all the world
Can convince me that You
No longer love me—
That You've given me the slip
And thrown me over?
Shall mounting pressures interfere
With my personal relationship with
  You?
Shall shadowy fears that plague my
  nights?
Shall a palpitating heart
Or a strange buzzing in my head
Or pounding pain
Or bitter tears?

Or what if people laugh at me and
  reject me
Until I feel utterly confused and
  alone?
Or what if I can no longer work
And unpaid bills pour over me
Like a deluge of crashing bricks?
Or what if an accident incapacitates
  me
And I must depend on others for
  personal care?
Or what if I can no longer
  remember names
And my blurry eyes see double
And my hands tremble?
Or what if an earthquake crumbles
  my home
And my furniture is buried in thick
  mud?
Or what if I am left alone
Without family or friends?
Am I finished then?
Does this end my small scene?

No, dear God.
Positively not!
In all these impossible circumstances
I know that nothing is impossible
  with You.
I am utterly assured that:
In weakness or sickness
Catastrophe or anxiety
Loneliness or despair
I am Yours and You are mine.
Nothing can separate me
From Your matchless love!

And I am convinced that nothing can ever separate us from his love. Death can't, and life can't. The angels can't, and the demons can't. Our fears for today, our worries about tomorrow, and even the powers of hell can't keep God's love away. Whether we are high above the sky or in the deepest ocean, nothing in all creation will ever be able to separate us from the love of God that is revealed in Christ Jesus our Lord. Romans 8:38-39, NLT

February 11

Once and for All

Lord

May I settle it once and for all

That I am dealing directly with You.

You need never apologize

For any plan You ordain for me

Since nothing but good

Can come from Your hand.

You are sufficient

For every *changing* circumstance

In my God-planned life—

For every *unchanging* circumstance as well.

The eyes of all look to you, and you give them their food at the proper time. You open your hand and satisfy the desires of every living thing.

Psalm 145:15-16, NIV

February 12

Practice Loving

It is so simple, dear Lord
So pleasant and comfortable
To sit in church on a Sunday
morning
Listening to a sermon about love—
Perhaps even speculating a bit
On whether my love surpasses the
love
Of the person to my right
Or the person to my left.
But to love with Your love
To practice loving, dear God
How uncomfortable the church
pew becomes
When I hear this ringing challenge
When I see Your gazing eyes.
Suddenly I remember the vicious
remarks
Of the woman who misjudged me.
I remember the unscrupulous
associate
Who finagled my husband's job.
I remember the careless driver
Who totaled our shining new car.
So quickly, Lord, I am faced
With a haunting parade
Of shameful, unloving attitudes.
God, You know me so much better
Than I know my own complex self
And still You continue to love me.
Give me, I pray, a fresh glimpse
Of Your vast, immeasurable love
For it is only out of gratitude for
Your love
That I shall finally learn
What it means to practice loving.

Dear children, let us not love with words or tongue but with actions and in truth.
1 John 3:18, NIV

February 13

Reflection

Lord
Again and again I have asked You
To robe me in splendor—
To spark my life with radiance
Until there burns within me
A soft unquenchable glow.
Now today as I read Your Word
Your answer to my longing is so direct:
"They looked to him and were radiant."

Lord, the mystery is solved!
I must look steadfastly to You
For my radiance can only be
A shimmering reflection of Yours.

And all of us have had that veil removed so that we can be mirrors that brightly reflect the glory of the Lord. 2 Corinthians 3:18, NLT

February 14

Morning Tribute

In all the years of my childhood, I doubt that we ever lived in a house where the sweet fragrance of roses didn't permeate the air.

I've never forgotten the summer ritual that made every breakfast a special event. Every morning my father would come in from the back yard with a freshly plucked rosebud—his token of love for my mother. Usually I'd be setting the table when Dad made his presentation. . . . "Here it is, sweetheart—your morning tribute."

One morning while sunbeams played leapfrog on our kitchen wall my mother stopped stirring oatmeal. She dropped her wooden spoon and threw her arms around my father. I'll never forget her words:

"There are ten thousand ways of loving and you know them all!"

Love knows no limit to its endurance; no end to its trust, no fading of its hope; it can outlast anything. It is, in fact, the one thing that still stands when all else has fallen.

If I could speak in any language in heaven or on earth but didn't love others, I would only be making meaningless noise like a loud gong or a clanging cymbal. 1 Corinthians 13:1, NLT

February 15

The Language of Love

Lord
I long so eagerly to love You more
Too often my love for You is
Cold
Calculating
Indifferent
And I so easily slip into apathy.
I dream nostalgically of might-have-beens
And often You seem a million miles away.
Frankly, I find it easier by far
To love my family and friends
Than to fervently love You.
I make this confession shamefully
And with the full knowledge
That You already know my heart's dullness.
Can You change me, Lord?
The disciples pleaded with You
To teach them to pray.
Right now I plead with You
To teach me to love.

The language of love, my child
Is always obedience
Search your heart with honesty.
Where are you shunning obedience?

But those who obey God's word really do love him. That is the way to know whether or not we live in him. Those who say they live in God should live their lives as Christ did. 1 John 2:5-6, NLT

February 16

Free Me Completely

O dear God
This aching desire!
My heart cries for it
Longs for it
With deep, throbbing intensity!
Yet in the depths of my soul
I know that what I ask
Is not Your highest
Or Your best for me.
I cannot come to You boldly
Nor can I make my request
In the Name of Your Son.
I dare not ask for a stone
When You offer me bread.
And so, my Lord
Though the longing clutches my heart
I yield it to You totally.
I ask not that You grant my desire
But that You free me completely
From desiring it.

Oh, what a miserable person I am! Who will free me from this life that is dominated by sin? Thank God! The answer is in Jesus Christ our Lord.

Romans 7:24-25, NLT

February 17

Inconsistency

Lord, forgive me

For telling You

I love You

When deep in my heart

I frantically fight

Against Your Will.

Search me, O God, and know my heart; test me and know my thoughts. Point out anything in me that offends you, and lead me along the path of everlasting life. Psalm 139:23-24, NLT

February 18

The Infallible Test

Lord
Often I have wondered
If my love for You is genuine.
Or do I flippantly mouth it
Like a small child
Saying grace at the table?
But today as I read Your Word
I discovered the one infallible test:
"The one who obeys me
Is the one who loves me."
Lord, never again need I wonder.
You have made it plain enough.

If you love me, you will obey what I command. John 14:15, NIV

February 19

Deduction

Lord, when You say
The same thing to me so often
I surely must need it
And You surely must mean it!
Help me to take You seriously.
May I remember that the one settled proof
That I have taken you seriously
Will always be—obedience.

Those who obey God's commandments live in fellowship with him, and he with them. And we know he lives in us because the Holy Spirit lives in us.
1 John 3:24, NLT

February 20

The Exception

Lord, too often I demand
From my family and friends
More love
More affirmation
More acceptance
Than they are capable of giving.
Today, dear God
I ask You to burn this truth
Into the depth of my inner being:
Nobody in all the world
Can ever love me
As much as I need to be loved—
Except You!

For as high as the heavens are above the earth, so great is his love for those who fear him.
Psalm 103:11, NIV

February 21

Grow Up

Picture it with me: a piece of gnarled bark tossed to and fro over the crashing breakers. First one direction, then another, back and forth, over and under. Aimless. No set purpose. Drifting . . . always drifting.

What an accurate picture of an immature Christian. Nothing but spiritual puttering. Up and down, in and out. One study group for a few weeks, then another. One church for a while, then another. Undisciplined, unsteady, one day soaring, the next day wading in self-pity. No consistency.

The apostle Paul tells us to grow up! Not grow older, but grow up into Christ. What we are today is more important to God than what we were yesterday. Our life journey with Jesus is now—this very day, this very hour. Why yearn for change if we've made no effort to follow the direction God has already given us?

To grow spiritually we must be single-minded. Our one goal? To be conformed to the image of Christ. He longs for our willingness to let him root us, cultivate us, water us. Above all, God wants our total commitment. He will take anything we give him except second place.

Don't copy the behavior and customs of this world, but let God transform you into a new person by changing the way you think. Then you will know what God wants you to do, and you will know how good and pleasing and perfect his will really is. Romans 12:2, NLT

February 22

Only a Feeling

Lord

I don't like feeling

Like a half-person.

My child

It is only a feeling.

You are complete in Me.

Have you never heard or understood? Don't you know that the Lord is the everlasting God, the Creator of all the earth? He never grows faint or weary. No one can measure the depths of his understanding.

Isaiah 40:28, NLT

February 23

Your Word

Your Word!

O God, how it pierces

The deepest recesses of my being.

It analyzes every secret emotion

And leaves me exposed and defenseless.

At times Your Word is like fire

Burning up my pettiness, my petulance.

Or like a steady hammer

Shattering to dust my tolerated conflicts.

At other times it is like a gentle voice

Spreading great calm over my restless mind.

O Lord, I can never be content

To dabble in a chapter here and there

Or skim a verse or two

For always You confront me personally

And I know that I am looking

Beyond earth and sky

Into the very face of God.

The law from your mouth is more precious to me than thousands of pieces of silver and gold. Psalm 119:72, NIV

February 24

I Don't Understand

Lord

I just don't understand

What in the world

You're doing in my life.

My child

Don't try to understand.

Just live it

For Me.

"My thoughts are completely different from yours," says the Lord. "And my ways are far beyond anything you could imagine. For just as the heavens are higher than the earth, so are my ways higher than your ways and my thoughts higher than your thoughts."

Isaiah 55:8-9, NLT

February 25

You Love Me

God
When I am wretched and weak
You love me.
When I am steady and strong
You love me.
When I am very right
Or terribly wrong
You love me.
When I talk too much
Or laugh too loud
Or sob too long
You love me.
When I am quiet and serene
You love me.
When I willingly obey
You love me.
When I insist on my own way
You love me.
When I fail to put You first
You love me.
When I come running back
  to You
You love me.
I need not beg You to love me
For You who are Love
Cannot exist without loving.

And yet this very day, dear God
I have no real assurance
Of Your love at all.
I wonder why?

Beloved child
The fact remains:
I love you.

See how very much our heavenly Father loves us, for he allows us to be called his children, and we really are! 1 John 3:1, NLT

February 26

At Last

At last there is One
With whom I am perfectly safe.
One who knows thoroughly
All the rubbled ruins of my heart.
At last I see that all that is
Riddled and distorted in me
Can still find God-planned fulfillment.
At last I need no longer explore
The deep, dark forest of my thoughts
For there is One who understands me
Far better than I understand myself.
One who stands with me
In the thick of the battle
One who supports me
On the slippery, ice-crested paths.
At last I have entrusted myself
To One who guarantees my wholeness
Someone whose love is immeasurable.
In all the world He alone can love me
As I need to be loved.
At last there is One—
My Lord and my God!

My soul finds rest in God alone; my salvation comes from him. He alone is my rock and my salvation; he is my fortress, I will never be shaken.

Psalm 62:1, NIV

February 27

Lost Shepherd

Sometimes, Lord
In my groping effort to find You
I have reversed the parable
Of the Shepherd and the sheep.
In my distorted concept
The Shepherd has been lost
And the sheep have trudged down
Dangerous mountain cliffs to find him.
How sadly prone I am to forget
That I would not be searching for You
If You were not first wanting me.
Let me remember always, Lord
How foolish it is
To stumble through darkness
Searching for You
When I need only to surrender
To Your search for me.

I am the good shepherd. The good shepherd lays down his life for the sheep.

John 10:11, NLT

February 28

The Lesson

God is teaching me a valuable lesson. I am beginning to grasp that one of the marks of total surrender is the quiet confidence that God is in control. We don't come into maturity in a day, a month, or a year. When we discover that we really *can* trust God's methods, he gives us the settled confidence that every process he takes us through is worth the wait.

Waiting! The most difficult of all God's requirements! I have sometimes argued, *God, I'm not waiting for a streetcar, or for a light to change, or for the rain to stop. This is a "life issue."* In kindness he reminds me that his ways are unsearchable, unfathomable.

Slowly I am beginning to sense that in waiting I am becoming more teachable, more flexible, more discerning. As I surrender to his wise plan, as I obey his instructions, I begin to discover that what God is doing *within* me as I wait is far more significant than what I am waiting for.

So I leave it there, believing that God's sovereignty is laced with his compassion and love. He doesn't need my personal analysis!

"My thoughts are not your thoughts, neither are your ways my ways," declares the Lord. "As the heavens are higher than the earth, so are my ways higher than your ways and my thoughts than your thoughts."

Isaiah 55:8-9, NIV

February 29

Settled Decision

God, it is my settled decision
Not to choose less
When You have chosen more for me.
Not to choose the worst
When You have chosen the best.
Not to stoop to defeat
When You have provided victory.
Not to let my emptiness
Close the door to Your fullness.

I listen carefully to what God the Lord is saying, for he speaks peace to his people, his faithful ones. But let them not return to their foolish ways.
Psalm 85:8, NLT

March

The Promise of Security

Hear God's word to you:

God is our refuge and strength,

an ever present help in trouble.

I will make you as secure as a fortified wall. . . . I will protect and deliver you. I, the Lord, have spoken!

Jeremiah 15:20, NLT

March 1

Plain Old Me

O Lord
Here I am again
Just plain old me
Coming to You
As I've come a thousand times—
And this is what always happens:
Your response is immediate
You open Your arms unhesitatingly
You draw me to Yourself
You clasp me to Your Father-heart.
Then You reaffirm my position:
I'm a child of the King
And all that is Yours is mine.
When I begin my stammering account
Of gross unworthiness
Your gentle smile hushes me.
With endless patience
You remind me once more
That my value never determines Your love.
Rather, Your love determines my value.

His son said to him, "Father, I have sinned against both heaven and you, and I am no longer worthy of being called your son." But his father said to the servants, "Quick! Bring the finest robe in the house and put it on him. Get a ring for his finger, and sandals for his feet."

Luke 15:21-22, NLT

March 2

Who Will Clap for Me?

I am often dramatic
Sometimes ecstatic
In the role I play
On the stage of Life.
I bow
And smile
And bask
In the limelight
Hoarding each moment
Of thunderous applause.
But when the curtain is pulled
For the last time
When the crowds have dispersed
And the stage is dark
Who will clap for me then, Lord?
You?

He humbled you, causing you to hunger and then feeding you with manna, which neither you nor your fathers had known, to teach you that man does not live on bread alone but on every word that comes from the mouth of the Lord. Deuteronomy 8:3, NIV

March 3

Like Now

There are black and dismal times, Lord
When there is nothing and no one but You
When encouragement from friends
(However sincere and honest)
Rings shallow and repetitious
When books seem nothing more
Than jumbled sentences
When music depresses
When food is offensive
When sleep is evasive
There are such times, Lord

Like now.

Though he slay me, yet will I hope in him. Job 13:15, NIV

March 4

Am I Growing?

"Consider the lilies of the field
How they grow . . ."
Yes, Lord, I know
They grow *in the dark.*
Just now it is dark
Very dark, Lord.

Am I growing?

You have tested us, O God; you have purified us like silver melted in a crucible.
Psalm 66:10, NLT

March 5

Minimoods

You amaze me, Lord
Really, You amaze me.
Again and again
I bring You my minimoods:
Moods of depression
Resentment
Fear.
With every conceivable mood
I kneel in Your Presence
Sometimes impatiently
Often desperately
Always longingly.

And then—
In ways I cannot comprehend
Or possibly explain
I begin to sense
The pressure of You:
Melting
Molding
Transforming
Until minimoods of confusion
Become maximoments of silent joy.
It is too wonderful, Lord—
Much too wonderful.

Nothing is too hard for You
Not even me.

You have turned my mourning into joyful dancing. You have taken away my clothes of mourning and clothed me with joy, that I might sing praises to you and not be silent. O Lord my God, I will give you thanks forever!
Psalm 30:11-12, NLT

March 6

Tell Me Again, Lord, I Forget

I don't want to get up this morning, Lord.
The day is cold and misty
I feel it
Even with the shades drawn.
My head aches
My heart skips beats
And my fingers tingle.
I just can't handle the pressure
Piled sky-high.
Lord
Do something
Say something
I'm scared.

Little one
I've already shown you
I've already told you
If you obey
You'll see.
If you refuse
I'm so sorry.

Tell me again, Lord
I forget.

The Lord hears his people when they call to him for help. He rescues them from all their troubles. The Lord is close to the brokenhearted; he rescues those who are crushed in spirit. Psalm 34:17-18, NLT

March 7

Worth the Waiting

Growing spiritually is such a long, slow process! It's painful, too. Every day at the turn of the road I become acquainted with new pitfalls and heartaches. Sometimes the pain backs me into a corner. For example: There is a woman I know who is so sarcastic, so curt and unkind. Am I ever excused? Is forgiveness always a part of my growth?

So often I feel like a spiritual midget while my husband and friends appear to be spiritual giants. I seem to shrink in my own home.

Another thing: I confess I'm a coward about pain. Emotional pain. Physical pain. The pain of loneliness, the pain of grief. Yet, again and again it is true. What I must learn in my pain is that it is leading to something positive, something beyond what I can see in the present darkness.

I do want to grow! I want to become more and more like Jesus. Even though it takes so long, surely it is worth the waiting!

Grow in the special favor and knowledge of our Lord and Savior Jesus Christ. To him be all glory and honor, both now and forevermore.

2 Peter 3:18, NLT

March 8

How Else?

O Lord
I am continually amazed
At Your willingness to work
Through my nothingness
And my simplicity.
I am always suggesting
That You wait
Until some future spring or fall
When I can offer You
A more polished, glittering self—
But the very things I struggle
To correct and improve
You want surrendered as they are.
You want to give Yourself
A magnificent reputation
By Your accomplishment in me.
So, dear Lord
Take my insignificance
And make it a shining emblem
Of Your creative power.
Do it all by Yourself.

Dear child, how else
Would it ever get done?

But by the grace of God I am what I am, and his grace to me was not without effect.
1 Corinthians 15:10, NIV

March 9

I Can't—You Can

O dear God

It comes to me

With sweet and gentle relief

That this thing in my life

Which I can't possibly handle

Is the one thing above all

That You *can* handle.

You can handle it totally

And You can handle it now.

Yes, dear child

Now let Me!

I am the Lord, the God of all the peoples of the world. Is anything too hard for me?
Jeremiah 32:27, NLT

March 10

All Will Be Well

O Lord God
In the midst of consuming sorrow
When despair and loneliness hedge me in
You understand my frailties—
My hesitancies, my fears.
As I scamper from doubt to doubt
You forgive so quickly my outbursts.
Never do You drive me away
When I rail against You
In peevish rebellion.
When I scream
"Don't You even care?"
You quiet my fragmented heart.
You work in me silently
Always planning in love.
You refine me in the white-flamed
Furnace of affliction.
In the silent darkness You whisper:
Trust Me—all will be well.

To you, O Lord, I lift up my soul; in you I trust, O my God.

Psalm 25:1-2, NIV

March 11

My Radiant Dawn

Dear God
The psalmist David said
He watched for You
As one who waits for the dawn.

I know, God
I know . . .

One who waits for the dawn
Waits in quivering darkness
In loneliness
In somber silence . . .
He waits for that
Which comes slowly—
Ever so slowly . . .
But, God
He waits for that
Which he *knows* will come
And when it comes
At last there is light!

I am waiting
As David waited.
O God
You *will* come—
My Radiant Dawn!

My soul waits for the Lord more than watchmen wait for the morning, more than watchmen wait for the morning. Psalm 130:6, NIV

March 12

At This Very Moment

O God

At this very moment

When I feel utterly abandoned

When I feel You are an enemy

And not my friend

When I feel You have turned Your face

And withdrawn Your love

At this very moment

I throw myself into Your arms

And stubbornly refuse to move.

What will You do with me now?

I waited patiently for the Lord to help me, and he turned to me and heard my cry. He lifted me out of the pit of despair, out of the mud and the mire. He set my feet on solid ground and steadied me as I walked along.

Psalm 40:1-2, NLT

March 13

Just Come Home

God, You are so good!
When at last I called to You
From my prison without Exit
You did not exact from me
A solemn promise to do better.
You did not insist
That I adhere to an endless set of rules
To guarantee Your acceptance of me.
Nor did You say with frightening sternness
"Stand on your own two feet."
Rather, with breathtaking simplicity
You unlocked prison doors
You invaded the very depths of me
You encompassed me with transforming love.
On the very spot where I groped and grappled
You turned me about toward a rugged cross.
You pointed to an empty tomb.
Then with gentle urging You said
"Your past is obliterated
Your future is secure
Just come home!"

He is so rich in kindness that he purchased our freedom through the blood of his Son, and our sins are forgiven. He has showered his kindness on us, along with all wisdom and understanding.

Ephesians 1:7-8, NLT

March 14

Has God Passed Me By?

We were sitting in our living room before a cheerful hearth fire, listening to the low March wind beat against our house. My pretty seventeen-year-old friend looked pensive. She said finally, "You'll probably think I sound morbid, but sometimes I just get the feeling that God has passed me by. He just doesn't seem personal. It's like being all alone in a huge computer universe where I don't really matter."

The doubts of a seventeen-year-old? If we're honest we'll all confess that we're prone to ask questions: Why life's tragedies? Why disease and pain and heartache? Why the sense of futility so often? Does it really matter to God about me?

What better evidence than the Cross? What better evidence than the Lord's promise, "I will never leave you nor forsake you." Our vast universe is in God's control. We are not governed by fate, but by our Father. Not chance, but his choice. Not a guessing game, but his guidance. He chose us to be the objects of his lavish love.

Cast down, perhaps—that we might learn to trust, regardless of circumstances. Tested, that we might claim God's unlimited resources. Passed by? Never!

God has said, "Never will I leave you; never will I forsake you." So we say with confidence, "The Lord is my helper; I will not be afraid."

Hebrews 13:5-6, NIV

March 15

It's Good

God, it's good to be loved by You!

The breathtaking knowledge

Of Your life-giving love

Rings chimes in my tremulous heart.

It fashions eternal declarations

Out of unsettled questions.

It creates a majestic life symphony

From a solitary note.

God, it's good to be loved by You!

I will sing of the Lord's great love forever; with my mouth I will make your faithfulness known through all generations. Psalm 89:1, NIV

March 16

The Mountain

Dear Lord

I see it more clearly now:

Again and again I've begged You

To remove my mountain of difficulty—

While You have been patiently waiting

To cleanse my cluttered doubts

And calm my frantic fears

So I may climb the mountain.

For I can do everything with the help of Christ who gives me the strength I need.

Philippians 4:13, NLT

March 17

The Exchange

O God
You are continually
Stripping me . . .
Stripping me . . .
Of all my natural plans
My dreams
My successes
My secret ambitions.
For so long, Lord
My natural achievements
Have been my one consuming thought.
And now they lie before me
In a paltry heap.
God, why?

My child
It is the only way
I can begin to shower you
With all the joys
Of the supernatural.
Do you resist that exchange?

Turn my heart toward your statutes and not toward selfish gain. Turn my eyes away from worthless things; preserve my life according to your word.
Psalm 119:36-37, NIV

March 18

What Is Your Schedule, God?

Lord
Many years ago Martin Luther said
"It is God's nature
To make something out of nothing.
That is why God cannot make anything
Out of him who is not yet nothing."

In ways I had never anticipated, Lord
Slowly but persistently
You continue Your hammering and crushing
In every hidden crevice of my life.
You seem determined
To reduce me to nothing
In order to make me something.
I wonder . . .
What is Your schedule, God?
As You creatively continue
To reshape and remake me
How long will the process last?
Lord, could You hurry a little?

And I am sure that God, who began the good work within you, will continue his work until it is finally finished on that day when Christ Jesus comes back again.
Philippians 1:6, NLT

March 19

How Is It, Lord?

How is it, Lord?

My friend is able
To speak with amazing assurance
About Your sustaining comfort
In times of heart-throbbing grief.
She expounds magnificently
About Your shining presence
In times of fear and despair.
Her smiling declarations
About Your healing power
In the midst of tormenting pain
Are intended to encourage, I'm sure.
But I'm puzzled, Lord.
How can she speak so confidently
When she is so comfortably settled?
When she has never lost one
More precious than life to her?
When her greatest obstacle
Is her lack of discipline?
When by her own admission
She has never been sick
A day in her life?

O Lord . . . ever-patient Friend
Forgive me for the times
I have foolishly attempted
To offer the solace
That You alone can give.

To all who mourn in Israel, he will give beauty for ashes, joy instead of mourning, praise instead of despair. For the Lord has planted them like strong and graceful oaks for his own glory. Isaiah 61:3, NLT

March 20

When Trouble Comes

My Lord . . . my dear Lord
Again this morning
As I read the words of the Psalmist
You refreshed my heart
And replenished my hope:
"When trouble comes He is the place to go."

Trouble!
Always I am unnerved
By its unannounced entrance
Into the secret corridors of my soul.
Pushing through with frightening force
It comes in sinister shapes and sizes.
I am never prepared for its onslaught.

Trouble!
Fashioned as pain it overwhelms me.
As sorrow it grieves me.
As disappointment it numbs me.
As failure it defeats me.
As anxiety it entangles me
In a perilous net of depression.

But God
I have boldly underlined David's words:
"When trouble comes He is the place to go."
How foolish to go running
From friend to friend
From place to place
When You have promised to deliver me.
It is in Your proximity
That my frantic fears dissolve.

"When trouble comes, He is the place to go."
In the margin of my Bible I have written:
Yes!
Yes!
Yes!

The Lord is a refuge for the oppressed, a stronghold in times of trouble. Those who know your name will trust in you, for you, Lord, have never forsaken those who seek you. Psalm 9:9-10, NIV

March 21

The Truant

What does God do with a truant who plays hooky from her heavenly Father? What are the options? One thing is sure: He doesn't pamper her. He knows she needs to stretch her spiritual muscles.

He doesn't shout, "Get up, foolish child!" She's so covered with mud she can't move. He doesn't condemn her, because his promise is "There is therefore now no condemnation."

In the end he does what he always does for any half-demolished child of his: He unlocks her handcuffed spirit with his key of infinite love. He checks her fluctuating heart with its spiritual irregularity. He gives her a fleeting glimpse of things as they could be. He accepts her confession. He thoroughly cleanses her, then he holds her close to his tender heart. He restores her joy and empowers her to obey.

Suddenly she knows with great gladness that her one safe fortress is the center of her Father's will.

At least so it is with one truant child: *me.*

If we confess our sins to him, he is faithful and just to forgive us and to cleanse us from every wrong. If we claim we have not sinned, we are calling God a liar and showing that his word has no place in our hearts.

1 John 1:9-10, NLT

March 22

I Will Wait

O Lord
Today I must face it honestly with
You
By pursuing the persistent
questions within me:

God, is there any gain at all by my
doubting?
Do doubts make me stronger?
Do they purify my heart? Fortify
my will?
Are my emotions firmly
established by my doubts?
Are my family and friends
encouraged?

On the other hand, God
Even though I see no possible way
out
Of the catastrophe I now face
Is there anything more pleasing
to You
Than my personal choice to trust
You?

I know it is true, Lord
I must rely on Your promises
in the end.
Would You be glorified, dear
God
If I trusted You now at the early
beginning?

O God, forgive me
For so limiting You.
Surely You know exactly what You
will do.
You are God, so You will not alter
Your Word.
Your power is instantly operative
In all the strange twisting of my
life.
You are God, so You are good.

I will hope
I will trust
I will wait
On the living God!

Yet the Lord longs to be gracious to you; he rises to show you compassion. For the Lord is a God of justice. Blessed are all who wait for him!
Isaiah 30:18, NIV

March 23

By You, Dear God

To be tattered and torn
Bit by bit, day in, day out
Or to be shattered totally
Like a crystal goblet
Flung fiercely against a giant rock.
To know the brutal intensity
Of pain and despair.
O God
How unbearable it seems
How intolerable as it happens.

But finally, finally
To stand against the storm
To stretch with the strain
To accept the pain
With a measure of quiet hope.
To look beyond the intrusion
And above the confusion
To catch a glimpse of rainbow
In an ocean of tears . . .

O great God
This is to trace at last
Your guiding hand—
To sense Your gentle touch.
This is to know Your presence—
More precious than
understanding—
To know Your compassion
Persists through the darkest night.
This is to walk courageously on
In the midst of a desolate
wilderness.
This is to be loved
To be held
To be kept
By the Sustainer of the universe.

To be loved
To be held
To be kept
By You, dear God
By You!

Those who live in the shelter of the Most High will find rest in the shadow of the Almighty. This I declare of the Lord: He alone is my refuge, my place of safety; he is my God, and I am trusting him.

Psalm 91:1-2, NLT

March 24

I Know You Best

God

So often I have

Seen and heard You

Between smiles

And singing

And laughter.

But I am beginning to see

I learn to know You best

Between sobs.

No discipline is enjoyable while it is happening—it is painful! But afterward there will be a quiet harvest of right living for those who are trained in this way. Hebrews 12:11, NLT

March 25

At Such Times

God, there are times
In the midst of heartache and heartbreak
When there is no comfort, no solace
Anywhere at all.
There are times
When in my crumbling state of mind
I feel I can no longer endure—
Not for a day, not even an hour.
It is at such times, O God
That I draw heavily
Upon Your unfathomable love.
At such times I implore
Your transforming peace.
At such times I live
By the power and promises
Of a Father who cares infinitely more
Than I can begin to grasp or comprehend.
Today, dear God, is a "such time."

Do not be afraid or discouraged, for the Lord is the one who goes before you. He will be with you; he will neither fail you nor forsake you.

Deuteronomy 31:8, NLT

March 26

Wrong Question

My faithful God

I see afresh this morning

The grave error of my question

"Don't You love me anymore?"

I ought always to ask instead

"How can You love me so continually

With such immeasurable love?"

Praise the Lord, all you nations; extol him, all you peoples. For great is his love toward us, and the faithfulness of the Lord endures forever. Praise the Lord.

Psalm 117:1-2, NIV

March 27

God, Why Do You Hide?

O God
Why do You hide from me
When I need You so much?
Why do You make it so difficult
For me to find You
When I know You are there?
When You have given me
Great and glorious promises
Why are none of them fulfilled?
When loneliness overwhelms me
Where is Your hand?
When I am depleted with fatigue
Where is Your rest?
O God, why do You hide from me?

Child of many questions
How can I answer
When you never stop asking?

Be still, and know that I am God. Psalm 46:10, NIV

March 28

Wonderful Joy Ahead

During the last three months of my mother's life, I was the willing caregiver for her as she battled a malignancy that seized her with brutal force. It robbed her of her zest, her gentle charm, her quick wit. I often walked aimlessly from room to room, pleading with God to release her from the intolerable pain.

Yet, in the midst of my mother's suffering, she called me to her bedside to remind me that Peter had told the early Christians to be truly glad—there is wonderful joy ahead, even though the going is rough down here for a while.

Frankly I could feel nothing of the wonderful joy ahead. I wanted an answer now.

Then one day when the pain subsided slightly, Mother began to pray aloud. I shall never forget her prayer: "God, I don't know how to interpret the sudden changes that have come so swiftly, nor can I explain the disappointment when so many plans seem unfinished. But I can still believe that to those who love you, you *always* bring ultimate joy." Then, with a kind of spiritual exuberance she added, "And dear Lord, you *know* how much I love you!"

At that moment I saw anew that though there are no pat answers, there is one who is the Answer—the Lord Jesus Christ!

We know that in all things God works for the good of those who love him.

Romans 8:28, NIV

March 29

I Often Forget

God

In the night's darkness

When sleep is evasive

I try with some semblance of clarity

To talk to You.

But I am troubled, dear Lord

After sleep finally beckons me

For by morning I often have forgotten what I prayed.

Never fear, weary child.

Though you forget

I always remember.

Can a mother forget the baby at her breast and have no compassion
or the child she has borne? Though she may forget, I will not
forget you! See, I have engraved you on the palms of my hands.

Isaiah 49:15-16, NIV

March 30

God, How Can I Describe You?

O God

How can I describe You?

To whom can You be compared?

Your Word says

No one in all the world

Can begin to fathom

The depths of Your understanding.

You sit above the circles of the earth.

You stretch out the heavens like a curtain.

You count the stars

To see that none of them have strayed.

You pick up the islands

As though they had no weight at all.

So why should I grapple

With a single lingering doubt

That You are powerful enough to hold me?

Look up into the heavens. Who created all the stars? He brings them out one after another, calling each by its name. And he counts them to see that none are lost or have strayed away. O Israel, how can you say the Lord does not see your troubles? How can you say God refuses to hear your case?

Isaiah 40:26-27, NLT

March 31

The Question

Yes, Lord, I know.

This is the way it will always be.

When You give me a definite promise

It is never a question

Of what *You* will do.

It is always a question

Of what *I* will do.

Without a single doubt

You will always keep Your word.

The question is—

Will I believe You?

"If you can?" said Jesus. "Everything is possible for him who believes." Immediately the boy's father exclaimed, "I do believe; help me overcome my unbelief!" Mark 9:23-24, NIV

April

The Promise of Peace

God promises:

He will keep in perfect peace

all those who trust in him.

Jesus said, "Come to me, all of you who are weary and carry heavy burdens, and I will give you rest. Take my yoke upon you. Let me teach you, because I am humble and gentle, and you will find rest for your souls."

Matthew 11:28-29, NLT

April 1

Winner

Lord

How did it happen

That You chose me

To belong to You?

Whatever the reason

One thing is certain:

I won.

You did not choose me, but I chose you and appointed you to go and bear fruit—fruit that will last. John 15:16, NIV

April 2

Walking Together

It would be sheer mockery, Lord
It would be subtle hypocrisy
For me to kneel
Anguished and weeping
Before Your Cross
Unless—

As I walk with You now
Down my personal Emmaus Road
I introduce You
With singing joy
To the broken and bound
The weary and worn
The depressed and defeated
Whom we meet on the way.

And, Lord, I observe
That as we walk together
Foot traffic thickens.

The King will reply, "I tell you the truth, whatever you did for one of the least of these brothers of mine, you did for me." Matthew 25:40, NIV

April 3

Eradication

Lord

I can no more

Eradicate my own guilt

Than I can

Sit on my own lap.

You alone can cleanse me.

While You accomplish the impossible

May I sit on Your lap?

Thank You for holding me, Lord.

I like it here.

My dear children, I am writing this to you so that you will not sin. But if you do sin, there is someone to plead for you before the Father. He is Jesus Christ, the one who pleases God completely. He is the sacrifice for our sins. He takes away not only our sins but the sins of all the world.

1 John 2:1-2, NLT

April 4

No Compromise

Walking home through fog and mist

Still pondering

Still puzzled and unsure

I desperately hoped we'd settle it.

That's why I said

"When I *know* I'll *do*."

But You wouldn't drop it, Lord

Not for a minute.

In fact, Your response was firm:

"When you *do* you'll *know*."

Then with soft gentleness You asked:

"When did I fail you last?"

By faith Abraham, when called to go to a place he would later receive as his inheritance, obeyed and went, even though he did not know where he was going.

Hebrews 11:8, NIV

April 5

My Delight

"You are My Delight . . ."

This, dear God

You said to Jesus

At the moment of His baptism

There in the river Jordan.

He is Your Son

I am Your child

Forever related to You through Him.

Baptize me, dear God

In the river of Your Love

Your Joy

Your Power

Until with deep and widening gladness

You can say to me

Your chosen child

"You are My delight."

The Lord delights in those who fear him, who put their hope in his unfailing love.
Psalm 147:11, NIV

April 6

Who Am I?

(Acts 17:28)

In Him
I live
I move
I have my being.
Therefore
Who am I?
I am in God.
In the
Great *I AM*
I am.

Thank You, Lord.
At last
I know
Who I am.

Therefore, if anyone is in Christ, he is a new creation; the old has gone, the new has come!
2 Corinthians 5:17, NIV

April 7

The God of Miracles

When she asked to speak to me, I noticed her glowing eyes. "Ruth, I just want to tell you that the God of miracles has worked an incredible miracle in my troubled heart.

"For weeks I attempted to force from God's control that which belongs only to him: *Vengeance!* Flames of resentment burned within me. With clenched fists I wanted to retaliate. Frankly, I hoped the offender was miserable! My words became stuttering syllables. I realized that the bondage of my own making was crippling my soul.

"Then one gray morning, without really thinking, I opened my Bible at random. The words on the page were clear and distinct: ' "It is mine to avenge. I will repay," says the Lord.'

"I was gripped with conviction. Suddenly I knew that healing was impossible unless I totally surrendered the pain to God. Slowly, my clenched fists became open hands. In a way I cannot explain, I began to pray for the one who had wronged me. I prayed with honest forgiveness.

"In a way I cannot explain, the flames of anger became charred embers. I was free! God took my sadness and gave me his gladness. He is indeed a God of miracles!"

Dear friends, never avenge yourselves. Leave that to God. For it is written, "I will take vengeance; I will repay those who deserve it," says the Lord. Romans 12:19, NLT

April 8

My Only Defense

The powerful reality grips me,
Lord
That when I kneel in Your
presence
To ask Your forgiveness
I am utterly stripped of facade.
You accept no big-name
references
No high-caliber
recommendations.
Extenuating circumstances
Crumble to dust
In Your court of appeal . . .
I am forgiven never
Because of inherited tendencies
Or emotional discomfort
Or nagging weakness . . .
I can never plead
Corrupt environment
Or life's strange twistings
Or my own unbelievable
stupidity . . .
Ultimately I have one solitary
defense.
Only one—
But always one:
Forgive me, God
For Jesus' sake.
Like a song unending
The words keep singing . . .
I am totally forgiven
I am continually cleansed
Just for Jesus' sake.

Then I said, "My destruction is sealed, for I am a sinful man and a member of a sinful race. Yet I have seen the King, the Lord Almighty!" Then one of the seraphim flew over to the altar, and he picked up a burning coal with a pair of tongs. He touched my lips with it and said, "See, this coal has touched your lips. Now your guilt is removed, and your sins are forgiven." Isaiah 6:5-7, NLT

April 9

All Gone

Thank You, Lord

For cleansing my heart's wound

With Living Water.

Thank You for Your bandage

Of pure, gentle love.

Thank You for the kiss of comfort.

At last the hurt is gone.

Praise the Lord, I tell myself, and never forget the good things he does for me. He forgives all my sins and heals all my diseases.

Psalm 103:2-3, NLT

April 10

Limping Home

Lord
With a crooked stick for a cane
I'm limping home.
Mocked and maligned
Stooped and stupid
Soiled and shabby
I limp toward You.
You could say, "I told you so."
You could say, "It's a little too late."
You could say, "Wait while I think it over."
You could sweep me under the rug—
We both know I deserve far less.
But when I see the Cross
And the Man who died there
Suddenly I know I limp
Toward unfathomable love
And there is forgiveness
Rushing toward me.
I don't ask for a banquet, Lord
Nor do I need a gold ring.
I'm so hungry
So thirsty
For You.

Then Jesus said, "Come to me, all of you who are weary and carry heavy burdens, and I will give you rest." Matthew 11:28, NLT

April 11

Change of Heart

One night
In black and bitter agony
I cried, "No, Lord!
No! No!"
Then suddenly
I saw Your Cross.
I saw You enduring
Intolerable pain.
I saw the nails
The thorns
The drops of blood.
I saw Love
Nailed willingly to a tree.
Slowly, slowly
My turmoil melted
Until at last
My throbbing heart sobbed
"Yes, Lord!
Yes! Yes!"

I will give you a new heart and put a new spirit in you; I will remove from you your heart of stone and give you a heart of flesh.

Ezekiel 36:26, NIV

April 12

I Love It, Lord

What in the world
Is going on today, Lord?
Why the big celebration?
The fragrance of lilacs
The shimmering sound of birds
The red-gold sky
The air blue and sweet
The sudden burst of pink bloom
A thirsty vine
The shout of mountains miles around . . .
Really, Lord
What's happening?

Is it—
Could it be
That Spring has made her debut?
Is that why
You've dressed all of Nature
In party clothes?

Whatever the reason
I love it, Lord.
Thank You!

Let them all praise the name of the Lord. For his name is very great; his glory towers over the earth and heaven! Psalm 148:13, NLT

April 13

Greater Than Sin

Lord, never before today
Have I so deeply understood
The ugliness of my sin.
But never before today
Have I been so completely submerged
In the ocean of Your grace.

But God showed his great love for us by sending Christ to die for us while we were still sinners. Romans 5:8, NLT

April 14

Easter Keeps Happening

Who can predict a single day ahead? (Isaiah 43:9)

The prophet Isaiah's question is agonizing. Who can? In one sweeping moment an ordinary day can become a grotesque nightmare. It can shatter our composure and torment us with grief. Adversity strikes when we least expect it. Seldom are we warned, never are we prepared.

But the chapter in Isaiah goes on to say, "From eternity to eternity I am God." This is the one glorious assurance. In the midst of a thousand puzzling questions, God is, he knows, he sees, he loves. The mysteries of both life and death are in his capable hands.

There is never a shortcut to the end of grief. Slowly, gradually it moves. We wait, even when waiting seems intolerable. The Bible explains it only partially. Jesus himself is our only complete explanation. Someday we will see beyond the mystery that now we must trustfully accept.

The glorious truth is—Jesus *did* walk out of the tomb. Easter keeps happening . . . and happening! We look ahead with glorious hope.

"You have been chosen to know me, believe in me, and understand that I alone am God. There is no other God; there never has been and never will be. I am the Lord, and there is no other Savior. First I predicted your deliverance; I declared what I would do, and then I did it—I saved you. . . . You are witnesses that I am the only God," says the Lord. "From eternity to eternity I am God."

Isaiah 43:10-13, NLT

April 15

Easter Morn

It was early dawn, Lord
And I was looking for You.
Looking
Looking
And weeping.
Within the dismal tomb
I searched
I called
I waited
But nowhere could I find You.

Then through the gray
There came a vibrant voice:
He's risen!
He's alive!
Rush toward joy!
You'll find Him everywhere
Outside the tomb—
But never, *never* there.

Startled and amazed
I left the tomb
To walk the path of praise—
Then looking up
I saw You by my side
And all of life became
An Easter morn.

You will go out in joy and be led forth in peace; the mountains and hills will burst into song before you, and the trees of the field will clap their hands.

Isaiah 55:12, NIV

April 16

Discoveries

Lord God

Today You have penetrated

My entire being

With three glorious discoveries:

When I am most weak

You are most strong.

When I am most fearful

You are utterly faithful.

When I am at my sinning worst

You are at Your saving best.

What can we say about such wonderful things as these? If God is for us, who can ever be against us?

Romans 8:31, NLT

April 17

I Have a Father

Lord, it was one humdinger of a
fight.
I wondered if it would ever end.
But three solid blows later
Little Loser limped toward his
home.
With his fists clenched he shouted:
"I'll tell my father on you!"
(I had a feeling he meant it.)
Then all of a sudden it happened—
Out the front door he walked
Calm and serene
His tall hefty father by his side.
Like a streak of jagged lightning
His frightened opponent was on
the run.

O Lord, what a reflection of me.
I too must do battle
With the adversary of my soul.
At times he comes masked
As an angel of light.
He thwarts and antagonizes.
He blinds and binds.
He harasses and accuses.
I'm no match for him, Lord.
The battle wages against
Principalities and powers.

But the great triumphant truth is—
I have a Father.
My Father protects and upholds
me.
He strengthens and supports me.
Nothing can happen to me
Outside my Father's will.
My Father is greater by far
Than he who is in the world.
Once and for all it was settled
On a rugged cross
On a lonely hill:
I have a Father.

And I will be your Father, and you will be my sons and daughters, says the Lord Almighty.
2 Corinthians 6:18, NLT

April 18

So Profound

O God

I want to sing and dance

I want to shout it from the hilltops:

There is absolutely nothing

In my wretched past

That can hinder You

From redeeming my future

Except my refusal to let You.

Thank You for invading my heart

With a truth so refreshing

So magnificent

So profound!

All honor to the God and Father of our Lord Jesus Christ, for it is by his boundless mercy that God has given us the privilege of being born again. Now we live with a wonderful expectation because Jesus Christ rose again from the dead. For God has reserved a priceless inheritance for his children. It is kept in heaven for you, pure and undefiled, beyond the reach of change and decay. 1 Peter 1:3-4, NLT

April 19

There Is Easter!

Death seems so wrong, dear Lord

Couldn't You have remedied it?

Have you forgotten, dear child?

There is Easter!

I will ransom them from the power of the grave; I will redeem them from death. Where, O death, are your plagues? Where, O grave, is your destruction?

Hosea 13:14, NIV

April 20

Ask Me Anything

I have to say it, Lord—
I just have to say it:
Sometimes You seem to be
Extremely inquisitive.
In orderly sequence You ask . . .
How are you spending your time?
What are your spiritual goals?
Why do you harbor secret
    resentment?
Where are you growing in depth?
When will you put Me first?
Lord, is nothing personal or
    private
In my day-by-day living?
Must I continually expose my
    heart?

Are You forever the "Hound
    of Heaven"
Seeking me out
Searching, sorting, pointing?

Child of my constant concern
If I withdrew from you
Leaving you totally alone
Would you be pleased?

O dear God
No, no!
Ask me anything—
Anything at all
But never let me go!

For the word of God is full of living power. It is sharper than the sharpest knife, cutting deep into our innermost thoughts and desires. It exposes us for what we really are. Nothing in all creation can hide from him. Everything is naked and exposed before his eyes. This is the God to whom we must explain all that we have done.

Hebrews 4:12-13, NLT

April 21

Even This

It was a long letter—pages of tear-stained script. "Even God doesn't care. . ." she wrote.

Perhaps you haven't put it in a letter, but has some overwhelming failure or fear obscured your sense of God's presence?

That was the catastrophe of the frightened disciples. The wind was boisterous, they had lost control . . . and Jesus went on sleeping.

We quickly identify with the shouting: "Don't you even care if we go under?" We've all shouted it, at least in attitude. Jesus quieted the sea that night, but his piercing question hits the target of our hearts: "Don't you *even yet* have confidence in me?"

The awe-filled disciples said among themselves, "Even the winds and the seas obey him."

"How wonderful," we say.

Then suddenly, often without warning, the winds of adversity beat against our personal lives, and we cry "*Lord, don't you even care?*"

Again he asks, "Don't you *even yet* have confidence in me? That habit that chains you. That fear that paralyzes you. That loss that numbs you . . . even this—*all of this* you may fling upon me!"

But it means more than half-heartedly singing, "He will break every fetter." It means surrendering to him completely. He knows your *every* need—*even this*.

[Jesus] rebuked the wind and said to the water, "Quiet down!" Suddenly the wind stopped, and there was a great calm. And he asked them, "Why are you so afraid? Do you still not have faith in me?"

Mark 4:39-40, NLT

April 22

Ecstasy of Joy

O dear God

What ecstasy of joy

That You took the whole of me

And made me wholly Yours!

You have made known to me the path of life; you will fill me with joy in your presence, with eternal pleasures at your right hand.

Psalm 16:11, NIV

April 23

The Secret

I couldn't help but watch her
As we sat in the service together
Last Sunday morning . . .
Her white hair so neatly coiffured
Her hands resting on her open Bible
Her smile so beautifully tranquil.
When the hymn was announced
She sang with a glowing smile.
Occasionally during the message
She nodded her head in assent.
(O Lord, what peace she portrays.)
After the service I spoke to her:
"You are an inspiration, my dear.
I hope I may sit with you again."
She thanked me profusely.
Then she added with shining joy
"Isn't it wonderful to know Jesus?
I mean—really KNOW Him!"
In that instant, dear God
I knew the secret of her radiance.

Yes, everything else is worthless when compared with the priceless gain of knowing Christ Jesus my Lord. Philippians 3:8, NLT

April 24

Long-ago Memories

Tonight, long-ago memories
Have been wandering down
Old familiar streets
And dark alleys
And dimly lit corridors.
With stubborn tenacity
They invade my carefully guarded defenses.
Sitting all alone watching dreams go by
I discover unexpectedly
That I am still susceptible to tears.
And then I recall vaguely
Part of an old song that says
"For these tears I died"
And my yearning heart, dear Lord
Reaches out for You.

Gladness and joy will overtake them, and sorrow and sighing will flee away. Isaiah 35:10, NIV

April 25

My Personal Rainbow

Lord, right now
I struggle with clutching fear.
Waves of agony pour over me
As I face the darkest moments
In my life's history.
But my conviction still stands firm:
You are my God!
And though I cannot predict my future
Or even tomorrow
I am sustained by the reminder
That the longest storm
The world has ever known . . .
And the worst . . .
Came to an end one clear-sky morning.
It was true for Noah
It will be true for me.
Though as yet I see no deliverance
I watch
I wait
I expect
My personal rainbow.

And we know that God causes everything to work together for the good of those who love God and are called according to his purpose for them.
Romans 8:28, NLT

April 26

Not Sure Yet

In our challenging discussion
I started to tell my college friend
That though I didn't understand electricity
I certainly accepted it.
With an impatient gesture he interrupted me.
"I don't want to hear about electricity.
I just want God."
"How much do you want Him?" I asked.
Nervous silence. Then finally a reply:
"I'm really not sure yet."

Lord, I don't know how long
My seeker-for-God friend
Will continue his flimsy excuses
Or linger in a state of noncommitment
But when he is sure enough to really seek You
He will surely find You.
This is Your personal promise.

Ask and it will be given to you; seek and you will find; knock and the door will be opened to you. For everyone who asks receives; he who seeks finds; and to him who knocks, the door will be opened.

Matthew 7:7-8, NIV

April 27

I Trust You

Lord, it was on an April morning

So many years ago

That You said to me so clearly

"Trust Me and you won't be disappointed."

Having heard You on that special morning

I simply cannot "unhear" you now.

I can't forget that morning

Nor do I think You want me to.

Because You live in an eternal Now

Your words are just as relevant today

As they were that long-ago morning.

I *trust* You. You will not disappoint me!

Jesus Christ is the same yesterday and today and forever.

Hebrews 13:8, NIV

April 28

Three Discoveries

I have made three overwhelming discoveries regarding God's reliable faithfulness:

The first: God will never let us go—*never!* We may fall flat on our faces. We may resist until we feel exhausted, but *nothing* can separate us from his matchless love.

The second: God will never let us down—*never!* He is forever faithful, even when we are faithless. He cannot deny himself. He will never leave us nor forsake us.

The third: He will never let us off—*never!* Whenever we give in to temptation, when we determine to have our own way—he says with all the love of his Father-heart, "I love you too much to excuse disobedience." Whom he loves, he chastens.

God is determined to bless us. He is eager to show us his kindness. He is glad to teach us the proper paths; but he *must* have access to our hearts. He will allow our guilt to become a burden until conviction comes, then confession, and finally renewed commitment!

May David's prayer be our prayer:

Teach me to do your will, for you are my God. May your gracious Spirit lead me forward on a firm footing. Psalm 143:10, NLT

April 29

Your Child, God

O God
With deep contrition
I shamefully confess
My small concept of You
My puny faith
My limited comprehension.
Forgive me, O God
And enlarge my narrow vision.
Stimulate my trust
As I concentrate on Your greatness.
Give me even now
A true perspective
Of Your majestic power
To totally transform the child
On whom You have set Your love—
The child whose name is engraved
On the palm of Your hand
The child who claims You
As her Maker and Master.
Your child, God!
Me!

Show me the path where I should walk, O Lord; point out the right road for me to follow. Lead me by your truth and teach me, for you are the God who saves me. All day long I put my hope in you.

Psalm 25:4-5, NLT

April 30

How Long Is Everlasting?

O dear God
How long will You ignore me?
How long must I continue to weep before You?
Will You forever keep silent
When I seek Your face?
Surely You know my desperation
And yet I cannot arouse Your attention.
Must I continually stumble
Through dense forests and dark valleys?
Does it matter to You about me?
I don't understand, Lord.
In the past You so lavishly blessed me.
Have I offended You?
Are there false motives that I cannot trace?
Are You searching me out?
O Lord, I cannot endure the thought
That You no longer love me.
Hear my cry, dear God.
Please speak to me.

Listen, dear child
Quietly listen.
I have loved you
With an everlasting love.
How long is everlasting?

But may all who seek you rejoice and be glad in you; may those who love your salvation always say, "The Lord be exalted!" Yet I am poor and needy; may the Lord think of me. You are my help and my deliverer; O my God, do not delay. Psalm 40:16-17, NIV

May

The Promise of Abundant Life

Lord, you always bring ultimate good

to those who love you. May I never surrender

to the false conclusion that you have no more

for me than what I already have.

You will show me the way of life, granting me the joy of your presence and the pleasures of living with you forever.

Psalm 16:11, NLT

May 1

Beautiful Belonging

Before I knew You, Lord
It was terribly important
To flaunt my culinary art
With a moist and tender roast.
Now that I'm Yours
It is far more important
To serve Your gentleness
To our guests.

Before I knew You
It was terribly important
To snatch every weed
From our meticulous yard.
Now that I'm Yours
It is far more important
To express neighborly concern
Over the back fence.

Before I knew You
It was terribly important
To check the television schedule
From night to night.
Now that I'm Yours
It is far more important
To check Your plan
From day to day.

What an incredible change—
This Beautiful Belonging!

But the Lord said to her, "My dear Martha, you are so upset over all these details! There is really only one thing worth being concerned about. Mary has discovered it—and I won't take it away from her."

Luke 10:41-42, NLT

May 2

Coincidences

Lord, I was intrigued
With the brilliant vocabulary
Of the patient sitting next to me
In the reception room.
I don't remember
The start of our conversation
But suddenly we were discussing
prayer.
I shared rather freely
Your pertinent answers
To my day-by-day requests.
Labeling himself a skeptic
He smiled and said courteously
"What you consider answered
prayer
I choose to call coincidence."
You know how it is with me,
Lord—
I'm always slightly ill at ease
In the Big Middle
Of a theological discussion.
I'm much more at home in my
kitchen
Mixing muffin batter
Or tossing green salads.
Frankly I was relieved
When the dentist called my name.
But one thing I do know, Lord
When I pray, "coincidences"
happen.
When I don't pray they stop . . .

So thank You again and again
For ten thousand "coincidences"
Always in the nick of time
When I pray.

And pray in the Spirit on all occasions with all kinds of prayers and requests.

Ephesians 6:18, NIV

May 3

Real Problem

Lord

Your dedicated servant said:

"Never doubt in the darkness

What God tells you in the light."

I've got a real problem, Lord.

I doubt even in the light.

Look at the birds. They don't need to plant or harvest or put food in barns because your heavenly Father feeds them. And you are far more valuable to him than they are. Can all your worries add a single moment to your life? Of course not. Matthew 6:26-27, NLT

May 4

I'm Drowning

Lord, I'm drowning
In a sea of perplexity.
Waves of confusion
Crash over me.
I'm too weak
To shout for help.
Either quiet the waves
Or lift me above them—
It's too late
To learn to swim.

Rise up! Come and help us! Save us because of your unfailing love.

Psalm 44:26, NLT

May 5

Courtesy

I tried to be
Very courteous.
I smiled and said
"No thank You, Lord."
You smiled back and said
"Omit the first word
And I'll be delighted
With your courtesy—
And more delighted
With your trust."
"Thank You, Lord."

Should we accept only good things from the hand of God and never anything bad? Job 2:10, NLT

May 6

This, Too, Is Faith

Lord, I am desperately afraid
Of tempestuous waves.
Had I been on the ship
The day you stilled the storm
I would have been the first
To scream for help—
This I shamelessly admit.
But, Lord, this too is faith:
Boldly expecting You
To do something about it.

Let us then approach the throne of grace with confidence, so that we may receive mercy and find grace to help us in our time of need.

Hebrews 4:16, NIV

May 7

Once in a While We Can

One bright Sunday when I was twelve, I didn't want to go to church. I wasn't coddling a pent-up rebellion. I simply pictured a leisurely day away from "have to" things.

How to explain and be understood! Finally I just blurted it out as Mother prepared breakfast. She listened attentively.

"Honey," she said calmly, "we can't always do what we feel like doing without hurting someone."

That settled it, I thought. I was sorry I had asked.

Suddenly I heard, "But once in a while we *can* do what we want to—just because we want to. You may stay home this Sunday."

The memory of that day is still vivid. Not because I stayed home from church, but because I learned a profound lesson: *Once in a while we can!*

Once in a while we can get away from alarm clocks, peanut-butter jars, milk cartons . . . away from the shattering pressures of our competitive society.

Once in a while we *need* to get away from work, family, friends, and pressing commitments. Often we lose the capacity for personal enjoyment.

Once in a while we need to walk, think, and meditate. Only God can satisfy our deepest longings. He longs for us to share our private secrets with him.

Once in a while we can.

The Lord is my shepherd; I have everything I need. He lets me rest in green meadows; he leads me beside peaceful streams. He renews my strength. He guides me along right paths, bringing honor to his name.

Psalm 23:1-3, NLT

May 8

Stay There

Lord

Please get me off

This emotional elevator

Which carries me so swiftly

From the basement of despair

To the tenth floor of exhilaration

And down to the basement again.

I'm hoarse from shouting

My fists are blue from pounding

I'm suffocating in this

Dark, windowless box.

Turn and look, dear child.

The door is wide open.

Walk straight into My waiting arms

And stay there.

Come, all you who are thirsty, come to the waters; and you who have no money, come, buy, and eat! Come, buy wine and milk without money and without cost. Why spend money on what is not bread, and you labor on what does not satisfy? Listen, listen to me, and eat what is good, and your soul will delight with the richest of fare.

Isaiah 55:1-2, NIV

May 9

Not As They Seem

It would seem, Lord
When You have been our dwelling place
In all generations . . .
When You have guided us
Undergirded us
And enveloped us with love . . .
When You are Bread for the hungry
Rest for the weary
Strength for the powerless
And Joy unspeakable . . .
It would seem, Lord
That we would have more to offer
Than lust
Greed
Hatred
War . . .

But that's precisely why
You came to die:
In the hearts of men
Things are not as they seem.

For God so loved the world that he gave his only Son, so that everyone who believes in him will not perish but have eternal life. God did not send his Son into the world to condemn it, but to save it.

John 3:16-17, NLT

May 10

Majestic Approval

O God

I'd love to keep

The beauty of this day

Forever and forever:

The sky incredibly blue

New leaves shining

Flowers swaying

In the gentle breeze

Birds with changeful wills

Darting here and there

The lake a sparkling jewel

Surrounded by spicy pines

And You looking down

At Your handiwork

With majestic approval.

The heavens tell of the glory of God. The skies display his marvelous craftsmanship.

Psalm 19:1, NLT

May 11

Forgive Me

Lord
So often I am
Fearful
Unbelieving
And apologetic about my faith.
I analyze
Whittle down
And tear apart
Your very words.
I conjure foolish reasons
For my lack of trust
As though You couldn't possibly mean
What You so clearly said.
Yet, all the while You wait for me
To believe *exactly* what You said—
Without exception
Without alteration.
Forgive me for treating You
Like someone who would lie.

God saved you by his special favor when you believed. And you can't take credit for this; it is a gift from God. Salvation is not a reward for the good things we have done, so none of us can boast about it.

Ephesians 2:8-9, NLT

May 12

You Did All the Rest

O Lord God!
I did what You asked me to do:
I just opened windows
Wide . . .
Wide . . .
And You did all the rest!
You poured into my heart
A blessed, blissful contentment.
You saturated my mind
With gigantic thoughts of You.
You struck an artesian well within me
Until sheer joy sprang forth.
You led me out of the valley of despair
Into a succession of incredible happenings.
Problems which seemed insurmountable
Melted like wax before my eyes.
Fears faded away like threatening clouds.
You startled me
You amazed me
With the glory of Your revelation.
It is true
Gloriously true—
I have literally walked and breathed with God.
I just opened windows
Wide . . .
Wide . . .
God, You did all the rest!

God is our refuge and strength, an ever-present help in trouble. Therefore we will not fear, though the earth give way and the mountains fall into the heart of the sea. Psalm 46:1-2, NIV

May 13

God's Searchlight

O God
If suddenly You were to reveal
To my family, my friends, my neighbors
Every real thought behind my courteous words
If You were to point to my clenched fist
While my other hand is openly extended
If You were to bring to light
Every masked motive, every selfish act
I would cringe with remorse
And beg You to remove Your light of revelation.
Yet, Lord, when the searchlight of the Holy Spirit
Begins to reveal me to *myself*
I so often close my eyes and turn my back
In a frantic but impossible effort
To escape Your penetrating gaze.
What a staggering contradiction, Lord
What appalling hypocrisy.
Apart from Your grace I am utterly shattered.
I ask You to sweep through me
Purify me, cleanse me completely.
From the depth of my penitent heart
I thank You for Your continual assurance
As I turn toward Your splintered cross:
Because of Your love I *became* Your child
Because of Your grace I *remain* Your child.

"Come now, let us reason together," says the Lord. "Though your sins be as scarlet, they shall be white as snow; though they are red as crimson, they shall be like wool."
Isaiah 1:18, NIV

May 14

Motherhood

Motherhood is *now!* The good and the bad of it. The rewards and the trials. Tremendous pressures are placed upon you as a mother, for you have been chosen to work with God in the awesome task of nurturing the priceless treasures God has given you.

As a mother, you accept your children's faltering steps toward independence with discipline, humor, patience, and a tremendous amount of trust. At times the struggles almost become an endurance contest. You wonder if you can handle all the confusion another day: the ringing phone, the broken dishes, the blaring television, the hurtful words. High temperatures, school conferences, dentist appointments, rebellious tears. Is there ever an end?

But suddenly in the midst of turmoil you catch a broad grin. You feel a warm hug. At bedtime somebody prays, "Thank you, God, for Mom and for chocolate-chip cookies . . . and for love."

You renew again your deep desire to create a genuine God-hunger in your children. God has chosen you for such a task as this.

Her children stand and bless her. Her husband praises her: "There are many virtuous and capable women in the world, but you surpass them all!"
Proverbs 31:28-29, NLT

May 15

This Beautiful Sunlit Morning

Dear God
On this beautiful sunlit
Morning in May
You've drenched me
With ecstatic joy.
I want to sing and shout
I want to soar with sheer delight.
At the same time I want to sob—
So utterly overwhelmed I am
With the magnitude of You.

O God, I know
I do know
With serene satisfaction
And confident certainty
That I belong to the God
Of the Universe—
To the Creator
Of all that exists.

I do know
That I, a mere mortal
Am forever linked to divine
destiny—
That my life has purpose and
dignity.
I do know
That You have chosen me
As the object of Your lavish love
That Your thoughts toward me
Are thoughts of kindness and
mercy
That You have inscribed me
In the palms of Your hands.

I do know
That all the Love of the Father
And the Life of the Son
And the Power of the Holy Spirit
Are freely, inseparably mine—
Now and through all eternity.
O God
On this beautiful sunlit
Morning in May
I do know.

To our God and Father be glory for ever and ever. Amen.

Philippians 4:20, NIV

May 16

Three Miserable Days

Lord

For three miserable days now

I have stubbornly resisted You.

I've balked and argued

I've looked for possible detours

I've shouted outrageous excuses

And I've tried in every possible way

To sidestep You.

All of this, only to discover

That my clenched-fist resistance

Has been far more unbearable

Than the obedience You required of me.

Lord, may I please have another chance?

When you bow down before the Lord and admit your dependence on him, he will lift you up and give you honor. James 4:10, NLT

May 17

Grief

Lord, You who permit my grief
Are the only One
Who can assuage it.
I wonder—
Do you permit grief
That I might learn
To be content
With nothing less
Than the comfort of God?
Whatever the reason
One thing I am learning:
You make useful to me
All that You permit.
So, dear God
Though a great ache
Wells within my heart
I ask You to grip my life.
Empower me to go
From depth to depth with You
Until I am a "wounded healer"
Bringing Your comfort to others
As You are now comforting me.

Even though the fig trees have no blossoms, and there are no grapes on the vine; even though the olive crop fails, and the fields lie empty and barren; even though the flocks die in the fields, and the cattle barns are empty, yet I will rejoice in the Lord! I will be joyful in the God of my salvation. The Sovereign Lord is my strength! He will make me as surefooted as a deer and bring me safely over the mountains.

Habakkuk 3:17-19, NLT

May 18

Forgiving Lord

Forgiving Lord
I long for her release—
My friend who churns
With memories of failure and
guilt.
She needs to feel sure and serene
Knowing You are holding her
fast.
She needs to understand
That her continual remorse
Is a sheer waste of energy and
time.
In no way can she change the past
Or relive it
Or rectify it.
Lord, she is torturing herself
In her circle of regret.

Please speak to her, God.
May she no longer censure herself
For what once happened.
Rather, direct her attention
To what is happening now.
May she stop berating herself
For her mismanaged past.
Empower her to concentrate
On managing the present.
Heal her, Lord!
She is so occupied
With morbid introspection.
Give her a fresh, breathtaking
glimpse
Of the joy that can be hers
When she is totally occupied with
You.

I lift up my eyes to the hills—where does my help come from?
My help comes from the Lord, the Maker of heaven and earth.

Psalm 121:1-2, NIV

May 19

New-born Ecstasy

When I resolve to come to You
Amid the chunks and cracks
Of all my mundane days—
When I resolve to listen
Really listen to Your gentle voice
Suddenly I know anew
That You are life
And life is joy!
Like a singing brook
Joy splashes over
All the common "dailies"
Until each empty space
Of my hungry heart
Is touched with new-born ecstasy.

Shout with joy to the Lord, O earth! Worship the Lord with gladness. Come before him, singing with joy. Acknowledge that the Lord is God! He made us, and we are his. We are his people, the sheep of his pasture. Psalm 100:1-3, NLT

May 20

All

O God

Thank You, thank You

For Your reiterated ALL. . . .

You have promised:

ALL my needs shall be supplied.

ALL grace shall abound toward me.

ALL the promises are mine.

ALL things asked I shall receive.

ALL sufficiency for ALL things.

You are with me always

ALL the days.

And today!

Give thanks to the Lord, for he is good! Psalm 136:1, NLT

May 21

Total Abandonment

With deep conviction I know I must habitually put to death every thought and every action that brings displeasure to God. I must daily come to grips with what my self demands. I must give up, and then give over every part of me that spells my name. Only then can I truly experience a radical soul release—which I need above all else.

When sin is continually indulged, it grows. At times slowly, but always surely. A gradual decline becomes obvious. Agony of soul begins to consume a previous longing for God. My hardened heart seeks every possible way to justify itself. An irrational dislike of others captures my distraught emotions. Distrust fosters bitterness. Finally life becomes empty, barren, dismal.

I genuinely thank God for letting me become so miserable with life that only one thing matters: Total abandonment to him, who calls me to himself. How relieving and releasing it is to recapture a renewed hunger and thirst for him, the true and living God. He alone is my heart's desire.

If you search for [the Lord] with all your heart and soul, you will find him.

Deuteronomy 4:29, NLT

May 22

Fed Up

Lord, I'm utterly fed up
With my foolish and futile attempt
To live a facsimile of genuine Christianity.
Like thousands of jagged Christians
I am just so "sick and tired
Of being sick and tired."
I want to withdraw my membership
From the Society of Self-Improvement
With its heavy dues and dismal news.
With all my breathless effort
I am no further improved
Than the day I joined.
So please take me as I am
And make me what I could never be
Apart from You: transparently real!

But now God has shown us a different way of being right in his sight—not by obeying the law but by the way promised in the Scriptures long ago. We are made right in God's sight when we trust in Jesus Christ to take away our sins. And we all can be saved in this same way, no matter who we are or what we have done.

Romans 3:21-22, NLT

May 23

Intimate Closeness

You promise, dear God
That when I draw close to You
You will draw close to me.
Lord, I give myself to You unreservedly.
Teach me more and more
Of intimate closeness
And fill my heart with You alone.
To walk arm-in-arm with You
Down every winding path
Seems to me
The dearest of all delights.

Come near to God and he will come near to you. James 4:8, NIV

May 24

Freedom

For so long, dear God
I stared with dreadful fascination
At the thick, heavy chains
Binding my burdened life
When all the while You were waiting
For my personal consent
To break the chains and set me free.
Oh, what liberating joy
When I finally said Yes!

Oh, what a miserable person I am! Who will free me from this life that is dominated by sin? Thank God! The answer is in Jesus Christ our Lord.

Romans 7:24-25, NLT

May 25

Never Too Late

Sometimes, dear Lord
You work so slowly!

Tell Me, dear child
Have I ever been too late?

Oh, the depth of the riches of the wisdom and knowledge of God! How unsearchable his judgments, and his paths beyond tracing out!

Romans 11:33, NIV

May 26

Very Different

Lord

Please put me

Where the talents and gifts

You've given me

Can be best used.

Put me, I pray

Where I can best serve You.

This is the deep longing

Of my heart.

My child

I will put you

Where you can best glorify Me.

This may be very different

Than all your present dreams.

Who is able to advise the Spirit of the Lord? Who knows enough to be his teacher or counselor? Isaiah 40:13, NLT

May 27

One Stupendous Thing

O dear God

If You love me at all

(And I want to believe You do)

I beg You to do one stupendous thing

For my torn and bleeding heart:

Please dear Lord

Take the place

Of what You've taken away.

I cannot survive

I cannot endure

Unless You grant this request.

And this same God who takes care of me will supply all your needs from his glorious riches, which have been given to us in Christ Jesus.

Philippians 4:19, NLT

May 28

One Early Evening

One early evening I knelt in the peaceful quiet of our blue-and-white bedroom and asked the Holy Spirit to permeate my life. My words were simple but honest: "Make me a woman after God's own heart."

I don't know what I expected exactly. Waves of ecstasy? Easter bells? A dramatic transformation? None of these things happened. I still washed dishes, baked cookies, washed clothes, and answered the phone in the same methodical way. When I grocery shopped, the money didn't miraculously stretch. When I stood on the scale I wasn't five pounds lighter.

But gradually, ever so gradually, as I trusted God's plan in fulfilling my request, I discovered old fears were disintegrating. A new confidence in God was emerging. I was less insistent about having my own way. Best of all, God's Word was becoming more *alive* as I read day after day.

I'm sure it's but the beginning. I have asked God to do whatever he needs to do to make me all he wants me to be. His promise captures my waiting heart:

For God is working in you, giving you the desire to obey him and the power to do what pleases him. Philippians 2:13, NLT

May 29

I Dare to Believe

"Out of the depths I cry to You,
O Lord."
On this day of remorse and
turmoil
The Psalmist's cry is my cry.
Trembling, crumbling, out of the
depths I cry.
And yet, in the throes of my
anguish, O God
I dare to believe
You see my groping and grasping.
You hear my sighs and sobs.
I dare to believe
You can break through the
emotional blockades
You can rebuild my broken
dreams.
Though my words seem drenched
with presumption
To those who march with illusive
courage
I dare to believe
Your love is unquenchable
Your faithfulness is inexhaustible.
I dare to believe
You delight to draw me to
Yourself
You long to silence my desperate
cry.
I dare to believe
I will yet hear Your gentle words
"I am your Father.
Come home."

Weeping child
It is true
That I am your Father.
Now dare to believe
You are home.

Humble yourselves, therefore, under God's mighty hand, that he may lift you up in due time. Cast all your anxiety on him because he cares for you.
1 Peter 5:6-7, NIV

May 30

Two Questions

O God
In my fear and frenzy
In my darkness and dread
My screaming question is
"Where *are* You?"

Wandering child
When things were going well
And you carelessly ignored Me
Where were you?

God has said, "I will never fail you. I will never forsake you."
Hebrews 13:5, NLT

May 31

I Can Settle for That

The word *rebellion* frightens me.
I always associate it with
Revolt . . . terrorism . . . riots . . .
death . . .
With economic and social
issues . . .
With the drug scene
That promotes life without
purpose.
I associate it with tempestuous
waves of change
That leap up like wild animals.
Like the disciples in the storm
I want to awaken You, Lord.
I wonder why You seem to be
sleeping.

But, Lord, maybe I don't
Really know You very well.
Maybe I don't let God be God.
After all, *You* are not frightened.
You do not hold Your hands up
in despair.
You never say, "You should have
come yesterday."
Nor do You say, "You're the
wrong age and color."
You never say, "You're too timid,
too slow."

You simply tell me to step out
Of my rocking boat.
You tell me to walk the waves with
You.
You assure me You are not asleep.
You tell me to show genuine love
To a desperately needy world.

You insist it is far better
To walk over the billows than to go
under them.
You tell me if I die in the attempt
At least I will die victoriously.
Then, facing me directly, You ask
"Can You settle for that?"
Lord, if You are with me
I can settle for that!

And so, dear brothers and sisters, I plead with you to give your bodies to God. Let them be a living and holy sacrifice—the kind he will accept. When you think of what he has done for you, is this too much to ask?

Romans 12:1, NLT

June

The Promise of Being Known

Though there is much about life that disturbs and puzzles us, there is one satisfying consolation: We know that God knows! And he can be trusted!

Trust in the Lord with all your heart; do not depend on your own understanding. Seek his will in all you do, and he will direct your paths. Proverbs 3:5-6, NLT

June 1

You're in My Way

This morning, Lord
I heard a distraught mother
Say to her lively son
"You're in my way—move."
This very same morning
You said to me
"You're in My way—stay."
How good it is
To be Your child.

Sing to him; yes, sing his praises. 1 Chronicles 16:9, NLT

June 2

When I Am with You

When I am with You, Lord
It is as though
I were given
A cup of cool water
Dipped from
An ever-flowing
Never-ceasing stream.
The water glistens
As a piece of clear ice
Tingles against
The side of my cup.
I want to drink
More
And more
And more
As though I could
Never drink enough—
And yet while I drink
I am satisfied
Completely.

What a strange and beautiful
Paradox!

Whoever drinks the water I give him will never thirst. Indeed, the water I give him will become in him a spring of water welling up to eternal life.
John 4:14, NIV

June 3

Painful

Lord

Too often my talents

Have been on display

For public inspection.

Now I am painfully learning

The only important thing:

Your reflection.

Who is Apollos, and who is Paul, that we should be the cause of such quarrels? Why, we're only servants. Through us God caused you to believe. Each of us did the work the Lord gave us.

1 Corinthians 3:5, NLT

June 4

Mountains—Molehills

Oh, Lord

You've done it again

You've turned

My flimsy little tune

Into a swelling crescendo.

But that's the way You are—

Always making mountains

Out of our molehills of joy.

The desert and the parched land will be glad; the wilderness will rejoice and blossom. Like the crocus, it wil burst into bloom; it will rejoice greatly and shout for joy. Isaiah 35:1-2, NIV

June 5

Resemblance

Lord, somewhere I read

That when two people

Love deeply

When they live together

Sharing

Caring

Giving

Forgiving

Eventually they begin

To resemble each other.

Lord, how long will it be

Before I look like *You*?

And we, who with unveiled faces all reflect the Lord's glory, are being transformed into his likeness with ever-increasing glory, which comes from the Lord, who is the Spirit. 2 Corinthians 3:18, NIV

June 6

Take Over

At first, Lord, I asked You
To take sides with me.
With David the Psalmist
I circled and underlined:
"The Lord is for me . . ."
"Maintain my rights, O Lord . . ."
"Let me stand above my foes . . ."
But with all my pleading
I lay drenched in darkness
Until in utter confusion I cried
"Don't take sides, Lord
Just take over."
And suddenly it was morning.

Teach me to do your will, for you are my God. May your gracious Spirit lead me forward on a firm footing. Psalm 143:10, NLT

June 7

A Friendship Observed

After my father's death, I sat in his quiet office sorting through years of sermons and journals. A few tears fell on the pages. My task was very personal. Hundreds of memories encircled the room.

I was amazed, yet pleased, when I began to compare my journals with my father's. Our groping and intense struggles, our affirmations and confessions were so often interlaced. It would never have occurred to us to share our journals while Dad was living. Diaries, letters, journals, and even phone calls were private.

Today I reflect upon my own record of life—page after page of spiritual encounters. Anguish, questions, purging, joy, discipline, insights, ecstasy, faith—*God's whispered secrets.*

Suddenly the early beginning became very much alive: A little girl, seven or eight, hearing her father say, "If you'll listen—really listen—God will whisper secrets to you!"

My father had said something very beautiful and strange. How did he know that God would whisper secrets to *me?*

But as I sorted through my father's careful recounting of his inner life and journey, it suddenly became very clear: *He, too, had heard God's secrets!*

"I know the plans I have for you," says the Lord. "They are plans for good and not for disaster, to give you a future and a hope. In those days when you pray, I will listen. If you look for me in earnest, you will find me when you seek me."

Jeremiah 29:11-13, NLT

June 8

A Better Way

A thousand times, dear Lord
In moments of fierce temptation
I have asked You to help me.
But at last I have learned a better way:
I no longer ask merely for help
I look up into Your gentle face
And ask You to do it all.

As a father has compassion on his children, so the Lord has compassion on those who fear him; for he knows how we are formed, he remembers that we are dust. Psalm 103:13-14, NIV

June 9

Rare Moments of Delight

Because You are God
And Your Word is unquestionable
There are things I assuredly know
Even when my heart is a brambled desert
And every ounce of emotion is drained:
I know Your love is everlasting
I know You will never forsake me
Nor will you leave me comfortless
I know I may come to you boldly
I know you will teach and instruct me
You will guide me with Your eye
I know my past is forgiven
And my future is secure.
But oh, dear God
How I praise You for the marvel
Of those rare, mysterious moments
When suddenly, without a flash or a sound
You add to my *knowing*
The ecstasy of *feeling*
And I am lifted to peaks of delight!

Be exalted, O God, above the highest heavens. May your glory shine over all the earth.
Psalm 108:5, NLT

June 10

I Know Who I Am

There he sat on his front porch
(Probably three or four years old)
And when he flashed a merry smile
I stopped to ask his name.
"I'm my daddy's boy," he said, grinning
And then he was off to play.
I still don't know his name, Lord
But it doesn't matter.
He knows who he is
And that makes everything all right.

Thank You, Lord
With all my heart
That I may say with genuine confidence
"I'm my Father's child."
That makes everything all right.

So you should not be like cowering, fearful slaves. You should behave instead like God's very own children, adopted into his family—calling him "Father, dear Father." For his Holy Spirit speaks to us deep in our hearts and tells us that we are God's children. Romans 8:15-16, NLT

June 11

Solution

Today, after hours of praying
For something that didn't come
Something I so desperately craved
I see anew, dear God
That with all my clamoring
And agonized pleading
I simply cannot change You.

No, dear child
But I can change you.

I the Lord do not change. Malachi 3:6, NIV

June 12

Overwhelmed

All day long, dear God
I have been overwhelmed
With my failure
And folly.
Now please overwhelm me
With Your faithfulness
And forgiveness.

Lord, if you kept a record of our sins, who, O Lord, could ever survive? But you offer forgiveness, that we might learn to fear you.

Psalm 130:3-4, NLT

June 13

Try Me

O Lord

Is there anyone

In all the world

Who really understands me?

Yes, dear child

Me.

O Lord, you have searched me and you know me. You know when I sit and when I rise; you perceive my thoughts from afar.

Psalm 139:1-2, NIV

June 14

Welcome Home

I remember so well the long-ago day when my brother of seven years wrote a note to my parents. He was anything but happy. So many alibis, so many collisions with trouble!

There had been an accumulation of things: He hadn't picked up his clothes. He's tracked mud on the carpeting. He had pinched his best friend to see how loud he would scream. One by one his privileges were taken away—so he wrote: *I'm running away. P.S. If I get hungry maybe I'll come back someday.*

"Someday" didn't take long. After an hour or so the young prodigal came home. He was penitent and hungry. There were tears and hugs. There was forgiveness. He was home!

So often I too run away: when prayers are unanswered . . . when God says no and I want him to say yes . . . when I want to go one way and he points to another.

Yet when I run from God I feel desolate, lonely. I hunger for his presence. When I finally begin the long walk home, he is waiting. With arms wide open he welcomes me. He forgives me. I discover again, there's no place like home!

Come, let us return to the Lord. Hosea 6:1, NLT

June 15

Which, Lord?

Lord

I always seem to be

The child in Your family

Who needs the most chastening.

Is it because

I'm so unmanageable

Or is it because

You love me so much?

My child, don't ignore it when the Lord disciplines you, and don't be discouraged when he corrects you. For the Lord corrects those he loves, just as a father corrects a child in whom he delights.

Proverbs 3:11-12, NLT

June 16

Increase My Enthusiasm

Lord, with gratitude

And genuine enthusiasm

I pray for those who love me.

But I must ask You now

To increase my enthusiasm

As I pray for those who don't.

Bless those who persecute you; bless and do not curse.

Romans 12:14, NIV

June 17

Intimacy

Dear God
May I live intimately close to You
Above the perplexities of Life
With the moon under my feet!
At the same time, God
Humble me, gentle me
Create in me a deepening awareness
So that I shall never miss
A cushion of violets hiding in the sod
Or the cry of a frightened child
Or the desperate sob of a lonely heart.

"'You must love the Lord your God with all your heart, all your soul, all your mind, and all your strength.' The second is equally important: 'Love your neighbor as yourself.' No other commandment is greater than these."
Mark 12:30-31, NLT

June 18

A Doubt

Sometimes, dear Lord

You don't seem

To love me at all.

Sometimes, dear child

You seem to ignore

The eternal facts.

He passed in front of Moses and said, "I am the Lord, I am the Lord, the merciful and gracious God. I am slow to anger and rich in unfailing love and faithfulness." Exodus 34:6, NLT

June 19

The Prayer

For so many anguished months
I've been waiting for You to
answer
The one longing desire of my
heart.
I've begged, pleaded, agonized.
I've prayed at times fumblingly
At other times intensely.
I've knelt and prayed.
I've buried my head in my pillow
and prayed.
I've prayed before breakfast
And after lunch.
I've prayed before dawn
And after dark.
I've prayed with spontaneous
outbursts
While tears washed my face.
I've prayed over our kitchen sink
And as I shopped for groceries.
I've prayed amid screeching traffic.
At times I've prayed with
confidence
At other times with fear.
And yet, Lord, though I have
waited
Though I have strained to listen
There is no answer.
I hear nothing . . . just nothing.
O God, I am so puzzled, so
bewildered.
A frightening thought haunts me.
Could it be true, Lord?
Don't You love me anymore?
My child
Because I love you so much
I wait for you to let Me
Remove the harmful desire.

Wait patiently for the Lord. Be brave and courageous. Yes, wait patiently for the Lord.
Psalm 27:14, NLT

June 20

New Beginning

O God

What shall I do?

I am at the total end

Of myself.

Wonderful, dear child!

Now start your new beginning

With Me.

He who was seated on the throne said, "I am making everything new!"
Revelation 21:5, NIV

June 21

A Woman Who Is Real

A woman who is real knows that in her family she must sometimes back off so God can move in.

A woman who is real continually builds a monument of healthy memories for her family. She believes that memories create security and establish values. Above all, they record a growing history of God's unwavering faithfulness.

A woman who is real refuses to let her life be cluttered with unconfessed guilts. She guards her tongue, knowing how quickly a little spark can ignite a huge fire.

A woman who is real listens well. She is careful not to break into an ongoing conversation to tell her own story.

A woman who is real sheds the masks of pretense. There are no dark corners in her heart—no credibility gap between who she is and how she accepts others.

A woman who is real feels no need to "prove" her Christianity; she herself is walking proof.

She is clothed with strength and dignity, and she laughs with no fear of the future. When she speaks, her words are wise, and kindness is the rule when she gives instructions. . . . Charm is deceptive, and beauty does not last; but a woman who fears the Lord will be greatly praised. Reward her for all she has done. Let her deeds publicly declare her praise.

Proverbs 31:25-31, NLT

June 22

The Living God

I place my whole confidence
In the Living God.
Not because things
Are going my way.
Not because I have what I want.
Not because I understand
All the inexplainables
Or because I am immune
To problems and pain and sorrow.
But despite my questions
My reversals, my disappointments
Despite my sorrow and tears
I place my whole confidence
In the Living God
For He alone can see me through.
He alone is worthy of my trust.

Whom have I in heaven but you? And earth has nothing I desire besides you. My flesh and my heart may fail, but God is the strength of my heart and my portion forever. Psalm 73:25-26, NIV

June 23

Always There

So often, Lord
I reach the bottom of the abyss.
So often I taste the dregs
Of my own helplessness.
Yet it is there, *exactly there*
That You come to my immediate rescue.
When I feel totally impoverished
Of all self-sufficiency
When I want to vanish into nowhere
From the depths of despair
I call Your name
And You are always there for me!

The Lord will guide you always; he will satisfy your needs in a sun-scorched land and will strengthen your frame. You will be like a well-watered garden, like a spring whose waters never fail.

Isaiah 58:11, NIV

June 24

Irreversible Yes

God, You have done
A beautiful thing for me.
You have freed me from the dissatisfaction
Of so many empty days and months.
Into my impoverished heart
You have poured life-changing thoughts of You
Making each new day gloriously rich.
You have struck a deep artesian well in my soul
As sheer joy springs forth.
All because in an act of honest surrender
When life had lost its challenge
I said an irreversible YES to You!

I am the bread of life. John 6:48, NIV

June 25

Life's Whys

Lord

If You were to answer

All of life's whys

Surely You would have started

With Your servant Job.

Instead, Your determined goal for Job

Was unrivaled loyalty and trust.

And so, dear God

As achingly difficult as it often is

Enable me to trust You

With such total abandonment

That You will hear no complaining

When I hear no explaining.

Blessed rather are those who hear the word of God and obey it.

Luke 11:28, NIV

June 26

Divided Heart

Lord
I am so often tormented
By my lack of clear direction—
So often disturbed
By my divided heart.

I am like a little child
Who wants to rock her doll
And jump rope at the same time.
I want to obey You in part
If I can choose the areas of
obedience.
I want to be real except at those
moments
When compromise is more
appealing.
I want to be half-motivated
And half-satisfied with things as
they are.

I want to walk a straight path
If now and then I can enjoy
A few side trips into the far
country.
I don't want to be a miserable
sinner
But neither do I feel excited
About being a stoic saint.
I want to be partly Yours
And partly my own.

But in the secret chamber
Of my divided heart
I am so often disquieted
By the pointed question:
"Why do you so foolishly
Mix weeds with seeds?"

Stop loving this evil world and all that it offers you, for when you love the world, you show that you do not have the love of the Father in you.

1 John 2:15, NLT

June 27

Soul Struggle

Her uncontrollable sobs know no respite.
"What is wrong with me"
She stammers convulsively
"That love has passed me by?
Am I so ugly, so stupidly plain?
Am I some kind of an oddity?
Doesn't God love me anymore?"

Lord, there are times when she hides
Behind a sophisticated facade
But today she is not pretending.
In her deep loneliness
There are no words to comfort her.
You alone can release her
From her shadowy world.
You alone can break the bleakness
And produce the firm conviction
Of Your measureless love.
Lord, my part in her soul's struggle
Is to reach for her hand.
Your part is to reach for her heart.

He tends his flock like a shepherd: He gathers the lambs in his arms and carries them close to his heart. Isaiah 40:11, NIV

June 28

Listening Love

Listening love is one of the greatest gifts we can give our mates, our families, and our friends. Too often we settle for surface talk or icy silences, for monologues or cutoffs, for defenses. What a difference when we follow the principles of listening love!

Listening love is courteous. It says . . .
I will strive not to interrupt or outguess you. I will not finish your sentences or break into your thoughts.

Listening love is attentive. It says . . .
I will give you my undivided attention. I will not turn you off or leave you isolated.

Listening love is patient. It says . . .
I will not rush you or insist on a right-now conclusion.

Listening love is kind. It says . . .
I will not shame you with sarcastic retorts. I will not belittle you.

Listening love is objective. It says . . .
I will try to be informative rather than opinionated. I will not attempt to think for you.

Listening love is unselfish. It says . . .
I will guard against overconfidence and trite "spiritual" answers.

Listening love is prayerful. It says . . .
I will pray for insight, for wisdom, and for gentle reactions.

May the words of my mouth and the meditation of my heart be pleasing in your sight, O Lord, my Rock and my Redeemer.

Psalm 19:14, NIV

June 29

Live by the Moment

O Lord
I am staggered by the enormity
Of the countless tasks
Flung at me today.
I simply don't know
How to tackle them all.
What shall I do first, Lord?
How shall I make room
For the interruptions
That are bound to come?
What shall I leave undone
When interruptions take priority?
Your Word clearly states
That You will guide me
With Your counsel.
You have promised Your wisdom
When my lack is so great.
I dare not plunge into the day
Without seeking Your guidance.
Lord, will You help me?

Anxious child
Live today
By the moment
Not by the year.

In repentance and rest is your salvation, in quietness and trust is your strength.
Isaiah 30:15, NIV

June 30

I Wait for You

O God

I have waited so long

Under dark clouds of trial and testing

And yet Your promise is clear and precise:

"Blessed are all those that wait for Him."

Though I see no glimmer of hope

Though my tears come unbidden

I am still waiting

For the clouds of trial

To break into refreshing showers of blessing.

Because You have promised, dear Lord

Surely my waiting cannot be in vain.

I wait for You . . . I wait for You . . . I wait.

But the Lord still waits for you to come to him so he can show you his love and compassion. For the Lord is a faithful God. Blessed are those who wait for him to help them. Isaiah 30:18, NLT

July

The Promise of Faithfulness

Lord, you assure me of two things:

You are God, and you are good.

God, who began the good work within you, will continue his work until it is finally finished. Philippians 1:6, NLT

July 1

The Task

Lord, You give me a task
So utterly impossible
So totally beyond comprehension—
The very thought of it
Startles me.
I want to run hide escape
Anything, Lord.

Then You electrify me
You invade and permeate me
You penetrate every fiber of me
Until the task is accomplished
By Your own magnificent power.

Then You praise the performance
Your creativity achieved
And You reward me beyond expectation—
As though I had done it
All by myself.
My Father.

"Not by might nor by power, but by my Spirit", says the Lord Almighty.

Zechariah 4:6, NIV

July 2

Illusive Dreams

Sometimes, Lord
I think I spend my entire life
Working toward illusive dreams.
I dream that someday things will be
Exactly as I want them:
I'll ride on the crest
Of my noble achievements.
With an easygoing independence
I'll keep my confident cool
My house will stay spotless
My budget will balance
My family will applaud me
My friends will acclaim me
I'll glow with charisma.
Lord, am I missing the mark?
Is there a chance for my dreams?

Child of My Plan
Seek first the Kingdom of God
And His righteousness
And every plan of Mine
Will exceed by far
All your illusive dreams.

But seek first his kingdom and his righteousness, and all these things will be given to you as well.
Matthew 6:33, NIV

July 3

You Are Free

O God
I read today
That the sons of Jacob
And their descendants
Had lived in Egypt 430 years.
But on the last day
Of the 430th year
Your people left Egypt
And the cruel bondage
They had painfully endured.
This was the time You selected.
God, what time have You selected
To free me from the cruel tyranny
That binds me without mercy to myself?

Chosen child
In My Son
You are even now
Completely free.
Accept your freedom!
Walk out this very moment
Into the radiant company
Of My people.

So now there is no condemnation for those who belong to Christ Jesus. For the power of the life-giving Spirit has freed you through Christ Jesus from the power of sin that leads to death.

Romans 8:1-2, NLT

July 4

Fourth of July

I was thinking, Lord—
Our Fourth of July pattern
Seldom varies;
Hot humid air
Hamburger fry
Tender corn
Fresh strawberry ice cream
Then finally
Those traditional sparklers
When darkness tiptoes in.

Funny thing about sparklers—
We never tire of their
Noiseless beauty . . .
Lord, now that I have signed
My Declaration of Dependence
Make me Your sparkler
Noiseless
But beautiful
Especially in the dark.

You are the light of the world—like a city on a mountain, glowing in the night for all to see. Don't hide your light under a basket! Instead, put it on a stand and let it shine for all. In the same way, let your good deeds shine out for all to see, so that everyone will praise your heavenly Father. Matthew 5:14-16, NLT

July 5

The Facts

Lord

When I feel I can't possibly make it

When I feel deluged with problems

When I feel helpless

Against the strange twistings of life

When I feel there is no way out

The FACT is

You have a Plan

You know what You're about.

The FACT is

The greater the strategy of the Enemy

The greater the assurance of victory.

The FACT is

The worst may seem to happen

But the best is on the way.

God, hold me to the facts.

Your word, O Lord, is eternal; it stands firm in the heavens. Your faithfulness continues through all generations; you established the earth, and it endures.

Psalm 119:89-90, NIV

July 6

Joy

Joy!

My favorite word.

Circumstances may determine my happiness

But, Lord, You determine my joy.

Joy is sweetly honest.

No wonder the minister said:

"You can't hide joy if you have it—

You can't fake it if you don't."

Who can manufacture it, Lord?

Joy is Your creation.

Who may have it?

Anyone who asks.

Thank You, Lord

For joy!

Don't be dejected and sad, for the joy of the Lord is your strength!

Nehemiah 8:10, NLT

July 7

It Takes a Lifetime

How I love the words of the apostle Paul.

"I don't mean to say . . . that I have already reached perfection! But I keep working toward that day when I will finally be all that Christ Jesus saved me for and wants me to be. No, dear brothers and sisters, I am still not all I should be, but I am focusing all my energies on this one thing: Forgetting the past and looking forward to what lies ahead, I strain to reach the end of the race and receive the prize for which God, through Christ Jesus, is calling us up to heaven" Philippians 3:12-14, NLT.

What tremendous encouragement! Paul, who knew Jesus Christ so intimately, whose consuming desire was to please him, who endured illness, imprisonment, shipwreck, beatings, mockery, and heartache all for the sake of Christ—this very same Paul confessed he hadn't "arrived." God was still growing him!

I see again, while my conversion took but a moment, my growth takes an entire lifetime. In God's great wisdom and knowledge he anticipates the finished product while he lovingly takes me through the long, long process.

I keep working toward that day when I will finally be all that Christ Jesus saved me for and wants me to be. Philippians 3:12, NLT

July 8

Destined

God, I am destined for You!

I was created for You!

Nothing I can ever do or think or feel

Can be separated from You.

With all my inner struggles

My self-absorption

My lethargy and fraud

I cannot alter to one degree

Your settled intention

Your divine purpose:

I was made to bring glory to You!

Long ago, even before he made the world, God loved us and chose us in Christ to be holy and without fault in his eyes. His unchanging plan has always been to adopt us into his own family by bringing us to himself through Jesus Christ. And this gave him great pleasure.

Ephesians 1:4-5, NLT

July 9

Finally—Immediately

Lord

You said so gently

So persistently

"Give Me your weariness

And I'll give you My rest."

I did—finally.

You did—immediately.

Then, Lord, I marveled

That I had waited so long.

Then Jesus said, "Come to me, all of you who are weary and carry heavy burdens, and I will give you rest." Matthew 11:28, NLT

July 10

Rivers and Rivers

O my Father
My heart longs for You!
Fill me to capacity with Your Spirit . . .
No, Father, I'm sorry—
That's not sufficient.
Fill me to *overflowing* with Your Spirit
And then increase my capacity
That there might be still more overflow.
Out of my life
May there flow rivers
And rivers
And still more rivers
Of Living Water
Bringing relief, release
And exhilarating refreshment
To a bruised and broken world
Where thirst can never be quenched
Apart from You.

If anyone is thirsty, let him come to me and drink. Whoever believes in me, as the Scripture has said, streams of living water will flow from within him.
John 7:37-38, NIV

July 11

He Can Be Trusted

If You, dear God
Could entrust
To Jesus, Your Son
The salvation of the world
Throughout all eternity
Then surely I can entrust
To Jesus, my Savior
The solution to my problem
Today.

Give your burdens to the Lord, and he will take care of you. He will not permit the godly to slip and fall. Psalm 55:22, NLT

July 12

I Trust You

O God, I trust You.
I don't understand
I cannot begin to comprehend
The wisdom of Your way
In my torn and tangled life
But I am steadfastly believing
That Your plan for me today
Must be—
Surely it *must* be
As kind
As loving
As profitable
As Your plan for me
In joyful days now past.
You are the same
Yesterday
And today
And forever
So, dear God
I trust You.

Jesus Christ is the same yesterday and today and forever.

Hebrews 13:8, NIV

July 13

Don't You Understand?

But Lord
Don't You understand?
If I can't, I *can't!*

But child
Don't you understand?
If I can, I can!
Things which are
Impossible with you
Are possible with Me.

For nothing is impossible with God. Luke 1:37, NLT

July 14

A Family Pledge

- We will permit God to use our conflicts and mixed emotions as lessons in quiet growth. With loving patience, without ridicule or judgment, we will support each other in the gradual untangling of built-in defenses.
- We will focus on each other as persons made in the image of God. We will seek to please rather than to pressure, to delight rather than to demand, to give rather than to get.
- We will share the humdrums as well as the highlights, the tears as well as the laughter, the defeats as well as the victories.
- We will not insist on perfection—rather we will anticipate growth. We will not compete for the mountaintop, rather we will climb the mountain together. We will wait for each other if one of us gets behind.
- We will lift our hearts in a celebration of gratitude for God's amazing love, which makes our family love possible.
- We will love each other as we do these things.

Anyone who listens to my teaching and obeys me is wise, like a person who builds a house on solid rock. Matthew 7:24, NLT

July 15

Until She Is Willing

Please, dear God
Assure her of my loving concern.
Help her to know I care for her
And genuinely long to befriend
her
But she is so frantically fretful
So steeped in self-pity
That any suggestion I casually make
Seems only to flame her hostility.

God, I want to understand her
limitations.
Guard me against being cheaply
cheerful.
I'll walk with her eagerly toward
health
No matter how steep the climb
Or how prolonged the effort.

I'll listen to her, pray with her
But until she is willing to change
I can no longer be her crutch.
She grasps so intensely
I sometimes feel strangled.
The more heavily she leans
The more locked-in she becomes.

Lord, I know only one thing to do:
I release her completely to You.
Speak to her festering heart
Find *some* way of letting her know
That You alone are her Answer—
You have no competitor.
Show her, dear God
That she'll never be free to step
out
Until she asks You to step in.

". . . Apart from me you can do nothing." John 15:5, NIV

July 16

What's Myself Doing to Myself?

With childish intensity she asked
"What's myself doing to myself?"
I couldn't help but smile
As she stood before the mirror
Struggling so impatiently
With a stubborn jacket zipper.

But I'm not smiling now, Lord
As I pass my own mirror
And glance at the tension
Etching my somber face.
I'm frightened, Lord.
Her innocent question clutches
me:
"What's myself doing to myself?"

Frustrated, frantic
So often breathless
Too many irons in the fire . . .
What am I doing to my body—
To my mind, my emotions?
What am I doing to my family?
What am I doing to Your Plan
For my personal fulfillment?
Why do I live like this, Lord
As though Your world
Couldn't exist without me?
Why do I so often
Tear myself from Your control?

Dear Lord, calm me.
Pull me off the merry-go-round
Of converging conflicts.
Give balance to my boggled mind.
This very hour, Lord
Infuse me with Your poise and
power
Until my total self
Is submerged in You—Yourself.
Only then will I be free
To be myself.

Don't worry about anything; instead, pray about everything. Tell God what you need, and thank him for all he has done. If you do this, you will experience God's peace, which is far more wonderful than the human mind can understand. His peace will guard your hearts and minds as you live in Christ Jesus. Philippians 4:6-7, NLT

July 17

Intrusions

A thousand intrusions
Have crowded in on my life today.
My reaction, Lord?
I've resented every one.
And now I read in Your Word
That I'm to put out the welcome sign!
In fact, I must welcome each intrusion
As a personal friend.
(Perhaps even serve tea, Lord?)
You assure me that You have a purpose
For their continual persistence:
My faith needs depth
My endurance needs development.

I have no argument with that, Lord
But I had hoped that an hour or two
Of trial and testing would suffice.
Or a day at most, dear God.
But again You remind me
That the process must continue
Until maturity becomes my password
And independence becomes my goal
And the Crown of Life becomes my reward.

No discipline is enjoyable while it is happening—it is painful! But afterward there will be a quiet harvest of right living for those who are trained in this way. Hebrews 12:11, NLT

July 18

Green Light

Thank You, dear Lord
That I need never
Push through jumbled traffic
Or maneuver around sudden detours
To get to Your Throne Room.
All the signal lights are green.

So let us come boldly to the throne of our gracious God. There we will receive his mercy, and we will find grace to help us when we need it.

Hebrews 4:16, NLT

July 19

The Next Thing

O Lord

I love what You said to me

In Your Word today:

"In the place

Where you have walked in defeat

There will I cause victory

To break forth."

Father, I look to You

To do that very thing.

You will not let me

Be ultimately defeated.

And when the battle is won

I must confidently ask

What is the next thing?

He holds victory in store for the upright, he is a shield to those whose walk is blameless, for he guards the course of the just and protects the way of his faithful ones.

Proverbs 2:7-8, NIV

July 20

A Quiet Tongue

Lord, a revealing fact
Began to surface today:
I talk more than I listen.
I seem to be thoroughly convinced
That my ideas
My inspiring experiences
My bits of wisdom
Are exactly what all my friends need.
Too often I break into conversations
Confident that my enlightened insight
Will solve the predicament—
Whatever it is.
Obviously, I feel more comfortable
When I'm expounding.

But this morning at a Bible study
I cringed when I read Your command
In the first chapter of James:
"Don't ever forget
That it is best to listen much
Speak little, and not become angry."
At first I wanted to run.
But as the words kept battering away
At my guilty heart
I finally circled them with red ink.
Now, Lord, please help me to obey them.
Remind me daily, hourly
That listening is a discipline
And a discipline always costs.

I know I must pay a price.
The price for me
Is a listening ear
And a quiet tongue.

My dear brothers and sisters, be quick to listen, slow to speak, and slow to get angry.

James 1:19, NLT

July 21

A Woman of Compassion

A woman of compassion seeks first, always first, the kingdom of God and his righteousness, knowing that all else will be given to her. She has one single purpose: to know and do the will of God. Often she narrows her interests in order to expand her heart for others.

She says to her troubled friend, "I feel your pain in my heart. I don't have a cure-all kit, but I will walk through the dark tunnel with you until the light breaks through again."

She says to her reserved husband, "I understand that you don't want to talk now, but I'm here for you if I can help."

She listens to the outbursts of her children in a way that makes them feel secure. She reminds them of their priceless individuality.

She opens her home as well as her heart. She knows that a cup of hot tea and an hour of concerned listening means so much more than "We want to have you for dinner someday."

A woman of compassion rests her total self on the reliability of the Word of God. Consequently she does not live in pieces—she lives in peace.

The Lord is good to all; he has compassion on all he has made.

Psalm 145:9, NIV

July 22

The You Means Me

O my Father, my Father!
At this crisis time of my life
When I feel trampled and battered
I know it is imperative
For me to remember
That the nature of my problem
Is not the significant thing.
The significant thing
Is the nature of You
My refuge. My rock.
My high tower.
There is no situation
Anytime, or anywhere
Of which I cannot confidently say
"For this I have Him."
But I am so quick to forget
And so prone to neglect.
Lord, may I get it settled
Once and for all
That when You say
"My peace I give unto you"
The *you* means *me!*

I am leaving you with a gift—peace of mind and heart. And the peace I give isn't like the peace the world gives. So don't be troubled or afraid.

John 14:27, NLT

July 23

God, Hold Me Close

O God

Hold me close

While I cry

For my freedom.

The louder I shout

The deeper my soul

Needs to know

You will never, never

Let me go.

If I rise on the wings of the dawn, if I settle on the far side of the sea, even there your hand will guide me, your right hand will hold me fast.

Psalm 139:9-10, NIV

July 24

Lost Argument

I read this morning
Your direct and piercing question
To the ancient Job:
"Do you still want to argue
With the Almighty?
Or will you yield?"
With thoughtful heart
I read Job's wise reply:
"I am nothing. . . .
How could I find the answers?
I lay my hand upon my mouth in silence."
You know so well that I do, God.
I continue to argue with You
As though I were in charge.
As though I could solve my own dilemma.
Finally in the end, broken and defeated
I yield to You, and then—peace.
Forgive me, dear God
For so foolishly ending
Where I should have begun.

Woe to him who quarrels with his Maker, to him who is but a potsherd among the potsherds on the ground. Does the clay say to the potter, "What are you making?" Does your work say, "He has no hands"?
Isaiah 45:9, NIV

July 25

Every Valley Exalted

Sometimes, Lord
It seems as though
You are the God of the hills
But not of the valleys.
For these past months
I have lived in a dark, lonely valley.
But then I remember Your promise
That every valley shall be exalted.
God, help me to persevere, to endure
Until my personal valley
Is gloriously exalted.

Every valley shall be raised up, every mountain and hill made low; the rough ground shall become level, the rugged places a plain. And the glory of the Lord will be revealed, and all mankind together will see it. For the mouth of the Lord has spoken. Isaiah 40:4-5, NIV

July 26

Immediately

Dear Lord
I'm so tired of living
In my little cramped vessel—
So weary of dangling my feet in the water
But never stepping out of the boat.
I want to walk the waves with You
Just as Peter did.
True, he took only a few steps
Before losing his courage
But at least he was heading toward You.
Lord, I'm coming, too!
If I begin to falter or sink
I trust You to catch me
Just as You caught Peter.
Remember, Lord?
You caught him *immediately.*

But when he looked around at the high waves, he was terrified and began to sink. "Save me, Lord!" he shouted. Instantly Jesus reached out his hand and grabbed him. "You don't have much faith," Jesus said. "Why did you doubt me?" Matthew 14:30-31, NLT

July 27

The Promise

O dear God, I continue to believe
Your personal promise still stands
Though every quivering emotion within
Shouts that it will be broken.
I am claiming Your help through the wilderness
Despite every frightening shadow and vale.
Often you do the most
When You seem to do the least.
Sometimes secretly
Sometimes quietly
Often slowly
But always most certainly
You are true to Your word.
And so, my Lord
Though I am weak, weary, and worn
Help me not to despair.
You see me, You hear me.
You know I am depending utterly
Upon Your unblemished integrity
Surely You will keep Your word.

The Lord is my shepherd, I shall not be in want. He makes me lie down in green pastures, he leads me beside quiet waters, he restores my soul. He guides me in paths of righteousness for his name's sake.

Psalm 23:1-3, NIV

July 28

Stephanie

More than anything else she wanted to play the piano. Her mother called to ask if I would give her lessons. "But I must tell you one thing: Stephanie is fighting an advanced malignancy. Her left arm has been amputated. Her future is critical."

I was startled. How could I teach a little girl with one arm to play the piano? Her mother's words kept echoing . . . "More than anything else she wants to take lessons from you."

God, please help me to teach her the music of love.

On her first lesson, she came with her shiny red book. Her eyes sparkled. She could hardly wait! Week after week we sat at the piano learning notes, playing melodies—she with her right hand, I with my left.

"I'm Mrs. Treble," she told me. "You're Mr. Bass." It was a happy joke between us.

"We're really good together," Stephanie said one day, "But you know what? I could never do it alone."

Stephanie taught me an incredible lesson: When I follow God's instructions, we make beautiful music together. *But I could never do it alone!*

Stephanie is with Jesus now. What joy it must be for her to play with both hands!

Jesus said, "Let the children come to me. Don't stop them! For the Kingdom of Heaven belongs to such as these." Matthew 19:14, NLT

July 29

O God . . . My God

O God . . . *My* God
Though You now seem totally hidden
I am clinging to You hopefully
Even confidently.
Someday, some way, You will make
All You are now permitting
Blessedly clear.
With fixed purpose, dear God
I am determined to wait, to trust
To rely upon Your faithfulness.
Despite the drain and strain
I anticipate new perspectives
And fresh depths of insight
Into all that is now so mysterious.
O God, in ways unanticipated
You are teaching me the great truth
Of Samuel Rutherford's words:
"I see that grace grows best in winter."
Thank You, dear God
Thank You for that!

And the God of all grace, who called you to his eternal glory in Christ, after you have suffered a little while, will himself restore you and make you strong, firm and steadfast. 1 Peter 5:10, NIV

July 30

Sudden Awe

My face wind-lashed
With stinging sand
Alone I trudge the beach
Filled with sudden awe
That You, O God
Are mightier by far
Than all the breakers
Pounding on the seashores
Of the world.

He gave the sea its boundaries and locked the oceans in vast reservoirs. Let everyone in the world fear the Lord, and let everyone stand in awe of him. For when he spoke, the world began! It appeared at his command. Psalm 33:7-9, NLT

July 31

The End of the Rope

O dear God

I feel as though I am clinging

To a rough, swinging rope.

Beneath me there is only emptiness.

My hands are bruised and bleeding.

There is no possible way

For me to tie a knot

At the end of the rope

And hang on.

O God, please help me.

Frightened child

Just let go.

I'll catch you.

Do not abandon me, Lord. Do not stand at a distance, my God.
Come quickly to help me, O Lord my savior. Psalm 38:21-22, NLT

August

The Promise of His Presence

God is:

- *Utterly trustworthy*
- *Supremely loving*
- *Always available*

Your Father already knows your needs. He will give you all you need from day to day if you make the Kingdom of God your primary concern. Luke 12:30-31, NLT

August 1

Why?

Standing here
At the kitchen sink
My hands immersed
In soapsuds
All of a sudden I know
With fresh, penetrating force
I am only really whole
When I am wholly Yours.
Yet with proud self-assertion
I often choose to be
Incomplete.
Why, Lord?

Yes, I am the vine; you are the branches. Those who remain in me, and I in them, will produce much fruit. For apart from me you can do nothing.
John 15:5, NLT

August 2

Morning Star

You who are

The Bright and Morning Star

Come in radiant splendor

And flood each shadowed crevice

Of my sullen heart

Until the world shall know

I've touched a Star.

God is light; in him there is no darkness at all. 1 John 1:5, NIV

August 3

Tic-Tac-Toe

Sometimes, Lord

I get the impression

We're playing a game

Of tic-tac-toe.

I draw my X

You draw Your O.

Then just as I contemplate

The next move

You draw a straight line

Which finishes the game.

You always win, Lord

Always.

Is it because Your circle

Is Whole

Complete

Total

Like You?

We may throw the dice, but the Lord determines how they fall.

Proverbs 16:33, NLT

August 4

Who, Me?

Lord
All of a sudden today
You picked me up
And hugged me
And hugged me
For no discernible reason.
I was puzzled.
After all—
I hadn't picked up my toys
Or practiced my lessons
Or brought You a daisy bouquet—

Hesitantly, I asked why.
You smiled and said:
I love you, that's all.
Then You added:
I long to hug you more often.
Why don't You, Lord?
You are too busy.
Too busy, Lord?
Too busy hugging yourself.

We love because he first loved us. 1 John 4:19, NIV

August 5

Superlatives

Lord

It's wonderful

That You see me

More wonderful

That You lead me

Most wonderful

That You love me.

Good, better, best?

No—with You

All is superlative:

Always best.

Whatever is good and perfect comes to us from God above, who created all heaven's lights. Unlike them, he never changes or casts shifting shadows.

James 1:17, NLT

August 6

Best Friends

Lord

Today I read

"And Abraham believed God . . .

And he was called

The friend of God."

Please, Lord, give me

A faith so strong

That we may be

Very best friends!

And so a whole nation came from this one man, Abraham, who was too old to have any children—a nation with so many people that, like the stars of the sky and the sand on the seashore, there is no way to count them.

Hebrews 11:12, NLT

August 7

Can You Sing in the Rain?

When I was a child I loved to take long walks with my tall, loving father. We trudged through meadows, we climbed rolling hills, and often we walked through tree-lined parks. As we walked, Dad would tell me stories about his childhood, and I would ask countless questions about my grandparents.

One day on a country road we walked under a gentle mist of rain. In the distance we saw a sparrow perched on a tree branch. The tiny bird was just singing away. My father asked a question: "Could you sing in the rain if nobody saw and nobody heard but God?"

Years have passed since that long-ago day. There have been wonderful days of joy. And there have been days of tears, too. Sometimes in the darkest night, during the most severe storm, God has enabled me to sing in the rain when nobody saw and nobody heard but God. Even through tears God has reminded me that the longest storm the world has ever known came to an end one sunny morning. And after the storm—a rainbow! God did it for Noah . . . and he does it for us!

Sing to him, sing praise to him; tell of all his wonderful acts.

Psalm 105:2, NIV

August 8

He Said—She Said

Another marriage is shattered, Lord.
The divorce will be final next week.

He said it was the breakdown of communication
And the subtle infiltration of boredom.
She said it was an accumulation of things.
He said she was unnecessarily preoccupied
With home and children and activities.
She said he stifled her dreams
And ignored her achievements.
He said he felt imprisoned, restricted—
That night after night he got the old push-away.
She said he was harsh and brutal
And he often embarrassed her in public.
He said her critical attitudes
Contributed to his sense of inadequacy.
She said she felt lonely and unappreciated
With no claim to personal identity.
He said she wallowed in self-pity
And refused to acknowledge her benefits.
She said he was thriftless and irresponsible.
He said she didn't understand.
She said he didn't care.

Lord, how tragic.
Through all the wearisome years
Neither of them asked what *You* said.

He did evil because he had not set his heart on seeking the Lord.
2 Chronicles 12:14, NIV

August 9

Direct Answer

O Lord

I've battled and struggled

I've dragged through

Tortured guilt-ridden hours

I've wept before You

Until there are no more tears.

What more can I do?

Dear child

You can begin to obey!

I assure you, anyone who obeys my teaching will never die!

John 8:51, NLT

August 10

"Have a Nice Forever"

Even at longest, Lord
Life is fleetingly short—
A mere breath
A withering flower
A shadow in pantomime.
It sobers me
That I am but a passing occupant
A temporary guest who says hello
Then so suddenly—good-bye.

But, Lord
You have chosen me
To be Your very own.
The instant You call my name
I shall be a permanent resident
In my Father's house.
Once again
With ecstatic joy
I shall say hello—
But never through all Eternity
Shall I have to say good-bye!

There are many rooms in my Father's home, and I am going to prepare a place for you. If this were not so, I would tell you plainly. When everything is ready, I will come and get you, so that you will always be with me where I am. John 14:2-3, NLT

August 11

Precious Treasure

O dear Lord

How can You know all about me—

Everything I've ever done—

And still love me so extravagantly?

You treat me as if I were

A precious treasure or something.

The beautiful part is—

To You I am!

For the Lord takes delight in his people; he crowns the humble with salvation.

Psalm 149:4, NIV

August 12

Beautiful Fact

Lord

There are countless things in my life

That are inexcusable.

There are things unaccountable

And things unexplainable.

There are things irrefutable

And things irresponsible.

But it comes to me with unutterable relief

That because of Your amazing love

Nothing in my life is unforgivable.

Our old sinful selves were crucified with Christ so that sin might lose its power in our lives. We are no longer slaves to sin. Romans 6:6, NLT

August 13

Spiritual Tug-of-War

Lord, I've waited long enough
No longer can I withstand
This spiritual tug-of-war between us.
Today I will do what You asked me to do.
I still don't want to, Lord—
Surely You know that.
I'm frightened and ill-at-ease.
I feel foolish and uncomfortable.
I almost feel put-upon.
What You've asked of me slaps at my pride.
Nevertheless, I choose to obey You
Simply because I love You.
Do You understand, dear Lord?
I wouldn't do this
For anyone in the world—but You.

You are good, and what you do is good; teach me your decrees.

Psalm 119:68, NIV

August 14

On the Way to the Airport

The women's retreat had ended, and I was on my way out the door. I had only a little while to get to the airport for my plane trip home. As I hurried toward the waiting car, a charming young wife followed me. I sensed her deep anxiety when she asked, "How can I live before my husband who wants nothing to do with God?"

From the car window I said, "Let me give you four DON'TS and four DO'S:

1. DON'T push.
2. DON'T preach.
3. DON'T pretend.
4. DON'T puncture his self-esteem.

1. DO permeate your home with love.
2. DO practice forgiving.
3. DO pay compliments to him often.
4. DO persist in prayer.

"Oh, yes, one more DON'T: Don't ever, ever, ever give up!"

The young woman reached inside her purse for her personal card. With gentle persuasion she asked, "Would you be willing to write all of that down for me when you get home?" I promised I would.

We've never seen each other again, but almost a year after the retreat I found her short note in our mailbox. Just three words and her name. "Thanks! It's working!"

Find out what is pleasing to the Lord. Ephesians 5:10, NLT

August 15

New Bible

This was an exciting day for me, Lord!
This morning I opened my new Bible.
Not a single word was circled
Not a single phrase underlined.
Now with each new day
I can circle and underline again
I can word-clutter the margins
And I know what will happen, Lord—
I'll be asking as I read
Why didn't I see that before?
But even with the joy of a new Bible
I'm going to miss my old one
With its tattered pages—
It's creased and torn edges.
Oh, how many personal notes
Are jotted on the margins
How many God-whispered secrets.
Yes, Lord, I'll miss it.
But thank You for a friend's reminder:
"If your Bible is falling apart
Chances are your life isn't."

Your word is a lamp for my feet and a light for my path.

Psalm 119:105, NLT

August 16

Need of Patience

O God
How pointedly You speak to my
heart
When You say, "You have need
of patience . . ."
Remorsefully I acknowledge Your
truth
For there is nothing I need more.
I am so easily disturbed, Lord
So many little things annoy me.
Patience is simply not a virtue
of mine.

I'm impatient with our neighbor
Who mows his lawn but once every
six weeks.
I'm impatient with our newsboy
Every time he misses our front
porch.
Yesterday a friend kept me waiting
And I robed my impatience in
self-pity.

Shoes pushed under the bed
An unrinsed coffee cup
An overly detailed story
Toys scattered on our lawn—
How I murmur and fret.
(Sometimes I explode.)

I'm impatient with myself, Lord
My foolish mistakes, my failures
And often I'm impatient with
You.
I am like a petulant child
Who insists on an answer—*now*.

Yes, God, I have need of patience.
But I will not be discouraged
Nor will I continue to flog myself.
Again Your Word speaks
pointedly:
"My God shall supply all your
need . . ."
The very need You know I have
Is the very need You will supply.
You will renew me in patience.
In You there is hope!

Since God chose you to be the holy people whom he loves, you must clothe yourselves with tenderhearted mercy, kindness, humility, gentleness, and patience. You must make allowance for each other's faults and forgive the person who offends you. Remember, the Lord forgave you, so you must forgive others. Colossians 3:12-13, NLT

August 17

You Name the Stars

God, I walked alone
In Your beautiful time
Called Night.
I lifted my face
To the soft-pillowed sky
And watched a shivering star
Fall out of bed—
And then I remembered:
That very star
You call by name!

He determines the number of the stars and calls them each by name. Great is our Lord and mighty in power; his understanding has no limit.
Psalm 147:4-5, NIV

August 18

The Difference

O dear God

Help me to grow

More like You

In spite of my circumstances.

Wounded child

You will grow

More like Me

Because of your circumstances.

Consider it pure joy, my brothers, whenever you face trials of many kinds, because you know that the testing of your faith develops perseverance.

James 1:2-3, NIV

August 19

Praise upon Praise

O Father
Through the years
You have permitted
Hurt upon hurt
In my God-planned life.
This early morning
Even before I greet the dawn
I offer You
Praise upon praise
For You are transforming every hurt
Into a holy hallmark—
A genuine guarantee
Of my permanent identification
With You.

Before I was afflicted I went astray, but now I obey your word.

Psalm 119:67, NIV

August 20

I Stake My Life

I stake my life totally
Completely
Permanently
On the integrity of Jesus.
Lord, Your integrity means
You will do all You promised.
You will see me through
Every fiery furnace
Every tempestuous storm.
If not, dear God
Then nothing in life
Makes any sense whatever.
Your part is to perform
What You promised.
My part is to trust and obey.

Obey me, and I will be your God and you will be my people.
Walk in all the ways I command you, that it may go well with you.

Jeremiah 7:23, NIV

August 21

He Is Enough

She lived in the most deprived section of the crowded city of New York, where there was never enough of anything—never enough food or clothing, never enough warmth or shelter, never enough compassion.

But one day a benevolent young couple invited her to spend a week at the seashore, to experience a piece of life she had never known. Hour by hour she breathed deeply as the crashing waves brushed against her small frame. She looked at the vast expanse of water—and then, without warning she began to sob. For the first time in her life she saw something of which there was enough!

Today I ask forgiveness for my limited concept of God. At times I've secretly felt cheated—as though somehow He was not enough to satisfy the longings of my heart. I need to learn and relearn that in Him there is enough faithfulness, enough love, enough grace, enough joy! May I never forget that God Himself is now and forever my great *enough!*

You will show me the way of life, granting me the joy of your presence and the pleasures of living with you forever. Psalm 16:11, NLT

August 22

Sane Estimate

Lord, help me to face with honesty
And genuine appreciation
The talents and abilities
You have given
As special gifts to me.
Give me a sane estimate of myself.
Neither exaggerated nor mud-crawling.
Just *sane*, as Your Word admonishes.
May I be joyfully satisfied
With Your unique plan for me.
When at times I'd secretly love to ride
On a colorful float
Beautifully adorned
Waving to cheering crowds
Smile at me, Lord.
With a twinkle in Your eye
Remind me again
That somebody has to build the float.

For by the grace given me I say to every one of you: Do not think of yourself more highly than you ought, but rather think of yourself with sober judgment, in accordance with the measure of faith God has given you.

Romans 12:3, NIV

August 23

Morbid Memories

Lord, I can't mow down morbid memories
Like my husband mows tall grass.
Mercilessly they take revenge
By tramping gleefully
Through my somber heart.
So, dear Lord
I ask YOU to shake them
In the sunlight of Your love.
Then may the gentle breeze
Of the Holy Spirit
Blow them all away—
Never to be found again.

Fix your thoughts on what is true and honorable and right. Think about things that are pure and lovely and admirable. Think about things that are excellent and worthy of praise. Philippians 4:8, NLT

August 24

Beautiful Things Happen

O God
Such beautiful things happen
When I meet You day by day
In quietness and confidence.
There is a deep inner wholeness
And the assurance of Your guidance.
I am not so easily disturbed
By changing circumstances.
I am less dependent on others
And more dependent on You.
My eyes may be full of tears
But my heart is full of joy.
In discovering Your hidden treasures
I learn how deeply I am treasured by You.
When day by day I am responsive
To Your whispered secrets
You do more for me in one day
Than I could do for myself in a lifetime.

You have given me greater joy than those who have abundant harvests of grain and wine. I will lie down in peace and sleep, for you alone, O Lord, will keep me safe. Psalm 4:7-8, NLT

August 25

Foolish Child

O God

Why do You play

A threatening game

Of hide-and-seek with me

When I know You are there?

Foolish child

It is not hide-and-seek.

It is only SEEK.

Seek Me with all your heart.

You will surely find Me.

Never do I play games

With My cherished children.

If you, then, though you are evil, know how to give good gifts to your children, how much more will your Father in heaven give good gifts to those who ask him!

Matthew 7:11, NIV

August 26

Relentless

God, You are relentless.

I have yielded

Everything to You—

Everything but one small exception—

An exception so small

I'm truly amazed

You would even take notice.

Yet it is invariably

To that one small exception

That You keep bringing me

Back, and back, and back.

Why does it matter so much to You?

My child

Why does it matter so much to you?

Then he said to the crowd, "If any of you wants to be my follower, you must put aside your selfish ambition, shoulder your cross daily, and follow me. If you try to keep your life for yourself, you will lose it. But if you give up your life for me, you will find true life."

Luke 9:23-24, NLT

August 27

So Slowly

Lord

I seem to grow so slowly

So *very* slowly.

So thank You for reminding me

That never has a Master Musician

Composed a lasting symphony

In an hour.

For God knew his people in advance, and he chose them to become like his Son, so that his Son would be the firstborn, with many brothers and sisters. Romans 8:29, NLT

August 28

Knowing God Intimately

How do we learn to know God so intimately that all of life takes on a new freshness?

We acknowledge that God is the instigator. We would not be wanting him if he did not first want us. Even a glimmer of spiritual desire is *his* desire planted in us.

We resign from our self-appointed office as president of the "Me First Club," which gives God the privilege of saying, "Good! Now I'll promote you."

We focus on Jesus Christ, God's Son. It is never a matter of how conspicuous we are. It only matters that he is conspicuous in us.

We make no promise of perfection. All the perfection we'll ever have is the perfection of Jesus living in us.

We let God's Word saturate our hearts. Five or ten minutes each day is far more helpful than three hours once a week.

We trust God to do within us what we cannot do, knowing that he is able to do immeasurably more than all we ask or imagine, according to his power that is at work within us.

To him who is able to do immeasurably more than all we ask or imagine, according to his power that is at work within us, to him be glory in the church and in Christ Jesus throughout all generations, for ever and ever! Amen. Ephesians 3:20-21, NIV

August 29

I'm Here

God, I cannot see You

But I wait for You.

My child

I can see you

And I'm here.

In the morning, O Lord, you hear my voice; in the morning I lay my requests before you and wait in expectation. Psalm 5:3, NIV

August 30

The Answer

Lord, my life seems
So full of things
I can't do anything about.

True, dear child
But I will do something
With *those things.*

Therefore, I urge you, brothers, in view of God's mercy, to offer you bodies as living sacrifices, holy and pleasing to God—this is your spiritual act of worship.
Romans 12:1, NIV

August 31

The Conclusion

Lord, Lord
I am not as brave
As You seem to think
Nor as strong
Nor as capable of standing firm
In the midst of affliction.
Lord, there is not a drop
Of emotional response in me.
No awareness of Your love
No comfort or joy in Your promises.
I have no deep conviction
That You are real.
There is no daylight in my heart
Nor even candlelight.
Nevertheless, with sheer determination
And perhaps a bit of spiritual grit
I have opted to throw my weight
On Your word *without*
Rather than my feelings *within.*
I don't know exactly when it happened
But I have reached the conclusion
That I would rather walk with You
In the dark of night
Than walk without You
In the light.

Come, people of Israel, let us walk in the light of the Lord!

Isaiah 2:5, NLT

September

The Promise of Stability

He will hold me in his steady hand.

No turn in the affairs of my life

can baffle him.

The Lord Almighty is here among us; the God of Israel is our fortress.
Psalm 46:11, NLT

September 1

John 15:5

Lord
Often You come in the nick of time
Before I collide with a crisis—

Yesterday
There I was
Rushing
Dashing madly
Company coming for dinner
The table unset
The salad half made
My hair in wild hysteria
And You interrupted
With Your quiet plea:
"Let Me help you."

It was better after that, Lord—
From boil to simmer
Far less hectic
My head stayed on.
Just one more incident
To prove I can't do anything
Without You.

You said so first.

In him we live and move and exist. Acts 17:28, NLT

September 2

Indelible Ink

I love her exuberance, Lord
Her refreshing spontaneity.
I smile when I think
How she rushed into the house
(Blue eyes aglow)
And thrust her new book
Into my hands:
"Please write my name on my book
In great big letters
So everybody knows
It belongs to me."

Yes, Lord
Yes.
I want that too.
Write Your name
On the chapters of my life—
My thoughts
Motives
Secret dreams . . .
Write Your name
On my total being
So everybody knows
I belong to You.

And Lord
Indelible ink, please.

You are not your own; you were bought at a price.

1 Corinthians 6:19-20, NIV

September 3

Method of Achievement

I said to You:
Lord, crush my resentment
Chisel my rebellion
Chain my self-centeredness
Crash my inconsistency
Stifle my fears.

You said to me:
I will cleanse you with My blood
I will melt you with My Love
I will flood you with Myself
Until you grasp anew—
Our intention is the same
But the method is Mine.

Who is able to advise the Spirit of the Lord? Who knows enough to be his teacher or counselor? Has the Lord ever needed anyone's advice? Does he need instruction about what is good or what is best?

Isaiah 40:13-14, NLT

September 4

Master Artist

There are days, Lord
Frightening and mysterious
When You seem to splash across
The canvas of my heart
With wasted strokes—
Like an amateur artist
Carelessly mixing pigment.
Frankly
Your colors appear unblended
Your strokes haphazard.
Instead of design
I see blobs of distortion.
Today, Lord
This very hour
Dissolve my apprehension
Renew my confidence
Settle my conviction
That You have planned
The total design.
Finally, Lord
When the finished canvas
Is luminously displayed
Make this my song of affirmation:
The pattern is perfectly clear.

"For I know the plans I have for you," says the Lord. "They are plans for good and not for disaster, to give you a future and a hope."

Jeremiah 29:11, NLT

September 5

Hold Me to My Yes

I'm frightened, Lord
Bewildered
What shall I do?
I could have sworn I was free—
Free from the sinister
temptation
So fiercely threatening me.
Months have passed
Even years
Not once have old memories
haunted me
Nor has ugliness plagued me
Until now.
Suddenly
Tauntingly
Daringly
Desire steals in
Like a midnight thief.
It clutches
Crushes
Until my thoughts reel
Until my breath is tight.

Lord, the day I said *yes* to You
My total being responded.
This You know.
Now while the enemy seeks
The target of my heart
Don't let me renege—
Hold me to my yes.

For this we both know:
To sacrifice the ultimate
For the immediate
Spells disaster
Despair
Defeat.

So, if you think you are standing firm, be careful that you don't fall! No temptation has seized you except what is common to man. And God is faithful; he will not let you be tempted beyond what you can bear. But when you are tempted, he will also provide a way out so that you can stand up under it. 1 Corinthians 10:12-13, NIV

September 6

Sacrilege

"That was great, my friend."

(Why wasn't I asked to do it?)

"Congratulations on your achievement."

(Why does he always succeed?)

"Your new home is charming."

(Some people have everything.)

Forgive me, God
For moments of sacrilege
When I have expressed good
While thinking evil.

A heart at peace gives life to the body, but envy rots the bones.
Proverbs 14:30, NIV

September 7

Competition with God

Often we must ask, what is my competition with God? When life seems to stand still, when my thoughts saunter through blind alleys, those very *thoughts* become my competition with God. When I embrace my personal desires instead of giving allegiance to God, *desire* becomes my competition with God. When I waste valuable time, ignoring God-assigned tasks, *time* becomes my competition with God. When personal possessions erase my concern for a desperately needy world, *possessions* become my competition with God.

If we allow a controversy in our lives, our praying may be with pretense, but it will not be with power. Walking the path of self-indulgence eventually leads to emptiness. Seeking *first* the Kingdom of God and his righteousness leads to freedom and joy.

You will hear a voice say, "This is the way; turn around and walk here." Isaiah 30:21, NLT

September 8

Why?

I'm singing today
In the midst of adversity—
Singing without reason for song.
Lord, do You want to know why?
Simply because I'm staunchly convinced
That as I continue my songs in the night
You'll create a new reason for singing.

He put a new song in my mouth, a hymn of praise to our God. Many will see and fear and put their trust in the Lord. Psalm 40:3, NIV

September 9

Moments of Leisure

Lord, thank You
For the moments of leisure
And peaceful solitude
I can legitimately snatch
Here and there
Without apologizing.
Thank You for assuring me
That I needn't condemn myself
When I spend some time
Reading or resting
Or shopping just for fun.
Thank You for convincing me
That there's no glory
In a rat race.
I've discovered, dear Lord
That an hour or two
"Away from it all"
Calms my inner muddle
And cuts through the confusion.
Without a driving sense of urgency
I think more clearly—
I plan more wisely.
I am more patient, more loving
More understanding with my
family.
I even accept with calmness
The multiple demands imposed
upon me.

Thank You so much, dear God
For the certain knowledge that
Jesus
(Who always obeyed the Father)
Went apart from the crowd to rest.
So must I!

He said to them, "Come with me by yourselves to a quiet place and get some rest." Mark 6:31, NIV

September 10

I Keep Running Back to You

You know how it is with me, Lord:
So often I mess up my days.
I judge harshly
I am critical and obstinate
I waste time and energy
I blame others for my failure.
There are people I try to avoid
And tasks I try to evade
And when I can't have my own way
I sulk in my own little corner.
Lord, I even turn my back on You
To escape Your penetrating gaze.

Then finally I get fed up with
myself.
The intolerable loneliness
frightens me
And I can no longer endure my
shame.
It always happens, Lord—
I keep running back to You!

Where else can I go?
Who else understands me so well
Or forgives me so totally?
Who else can save me from foolish
pride?
No one, Lord, but You.
So thank You for accepting me
For loving me
For always welcoming me.
I just can't help it, Lord
I keep running back to You!

He tends his flock like a shepherd: He gathers the lambs in his arms and carries them close to his heart; he gently leads those that have young.
Isaiah 40:11, NIV

September 11

One of the Two

Dear God

Please help me.

I'm encumbered with problems

Too heavy to handle.

Dear child

Why should two of us

Carry the weight of your burden

When one of the two is Me?

Cast all your anxiety on him because he cares for you. 1 Peter 5:7, NIV

September 12

Seek First

O Lord
How futile, how foolish
To attempt to keep up with the Joneses
On the gold-studded ladder of success.
Even if we make it
(Setting high, competitive goals)
We awake one dismal morning
To discover the Smiths have bypassed the Joneses
So it starts again—the goading competition.

God, Your objective is far more rewarding.
You want us to "keep up" with Your Plan
For our individual lives.
"Seek first the Kingdom of God"
Is Your shining word to us.
Forgive us for moments and days
(Even months)
When our love of money
Has exceeded our love for You.
Please, God
Be our Financial Advisor
And deliver us from a thousand "if onlys."
May we never be defeated
By the lack of money
Or captivated by the lure of it.

So if we have enough food and clothing, let us be content. But people who long to be rich fall into temptation and are trapped by many foolish and harmful desires that plunge them into ruin and destruction. 1 Timothy 6:8-9, NLT

September 13

Lord, Remind Me Often Today

Lord, remind me often today . . .

That if there is some area in my life
Not fully surrendered to You
That is always the area
In which I will be most severely tried.

Lord, remind me often today . . .

That You've already done Your part:
You've provided a way of escape
Against every temptation I shall face.
I must *choose* Your escape-door.

Lord, remind me often today . . .

That You want more than first place
In my heart and life.
You want all of me, always.
Surrender means every detail of my life
Under your careful scrutiny.

Lord, remind me often today . . .

That You alone are my Source.
Only God
Always God
Totally God
You alone are my Source.

He must become greater; I must become less. John 3:30, NIV

September 14

The God Who Never Changes

It is irrefutably true: We have lost many opportunities that can never be retrieved. We have made foolish choices that can never be rectified. But we dare not live life in a spirit of despair and defeat.

As children of God we need to understand that all God's discipline has but one objective: To bring us to the end of ourselves and back to him! His desire is always to restore us, never to reject us. His goal is always to use us, never to ignore us.

With confession, renewed surrender, and a heart that is fixed on him, God will do in us whatever he needs to do to make us whatever he wants us to be. Every necessary change God chooses to make is wonderfully possible because of Jesus, who never changes.

Jesus Christ is the same yesterday, today, and forever.

Hebrews 13:8, NLT

September 15

The Challenge

It may be true, dear God
That my husband and I had more to live on
A year ago than we have today
But it is equally true
That we have just as much to live *for.*
The real values of our lives remain
Solid, stable, unshifting.
Our financial loss has in no way
Diminished the value of a single friendship.
We have lost nothing of human dignity
And we are discovering spiritual realities
Full of wonder and sheer delight.
Our faith in Your loving-kindness
Adds growing serenity to our guided lives.
You are making us increasingly aware
That what we *are* is vastly more vital
Than our fondest possessions.
Above all, You are teaching us
That a limited salary is our shining challenge
To trust and exalt our limitless God!

So don't worry about having enough food or drink or clothing. Why be like the pagans who are so deeply concerned about these things? Your heavenly Father already knows all your needs, and he will give you all you need from day to day if you live for him and make the Kingdom of God your primary concern. Matthew 6:31-33, NLT

September 16

Permanent Hookup

God

I am always getting one thing

Straightened out with You

And then another lion

Jumps out of the jungle.

Why couldn't You create

Some kind of permanent hookup

So life would stay

Settled, serene

And ecstatically spiritual?

Dear child

I have.

It's called Heaven.

And they will see his face, and his name will be written on their foreheads. And there will be no night there—no need for lamps or sun—for the Lord God will shine on them. And they will reign forever and ever.

Revelation 22:4-5, NLT

September 17

That Little

O dear God

There is within me

A deep, intense longing

To use whatever gifts

You've entrusted to me.

But, Lord, they seem so small.

There's so little I can do

So little I can say.

My timid child

It is just "that little"

That I ask from you.

Hear what I say:

OBEY!

It is the Lord your God you must follow, and him you must revere. Keep his commands and obey him; serve him and hold fast to him.

Deuteronomy 13:4, NIV

September 18

Fear Not

Again and again, dear Lord
I read Your words, "Fear not."
Surely You would not say it so often
If there were any reason to fear.
Nor would You command it so explicitly
If You could not keep me from fearing.
God, You have given me a *Fear Not*
For every puzzling circumstance
For every possible emergency
For every trial and testing
Real or imagined.
Yet I confess wasted hours—
Even days, dear Lord
When fear clutches and clobbers me
Until I am physically and emotionally spent.
Lord, when David cried to You
You delivered him from all his fears.
On this gray-sky morning
I kneel before You with David's cry.
O my Father, I cannot believe
You would be less kind to me
Than You were to David.

Those who look to him for help will be radiant with joy; no shadow of shame will darken their faces. I cried out to the Lord in my suffering, and he heard me. He set me free from all my fears. Psalm 34:5-6, NLT

September 19

Greater Understanding

O God
With greater understanding
My heart proclaims
Your own words:
"For my thoughts are not your thoughts
Neither are your ways my ways . . ."

What so often seems to me
An enormous trial
Crushing, mangling
Tearing me to shreds
Represents to You
An enormous transformation
Of my total self—
Purging, renewing
Liberating me
Until my soul soars!

"For my thought are not your thoughts, neither are your ways my ways," declares the Lord. "As the heavens are higher than the earth, so are my ways higher than your ways and my thoughts than your thoughts."

Isaiah 55:8-9, NIV

September 20

Commonplace Days

Lord of my commonplace days
Forgive me for foolishly waiting
For "divine inspiration"
Before moving in on the tasks
Personally assigned to me.
Hopefully I am learning
To face with greater determination
The day-by-day drudgery
The trite, mundane tasks
The pushing-pulling glamourless duties.
Lord, even when I think
I'm getting no place
Keep me pushing on and on
With purpose and direction.
Grab my heart and quiet me
When I begin to whine and whimper.
Despite the daily drain
I think I see it more clearly now:
It is only when I begin to *do*
That You begin to *bless.*

And whatever you do, whether in word or deed, do it all in the name of the Lord Jesus, giving thanks to God the Father through him.

Colossians 3:17, NIV

September 21

A Listening Heart

I remember vividly the lesson I learned from my husband one day as he came home from his office weary and depleted. It had been a difficult day. He needed to talk.

My day had been difficult, too. Countless interruptions, phone calls, guests coming for brunch the next day. I wanted to listen, so I suggested that he follow me from room to room while I dusted furniture.

We tried it. While I dusted the piano, he talked. When I cleaned the clanging piano keys he continued, but with a trace of impatience. Next the stereo, then the tables. When I moved, he moved. Suddenly he grabbed my shoulders. "Please listen to me!"

Frankly I was shocked. "Honey, I heard every word you said."

"I mean listen with your *heart!*" I dropped the dust cloth. We sat down, and I gave my full attention. No body signals, no folded arms, no finger tapping. I was again aware of the tremendous responsibilities my husband carried. He needed my understanding. He thanked me profusely for listening.

That night I remembered how often God had said to the children of Israel, "If my people would only listen." I thought of God's yearning for an intimate relationship with us. He waits for our response to his still small voice. He longs for our listening hearts. How we must grieve him when we don't listen!

Be still, and know that I am God. Psalm 46:10, NIV

September 22

I Sing in the Rain

One cold, misty day
When I was nine years old
I walked hand-in-hand
Through a wooded forest
With my strong, gentle father.
"Listen to the stillness," he whispered.
"Stillness makes beautiful music."
Suddenly he pointed to a tiny bird
Perched on a limb of a bending tree.
"The bird doesn't know we're here
But he's singing his heart out."
Then smiling down at me he asked
"Could you sing in the rain
If nobody heard you but God?"

Lord, though many years have passed
Since I walked with my father
I have never forgotten his question.
Today I am alone—
Yet not alone, for YOU are here.
Though my heart is grief drenched
I know You are worthy of praise.
Help me, please help me
To sing my feeble song in the rain
Though nobody hears but You.

Answer me when I call to you, O my righteous God. Give me relief from my distress; be merciful to me and hear my prayer. Psalm 4:1, NIV

September 23

Now

My great, strong God!
All the fight
Is drained out of me.
In my debilitating weakness
I can't even hold on to You.
But Your own words
Keep my hope stirring:
"For I your God
Am firmly grasping
Your right hand.
I am saying unto you
Do not fear.
I have become your helper."
Now, dear Lord!
Now!

The Lord is a shelter for the oppressed, a refuge in times of trouble. Those who know your name trust in you, for you, O Lord, have never abandoned anyone who searches for you. Psalm 9:9-10, NLT

September 24

Relationship

Lord

As You show me

That You are my Father

By instructing me

May I show You

That I am Your child

By obeying You.

This is love for God: to obey his commands. 1 John 5:3, NIV

September 25

Excuses

O God
I've become a self-educated master
Of a thousand polished excuses.
Hoping to avoid Your penetrating gaze
I clutch them to me like valuable gems.
When I think I have myself thoroughly covered
I'm caught short with the realization
That You see right through me.
My flimsy excuses are never really hidden.
I find an excuse for all my failures
Wrong choices
Late appointments
Wasted time.
I excuse my foolish blunders, my laziness
My broken resolves, my unreached goals.
I need Your help, Lord!
To hide from You is as foolish
As the Grand Canyon
Attempting to hide from the sky.
O God, my only hope
Lies in Your invincible power
To make me what I am not yet
But what You know I can become.
Strengthen my will, Lord.
Make me firm, steadfast, consistent.
Control my impulses, my emotions.
May I keep pursuing and never quit.

Let us fix our eyes on Jesus, the author and perfecter of our faith,
who for the joy set before him endured the cross, scorning its shame,
and sat down at the right hand of the throne of God. Hebrews 12:2, NIV

September 26

Three Unalterable Truths

Lord, through the years
Of walking hand-in-hand with You
I have learned three unalterable truths:
First, what You command me to do
You consistently expect me to do.
Never do You say, "Give the command a fair try."
Nor do You say, "Consider and then decide."
My natural weakness is never
An acceptable excuse.
Nor is my inability
To reach unreachable standards.
Rather, You tell me to *seek*
And then to *keep* Your commands.
Second, all of Your commands
Are always for my ultimate good.
"Obey Me," Your Word says
"So that I can do for you
All the wonderful things I promised. . . ."
"In the keeping of My Word
There is great reward."
Third, whatever You command me to do
You fully enable me to do.
As You give light to reveal a command
So You give grace to fulfill it.
Your divine energy is always at my disposal.
The choice to obey is always mine.
The power to obey is always Yours.

May I be blameless in keeping your principles; then I will never have to be ashamed. Psalm 119:80, NLT

September 27

Free Choice

My Lord

Because You have given me

The irrevocable power of free choice

You will not force me

To do something

I selfishly don't want to do.

But I have made

A grave and painful discovery:

You can certainly

Make me wish I had done it.

All of us have strayed away like sheep. We have left God's paths to follow our own. Yet the Lord laid on him the guilt and sins of us all.

Isaiah 53:6, NLT

September 28

An Honest Appraisal

I must answer honestly. . . .
Am I often so exhausted that I want to be left alone?
Are my outside activities crowding my availability at home?
Am I tense, irritable, tied in knots?
Am I sometimes preoccupied?
Do I answer questions sharply?
Do I vacillate in my decisions?
Am I unable to cope with simple tasks without showing panic?

If I must answer yes to any or all of the above, I am too busy. I am burdening my family. I am puzzling my friends. I am endangering my mental and physical stamina. I am ignoring God's agenda.

The solution . . .
I must accept the fact that the little word *no* is often more honoring to God and to those I care about than an impulsive *yes.*

The threatening question . . .
Will I begin to make changes *today?*

I can do everything with the help of Christ who gives me the strength I need.
Philippians 4:13, NLT

September 29

At Long Last

O Lord

At long last

I have placed in Your hands

The strong and aching desire

Which for so many months

Completely absorbed me.

Now to my surprise and delight

I have made the joyful discovery

That all my tenacious resistance

Was far more painful, more agonizing

Than a total letting go

In obedience to Your command.

My child

So it will always be.

Seek the Lord, all you humble of the land, you who do what he commands. Seek righteousness, seek humility. Zephaniah 2:3, NIV

September 30

So Demanding

God, Your Word is so demanding.
It demands great stretches of my
time—
Not just occasionally
But day after day, year after year.
I can't just grab a bite of it
With one hand in the dishwater
Or on the steering wheel
While I'm backing out of the
garage.
Your Word insists that I ponder
That I contemplate and meditate
That I seriously apply it to my life.
It insists on obedience and
forgiveness
On gentleness and love.
Its claim upon me is absolute.
Only as I obey
Can I know the peace
That passes all understanding.

But God
Its very insistence transforms me
For it proclaims Your faithfulness
In superlative terms.
As I give it my fixed, steady
attention
My composure increases
My anxiety decreases
And I am supported on every side.
Jeremiah said, " . . . your word was
unto me
The joy and rejoicing of my
heart."

And in the margin of my Bible
Next to the words of the prophet
There is my own personal
notation:
"My heart, too!"

Heaven and earth will disappear, but my words will remain forever.
Matthew 24:35, NLT

October

The Promise of Endurance

Lord, help me to avoid stumbling from worry to worry

by teaching me to soar from prayer to prayer.

Those who wait on the Lord will find new strength.
They will fly high on wings like eagles. They will run
and not grow weary. They will walk and not faint.

Isaiah 40:31, NLT

October 1

In the Morning

"Joy comes with the morning" (Psalm 30:5).

Today, Lord
I have an unshakable conviction
A positive resolute assurance
That what You have spoken
Is unalterably true.

But today, Lord
My sick body feels stronger
And the stomping pain quietly subsides.
Tomorrow . . .

And then tomorrow
If I must struggle again
With aching exhaustion
With twisting pain
Until I am breathless
Until I am utterly spent
Until fear eclipses the last vestige of hope
Then, Lord
Then grant me the enabling grace
To believe without feeling
To know without seeing
To clasp Your invisible hand
And wait with invincible trust

For the morning.

Weeping may go on all night, but joy comes with the morning.

Psalm 30:5, NLT

October 2

Ten to One

Lord, I ask more questions
Than You ask.
The ratio, I would suppose
Is ten to one.

I ask:
Why do You permit this anguish?
How long can I endure it?
What possible purpose does it serve?
Have You forgotten to be gracious?
Have I wearied You?
Have I offended You?
Have You cast me off?
Where did I miss Your guidance?
When did I lose the way?
Do You see my utter despair?

You ask:
Are you trusting me?

Do not abandon me, Lord. Do not stand at a distance, my God. Come quickly to help me, O Lord my savior. Psalm 38:21-22, NLT

October 3

I Have You

Sick depressed anxious

Fatigued frustrated

Puzzled perplexed lonely

Desperate despairing

Lord, for this I have You.

As for me, I am poor and needy, but the Lord is thinking about me right now. You are my helper and my savior. Do not delay, O my God.

Psalm 40:17, NLT

October 4

Big Switch

Once again I have utterly failed.
This time I thought I would make it.
I honestly thought I could cut it.
I thought it was all sewed up.
But here alone in my silent room
Your message rings loud and clear:
"Turn yourself in
And I will take over."
Could we make the Big Switch
Now, Lord?

The Lord is good. When trouble comes, he is a strong refuge. And he knows everyone who trusts in him. Nahum 1:7, NLT

October 5

The Reason

Lord, we both know
I come to You
Boldly
Persistently
Expectantly
Day after day
Need after need
As if everything
In my entire life
Depended upon it.
There's a reason, Lord—
It does.

Blessed is he whose help is the God of Jacob, whose hope is in the Lord his God, the Maker of heaven and earth, the sea, and everything in them—the Lord, who remains faithful forever. Psalm 146:5-6, NIV

October 6

Keep

I sit here at my desk
With Your Word before me—
A red pencil in my hand.
Suddenly the word *keep*
Looms from the page
Black and bold:
"He will *keep*
Keep
Keep
That which I have committed . . ."
Really, Lord?
This haunting anxiety?
This brick barrier which is
Blocking my peace?
This sinister intrusion?
It's so heavy, Lord
The weight of it is breaking me.
But You said You'd *keep*
So I give it to You now
Palms down.

Release!
Relief!
Laughter!
Joy!

And that is why I am suffering here in prison. But I am not ashamed of it, for I know the one in whom I trust, and I am sure that he is able to guard what I have entrusted to him until the day of his return.

2 Timothy 1:12, NLT

October 7

I Asked for a Sign

Even as I answer your letter, you are perhaps still waiting while God sends only silence. There is no sudden hailstorm, no writing in the sky. The crisis is real, and you don't want to be presumptuous. Like Gideon in Judges 6, you want to feel the wet fleece. Or the dry fleece—you don't care which one. You just want to *know!*

You don't stand alone! All of us who walk with God face conflicts that involve urgent decisions. God is not a God of confusion. We *can* know his will. When our faith is very new, he may send a sign to fortify us. However, I am convinced that God's highest intention is to free us from unnecessary "props." He wants to buttress us, not baby us. Above all, he wants us to trust his Word, not the wool! When he encourages us to hope in a promise, that hope may be our *only* evidence.

At this moment you can't see ahead. However, you can still be incorrigibly hopeful! You can anticipate as you wait, knowing that God will never disappoint the hope he himself implants. He is never too late. Remember: Not the wool but his Word!

Give your burdens to the Lord, and he will take care of you. He will not permit the godly to slip and fall. Psalm 55:22, NLT

October 8

You Wait for Me

Lord
I am so prone to
Extravagant extremes:
I either foolishly
Justify my imperfections
Or I frantically bemoan them.
All the while You wait for me
To release them—to You.

If we confess our sins, he is faithful and just and will forgive us our sins and purify us from all unrighteousness. If we claim we have not sinned, we make him out to be a liar and his word has no place in our lives.

1 John 1:9-10, NIV

October 9

Promotion

Dear God:

I resign.

Dear child:

Good!

Now I'll promote you.

Many are the plans in a man's heart, but it is the Lord's purpose that prevails.

Proverbs 19:21, NIV

October 10

Beginning

Lord

I'm at the end

Of all my resources.

Child

You're just at the beginning

Of Mine.

Surely God is my help; the Lord is the one who sustains me.

Psalm 54:4, NIV

October 11

Failure

Sometimes, God

I feel like a failure

In everyone's sight but Yours.

Dear child

Be glad it isn't reversed.

Your approval or disapproval means nothing to me. John 5:41, NLT

October 12

You Love Me

Yesterday, God, I was soaring
Like a graceful eagle
And You loved me.
Today I feel like a blob
And You love me.
Tomorrow I may ask
"Whatever happened
To disturb me yesterday?"
And You'll love me.

God, there are innumerable things
I cannot begin to comprehend
But the one great certainty
In all my life is this:
I know that You love me.

For the Lord is good and his love endures forever; his faithfulness continues through all generations. Psalm 100:5, NIV

October 13

I Will Let You

Early this morning, Lord
An hour or so before dawn
You whispered a secret
Within my trembling heart . . .

You said, "If you will let Me
I will make this seeming tragedy
The most valuable experience
Of your entire life.
I will blaze a luminous trail
Through the vast wilderness.
Where there is sand and tumbleweed
I will cultivate a fertile valley.
I will plant green trees by still waters.
If you will let Me."

O Lord, Yes!
I will let You!

Even the wilderness will rejoice in those days. The desert will blossom with flowers. Yes, there will be an abundance of flowers and singing and joy! The deserts will become as green as the mountains of Lebanon, as lovely as Mount Carmel's pastures and the plain of Sharon. There the Lord will display his glory, the splendor of our God.

Isaiah 35:1-2, NLT

October 14

The Lesson of the Windmill

Lorraine, Kansas, where I grew up, was known as the City of Windmills. I loved having one in our backyard. I was sure that if I climbed to the very top I could touch God! If only I was brave enough to try! My brother, two years younger than I, was usually eager to please me, so I begged him until he finally agreed. He stepped on the first rung, the second, the third and fourth.

"I'm proud of you!" I shouted.

Another rung . . . and another . . . and almost to the top. Then he looked down—and froze. Our mother heard his screams. When she saw her young son on the ladder, she calmly silenced his screams while I ran for our neighbor. In moments Johnnie was rescued. I knew he was angry. "You said if I climbed to the top I could touch God, but I didn't even see him."

Often God has used the memory of the windmill to remind me that we never reach God by climbing. Again and again we attempt to climb the rung of good works, the rung of prestige and success—until we discover anew that the *only* way to reach God is by kneeling at the foot of the Cross. He waits for us there!

It is by grace you have been saved, through faith—and this not from yourselves, it is the gift of God—not by works, so that no one can boast. Ephesians 2:8-9, NIV

October 15

The Time Is Now

O God

No temptation is irresistible.

I can absolutely trust You

To keep the temptation

From becoming so strong

That I can't stand against it.

You've promised this

And You will do what you say.

But I don't need the promise

For yesterday or tomorrow, Lord.

I need it today. Desperately.

This very moment.

Because he himself suffered when he was tempted, he is able to help those who are being tempted.
Hebrews 2:18, NIV

October 16

Don't Stop, Lord

Lord
In asking You
To make me whole
I certainly didn't know
What I was in for.
You have ransacked me
Until I sometimes feel
There is nothing left.
But don't stop, Lord
Please don't stop!
I'm trusting that the product
Will be worth the process.

These trials are only to test your faith, to show that it is strong and pure. It is being tested as fire tests and purifies gold—and your faith is far more precious to God than mere gold. So if your faith remains strong after being tried by fiery trials, it will bring you much praise and glory and honor on the day when Jesus Christ is revealed to the whole world. 1 Peter 1:7, NLT

October 17

Patience

Lord, as I read Your Word today
I underlined these words:
"Don't be impatient for the Lord to act.
Keep traveling steadily along his pathway
And in due season he will honor you
With every blessing."
I know I need more patience, Lord
But I simply cannot create it.
I plead with You to do it for me.
And, Lord, could You hurry a little?

But when the Holy Spirit controls our lives, he will produce this kind of fruit in us: love, joy, peace, patience, kindness, goodness, faithfulness, gentleness, and self-control. Here there is no conflict with the law.

Galatians 5:22-23, NLT

October 18

Could You Hurry a Little

Lord, I know there are countless times
When I must wait patiently for You.
Waiting develops endurance.
It strengthens my faith
And deepens my dependence upon You.
I know You are Sovereign God—
Not an errand boy
Responding to the snap of my finger.
I know Your timing is neatly wrapped
In Your incomparable wisdom.
But, Lord
You have appointed prayer
To obtain answers!
Even David the Psalmist cried
With confident boldness:
"It is time, O Lord, for you to act."
God, on this silent sunless morning
When I am hedged in on every side
I too cry boldly.
You are my Father, and I am Your child.
So, Lord, could You hurry a little?

But you, O Lord, be not far off; O my Strength, come quickly to help me. Psalm 22:19, NIV

October 19

Only Goodness

What glorious words of wonder
Come from the Apostle Peter.
He wrote, "But we are looking forward
To God's promise of new heavens
And a new earth afterwards
Where there will be only goodness."

O dear God
"Where there will be only goodness."
After centuries of war, greed, and lust
After indulgences shamelessly practiced
After hatred, hostility
Jealousy and abuse.
Murder and martyrdom
Crime and cruelty
Curses and rebellion.
After whimpering cries from starving children
After tragedy and catastrophe
Loneliness and despair
At last . . . at long last
"There will be only goodness."
O dear Lord
Your promise is Your guarantee
But please hurry a little!

I heard a loud shout from the throne, saying, "Look, the home of God is now among his people! He will live with them, and they will be his people. God himself will be with them. He will remove all of their sorrows, and there will be no more death or sorrow or crying or pain. For the old world and its evils are gone forever." Revelation 21:3-4, NLT

October 20

Autumn Glow

Lord, if You will make
The autumn of my life
As lovely as this
Golden autumn morning
I will not look back to grieve
The passing days of summer.
Of all the regal seasons
Autumn is most brilliant.
Make my life brilliant, too!

But I trust in you, O Lord; I say, "You are my God." My times are in your hands.

Psalm 31:14-15, NIV

October 21

Nobody Can Possibly Help Me

How wonderful! You can shake hands with a king. His name is Jehoshaphat, and his story reads like a letter from someone who feels desperate—maybe like you feel right now. You don't know where to turn. Neither did he. Jehoshaphat had no forces to oppose the "great company" marching against him.

Standing achingly helpless (as you are), what did he do? He literally threw himself on God. He prayed, "O our God, we have no power to face this vast army attacking us. We don't know what to do, but our eyes are upon you." (You'll find the story in 2 Chronicles 20.)

Do you see yourself in the mirror of the story? Do you feel overpowered by a "great company" of temptations. Are you stumbling through confused days and tossing through sleepless nights.

What is the answer? Stoic endurance? No. That brings only deeper despair. But you *can* pray Jehoshaphat's prayer! His God is your God if your faith is in Jesus Christ. You can plead with God on the grounds of his great power, his promises, and his love. And all the while *you can keep your eyes steadfastly on him.*

The result? As you trust, you will one day say as Jehoshaphat said, "The Lord has given me cause to rejoice."

"O Lord, God of our fathers, are you not the God who is in heaven? You rule over all the kingdoms of the nations. Power and might are in your hand, and no one can withstand you. . . . O our God. . . . We do not know what to do, but our eyes are upon you."

2 Chronicles 20:6, 12, NIV

October 22

I Shout for Joy

Sometimes, Lord

You seem a million miles away

And then I remember Your unfailing words:

"I will never, never let go of your hand."

Once again I shout for joy

That what *seems* to be

Is not always what is.

Come, everyone, and clap your hands for joy! Shout to God with joyful praise! For the Lord Most High is awesome. He is the great King of all the earth. Psalm 47:1-2, NLT

October 23

The Hardest Thing

O God
In these crisis days
Of piercing pain
And emotional fatigue
Do a brand new thing in me.
Give me water in the wilderness
And streams in my desert.
You have promised to be my God
Through all my lifetime.
Surely You will keep Your word!

As You promised
Give me rest from my sorrow
And from my fear
And from the bondage
That binds me.
One thing more, dear Lord:
Enable me to praise You
When to praise
Is the hardest thing of all.

Then maidens will dance and be glad, young men and old as well. I will turn their mourning into gladness; I will give them comfort and joy instead of sorrow. Jeremiah 31:13, NIV

October 24

Soundproof

God of penitent hearts

The moment Your prophet Isaiah

Knew You had cleansed his sin

At that very moment

He heard Your Voice

Addressed directly to him.

Lord, thank You

For the revealing discovery

That only one thing

Makes me soundproof

Against Your Voice:

My refusal to relinquish my sin.

Then I said, "My destruction is sealed, for I am a sinful man and a member of a sinful race. Yet I have seen the King, the Lord Almighty!"

Isaiah 6:5, NLT

October 25

The Pain of Growth

O God
Growth is a painful process.
I frankly confess
I am a coward about pain.
I don't like it, Lord.
I never pray for it
Or get excited over it.
In fact, I often resist it:
The pain of emotional trauma
So overwhelming
So baffling and crushing.
The deep-cutting pain
Of a broken relationship.
Physical pain that goes on and on
Until my entire body screams.
The pain of cruel cutting words.
The pain of loneliness, rejection
Or financial ruin.
The pain of being misunderstood.
Lord, the very thought of pain
Frightens and unnerves me.
Yet it is true—
Again and again it is true:
My greatest spiritual growth
Has come through pain.
Through heartache
And anguish.
And very often in my suffering
When I sadly thought
You were doing absolutely nothing
At that very moment
You were doing more *within* me
Than I ever dreamed or hoped.

I know, O Lord, that your laws are righteous, and in faithfulness you have afflicted me. May your unfailing love be my comfort, according to your promise to your servant. Psalm 119:75-76, NIV

October 26

My Glorious Enough

Oh, how I love You, my Lord
But not enough.
How I hunger and thirst for You
But not enough.
How I rejoice in Your inimitable goodness
But not enough.
Pour Yourself lavishly, dear God
Into every vacant hollow
Into every cluttered chamber
Of my longing heart.
Free me from every shallow substitute
From every hidden pretense
Until I shall know
With deep, consuming conviction
That You are my Glorious Enough.

Blessed are those who hunger and thirst for righteousness, for they will be filled. Matthew 5:6, NIV

October 27

I Am Sure of You

Lord, I was sure of my faith
Just long enough
To watch it collapse.
Now I am sure of *You*
And You will not collapse.

The name of the Lord is a strong fortress; the godly run to him and are safe.

Proverbs 18:10, NLT

October 28

I Do Know

There is much I cannot begin to fathom concerning the vast, indescribable universe created by our majestic God. There is much I will never comprehend. I want to sing and shout, so utterly overwhelmed I am with the magnitude of God.

But I do know with confident certainty that I belong to the God of the universe—the Creator of all that exists. I know that I, a mere mortal, am forever linked to divine destiny. I know that my life has purpose and dignity. I know that God has chosen me as the object of his lavish love; that his thoughts toward me are thoughts of kindness and mercy; that he has inscribed me in the palms of his hands. I know that all the love of the Father, and the life of the Son, and the power of the Holy Spirit are freely, inseparably mine—now and throughout all eternity.

This I do *know*!

I know the one in whom I trust, and I am sure that he is able to guard what I have entrusted to him until the day of his return.

2 Timothy 1:12, NLT

October 29

Nevertheless

Lord, right now

My life is one gigantic puzzle.

None of the pieces fit together.

None of them, Lord!

In my stupor and confusion

I confess I don't understand Your hand.

Nevertheless, My child

You can always trust My heart.

O Sovereign Lord, you are God! Your words are trustworthy, and you have promised these good things to your servant. 2 Samuel 7:28, NIV

October 30

Unexplainable Mystery

Mysterious God
Today I am desolate
I am puzzled
I am heartsick
That I must wait so long
When You have promised so much.
At the same time
I am conscience-stricken
That I should feel such bitter rebellion.
Yet, to try to hide my emotions
Would only build up a pretense
That would eventually be exposed.
I suppose, O God
In the great perplexities
Of my unpredictable life
One of two things will always happen:
Either I will crowd You out
(Slowly but surely)
Or I will acknowledge Your sovereignty
In every area of my bewildered life.
To offer myself to You
Regardless of circumstances
May always bring unexplainable mystery.
But rejecting You totally
Brings the depth of despair.

May my cry come before you, O Lord; give me understanding according to your word. May my supplication come before you; deliver me according to your promise.
Psalm 119:169-170, NIV

October 31

Enormous Rewards

O dear God

Thank You for teaching me

The enormous rewards

Of walking obediently with You:

There is joy without guilt

Freedom without fear

Satisfaction without sordidness

Purpose without confusion

Friendship without compromise

Forgiveness without penance

Fulfillment without disappointment.

Now to him who is able to do immeasurably more than all we ask or imagine, according to his power that is at work within us, to him be glory in the church and in Christ Jesus throughout all generations, for ever and ever! Amen.

Ephesians 3:20, NIV

November

The Promise of Help

When I finally confess my inability to make it alone,

God whispers, "That's why you have me!"

God is my helper. The Lord is the one who keeps me alive! Psalm 54:4, NLT

November 1

Worst—Best

O God

It is difficult for me to think coherently

To pray with any kind of sequence today.

I am so weary, so worn, so fragmented.

But, Lord, perhaps to Your ears

Sometimes my worst praying

Is really my best.

I trust so . . . I trust so.

One thing I do know:

All my desire is before You!

And the Holy Spirit helps us in our distress. For we don't even know what we should pray for, nor how we should pray. But the Holy Spirit prays for us with groanings that cannot be expressed in words. And the Father who knows all hearts knows what the Spirit is saying, for the Spirit pleads for us believers in harmony with God's own will.

Romans 8:26-27, NLT

November 2

Busy Day

Lord, this is one of the days
I must ask You to preserve my sanity
In the midst of turmoil.
I'm so pressed by commitments—
Plus a thousand trivial tasks—
That I can scarcely see over my head.
So I plead for enough wisdom
To sort my priorities carefully.
Regardless of my frenzied schedule
May I keep my sense of humor
And even enjoy a hearty chuckle or two.

Calm my quivering nerves
With mental flashes from Your Word.
Help me to maintain
At least a semblance
Of Mary-Martha balance.
And tonight when we're together again
Should my husband confront me with
"What have you been doing today?"
May my answer be genuine and gentle:
"Part of the time, darling
I've thanked God for you."

But the Lord said to her, "My dear Martha, you are so upset over all these details!" Luke 10:41, NLT

November 3

Feeling Spiritual

Lord, I keep remembering
Our happy time last night—
Just You and me
In the quiet of our family room.
I had been reading a devotional book
Very "spiritual"
Very inspirational
So challenging
I doubted that I'd ever reach the goal.
Suddenly the book felt heavy
Sentences twirled
Words collided
And with all my valiant effort
I simply could not feel "spiritual."
Then, glancing at a Charlie Brown book
I thought I heard You say
"Let's read it together—
You and me."
I was delighted.
We read and laughed
And read and laughed . . .
And just as we finished the last page
You said what I needed most to hear:
"Never worry about feeling 'spiritual.'
Just share *everything* with me."

Now the Lord is the Spirit, and where the Spirit of the Lord is, there is freedom.
2 Corinthians 3:17, NIV

November 4

Lord, You Love to Say Yes

Lord, I asked You for abundant life
Rich, challenging, full of adventure
And You said Yes.
I asked You for an undisturbable joy
Independent of transitory change
And You said Yes.
I asked You to thread my tears into a song
When I was shattered and torn with grief
And You said Yes.
I asked You to steady me when I staggered—
To hold me when I struggled
To seize me when I resisted
And You said Yes.
I asked You to forgive my vain grasping
My foolish fears, my willful pride
And You said Yes.
I asked You to be my Helper, my Friend
My Light in the darkness
And You said Yes.
I asked You to guide me all my life
With Your wisdom, Your counsel
Your captivating love
And You said Yes.
Sometimes, Lord
I feel like a spoiled child
Who gets whatever he asks for.
You overwhelm me with joy
For *You love to say Yes!*

He fills my life with good things. My youth is renewed like the eagle's!
Psalm 103:5, NLT

November 5

Romans 8—to Me

God
I may fall flat on my face
I may fail until I feel
Old and beaten and done in
Yet Your love for me is changeless.
All the music may go out of my
    life
My private world may shatter to
    dust
Even so You will hold me
In the palm of Your steady hand.
No turn in the affairs
Of my fractured life
Can baffle You.
Satan with all his braggadocio
Cannot distract You.
Nothing can separate me
From Your measureless love:

Pain can't
Disappointments can't
Anguish can't.
Yesterday, today, tomorrow can't.
The loss of my dearest love can't.

Death can't.
Life can't.
Riots war insanity unidentity
Hunger neurosis disease—
None of these things
Nor all of them heaped together
Can budge the fact
That I am dearly loved.
Completely forgiven
And forever free
Through Jesus Christ
Your beloved Son.

And I am convinced that nothing can ever separate us from his love. Death can't, and life can't. The angels can't, and the demons can't. Our fears for today, our worries about tomorrow, and even the powers of hell can't keep God's love away. Whether we are high above the sky or in the deepest ocean, nothing in all creation will ever be able to separate us from the love of God that is revealed in Christ Jesus our Lord.

Romans 8:38-39, NLT

November 6

Last Word

I read, "In everything give thanks."
I said, "Lord, I'm in deep trouble—
You know I can't thank You for this."
You said, "My word is a command
And not a suggestion, dear child."

I read, "Your sins are forgiven you."
I said, "Thank you for forgiving me—
I repeat the same sin so often."
You said, "I can deliver, as well as forgive."

I read, "Trust in the Lord at all times."
I said, "You know how earnestly I try."
You said, "My Word says Trust."

Lord, it seems to me
You always have
The last word.

For the word of God is full of living power. It is sharper than the sharpest knife, cutting deep into our innermost thoughts and desires. It exposes us for what we really are. Hebrews 4:12, NLT

November 7

Discipline

It was a chilly morning. The warm blankets felt wonderful. After a two-minute struggle, I surrendered. In less than a minute I was asleep again.

For weeks I had been getting up at six o'clock. With my Bible and my journal I had spent uninterrupted time with God. The spiritual value far surpassed the discomfort of a cold morning. Why had I disrupted the habit? God wasn't shaking his finger, but why had I cheated myself?

Not wanting to miss out entirely, I opened my Bible to the book of Proverbs. One verse held my attention:

> I will teach you wisdom's ways and lead you in straight paths. (Proverbs 4:11)

Later in the day as I glanced out the window I saw her: Our eighty-year-old neighbor taking her three-mile walk. Rain or shine she walked.

One day I finally asked, "Kay, is it hard for you to walk three miles every day?"

"It's *very* hard," she said. "But not nearly as hard on my disposition as being undisciplined!"

Clearly I saw it! The purpose of discipline is to *free* us, not to enslave us.

Cry out for insight and understanding. Search for them as you would for lost money or hidden treasure. Then you will understand what it means to fear the Lord, and you will gain knowledge of God.

Proverbs 2:3-5, NLT

November 8

Reversal

Lord
For so long
I thought Your love
Demanded that I change.
At last
I am beginning to understand
That Your love
Changes me.

God demonstrates his own love for us in this: While we were still sinners, Christ died for us.

Romans 5:8, NIV

November 9

Celebration

When I think of Your lavish goodness
The longings You've satisfied
The forgiveness You've granted
The promises You've kept
When I think of Your irresistible love
Your ceaseless care
Your unfailing protection . . .

O Lord God
I want to raise flags
And fly banners
And sound bugles.
I want to run with lighted torches
And praise You
From the mountaintop.
I want to write symphonies
And shout for joy.
I want to throw a festive party
For ten thousand guests.
I want to celebrate with streamers
And bright lights
And an elaborate banquet.

Fine, dear child.
I'm ready.

I will exalt you, my God the King; I will praise your name for ever and ever. Every day I will praise you and extol your name for ever and ever.
Psalm 145:1-2, NIV

November 10

Just Cry

Lord, the sky is black and ominous
And all sense of Your presence is gone.
I am utterly devoid of energy
I am thwarted at every turn
My fragmented thoughts
Refuse to form words
All I can bring to You
Is my anguished cry.

Then cry, dear child
Just cry.

I cry aloud to the Lord; I lift up my voice to the Lord for mercy.
I pour out my complaint before him; before him I tell my trouble.
Psalm 142:1-2, NIV

November 11

The Reason

God, why am I so often defeated?
Why am I so full of dread and anxiety?
Why am I so lamentably weak—
So perilously susceptible to temptation?
Why am I often inhospitable
So intolerant of the needs of others?
Why am I so undisciplined
So restless and dissatisfied?
Why do I protest so violently?
Above all, God
Why do I so frequently lose
The sense of Your shining Presence?
God, why?
Why?

Because you pray so little.

Keep on praying. 1 Thessalonians 5:17, NLT

November 12

Too Sleepy

When I awoke this morning
You said so clearly
"Don't worry about anything
Instead, pray about everything . . ."
So, dear Lord, all day long
Will You keep me so prayerfully occupied
With Your assigned tasks
That I will find no time to worry?
Then tonight, when I finally lie down
And stretch out on my comfortable bed
Please silence my clamoring thoughts
And make me too sleepy to worry.

Do not be anxious about anything, but in everything, by prayer and petition, with thanksgiving, present your requests to God. And the peace of God, which transcends all understanding, will guard your hearts and your minds in Christ Jesus. Philippians 4:6-7, NIV

November 13

I Try

Lord

Never in a million years

Could I adequately thank You

For Your amazing goodness

Your matchless love—

But I like to try!

I will give thanks to the Lord because of his righteousness and will sing praise to the name of the Lord Most High. Psalm 7:17, NIV

November 14

It Happened to Me

It may be a question you'd rather not face. You've struggled with it for so long. A resentment, perhaps, or a seething rebellion . . . or an ugly jealousy that keeps churning. There may be someone you haven't forgiven, despite a whole string of resolutions. Day after day, in fact week after week, you live with no sense of fulfillment, no recharge of joy, no happy expectations. You long for a deeper understanding of God's will for your life. Your heart feels empty, your soul feels weary.

Do you wonder if there is a way out? If other Christians have found the secret? Oh, yes! Assuredly YES! Let me tell you *when!* When they were *desperate* enough to trust the Holy Spirit to do what they could not do. When they were *simple* enough to trust God's promise: "I will put my Spirit within you." When they were *willing* enough to open their hearts and give it all over to God.

Do you wonder why I am so joyfully sure? *It happened to me!*

I will give you a new heart with new and right desires, and I will put a new spirit in you. I will take out your stony heart of sin and give you a new, obedient heart. Ezekiel 36:26, NLT

November 15

I Praise You

I praise You, my Lord!
I praise You for all things:
For this very moment
For future days
For the past
Often so reckless
On my part
So filled with
Foolish fantasies.
But so gracious
On Your part
So loving
And so totally forgiving.
I praise You!

I will praise you, my God and King, and bless your name forever and ever. I will bless you every day, and I will praise you forever.

Psalm 145:1-2, NLT

November 16

Wrong Center

Lord, I'm so discouraged.

Again and again I've struggled

To get hold of myself

But I simply can't do it.

Weary child

Your center is wrong.

The secret is—

Get hold of Me.

I wait quietly before God, for my salvation comes from him. He alone is my rock and my salvation, my fortress where I will never be shaken.

Psalm 62:1-2, NLT

November 17

Not Tomorrow

Lord

You have promised forgiveness

To my sincere repentance.

With all my heart

I praise You for that.

But may I never reject

The unalterable truth

That You have not promised tomorrow

To my procrastination.

A lazy person sleeps soundly—and goes hungry. Proverbs 19:15, NLT

November 18

Release

You are showing me, Lord
That when I cling to negative thoughts
Regarding the actions of my family
I thwart Your divine purpose
And turn their actions upon myself.
I am beginning to grasp
That I must *release* to You
What I too often *resent* in others.

If you forgive those who sin against you, your heavenly Father will forgive you. But if you refuse to forgive others, your Father will not forgive your sins.
Matthew 6:14-15, NLT

November 19

Unnecessary

How patiently You wait, dear God
Until having battered myself
Against the impregnable wall
Of my own selfishness and rebellion
I turn at last
Broken and bruised
Into Your wide-open arms.
It is then that I learn
That all my struggling, my panic
My foolish pretenses were unnecessary—
Had I simply fallen trustingly
Into Your waiting arms
At the very beginning.

Even youths grow tired and weary, and young men stumble and fall; but those who hope in the Lord will renew their strength. They will soar on wings like eagles; they will run and not grow weary, they will walk and not be faint.

Isaiah 40:30-31, NIV

November 20

Turnabout

God, for so long
I thought that by praying
I could change Your mind.
Often I prayed
Fervently, pleadingly
Until I felt
Emotionally pulverized.
Then I gradually began to grasp
That the purpose of prayer
Is to find *Your* mind
And let You change mine.
Little by little
The turnabout is renewing me.
Slowly I begin to feel
A settling quietness.
I wait while You woo me
To Your will, dear Lord.
I wait until my thoughts
Harmonize with Yours.
For in my deepest heart
Despite my guarded resistance
I somehow sense
That what You want for me
Is stupendously more
Than anything I could
Dream or wish or want
For myself.

Search me, O God, and know my heart; test me and know my anxious thoughts. See if there is any offensive way in me, and lead me in the way everlasting.
Psalm 139:23-24, NIV

November 21

The "Someday" Syndrome

The "Someday" Syndrome! How prevalent it has become in our "advanced" society. How thought-consuming; how time-consuming. "Someday" when we've bought a bigger house, when we've installed our swimming pool, when we've taken another trip or two . . .

"Someday" we'll be able to give more to the hungry, to the needy. But right now there are so many pressing demands, so many social events that consume both time and money. "Someday" the struggle will be less taxing.

However, it doesn't really work that way. "Someday" never seems to happen. It's only when giving becomes primary and getting becomes secondary that we begin to see things from God's point of view.

When we obey God's Word, his giving never stops. We need to be spiritually prepared to catch his gifts!

If you give, you will receive. Your gift will return to you in full measure, pressed down, shaken together to make room for more, and running over. Whatever measure you use in giving—large or small—it will be used to measure what is given back to you. Luke 6:38, NLT

November 22

Suddenly or Finally

Right now, dear God
In my bewildering day of turmoil
I call upon You
With unashamed boldness.
I come to You directly
Before seeking out family or friends.
You have promised to extricate me
According to Your infallible Word.
I offer You now my sacrifice of praise
For I know my deliverance will come.
"He is faithful that promised."
And, dear Lord, when You do deliver me
Whether it be suddenly or finally
I pledge my continual gratitude.
In fact, You'll never hear the end of it!

Let us hold unswervingly to the hope we profess, for he who promised is faithful.
Hebrews 10:23, NIV

November 23

Thanksgiving Day Dream

On this fragrant, frosty Thanksgiving Day
The huge turkey browns beautifully
In our king-size oven.
The tender yams are evenly candied;
The corn soufflé is beginning to bubble;
The congealed salad is ready to unmold.
The homemade bread with its crunchy texture
Is wrapped in foil for reheating.
The ice cubes are bagged in plastic;
The relishes are artistically arranged
On a round crystal plate.
The pumpkin pies are still slightly warm.
Fresh yellow chrysanthemums
Grace the long, colorful table.
The house glistens and shines.
My makeup is evenly applied. . . .

So, dear family
How about settling down
In our favorite chairs
For an hour of relaxation
Before our guests arrive!

Lord, I dream of this happening
Some ethereal Thanksgiving Day!

Then the King will say to those on the right, "Come, you who are blessed by my Father, inherit the Kingdom prepared for you from the foundation of the world. For I was hungry, and you fed me. I was thirsty, and you gave me a drink. I was a stranger, and you invited me into your home."

Matthew 25:34-35, NLT

November 24

Disciplined One

Today I promised myself
I wouldn't eat a bite of candy—
Not a single bite.
I kept that promise.
I promised myself
I'd walk two miles
And I walked almost three.
I kept that promise.
I promised myself
I'd clean the messy refrigerator.
I kept that promise.
I promised myself
I'd read a magazine article
About choosing priorities.
I kept that promise.
I promised myself
There would be no bedtime snack.
I cheated. I failed.
I just couldn't resist
Those crackers with the tangy
    cheese.
(At least I *didn't* resist.)
Well, four out of five promises
    kept—
That's at least better than yesterday.

O Lord
I struggle so with discipline!
Sometimes the very word
    depresses me.
Nevertheless, keep turning me
Toward the right direction.
Even though a detour from time
    to time
Doesn't mean total defeat
I do so long for the rugged
    strength
That discipline always builds.
Forcefully remind me, dear God
That unbridled behavior
Always leads to discontent.
I really want to follow You, Lord
And a disciple is a disciplined
    one!

But since we belong to the day, let us be self-controlled, putting on faith and love as a breastplate, and the hope of salvation as a helmet.

1 Thessalonians 5:8, NIV

November 25

There Are No Words

How can I put into words, my Lord
The flooding, transforming power
That sweeps my life because of You?
How can I explain to anyone
The soaring, surging peace
That You alone can give?
All the wonder-filled things in my life
All the joyful, glorious things
I owe to Your goodness, Your grace, Your love.
Nothing is ever the same since knowing You
And the longer I know You
The deeper my love.

Now, our God, we give you thanks, and praise your glorious name.
1 Chronicles 29:13, NIV

November 26

Thanksgiving Morning

Early on Thanksgiving morning
Before my family awakened
I began to form a list entitled
Reasons for Gratitude.
Then, halfway down the page
I pensively wondered—
Lord, do I give You any reasons
To be thankful for me?

Give thanks to the Lord, for he is good; his love endures forever.

Psalm 118:1, NIV

November 27

Dead Giveaway

O dear God
My heart overflows
With proclamations of joy!
You are so good
So faithful
Your loving-kindness is so great.
I long for my continual gratitude
To be a dead giveaway
Of my deepening love for You.

I will thank you, Lord, with all my heart; I will tell of all the marvelous things you have done. I will be filled with joy because of you. I will sing praises to your name, O Most High.

Psalm 9:1-2, NLT

November 28

Fiery Trials

God is teaching me incredible lessons regarding growth. I see with undeniable evidence that growth means pruning, and pruning means pain. I confess, I'm actually a coward about pain. I certainly never pray for it. I don't anticipate or look for it. I do only one thing. I ask God to steady me, since the Bible so clearly states that trials are a part of our lifewalk with him.

In all honesty I would prefer to escape the testing. I don't like the pain of emotional trauma, which can be so overwhelming and baffling. I don't like the deep cutting pain that goes on and on without relief. The pain of loneliness frightens me, the pain of losing someone dear to me grieves me.

Nevertheless, I am praying for an open heart. I can't begin to contemplate what fiery ordeals God may choose for my testing and growth, but I do long for my *yieldedness* to prove my *willingness* to be conformed to the image of his dear Son.

Dear friends, don't be surprised at the fiery trials you are going through, as if something strange were happening to you.

1 Peter 4:12, NLT

November 29

The Deliberate No

O God, teach me to say
The deliberate and releasing word *no*
Without a spiritual tug-of-war
Between variations of false guilt.
May I say it tactfully
Kindly and gently
But enable me to *say* it!
If on occasions I am forced
To confront an honest doubt
May I wait patiently
For Your clear guidance.
May this powerful truth
Penetrate the inner chambers of my being:
It is better to say a God-guided no
Than a self-guided yes.
Lord, remind me often
That a squirrel cage
Can be mighty confining.
So can a heart attack
And a hospital bed.

So now there is no condemnation for those who belong to Christ Jesus. For the power of the life-giving Spirit has freed you through Christ Jesus from the power of sin that leads to death.

Romans 8:1-2, NLT

November 30

Renewed Commitment

Forgive me, dear Lord
For too often
Letting the painful memories
Of my yesterdays
Crowd out the glad tomorrows
You graciously offer me.
I know I cannot rekindle
The charred embers
Of the past year.
I cannot erase the blunders
Made so impulsively
Nor can I regain the opportunities
That are forever lost.
I cannot retract the impetuous words
I wish I had not spoken
Or replace the shallow choices
I should not have made.
But I *can* open my wayward heart
To Your cleansing power.
With honest determination
I *can* renew my broken vows.
And I *can* begin to praise You
This very day
For the joy of beginning again.

You turned my wailing into dancing; you removed my sackcloth and clothed me with joy, that my heart may sing to you and not be silent.

Psalm 30:11-12, NIV

December

The Promise of Belonging

Home for Christmas!

Home to look with swelling gratitude into

the loving face of the Savior who came

to make his home in our hearts.

Home for Christmas because of him!

[If] you belong to Christ, you are . . . his heirs, and now all the promises God gave to him belong to you.

Galatians 3:29, NLT

December 1

The Gift

It's Christmas, Lord
It's Your birthday.
What can I give You—
You who have given
So much to me?
I search and search
Through my talents
My possessions
My friendships
My loves
But with all my searching
I find nothing new.
Strangely—
Whatever I could offer
Is always that
Which You have first
Given me.
And now in the soft silence
I hear You say
What I want from you—
Is you.

See how very much our heavenly Father loves us, for he allows us to be called his children, and we really are! 1 John 3:1, NLT

December 2

Christmas

The stable—my heart

The guiding star—Your perfect plan

The Song—"Just As I Am"

The gift—my irrevocable Yes

The joy—Your immeasurable love

The hope—the King is coming

Lord, this is my personal paraphrase

Of Christmas.

Long live the king! May the gold of Sheba be given to him.

Psalm 72:15, NLT

December 3

A Better Way

Lord, I'm utterly exhausted
From standing on tiptoe
Shouting my numerous wants.
My lips are dry
My eyes burn
My muscles ache
My nerves are tense.
I'm beginning to wonder
If it would be better
For me to relax
While You lean down
And whisper to me.

And after the earthquake there was a fire, but the Lord was not in the fire. And after the fire there was the sound of a gentle whisper. When Elijah heard it, he wrapped his face in his cloak and went out and stood at the entrance of the cave. And a voice said, "What are you doing here, Elijah?" 1 Kings 19:12-13, NLT

December 4

Forever Worthy

Dear God

I have sinned

Against Heaven

And against You.

I am no longer worthy

To be called Your child.

Child, I know . . . I know . . .

But My Son

Is forever worthy

To be called your Savior.

We had to celebrate this happy day. For your brother was dead and has come back to life! He was lost, but now he is found!

Luke 15:32, NLT

December 5

Reversal

I said: Lord, look at me
Just look at me
All of life upside down—
Tangled emotions smeared with
  fear
Guilt
Despair
Disgust
A prisoner of myself.
The hopeless thing is that
It's all decided.
I'm defenseless
At the end of my rope
Locked in
And I've tried, Lord
Tried desperately.
But how does one see without eyes
Or walk without feet?
How, Lord?

You said: Come unto Me.
You need not cringe
Nor climb
Nor compete
Nor change
Come even without feeling
Without tokens
Without merit or hope

But come.
Come now.
I came
And all of life
Turned right side up.

In my anguish I cried to the Lord, and he answered by setting me free.
Psalm 118:5, NIV

December 6

The Time Is Now

Lord

I see with startling clarity

That life is never long enough

To put You off

Until tomorrow.

The things that are before

Are all too soon behind.

I can never pick up

The years I've put down.

If I intend

To walk with You tomorrow

I must start today.

Another said, "Yes, Lord, I will follow you, but first let me say good-bye to my family." But Jesus told him, "Anyone who puts a hand to the plow and then looks back is not fit for the Kingdom of God."

Luke 9:61-62, NLT

December 7

The Man God Honors

There are thousands of men in the world. Men come in assorted sizes—tall and short, wide and lean. There are bankers, salesmen, politicians, mechanics, lawyers, teachers. But the man God honors is marked by at least five characteristics:

FIRST: He is a man totally committed to God, and his concern is that he will obey God's Word, whatever the cost.

SECOND: He is a man whose faith can be defined as confident trust. His high priority is prayer, knowing that a supernatural God works in supernatural ways.

THIRD: He rests his past, present, and future in the hands of an all-loving God, even in times of turbulence, uncertainty, agony, misunderstanding, and pain, assured that his times are in God's hands.

FOURTH: He believes with all his heart that, as he keeps steadily traveling along God's pathway, God will honor him with every blessing.

FIFTH: He has one consistent desire: "God, make me a man after your own heart."

Oh, the joys of those who do not follow the advice of the wicked, or stand around with sinners, or join in with scoffers. But they delight in doing everything the Lord wants; day and night they think about his law.

Psalm 1:1-2, NLT

December 8

Now

Lord
I don't ask You to renovate me
Nor do I ask You to reconstruct me
Or make me over.
I don't even ask You to patch me up
Or pare out the bruised spots
Or gloss over the tin and tarnish.
Rather, dear Lord, I ask You
To make a new species—
Something that never before existed.
Impart to me Your very own Life.
After all, Lord
It is such a simple thing for You
To create something beautiful
From a shapeless, chaotic mass.
It is such a simple thing for You
To divide light from darkness.
Please do it for me—now.

Child of My Infinite Plan
Two thousand years ago
All you have asked I did.
Please accept it from Me—now.

Therefore, if anyone is in Christ, he is a new creation; the old has gone, the new has come! 2 Corinthians 5:17, NIV

December 9

Gift Exchange

Dear God

This Christmas

I want to give You me.

I come just as I am

Unboxed

Unribboned

Without glitter

Or glamour.

On the name tag of my heart

I've written

"To God with love."

Do with me exactly as you choose.

Dear child

I choose to give you Me.

To him who loves us and has freed us from our sins by his blood, and has made us to be a kingdom and priests to serve his God and Father—to him be glory and power for ever and ever! Amen.

Revelation 1:5-6, NIV

December 10

I Will Be Pleased

Lord, this fresh early morning
As I sit in our quiet living room
You've just reminded me
Through David the Psalmist
That there is incomparable joy
For those who delight to please You—
For those who are thinking about ways
To follow You more closely.
Lord, the day stretches out before me.
In a few brief moments I must arouse my family
And face again the noise, the distraction
The hubbub of confusion.
But while we are still alone
Just the two of us, my Lord
While Your peace floods my tranquil heart
Please tell me what I can do
This duty-packed day
To follow You more closely.

Dearly loved child
Praise me joyfully
Talk with me intimately
Trust me totally
And I will be pleased.

Blessed are those who have learned to acclaim you, who walk in the light of your presence, O Lord. Psalm 89:15, NIV

December 11

An Echo

God, may I never be content

To be but the echo

Of my environment.

Empower me day by day

To be the echo

Of Your amazing love

In my God-guarded life!

But thanks be to God, who made us his captives and leads us along in Christ's triumphal procession. Now wherever we go he uses us to tell others about the Lord and to spread the Good News like a sweet perfume.

2 Corinthians 2:14, NLT

December 12

You Cannot Be Hid

Lord, I've discovered it's never a secret
When You live in a home
For You simply cannot be hid.
The neighbors soon know You are there
Even strangers learn of Your presence.
When You are the Great First in a home
There is a radiance that speaks of joy
There is gentleness, kindness
Laughter and love.
There is commotion mixed with contentment
There are problems mixed with prayer.
Lord, Your own Word says it so vividly:
"It was known that He was in the house."

You are the light of the world—like a city on a mountain, glowing in the night for all to see. Don't hide your light under a basket! Instead, put it on a stand and let it shine for all. Matthew 5:14-15, NLT

December 13

Book of All Books

Lord, I am overwhelmed
As I read Your living Word.
What power, what pungency
I find within its pages.
It stirs me, burns within me
It challenges me, invigorates me
And often disturbs me.
When I obey its commands
The results are what You claim:
Darkness becomes light
Crooked places become straight
The more I seek, the more I find.
Within its pages, God
I see beyond mere philosophy
I see beyond a neat package of ethics.
I crash head-on with a living Person
The One who makes all things new.
No other book can claim as much.

The word of God is living and active. Sharper than any two-edged sword, it penetrates even to dividing soul and spirit, joints and marrow; it judges the thoughts and attitudes of the heart.

Hebrews 4:12, NIV

December 14

Haunted House

When I opened the door to my young friend, I knew she had been crying. She carried a small suitcase, and before I could invite her in she said, "I'm coming to live with you."

As we sat at the kitchen table drinking hot chocolate, she repeated the story of her dysfunctional home. She had shared it often before. I ached for her, yet I felt so helpless. After an hour I said, "Now I must call your mother. She'll be worried about you. I'm sure she wants you to come home."

Again the tears and stumbling words: "I don't live in a home. I live in a haunted house."

My friend is an adult now, making her way in the world as best she can. But I never think of her without remembering that throughout our vast nation there are countless families who live in "haunted houses." Houses haunted by bitterness, rebellion, alcohol, and drugs . . . haunted by disgraceful abuse and neglect.

There is *no* substitute for an authentic home. A home where character and values and love and laughter add joy to living. A home where God is invited to live. God longs to empower us to remake what we have allowed the adversary to break!

Choose today whom you will serve. . . . As for me and my family, we will serve the Lord.
Joshua 24:15, NLT

December 15

The Most—The Least

Lord, when I feel exuberant
Bursting with energy and strength
When everything in my life
Seems to be going amazingly well
Then, dear God
I think I can accomplish anything for You.
In fact, *everything*.
I'm ready to go for it!
But when pain and depression grab me
And trials clobber me unmercifully
When I am hurt by criticism
Or neglected by my family
Or burdened with numerous demands
Then I am convinced
I can serve You in no way at all.

Often, dear child
When you think
You are doing the most
You are serving the least.
And when you think
You are doing the least
As you rest in my love
You are serving Me best.

"Why are you crying?" Jesus asked her. "Who are you looking for?" She thought he was the gardener. "Sir," she said, "if you have taken him away, tell me where you have put him, and I will go and get him." "Mary!" Jesus said. She turned toward him and exclaimed, "Teacher!"

John 20:15-16, NLT

December 16

I Cannot Imagine

God of my pensive heart

I cannot imagine

A day without the dawn

Or the sky without a star

Or a bird without a song

Or my life without You.

For to me, to live is Christ and to die is gain. Philippians 1:21, NIV

December 17

Slow Growth

In my fretful impatience
I am so often inclined to ask
"Why can't she change?"
"Why is he always so slow?"
"Will they ever learn from past mistakes?"
And then You begin to impress me
With my own slow progress upward.
I see Your stretched-out patience.
I remember how long You've waited for me.
And I grieve that my attitude
Is so often intolerant.
O God, keep fresh the imprint
Of my own need to grow
And make me more flexible
More understanding
And always more loving.

Be kind and compassionate to one another, forgiving each other, just as in Christ God forgave you. Ephesians 4:32, NIV

December 18

In the End

God, it is not always easy
To know and do Your will.
But of this I am wholly convinced:
In the end, nothing else matters.

He went on a little farther and fell face down on the ground, praying, "My Father! If it is possible, let this cup of suffering be taken away from me. Yet I want your will, not mine." Matthew 26:39, NLT

December 19

You Show Yourself Strong

Dear Lord, Your Word says
Your eyes search back and forth
Across the whole earth
To show Yourself strong
On behalf of those
Whose hearts are in harmony with Yours.
As You search back and forth
At six o'clock each morning, dear God,
I know You see me
As I reluctantly crawl
From under the soft blankets
And stumble in the dark
Toward my living room trysting place.
It isn't easy to cater
To the clanging alarm
Especially on cold winter mornings
When my will is so weak
And the bed feels so warm.
But after an hour of meditation and prayer
You miraculously renew me
And my spirit is wonderfully restored.
Thank You for showing Yourself strong
On my behalf, dear Lord
As I sit in my brown chair
Reading Your Word and
Hearing Your voice
At six o'clock in the morning.

For the eyes of the Lord range throughout the earth to strengthen those whose hearts are fully committed to him. 2 Chronicles 16:9, NIV

December 20

Christmas Gratitude

Lord
As I stand at the kitchen sink
Mixing batter for Christmas
cookies
The scent of spicy pine
Permeates our house.
Already everyone is rushing in our
town!
I remember that it started years
ago
When the startled shepherds
Came with haste
To find the newborn Baby.

Dear God
As I bake enormous batches of
cookies
This beautiful Christmas season
I pray for sufficient strength
To go with haste
To the frightened and lonely
To the worn and weary
To those without courage and
hope.
Lord, may each batch of cookies
Be mixed with love—
Not just mine, but Yours!

Right now, dear God
With flour smudging my face
And dough clinging to my fingers
I praise You with all my heart
For loving us enough
To give the very best—
The gift of Your only begotten
Son.

They ran to the village and found Mary and Joseph. And there was the baby, lying in the manger. Then the shepherds told everyone what had happened and what the angel had said to them about this child.

Luke 2:16-17, NLT

December 21

The Wonder of It All!

It happened at a popular department store several years ago. The store was charged with excitement. Parents and children rushed madly, pushing into elevators and slow-moving escalators. At noon Santa was coming to the store in a helicopter!

The huge clock on the main floor moved slowly. Eleven-thirty . . . eleven-forty-five . . . then five minutes to twelve. Milling crowds pushed through the doors to get to the parking lot. Hundreds of excited eyes looked skyward. Santa was on time! The joy was almost too great to bear.

Suddenly above the excitement the high-pitched voice of one little boy was heard: "Mommy, Mommy, look! Santa is waving, and he's waving to *me!*" For one little boy, Santa's wave was personal.

That's the wonder of it all! Not because we have a Santa-God, but because we have a personal God who literally stepped from eternity to take on humanity. Over against the world's darkness there is Jesus Christ, the Son of God! In every village, every city, and every faraway country, the cry of triumph can be "He came for *me!* He died for *me!* He rose for *me!*"

That's the glory of Christmas!

God so loved the world that he gave his only Son, so that everyone who believes in him will not perish but have eternal life.

John 3:16, NLT

December 22

Memories

Dear God
How I thank You
For thousands of beautiful memories
That have become a growing history
Of Your supreme goodness in my life.
Thank You for many memories
Flaming memories, trailing memories.
Thank You for throbbing memories
Quiet, gentle memories
Pink-tinted memories
That live on and on
To gladden somber days.
Thank You for memories that have rooted me
Stabilized me, sensitized me
And toughened the inner fiber of my being.
In Your honor, dear God
I erect my *Monument of Memories.*
For Your glory . . . You who are
My "living bright Reality."

I remember the days of long ago; I meditate on all your works and consider what your hands have done. I spread out my hands to you; my soul thirsts for you like a parched land. Psalm 143:5-6, NIV

December 23

Explanation

Just this week
I read a newspaper account
Of a thirteen-year-old boy
Who saved his brother's life
By driving him to a hospital
In his father's car.
Never having driven before
His explanation was simple:
"I just did what I saw my father do."

O dear God
Please empower me to bring life
To a sick, wounded world
With the simple explanation:
"I do what my Father does."

The world must learn that I love the Father and that I do exactly what my Father has commanded me.
John 14:31, NIV

December 24

The Gift

Lord

The shopping is finished

The gifts, beautifully wrapped

Are placed with gentleness

Under our smiling tree.

We chose carefully, Lord

Just the right gifts

For those who are so dear to us.

Today I am suddenly aware

That long years ago

In the fullness of time

You sent the Gift of Your Son

Because we are so dear to You!

O God, thank You!

But when the right time came, God sent his Son, born of a woman, subject to the law. God sent him to buy freedom for us who were slaves to the law, so that he could adopt us as his very own children.

Galatians 4:4-5, NLT

December 25

It's Christmas

It's Christmas!

Sing!
Rejoice!
Celebrate!

Let God create in you
Colorful explosions
Of joy and excitement.
Smile away fears, push away tears.
Out with pretense, in with praise.

It's Christmas!

Open your heart to light
To trust, to love, to hope.
Awaken slumbering memories
Stir up stupendous dreams
Anticipate surprises
Open your arms wide.

It's Christmas!

Time for candles and cards
For carols and cookies
For brightly lit trees
With the fragrance of pine.
Time to hug and hold
To think and thank
Time to greet the world
With the Good News.

It's Christmas!

Thank God for life
Thank Him for the manger
For the splintered cross
For the empty tomb.
Thank Him for His only Son
The Savior of the world.

Shout!
Laugh!
Share!
Care!

And say to God
On Christmas morning:
"I entrust myself anew
To You."

The Word became flesh and made his dwelling among us. We have seen his glory, the glory of the one and only Son, who came from the Father, full of grace and truth. John 1:14, NIV

December 26

The Song I Sing

O dear God
Make me a woman of concern
And deep, deep compassion.
There is so much loneliness
So much despair and neglect
So much pain and disappointment
In the world today.
I see it all around me, Lord.
In my block, my church
In the homes of families and friends.
Make me achingly aware.
Let me care, let me share.
Lord, may I be at least one chord
Of beautiful music
In the heart of a mother
Or a father or a precious child
Where the longing for harmony
Lies so deeply hidden.
Above all, my Lord
Channel through me
Your matchless love
For You are the Song I joyfully sing.

For God, who said, "Let there be light in the darkness," has made us understand that this light is the brightness of the glory of God that is seen in the face of Jesus Christ. But this precious treasure—this light and power that now shine within us—is held in perishable containers, that is, in our weak bodies. So everyone can see that our glorious power is from God and is not our own. 2 Corinthians 4:6-7, NLT

December 27

The Promise (2 Samuel 22:29, TLB)

And the Lord will lighten my darkness . . .

O Lord, how I needed to read this promise
In Your Word this very day.
You will lighten my darkness.
You will *personally* do it.
I cannot, nor can my family.
My friends cannot
Nor can the one dearest to me.
You alone can lighten my darkness.
Though it is pitch black
Though clouds pile heavy and high
Though thunder roars
Though I see only confusion
You will lighten my darkness.
My hope is in You.
I look for You. I wait for You.
Nothing will prevent it.
You will lighten my darkness.

For you are the fountain of life, the light by which we see.

Psalm 36:9, NLT

December 28

Five Days of Journaling

SUNDAY

Lord, today I wish I were a cheerleader running and waving colorful pom-poms in tribute to your majesty. All of nature exalts you—from the newest blade of grass to the tallest mountain peak. And I? I lift my heart in praise for the wonder of it all.

MONDAY

Today, Lord, I asked how I could know if my surrender was complete. You said so quickly, "How is it *now,* this moment? Settle it each moment, and you won't need to ask."

TUESDAY

This afternoon at the sunny beach I sent a thousand thoughts tumbling into the crashing breakers. I heard you say, "My boundless love surrounds you. . . ."

WEDNESDAY

When I was washing windows today I was thinking how variable my life is . . . high moments and low moments. Deep joy, and then when I least expect it, a crushing blow. It happens often in my life. God, do you want to explain it or must I just keep on—you know—TRUSTING?

THURSDAY

God, you know more about my needs than I do. You know my hopes, my longings, my dreams. Even when you seem to be silent, surely it must mean that you are always in pursuit of solutions not yet apparent.

Give thanks to the Lord and proclaim his greatness. Let the whole world know what he has done. Sing to him; yes, sing his praises. Tell everyone about his miracles. Psalm 105:1-2, NLT

December 29

I Promise You

My Father
How You will send Your help
I don't know.
But as certain as You are Love
Your help will come!
As surely as You keep Your word
You will supply my need.
I don't know what to do
But my eyes are on You.
You have said
"I promise you."

As we know Jesus better, his divine power gives us everything we need for living a godly life. He has called us to receive his own glory and goodness! And by that same mighty power, he has given us all of his rich and wonderful promises. 2 Peter 1:3-4, NLT

December 30

Listen Trustingly

Lord, I'm listening.

Why don't I hear You?

Fretful child

You listen

Strenuously

Anxiously

Laboriously.

Rest in Me

And listen

Trustingly.

I am talking

All the time.

But the Counselor, the Holy Spirit, whom the Father will send in my name, will teach you all things and will remind you of everything I have said to you. Peace I leave with you; my peace I give you. I do not give to you as the world gives. Do not let your hearts be troubled and do not be afraid.

John 14:26-27, NIV

December 31

Day of Rejoicing

Lord, all day long
We've been laughing and singing.
We've been shouting and praising.
After weeks and months
Of waiting and pleading
You have wonderfully answered our prayers.
Our hearts are filled with unspeakable joy.
You promised that those
Who sow in tears
Shall reap in joy.
It is happening, dear Lord
To us . . . to *us!*

Those who sow in tears will reap with songs of joy. He who goes out weeping, carrying seed to sow, will return with songs of joy, carrying sheaves with him.
Psalm 126:5-6, NIV

The One Year Book
OF
Bible Readings

THE ONE YEAR®

book of

Bible Readings

TYNDALE HOUSE PUBLISHERS, INC.
WHEATON, ILLINOIS

Visit Tyndale's exciting Web site at www.tyndale.com

The readings in *The One Year Book of Bible Readings* are taken from *In Touch,* a compilation created by Edythe Draper.

Notes are taken from the *Life Application Bible. Life Application* is a registered trademark of Tyndale House Publishers, Inc.

ISBN 0-8423-5387-9

Printed in China

05 04 03
6 5 4 3

Publisher's Note

The One Year Book of Bible Readings has been prepared to help you in the discipline of daily devotional Bible reading. Each day's reading is a short compilation of several topically related Scriptures. The passages included are referenced at the bottom of each page so that favorite verses can be easily located in your Bible.

Each day's reading is introduced by a special thought that speaks to pressing needs and concerns that everyone has experienced. This thought is followed by Scripture passages that speak to these issues, bringing God's perspective and power into the problems, fears, and joys of everyday life. And each reading includes a powerful application note taken from the *Life Application Bible.*

This book will help you get in touch with God, who is able to solve even the deepest of problems. Each reading is filled with the hope, comfort, and wisdom that God offers to all who are willing to look to him for guidance and help. May this year and every year be enriched as you enjoy these daily portions from God's holy Word.

And now, just as you accepted Christ Jesus as your Lord, you must continue to live in obedience to him. Let your roots grow down into him and draw up nourishment from him, so you will grow in faith, strong and vigorous in the truth you were taught. Let your lives overflow with thanksgiving for all he has done.

Colossians 2:6-7

January

All Things New

Another year of promise and of blessings
A year of uncertainties and of unknowns
A year for seeking God's heart

Whether you are looking forward to the excitement and possibilities of a new job, relationship, discovery, or any other new event, God desires to share each step of the way with you. Take his hand, and begin a new year full of God's abundant life!

January 1

Do not be afraid or discouraged, for the LORD is the one who goes before you. He will be with you; he will neither fail you nor forsake you.

I know, LORD, that a person's life is not his own. No one is able to plan his own course. ❖ If you don't go with us personally, don't let us move a step from this place.

The steps of the godly are directed by the LORD. He delights in every detail of their lives. Though they stumble, they will not fall, for the LORD holds them by the hand.

Yet I still belong to you; you are holding my right hand. You will keep on guiding me with your counsel, leading me to a glorious destiny. ❖ And I am convinced that nothing can ever separate us from his love. Death can't, and life can't. The angels can't, and the demons can't. Our fears for today, our worries about tomorrow, and even the powers of hell can't keep God's love away. Whether we are high above the sky or in the deepest ocean, nothing in all creation will ever be able to separate us from the love of God that is revealed in Christ Jesus our Lord.

The person in whom God delights is one who follows God, trusts him, and tries to do his will. God watches over and makes firm every step that person takes. If you would like to have God direct your way, then seek his advice before you step out. *LAB note for Psalm 37:23-24*

(DEUTERONOMY 31:8) (JEREMIAH 10:23) (EXODUS 33:15) (PSALM 37:23-24) (PSALM 73:23-24) (ROMANS 8:38-39)

January 2

Sing a new song to the LORD! Sing his praises from the ends of the earth!

Sing praises to God, our strength. Sing to the God of Israel. Sing! Beat the tambourine. Play the sweet lyre and harp. ▪ He has given me a new song to sing, a hymn of praise to our God. Many will see what he has done and be astounded. They will put their trust in the LORD.

I command you—be strong and courageous! Do not be afraid or discouraged. For the LORD your God is with you wherever you go. ▪ The joy of the LORD is your strength! ▪ Paul . . . thanked God and took courage.

The night is almost gone; the day of salvation will soon be here. So don't live in darkness. Get rid of your evil deeds. Shed them like dirty clothes. Clothe yourselves with the armor of right living, as those who live in the light. We should be decent and true in everything we do, so that everyone can approve of our behavior. Don't participate in wild parties and getting drunk, or in adultery and immoral living, or in fighting and jealousy. But let the Lord Jesus Christ take control of you, and don't think of ways to indulge your evil desires.

Look at all the Lord will do for us and through us! Majestic works prompt majestic responses. Do you really appreciate the good things that God does for you and through you? If so, let your praise to him reflect how you really feel. *LAB note for Isaiah 42:10*

(ISAIAH 42:10) (PSALM 81:1-2) (PSALM 40:3) (JOSHUA 1:9) (NEHEMIAH 8:10) (ACTS 28:15) (ROMANS 13:12-14)

January 3

I will not fail you or abandon you.

All of the good promises that the LORD had given Israel came true.

God is not a man, that he should lie. He is not a human, that he should change his mind. Has he ever spoken and failed to act? Has he ever promised and not carried it through?

Understand, therefore, that the LORD your God is indeed God. He is the faithful God who keeps his covenant for a thousand generations and constantly loves those who love him and obey his commands. ◆ He always remembers his covenant. ◆ So don't worry about tomorrow, for tomorrow will bring its own worries. Today's trouble is enough for today.

Can a mother forget her nursing child? Can she feel no love for a child she has borne? But even if that were possible, I would not forget you! See, I have written your name on my hand.

The LORD your God has arrived to live among you. He is a mighty savior. He will rejoice over you with great gladness. With his love, he will calm all your fears. He will exult over you by singing a happy song.

The more we learn of the promises God has fulfilled and continues to fulfill, the easier it is to hope for those yet to come. Sometimes we become impatient, wanting God to act in a certain way now. Instead, we should faithfully do what we know he wants us to do and trust him for the future. *LAB note for Joshua 21:43-45*

(JOSHUA 1:5) (JOSHUA 21:45) (NUMBERS 23:19) (DEUTERONOMY 7:9) (PSALM 111:5) (MATTHEW 6:34) (ISAIAH 49:15-16) (ZEPHANIAH 3:17)

January 4

You will keep in perfect peace all who trust in you, whose thoughts are fixed on you!

Give your burdens to the LORD, and he will take care of you. He will not permit the godly to slip and fall. ▪ I will trust in him and not be afraid. The LORD God is my strength and my song; he has become my salvation.

Why are you afraid? You have so little faith! ▪ Don't worry about anything; instead, pray about everything. Tell God what you need, and thank him for all he has done. If you do this, you will experience God's peace, which is far more wonderful than the human mind can understand. His peace will guard your hearts and minds as you live in Christ Jesus. ▪ In quietness and confidence is your strength.

Righteousness will bring peace. Quietness and confidence will fill the land forever. ▪ I am leaving you with a gift—peace of mind and heart. And the peace I give isn't like the peace the world gives. So don't be troubled or afraid. ▪ Grace and peace from the one who is, who always was, and who is still to come.

We can never avoid strife in the world around us, but when we fix our thoughts on God, we can know perfect peace even in turmoil. As we focus our mind on God and his Word, we become steady and stable. Supported by God's unchanging love and mighty power, we are not shaken by the surrounding chaos. *LAB note for Isaiah 26:3*

(ISAIAH 26:3) (PSALM 55:22) (ISAIAH 12:2) (MATTHEW 8:26) (PHILIPPIANS 4:6-7) (ISAIAH 30:15) (ISAIAH 32:17) (JOHN 14:27) (REVELATION 1:4)

January 5

Jesus asked the man, "What do you want me to do for you?" "Lord," he pleaded, "I want to see!"

Open my eyes to see the wonderful truths in your law.

Then he opened their minds to understand these many Scriptures. ▪ When the Father sends the Counselor as my representative—and by the Counselor I mean the Holy Spirit—he will teach you everything and will remind you of everything I myself have told you. ▪ Whatever is good and perfect comes to us from God above, who created all heaven's lights. Unlike them, he never changes or casts shifting shadows.

God, the glorious Father of our Lord Jesus Christ . . . give you spiritual wisdom and understanding, so that you might grow in your knowledge of God. I pray that your hearts will be flooded with light so that you can understand the wonderful future he has promised to those he called. I want you to realize what a rich and glorious inheritance he has given to his people. I pray that you will begin to understand the incredible greatness of his power for us who believe him. This is the same mighty power that raised Christ from the dead and seated him in the place of honor at God's right hand in the heavenly realms.

Most of us chafe under rules, for we think they restrict us from doing what we want. But God's laws were given to free us to be all he wants us to be. They help us follow his path and avoid paths that lead to destruction. *LAB note for Psalm 119:12-24*

(LUKE 18:41) (PSALM 119:18) (LUKE 24:45) (JOHN 14:26) (JAMES 1:17) (EPHESIANS 1:17-20)

January 6

Take control of what I say, O LORD, and keep my lips sealed.

LORD, if you kept a record of our sins, who, O Lord, could ever survive?

You are not defiled by what you eat; you are defiled by what you say and do.

Gossip separates the best of friends. ▪ Some people make cutting remarks, but the words of the wise bring healing. Truth stands the test of time; lies are soon exposed. ▪ No one can tame the tongue. It is an uncontrollable evil, full of deadly poison. Blessing and cursing come pouring out of the same mouth. Surely, my brothers and sisters, this is not right!

Now is the time to get rid of anger, rage, malicious behavior, slander, and dirty language. Don't lie to each other, for you have stripped off your old evil nature and all its wicked deeds. ▪ God wants you to be holy.

Gentle words bring life and health.

Even though we may not achieve perfect control of our tongues, the Holy Spirit will help us learn self-control, giving us increasing power to monitor and control what we say. Then when we are criticized, the Spirit will heal the hurt and help us not to lash out. *LAB note for James 3:8*

(PSALM 141:3) (PSALM 130:3) (MATTHEW 15:11) (PROVERBS 16:28)
(PROVERBS 12:18-19) (JAMES 3:8, 10) (COLOSSIANS 3:8-9)
(1 THESSALONIANS 4:3) (PROVERBS 15:4)

January 7

You have raised a banner for those who honor you—a rallying point in the face of attack.

The LORD Is My Banner. ■ They will respect and glorify the name of the LORD throughout the world. For he will come like a flood tide driven by the breath of the LORD.

May we shout for joy when we hear of your victory, flying banners to honor our God. May the LORD answer all your prayers. ■ The LORD has vindicated us. Come, let us announce in Jerusalem everything the LORD our God has done. ■ Overwhelming victory is ours through Christ, who loved us. ■ How we thank God, who gives us victory over sin and death through Jesus Christ our Lord! ■ Jesus . . . a perfect leader.

Be strong with the Lord's mighty power. ■ Prove yourself to be a real warrior by fighting the LORD's battles. ■ Take courage and work, for I am with you, says the LORD Almighty. . . . Do not be afraid. ■ Look around you! Vast fields are ripening all around us and are ready now for the harvest.

In the Christian life we battle against rulers and authorities. To withstand their attacks, we must depend on God's strength and use every piece of his armor. As you do battle against the "mighty powers of darkness," ask for the Holy Spirit's help in the fight.

LAB note for Ephesians 6:10-17

(PSALM 60:4) (EXODUS 17:15) (ISAIAH 59:19) (PSALM 20:5) (JEREMIAH 51:10) (ROMANS 8:37) (1 CORINTHIANS 15:57) (HEBREWS 2:10) (EPHESIANS 6:10) (1 SAMUEL 18:17) (HAGGAI 2:4-5) (JOHN 4:35)

January 8

There is really only one thing worth being concerned about.

Many people say, "Who will show us better times?" Let the smile of your face shine on us, LORD. You have given me greater joy than those who have abundant harvests of grain and wine.

As the deer pants for streams of water, so I long for you, O God. I thirst for God, the living God. ▪ O God, you are my God; I earnestly search for you. My soul thirsts for you; my whole body longs for you in this parched and weary land where there is no water.

"I am the bread of life. No one who comes to me will ever be hungry again. Those who believe in me will never thirst." "Sir . . . give us that bread every day of our lives." ▪ Mary . . . sat at the Lord's feet, listening to what he taught. ▪ The one thing I ask of the LORD—the thing I seek most—is to live in the house of the LORD all the days of my life, delighting in the LORD's perfections and meditating in his Temple. ▪ Surely your goodness and unfailing love will pursue me all the days of my life, and I will live in the house of the LORD forever.

As the life of a deer depends upon water, so our lives depend upon God. Those who seek him and long to understand him find eternal life. When you feel separated from God, you shouldn't rest until you have restored your relationship with God. Your very life depends on it.

LAB note for Psalm 42:1-2

(LUKE 10:42) (PSALM 4:6-7) (PSALM 42:1-2) (PSALM 63:1) (JOHN 6:35, 34) (LUKE 10:39) (PSALM 27:4) (PSALM 23:6)

January 9

Oh, that you would burst from the heavens and come down!

Come quickly, my love! Move like a swift gazelle or a young deer on the mountains of spices. ▪ Even we Christians, although we have the Holy Spirit within us as a foretaste of future glory, also groan to be released from pain and suffering. We, too, wait anxiously for that day when God will give us our full rights as his children, including the new bodies he has promised us. ▪ Bend down the heavens, LORD, and come down. Touch the mountains so they billow smoke.

Jesus has been taken away from you into heaven. And someday . . . he will return. ▪ He will come again but not to deal with our sins again. This time he will bring salvation to all those who are eagerly waiting for him. ▪ In that day the people will proclaim, "This is our God. We trusted in him, and he saved us. This is the LORD, in whom we trusted. Let us rejoice in the salvation he brings!"

He who is the faithful witness to all these things says, "Yes, I am coming soon!" Amen! Come, Lord Jesus! ▪ We look forward to that wonderful event when the glory of our great God and Savior, Jesus Christ, will be revealed. ▪ We are citizens of heaven, where the Lord Jesus Christ lives.

Because Christ died and rescued us from sin, we are free from sin's control. God gives us the power and understanding to live according to his will and do good. Then we will look forward to Christ's wonderful return with eager expectation and hope. *LAB note for Titus 2:11-14*

(ISAIAH 64:1) (SONG OF SONGS 8:14) (ROMANS 8:23) (PSALM 144:5) (ACTS 1:11) (HEBREWS 9:28) (ISAIAH 25:9) (REVELATION 22:20) (TITUS 2:13) (PHILIPPIANS 3:20)

January 10

Don't sin by letting anger gain control over you.

"If another believer sins against you, go privately and point out the fault. If the other person listens and confesses it, you have won that person back." "Lord, how often should I forgive someone who sins against me? Seven times?" "No!" Jesus replied, "seventy times seven!"

When you are praying, first forgive anyone you are holding a grudge against, so that your Father in heaven will forgive your sins, too.

Since God chose you to be the holy people whom he loves, you must clothe yourselves with tenderhearted mercy, kindness, humility, gentleness, and patience. You must make allowance for each other's faults and forgive the person who offends you. Remember, the Lord forgave you, so you must forgive others. Be kind to each other, tenderhearted, forgiving one another, just as God through Christ has forgiven you.

The key to forgiving others is remembering how much God has forgiven you. Is it difficult for you to forgive someone who has wronged you a little when God has forgiven you so much? Realizing God's infinite love and forgiveness can help you love and forgive others.

LAB note for Colossians 3:13

(Ephesians 4:26) (Matthew 18:15, 21-22) (Mark 11:25)
(Colossians 3:12-13) (Ephesians 4:32)

January 11

I lie in the dust, completely discouraged; revive me by your word.

Since you have been raised to new life with Christ, set your sights on the realities of heaven, where Christ sits at God's right hand in the place of honor and power. Let heaven fill your thoughts. Do not think only about things down here on earth. For you died when Christ died, and your real life is hidden with Christ in God. ▪ We are citizens of heaven, where the Lord Jesus Christ lives. And we are eagerly waiting for him to return as our Savior. He will take these weak mortal bodies of ours and change them into glorious bodies like his own, using the same mighty power that he will use to conquer everything, everywhere.

The old sinful nature loves to do evil, which is just opposite from what the Holy Spirit wants. ▪ Dear brothers and sisters, you have no obligation whatsoever to do what your sinful nature urges you to do. For if you keep on following it, you will perish. But if through the power of the Holy Spirit you turn from it and its evil deeds, you will live. ▪ You are foreigners and aliens here. So I warn you to keep away from evil desires because they fight against your very souls.

Setting your sights on heaven means striving to put heaven's priorities into daily practice. Letting heaven fill our thoughts means concentrating on the eternal rather than the temporal.

LAB note for Colossians 3:1–2

(PSALM 119:25) (COLOSSIANS 3:1–3) (PHILIPPIANS 3:20–21) (GALATIANS 5:17) (ROMANS 8:12–13) (1 PETER 2:11)

January 12

Be honest in your estimate of yourselves, measuring your value by how much faith God has given you.

[He is] weak in faith. ▪ His faith grew stronger, and in this he brought glory to God.

"You don't have much faith," Jesus said. "Why did you doubt me?" ▪ Your faith is great. Your request is granted.

"Do you believe I can make you see?" "Yes, Lord," they told him, "we do." "Because of your faith, it will happen."

We need more faith. ▪ Continue to build your lives on the foundation of your holy faith. ▪ Let your roots grow down into him and draw up nourishment from him, so you will grow in faith, strong and vigorous in the truth you were taught. ▪ It is God who gives us, along with you, the ability to stand firm for Christ. ▪ After you have suffered a little while, he will restore, support, and strengthen you, and he will place you on a firm foundation.

We must be considerate of the doubts and fears of [others]. . . . We should please others. ▪ Don't condemn each other anymore. Decide instead to live in such a way that you will not put an obstacle in another Christian's path.

Although we start out with good intentions, sometimes our faith falters. But we can be afraid and still look to Christ. When you are apprehensive about the troubles around you and doubt Christ's presence or ability to help, remember that he is always with you and is the only one who can really help. *LAB note for Matthew 14:30-31*

(ROMANS 12:3) (ROMANS 14:1) (ROMANS 4:20) (MATTHEW 14:31) (MATTHEW 15:28) (MATTHEW 9:28-29) (LUKE 17:5) (JUDE 20) (COLOSSIANS 2:7) (2 CORINTHIANS 1:21) (1 PETER 5:10) (ROMANS 15:1) (ROMANS 14:13)

January 13

You have rescued me from death and have forgiven all my sins.

God showed how much he loved us by sending his only Son into the world so that we might have eternal life through him. This is real love. It is not that we loved God, but that he loved us and sent his Son as a sacrifice to take away our sins.

Where is another God like you, who pardons the sins of the survivors among his people? You cannot stay angry with your people forever, because you delight in showing mercy. Once again you will have compassion on us. You will trample our sins under your feet and throw them into the depths of the ocean! ▪ O LORD my God, I cried out to you for help, and you restored my health. You brought me up from the grave, O LORD. You kept me from falling into the pit of death. ▪ When I had lost all hope, I turned my thoughts once more to the LORD. And my earnest prayer went out to you in your holy Temple. ▪ I waited patiently for the LORD to help me, and he turned to me and heard my cry. He lifted me out of the pit of despair, out of the mud and the mire. He set my feet on solid ground and steadied me as I walked along.

God delights to show mercy! He does not forgive grudgingly but is glad when we repent, and he offers forgiveness to all who come back to him. Today you can confess your sins and receive his loving forgiveness.

LAB note for Micah 7:18

(ISAIAH 38:17) (1 JOHN 4:9-10) (MICAH 7:18-19) (PSALM 30:2-3) (JONAH 2:7) (PSALM 40:1-2)

*J*anuary 14

All that I know now is partial and incomplete.

Now we see things imperfectly as in a poor mirror, but then we will see everything with perfect clarity. . . . Then I will know everything completely, just as God knows me now.

We have even greater confidence in the message proclaimed by the prophets. Pay close attention to what they wrote, for their words are like a light shining in a dark place—until the day Christ appears and his brilliant light shines in your hearts. ▪ Your word is a lamp for my feet and a light for my path.

You, my dear friends, must remember what the apostles of our Lord Jesus Christ told you, that in the last times there would be scoffers. ▪ The Holy Spirit tells us clearly that in the last times some will turn away from what we believe; they will follow lying spirits and teachings that come from demons.

Dear children, the last hour is here. ▪ The night is almost gone; the day of salvation will soon be here. . . . Clothe yourselves with the armor of right living, as those who live in the light.

We have the hope that one day we will be complete when we see God face-to-face. This truth should strengthen our faith. We don't have all the answers now, but one day we will. Someday we will meet Christ in person and be able to see with God's perspective.

LAB note for 1 Corinthians 13:12

(1 CORINTHIANS 13:12) (1 CORINTHIANS 13:12) (2 PETER 1:19) (PSALM 119:105) (JUDE 1:17-18) (1 TIMOTHY 4:1) (1 JOHN 2:18) (ROMANS 13:12)

January 15

Serve each other in humility.

Whoever wants to be a leader among you must be your servant, and whoever wants to be first must become your slave. For even I, the Son of Man, came here not to be served but to serve others, and to give up my life as a ransom for many.

If you think you are too important to help someone in need, you are only fooling yourself. You are really a nobody. ■ As God's messenger, I give each of you this warning: Be honest in your estimate of yourselves, measuring your value by how much faith God has given you. ■ When you obey me, you should say, "We are not worthy of praise. We are servants who have simply done our duty."

When we are weighed down with troubles, it is for your benefit and salvation! For when God comforts us, it is so that we, in turn, can be an encouragement to you. Then you can patiently endure the same things we suffer. We are confident that as you share in suffering, you will also share God's comfort. ■ This precious treasure—this light and power that now shine within us—is held in perishable containers, that is, in our weak bodies. So everyone can see that our glorious power is from God and is not our own.

A real leader has a servant's heart. Servant leaders appreciate others' worth and realize that they're not above any job. If you see something that needs to be done, don't wait to be asked. Take the initiative and do it like a faithful servant. *LAB note for Matthew 20:27*

(1 PETER 5:5) (MATTHEW 20:26-28) (GALATIANS 6:3) (ROMANS 12:3) (LUKE 17:10) (2 CORINTHIANS 1:6-7) (2 CORINTHIANS 4:7)

January 16

His special possession.

You belong to Christ, and Christ belongs to God. ▩ I am my lover's, the one he desires. ▩ I am his. ▩ The Son of God . . . loved me and gave himself for me.

You do not belong to yourself, for God bought you with a high price. So you must honor God with your body. ▩ Remember that the LORD rescued you . . . to become his own people and special possession; that is what you are today.

You are God's field, God's building. ▩ But Christ, the faithful Son, was in charge of the entire household. And we are God's household, if we keep up our courage and remain confident in our hope in Christ. ▩ God is building you, as living stones, into his spiritual temple.

"They will be my people," says the LORD Almighty. "On the day when I act, they will be my own special treasure." ▩ And all of them, since they are mine, belong to you; and you have given them back to me, so they are my glory!

What did Paul mean when he said that our body belongs to God? Many people say they have the right to do whatever they want with their own bodies. But when we become Christians, the Holy Spirit comes to live in us. Therefore we no longer own our bodies.

LAB note for 1 Corinthians 6:19-20

(DEUTERONOMY 32:9) (1 CORINTHIANS 3:23) (SONG OF SONGS 7:10) (SONG OF SONGS 2:16) (GALATIANS 2:20) (1 CORINTHIANS 6:19-20) (DEUTERONOMY 4:20) (1 CORINTHIANS 3:9) (HEBREWS 3:6) (1 PETER 2:5) (MALACHI 3:17) (JOHN 17:10)

January 17

He prunes the branches that do bear fruit so they will produce even more.

He will be like a blazing fire that refines metal or like a strong soap that whitens clothes. He will sit and judge like a refiner of silver, watching closely as the dross is burned away.

We can rejoice, too, when we run into problems and trials, for we know that they are good for us—they help us learn to endure. And endurance develops strength of character in us, and character strengthens our confident expectation of salvation. And this expectation will not disappoint us. For we know how dearly God loves us, because he has given us the Holy Spirit to fill our hearts with his love. ▪ As you endure this divine discipline, remember that God is treating you as his own children. Whoever heard of a child who was never disciplined? If God doesn't discipline you as he does all of his children, it means that you are illegitimate and are not really his children after all. No discipline is enjoyable while it is happening—it is painful! But afterward there will be a quiet harvest of right living for those who are trained in this way. So take a new grip with your tired hands and stand firm on your shaky legs.

Christ is the vine, and God is the gardener who cares for the branches to make them fruitful. The branches are all those who claim to be followers of Christ. The fruitful branches are true believers who by their living union with Christ produce much fruit. *LAB note for John 15:1ff.*

(JOHN 15:2) (MALACHI 3:2-3) (ROMANS 5:3-5) (HEBREWS 12:7-8, 11-12)

January 18

He is our God forever and ever, and he will be our guide until we die.

O LORD, I will honor and praise your name, for you are my God. You do such wonderful things! You planned them long ago, and now you have accomplished them. ▪ LORD, you alone are my inheritance, my cup of blessing. You guard all that is mine.

He renews my strength. He guides me along right paths, bringing honor to his name. Even when I walk through the dark valley of death, I will not be afraid, for you are close beside me. ▪ You are holding my right hand. You will keep on guiding me with your counsel, leading me to a glorious destiny. Whom have I in heaven but you? I desire you more than anything on earth. My health may fail, and my spirit may grow weak, but God remains the strength of my heart; he is mine forever. ▪ In him our hearts rejoice, for we are trusting in his holy name. ▪ The LORD will work out his plans for my life—for your faithful love, O LORD, endures forever. Don't abandon me, for you made me.

As we struggle with decisions, we need both a map that gives us directions and a constant companion who has an intimate knowledge of the way and will make sure we interpret the map correctly. The Bible is such a map, and the Holy Spirit is our constant companion and guide. As you make your way through life, use both. *LAB note for Psalm 48:14*

(PSALM 48:14) (ISAIAH 25:1) (PSALM 16:5) (PSALM 23:3-4) (PSALM 73:23-26) (PSALM 33:21) (PSALM 138:8)

January 19

When doubts filled my mind, your comfort gave me renewed hope and cheer.

My heart is overwhelmed. Lead me to the towering rock of safety.

I am in trouble, Lord. Help me! ▪ Give your burdens to the LORD, and he will take care of you. He will not permit the godly to slip and fall.

I am like a little child who doesn't know his way around. ▪ If you want to know what God wants you to do—ask him, and he will gladly tell you.

Who is adequate for such a task? ▪ I am rotten through and through so far as my old sinful nature is concerned. ▪ My gracious favor is all you need. My power works best in your weakness.

"Take heart, son! Your sins are forgiven." "Daughter, be encouraged! Your faith has made you well."

You satisfy me more than the richest of foods. I will praise you with songs of joy. I lie awake thinking of you, meditating on you through the night. I think how much you have helped me; I sing for joy in the shadow of your protecting wings. I follow close behind you; your strong right hand holds me securely.

Who is adequate for the task of representing Christ? Our adequacy is always from God, who has already commissioned and sent us. As we realize that God has equipped us, we can overcome our feelings of inadequacy. Serving Christ, therefore, requires that we focus on what he can do through us, not on what we can't do by ourselves.

LAB note for 2 Corinthians 2:16–17

(PSALM 94:19) (PSALM 61:2) (ISAIAH 38:14) (PSALM 55:22) (1 KINGS 3:7) (JAMES 1:5) (2 CORINTHIANS 2:16) (ROMANS 7:18) (2 CORINTHIANS 12:9) (MATTHEW 9:2, 22) (PSALM 63:5–8)

January 20

The fact that I am still being persecuted proves that I am still preaching salvation through the cross of Christ alone.

If any of you wants to be my follower, you must put aside your selfish ambition, shoulder your cross, and follow me.

Don't you realize that friendship with this world makes you an enemy of God? I say it again, that if your aim is to enjoy this world, you can't be a friend of God. ▩ They must enter into the Kingdom of God through many tribulations.

Anyone who believes in him will not be disappointed. ▩ He is very precious to you who believe.

God forbid that I should boast about anything except the cross of our Lord Jesus Christ. Because of that cross, my interest in this world died long ago, and the world's interest in me is also long dead. ▩ I have been crucified with Christ. ▩ Those who belong to Christ Jesus have nailed the passions and desires of their sinful nature to his cross and crucified them there.

If we endure hardship, we will reign with him. If we deny him, he will deny us.

God is faithful to his children, and although we may suffer great hardships here, God promises that someday we will live eternally with him. Are you facing hardships? Don't turn away from God—he promises you a wonderful future with him. *LAB note for 2 Timothy 2:11-13*

(GALATIANS 5:11) (MATTHEW 16:24) (JAMES 4:4) (ACTS 14:22) (ROMANS 9:33) (1 PETER 2:7) (GALATIANS 6:14) (GALATIANS 2:19) (GALATIANS 5:24) (2 TIMOTHY 2:12)

January 21

The Lord is coming soon.

The Lord himself will come down from heaven with a commanding shout, with the call of the archangel, and with the trumpet call of God. First, all the Christians who have died will rise from their graves. Then, together with them, we who are still alive and remain on the earth will be caught up in the clouds to meet the Lord in the air and remain with him forever. So comfort and encourage each other with these words. ▪ He who is the faithful witness to all these things says, "Yes, I am coming soon!" Amen! Come, Lord Jesus!

Dear friends, while you are waiting for these things to happen, make every effort to live a pure and blameless life. And be at peace with God. ▪Keep away from every kind of evil. Now may the God of peace make you holy in every way, and may your whole spirit and soul and body be kept blameless until that day when our Lord Jesus Christ comes again. God, who calls you, is faithful; he will do this.

Be patient. And take courage, for the coming of the Lord is near.

Because Jesus Christ came back to life, so will all believers. All Christians, including those living when Christ returns, will live with Christ forever. All believers throughout history will stand reunited in God's very presence, safe and secure. *LAB note for 1 Thessalonians 4:15-18*

(Philippians 4:5) (1 Thessalonians 4:16-18) (Revelation 22:20)
(2 Peter 3:14) (1 Thessalonians 5:22-24) (James 5:8)

January 22

A choice vine.

My beloved has a vineyard on a rich and fertile hill. He plowed the land, cleared its stones, and planted it with choice vines. . . . Then he waited for a harvest of sweet grapes, but the grapes that grew were wild and sour. ▩ How could this happen? When I planted you, I chose a vine of the purest stock—the very best. How did you grow into this corrupt wild vine?

When you follow the desires of your sinful nature, your lives will produce these evil results: sexuality immorality, impure thoughts, eagerness for lustful pleasure, . . . envy, drunkenness, wild parties, and other kinds of sin. . . . But when the Holy Spirit controls our lives, he will produce this kind of fruit in us: love, joy, peace, patience, kindness, goodness, faithfulness, gentleness, and self-control.

I am the true vine, and my Father is the gardener. He cuts off every branch that doesn't produce fruit, and he prunes the branches that do bear fruit so they will produce even more. Remain in me, and I will remain in you. My true disciples produce much fruit. This brings great glory to my Father.

Jesus makes a distinction between cutting off and cutting back branches. Fruitful branches are cut back to promote growth (meaning God must sometimes discipline us to strengthen our character and faith). But branches that don't bear fruit are cut off at the trunk (meaning people who don't bear fruit for God or who try to block the efforts of God's followers will be cut off from his life-giving power). *LAB note for John 15:2-3*

(Genesis 49:11) (Isaiah 5:1-2) (Jeremiah 2:21) (Galatians 5:19, 21-23) (John 15:1-2, 4, 8)

January 23

We are made right in God's sight when we trust in Jesus Christ to take away our sins.

For God made Christ, who never sinned, to be the offering for our sin, so that we could be made right with God through Christ. ▪ Christ . . . took upon himself the curse for our wrongdoing. ▪ God alone made it possible for you to be in Christ Jesus. For our benefit God made Christ to be wisdom itself. He is the one who made us acceptable to God. He made us pure and holy, and he gave himself to purchase our freedom. ▪ He saved us, not because of the good things we did, but because of his mercy. He washed away our sins and gave us a new life through the Holy Spirit. He generously poured out the Spirit upon us because of what Jesus Christ our Savior did.

Everything else is worthless when compared with the priceless gain of knowing Christ Jesus my Lord. I have discarded everything else, counting it all as garbage, so that I may have Christ and become one with him. I no longer count on my own goodness or my ability to obey God's law, but I trust Christ to save me. For God's way of making us right with himself depends on faith.

There is a way to be declared not guilty—by trusting Jesus Christ to take away our sins. Trusting means putting our confidence in Christ to forgive our sins, to make us right with God, and to empower us to live the way he taught us.

LAB note for Romans 3:21–29

(Romans 3:22) (2 Corinthians 5:21) (Galatians 3:13) (1 Corinthians 1:30) (Titus 3:5–6) (Philippians 3:8–9)

January 24

Adopted into his family—calling him "Father, dear Father."

Jesus . . . looked up to heaven and said, "Father . . . Holy Father . . . righteous Father." ■ Because you Gentiles have become his children, God has sent the Spirit of his Son into your hearts, and now you can call God your dear Father. ■ All of us, both Jews and Gentiles, may come to the Father through the same Holy Spirit because of what Christ has done for us. So now you Gentiles are no longer strangers and foreigners. You are citizens along with all of God's holy people. You are members of God's family.

I will go home to my father and say, "Father, I have sinned against both heaven and you, and I am no longer worthy of being called your son. Please take me on as a hired man." So he returned home to his father. And while he was still a long distance away, his father saw him coming. Filled with love and compassion, he ran to his son, embraced him, and kissed him.

Surely you are still our Father! . . . You are our Redeemer from ages past.

As adopted children of God, we share with Jesus all rights to God's resources. As God's heirs, we can claim what he has provided for us—our full identity as his children. *LAB note for Galatians 4:5-7*

(ROMANS 8:15) (JOHN 17:1, 11, 25) (GALATIANS 4:6) (EPHESIANS 2:18-19) (LUKE 15:18-20) (ISAIAH 63:16)

January 25

Let us go out to him outside the camp and bear the disgrace he bore. For this world is not our home; we are looking forward to our city in heaven, which is yet to come.

Dear friends, don't be surprised at the fiery trials you are going through, as if something strange were happening to you. Instead, be very glad—because these trials will make you partners with Christ in his suffering, and afterward you will have the wonderful joy of sharing his glory when it is displayed to all the world. ▪ We are confident that as you share in suffering, you will also share God's comfort.

Be happy if you are insulted for being a Christian, for then the glorious Spirit of God will come upon you.

The apostles left the high council rejoicing that God had counted them worthy to suffer dishonor for the name of Jesus. ▪ Moses . . . chose to share the oppression of God's people instead of enjoying the fleeting pleasures of sin. He thought it was better to suffer for the sake of the Messiah than to own the treasures of Egypt, for he was looking ahead to the great reward that God would give him.

It is easy to be deceived by the temporary benefits of wealth, popularity, status, and achievement, and to be blind to the long-range benefits of God's Kingdom. Faith helps us look beyond the world's value system to see the eternal values of God's Kingdom.

LAB note for Hebrews 11:24–28

(Hebrews 13:13–14) (1 Peter 4:12–13) (2 Corinthians 1:7) (1 Peter 4:14) (Acts 5:41) (Hebrews 11:24–26)

January 26

May your strength match the length of your days!

When you are arrested and stand trial, don't worry about what to say in your defense. Just say what God tells you to. Then it is not you who will be speaking, but the Holy Spirit. ▨ Don't worry about tomorrow, for tomorrow will bring its own worries. Today's trouble is enough for today.

The God of Israel gives power and strength to his people. Praise be to God! ▨ He gives power to those who are tired and worn out; he offers strength to the weak.

"My gracious favor is all you need. My power works best in your weakness." So now I am glad to boast about my weaknesses, so that the power of Christ may work through me. Since I know it is all for Christ's good, I am quite content with my weaknesses and with insults, hardships, persecutions, and calamities. For when I am weak, then I am strong. ▨ For I can do everything with the help of Christ who gives me the strength I need. ▨ March on, my soul, with courage!

The fact that God's power is displayed in our weaknesses should give us courage and hope. As we recognize our limitations, we will depend more on God for our effectiveness rather than on our own energy, effort, or talent.

LAB note for 2 Corinthians 12:9

(Deuteronomy 33:25) (Mark 13:11) (Matthew 6:34) (Psalm 68:35) (Isaiah 40:29) (2 Corinthians 12:9–10) (Philippians 4:13) (Judges 5:21)

January 27

Don't be discouraged when he corrects you.

No discipline is enjoyable while it is happening—it is painful! But afterward there will be a quiet harvest of right living for those who are trained in this way. ■ The Holy Spirit . . . will produce fruit in us.

The LORD is like a father to his children, tender and compassionate to those who fear him.

Though our bodies are dying, our spirits are being renewed every day. For our present troubles are quite small and won't last very long. Yet they produce for us an immeasurably great glory that will last forever! So we don't look at the troubles we can see right now; rather, we look forward to what we have not yet seen. For the troubles we see will soon be over, but the joys to come will last forever.

Even though Jesus was God's Son, he learned obedience from the things he suffered. ■ He faced all of the same temptations we do, yet he did not sin.

We may respond to discipline in several ways: (1) We can accept it with resignation; (2) we can accept it with self-pity, thinking we really don't deserve it; (3) we can be angry and resentful toward God; or (4) we can accept it gratefully, as the appropriate response we owe a loving Father.

LAB note for Hebrews 12:11

(PROVERBS 3:11) (HEBREWS 12:11) (GALATIANS 5:22) (PSALM 103:13) (2 CORINTHIANS 4:16-18) (HEBREWS 5:8) (HEBREWS 4:15)

January 28

The God who sees me.

O LORD, you have examined my heart and know everything about me. You know when I sit down or stand up. You know my every thought when far away. You chart the path ahead of me and tell me where to stop and rest. Every moment you know where I am. You know what I am going to say even before I say it, LORD. Such knowledge is too wonderful for me, too great for me to know! I can never escape from your spirit! I can never get away from your presence!

The LORD is watching everywhere, keeping his eye on both the evil and the good. ▪ For the LORD sees clearly what a man does, examining every path he takes. ▪ You like to look good in public, but God knows your evil hearts. What this world honors is an abomination in the sight of God. ▪ The eyes of the LORD search the whole earth in order to strengthen those whose hearts are fully committed to him.

Jesus . . . knew what people were really like. No one needed to tell him about human nature. ▪ Lord, you know everything. ▪ You know I love you.

God already knows everything about us, and still he accepts and loves us. He is with us through every situation, in every trial—protecting, loving, guiding. He knows and loves us completely. *LAB note for Psalm 139:1-5*

(GENESIS 16:13) (PSALM 139:1-4, 6-7) (PROVERBS 15:3) (PROVERBS 5:21) (LUKE 16:15) (2 CHRONICLES 16:9) (JOHN 2:24-25) (JOHN 21:17) (JOHN 21:16)

January 29

When the Holy Spirit controls our lives, he will produce . . . self-control.

All athletes practice strict self-control. They do it to win a prize that will fade away, but we do it for an eternal prize. So I run straight to the goal with purpose in every step. I am not like a boxer who misses his punches. I discipline my body like an athlete, training it to do what it should. Otherwise, I fear that after preaching to others I myself might be disqualified.

Don't be drunk with wine, because that will ruin your life. Instead, let the Holy Spirit fill and control you.

If any of you wants to be my follower, you must put aside your selfish ambition, shoulder your cross, and follow me.

Be on your guard, not asleep like the others. Stay alert and be sober. Night is the time for sleep and the time when people get drunk. But let us who live in the light think clearly. ❖ We are instructed to turn from godless living and sinful pleasures. We should live in this evil world with self-control, right conduct, and devotion to God.

At times we must even give up something good in order to do what God wants. Without a goal, discipline is nothing but self-punishment. With the goal of pleasing God, our denial seems like nothing compared to the eternal imperishable reward that will be ours.

LAB note for 1 Corinthians 9:25

(GALATIANS 5:22-23) (1 CORINTHIANS 9:25-27) (EPHESIANS 5:18) (MATTHEW 16:24) (1 THESSALONIANS 5:6-8) (TITUS 2:12)

January 30

Let us run with endurance the race that God has set before us. We do this by keeping our eyes on Jesus, on whom our faith depends from start to finish.

If any of you wants to be my follower, you must put aside your selfish ambition, shoulder your cross daily, and follow me. ▪ No one can become my disciple without giving up everything for me. ▪ Don't live in darkness. Get rid of your evil deeds.

All athletes practice strict self-control. They do it to win a prize that will fade away, but we do it for an eternal prize. I discipline my body like an athlete, training it to do what it should. ▪ I am still not all I should be, but I am focusing all my energies on this one thing: Forgetting the past and looking forward to what lies ahead, I strain to reach the end of the race and receive the prize for which God, through Christ Jesus, is calling us up to heaven. ▪ Oh, that we might know the LORD! Let us press on to know him! Then he will respond to us as surely as the arrival of dawn or the coming of rains in early spring.

The Christian life involves hard work. It requires us to give up whatever endangers our relationship with God, to run patiently, and to struggle against sin with the power of the Holy Spirit. To live effectively, we must keep our eyes on Jesus. *LAB note for Hebrews 12:1-4*

(HEBREWS 12:1-2) (LUKE 9:23) (LUKE 14:33) (ROMANS 13:12) (1 CORINTHIANS 9:25, 27) (PHILIPPIANS 3:13-14) (HOSEA 6:3)

January 31

It is good for the young to submit to the yoke of his discipline.

Teach your children to choose the right path, and when they are older, they will remain upon it.

Since we respect our earthly fathers who disciplined us, should we not all the more cheerfully submit to the discipline of our heavenly Father and live forever? For our earthly fathers disciplined us for a few years, doing the best they knew how. But God's discipline is always right and good for us because it means we will share in his holiness.

LORD, in distress we searched for you. We were bowed beneath the burden of your discipline. ▪ I used to wander off until you disciplined me; but now I closely follow your word. The suffering you sent was good for me, for it taught me to pay attention to your principles.

"I know the plans I have for you," says the LORD. "They are plans for good and not for disaster, to give you a future and a hope." ▪ Humble yourselves under the mighty power of God, and in his good time he will honor you.

When parents teach a child how to make decisions, they don't have to watch every step he or she takes. They know their children will remain on the right path because they have made the choice themselves.

LAB note for Proverbs 22:6

(LAMENTATIONS 3:27) (PROVERBS 22:6) (HEBREWS 12:9-10) (ISAIAH 26:16) (PSALM 119:67, 71) (JEREMIAH 29:11) (1 PETER 5:6)

February

Above All . . . Love

Love speaks honestly and pardons graciously.
Love rejoices in victories and comforts in sorrows.
Love overcomes circumstances.

God is the giver of true love. He created it, and he rejoices in seeing us learn it from him. May you experience more of God's perfect love this year so that your peace and joy will inspire others.

February 1

How kind and gracious the Lord was! He filled me completely with faith and the love of Christ Jesus.

You know how full of love and kindness our Lord Jesus Christ was. Though he was very rich, yet for your sakes he became poor, so that by his poverty he could make you rich. ▩ As people sinned more and more, God's wonderful kindness became more abundant.

God saved you by his special favor when you believed. And you can't take credit for this; it is a gift from God. Salvation is not a reward for the good things we have done, so none of us can boast about it. ▩ We have believed in Christ Jesus, that we might be accepted by God because of our faith in Christ—and not because we have obeyed the law. For no one will ever be saved by obeying the law. ▩ He saved us, not because of the good things we did, but because of his mercy. He washed away our sins and gave us a new life through the Holy Spirit. He generously poured out the Spirit upon us because of what Jesus Christ our Savior did.

Jesus did not give up his eternal power when he became human, but he did set aside his glory and his rights. He became "poor" when he became human because he set aside so much. Yet by doing so, he made us "rich" because we received salvation and eternal life.

LAB note for 2 Corinthians 8:9

(1 TIMOTHY 1:14) (2 CORINTHIANS 8:9) (ROMANS 5:20) (EPHESIANS 2:8-9) (GALATIANS 2:16) (TITUS 3:5-6)

February 2

If someone sins against another person, God can mediate for the guilty party. But if someone sins against the LORD, who can intercede?

If you do sin, there is someone to plead for you before the Father. He is Jesus Christ, the one who pleases God completely. He is the sacrifice for our sins. He takes away not only our sins but the sins of all the world. For God sent Jesus to take the punishment for our sins and to satisfy God's anger against us. We are made right with God when we believe that Jesus shed his blood, sacrificing his life for us. God was being entirely fair and just when he did not punish those who sinned in former times. And he is entirely fair and just in this present time when he declares sinners to be right in his sight because they believe in Jesus.

What can we say about such wonderful things as these? If God is for us, who can ever be against us? Who dares accuse us whom God has chosen for his own? Will God? No! He is the one who has given us right standing with himself. Who then will condemn us? Will Christ Jesus? No, for he is the one who died for us and was raised to life for us and is sitting at the place of highest honor next to God, pleading for us.

When you feel guilty and condemned, don't give up hope—the best defense attorney in the universe is pleading your case. Jesus Christ, your defender, has already suffered your penalty in your place. You can't be tried for a case that is no longer on the docket. *LAB note for 1 John 2:1-2*

(1 SAMUEL 2:25) (1 JOHN 2:1-2) (ROMANS 3:25-26) (ROMANS 8:31, 33-34)

February 3

The stars differ from each other in their beauty and brightness.

They had been arguing about which one of them was the greatest. He sat down and called the twelve disciples over to him. Then he said, "Anyone who wants to be the first must take last place and be the servant of everyone else." ❧ Serve each other in humility, for "God sets himself against the proud, but he shows favor to the humble." So humble yourselves under the mighty power of God, and in his good time he will honor you.

Your attitude should be the same that Christ Jesus had. Though he was God . . . he took the humble position of a slave and appeared in human form. Because of this, God raised him up to the heights of heaven and gave him a name that is above every other name, so that at the name of Jesus every knee will bow, in heaven and on earth and under the earth, and every tongue will confess that Jesus Christ is Lord, to the glory of God the Father.

Those who are wise will shine as bright as the sky, and those who turn many to righteousness will shine like stars forever.

If we say we follow Christ, we must also say we want to live as he lived. We should develop his attitude of humility as we serve, even when we are not likely to get recognition for our efforts. Are you selfishly clinging to your rights, or are you willing to serve? *LAB note for Philippians 2:5-11*

(1 Corinthians 15:41) (Mark 9:34-35) (1 Peter 5:5-6) (Philippians 2:5-7, 9-10) (Daniel 12:3)

February 4

Take courage and work, for I am with you, says the LORD Almighty.

I am the vine; you are the branches. Those who remain in me, and I in them, will produce much fruit. For apart from me you can do nothing. ▪ I can do everything with the help of Christ who gives me the strength I need. ▪ Be strong with the Lord's mighty power. ▪ The joy of the LORD is your strength!

This is what the LORD Almighty says: "Take heart and finish the task! You have heard what the prophets have been saying." ▪ Strengthen those who have tired hands, and encourage those who have weak knees. Say to those who are afraid, "Be strong, and do not fear, for your God is coming to destroy your enemies. He is coming to save you." ▪ The LORD . . . said, "Go with the strength you have."

If God is for us, who can ever be against us? ▪ And so, since God in his mercy has given us this wonderful ministry [of telling his Good News to others], we never give up.

So don't get tired of doing what is good. Don't get discouraged and give up, for we will reap a harvest of blessing at the appropriate time. ▪ How we thank God, who gives us victory over sin and death through Jesus Christ our Lord!

It is discouraging to continue to do right and receive no word of thanks or see any tangible results. But we must keep on doing good and trust God for the results. In due time we will reap a harvest of blessing.

LAB note for Galatians 6:9–10

(HAGGAI 2:4) (JOHN 15:5) (PHILIPPIANS 4:13) (EPHESIANS 6:10) (NEHEMIAH 8:10) (ZECHARIAH 8:9) (ISAIAH 35:3–4) (JUDGES 6:14) (ROMANS 8:31) (2 CORINTHIANS 4:1) (GALATIANS 6:9) (1 CORINTHIANS 15:57)

February 5

Even in darkness I cannot hide from you.

God carefully watches the way people live; he sees everything they do. No darkness is thick enough to hide the wicked from his eyes. ▪ Can anyone hide from me? Am I not everywhere in all the heavens and the earth?

Do not be afraid of the terrors of the night, nor fear the dangers of the day, nor dread the plague that stalks in darkness, nor the disaster that strikes at midday. If you make the LORD your refuge, if you make the Most High your shelter, no evil will conquer you; no plague will come near your dwelling. ▪ He will not let you stumble and fall; the one who watches over you will not sleep.

The LORD himself watches over you! The LORD stands beside you as your protective shade. The sun will not hurt you by day, nor the moon at night. The LORD keeps you from all evil and preserves your life.

Even though I walk through the dark valley of death, I will not be afraid, for you are close beside me. Your rod and your staff protect and comfort me.

We should never trust a lesser power than God himself. Not only is he all-powerful, he also watches over us. Nothing diverts or deters him. We are safe. We never outgrow our need for God's untiring watch over our life. *LAB note for Psalm 121:1ff.*

(PSALM 139:12) (JOB 34:21-22) (JEREMIAH 23:24) (PSALM 91:5-6, 9-10) (PSALM 121:3) (PSALM 121:5-7) (PSALM 23:4)

February 6

Never return.

If they had meant the country they came from, they would have found a way to go back. But they were looking for a better place, a heavenly homeland. Moses . . . chose to share the oppression of God's people instead of enjoying the fleeting pleasures of sin. He thought it was better to suffer for the sake of the Messiah than to own the treasures of Egypt. ▪ A righteous person will live by faith. But I will have no pleasure in anyone who turns away. ▪ Anyone who puts a hand to the plow and then looks back is not fit for the Kingdom of God.

God forbid that I should boast about anything except the cross of our Lord Jesus Christ. Because of that cross, my interest in this world died long ago, and the world's interest in me is also long dead. ▪ Therefore come out from them and separate yourselves from them, says the Lord. Don't touch their filthy things, and I will welcome you.

I am sure that God, who began the good work within you, will continue his work until it is finally finished on that day when Christ Jesus comes back again.

What does Jesus want from us? Total dedication, not halfhearted commitment. We can't pick and choose among Jesus' ideas and follow him selectively; we have to accept the cross along with the crown, judgment as well as mercy.

LAB note for Luke 9:62

(Deuteronomy 17:16) (Hebrews 11:15-16, 24-26) (Hebrews 10:38) (Luke 9:62) (Galatians 6:14) (2 Corinthians 6:17) (Phlippians 1:6)

February 7

My purpose is to give life in all its fullness.

The wages of sin is death, but the free gift of God is eternal life through Christ Jesus our Lord. ◾ The sin of this one man, Adam, caused death to rule over us, but all who receive God's wonderful, gracious gift of righteousness will live in triumph over sin and death through this one man, Jesus Christ. ◾ Just as death came into the world through a man, Adam, now the resurrection from the dead has begun through another man, Christ. Everyone dies because all of us are related to Adam, the first man. But all who are related to Christ, the other man, will be given new life. ◾ Christ Jesus, our Savior . . . broke the power of death and showed us the way to everlasting life through the Good News.

And this is what God has testified: He has given us eternal life, and this life is in his Son. So whoever has God's Son has life; whoever does not have his Son does not have life. ◾ God did not send his Son into the world to condemn it, but to save it.

The life Jesus gives right now is abundantly rich and full. It is eternal, yet it begins immediately. Life in Christ is lived on a higher plane because of his overflowing forgiveness, love, and guidance. Have you taken Christ's offer of life? *LAB note for John 10:10*

(John 10:10) (Romans 6:23) (Romans 5:17) (1 Corinthians 15:21–22) (2 Timothy 1:10) (1 John 5:11–12) (John 3:17)

February 8

If you fail to drive out the people who live in the land, those who remain will be like splinters in your eyes and thorns in your sides.

Fight the good fight for what we believe. ▪ We use God's mighty weapons, not mere worldly weapons, to knock down the Devil's strongholds. With these weapons we break down every proud argument that keeps people from knowing God. With these weapons we conquer their rebellious ideas, and we teach them to obey Christ.

Dear brothers and sisters, you have no obligation whatsoever to do what your sinful nature urges you to do. For if you keep on following it, you will perish. But if through the power of the Holy Spirit you turn from it and its evil deeds, you will live.

The old sinful nature loves to do evil, which is just opposite from what the Holy Spirit wants. And the Spirit gives us desires that are opposite from what the sinful nature desires. These two forces are constantly fighting each other, and your choices are never free from this conflict. ▪ But there is another law at work within me that is at war with my mind. ▪ Despite all these things, overwhelming victory is ours through Christ, who loved us.

Some think Christianity is a passive religion that advocates waiting for God to act. On the contrary, we must have an active faith, obeying God with courage and doing what we know is right. Is it time for action on your part? Don't wait—get going! *LAB note for 1 Timothy 6:11-12*

(NUMBERS 33:55) (1 TIMOTHY 6:12) (2 CORINTHIANS 10:4-5) (ROMANS 8:12-13) (GALATIANS 5:17) (ROMANS 7:23) (ROMANS 8:37)

February 9

When you have eaten your fill, praise the LORD your God for the good land he has given you.

Beware that in your plenty you do not forget the LORD your God. ▪ One of them, when he saw that he was healed, came back to Jesus, shouting, "Praise God, I'm healed!" He fell face down on the ground at Jesus' feet, thanking him for what he had done. This man was a Samaritan. Jesus asked, "Didn't I heal ten men? Where are the other nine? Does only this foreigner return to give glory to God?"

Since everything God created is good, we should not reject any of it. We may receive it gladly, with thankful hearts. For it is made holy by the word of God and prayer. ▪ The blessing of the LORD makes a person rich, and he adds no sorrow with it.

Praise the LORD, I tell myself; with my whole heart, I will praise his holy name. Praise the LORD, I tell myself, and never forget the good things he does for me. He forgives all my sins and heals all my diseases. He ransoms me from death and surrounds me with love and tender mercies. He fills my life with good things. My youth is renewed like the eagle's!

It is easy to get so busy collecting and managing wealth that we push God right out of our lives. But it is God who gives us everything we have, and it is God who asks us to manage it for him.

LAB note for Deuteronomy 8:11–20

(DEUTERONOMY 8:10) (DEUTERONOMY 8:11) (LUKE 17:15–18)
(1 TIMOTHY 4:4–5) (PROVERBS 10:22) (PSALM 103:1–5)

February 10

He had compassion on them.

Jesus Christ is the same yesterday, today, and forever. ▩ We have a High Priest who has gone to heaven, Jesus the Son of God. Let us cling to him and never stop trusting him. This High Priest of ours understands our weaknesses, for he faced all of the same temptations we do, yet he did not sin. ▩ Because he is human, he is able to deal gently with the people, though they are ignorant and wayward. For he is subject to the same weaknesses they have. ▩ Then he returned and found the disciples asleep. "Simon!" he said to Peter. "Are you asleep? Couldn't you stay awake and watch with me even one hour? Keep alert and pray. Overwise temptation will overpower you. For though the spirit is willing enough, the body is weak."

The LORD is like a father to his children, tender and compassionate to those who fear him. For he understands how weak we are; he knows we are only dust.

You, O Lord, are a merciful and gracious God, slow to get angry, full of unfailing love and truth. Look down and have mercy on me. Give strength to your servant; yes, save me, for I am your servant.

Jesus is like us because he experienced a full range of temptations throughout his life as a human being. We can be comforted, knowing that Jesus faced temptation—he can sympathize with us. We can be encouraged, knowing that Jesus faced temptation without giving in to sin.

LAB note for Hebrews 4:15

(MATTHEW 14:14) (HEBREWS 13:8) (HEBREWS 4:14-15) (HEBREWS 5:2) (MARK 14:37-38) (PSALM 103:13-14) (PSALM 86:15-16)

February 11

Your eye is a lamp for your body. A pure eye lets sunshine into your soul.

People who aren't Christians can't understand these truths from God's Spirit. It all sounds foolish to them because only those who have the Spirit understand what the Spirit means. ▪ Open my eyes to see the wonderful truths in your law.

I am the light of the world. If you follow me, you won't be stumbling through the darkness, because you will have the light that leads to life. ▪ All of us have had that veil removed so that we can be mirrors that brightly reflect the glory of the Lord. And as the Spirit of the Lord works within us, we become more and more like him and reflect his glory even more. ▪ For God, who said, "Let there be light in the darkness," has made us understand that this light is the brightness of the glory of God that is seen in the face of Jesus Christ.

God, the glorious Father of our Lord Jesus Christ, . . . give you spiritual wisdom and understanding, so that you might grow in your knowledge of God . . . [and] understand the wonderful future he has promised to those he called.

Jesus Christ is the Creator of life, and his life brings light to humankind. In his light we see ourselves as we really are (sinners in need of a Savior). When we follow Jesus, he lights the path ahead of us so we can see how to live. He removes the darkness of sin from our lives.

LAB note for John 1:4–5

(LUKE 11:34) (1 CORINTHIANS 2:14) (PSALM 119:18) (JOHN 8:12) (2 CORINTHIANS 3:18) (2 CORINTHIANS 4:6) (EPHESIANS 1:17–18)

February 12

Who can say, "I have cleansed my heart; I am pure and free from sin"?

The LORD looks down from heaven on the entire human race; he looks to see if there is even one with real understanding, one who seeks for God. But no, all have turned away from God; all have become corrupt. ❖ Those who are still under the control of their sinful nature can never please God.

I know I am rotten through and through so far as my old sinful nature is concerned. No matter which way I turn, I can't make myself do right. I want to, but I can't. ❖ We are all infected and impure with sin. When we proudly display our righteous deeds, we find they are but filthy rags.

If the law could have given us new life, we could have been made right with God by obeying. But the Scriptures have declared that we are all prisoners of sin, so the only way to receive God's promise is to believe in Jesus Christ. ❖ For God was in Christ, reconciling the world to himself, no longer counting people's sins against them.

If we say we have no sin, we are only fooling ourselves and refusing to accept the truth. But if we confess our sins to him, he is faithful and just to forgive us and to cleanse us from every wrong.

No one is without sin. We all need ongoing cleansing, moment by moment. Thank God he provides forgiveness by his mercy when we ask for it. Make confession and repentance a regular part of your talks with God. Rely on him moment by moment for the cleansing you need.

LAB note for Proverbs 20:9

(PROVERBS 20:9) (PSALM 14:2-3) (ROMANS 8:8) (ROMANS 7:18) (ISAIAH 64:6) (GALATIANS 3:22) (2 CORINTHIANS 5:19) (1 JOHN 1:8-9)

February 13

I am your inheritance and your share.

Whom have I in heaven but you? I desire you more than anything on earth. My health may fail, and my spirit may grow weak, but God remains the strength of my heart; he is mine forever. LORD, you alone are my inheritance, my cup of blessing. You guard all that is mine. The land you have given me is a pleasant land. What a wonderful inheritance!

I say to myself, "The LORD is my inheritance; therefore, I will hope in him!"

Your decrees are my treasure; they are truly my heart's delight.

O God, you are my God; I earnestly search for you. My soul thirsts for you; my whole body longs for you in this parched and weary land where there is no water. You satisfy me more than the richest of foods. I will praise you with songs of joy. I lie awake thinking of you, meditating on you through the night. I think how much you have helped me; I sing for joy in the shadow of your protecting wings.

My lover is mine, and I am his.

If you are lonely or thirsty for something lasting in your life, remember David's prayer: "O God . . . my soul thirsts for you . . . in this parched and weary land." God alone can satisfy our deepest longings!

LAB note for Psalm 63:1-5

(Numbers 18:20) (Psalm 73:25-26) (Psalm 16:5-6) (Lamentations 3:24) (Psalm 119:111) (Psalm 63:1, 5-7) (Song of Songs 2:16)

February 14

Those who feared the LORD spoke with each other, and the LORD listened to what they said. In his presence, a scroll of remembrance was written to record the names of those who feared him and loved to think about him.

Suddenly, Jesus himself came along and joined them and began walking beside them. ▩ For where two or three gather together because they are mine, I am there among them.

Let the words of Christ, in all their richness, live in your hearts and make you wise. Use his words to teach and counsel each other. Sing psalms and hymns and spiritual songs to God with thankful hearts. ▩ You must warn each other every day, as long as it is called "today," so that none of you will be deceived by sin and hardened against God. ▩ Talk about [God's Word] when you are at home and when you are away on a journey, when you are lying down and when you are getting up again.

I tell you this, that you must give an account on judgment day of every idle word you speak. The words you say now reflect your fate then; either you will be justified by them or you will be condemned.

I will tell about your righteous deeds all day long.

What kinds of words come from your mouth? That is an indication of what is in your heart. You can't solve your heart problem, however, just by cleaning up your speech. You must allow the Holy Spirit to fill you with new attitudes and motives. *LAB note for Matthew 12:34-36*

(MALACHI 3:16) (LUKE 24:15) (MATTHEW 18:20) (COLOSSIANS 3:16) (HEBREWS 3:13) (DEUTERONOMY 6:7) (MATTHEW 12:36-37) (PSALM 71:24)

February 15

The mighty oceans have roared, O LORD.

Mightier than the violent raging of the seas, mightier than the breakers on the shore—the LORD above is mightier than these! ▧ O LORD God Almighty! Where is there anyone as mighty as you, LORD? Faithfulness is your very character. You are the one who rules the oceans. When their waves rise in fearful storms, you subdue them.

Do you have no respect for me? Why do you not tremble in my presence? I, the LORD, am the one who defines the ocean's sandy shoreline, an everlasting boundary that the waters cannot cross. The waves may toss and roar, but they can never pass the bounds I set.

When you go through deep waters and great trouble, I will be with you. When you go through rivers of difficulty, you will not drown!

Peter went over the side of the boat and walked on the water toward Jesus. But when he looked around at the high waves, he was terrified and began to sink. "Save me, Lord!" he shouted. Instantly Jesus reached out his hand and grabbed him. "You don't have much faith," Jesus said. "Why did you doubt me?"

When I am afraid, I put my trust in you.

What is your attitude when you come into God's presence? We should come with respect and trembling because God sets the boundaries of the roaring seas and sends the rain, assuring us of plentiful harvests.

LAB note for Jeremiah 5:22-24

(PSALM 93:3) (PSALM 93:4) (PSALM 89:8-9) (JEREMIAH 5:22) (ISAIAH 43:2) (MATTHEW 14:29-31) (PSALM 56:3)

February 16

How fragrant your cologne, and how pleasing your name!

Christ . . . loved you and gave himself as a sacrifice to take away your sins. And God was pleased, because that sacrifice was like sweet perfume to him. ▪ He is very precious to you who believe. ▪ God raised him up to the heights of heaven and gave him a name that is above every other name, so that at the name of Jesus every knee will bow, in heaven and on earth and under the earth. ▪ For in Christ the fullness of God lives in a human body.

If you love me, obey my commandments. ▪ We know how dearly God loves us, because he has given us the Holy Spirit to fill our hearts with his love. ▪ Our lives are a fragrance presented by Christ to God. But this fragrance is perceived differently by those being saved and by those perishing.

O LORD, our Lord, the majesty of your name fills the earth! Your glory is higher than the heavens. ▪ Immanuel . . . God is with us. ▪ These will be his royal titles: Wonderful Counselor, Mighty God, Everlasting Father, Prince of Peace. ▪ The LORD is a strong fortress; the godly run to him and are safe.

Just as children imitate their parents, we should follow God's example. His great love for us led him to sacrifice himself so that we might live. Our love for others should be of the same kind—a love that goes beyond affection to self-sacrificing service. *LAB note for Ephesians 5:1-2*

(SONG OF SONGS 1:3) (EPHESIANS 5:2) (1 PETER 2:7) (PHILIPPIANS 2:9-10) (COLOSSIANS 2:9) (JOHN 14:15) (ROMANS 5:5) (2 CORINTHIANS 2:15) (PSALM 8:1) (MATTHEW 1:23) (ISAIAH 9:6) (PROVERBS 18:10)

February 17

LORD, do not desert me now! You alone are my hope.

Many people say, "Who will show us better times?" Let the smile of your face shine on us, LORD. ▪ I will sing about your power. I will shout with joy each morning because of your unfailing love. For you have been my refuge, a place of safety in the day of distress.

When I was prosperous I said, "Nothing can stop me now!" Your favor, O LORD, made me as secure as a mountain. Then you turned away from me, and I was shattered. I cried out to you, O LORD. I begged the Lord for mercy, saying, "What will you gain if I die, if I sink down into the grave? Can my dust praise you from the grave? Can it tell the world of your faithfulness? Hear me, LORD, and have mercy on me. Help me, O LORD."

"For a brief moment I abandoned you, but with great compassion I will take you back. In a moment of anger I turned my face away for a little while. But with everlasting love I will have compassion on you," says the LORD, your Redeemer. ▪ Your grief will suddenly turn to wonderful joy. ▪ Weeping may go on all night, but joy comes with the morning.

The God we serve is holy, and he cannot tolerate sin. But if we confess our sin and repent, then God will forgive us. Have you ever been separated from a loved one and then experienced joy when that person returned? That is like the joy God experiences when you repent and return to him. *LAB note for Isaiah 54:6-8*

(JEREMIAH 17:17) (PSALM 4:6) (PSALM 59:16) (PSALM 30:6-10) (ISAIAH 54:7-8) (JOHN 16:20) (PSALM 30:5)

February 18

God's law was given so that all people could see how sinful they were.

Who can create purity in one born impure? ▪ For I was born a sinner—yes, from the moment my mother conceived me.

Once you were dead, doomed forever because of your many sins. We were born with an evil nature, and we were under God's anger just like everyone else. ▪ I don't understand myself at all, for I really want to do what is right, but I don't do it. Instead, I do the very thing I hate. I know I am rotten through and through so far as my old sinful nature is concerned. No matter which way I turn, I can't make myself do right.

When Adam sinned, sin entered the entire human race. Adam's sin brought death, so death spread to everyone, for everyone sinned. What a contrast between Adam and Christ, who was yet to come! This other man, Jesus Christ, brought forgiveness to many through God's bountiful gift. Because one person disobeyed God, many people became sinners. But because one other person obeyed God, many people will be made right in God's sight.

For the power of the life-giving Spirit has freed you through Christ Jesus from the power of sin that leads to death.

How we thank God, who gives us victory over sin and death through Jesus Christ our Lord!

As a sinner separated from God, you see his law from below, as a ladder to be climbed to get to God. What relief it is to see Jesus' open arms offering to lift you above the ladder of the law and take you directly to God!

LAB note for Romans 5:20

(ROMANS 5:20) (JOB 14:4) (PSALM 51:5) (EPHESIANS 2:1, 3) (ROMANS 7:15, 18) (ROMANS 5:12, 14–15, 19) (ROMANS 8:2) (1 CORINTHIANS 15:57)

February 19

The LORD grants wisdom! From his mouth come knowledge and understanding.

Trust in the LORD with all your heart; do not depend on your own understanding. ▪ If you need wisdom—if you want to know what God wants you to do—ask him, and he will gladly tell you. He will not resent your asking. ▪ God is far wiser than the wisest of human plans, and God's weakness is far stronger than the greatest of human strength. God chose things despised by the world, things counted as nothing at all, and used them to bring to nothing what the world considers important, so that no one can ever boast in the presence of God.

As your words are taught, they give light; even the simple can understand them. ▪ I have hidden your word in my heart, that I might not sin against you.

All who were there spoke well of him and were amazed by the gracious words that fell from his lips. ▪ We have never heard anyone talk like this! ▪ God alone made it possible for you to be in Christ Jesus.

Wisdom comes in two ways: It is a God-given gift and also the result of an energetic search. Wisdom's starting point is God and his revealed Word, the source of "knowledge and understanding."

LAB note for Proverbs 2:3-6

(PROVERBS 2:6) (PROVERBS 3:5) (JAMES 1:5) (1 CORINTHIANS 1:25, 28-29) (PSALM 119:130) (PSALM 119:11) (LUKE 4:22) (JOHN 7:46) (1 CORINTHIANS 1:30)

February 20

Don't harden your hearts against him as Israel did when they rebelled, when they tested God's patience in the wilderness.

In the wilderness, their desires ran wild, testing God's patience in that dry land.

Jesus, full of the Holy Spirit, left the Jordan River. He was led by the Spirit to go out into the wilderness, where the Devil tempted him for forty days. He ate nothing all that time and was very hungry. Then the Devil said to him, "If you are the Son of God, change this stone into a loaf of bread." But Jesus told him, "No! The Scriptures say, 'People need more than bread for their life.'"

No one who wants to do wrong should ever say, "God is tempting me." God is never tempted to do wrong, and he never tempts anyone else either. Temptation comes from the lure of our own evil desires. These evil desires lead to evil actions, and evil actions lead to death.

Since he himself has gone through suffering and temptation, he is able to help us when we are being tempted. ▪ Simon, Simon, Satan has asked to have all of you, to sift you like wheat. But I have pleaded in prayer for you, Simon, that your faith should not fail.

In many places the Bible warns us not to "harden" our hearts. This means stubbornly setting ourselves against God so that we are no longer able to turn to him for forgiveness. Be careful to obey God's Word, and do not allow your heart to become hardened. *LAB note for Exodus 3:7-15*

(HEBREWS 3:8) (PSALM 106:14) (LUKE 4:1-4) (JAMES 1:13-15) (HEBREWS 2:18) (LUKE 22:31-32)

February 21

Light shines on the godly, and joy on those who do right.

Those who plant in tears will harvest with shouts of joy. They weep as they go to plant their seed, but they sing as they return with the harvest. ▩ Plant the good seeds of righteousness, and you will harvest a crop of my love.

All honor to the God and Father of our Lord Jesus Christ, for it is by his boundless mercy that God has given us the privilege of being born again. Now we live with a wonderful expectation because Jesus Christ rose again from the dead. So be truly glad! There is wonderful joy ahead, even though it is necessary for you to endure many trials for a while. These trials are only to test your faith, to show that it is strong and pure. It is being tested as fire tests and purifies gold—and your faith is far more precious to God than mere gold. So if your faith remains strong after being tried by fiery trials, it will bring you much praise and glory and honor on the day when Jesus Christ is revealed to the whole world.

Don't get discouraged and give up, for we will reap a harvest of blessing at the appropriate time.

God's ability to restore life is beyond our understanding. Our tears can be seeds that will grow into a harvest of joy because God is able to bring good out of tragedy. When burdened by sorrow, know that your times of grief will end and you will again find God's harvest of joy.

LAB note for Psalm 126:5-6

(PSALM 97:11) (PSALM 126:5-6) (HOSEA 10:12) (1 PETER 1:3, 6-7) (GALATIANS 6:9)

February 22

Who are those who fear the LORD? He will show them the path they should choose.

The LORD guided them by a pillar of cloud during the day and a pillar of fire at night.

Your word is a lamp for my feet and a light for my path. ▪ You will hear a voice say, "This is the way; turn around and walk here." ▪ The LORD says, "I will guide you along the best pathway for your life. I will advise you and watch over you. Do not be like a senseless horse or mule that needs a bit and bridle to keep it under control." Many sorrows come to the wicked, but unfailing love surrounds those who trust the LORD. So rejoice in the LORD and be glad, all you who obey him! ▪ The LORD leads with unfailing love and faithfulness all those who keep his covenant and obey his decrees.

I know, LORD, that a person's life is not his own. No one is able to plan his own course. ▪ Show me the path where I should walk, O LORD; point out the right road for me to follow.

To fear the Lord is to recognize God's attributes: He is holy, almighty, righteous, pure, all-knowing, all-powerful, and all-wise. When we recognize who God is and who we are, we will fall at his feet in humble respect. Only then will he show us how to choose his way.

LAB note for Psalm 25:12

(PSALM 25:12) (EXODUS 13:21) (PSALM 119:105) (ISAIAH 30:21) (PSALM 32:8-11) (PSALM 25:10) (JEREMIAH 10:23) (PSALM 25:4)

February 23

You can lie down without fear and enjoy pleasant dreams.

Soon a fierce storm arose. High waves began to break into the boat until it was nearly full of water. Jesus was sleeping at the back of the boat with his head on a cushion.

Don't worry about anything; instead, pray about everything. Tell God what you need, and thank him for all he has done. If you do this, you will experience God's peace, which is far more wonderful than the human mind can understand. His peace will guard your hearts and minds as you live in Christ Jesus.

I will lie down in peace and sleep, for you alone, O LORD, will keep me safe. ▪ God gives rest to his loved ones.

As they stoned him, Stephen prayed, "Lord Jesus, receive my spirit." And he fell to his knees, shouting, "Lord, don't charge them with this sin!" And with that, he died. ▪ We are fully confident, and we would rather be away from these bodies, for then we will be at home with the Lord.

Imagine never worrying about anything! It seems like an impossibility; we all have worries on the job, in our homes, at school. But if you want to worry less, pray more! Whenever you start to worry, stop and pray.

LAB note for Philippians 4:6–7

(PROVERBS 3:24) (MARK 4:37–38) (PHILIPPIANS 4:6–7) (PSALM 4:8) (PSALM 127:2) (ACTS 7:59–60) (2 CORINTHIANS 5:8)

February 24

Who can comprehend the power of your anger?

At noon, darkness fell across the whole land until three o'clock. At about three o'clock, Jesus called out with a loud voice, "Eli, Eli, lema sabachthani?" which means, "My God, my God, why have you forsaken me?" ▪ The LORD laid on him the guilt and sins of us all.

So now there is no condemnation for those who belong to Christ Jesus. ▪ Since we have been made right in God's sight by faith, we have peace with God because of what Jesus Christ our Lord has done for us. ▪ Christ has rescued us from the curse pronounced by the law. When he was hung on the cross, he took upon himself the curse for our wrongdoing.

God showed how much he loved us by sending his only Son into the world so that we might have eternal life through him. This is real love. It is not that we loved God, but that he loved us and sent his Son as a sacrifice to take away our sins. ▪ He declares sinners to be right in his sight because they believe in Jesus.

"Not guilty; let him go free." What would those words mean to you if you were on death row? The whole human race is on death row, justly condemned for repeatedly breaking God's holy law. But thank God! He has declared us not guilty and has offered us freedom from sin and power to do his will. *LAB note for Romans 8:1*

(PSALM 90:11) (MATTHEW 27:45-46) (ISAIAH 53:6) (ROMANS 8:1) (ROMANS 5:1) (GALATIANS 3:13) (1 JOHN 4:9-10) (ROMANS 3:26)

February 25

The Sovereign LORD says, I am ready to hear . . . and . . . grant them their requests.

The reason you don't have what you want is that you don't ask God for it.

Keep on asking, and you will be given what you ask for. Keep on looking, and you will find. Keep on knocking, and the door will be opened. For everyone who asks, receives. Everyone who seeks, finds. And the door is opened to everyone who knocks. ▪ We can be confident that he will listen to us whenever we ask him for anything in line with his will. And if we know he is listening when we make our requests, we can be sure that he will give us what we ask for. ▪ If you need wisdom—if you want to know what God wants you to do—ask him, and he will gladly tell you. He will not resent your asking.

The eyes of the LORD watch over those who do right; his ears are open to their cries for help. The LORD hears his people when they call to him for help. He rescues them from all their troubles.

Ask in my name. I'm not saying I will ask the Father on your behalf, for the Father himself loves you dearly because you love me.

When you talk to God, what do you talk about? Do you ask only to satisfy your desires? Do you seek God's approval for what you already plan to do? Your prayers will become powerful when you allow God to change your desires so that they perfectly correspond to his will for you.

LAB note for James 4:2-3

(EZEKIEL 36:37) (JAMES 4:2) (MATTHEW 7:7-8) (1 JOHN 5:14-15) (JAMES 1:5) (PSALM 34:15, 17) (JOHN 16:26-27)

February 26

Should we accept only good things from the hand of God and never anything bad?

I know, O LORD, that your decisions are fair; you disciplined me because I needed it. ▪ LORD, you are our Father. We are the clay, and you are the potter. We are all formed by your hand. ▪ It is the LORD's will. . . . Let him do what he thinks best.

He will sit and judge like a refiner of silver, watching closely as the dross is burned away. ▪ For the Lord disciplines those he loves, and he punishes those he accepts as his children. ▪ The student shares the teacher's fate. The servant shares the master's fate. ▪ Even though Jesus was God's Son, he learned obedience from the things he suffered.

Be very glad—because these trials will make you partners with Christ in his suffering, and afterward you will have the wonderful joy of sharing his glory when it is displayed to all the world. ▪ He said to me, "These are the ones coming out of the great tribulation. They washed their robes in the blood of the Lamb and made them white."

Many people think that believing in God protects them from trouble, so when calamity comes, they question God's goodness and justice. But you should not give up on God because he allows you to have bad experiences. God is capable of rescuing us from suffering, but he may also allow suffering to come for reasons we cannot understand.

LAB note for Job 2:10

(JOB 2:10) (PSALM 119:75) (ISAIAH 64:8) (1 SAMUEL 3:18) (MALACHI 3:3) (HEBREWS 12:6) (MATTHEW 10:25) (HEBREWS 5:8) (1 PETER 4:13) (REVELATION 7:14)

February 27

Resist the Devil, and he will flee from you.

"Get out of here, Satan," Jesus told him. "For the Scriptures say, 'You must worship the Lord your God; serve only him.'" Then the Devil went away, and angels came and cared for Jesus.

Be strong with the Lord's mighty power. Put on all of God's armor so that you will be able to stand firm against all strategies and tricks of the Devil. ▪ Take no part in the worthless deeds of evil and darkness; instead, rebuke and expose them. ▪ Satan will not outsmart us. For we are very familiar with his evil schemes. ▪ Be careful! Watch out for attacks from the Devil, your great enemy. He prowls around like a roaring lion, looking for some victim to devour. Take a firm stand against him, and be strong in your faith. Remember that your Christian brothers and sisters all over the world are going through the same kind of suffering you are. ▪ Every child of God defeats this evil world by trusting Christ to give the victory.

I am convinced that nothing can ever separate us from his love. Death can't, and life can't. The angels can't, and the demons can't. . . . Even the powers of hell can't keep God's love away.

Although God and the Devil are at war, we don't have to wait until the end to see who will win. God has already defeated Satan, and when Christ returns, the Devil and all he stands for will be eliminated forever. With the Holy Spirit's power we can resist the Devil, and he will flee from us. *LAB note for James 4:7*

(JAMES 4:7) (MATTHEW 4:10-11) (EPHESIANS 6:10-11) (EPHESIANS 5:11) (2 CORINTHIANS 2:11) (1 PETER 5:8-9) (1 JOHN 5:4) (ROMANS 8:38)

February 28

The glow of an emerald circled his throne like a rainbow.

I am giving you a sign as evidence of my eternal covenant with you and all living creatures. I have placed my rainbow in the clouds. It is the sign of my permanent promise to you and to all the earth. When I see the rainbow in the clouds, I will remember the eternal covenant between God and every living creature on earth. ◆ An everlasting covenant . . . eternal, final, sealed. ◆ God has given us both his promise and his oath. These two things are unchangeable because it is impossible for God to lie. Therefore, we who have fled to him for refuge can take new courage, for we can hold on to his promise with confidence. This confidence is like a strong and trustworthy anchor for our souls. It leads us through the curtain of heaven into God's inner sanctuary. Jesus has already gone in there for us. He has become our eternal High Priest in the line of Melchizedek. ◆ In this man Jesus there is forgiveness for your sins. Everyone who believes in him is freed from all guilt and declared right with God.

Jesus Christ is the same yesterday, today, and forever.

Because God is truth, you can be secure in his promises; you don't need to wonder if he will change his plans. Our hope is secure and immovable, anchored in God. This truth should give you encouragement, assurance, and confidence. *LAB note for Hebrews 6:18-19*

(REVELATION 4:3) (GENESIS 9:12-13, 16) (2 SAMUEL 23:5) (HEBREWS 6:18-20) (ACTS 13:38-39) (HEBREWS 13:8)

February 29

God . . . always does just what he says, and he is the one who invited you into this wonderful friendship with his Son, Jesus Christ our Lord.

Without wavering, let us hold tightly to the hope we say we have, for God can be trusted to keep his promise. ▪ We are the temple of the living God. As God said: "I will live in them and walk among them. I will be their God, and they will be my people." ▪ You may have fellowship with us. And our fellowship is with the Father and with his Son, Jesus Christ. ▪ Be very glad—because these trials will make you partners with Christ in his suffering, and afterward you will have the wonderful joy of sharing his glory when it is displayed to all the world.

I pray that Christ will be more and more at home in your hearts as you trust in him. May your roots go down deep into the soil of God's marvelous love. And may you have the power to understand, as all God's people should, how wide, how long, how high, and how deep his love really is. May you experience the love of Christ, though it is so great you will never fully understand it. Then you will be filled with the fullness of life and power that comes from God.

We have significant privileges associated with our new life in Christ: (1) we have personal access to God through Christ; (2) we may grow in faith, overcome doubts and questions, and deepen our relationship with him; (3) we may enjoy encouragement from one another; (4) we may worship together. *LAB note for Hebrews 10:22–25*

(1 Corinthians 1:9) (Hebrews 10:23) (2 Corinthians 6:16) (1 John 1:3) (1 Peter 4:13) (Ephesians 3:17–19)

March

New Life in Spring

Abundant life and new beginnings
Warm sunny days and cool rainy evenings
Spring brings a sense of refreshment and peace.

Take a moment each morning to pause outside your door and breathe deeply of the scent of fresh air and new life. Listen for the chirping of birds, and revel in the gift of the season.

*M*arch 1

The LORD made the heavens, the earth, the sea, and everything in them.

The heavens tell of the glory of God. The skies display his marvelous craftsmanship. ▪ The LORD merely spoke, and the heavens were created. He breathed the word, and all the stars were born. He gave the sea its boundaries and locked the oceans in vast reservoirs. When he spoke, the world began! It appeared at his command. ▪ All the nations of the world are nothing in comparison with him. They are but a drop in the bucket, dust on the scales. He picks up the islands as though they had no weight at all.

Who else has held the oceans in his hand? Who has measured off the heavens with his fingers? Who else knows the weight of the earth or has weighed out the mountains and the hills?

By faith we understand that the entire universe was formed at God's command, that what we now see did not come from anything that can be seen.

When I look at the night sky and see the work of your fingers—the moon and the stars you have set in place—what are mortals that you should think of us, mere humans that you should care for us?

As God reveals himself through nature, we learn about his power and our finiteness. As God reveals himself through Scripture, we learn about his holiness and our sinfulness. As God reveals himself through daily experiences, we learn about his gracious forgiveness that frees us from guilt. *LAB note for Psalm 19:1ff.*

(EXODUS 20:11) (PSALM 19:1) (PSALM 33:6-7, 9) (ISAIAH 40:15) (ISAIAH 40:12) (HEBREWS 11:3) (PSALM 8:3-4)

*M*arch 2

Don't brag about tomorrow, since you don't know what the day will bring.

At just the right time, I heard you. On the day of salvation, I helped you. ▪ My light will shine out for you just a little while longer. Walk in it while you can, so you will not stumble when the darkness falls. If you walk in the darkness, you cannot see where you are going. Believe in the light while there is still time; then you will become children of the light.

Whatever you do, do well. For when you go to the grave, there will be no work or planning or knowledge or wisdom.

And I'll sit back and say to myself, "My friend, you have enough stored away for years to come. Now take it easy! Eat, drink, and be merry!" But God said to him, "You fool! You will die this very night. Then who will get it all?" Yes, a person is a fool to store up earthly wealth but not have a rich relationship with God.

Your life is like the morning fog—it's here a little while, then it's gone. ▪ This world is fading away, along with everything it craves. But if you do the will of God, you will live forever.

Life is short, no matter how many years we live. Don't be deceived into thinking that you have lots of remaining time to live for Christ, to enjoy your loved ones, or to do what you know you should. Live for God today! Then no matter when your life ends, you will have fulfilled God's plan for you. *LAB note for James 4:14*

(PROVERBS 27:1) (2 CORINTHIANS 6:2) (JOHN 12:35-36) (ECCLESIASTES 9:10) (LUKE 12:19-21) (JAMES 4:14) (1 JOHN 2:17)

M a r c h 3

You are always the same; your years never end.

Before the mountains were created, before you made the earth and the world, you are God, without beginning or end.

I am the LORD, and I do not change. That is why you descendants of Jacob are not already completely destroyed. ■ Jesus Christ is the same yesterday, today, and forever.

Whatever is good and perfect comes to us from God above, who created all heaven's lights. Unlike them, he never changes or casts shifting shadows. ■ God's gifts and his call can never be withdrawn.

God is not a man, that he should lie. He is not a human, that he should change his mind. ■ The unfailing love of the LORD never ends! By his mercies we have been kept from complete destruction.

Jesus remains a priest forever; his priesthood will never end. Therefore he is able, once and forever, to save everyone who comes to God through him. He lives forever to plead with God on their behalf. ■ Don't be afraid! I am the First and the Last.

Though human leaders have much to offer, we must keep our eyes on Christ, our ultimate leader. Unlike any human leaders, he will never change. Christ has been and will be the same forever. In a changing world we can trust our unchanging Lord. *LAB note for Hebrews 13:8*

(PSALM 102:27) (PSALM 90:2) (MALACHI 3:6) (HEBREWS 13:8) (JAMES 1:17) (ROMANS 11:29) (NUMBERS 23:19) (LAMENTATIONS 3:22) (HEBREWS 7:24-25) (REVELATION 1:17)

March 4

The LORD Is My Banner.

If God is for us, who can ever be against us? ▪ The LORD is for me, so I will not be afraid. What can mere mortals do to me?

You have raised a banner for those who honor you—a rallying point in the face of attack.

The LORD is my light and my salvation—so why should I be afraid? The LORD protects me from danger—so why should I tremble? Though a mighty army surrounds me, my heart will know no fear. Even if they attack me, I remain confident.

God is with us. He is our leader. ▪ The LORD Almighty is here among us; the God of Israel is our fortress.

They will wage war against the Lamb, but the Lamb will defeat them.

Why do the nations rage? Why do the people waste their time with futile plans? The one who rules in heaven laughs. The Lord scoffs at them. ▪ Call your councils of war, develop your strategies, prepare your plans of attack—and then die! For God is with us!

We can conquer fear by using the bright liberating light of the Lord, who brings salvation. If we want to dispel the darkness of fear, let us remember with the psalmist that "the LORD is my light and my salvation."

LAB note for Psalm 27:1

(EXODUS 17:15) (ROMANS 8:31) (PSALM 118:6) (PSALM 60:4) (PSALM 27:1, 3) (2 CHRONICLES 13:12) (PSALM 46:7) (REVELATION 17:14) (PSALM 2:1, 4) (ISAIAH 8:10)

*M*arch 5

Trust in the LORD with all your heart; do not depend on your own understanding.

Seek his will in all you do, and he will direct your paths. ▪ O my people, trust in him at all times. Pour out your heart to him, for God is our refuge.

The LORD says, "I will guide you along the best pathway for your life. I will advise you and watch over you. Do not be like a senseless horse or mule that needs a bit and bridle to keep it under control." Many sorrows come to the wicked, but unfailing love surrounds those who trust the LORD. ▪ You will hear a voice say, "This is the way; turn around and walk here." ▪ The LORD will guide you continually, watering your life when you are dry and keeping you healthy, too. You will be like a well-watered garden, like an ever-flowing spring.

I know, LORD, that a person's life is not his own. No one is able to plan his own course. ▪ If you don't go with us personally, don't let us move a step from this place.

When we have an important decision to make, we sometimes feel that we can't trust anyone—not even God. But God knows what is best for us. He is a better judge of what we want than we are! We must trust him completely in every choice we make. *LAB note for Proverbs 3:5-6*

(PROVERBS 3:5) (PROVERBS 3:6) (PSALM 32:8-10) (ISAIAH 30:21) (ISAIAH 58:11) (JEREMIAH 10:23) (EXODUS 33:15)

March 6

The prize for which God, through Christ Jesus, is calling us up to heaven.

You will have treasure in heaven. . . . Come, follow me. ▩ Your reward will be great.

The master was full of praise. "Well done, my good and faithful servant. You have been faithful in handling this small amount, so now I will give you many more responsibilities. Let's celebrate together!" ▩ They will reign forever and ever.

Your reward will be a never-ending share in his glory and honor. ▩ [You] will receive the crown of life. ▩ An eternal prize.

Father, I want these whom you've given me to be with me, so they can see my glory. You gave me the glory because you loved me even before the world began! ▩ We who are still alive . . . will be caught up in the clouds . . . and remain with him forever.

What we suffer now is nothing compared to the glory he will give us later.

"No eye has seen, no ear has heard, and no mind has imagined what God has prepared for those who love him." But we know these things because God has revealed them to us by his Spirit.

God's crown of life is not glory and honor here on earth but the reward of eternal life—living with God forever. The way to be in God's winners' circle is by loving him and staying faithful even under pressure.

LAB note for James 1:12

(Philippians 3:14) (Matthew 19:21) (Genesis 15:1) (Matthew 25:21) (Revelation 22:5) (1 Peter 5:4) (James 1:12) (1 Corinthians 9:25) (John 17:24) (1 Thessalonians 4:17) (Romans 8:18) (1 Corinthians 2:9-10)

*M*arch 7

He will bend his shoulder to the task.

For examples of patience in suffering, dear brothers and sisters, look at the prophets who spoke in the name of the Lord. ■ All these events happened to them as examples for us. They were written down to warn us, who live at the time when this age is drawing to a close.

Should we accept only good things from the hand of God and never anything bad? ■ Job is an example of a man who endured patiently. From his experience we see how the Lord's plan finally ended in good, for he is full of tenderness and mercy. ■ It is the LORD's will. . . . Let him do what he thinks best.

Give your burdens to the LORD, and he will take care of you. He will not permit the godly to slip and fall. ■ It was our weaknesses he carried; it was our sorrows that weighed him down.

Come to me, all of you who are weary and carry heavy burdens, and I will give you rest. Take my yoke upon you. Let me teach you, because I am humble and gentle, and you will find rest for your souls. For my yoke fits perfectly, and the burden I give you is light.

Jesus frees people from burdens. The rest that Jesus promises is love, healing, and peace with God, not the end of all labor. A relationship with God changes meaningless, wearisome toil into spiritual productivity and purpose. *LAB note for Matthew 11:28-30*

(GENESIS 49:15) (JAMES 5:10) (1 CORINTHIANS 10:11) (JOB 2:10) (JAMES 5:11) (1 SAMUEL 3:18) (PSALM 55:22) (ISAIAH 53:4) (MATTHEW 11:28-30)

March 8

I am in trouble, Lord. Help me!

I lift my eyes to you, O God, enthroned in heaven. We look to the LORD our God for his mercy, just as servants keep their eyes on their master, as a slave girl watches her mistress for the slightest signal. ▪ O God, listen to my cry! Hear my prayer! From the ends of the earth, I will cry to you for help, for my heart is overwhelmed. Lead me to the towering rock of safety, for you are my safe refuge, a fortress where my enemies cannot reach me. Let me live forever in your sanctuary, safe beneath the shelter of your wings! ▪ To the poor, O LORD, you are a refuge from the storm. To the needy in distress, you are a shelter from the rain and the heat.

Christ, who suffered for you, is your example. Follow in his steps. He never sinned, and he never deceived anyone. He did not retaliate when he was insulted. When he suffered, he did not threaten to get even. He left his case in the hands of God, who always judges fairly. ▪ This High Priest of ours understands our weaknesses, for he faced all of the same temptations we do, yet he did not sin. So let us come boldly to the throne of our gracious God. There we will receive his mercy, and we will find grace to help us when we need it.

The psalmist lifted his eyes to God, waiting and watching for God to send his mercy. The more he waited, the more he cried out to God, because he knew that the evil and proud offered no help—they had only contempt for God. *LAB note for Psalm 123:1ff.*

(ISAIAH 38:14) (PSALM 123:1-2) (PSALM 61:1-4) (ISAIAH 25:4) (1 PETER 2:21-23) (HEBREWS 4:15-16)

March 9

Fight the good fight.

Outside there there was conflict from every direction, and inside there was fear. ▪ Don't be afraid! . . . For there are more on our side than on theirs! ▪ Be strong with the Lord's mighty power.

You come to me with sword, spear, and javelin, but I come to you in the name of the LORD Almighty—the God of the armies of Israel, whom you have defied. ▪ God is my strong fortress. . . . He prepares me for battle; he strengthens me to draw a bow of bronze. ▪ Our only power and success come from God.

The angel of the LORD guards all who fear him, and he rescues them. ▪ "O LORD, open his eyes and let him see!" The LORD opened his servant's eyes, and when he looked up, he saw that the hillside around Elisha was filled with horses and chariots of fire.

How much more do I need to say? It would take too long to recount the stories. . . . By faith these people overthrew kingdoms. . . . Their weakness was turned to strength. They became strong in battle and put whole armies to flight.

When you face difficulties that seem insurmountable, remember that spiritual resources are there even if you can't see them. Look through the eyes of faith, and let God show you his resources. *LAB note for 2 Kings 6:16*

(1 TIMOTHY 6:12) (2 CORINTHIANS 7:5) (2 KINGS 6:16) (EPHESIANS 6:10) (1 SAMUEL 17:45) (2 SAMUEL 22:33, 35) (2 CORINTHIANS 3:5) (PSALM 34:7) (2 KINGS 6:17) (HEBREWS 11:32-34)

March 10

He guards the paths of justice and protects those who are faithful to him.

The LORD your God . . . goes before you looking for the best places to camp, guiding you by a pillar of fire at night and a pillar of cloud by day. ▪ Like an eagle that rouses her chicks and hovers over her young, so he spread his wings to take them in and carried them aloft on his pinions. The LORD alone guided them. ▪ The steps of the godly are directed by the LORD. He delights in every detail of their lives. Though they stumble, they will not fall, for the LORD holds them by the hand. ▪ The righteous face many troubles, but the LORD rescues them from each and every one. ▪ For the LORD watches over the path of the godly, but the path of the wicked leads to destruction. ▪ And we know that God causes everything to work together for the good of those who love God and are called according to his purpose for them. ▪ We have the LORD our God to help us and to fight our battles for us!

The LORD your God has arrived to live among you. He is a mighty savior. He will rejoice over you with great gladness.

The Israelites had no excuse for abandoning God. He had been the encircling protector, like a mother eagle who protects her young. The Lord alone had led them. And he alone leads us. Let us remember to trust in him. *LAB note for Deuteronomy 32:10-11*

(PROVERBS 2:8) (DEUTERONOMY 1:32-33) (DEUTERONOMY 32:11-12) (PSALM 37:23-24) (PSALM 34:19) (PSALM 1:6) (ROMANS 8:28) (2 CHRONICLES 32:8) (ZEPHANIAH 3:17)

March 11

You . . . have forgiven all my sins.

Where is another God like you, who pardons the sins of the survivors among his people? You cannot stay angry with your people forever, because you delight in showing mercy. Once again you will have compassion on us. You will trample our sins under your feet and throw them into the depths of the ocean!

"For a brief moment I abandoned you, but with great compassion I will take you back. In a moment of anger I turned my face away for a little while. But with everlasting love I will have compassion on you," says the LORD, your Redeemer. ▪ I will forgive their wickedness and will never again remember their sins.

Oh, what joy for those whose rebellion is forgiven, whose sin is put out of sight! Yes, what joy for those whose record the LORD has cleared of sin, whose lives are lived in complete honesty! ▪ The blood of Jesus, his Son, cleanses us from every sin. If we say we have no sin, we are only fooling ourselves and refusing to accept the truth. But if we confess our sins to him, he is faithful and just to forgive us and to cleanse us from every wrong.

Prayer brings deliverance, forgiveness, and good from even a bitter experience. The next time you have difficult struggles, pray for God's help to gain something beneficial from them.

LAB note for Isaiah 38:16-18

(ISAIAH 38:17) (MICAH 7:18-19) (ISAIAH 54:7-8) (JEREMIAH 31:34) (PSALM 32:1-2) (1 JOHN 1:7-9)

March 12

I know the one in whom I trust, and I am sure that he is able to guard what I have entrusted to him until the day of his return.

He is able to accomplish infinitely more than we would ever dare to ask or hope.

God will generously provide all you need. Then you will always have everything you need and plenty left over to share with others.

He is able to help us when we are being tempted.

He is able, once and forever, to save everyone who comes to God through him. He lives forever to plead with God on their behalf.

God . . . is able to keep you from stumbling, and . . . will bring you into his glorious presence innocent of sin and with great joy.

He is able to guard what I have entrusted to him until the day of his return.

He will take these weak mortal bodies of ours and change them into glorious bodies like his own, using the same mighty power that he will use to conquer everything, everywhere.

"Do you believe?" . . . "Yes, Lord," they told him, "we do." . . . "Because of your faith, it will happen!"

Even in prison, the apostle Paul knew that God was still in control. No matter what setbacks or problems we face, we can trust fully in God. *LAB note for 2 Timothy 1:12*

(2 Timothy 1:12) (Ephesians 3:20) (2 Corinthians 9:8) (Hebrews 2:18) (Hebrews 7:25) (Jude 1:24) (2 Timothy 1:12) (Philippians 3:21) (Matthew 9:28-29)

March 13

The LORD Will Provide.

I trust in you, my God! Do not let me be disgraced, or let my enemies rejoice in my defeat.

The LORD is not too weak to save you, and he is not becoming deaf. He can hear you when you call. ▨ A Deliverer will come from Jerusalem.

Happy are those who have the God of Israel as their helper, whose hope is in the LORD their God. ▨ The LORD watches over those who fear him, those who rely on his unfailing love. He rescues them from death and keeps them alive in times of famine.

This same God who takes care of me will supply all your needs from his glorious riches, which have been given to us in Christ Jesus. ▨ For God has said, "I will never fail you. I will never forsake you." That is why we can say with confidence, "The Lord is my helper, so I will not be afraid. What can mere mortals do to me?" ▨ The LORD is my strength, my shield from every danger. I trust in him with all my heart. He helps me, and my heart is filled with joy. I burst out in songs of thanksgiving. The LORD protects his people.

We do not have an ironclad guarantee that all believers will be delivered from death and starvation. God can (and often does) miraculously deliver his followers from pain and death; although sometimes, for purposes known only to him, he chooses not to.

LAB note for Psalm 33:18-19

(GENESIS 22:14) (PSALM 25:2) (ISAIAH 59:1) (ROMANS 11:26) (PSALM 146:5) (PSALM 33:18-19) (PHILIPPIANS 4:19) (HEBREWS 13:5-6) (PSALM 28:7-8)

*M*arch 14

The things that please him.

It is impossible to please God without faith. ▪ Those who are still under the control of their sinful nature can never please God. ▪ The LORD delights in his people; he crowns the humble with salvation.

God is pleased with you when, for the sake of your conscience, you patiently endure unfair treatment. Of course, you get no credit for being patient if you are beaten for doing wrong. But if you suffer for doing right and are patient beneath the blows, God is pleased with you. ▪ You should be known for the beauty that comes from within, the unfading beauty of a gentle and quiet spirit, which is so precious to God.

Giving thanks is a sacrifice that truly honors me. If you keep to my path, I will reveal to you the salvation of God. ▪ Then I will praise God's name with singing, and I will honor him with thanksgiving. For this will please the LORD more than sacrificing an ox or presenting a bull with its horns and hooves.

Dear brothers and sisters, I plead with you to give your bodies to God. Let them be a living and holy sacrifice—the kind he will accept. When you think of what he has done for you, is this too much to ask?

God wants us to offer ourselves as living sacrifices—daily laying aside our own desires to follow him, putting all our energy and resources at his disposal, and trusting him to guide us. We do this out of gratitude that our sins have been forgiven. *LAB note for Romans 12:1*

(1 JOHN 3:22) (HEBREWS 11:6) (ROMANS 8:8) (PSALM 149:4) (1 PETER 2:19-20) (1 PETER 3:4) (PSALM 50:23) (PSALM 69:30-31) (ROMANS 12:1)

March 15

I am deeply discouraged.

You will keep in perfect peace all who trust in you, whose thoughts are fixed on you! Trust in the LORD always, for the LORD GOD is the eternal Rock.

Give your burdens to the LORD, and he will take care of you. He will not permit the godly to slip and fall. ▪ He has not ignored the suffering of the needy. He has not turned and walked away. He has listened to their cries for help. ▪ Are any among you suffering? They should keep praying about it.

Don't be troubled or afraid. ▪ Don't worry about everyday life—whether you have enough food, drink, and clothes. Doesn't life consist of more than food and clothing? Look at the birds. They don't need to plant or harvest or put food in barns because your heavenly Father feeds them. And you are far more valuable to him than they are. Can all your worries add a single moment to your life? Of course not. And why worry about your clothes? Look at the lilies and how they grow. They don't work or make their clothing, yet Solomon in all his glory was not dressed as beautifully as they are. And if God cares so wonderfully for flowers that are here today and gone tomorrow, won't he more surely care for you? ▪ Don't be faithless any longer. Believe! ▪ I am with you always.

Sin, fear, uncertainty, doubt, and numerous other forces are at war within us. The peace of God moves into our hearts and lives to restrain these hostile forces and offer comfort in place of conflict. Jesus says he will give us that peace if we are willing to accept it from him.

LAB note for John 14:27–29

(PSALM 42:6) (ISAIAH 26:3-4) (PSALM 55:22) (PSALM 22:24) (JAMES 5:13) (JOHN 14:27) (MATTHEW 6:25-30) (JOHN 20:27) (MATTHEW 28:20)

March 16

Don't hide your light under a basket! Instead, put it on a stand and let it shine for all. In the same way, let your good deeds shine out for all to see, so that everyone will praise your heavenly Father.

Live in a manner worthy of the Good News about Christ, as citizens of heaven. ▩ Keep away from every kind of evil. ▩ Be happy if you are insulted for being a Christian, for then the glorious Spirit of God will come upon you. If you suffer, however, it must not be for murder, stealing, making trouble, or prying into other people's affairs. ▩ In everything you do, stay away from complaining and arguing, so that no one can speak a word of blame against you. You are to live clean, innocent lives as children of God in a dark world full of crooked and perverse people. Let your lives shine brightly before them. ▩ Make the teaching about God our Savior attractive in every way.

Never let loyalty and kindness get away from you! Wear them like a necklace; write them deep within your heart. Then you will find favor with both God and people, and you will gain a good reputation. Trust in the LORD with all your heart; do not depend on your own understanding. ▩ Fix your thoughts on what is true and honorable and right. Think about things that are pure and lovely and admirable. Think about things that are excellent and worthy of praise.

Can you hide a city that is sitting on top of a mountain? Its light at night can be seen for miles. If we live for Christ, we will glow like lights, showing others what Christ is like. Be a beacon of truth—don't shut your light off from the rest of the world. *LAB note for Matthew 5:14-16*

(MATTHEW 5:15-16) (PHILIPPIANS 1:27) (1 THESSALONIANS 5:22) (1 PETER 4:14-15) (PHILIPPIANS 2:14-15) (TITUS 2:10) (PROVERBS 3:3-5) (PHILIPPIANS 4:8)

March 17

The LORD Is Our Righteousness.

We are all infected and impure with sin. When we proudly display our righteous deeds, we find they are but filthy rags.

I will praise your mighty deeds, O Sovereign LORD. I will tell everyone that you alone are just and good. ■ I am overwhelmed with joy in the LORD my God! For he has dressed me with the clothing of salvation and draped me in a robe of righteousness. I am like a bridegroom in his wedding suit or a bride with her jewels.

Bring the finest robe in the house and put it on. ■ Wear the finest white linen. (Fine linen represents the good deeds done by the people of God.)

Everything else is worthless when compared with the priceless gain of knowing Christ Jesus my Lord. I have discarded everything else, counting it all as garbage, so that I may have Christ and become one with him. I no longer count on my own goodness or my ability to obey God's law, but I trust Christ to save me. For God's way of making us right with himself depends on faith.

Sin makes us unclean so that we cannot approach God any more than a beggar in filthy rags could dine at a king's table. Our best efforts are still infected with sin. Our only hope, therefore, is faith in Jesus Christ, who can cleanse us and bring us into God's presence. *LAB note for Isaiah 64:6*

(JEREMIAH 23:6) (ISAIAH 64:6) (PSALM 71:16) (ISAIAH 61:10) (LUKE 15:22) (REVELATION 19:8) (PHILIPPIANS 3:8-9)

March 18

Through the suffering of Jesus, God made him a perfect leader.

"My soul is crushed with grief to the point of death. Stay here and watch with me." He went on a little farther and fell face down on the ground, praying, "My Father! If it is possible, let this cup of suffering be taken away from me. Yet I want your will, not mine." ▩ He prayed more fervently, and he was in such agony of spirit that his sweat fell to the ground like great drops of blood.

Death had its hands around my throat; the terrors of the grave overtook me. I saw only trouble and sorrow. ▩ Their insults have broken my heart, and I am in despair. If only one person would show some pity; if only one would turn and comfort me. ▩ No one gives me a passing thought! No one will help me; no one cares a bit what happens to me.

He was despised and rejected—a man of sorrows, acquainted with bitterest grief. We turned our backs on him and looked the other way when he went by. He was despised, and we did not care. But he was wounded and crushed for our sins. He was beaten that we might have peace. He was whipped, and we were healed! He was oppressed and treated harshly, yet he never said a word.

I will give him the honors of one who is mighty and great, because he exposed himself to death.

The man of sorrows was despised and rejected by those around him, and he is still despised and rejected by many today. Some reject Christ by standing against him. Others despise Christ and his great gift of forgiveness. Do you despise him, reject him, or accept him?

LAB note for Isaiah 53:3

(HEBREWS 2:10) (MATTHEW 26:38-39) (LUKE 22:44) (PSALM 116:3) (PSALM 69:20) (PSALM 142:4) (ISAIAH 53:3, 5, 7) (ISAIAH 53:12)

*M*arch 19

The LORD's searchlight penetrates the human spirit, exposing every hidden motive.

"All right, stone her. But let those who have never sinned throw the first stones!" When the accusers heard this, they slipped away one by one, beginning with the oldest.

"Who told you that you were naked?" the LORD God asked. "Have you eaten the fruit I commanded you not to eat?"

It is sin to know what you ought to do and then not do it. ▪ We will be confident when we stand before the Lord, even if our hearts condemn us. For God is greater than our hearts, and he knows everything. Dear friends, if our conscience is clear, we can come to God with bold confidence.

There is nothing wrong with these things in themselves. But it is wrong to eat anything if it makes another person stumble. Blessed are those who do not condemn themselves by doing something they know is all right.

Search me, O God, and know my heart; test me and know my thoughts. Point out anything in me that offends you, and lead me along the path of everlasting life.

We tend to think that doing wrong is sin. But sin is also not doing right. If God has directed you to do a kind act, to render a service, or to restore a relationship, do it. You will experience a renewed vitality in your Christian faith. *LAB note for James 4:17*

(PROVERBS 20:27) (JOHN 8:7, 9) (GENESIS 3:11) (JAMES 4:17) (1 JOHN 3:19-21) (ROMANS 14:20, 22) (PSALM 139:23-24)

*M*arch 20

I will pray in the spirit, and I will pray in words I understand. I will sing in the spirit, and I will sing in words I understand.

Let the Holy Spirit fill and control you. Then you will sing psalms and hymns and spiritual songs among yourselves, making music to the Lord in your hearts. ▪ Let the words of Christ, in all their richness, live in your hearts and make you wise. Use his words to teach and counsel each other. Sing psalms and hymns and spiritual songs to God with thankful hearts.

I will praise the LORD, and everyone on earth will bless his holy name forever and forever.

How good it is to sing praises to our God! How delightful and how right! Sing out your thanks to the LORD; sing praises to our God, accompanied by harps.

I heard a sound from heaven like the roaring of a great waterfall or the rolling of mighty thunder. It was like the sound of many harpists playing together. ▪ Then I saw in heaven another significant event. . . . They were all holding harps that God had given them. And they were singing the song of Moses, the servant of God, and the song of the Lamb: "Great and marvelous are your actions, Lord God Almighty. Just and true are your ways, O King of the nations."

In praying and singing, both the mind and the spirit are to be fully engaged. When we sing, we should also think about the meaning of the words. When we pour out our feelings to God in prayer, we should not turn off our capacity to think. *LAB note for 1 Corinthians 14:15*

(1 CORINTHIANS 14:15) (EPHESIANS 5:18-19) (COLOSSIANS 3:16) (PSALM 145:21) (PSALM 147:1, 7) (REVELATION 14:2) (REVELATION 15:1-3)

*M*arch 21

God in all his fullness was pleased to live in Christ.

The Father loves his Son, and he has given him authority over everything. ▪ God raised him up to the heights of heaven and gave him a name that is above every other name, so that at the name of Jesus every knee will bow, in heaven and on earth and under the earth, and every tongue will confess that Jesus Christ is Lord, to the glory of God the Father. ▪ Now he is far above any ruler or authority or power or leader or anything else in this world or in the world to come. ▪ Christ is the one through whom God created everything in heaven and earth. He made the things we can see and the things we can't see—kings, kingdoms, rulers, and authorities. Everything has been created through him and for him.

Christ died and rose again for this very purpose, so that he might be Lord of those who are alive and of those who have died. ▪ You are complete through your union with Christ. He is the Lord over every ruler and authority in the universe. ▪ We have all benefited from the rich blessings he brought to us—one gracious blessing after another.

Christ was fully human; he was also fully divine. Christ has always been God and always will be God. When we have Christ, we have all of God in human form. Don't diminish any aspect of Christ—either his humanity or his divinity.

LAB note for Colossians 1:19

(COLOSSIANS 1:19) (JOHN 3:35) (PHLIPPIANS 2:9-11) (EPHESIANS 1:21) (COLOSSIANS 1:16) (ROMANS 14:9) (COLOSSIANS 2:10) (JOHN 1:16)

March 22

He faced all of the same temptations we do, yet he did not sin.

The fruit looked so fresh and delicious, and it would make her so wise! So she ate some of the fruit. She also gave some to her husband, who was with her. Then he ate it, too. ▪ Stop loving this evil world and all that it offers you, for when you love the world, you show that you do not have the love of the Father in you.

Then the Devil came and said to him, "If you are the Son of God, change these stones into loaves of bread." But Jesus told him, "No! The Scriptures say, 'People need more than bread for their life; they must feed on every word of God.'" Next the Devil took him to the peak of a very high mountain and showed him the nations of the world and all their glory. "I will give it all to you," he said, "if you will only kneel down and worship me." "Get out of here, Satan," Jesus told him. ▪ The world offers only the lust for physical pleasure, the lust for everything we see, and pride in our posessions. These are not from the Father. They are from this evil world.

Since he himself has gone through suffering and temptation, he is able to help us when we are being tempted.

God blesses the people who patiently endure testing.

Prepare yourself for the attractive temptations that may come your way. We cannot always prevent temptation, but there is always a way of escape. Use God's Word and God's people to help you stand against it.

LAB note for Genesis 3:6

(HEBREWS 4:15) (GENESIS 3:6) (1 JOHN 2:15) (MATTHEW 4:3-4, 8-10) (1 JOHN 2:16) (HEBREWS 2:18) (JAMES 1:12)

March 23

My eyes grew tired of looking to heaven for help.

Have compassion on me, LORD, for I am weak. Heal me, LORD, for my body is in agony. I am sick at heart. How long, O LORD, until you restore me? Return, O LORD, and rescue me. Save me because of your unfailing love. ▪ My heart is in anguish. The terror of death overpowers me. Fear and trembling overwhelm me. I can't stop shaking. Oh, how I wish I had wings like a dove; then I would fly away and rest!

Patient endurance is what you need now, so you will continue to do God's will. ▪ Don't get tired of doing what is good. Don't get discouraged and give up, for we will reap a harvest of blessing at the appropriate time.

As they were straining their eyes to see him, two white-robed men suddenly stood there among them. They said, "Men of Galilee, why are you standing here staring at the sky? Jesus has been taken away from you into heaven. And someday, just as you saw him go, he will return!" ▪ We are citizens of heaven, where the Lord Jesus Christ lives. And we are eagerly waiting for him to return as our Savior. ▪ We look forward to that wonderful event when the glory of our great God and Savior, Jesus Christ, will be revealed.

Don't abandon your faith in times of persecution, but show by your endurance that your faith is real. Faith means resting in what Christ has done for us in the past, but it also means trusting him for what he will do for us in the present and in the future. *LAB note for Hebrews 10:35-38*

(ISAIAH 38:14) (PSALM 6:2-4) (PSALM 55:4-6) (HEBREWS 10:36) (GALATIANS 6:9) (ACTS 1:10-11) (PHILIPPIANS 3:20) (TITUS 2:13)

March 24

When God raised up his servant, he sent him . . . to bless you by turning each of you back from your sinful ways.

All honor to the God and Father of our Lord Jesus Christ, for it is by his boundless mercy that God has given us the privilege of being born again. Now we live with a wonderful expectation because Jesus Christ rose again from the dead.

Our great God and Savior, Jesus Christ . . . gave his life to free us from every kind of sin, to cleanse us, and to make us his very own people, totally committed to doing what is right. ▪ Be holy in everything you do, just as God—who chose you to be his children—is holy. For he himself has said, "You must be holy because I am holy."

God, the Father of our Lord Jesus Christ . . . has blessed us with every spiritual blessing in the heavenly realms because we belong to Christ. ▪ For in Christ the fullness of God lives in a human body, and you are complete through your union with Christ. ▪ We have all benefited from the rich blessings he brought to us—one gracious blessing after another.

Since God did not spare even his own Son but gave him up for us all, won't God, who gave us Christ, also give us everything else?

Christ's freeing us from sin opens the way for him to purify us. He freed us from sin (redeemed us) by purchasing our release from the captivity of sin with a ransom. We are not only free from the sentence of death for our sin, but we are also purified from sin's influence as we grow in Christ. *LAB note for Titus 2:14*

(ACTS 3:26) (1 PETER 1:3) (TITUS 2:13-14) (1 PETER 1:15-16) (EPHESIANS 1:3) (COLOSSIANS 2:9-10) (JOHN 1:16) (ROMANS 8:32)

*M*arch 25

Encourage me by your word.

Remember your promise to me, for it is my only hope. ▪ I am in trouble, Lord. Help me!

Heaven and earth will disappear, but my words will remain forever. ▪ Deep in your hearts you know that every promise of the LORD your God has come true.

Don't be afraid, for I am with you. Do not be dismayed, for I am your God. I will strengthen you. I will help you. I will uphold you with my victorious right hand. ▪ Take courage and work, for I am with you, says the LORD Almighty. ▪ Not by force nor by strength, but by my Spirit, says the LORD Almighty. ▪ Study this Book of the Law continually. Meditate on it day and night so you may be sure to obey all that is written in it. Only then will you succeed. I command you—be strong and courageous! Do not be afraid or discouraged. For the LORD your God is with you wherever you go.

Be strong with the Lord's mighty power.

To succeed you must (1) be strong and courageous, (2) obey God's law, and (3) constantly read and study God's Word. You may not succeed by the world's standards, but you will be a success in God's eyes—and his opinion lasts forever. *LAB note for Joshua 1:6-8*

(PSALM 119:28) (PSALM 119:49) (ISAIAH 38:14) (LUKE 21:33) (JOSHUA 23:14) (ISAIAH 41:10) (HAGGAI 2:4) (ZECHARIAH 4:6) (JOSHUA 1:8-9) (EPHESIANS 6:10)

*M*arch 26

Wake up! Strengthen what little remains, for even what is left is at the point of death.

The end of the world is coming soon. Therefore, be earnest and disciplined in your prayers. ▪ Be careful! Watch out for attacks from the Devil, your great enemy. He prowls around like a roaring lion, looking for some victim to devour. ▪ Watch out! Be very careful never to forget what you have seen the LORD do for you. Do not let these things escape from your mind as long as you live! ▪ A righteous person will live by faith. But I will have no pleasure in anyone who turns away. . . . We have faith that assures our salvation.

Keep a sharp lookout! For you do not know when the homeowner will return—at evening, midnight, early dawn, or late daybreak. Don't let him find you sleeping when he arrives without warning. What I say to you I say to everyone: Watch for his return!

Don't be afraid, for I am with you. Do not be dismayed, for I am your God. I will strengthen you. I will help you. I will uphold you with my victorious right hand. I am holding you by your right hand—I, the LORD your God. And I say to you, "Do not be afraid. I am here to help you."

We should live expectantly because Christ is coming soon. Getting ready to meet Christ involves continually growing in love for God and for others. It is important to pray regularly and to reach out to needy people. Invest your time and talents where they will make an eternal difference. *LAB note for 1 Peter 4:7-9*

(REVELATION 3:2) (1 PETER 4:7) (1 PETER 5:8) (DEUTERONOMOY 4:9) (HEBREWS 10:38-39) (MARK 13:35-37) (ISAIAH 41:10, 13)

March 27

Is his unfailing love gone forever?

He remembered our utter weakness. His faithful love endures forever. ▪ The LORD is slow to anger and rich in unfailing love, forgiving every kind of sin and rebellion. ▪ Where is another God like you, who pardons the sins of the survivors among his people? You cannot stay angry with your people forever, because you delight in showing mercy. Once again you will have compassion on us. You will trample our sins under your feet and throw them into the depths of the ocean! ▪ He saved us, not because of the good things we did, but because of his mercy. He washed away our sins and gave us a new life through the Holy Spirit.

All praise to the God and Father of our Lord Jesus Christ. He is the source of every mercy and the God who comforts us. He comforts us in all our troubles.

Our merciful and faithful High Priest before God . . . could offer a sacrifice that would take away the sins of the people. Since he himself has gone through suffering and temptation, he is able to help us when we are being tempted.

Here are several unchanging characteristics of God we can rely on: (1) God is immensely patient; (2) God's love is one promise we can always count on; (3) God forgives again and again; (4) God is merciful, listening to and answering our requests. *LAB note for Micah 14:17-20*

(PSALM 77:8) (PSALM 136:23) (NUMBERS 14:18) (MICAH 7:18-19) (TITUS 3:5) (2 CORINTHIANS 1:3-4) (HEBREWS 2:17-18)

March 28

Lot took a long look at the fertile plains of the Jordan Valley in the direction of Zoar. The whole area was well watered everywhere, like the garden of the LORD or the beautiful land of Egypt. (This was before the LORD had destroyed Sodom and Gomorrah.) Lot chose that land for himself—the Jordan Valley to the east of them.

Lot . . . was a good man.

Don't be misled. Remember that you can't ignore God and get away with it. You will always reap what you sow! ▪ Remember what happened to Lot's wife!

Don't team up with those who are unbelievers. How can goodness be a partner with wickedness? How can light live with darkness? Therefore, come out from them and separate yourselves from them, says the Lord. Don't touch their filthy things, and I will welcome you. ▪ Don't participate in the things these people do. For though your hearts were once full of darkness, now you are full of light from the Lord, and your behavior should show it! Try to find out what is pleasing to the Lord. Take no part in the worthless deeds of evil and darkness; instead, rebuke and expose them. ▪ Knowing God leads to self-control. Self-control leads to patient endurance, and patient endurance leads to godliness. The more you grow like this, the more you will become productive and useful in your knowledge of our Lord Jesus Christ.

Just as God rescued Lot from Sodom, so he is able to rescue us from the temptations and trials we face in a wicked world. Lot was not sinless, but he put his trust in God and was spared when Sodom was destroyed. *LAB note for 2 Peter 2:7-9*

(GENESIS 13:10-11) (2 PETER 2:7) (GALATIANS 6:7) (LUKE 17:32) (2 CORINTHIANS 6:14, 17) (EPHESIANS 5:7-8, 10-11) (2 PETER 1:6, 8)

March 29

Holy, holy, holy is the Lord God Almighty.

The praises of Israel surround your throne. ▪ "Do not come any closer," God told him. "Take off your sandals, for you are standing on holy ground." Then he said, "I am the God of your ancestors—the God of Abraham, the God of Isaac, and the God of Jacob." When Moses heard this, he hid his face in his hands because he was afraid to look at God. ▪ "To whom will you compare me? Who is my equal?" asks the Holy One. ▪ I am the LORD, your God, the Holy One of Israel, your Savior. There is no other God.

Now you must be holy in everything you do, just as God—who chose you to be his children—is holy. For he himself has said, "You must be holy because I am holy." ▪ Don't you know that your body is the temple of the Holy Spirit, who lives in you and was given to you by God? You do not belong to yourself.

And so . . . I plead with you to give your bodies to God. Let them be a living and holy sacrifice—the kind he will accept. When you think of what he has done for you, is this too much to ask?

God is our friend, but he is also our sovereign Lord. To approach him frivolously shows a lack of respect and sincerity. When you come to God in worship, do you approach him casually, or do you come as though you were an invited guest before a king? *LAB note for Exodus 3:5-6*

(REVELATION 4:8) (PSALM 22:3) (EXODUS 3:5-6) (ISAIAH 40:25) (ISAIAH 43:3, 10) (1 PETER 1:15-16) (1 CORINTHIANS 6:19) (ROMANS 12:1)

*M*arch 30

I will never fail you. I will never forsake you.

That is why we can say with confidence, "The Lord is my helper, so I will not be afraid. What can mere mortals do to me?"

I will be with you, and I will protect you wherever you go. I will someday bring you safely back to this land. I will be with you constantly until I have finished giving you everything I have promised. ▪ Be strong and courageous! Do not be afraid of them! The LORD your God will go ahead of you. He will neither fail you nor forsake you.

Demas has deserted me because he loves the things of this life. The first time I was brought before the judge, no one was with me. Everyone had abandoned me. I hope it will not be counted against them. But the Lord stood with me and gave me strength, that I might preach the Good News in all its fullness for all the Gentiles to hear. ▪ Even if my father and mother abandon me, the LORD will hold me close.

I am with you always, even to the end of the age. ▪ I am the living one who died. Look, I am alive forever and ever! ▪ I will not abandon you as orphans—I will come to you. ▪ I am leaving you with a gift—peace of mind and heart.

When Jesus said, "I will come to you," he meant it. Although Jesus ascended to heaven, he sent the Holy Spirit to live in believers, and to have the Holy Spirit is to have Jesus himself. *LAB note for John 14:18*

(HEBREWS 13:5) (HEBREWS 13:6) (GENESIS 28:15) (DEUTERONOMY 31:6) (2 TIMOTHY 4:10, 16-17) (PSALM 27:10) (MATTHEW 28:20) (REVELATION 1:18) (JOHN 14:18) (JOHN 14:27)

March 31

The Kingdom of Heaven can be illustrated by the story of a man going on a trip. He called together his servants and gave them money to invest for him while he was gone . . . dividing it in proportion to their abilities.

Don't you realize that whatever you choose to obey becomes your master? You can choose sin, which leads to death, or you can choose to obey God and receive his approval.

It is the one and only Holy Spirit who distributes these gifts. He alone decides which gift each person should have. A spiritual gift is given to each of us as a means of helping the entire church. ❖ God has given gifts to each of you from his great variety of spiritual gifts. Manage them well so that God's generosity can flow through you. ❖ A person who is put in charge as a manager must be faithful. ❖ Much is required from those to whom much is given, and much more is required from those to whom much more is given.

Who is adequate for such a task as this? ❖ I can do everything with the help of Christ who gives me the strength I need.

God gives us time, gifts, and other resources according to our abilities, and he expects us to invest them wisely until he returns. We are responsible to use well what God has given us. The issue is not how much we have but how well we use what we have. *LAB note for Matthew 25:15*

(MATTHEW 25:14-15) (ROMANS 6:16) (1 CORINTHIANS 12:11, 7) (1 PETER 4:10) (1 CORINTHIANS 4:2) (LUKE 12:48) (2 CORINTHIANS 2:16) (PHILIPPIANS 4:13)

April

One Sunday Morning

One of a kind, timeless significance
From devastating tragedy to extraordinary blessing
No other day means more than this one.

This Easter season may you gain a fresh awareness of God's wondrous plan offered for you! Such enormous grace shown to imperfect people—that is treasure beyond words.

April 1

When the Holy Spirit controls our lives, he will produce . . . love.

We know how much God loves us, and we have put our trust in him. ▪ How dearly God loves us, because he has given us the Holy Spirit to fill our hearts with his love. ▪ He is very precious to you who believe. ▪ We love each other as a result of his loving us first. ▪ Whatever we do, it is because Christ's love controls us. Since we believe that Christ died for everyone, we also believe that we have all died to the old life we used to live. He died for everyone so that those who receive his new life will no longer live to please themselves. Instead, they will live to please Christ, who died and was raised for them.

God himself has taught you to love one another. ▪ I command you to love each other in the same way that I love you. ▪ Most important of all, continue to show deep love for each other, for love covers a multitude of sins. ▪ Live a life filled with love for others, following the example of Christ, who loved you and gave himself as a sacrifice to take away your sins. And God was pleased, because that sacrifice was like sweet perfume to him.

Since Christ's love controls our lives and he died for us, we are dead to our old life. We should no longer live to please ourselves; we should spend our life pleasing Christ, who died for us and rose again from the grave. *LAB note for 2 Corinthians 5:13–15*

(Galatians 5:22) (1 John 4:16) (Romans 5:5) (1 Peter 2:7) (1 John 4:19) (2 Corinthians 5:14–15) (1 Thessalonians 4:9) (John 15:12) (1 Peter 4:8) (Ephesians 5:2)

April 2

The reward of the godly will last.

After a long time their master returned from his trip and called them to give an account of how they had used his money. The servant to whom he had entrusted the five bags of gold said, "Sir, you gave me five bags of gold to invest, and I have doubled the amount." The master was full of praise. "Well done, my good and faithful servant. You have been faithful in handling this small amount, so now I will give you many more responsibilities. Let's celebrate together!"

We must all stand before Christ to be judged. We will each receive whatever we deserve for the good or evil we have done in our bodies.

I have fought a good fight, I have finished the race, and I have remained faithful. And now the prize awaits me—the crown of righteousness that the Lord, the righteous Judge, will give me on that great day of his return. And the prize is not just for me but for all who eagerly look forward to his glorious return.

I am coming quickly. Hold on to what you have, so that no one will take away your crown.

While eternal life is a free gift given on the basis of God's grace, each of us will still be judged by Christ. All Christians must give account on the day of judgment, and Christ will reward us for how we have lived.

LAB note for 2 Corinthians 5:9–10

(PROVERBS 11:18) (MATTHEW 25:19–21) (2 CORINTHIANS 5:10)
(2 TIMOTHY 4:7–8) (REVELATION 3:11)

April 3

God is faithful.

God is not a man, that he should lie. He is not a human, that he should change his mind. . . . Has he ever promised and not carried it through? ▩ The Lord has taken an oath and will not break his vow.

God also bound himself with an oath, so that those who received the promise could be perfectly sure that he would never change his mind. So God has given us both his promise and his oath. These two things are unchangeable because it is impossible for God to lie. Therefore, we who have fled to him for refuge can take new courage, for we can hold on to his promise with confidence. ▩ So if you are suffering according to God's will, keep on doing what is right, and trust yourself to the God who made you, for he will never fail you.

I know the one in whom I trust, and I am sure that he is able to guard what I have entrusted to him until the day of his return. ▩ God, who calls you, is faithful; he will do this. ▩ All of God's promises have been fulfilled in him. That is why we say "Amen" when we give glory to God through Christ.

All of God's promises of what the Messiah would be like are fulfilled in Christ. Jesus was completely faithful in his ministry; he never sinned; he faithfully died for us; and now he faithfully intercedes for us.

LAB note for 2 Corinthians 1:19–20

(1 Corinthians 10:13) (Numbers 23:19) (Hebrews 7:21) (Hebrews 6:17–18) (1 Peter 4:19) (2 Timothy 1:12) (1 Thessalonians 5:24) (2 Corinthians 1:20)

April 4

Be strong and courageous!

The LORD is my light and my salvation—so why should I be afraid? ▪ He gives power to those who are tired and worn out; he offers strength to the weak. Even youths will become exhausted, and young men will give up. But those who wait on the LORD will find new strength. They will fly high on wings like eagles. They will run and not grow weary. They will walk and not faint. ▪ My health may fail, and my spirit may grow weak, but God remains the strength of my heart; he is mine forever.

What can we say about such wonderful things as these? If God is for us, who can ever be against us? Since God did not spare even his own Son but gave him up for us all, won't God, who gave us Christ, also give us everything else? ▪ The LORD is for me, so I will not be afraid. What can mere mortals do to me? ▪ Only by your power can we push back our enemies; only in your name can we trample our foes. ▪ Overwhelming victory is ours through Christ, who loved us.

May the LORD be with you and give you success. Be strong and courageous; do not be afraid or lose heart!

When God commissioned Joshua, he was told three times to be strong and courageous! Apparently he took God's message to heart. The next time you are afraid to do what you know is right, remember that strength and courage are readily available from God. *LAB note for Joshua 1:18*

(JOSHUA 1:18) (PSALM 27:1) (ISAIAH 40:29-31) (PSALM 73:26) (ROMANS 8:31-32) (PSALM 118:6) (PSALM 44:5) (ROMANS 8:37) (1 CHRONICLES 22:11, 13)

April 5

Riches don't last forever, and the crown might not be secure for the next generation.

We are merely moving shadows, and all our busy rushing ends in nothing. We heap up wealth for someone else to spend. ▩ Let heaven fill your thoughts. Do not think only about things down here on earth. ▩ Don't store up treasures here on earth, where they can be eaten by moths and get rusty, and where thieves break in and steal. Store your treasures in heaven, where they will never become moth-eaten or rusty and where they will be safe from thieves. Wherever your treasure is, there your heart and thoughts will be also.

All athletes practice strict self-control. They do it to win a prize that will fade away, but we do it for an eternal prize. ▩ So we don't look at the troubles we can see right now; rather, we look forward to what we have not yet seen. ▩ The reward of the godly will last. ▩ Now the prize awaits me—the crown of righteousness that the Lord, the righteous Judge, will give me on that great day of his return. And the prize is not just for me but for all who eagerly look forward to his glorious return. ▩ Your reward will be a never-ending share in his glory and honor.

Because life is uncertain, we should be all the more diligent in preparing for the future. We should act with foresight, giving responsible attention to our home, our family, and our career. Thinking ahead is a duty, not an option, for God's people. *LAB note for Proverbs 27:23-27*

(PROVERBS 27:24) (PSALM 39:6) (COLOSSIANS 3:2) (MATTHEW 6:19-21) (1 CORINTHIANS 9:25) (2 CORINTHIANS 4:18) (PROVERBS 11:18) (2 TIMOTHY 4:8) (1 PETER 5:4)

April 6

Isaac . . . was taking a walk out in the fields, meditating.

May the words of my mouth and the thoughts of my heart be pleasing to you, O LORD, my rock and my redeemer.

When I look at the night sky and see the work of your fingers—the moon and the stars you have set in place—what are mortals that you should think of us, mere humans that you should care for us? ❖ I will thank the LORD with all my heart as I meet with his godly people. How amazing are the deeds of the LORD! All who delight in him should ponder them.

Oh, the joys of those who do not follow the advice of the wicked, or stand around with sinners, or join in with scoffers. But they delight in doing everything the LORD wants; day and night they think about his law. ❖ Study this Book of the Law continually. Meditate on it day and night so you may be sure to obey all that is written in it. ❖ I will praise you with songs of joy. I lie awake thinking of you, meditating on you through the night. I think how much you have helped me; I sing for joy in the shadow of your protecting wings. I follow close behind you; your strong right hand holds me securely.

Would you change the way you live if you knew that every word and thought would be examined by God first? As you begin each day, determine that God's love will guide what you say and how you think.

LAB note for Psalm 19:14

(GENESIS 24:62-63) (PSALM 19:14) (PSALM 8:3-4) (PSALM 111:1-2) (PSALM 1:1-2) (JOSHUA 1:8) (PSALM 63:5-8)

April 7

O LORD, how long will you forget me? Forever? How long will you look the other way?

Whatever is good and perfect comes to us from God above, who created all heaven's lights. Unlike them, he never changes or casts shifting shadows. ▪ Yet Jerusalem says, "The LORD has deserted us; the Lord has forgotten us." "Never! Can a mother forget her nursing child? Can she feel no love for a child she has borne? But even if that were possible, I would not forget you!"

I will not forget to help you. I have swept away your sins like the morning mists.

Although Jesus loved Martha, Mary, and Lazarus, he stayed where he was for the next two days and did not go to them. ▪ A Gentile woman . . . came to him, pleading, "Have mercy on me, O Lord, Son of David! . . ." But Jesus gave her no reply—not even a word.

These trials are only to test your faith, to show that it is strong and pure. It is being tested as fire tests and purifies gold—and your faith is far more precious to God than mere gold. So if your faith remains strong after being tried by fiery trials, it will bring you much praise and glory and honor on the day when Jesus Christ is revealed to the whole world.

Why is God sometimes slow to act? Why does he allow evil and suffering to go seemingly unchecked? The psalmist David affirmed that he would continue to trust God, no matter how long he had to wait for God's justice to be realized. When you feel impatient, remember David's steadfast faith in God's unfailing love. *LAB note for Psalm 13:1-5*

(PSALM 13:1) (JAMES 1:17) (ISAIAH 49:14-15) (ISAIAH 44:21-22) (JOHN 11:5-6) (MATTHEW 15:22-23) (1 PETER 1:7)

April 8

This same God who takes care of me will supply all your needs from his glorious riches, which have been given to us in Christ Jesus.

Your heavenly Father already knows all your needs, and he will give you all you need from day to day if you live for him and make the Kingdom of God your primary concern. ▪ Since God did not spare even his own Son but gave him up for us all, won't God, who gave us Christ, also give us everything else? ▪ Everything belongs to you: . . . the whole world and life and death; the present and the future. Everything belongs to you, and you belong to Christ, and Christ belongs to God. ▪ We own nothing, and yet we have everything.

The LORD is my shepherd; I have everything I need. ▪ For the LORD God is our light and protector. He gives us grace and glory. No good thing will the LORD withhold from those who do what is right. ▪ The living God . . . richly gives us all we need for our enjoyment. ▪ God will generously provide all you need. Then you will always have everything you need and plenty left over to share with others.

God will always meet our needs. However, there is a difference between wants and needs. Most people want to feel good and avoid pain. We may not get all that we want. But by trusting in Christ, our attitudes and appetites can change from wanting everything to accepting his provision and power to live in him. *LAB note for Philippians 4:19*

(PHILIPPIANS 4:19) (MATTHEW 6:32-33) (ROMANS 8:32) (1 CORINTHIANS 3:21-23) (2 CORINTHIANS 6:10) (PSALM 23:1) (PSALM 84:11) (1 TIMOTHY 6:17) (2 CORINTHIANS 9:8)

April 9

How can goodness be a partner with wickedness?

They loved the darkness more than the light, for their actions were evil. ❖ You are all children of the light and of the day; we don't belong to darkness and night.

Your word is a lamp for my feet and a light for my path.

The land is full of darkness and violence! ❖ Love comes from God. Anyone who loves is born of God and knows God. But anyone who does not love does not know God—for God is love.

The way of the wicked is like complete darkness. The way of the righteous is like the first gleam of dawn, which shines ever brighter until the full light of day.

I have come as a light to shine in this dark world, so that all who put their trust in me will no longer remain in the darkness. ❖ Though your hearts were once full of darkness, now you are full of light from the Lord, and your behavior should show it! For this light within you produces only what is good and right and true. Try to find out what is pleasing to the Lord.

For those who have discovered God's light, there can be no fellowship or compromise with darkness. Does your behavior shine like a light in the darkness, or is it being obscured by the darkness around you?

LAB note for 2 Corinthians 6:14–15

(2 Corinthians 6:14) (John 3:19) (1 Thessalonians 5:5) (Psalm 119:105) (Psalm 74:20) (1 John 4:7–8) (Proverbs 4:19, 18) (John 12:46) (Ephesians 5:8–10)

April 10

If you are really serious about wanting to return to the LORD, get rid of your foreign gods and your images of Ashtoreth. Determine to obey only the LORD.

Dear children, keep away from anything that might take God's place in your hearts. ▪ Therefore come out from them and separate yourselves from them, says the Lord. Don't touch their filthy things, and I will welcome you. And I will be your Father, and you will be my sons and daughters, says the Lord Almighty. ▪ You cannot serve both God and money.

You must worship no other gods, but only the LORD, for he is a God who is passionate about his relationship with you. ▪ Worship and serve him with your whole heart and with a willing mind. For the LORD sees every heart and understands and knows every plan and thought.

You desire honesty from the heart, so you can teach me to be wise in my inmost being. ▪ People judge by outward appearance, but the LORD looks at a person's thoughts and intentions. ▪ Dear friends, if our conscience is clear, we can come to God with bold confidence. ▪ Cling tightly to your faith in Christ, and always keep your conscience clear.

Do you ever feel as if God has abandoned you? Check to see if there is anything he has already told you to do. You may not receive new guidance from God until you have acted on his previous directions. How easy it is for us to complain about our problems, even to God, while we refuse to act, change, and do what he requires! *LAB note for 1 Samuel 7:2-3*

(1 SAMUEL 7:3) (1 JOHN 5:21) (2 CORINTHIANS 6:17-18) (MATTHEW 6:24) (EXODUS 34:14) (1 CHRONICLES 28:9) (PSALM 51:6) (1 SAMUEL 16:7) (1 JOHN 3:21) (1 TIMOTHY 1:19)

April 11

You must not forget, dear friends, that a day is like a thousand years to the Lord, and a thousand years is like a day.

"My thoughts are completely different from yours," says the LORD. "And my ways are far beyond anything you could imagine. For just as the heavens are higher than the earth, so are my ways higher than your ways and my thoughts higher than your thoughts. The rain and snow come down from the heavens and stay on the ground to water the earth. . . . It is the same with my word. I send it out, and it always produces fruit. It will accomplish all I want it to, and it will prosper everywhere I send it."

God has imprisoned all people in their own disobedience so he could have mercy on everyone. Oh, what a wonderful God we have! How great are his riches and wisdom and knowledge! How impossible it is for us to understand his decisions and his methods! For who can know what the Lord is thinking? Who knows enough to be his counselor? And who could ever give him so much that he would have to pay it back? For everything comes from him; everything exists by his power and is intended for his glory. To him be glory evermore.

So be on your guard, not asleep like the others. Stay alert and be sober. No matter what happens, always be thankful, for this is God's will for you who belong to Christ Jesus.

No one has fully understood the mind of the Lord. No one has been his counselor. And God owes nothing to any one of us. God alone is the possessor of absolute power and absolute wisdom.

LAB note for Romans 11:34-35

(2 PETER 3:8) (ISAIAH 55:8-11) (ROMANS 11:32-36) (1 THESSALONIANS 5:6, 18)

April 12

Lead me to the towering rock of safety.

Don't worry about anything; instead, pray about everything. Tell God what you need, and thank him for all he has done. If you do this, you will experience God's peace, which is far more wonderful than the human mind can understand. His peace will guard your hearts and minds as you live in Christ Jesus.

I am overwhelmed, and you alone know the way I should turn. ▪ He knows where I am going. And when he has tested me like gold in a fire, he will pronounce me innocent. ▪ Lord, through all the generations you have been our home! ▪ To the poor, O LORD, you are a refuge from the storm. To the needy in distress, you are a shelter from the rain and the heat.

For who is God except the LORD? Who but our God is a solid rock? ▪ They will never perish. No one will snatch them away from me. ▪ Lord, sustain me as you promised, that I may live! Do not let my hope be crushed. ▪ This confidence is like a strong and trustworthy anchor for our souls. It leads us through the curtain of heaven into God's inner sanctuary.

God is concerned for the poor and is a refuge for them. When we are disadvantaged or oppressed, we can turn to God for comfort and help. Jesus said that the Kingdom of God belongs to the poor.

LAB note for Isaiah 25:4

(PSALM 61:2) (PHILIPPIANS 4:6-7) (PSALM 142:3) (JOB 23:10) (PSALM 90:1) (ISAIAH 25:4) (PSALM 18:31) (JOHN 10:28) (PSALM 119:116) (HEBREWS 6:19)

April 13

My future is in your hands.

Your holy ones are in your hands. ■ Then the LORD said to Elijah, "Go to the east and hide by Kerith Brook at a place east of where it enters the Jordan River. Drink from the brook and eat what the ravens bring you, for I have commanded them to bring you food." Then the LORD said to Elijah, "Go and live in the village of Zarephath, near the city of Sidon. There is a widow there who will feed you. I have given her my instructions."

Don't worry about everyday life—whether you have enough food, drink, and clothes. Doesn't life consist of more than food and clothing? Your heavenly Father already knows all your needs, and he will give you all you need from day to day if you live for him and make the Kingdom of God your primary concern. So don't worry about tomorrow, for tomorrow will bring its own worries. Today's trouble is enough for today.

Trust in the LORD with all your heart; do not depend on your own understanding. Seek his will in all you do, and he will direct your paths. ■ Give all your worries and cares to God, for he cares about what happens to you.

In saying, "My future is in your hands," David was expressing his belief that all of life's circumstances are under God's control. Knowing that God loves and cares for us enables us to keep steady in our faith, regardless of our circumstances. *LAB note for Psalm 31:14–15*

(PSALM 31:15) (DEUTERONOMY 33:3) (1 KINGS 17:2-4, 8-9) (MATTHEW 6:25, 32-34) (PROVERBS 3:5-6) (1 PETER 5:7)

April 14

He is able, once and forever, to save everyone who comes to God through him. He lives forever to plead with God on their behalf.

Who then will condemn us? Will Christ Jesus? No, for he is the one who died for us . . . and is sitting at the place of highest honor next to God, pleading for us. ▪ Christ has entered into heaven itself to appear now before God as our Advocate.

If you do sin, there is someone to plead for you before the Father. He is Jesus Christ, the one who pleases God completely. ▪ There is only one God and one Mediator who can reconcile God and people. He is the man Christ Jesus.

We have a great High Priest who has gone to heaven, Jesus the Son of God. Let us cling to him and never stop trusting him. This High Priest of ours understands our weaknesses, for he faced all of the same temptations we do, yet he did not sin. So let us come boldly to the throne of our gracious God. There we will receive his mercy, and we will find grace to help us when we need it.

All of us . . . may come to the Father through the same Holy Spirit because of what Christ has done for us.

As our High Priest, Christ is our Advocate, the mediator between us and God. He looks after our interests and intercedes for us with God. Christ's continual presence with the Father in heaven assures us that our sins have been paid for and forgiven. *LAB note for Hebrews 7:25*

(HEBREWS 7:25) (ROMANS 8:34) (HEBREWS 9:24) (1 JOHN 2:1) (1 TIMOTHY 2:5) (HEBREWS 4:14-16) (EPHESIANS 2:18)

April 15

Those who know your name trust in you, for you, O LORD, have never abandoned anyone who searches for you.

This is his name: "The LORD Is Our Righteousness." ▪ I will praise your mighty deeds, O Sovereign LORD. I will tell everyone that you alone are just and good.

His royal titles: Wonderful Counselor. ▪ I know, LORD, that a person's life is not his own. No one is able to plan his own course.

Mighty God, Everlasting Father. ▪ I know the one in whom I trust, and I am sure that he is able to guard what I have entrusted to him until the day of his return.

Prince of Peace. ▪ Christ himself has made peace between us. ▪ Since we have been made right in God's sight by faith, we have peace with God because of what Jesus Christ our Lord has done for us.

The name of the LORD is a strong fortress; the godly run to him and are safe. ▪ Destruction is certain for those who look to Egypt for help, trusting their cavalry and chariots instead of looking to the LORD, the Holy One of Israel. ▪ There is no one like the God of Israel. He rides across the heavens to help you, across the skies in majestic splendor. The eternal God is your refuge, and his everlasting arms are under you.

God will never abandon those who seek him. God's promise does not mean that if we trust in him we will escape loss or suffering; it means that God himself will never leave us no matter what we face.

LAB note for Psalm 9:10

(PSALM 9:10) (JEREMIAH 23:6) (PSALM 71:16) (ISAIAH 9:6) (JEREMIAH 10:23) (ISAIAH 9:6) (2 TIMOTHY 1:12) (ISAIAH 9:6) (EPHESIANS 2:14) (ROMANS 5:1) (PROVERBS 18:10) (ISAIAH 31:1) (DEUTERONOMY 33:26-27)

April 16

Let us . . . work toward complete purity because we fear God.

Let us cleanse ourselves from everything that can defile our body or spirit.

You desire honesty from the heart, so you can teach me to be wise in my inmost being. ▪ We are instructed to turn from godless living and sinful pleasures. We should live in this evil world with self-control, right conduct, and devotion to God. ▪ Don't hide your light under a basket! Instead, put it on a stand and let it shine for all. In the same way, let your good deeds shine out for all to see, so that everyone will praise your heavenly Father. ▪ I don't mean to say that I have already achieved these things or that I have already reached perfection!

When he comes we will be like him, for we will see him as he really is. And all who believe this will keep themselves pure, just as Christ is pure.

God himself has prepared us for this, and as a guarantee he has given us his Holy Spirit. ▪ He is the one who gave these gifts to the church. . . . Their responsibility is to equip God's people to do his work and build up the church, the body of Christ, until we come to such unity in our faith and knowledge of God's Son that we will be mature and full grown in the Lord, measuring up to the full stature of Christ.

Cleansing is a twofold action: turning away from sin and turning toward God. Have nothing to do with paganism. Make a clean break with your past and give yourself to God alone. *LAB note for 2 Corinthians 7:1*

(2 Corinthians 7:1) (2 Corinthians 7:1) (Psalm 51:6) (Titus 2:12) (Matthew 5:15-16) (Philippians 3:12) (1 John 3:2-3) (2 Corinthians 5:5) (Ephesians 4:11-13)

April 17

He has enriched your church.

When we were utterly helpless, Christ came at just the right time and died for us sinners. ▪ Since God did not spare even his own Son but gave him up for us all, won't God, who gave us Christ, also give us everything else?

In Christ the fullness of God lives in a human body, and you are complete through your union with Christ. He is the Lord over every ruler and authority in the universe.

Remain in me, and I will remain in you. For a branch cannot produce fruit if it is severed from the vine, and you cannot be fruitful apart from me. Yes, I am the vine; you are the branches. Those who remain in me, and I in them, will produce much fruit. For apart from me you can do nothing. ▪ He has given each one of us a special gift according to the generosity of Christ.

If you stay joined to me and my words remain in you, you may ask any request you like, and it will be granted! ▪ Let the words of Christ, in all their richness, live in your hearts and make you wise.

"In Christ the fullness of God lives in a human body" means that all of God was in Christ's human body. When we have Christ, we have everything we need for salvation and right living. *LAB note for Colossians 2:9*

(1 Corinthians 1:5) (Romans 5:6) (Romans 8:32) (Colossians 2:9-10) (John 15:4-5) (Ephesians 4:7) (John 15:7) (Colossians 3:16)

April 18

I will tell of the LORD's unfailing love. I will praise the LORD for all he has done. I will rejoice in his great goodness.

He lifted me out of the pit of despair, out of the mud and the mire. He set my feet on solid ground and steadied me as I walked along. ❖ The Son of God . . . loved me and gave himself for me. ❖ Since God did not spare even his own Son but gave him up for us all, won't God, who gave us Christ, also give us everything else? ❖ God showed his great love for us by sending Christ to die for us while we were still sinners.

He has identified us as his own by placing the Holy Spirit in our hearts as the first installment of everything he will give us. ❖ The Spirit is God's guarantee that he will give us everything he promised and that he has purchased us to be his own people.

God is so rich in mercy, and he loved us so very much, that even while we were dead because of our sins, he gave us life when he raised Christ from the dead. (It is only by God's special favor that you have been saved!) For he raised us from the dead along with Christ, and we are seated with him in the heavenly realms—all because we are one with Christ Jesus.

Through faith in Christ we stand acquitted, or not guilty, before God. But God does not take us out of the world or make us robots—we will still feel like sinning, and sometimes we will sin. The difference is that before we became Christians, we were dead in sin and were slaves to our sinful nature. But now we are alive in Christ. *LAB note for Ephesians 2:4-5*

(ISAIAH 63:7) (PSALM 40:2) (GALATIANS 2:20) (ROMANS 8:32) (ROMANS 5:8) (2 CORINTHIANS 1:22) (EPHESIANS 1:14) (EPHESIANS 2:4-6)

April 19

Don't talk too much, for it fosters sin. Be sensible and turn off the flow!

Dear brothers and sisters, be quick to listen, slow to speak, and slow to get angry. ▪ It is better to be patient than powerful; it is better to have self-control than to conquer a city. ▪ Those who control their tongues can also control themselves in every other way. ▪ The words you say now reflect your fate then; either you will be justified by them or you will be condemned. ▪ Take control of what I say, O LORD, and keep my lips sealed.

Christ, who suffered for you, is your example. Follow in his steps. He never sinned, and he never deceived anyone. He did not retaliate when he was insulted. When he suffered, he did not threaten to get even. He left his case in the hands of God, who always judges fairly. ▪ Think about all he endured when sinful people did such terrible things to him, so that you don't become weary and give up. ▪ Gentle words bring life and health.

No falsehood can be charged against them; they are blameless.

When we talk too much and listen too little, we communicate to others that we think our ideas are much more important than theirs. Instead, reverse the process. Put a mental stopwatch on your conversations, and keep track of how much you talk and how much you listen.

LAB note for James 1:19

(PROVERBS 10:19) (JAMES 1:19) (PROVERBS 16:32) (JAMES 3:2) (MATTHEW 12:37) (PSALM 141:3) (1 PETER 2:21-23) (HEBREWS 12:3) (PROVERBS 15:4) (REVELATION 14:5)

April 20

Teach me how to live, O LORD.

The LORD says, "I will guide you along the best pathway for your life. I will advise you and watch over you." ▩ The LORD is good and does what is right; he shows the proper path to those who go astray. He leads the humble in what is right, teaching them his way.

Yes, I am the gate. Those who come in through me will be saved. Wherever they go, they will find green pastures.

Jesus told him, "I am the way, the truth, and the life. No one can come to the Father except through me." ▩ We can boldly enter heaven's Most Holy Place because of the blood of Jesus. This is the new, life-giving way that Christ has opened up for us through the sacred curtain, by means of his death for us. And since we have a great High Priest who rules over God's people, let us go right into the presence of God, with true hearts fully trusting him.

Oh, that we might know the LORD! Let us press on to know him! ▩ The LORD leads with unfailing love and faithfulness all those who keep his covenant and obey his decrees.

We are bombarded today with relentless appeals to go in various directions. Add to that the dozens of decisions we must make concerning our job, our family, our money, and our society, and we become desperate for someone to show us the right way. If you find yourself pulled in several directions, remember that God teaches the humble his way.

LAB note for Psalm 25:8-11

(PSALM 27:11) (PSALM 32:8) (PSALM 25:8-9) (JOHN 10:9) (JOHN 14:6) (HEBREWS 10:19-22) (HOSEA 6:3) (PSALM 25:10)

April 21

When God's children are in need, be the one to help them out.

One day David began wondering if anyone in Saul's family was still alive, for he had promised Jonathan that he would show kindness to them.

Come, you who are blessed by my Father, inherit the Kingdom prepared for you from the foundation of the world. For I was hungry, and you fed me. I was thirsty, and you gave me a drink. I was a stranger, and you invited me into your home. I was naked, and you gave me clothing. I was sick, and you cared for me. I was in prison, and you visited me. When you did it to one of the least of these my brothers and sisters, you were doing it to me! ▪ And if you give even a cup of cold water to one of the least of my followers, you will surely be rewarded.

Don't forget to do good and to share what you have with those in need, for such sacrifices are very pleasing to God. ▪ For God is not unfair. He will not forget how hard you have worked for him and how you have shown your love to him by caring for other Christians, as you still do. Our great desire is that you will keep right on loving others as long as life lasts, in order to make certain that what you hope for will come true.

Entertaining focuses on the host and setting; Christian hospitality focuses on the guests' needs. It can happen around a dinner table where the main dish is canned soup. Don't hesitate to offer hospitality just because you are too tired, too busy, or not wealthy enough to entertain. *LAB note for Romans 12:13*

(ROMANS 12:13) (2 SAMUEL 9:1) (MATTHEW 25:34-36, 40) (MATTHEW 10:42) (HEBREWS 13:16) (HEBREWS 6:10-11)

April 22

Are you seeking great things for yourself? Don't do it!

Take my yoke upon you. Let me teach you, because I am humble and gentle, and you will find rest for your souls. ■ Your attitude should be the same that Christ Jesus had. Though he was God, he did not demand and cling to his rights as God. He made himself nothing; he took the humble position of a slave and appeared in human form. And in human form he obediently humbled himself even further by dying a criminal's death on a cross.

If you refuse to take up your cross and follow me, you are not worthy of being mine. ■ Christ, who suffered for you, is your example. Follow in his steps. ■ Many who seem to be important now will be the least important then, and those who are considered least here will be the greatest then.

True religion with contentment is great wealth. After all, we didn't bring anything with us when we came into the world, and we certainly cannot carry anything with us when we die. So if we have enough food and clothing, let us be content. ■ I have learned how to get along happily whether I have much or little.

It is easy to lose the joy of serving God when we take our eyes off him. The more we look away from God's purposes toward our own sacrifices, the more frustrated we will become. As you serve God, look at him rather than at yourself. *LAB note for Jeremiah 45:5*

(Jeremiah 45:5) (Matthew 11:29) (Philippians 2:5-8) (Matthew 10:38) (1 Peter 2:21) (Matthew 19:30) (1 Timothy 6:6-8) (Philippians 4:11)

April 23

Stay true to the Lord.

I have stayed in God's paths; I have followed his ways and not turned aside. ▪ The LORD loves justice, and he will never abandon the godly. ▪ The LORD keeps you from all evil and preserves your life.

A righteous person will live by faith. But I will have no pleasure in anyone who turns away. But we are not like those who turn their backs on God and seal their fate. We have faith that assures our salvation. ▪ These people left our churches because they never really belonged with us; otherwise they would have stayed with us. When they left us, it proved that they do not belong with us.

You are truly my disciples if you keep obeying my teachings. ▪ Those who endure to the end will be saved. ▪ Be on guard. Stand true to what you believe. Be courageous. Be strong. ▪ Hold on to what you have, so that no one will take away your crown. ▪ All who are victorious will be clothed in white. I will never erase their names from the Book of Life, but I will announce before my Father and his angels that they are mine.

How do we "stay true to the Lord"? The way to stay true is to keep our eyes on Christ, to remember that this world is not our home, and to focus on the fact that Christ will bring everything under his control.

LAB note for Philippians 4:1

(PHILIPPIANS 4:1) (JOB 23:11) (PSALM 37:28) (PSALM 121:7) (HEBREWS 10:38-39) (1 JOHN 2:19) (JOHN 8:31) (MATTHEW 24:13) (1 CORINTHIANS 16:13) (REVELATION 3:11) (REVELATION 3:5)

April 24

Our Lord Jesus . . . Though he was very rich, yet for your sakes he became poor, so that by his poverty he could make you rich.

For God in all his fullness was pleased to live in Christ. ▪ The Son reflects God's own glory, and everything about him represents God exactly. He sustains the universe by the mighty power of his command. After he died to cleanse us from the stain of sin, he sat down in the place of honor at the right hand of the majestic God of heaven. This shows that God's Son is far greater than the angels, just as the name God gave him is far greater than their names. ▪ Though he was God, he did not demand and cling to his rights as God. He made himself nothing; he took the humble position of a slave and appeared in human form.

Foxes have dens to live in, and birds have nests, but I, the Son of Man, have no home of my own, not even a place to lay my head.

Everything belongs to you . . . the whole world and life and death; the present and the future. Everything belongs to you, and you belong to Christ, and Christ belongs to God.

Jesus became poor by giving up his rights as God and voluntarily becoming human. In response to the Father's will, he limited his power and knowledge. Yet by doing so, he made us "rich" because we received salvation and eternal life. *LAB note for 2 Corinthians 8:9*

(2 Corinthians 8:9) (Colossians 1:19) (Hebrews 1:3-4) (Philippians 2:6-7) (Matthew 8:20) (1 Corinthians 3:21-23)

April 25

The time that remains is very short.

How frail is humanity! How short is life, and how full of trouble! Like a flower, we blossom for a moment and then wither. Like the shadow of a passing cloud, we quickly disappear. ▪ This world is fading away, along with everything it craves. But if you do the will of God, you will live forever. ▪ Everyone dies because all of us are related to Adam, the first man. But all who are related to Christ, the other man, will be given new life. Death is swallowed up in victory. ▪ While we live, we live to please the Lord. And when we die, we go to be with the Lord. So in life and in death, we belong to the Lord.

For to me, living is for Christ, and dying is even better.

Do not throw away this confident trust in the Lord, no matter what happens. Remember the great reward it brings you! Patient endurance is what you need now, so you will continue to do God's will. Then you will receive all that he has promised. "For in just a little while, the Coming One will come and not delay." ▪ The night is almost gone; the day of salvation will soon be here. So don't live in darkness. Get rid of your evil deeds. Shed them like dirty clothes. Clothe yourselves with the armor of right living, as those who live in the light. ▪ The end of the world is coming soon. Therefore, be earnest and disciplined in your prayers.

All believers should make the most of their time before Christ's return. Every person in every generation should have this sense of urgency about telling the Good News to others. Life is short—there's not much time! *LAB note for 1 Corinthians 7:29*

(1 Corinthians 7:29) (Job 14:1-2) (1 John 2:17) (1 Corinthians 15:22, 54) (Romans 14:8) (Philippians 1:21) (Hebrews 10:35-37) (Romans 13:12) (1 Peter 4:7)

April 26

We look forward to that wonderful event when the glory of our great God and Savior, Jesus Christ, will be revealed.

This confidence is like a strong and trustworthy anchor for our souls. It leads us through the curtain of heaven into God's inner sanctuary. Jesus has already gone in there for us. He has become our eternal High Priest in the line of Melchizedek. ▪ For he must remain in heaven until the time for the final restoration of all things, as God promised long ago through his prophets. ▪ When he comes to receive glory and praise from his holy people.

We know that all creation has been groaning as in the pains of childbirth right up to the present time. And even we Christians . . . also groan to be released from pain and suffering. We, too, wait anxiously for that day when God will give us our full rights as his children, including the new bodies he has promised us. ▪ Dear friends, we are already God's children, and we can't even imagine what we will be like when Christ returns. But we do know that when he comes we will be like him, for we will see him as he really is. ▪ When Christ, who is your real life, is revealed to the whole world, you will share in all his glory.

"Yes, I am coming soon!" Amen! Come, Lord Jesus!

Christ gives us power to live for him now, and he gives us hope for the future—he will return. Christians should act now in order to be prepared for Christ's return. *LAB note for Colossians 3:4*

(Titus 2:13) (Hebrews 6:19-20) (Acts 3:21) (2 Thessalonians 1:10) (Romans 8:22-23) (1 John 3:2) (Colossians 3:4) (Revelation 22:20)

April 27

Those who obey God's word really do love him.

May the God of peace, who brought again from the dead our Lord Jesus, equip you with all you need for doing his will. May he produce in you, through the power of Jesus Christ, all that is pleasing to him. Jesus is the great Shepherd of the sheep by an everlasting covenant, signed with his blood. To him be glory forever and ever. Amen.

How can we be sure that we belong to him? By obeying his commandments. ▧ All those who love me will do what I say. My Father will love them, and we will come to them and live with them. ▧ If we continue to live in him, we won't sin either. But those who keep on sinning have never known him or understood who he is. Dear children, don't let anyone deceive you about this: When people do what is right, it is because they are righteous, even as Christ is righteous.

As we live in God, our love grows more perfect. So we will not be afraid on the day of judgment, but we can face him with confidence because we are like Christ here in this world.

How can you be sure that you belong to Christ? If you do what Christ says and live as Christ wants. True Christian faith results in loving behavior; that is why the way we act can give us assurance that we belong to Christ. *LAB note for 1 John 2:3-6*

(1 JOHN 2:5) (HEBREWS 13:20-21) (1 JOHN 2:3) (JOHN 14:23) (1 JOHN 3:6-7) (1 JOHN 4:17)

April 28

Those who control their anger have great understanding.

He passed in front of Moses and said, "I am the LORD, I am the LORD, the merciful and gracious God. I am slow to anger and rich in unfailing love and faithfulness."

Follow God's example in everything you do, because you are his dear children. ▪ When the Holy Spirit controls our lives, he will produce this kind of fruit in us: love, joy, peace, patience, kindness, goodness, faithfulness, gentleness, and self-control. ▪ God is pleased with you when, for the sake of your conscience, you patiently endure unfair treatment. Of course, you get no credit for being patient if you are beaten for doing wrong. But if you suffer for doing right and are patient beneath the blows, God is pleased with you. This suffering is all part of what God has called you to. Christ, who suffered for you, is your example. Follow in his steps. He never sinned, and he never deceived anyone. He did not retaliate when he was insulted. When he suffered, he did not threaten to get even. He left his case in the hands of God, who always judges fairly.

"Don't sin by letting anger gain control over you." Don't let the sun go down while you are still angry, for anger gives a mighty foothold to the Devil.

When you feel yourself getting angry, look for the cause. Are you reacting to an evil situation that you are going to set right? Or are you responding selfishly to a personal insult? Pray that God will help you control a quick temper, channeling your feelings into effective action and conquering selfish anger through humility and repentance.

LAB note for Proverbs 14:29

(PROVERBS 14:29) (EXODUS 34:6) (EPHESIANS 5:1) (GALATIANS 5:22-23) (1 PETER 2:19-23) (EPHESIANS 4:26)

April 29

The LORD is in this place.

Where two or three gather together because they are mine, I am there among them. ▪ I am with you always, even to the end of the age. ▪ I will personally go with you. . . . I will give you rest—everything will be fine for you.

I can never escape from your spirit! I can never get away from your presence! If I go up to heaven, you are there; if I go down to the place of the dead, you are there. If I ride the wings of the morning, if I dwell by the farthest oceans, even there your hand will guide me, and your strength will support me. I could ask the darkness to hide me and the light around me to become night—but even in darkness I cannot hide from you. To you the night shines as bright as day. ▪ "Am I a God who is only in one place?" asks the LORD. "Do they think I cannot see what they are doing? Can anyone hide from me? Am I not everywhere in all the heavens and earth?"

Will God really live on earth? Why, even the highest heavens cannot contain you. How much less this Temple I have built! ▪ The high and lofty one who inhabits eternity, the Holy One, says this: "I live in that high and holy place with those whose spirits are contrite and humble. I refresh the humble and give new courage to those with repentant hearts."

Jesus looked ahead to a new day when he would be present with his followers, not in body but through his Holy Spirit. In the body of believers (the church) the sincere agreement of two people in prayer is powerful because Christ's Holy Spirit is with them.

LAB note for Matthew 18:19-20

(GENESIS 28:16) (MATTHEW 18:20) (MATTHEW 28:20) (EXODUS 33:14) (PSALM 139:7-12) (JEREMIAH 23:23-24) (ISAIAH 57:15)

April 30

Keep away from anything that might take God's place in your hearts.

O my son, give me your heart. May your eyes delight in my ways of wisdom. ▩ Let heaven fill your thoughts. Do not think only about things down here on earth.

Son of man, these leaders have set up idols in their hearts. . . . Why should I let them ask me anything? ▩ Put to death the sinful, earthly things lurking within you. Have nothing to do with sexual sin, impurity, lust, and shameful desires. Don't be greedy for the good things of this life, for that is idolatry. ▩ People who long to be rich fall into temptation and are trapped by many foolish and harmful desires that plunge them into ruin and destruction. For the love of money is at the root of all kinds of evil. And some people, craving money, have wandered from the faith and pierced themselves with many sorrows. But you . . . belong to God; so run from all these evil things, and follow what is right and good. Pursue a godly life, along with faith, love, perseverance, and gentleness. ▩ Don't try to get rich by extortion or robbery. ▩ My gifts are better than the purest gold, my wages better than sterling silver!

Wherever your treasure is, there your heart and thoughts will also be. ▩ The LORD looks at a person's thoughts and intentions.

Many things can take God's place in our life. This includes anything that substitutes for the true faith, anything that robs Christ of his full deity and humanity, any human idea that claims to be more authoritative than the Bible, or any loyalty that replaces God at the center of our life.

LAB note for 1 John 5:21

(1 JOHN 5:21) (PROVERBS 23:26) (COLOSSIANS 3:2) (EZEKIEL 14:3) (COLOSSIANS 3:5) (1 TIMOTHY 6:9-11) (PSALM 62:10) (PROVERBS 8:19) (MATTHEW 6:21) (1 SAMUEL 16:7)

May

Only a Mother's Love

A mother's love is encouraging but not overbearing.
It is both sheltering and freeing.
A mother's love is a reflection of God's character.

It is often said that a mother's work is never done, and that is true. A mother never forgets her child's small victories and character-building experiences that helped mold him or her into a mature adult. May your heart be filled with the joy and peace of a mother's love.

May 1

I will comfort you there as a child is comforted by its mother.

Can a mother forget her nursing child? Can she feel no love for a child she has borne? But even if that were possible, I would not forget you!

[I give] the barren woman a home, so that she becomes a happy mother. Praise the Lord! ▪ She extends a helping hand to the poor and opens her arms to the needy. ▪ She is clothed with strength and dignity, and she laughs with no fear of the future. When she speaks, her words are wise, and kindness is the rule when she gives instructions. She carefully watches all that goes on in her household and does not have to bear the consequences of laziness.

Her children stand and bless her. Her husband praises her: "There are many virtuous and capable women in the world, but you surpass them all!"

Charm is deceptive, and beauty does not last; but a woman who fears the Lord will be greatly praised. Reward her for all she has done. Let her deeds publicly declare her praise.

God will never forget you, just as a loving mother would not forget her little child. *adapted from LAB note for Isaiah 49:15*

(Isaiah 66:13) (Isaiah 49:15) (Psalm 113:9)
(Proverbs 31:20) (Proverbs 31:25-31)

May 2

Thank you for making me so wonderfully complex!

I have stilled and quieted myself, just as a small child is quiet with its mother. Yes, like a small child is my soul within me. ▪ You have been with me from birth; from my mother's womb you have cared for me. No wonder I am always praising you! ▪ You made all the delicate, inner parts of my body and knit me together in my mother's womb. Your workmanship is marvelous—and how well I know it. ▪ You both precede and follow me. You place your hand of blessing on my head. Such knowledge is too wonderful for me, too great for me to know! I can never escape from your spirit! I can never get away from your presence! If I go up to heaven, you are there; if I go down to the place of the dead, you are there. If I ride the wings of the morning, if I dwell by the farthest oceans, even there your hand will guide me, and your strength will support me.

God's character goes into the creation of every person. When you feel worthless or even begin to hate yourself, remember that God's Spirit is ready and willing to work within you. *LAB note for Psalm 139:13-14*

(PSALM 139:14) (PSALM 131:2) (PSALM 71:6)
(PSALM 139:13-14) (PSALM 139:5-10)

May 3

Keep none of the plunder.

Come out from them and separate yourselves from them, says the Lord. Don't touch their filthy things. ▩ Dear brothers and sisters, you are foreigners and aliens here. So I warn you to keep away from evil desires because they fight against your very souls. ▩ Be careful that you aren't contaminated by their sins.

We are already God's children, and we can't even imagine what we will be like when Christ returns. But we do know that when he comes we will be like him, for we will see him as he really is. And all who believe this will keep themselves pure, just as Christ is pure. ▩ For the grace of God has been revealed, bringing salvation to all people. And we are instructed to turn from godless living and sinful pleasures. We should live in this evil world with self-control, right conduct, and devotion to God, while we look forward to that wonderful event when the glory of our great God and Savior, Jesus Christ, will be revealed. He gave his life to free us from every kind of sin, to cleanse us, and to make us his very own people, totally committed to doing what is right.

Separation from the world involves more than keeping our distance from sinners; it means staying close to God. There is no way to separate ourselves totally from all sinful influences. Nevertheless, we are to resist the sin around us, without either giving up or giving in.

LAB note for 2 Corinthians 6:17

(Deuteronomy 13:17) (2 Corinthians 6:17) (1 Peter 2:11) (Jude 1:23) (1 John 3:2-3) (Titus 2:11-14)

May 4

The LORD spread out a cloud above them as a covering and gave them a great fire to light the darkness.

The LORD is like a father to his children, tender and compassionate to those who fear him. For he understands how weak we are; he knows we are only dust.

The sun will not hurt you by day, nor the moon at night. ▪ It will be a shelter from daytime heat and a hiding place from storms or rain.

The LORD himself watches over you! The LORD stands beside you as your protective shade. The LORD keeps watch over you as you come and go, both now and forever. ▪ He found them in a desert land, in an empty, howling wasteland. He surrounded them and watched over them; he guarded them as his most precious possession. ▪ In your great mercy you did not abandon them to die in the wilderness. The pillar of cloud still led them forward by day, and the pillar of fire showed them the way through the night. You sent your good Spirit to instruct them, and you did not stop giving them bread from heaven or water for their thirst. For forty years you sustained them in the wilderness. They lacked nothing in all that time. Their clothes did not wear out, and their feet did not swell! ▪ With unfailing love you will lead this people whom you have ransomed. You will guide them in your strength to the place where your holiness dwells.

Jesus Christ is the same yesterday, today, and forever.

Seeing how God continued to be with his people shows that his patience is amazing! In spite of our repeated failings, pride, and stubbornness, he is always ready to pardon, and his Spirit is always ready to instruct.

LAB note for Nehemiah 9:16–21

(PSALM 105:39) (PSALM 103:13–14) (PSALM 121:6) (ISAIAH 4:6) (PSALM 121:5, 8) (DEUTERONOMY 32:10) (NEHEMIAH 9:19–21) (EXODUS 15:13) (HEBREWS 13:8)

*M*ay 5

Wars will break out near and far, but don't panic. Yes, these things must come, but the end won't follow immediately.

God is our refuge and strength, always ready to help in times of trouble. So we will not fear, even if earthquakes come and the mountains crumble into the sea. Let the oceans roar and foam. Let the mountains tremble as the waters surge! ▪ Go home, my people, and lock your doors! Hide until the LORD's anger against your enemies has passed. Look! The LORD is coming from heaven to punish the people of the earth for their sins. ▪ I will hide beneath the shadow of your wings until this violent storm is past. ▪ Your real life is hidden with Christ in God.

Happy are those who fear the LORD. Yes, happy are those who delight in doing what he commands. Such people will not be overcome by evil circumstances. Those who are righteous will be long remembered. They do not fear bad news; they confidently trust the LORD to care for them.

I have told you all this so that you may have peace in me. Here on earth you will have many trials and sorrows. But take heart, because I have overcome the world.

It seems impossible to consider the end of the world without becoming consumed by fear, but the Bible is clear—God is our refuge even in the midst of total destruction. He is not merely a temporary retreat; he is our eternal refuge and can provide strength in any circumstance.

LAB note for Psalm 46:1-3

(MATTHEW 24:6) (PSALM 46:1-3) (ISAIAH 26:20-21) (PSALM 57:1) (COLOSSIANS 3:3) (PSALM 112:1, 6-7) (JOHN 16:33)

May 6

Come to your senses and stop sinning.

You are all children of the light and of the day; we don't belong to darkness and night. So be on your guard, not asleep like the others. Stay alert and be sober.

Another reason for right living is that you know how late it is; time is running out. Wake up, for the coming of our salvation is nearer now than when we first believed. The night is almost gone; the day of salvation will soon be here. So don't live in darkness. Get rid of your evil deeds. Shed them like dirty clothes. Clothe yourselves with the armor of right living, as those who live in the light. ▪ Use every piece of God's armor to resist the enemy in the time of evil, so that after the battle you will still be standing firm. ▪ Turn from your sins! Don't let them destroy you! Put all your rebellion behind you, and get for yourselves a new heart and a new spirit. ▪ Get rid of all the filth and evil in your lives, and humbly accept the message God has planted in your hearts, for it is strong enough to save your souls.

Now, dear children, continue to live in fellowship with Christ so that when he returns, you will be full of courage and not shrink back from him in shame.

If we renounce our life's direction of sin and rebellion and turn to God, he will give us a new direction, a new love, and a new power to change. You can begin by faith, trusting in God's power to change your heart and mind. Then determine to live each day with him in control.

LAB note for Ezekiel 18:30-32

(1 CORINTHIANS 15:34) (1 THESSALONIANS 5:5-6) (ROMANS 13:11-12) (EPHESIANS 6:13) (EZEKIEL 18:30-31) (JAMES 1:21) (1 JOHN 2:28)

May 7

Their insults have broken my heart.

He's just a carpenter's son. ▩ Nazareth! . . . Can anything good come from there? ▩ He can cast out demons because he is empowered by the prince of demons. ▩ We know Jesus is a sinner. ▩ He's nothing but a fraud, deceiving the people. ▩ Blasphemy! This man talks like he is God! ▩ I, the Son of Man, feast and drink, and you say, "He's a glutton and a drunkard, and a friend of the worst sort of sinners!"

God is pleased with you when, for the sake of your conscience, you patiently endure unfair treatment. Of course, you get no credit for being patient if you are beaten for doing wrong. But if you suffer for doing right and are patient beneath the blows, God is pleased with you. This suffering is all part of what God has called you to. Christ, who suffered for you, is your example. Follow in his steps. He never sinned, and he never deceived anyone. He did not retaliate when he was insulted. When he suffered, he did not threaten to get even. He left his case in the hands of God, who always judges fairly. ▩ Be happy if you are insulted for being a Christian, for then the glorious Spirit of God will come upon you.

The student shares the teacher's fate. The servant shares the master's fate.

Good is sometimes labeled evil. If Jesus, who is perfect, was called evil, his followers should expect that similar accusations will be directed at them. But those who endure will be vindicated. *LAB note for Matthew 10:25*

(PSALM 69:20) (MATTHEW 13:55) (JOHN 1:46) (MATTHEW 9:34) (JOHN 9:24) (JOHN 7:12) (MATTHEW 9:3) (MATTHEW 11:19) (1 PETER 2:19-23) (1 PETER 4:14) (MATTHEW 10:25)

May 8

I want men to pray with holy hands lifted up to God, free from anger and controversy.

True worshipers will worship the Father in spirit and in truth. The Father is looking for anyone who will worship him that way. For God is Spirit, so those who worship him must worship in spirit and in truth. ▪ When you call, the LORD will answer. "Yes, I am here." ▪ When you are praying, first forgive anyone you are holding a grudge against, so that your Father in heaven will forgive your sins, too.

It is impossible to please God without faith. Anyone who wants to come to him must believe that there is a God and that he rewards those who sincerely seek him. ▪ When you ask him, be sure that you really expect him to answer, for a doubtful mind is as unsettled as a wave of the sea that is driven and tossed by the wind. People like that should not expect to receive anything from the Lord.

If I had not confessed the sin in my heart, my Lord would not have listened. ▪ My dear children, I am writing this to you so that you will not sin. But if you do sin, there is someone to plead for you before the Father. He is Jesus Christ, the one who pleases God completely.

Besides displeasing God, anger and controversy make prayer difficult. That is why Jesus said that we should interrupt our prayers, if necessary, to make peace with others. God wants us to obey him immediately and thoroughly. *LAB note for 1 Timothy 2:8*

(1 TIMOTHY 2:8) (JOHN 4:23-24) (ISAIAH 58:9) (MARK 11:25) (HEBREWS 11:6) (JAMES 1:6-7) (PSALM 66:18) (1 JOHN 2:1)

May 9

My heart beats wildly, my strength fails.

O God, listen to my cry! Hear my prayer! From the ends of the earth, I will cry to you for help, for my heart is overwhelmed. Lead me to the towering rock of safety.

"My gracious favor is all you need. My power works best in your weakness." So now I am glad to boast about my weaknesses, so that the power of Christ may work through me. Since I know it is all for Christ's good, I am quite content with my weaknesses and with insults, hardships, persecutions, and calamities. For when I am weak, then I am strong.

When he [Peter] looked around at the high waves, he was terrified and began to sink. "Save me, Lord!" he shouted. Instantly Jesus reached out his hand and grabbed him. "You don't have much faith," Jesus said. "Why did you doubt me?" ▪ If you fail under pressure, your strength is not very great. ▪ He gives power to those who are tired and worn out; he offers strength to the weak. ▪ The eternal God is your refuge, and his everlasting arms are under you. ▪ We also pray that you will be strengthened with his glorious power so that you will have all the patience and endurance you need.

Even the strongest people get tired at times, but God's power and strength never diminish. He is never too tired or too busy to help and listen. When you feel all of life crushing you and you cannot go another step, remember that you can call upon God to renew your strength.

LAB note for Isaiah 40:29–31

(Psalm 38:10) (Psalm 61:1–2) (2 Corinthians 12:9–10) (Matthew 14:30–31) (Proverbs 24:10) (Isaiah 40:29) (Deuteronomy 33:27) (Colossians 1:11)

May 10

I will bless the LORD who guides me.

Wonderful Counselor. ▪ Good advice and success belong to me. Insight and strength are mine. ▪ Your word is a lamp for my feet and a light for my path. ▪ Trust in the LORD with all your heart; do not depend on your own understanding. Seek his will in all you do, and he will direct your paths.

I know, LORD, that a person's life is not his own. No one is able to plan his own course. ▪ You will hear a voice say, "This is the way; turn around and walk here." ▪ Commit your work to the LORD, and then your plans will succeed. ▪ How can we understand the road we travel? It is the LORD who directs our steps.

You will keep on guiding me with your counsel, leading me to a glorious destiny. ▪ Even when I walk through the dark valley of death, I will not be afraid, for you are close beside me. Your rod and your staff protect and comfort me. ▪ For that is what God is like. He is our God forever and ever, and he will be our guide until we die.

We must not be wise in our own eyes but be willing to listen to and be corrected by God's Word and wise counselors. Bring your decisions to God in prayer; use the Bible as your guide; and then follow God's leading. He will direct your paths by both guiding and protecting you.

LAB note for Proverbs 3:5-6

(PSALM 16:7) (ISAIAH 9:6) (PROVERBS 8:14) (PSALM 119:105) (PROVERBS 3:5-6) (JEREMIAH 10:23) (ISAIAH 30:21) (PROVERBS 16:3) (PROVERBS 20:24) (PSALM 73:24) (PSALM 23:4) (PSALM 48:14)

*M*ay 11

I am the LORD your God. . . . Follow my laws, pay attention to my instructions.

Now you must be holy in everything you do, just as God—who chose you to be his children—is holy. ▪ Those who say they live in God should live their lives as Christ did.

It is not that we think we can do anything of lasting value by ourselves. Our only power and success come from God. ▪ Remain in me, and I will remain in you. For a branch cannot produce fruit if it is severed from the vine, and you cannot be fruitful apart from me.

Be even more careful to put into action God's saving work in your lives, obeying God with deep reverence and fear. For God is working in you, giving you the desire to obey him and the power to do what pleases him. ▪ May the God of peace, who brought again from the dead our Lord Jesus, equip you with all you need for doing his will. May he produce in you, through the power of Jesus Christ, all that is pleasing to him. Jesus is the great Shepherd of the sheep by an everlasting covenant, signed with his blood.

He is a God of mercy and justice who cares personally for each of his followers. Our holy God expects us to imitate him by following his high moral standards and by being both merciful and just.

LAB note for 1 Peter 1:15

(EZEKIEL 20:19) (1 PETER 1:15) (1 JOHN 2:6) (2 CORINTHIANS 3:5) (JOHN 15:4) (PHILIPPIANS 2:12-13) (HEBREWS 13:20-21)

May 12

The Father has life in himself, and he has granted his Son to have life in himself.

Christ Jesus, our Savior . . . broke the power of death and showed us the way to everlasting life through the Good News. ▪ I am the resurrection and the life. Those who believe in me, even though they die like everyone else, will live again. ▪ I will live again, and you will, too. ▪ We will share in all that belongs to Christ. ▪ "The first man, Adam, became a living person." But the last Adam—that is, Christ—is a life-giving Spirit. But let me tell you a wonderful secret God has revealed to us. Not all of us will die, but we will all be transformed. It will happen in a moment, in the blinking of an eye, when the last trumpet is blown. For when the trumpet sounds, the Christians who have died will be raised with transformed bodies. And then we who are living will be transformed so that we will never die. For our perishable earthly bodies must be transformed into heavenly bodies that will never die.

Holy, holy, holy is the Lord God Almighty—the one who always was, who is, and who is still to come . . . the one who lives forever and ever. ▪ The blessed and only almighty God, the King of kings and Lord of lords. ▪ Glory and honor to God forever and ever. He is the eternal King, the unseen one who never dies; he alone is God. Amen.

God is the source and Creator of life, for there is no life apart from God, here or hereafter. The life in us is a gift from him. Because Jesus is eternally existent with God, the Creator, he, too, is "the life" through whom we may live eternally. *LAB note for John 5:26*

(JOHN 5:26) (2 TIMOTHY 1:10) (JOHN 11:25) (JOHN 14:19) (HEBREWS 3:14) (1 CORINTHIANS 15:45, 51-53) (REVELATION 4:8-9) (1 TIMOTHY 6:15) (1 TIMOTHY 1:17)

May 13

Let us not become conceited, or irritate one another, or be jealous of one another.

Gideon replied, ". . . I have one request. Each of you can give me an earring out of the treasures you collected from your fallen enemies." (The enemies, being Ishmaelites, all wore gold earrings.) "Gladly!" they replied. They spread out a cloak, and each one threw in a gold earring he had gathered. Gideon made a sacred ephod from the gold and put it in Ophrah, his hometown. But soon all the Israelites prostituted themselves by worshiping it, and it became a trap for Gideon and his family.

Are you seeking great things for yourself? Don't do it! ▪ I have received wonderful revelations from God. But to keep me from getting puffed up, I was given a thorn in my flesh, a messenger from Satan to torment me and keep me from getting proud. Now I am glad to boast about my weaknesses, so that the power of Christ may work through me.

Don't be selfish; don't live to make a good impression on others. Be humble, thinking of others as better than yourself. ▪ Love is patient and kind. Love is not jealous or boastful or proud or rude. Love does not demand its own way.

Take my yoke upon you. Let me teach you. . . . For my yoke fits perfectly.

Everyone needs a certain amount of approval from others. But those who go out of their way to secure honors or to win popularity with a lot of people become conceited. Those who look to God for approval won't need to envy others. *LAB note for Galatians 5:26*

(Galatians 5:26) (Judges 8:23-25, 27) (Jeremiah 45:5) (2 Corinthians 12:7, 9) (Philippians 2:3) (1 Corinthians 13:4-5) (Matthew 11:29-30)

May 14

Keep a close watch on yourself and on your teaching.

All athletes practice strict self-control. They do it to win a prize that will fade away, but we do it for an eternal prize. So I run straight to the goal with purpose in every step. I am not like a boxer who misses his punches. I discipline my body like an athlete, training it to do what it should. Otherwise, I fear that after preaching to others I myself might be disqualified.

Put on all of God's armor so that you will be able to stand firm against all strategies and tricks of the Devil. For we are not fighting against people made of flesh and blood, but against the evil rulers and the authorities of the unseen world, against those mighty powers of darkness who rule this world, and against wicked spirits in the heavenly realms.

Those who belong to Christ Jesus have nailed their passions and desires of their sinful nature to his cross and crucified them there. If we are living now by the Holy Spirit, let us follow the Holy Spirit's leading in every part of our lives.

We must be on constant guard against falling into sin, which can so easily destroy us. Yet we must watch what we believe just as closely. Wrong beliefs can quickly lead us into sin and heresy. We should be on guard against those who would persuade us that how we live is more important than what we believe. *LAB note for 1 Timothy 4:16*

(1 Timothy 4:16) (1 Corinthians 9:25-27) (Ephesians 6:11-12) (Galatians 5:24-25)

May 15

The Holy Spirit helps us in our distress.

The Counselor . . . the Holy Spirit. ▩ Don't you know that your body is the temple of the Holy Spirit, who lives in you and was given to you by God? ▩ God is working in you.

The Holy Spirit helps us in our distress. For we don't even know what we should pray for, nor how we should pray. But the Holy Spirit prays for us with groanings that cannot be expressed in words. And the Father who knows all hearts knows what the Spirit is saying, for the Spirit pleads for us believers in harmony with God's own will.

He knows we are only dust. ▩ He will not crush those who are weak or quench the smallest hope.

Though the spirit is willing enough, the body is weak!

The LORD is my shepherd; I have everything I need. He lets me rest in green meadows; he leads me beside peaceful streams. He renews my strength. He guides me along right paths, bringing honor to his name. Even when I walk through the dark valley of death, I will not be afraid, for you are close beside me. Your rod and your staff protect and comfort me.

As a believer, you are not left to your own resources to cope with problems. Even when you don't know the right words to pray, the Holy Spirit prays with and for you, and God answers. So don't be afraid to ask the Holy Spirit to intercede for you "in harmony with God's own will."

LAB note for Romans 8:26-27

(ROMANS 8:26) (JOHN 14:26) (1 CORINTHIANS 6:19) (PHILIPPIANS 2:13) (ROMANS 8:26-27) (PSALM 103:14) (ISAIAH 42:3) (MATTHEW 26:41) (PSALM 23:1-4)

May 16

When they call on me, I will answer; I will be with them in trouble. I will rescue them and honor them.

Jabez . . . prayed to the God of Israel, "Oh, that you would bless me and extend my lands! Please be with me in all that I do, and keep me from all trouble and pain!" And God granted him his request. ▪ God appeared to Solomon in a dream and said, "What do you want? Ask, and I will give it to you!" Solomon replied to God, "You have been so faithful and kind to my father, David, and now you have made me king in his place. Give me wisdom and knowledge to rule them properly, for who is able to govern this great nation of yours?" ▪ God gave Solomon great wisdom and understanding, and knowledge too vast to be measured. In fact, his wisdom exceeded that of all the wise men of the East and the wise men of Egypt.

Asa deployed his armies for battle. . . . Then Asa cried out to the LORD his God, "O LORD, no one but you can help the powerless against the mighty! Help us, O LORD our God, for we trust in you alone. It is in your name that we have come against this vast horde. O LORD, you are our God; do not let mere men prevail against you!" So the LORD defeated the Ethiopians in the presence of Asa and the army of Judah, and the enemy fled.

You answer our prayers, and to you all people will come.

Jabez is remembered for a prayer request rather than a heroic act. When we pray for God's blessing, we should also ask him to take his rightful position as Lord over our work, our family time, and our recreation. Obeying him in daily responsibilities is heroic living.

LAB note for 1 Chronicles 4:9-10

(PSALM 91:15) (1 CHRONICLES 4:9-10) (2 CHRONICLES 1:7-8, 10) (1 KINGS 4:29-30) (2 CHRONICLES 14:10-12) (PSALM 65:2)

May 17

Clothe yourselves with the armor of right living.

Let the Lord Jesus Christ take control of you. ▪ I have discarded everything else, counting it all as garbage, so that I may have Christ and become one with him. I no longer count on my own goodness or my ability to obey God's law, but I trust Christ to save me. For God's way of making us right with himself depends on faith. ▪ We are made right in God's sight when we trust in Jesus Christ to take away our sins. And we all can be saved in this same way, no matter who we are or what we have done.

He has dressed me with the clothing of salvation and draped me in a robe of righteousness. ▪ I will tell everyone that you alone are just and good.

For though your hearts were once full of darkness, now you are full of light from the Lord, and your behavior should show it! Take no part in the worthless deeds of evil and darkness; instead, rebuke and expose them. But when the light shines on them, it becomes clear how evil these things are. And where your light shines, it will expose their evil deeds. This is why it is said, "Awake, O sleeper, rise up from the dead, and Christ will give you light."

Attitudes are as important as actions. Just as hatred leads to murder, so jealousy leads to strife and lust to adultery. When Christ returns, he wants to find his people clean on the inside as well as on the outside. *LAB note for Romans 13:12-14*

(Romans 13:12) (Romans 13:14) (Philippians 3:8-9) (Romans 3:22) (Isaiah 61:10) (Psalm 71:16) (Ephesians 5:8, 11, 13-15)

May 18

Your goodness is so great! You have stored up great blessings for those who honor you.

Since the world began, no ear has heard, and no eye has seen a God like you, who works for those who wait for him! ▪ No eye has seen, no ear has heard, and no mind has imagined what God has prepared for those who love him. But we know these things because God has revealed them to us by his Spirit, and his Spirit searches out everything and shows us even God's deep secrets. ▪ You will show me the way of life, granting me the joy of your presence and the pleasures of living with you forever.

How precious is your unfailing love, O God! All humanity finds shelter in the shadow of your wings. You feed them from the abundance of your own house, letting them drink from your rivers of delight.

Spend your time and energy in training yourself for spiritual fitness. Physical exercise has some value, but spiritual exercise is much more important, for it promises a reward in both this life and the next.

We cannot imagine all that God has in store for us, both in this life and for eternity. Knowing the wonderful and eternal future that awaits us gives us hope and courage to press on in this life, to endure hardship, and to avoid giving in to temptation. The best is yet to come.

LAB note for 1 Corinthians 2:9

(Psalm 31:19) (Isaiah 64:4) (1 Corinthians 2:9-10) (Psalm 16:11) (Psalm 36:7-8) (1 Timothy 4:7-8)

May 19

The Son of God, whose eyes are bright like flames of fire.

The human heart is most deceitful and desperately wicked. Who really knows how bad it is? But I know! I, the LORD, search all hearts and examine secret motives. I give all people their due rewards, according to what their actions deserve. ▩ You spread out our sins before you—our secret sins—and you see them all. ▩ The Lord turned and looked at Peter. . . . And Peter left the courtyard, crying bitterly.

Jesus didn't trust them, because he knew what people were really like. No one needed to tell him about human nature. ▩ He knows we are only dust. ▩ He will not crush those who are weak or quench the smallest hope.

The Lord knows those who are his. ▩ I am the good shepherd; I know my own sheep, and they know me. My sheep recognize my voice; I know them, and they follow me. I give them eternal life, and they will never perish. No one will snatch them away from me, for my Father has given them to me, and he is more powerful than anyone else. So no one can take them from me.

God makes it clear why we sin—it's a matter of the heart. Our heart is inclined toward sin from the time we are born. But we can still choose whether or not to continue in sin. We can ask God to help us resist temptation when it comes. *LAB note for Jeremiah 17:9-10*

(REVELATION 2:18) (JEREMIAH 17:9-10) (PSALM 90:8) (LUKE 22:61-62) (JOHN 2:24-25) (PSALM 103:14) (ISAIAH 42:3) (2 TIMOTHY 2:19) (JOHN 10:14, 27-29)

*M*ay 20

Jesus is the great Shepherd of the sheep.

The head Shepherd. ▪ I am the good shepherd; I know my own sheep, and they know me. My sheep recognize my voice; I know them, and they follow me. I give them eternal life, and they will never perish. No one will snatch them away from me. I have other sheep, too, that are not in this sheepfold. I must bring them also, and they will listen to my voice.

The LORD is my shepherd; I have everything I need. He lets me rest in green meadows; he leads me beside peaceful streams. He renews my strength. He guides me along right paths, bringing honor to his name.

All of us have strayed away like sheep. We have left God's paths to follow our own. Yet the LORD laid on him the guilt and sins of us all. ▪ I am the good shepherd. The good shepherd lays down his life for the sheep. ▪ I will search for my lost ones who strayed away, and I will bring them safely home again. I will bind up the injured and strengthen the weak. ▪ Once you were wandering like lost sheep. But now you have turned to your Shepherd, the Guardian of your souls.

A hired hand tends the sheep for money, while the shepherd does it out of love. The shepherd owns the sheep and is committed to them. Jesus is not merely doing a job; he is committed to love us and even lay down his life for us. *LAB note for John 10:11-12*

(HEBREWS 13:20) (1 PETER 5:4) (JOHN 10:14, 27-28, 16) (PSALM 23:1-3) (ISAIAH 53:6) (JOHN 10:11) (EZEKIEL 34:16) (1 PETER 2:25)

May 21

The city has no need of sun or moon, for the glory of God illuminates the city, and the Lamb is its light.

A light from heaven brighter than the sun shone down on me and my companions. "Who are you, sir?" I asked. And the Lord replied, "I am Jesus, the one you are persecuting." ▪ Jesus took Peter and the two brothers, James and John, and led them up a high mountain. As the men watched, Jesus' appearance changed so that his face shone like the sun, and his clothing beame dazzling white. ▪ No longer will you need the sun or moon to give you light, for the LORD your God will be your everlasting light, and he will be your glory. The sun will never set; the moon will not go down. For the LORD will be your everlasting light. Your days of mourning will come to an end.

After you have suffered a little while, he will restore, support, and strengthen you, and he will place you on a firm foundation. All power is his forever and ever. ▪ So be truly glad! There is wonderful joy ahead, even though it is necessary for you to endure many trials for a while.

The Transfiguration was a vision, a brief glimpse of the true glory of the King. This was a special revelation of Jesus' divinity to three of the disciples, and it was God's divine affirmation of everything Jesus had done and was about to do. *LAB note for Matthew 17:1ff.*

(REVELATION 21:23) (ACTS 26:13, 15) (MATTHEW 17:1-2) (ISAIAH 60:19-20) (1 PETER 5:10-11) (1 PETER 1:6)

May 22

The LORD is good. When trouble comes, he is a strong refuge. And he knows everyone who trusts in him.

Give thanks to the LORD Almighty, for the LORD is good. His faithful love endures forever! ■ God is our refuge and strength, always ready to help in times of trouble. ■ This I declare of the LORD: He alone is my refuge, my place of safety; he is my God, and I am trusting him. ■ How blessed you are, O Israel! Who else is like you, a people saved by the LORD? He is your protecting shield and your triumphant sword! ■ As for God, his way is perfect. All the LORD's promises prove true. He is a shield for all who look to him for protection. For who is God except the LORD?

The person who loves God is the one God knows and cares for. ■ God's truth stands firm like a foundation stone with this inscription: "The Lord knows those who are his," and "Those who claim they belong to the Lord must turn away from all wickedness." ■ The LORD watches over the path of the godly, but the path of the wicked leads to destruction. ■ You have found favor with me, and you are my friend.

To people who refuse to believe, God's punishment is like an angry fire. To those who love him, his mercy is a refuge, providing for all their needs without diminishing his supply. The relationship we have with God is up to us. What kind of relationship will you choose?

LAB note for Nahum 1:7

(NAHUM 1:7) (JEREMIAH 33:11) (PSALM 46:1) (PSALM 91:2) (DEUTERONOMY 33:29) (2 SAMUEL 22:31-32) (1 CORINTHIANS 8:3) (2 TIMOTHY 2:19) (PSALM 1:6) (EXODUS 33:17)

May 23

I want you to be free from the concerns of this life.

Give all your worries and cares to God, for he cares about what happens to you. ▪ The eyes of the LORD search the whole earth in order to strengthen those whose hearts are fully committed to him.

Taste and see that the LORD is good. Oh, the joys of those who trust in him! Even strong young lions sometimes go hungry, but those who trust in the LORD will never lack any good thing. ▪ Don't worry about everyday life—whether you have enough food, drink, and clothes. Doesn't life consist of more than food and clothing? Look at the birds. They don't need to plant or harvest or put food in barns because your heavenly Father feeds them. And you are far more valuable to him than they are. ▪ Don't worry about anything; instead, pray about everything. Tell God what you need, and thank him for all he has done. If you do this, you will experience God's peace, which is far more wonderful than the human mind can understand. His peace will guard your hearts and minds as you live in Christ Jesus.

How many ill effects of worry are you experiencing? It damages your health, disrupts your productivity, negatively affects the way you treat others, and reduces your ability to trust in God. Here is the difference between worry and genuine concern—worry immobilizes, but concern moves you to action. *LAB note for Matthew 6:25*

(1 CORINTHIANS 7:32) (1 PETER 5:7) (2 CHRONICLES 16:9) (PSALM 34:8, 10) (MATTHEW 6:25-26) (PHILIPPIANS 4:6-7)

May 24

Continue to live in fellowship with Christ.

A doubtful mind is as unsettled as a wave of the sea that is driven and tossed by the wind. People like that should not expect to receive anything from the Lord. They can't make up their minds. They waver back and forth in everything they do.

I am shocked that you are turning away so soon from God, who in his love and mercy called you to share the eternal life he gives through Christ. You are already following a different way.

If you are trying to make yourselves right with God by keeping the law, you have been cut off from Christ! You have fallen away from God's grace. You were getting along so well. Who has interfered with you to hold you back from following the truth?

Remain in me, and I will remain in you. For a branch cannot produce fruit if it is severed from the vine, and you cannot be fruitful apart from me. But if you stay joined to me and my words remain in you, you may ask any request you like, and it will be granted! For all of God's promises have been fulfilled in him. That is why we say "Amen" when we give glory to God through Christ.

Because true faith always results in good deeds, those who claim to have faith and who consistently do what is right are true believers. Good deeds cannot produce salvation, but they are necessary proof that true faith is actually present. *LAB note for 1 John 2:28–29*

(1 John 2:28) (James 1:6–8) (Galatians 1:6) (Galatians 5:4, 7) (John 15:4, 7) (2 Corinthians 1:20)

May 25

I am God Almighty; serve me faithfully and live a blameless life.

I [Paul] don't mean to say that I have already achieved these things or that I have already reached perfection! But I keep working toward that day when I will finally be all that Christ Jesus saved me for and wants me to be. No, dear brothers and sisters, I am still not all I should be, but I am focusing all my energies on this one thing: Forgetting the past and looking forward to what lies ahead, I strain to reach the end of the race and receive the prize for which God, through Christ Jesus, is calling us up to heaven.

Grow in the special favor and knowledge of our Lord and Savior Jesus Christ. ▪ All of us have had that veil removed so that we can be mirrors that brightly reflect the glory of the Lord. And as the Spirit of the Lord works within us, we become more and more like him and reflect his glory even more. ▪ The way of the righteous is like the first gleam of dawn, which shines ever brighter until the full light of day.

Jesus . . . looked up to heaven and said, ". . . I'm not asking you to take them out of the world, but to keep them safe from the evil one. I in them and you in me, all being perfected into one."

We are to obey the Lord in every respect because he is God—that is reason enough. If you don't think the benefits of obedience are worth it, consider who God is—the only one with the power and ability to meet your every need.

LAB note for Genesis 17:1

(Genesis 17:1) (Philippians 3:12-14) (2 Peter 3:18) (2 Corinthians 3:18) (Proverbs 4:18) (John 17:1, 15, 23)

May 26

Do not bring sorrow to God's Holy Spirit by the way you live.

Love . . . given to you by the Holy Spirit. ▪ The Counselor . . . the Holy Spirit. ▪ In all their suffering he also suffered, and he personally rescued them. In his love and mercy he redeemed them. He lifted them up and carried them through all the years.

God has given us his Spirit as proof that we live in him and he in us. ▪ He identified you as his own by giving you the Holy Spirit, whom he promised long ago. The Spirit is God's guarantee that he will give us everything he promised and that he has purchased us to be his own people. This is just one more reason for us to praise our glorious God. ▪ I advise you to live according to your new life in the Holy Spirit. Then you won't be doing what your sinful nature craves. The old sinful nature loves to do evil, which is just opposite from what the Holy Spirit wants. And the Spirit gives us desires that are opposite from what the sinful nature desires.

The Holy Spirit helps us in our distress.

Are you bringing sorrow to God—or pleasing him with your attitudes and actions? Act in love toward your brothers and sisters in Christ, just as Christ acted in love by sending his Son to die for your sins.

LAB note for Ephesians 4:28–32

(EPHESIANS 4:30) (ROMANS 15:30) (JOHN 14:26) (ISAIAH 63:9) (1 JOHN 4:13) (EPHESIANS 1:13–14) (GALATIANS 5:16–17) (ROMANS 8:26)

May 27

When you obey me, you should say, "We are not worthy of praise. We are servants who have simply done our duty."

Can we boast, then, that we have done anything to be accepted by God? No, because our acquittal is not based on our good deeds. It is based on our faith. ▪ What makes you better than anyone else? What do you have that God hasn't given you? And if all you have is from God, why boast as though you have accomplished something on your own? ▪ God saved you by his special favor when you believed. And you can't take credit for this; it is a gift from God. Salvation is not a reward for the good things we have done, so none of us can boast about it. For we are God's masterpiece. He has created us anew in Christ Jesus, so that we can do the good things he planned for us long ago.

But whatever I am now, it is all because God poured out his special favor on me. ▪ For everything comes from him; everything exists by his power and is intended for his glory. ▪ Everything we have has come from you, and we give you only what you have already given us!

Do you sometimes feel you deserve extra credit for serving God? Obedience is not something extra we do; it is our duty. Jesus is not suggesting our service is meaningless or useless, nor is he advocating doing away with rewards. He is attacking unwarranted self-esteem and spiritual pride.

LAB note for Luke 17:7-10

(LUKE 17:10) (ROMANS 3:27) (1 CORINTHIANS 4:7) (EPHESIANS 2:8-10) (1 CORINTHIANS 15:10) (ROMANS 11:36) (1 CHRONICLES 29:14)

*M*ay 28

Forgive all my sins.

"Come now, let us argue this out," says the LORD. "No matter how deep the stain of your sins, I can remove it. I can make you as clean as freshly fallen snow. Even if you are stained as red as crimson, I can make you as white as wool."

Take heart, son! Your sins are forgiven. ▪ I—yes, I alone—am the one who blots out your sins for my own sake and will never think of them again.

He is so rich in kindness that he purchased our freedom through the blood of his Son, and our sins are forgiven. ▪ He saved us, not because of the good things we did, but because of his mercy. He washed away our sins and gave us a new life through the Holy Spirit. He generously poured out the Spirit upon us because of what Jesus Christ our Savior did. ▪ He forgave all our sins. He canceled the record that contained the charges against us. He took it and destroyed it by nailing it to Christ's cross.

Praise the LORD, I tell myself. . . . He forgives all my sins.

The stain of sin seems permanent, but God can remove that stain from our life. We don't have to go through life permanently soiled. God's Word assures us that if we are willing and obedient, Christ will forgive and remove our most indelible stains. *LAB note for Isaiah 1:18*

(PSALM 25:18) (ISAIAH 1:18) (MATTHEW 9:2) (ISAIAH 43:25) (EPHESIANS 1:7) (TITUS 3:5-6) (COLOSSIANS 2:13-14) (PSALM 103:2-3)

May 29

This younger son packed all his belongings and took a trip to a distant land, and there he wasted all his money on wild living.

There was a time when some of you were just like that, but now your sins have been washed away, and you have been set apart for God. You have been made right with God because of what the Lord Jesus Christ and the Spirit of our God have done for you. ▪ All of us used to live that way, following the passions and desires of our evil nature. We were born with an evil nature, and we were under God's anger just like everyone else. But God is so rich in mercy, and he loved us so very much, that even while we were dead because of our sins, he gave us life when he raised Christ from the dead. (It is only by God's special favor that you have been saved!) For he raised us from the dead along with Christ, and we are seated with him in the heavenly realms—all because we are one with Christ Jesus.

This is real love. It is not that we loved God, but that he loved us and sent his Son as a sacrifice to take away our sins. ▪ God showed his great love for us by sending Christ to die for us while we were still sinners. For since we were restored to friendship with God by the death of his Son while we were still his enemies, we will certainly be delivered from eternal punishment by his life.

Nothing sinful or evil can exist in God's presence. He is absolute goodness. He cannot overlook, condone, or excuse sin as though it never happened. He loves us, but his love does not make him morally lax. If we trust in Christ, however, we will be acquitted by his atoning sacrifice.

LAB note for 1 John 4:10

(LUKE 15:13) (1 CORINTHIANS 6:11) (EPHESIANS 2:3-6)
(1 JOHN 4:10) (ROMANS 5:8, 10)

May 30

He returned home to his father. And while he was still a long distance away, his father saw him coming. Filled with love and compassion, he ran to his son, embraced him, and kissed him.

The LORD is merciful and gracious; he is slow to get angry and full of unfailing love. He will not constantly accuse us, nor remain angry forever. He has not punished us for all our sins, nor does he deal with us as we deserve. For his unfailing love toward those who fear him is as great as the height of the heavens above the earth. He has removed our rebellious acts as far away from us as the east is from the west. The LORD is like a father to his children, tender and compassionate to those who fear him.

So you should not be like cowering, fearful slaves. You should behave instead like God's very own children, adopted into his family—calling him "Father, dear Father." For his Holy Spirit speaks to us deep in our hearts and tells us that we are God's children. ▪ Now you belong to Christ Jesus. Though you once were far away from God, now you have been brought near to him because of the blood of Christ. So now you Gentiles are no longer strangers and foreigners. You are citizens along with all of God's holy people. You are members of God's family.

We are fragile, but God's care is eternal. When God examines our lives, he remembers our human condition. But our weakness should never be used as a justification for sin. His mercy takes everything into account. God will deal with you compassionately. Trust him.

LAB note for Psalm 103:13–14

(LUKE 15:20) (PSALM 103:8–13) (ROMANS 8:15–16) (EPHESIANS 2:13, 19)

May 31

Remember, the Lord forgave you, so you must forgive others.

Then Jesus told him this story: "A man loaned money to two people—five hundred pieces of silver to one and fifty pieces to the other. But neither of them could repay him, so he kindly forgave them both, canceling their debts." ■ I forgave you that tremendous debt because you pleaded with me. Shouldn't you have mercy on your fellow servant, just as I had mercy on you?

But when you are praying, first forgive anyone you are holding a grudge against, so that your Father in heaven will forgive your sins, too. ■ Since God chose you to be the holy people whom he loves, you must clothe yourselves with tenderhearted mercy, kindness, humility, gentleness, and patience. You must make allowance for each other's faults and forgive the person who offends you.

"Lord, how often should I forgive someone who sins against me? Seven times?" "No!" Jesus replied, "seventy times seven!"

The most important piece of clothing you must wear is love. ■ Oh, how kind and gracious the Lord was! He filled me completely with faith and the love of Christ Jesus.

The rabbis taught that people should forgive those who offend them—but only three times. But Jesus said, "Seventy times seven," meaning we shouldn't even keep track of how many times we forgive someone. We should always forgive those who are truly repentant, no matter how many times they ask.

LAB note for Matthew 18:22

(Colossians 3:13) (Luke 7:41-42) (Matthew 18:32-33) (Mark 11:25) (Colossians 3:12-13) (Matthew 18:21-22) (Colossians 3:14) (1 Timothy 1:14)

June

A Man among Men

Bike rides and baseball games, tree houses
and camping trips
Lighthearted fun times and spontaneous
teaching moments
One can never overestimate the importance
of a father's involvement.

A father is a wonderful balance of security and patience, wisdom and integrity, encouragement and inspiration. He has the unique and essential role of reflecting the heavenly Father's unconditional love for his children. May you be blessed by a fatherly man in your life.

June 1

I will be your Father, and you will be my sons and daughters, says the Lord Almighty.

See how very much our heavenly Father loves us, for he allows us to be called his children, and we really are! But the people who belong to this world don't know God, so they don't understand that we are his children. ▪ Everyone who believes that Jesus is the Christ is a child of God. And everyone who loves the Father loves his children, too. ▪ And because you . . . have become his children, God has sent the Spirit of his Son into your hearts, and now you can call God your dear Father. ▪ Now all of us . . . may come to the Father through the same Holy Spirit because of what Christ has done for us. ▪ He said to Jesus: "You are my Son. Today I have become your Father." And again God said, "I will be his Father, and he will be my Son."

As God's heirs, we can claim what he has provided for us—our full identity as his children. *LAB note for Galatians 4:6*

(2 Corinthians 6:18) (1 John 3:1) (1 John 5:1) (Galatians 4:6) (Ephesians 2:18) (Hebrews 1:5)

June 2

Now a word to you fathers. Don't make your children angry by the way you treat them. Rather, bring them up with the discipline and instruction approved by the Lord.

My children, listen to me. Listen to your father's instruction. Pay attention and grow wise, for I am giving you good guidance. Don't turn away from my teaching. For I, too, was once my father's son, tenderly loved by my mother as an only child.

My father told me, Take my words to heart. Follow my instructions and you will live. Learn to be wise, and develop good judgment. Don't forget or turn away from my words. ▪ Let those who are wise listen to these proverbs and become even wiser. And let those who understand receive guidance. ▪ Listen, my child, to what your father teaches you. ▪ For wisdom will enter your heart, and knowledge will fill you with joy. Wise planning will watch over you. Understanding will keep you safe. ▪ The Lord is like a father to his children, tender and compassionate to those who fear him. ▪ The Lord corrects those he loves, just as a father corrects a child in whom he delights. ▪ Now glory be to God our Father forever and ever.

The purpose of parental discipline is to help children grow, not to exasperate and provoke them to anger or discouragement. Parenting is not easy—it takes lots of patience to raise children. *LAB note for Ephesians 6:4*

(Ephesians 6:4) (Proverbs 4:1-5) (Proverbs 1:5) (Proverbs 1:8) (Proverbs 2:10-11) (Psalm 103:13) (Proverbs 3:12) (Philippians 4:20)

June 3

I am making all things new!

I assure you, unless you are born again, you can never see the Kingdom of God. ▪ Those who become Christians become new persons. They are not the same anymore, for the old life is gone. A new life has begun!

I will sprinkle clean water on you, and you will be clean. Your filth will be washed away, and you will no longer worship idols. And I will give you a new heart with new and right desires, and I will put a new spirit in you. I will take out your stony heart of sin and give you a new, obedient heart. And I will put my Spirit in you so you will obey my laws and do whatever I command. ▪ You must display a new nature because you are a new person, created in God's likeness—righteous, holy, and true.

The LORD will give you a new name. The LORD will hold you in his hands for all to see—a splendid crown in the hands of God.

I am creating new heavens and a new earth—so wonderful that no one will even think about the old ones anymore. ▪ Since everything around us is going to melt away, what holy, godly lives you should be living!

Christians are brand-new people on the inside. The Holy Spirit gives them new life, and they are not the same anymore. We are not reformed, rehabilitated, or reeducated—we are re-created (new creations), living in vital union with Christ. *LAB note for 2 Corinthians 5:17*

(REVELATION 21:5) (JOHN 3:3) (2 CORINTHIANS 5:17) (EZEKIEL 36:25-27) (EPHESIANS 4:24) (ISAIAH 62:2-3) (ISAIAH 65:17) (2 PETER 3:11)

June 4

We can be dead to sin and live for what is right.

Throw off your old evil nature and your former way of life, which is rotten through and through, full of lust and deception. Instead, there must be a spiritual renewal of your thoughts and attitudes. You must display a new nature because you are a new person, created in God's likeness—righteous, holy, and true.

You died when Christ died, and your real life is hidden with Christ in God. ▪ We died and were buried with Christ by baptism. And just as Christ was raised from the dead by the glorious power of the Father, now we also may live new lives. Our old sinful selves were crucified with Christ so that sin might lose its power in our lives. We are no longer slaves to sin. For when we died with Christ, we were set free from the power of sin. So you should consider yourselves dead to sin and able to live for the glory of God through Christ Jesus. Do not let any part of your body become a tool of wickedness, to be used for sinning. Instead, give yourselves completely to God since you have been given new life. And use your whole body as a tool to do what is right for the glory of God.

Christ died for our sins in our place, so we would not have to suffer the punishment we deserve. This is called "substitionary atonement." Since Christ has done this for us, we must choose to do right daily and to walk in his footsteps. *LAB note for 1 Peter 2:24*

(1 PETER 2:24) (EPHESIANS 4:22-24) (COLOSSIANS 3:3) (ROMANS 6:4, 6-7, 11, 13)

June 5

Remain in me, and I will remain in you.

I have been cruciified with Christ. I myself no longer live, but Christ lives in me. So I live my life in this earthly body by trusting in the Son of God, who loved me and gave himself for me.

I know I am rotten through and through so far as my old sinful nature is concerned. No matter which way I turn, I can't make myself do right. I want to, but I can't. Oh, what a miserable person I am! Who will free me from this life that is dominated by sin? Thank God! The answer is in Jesus Christ our Lord. ▪ Since Christ lives within you, even though your body will die because of sin, your spirit is alive because you have been made right with God. ▪ But you must continue to believe this truth and stand in it firmly. Don't drift away from the assurance you received when you heard the Good News.

And now, dear children, continue to live in fellowship with Christ so that when he returns, you will be full of courage and not shrink back from him in shame. ▪ Those who say they live in God should live their lives as Christ did.

In our daily life we must regularly crucify sinful desires that keep us from following Christ. And yet the focus of Christianity is not dying but living. Because we have been crucified with Christ, we have also been raised with him. *LAB note for Galatians 2:20*

(John 15:4) (Galatians 2:20) (Romans 7:18, 24–25) (Romans 8:10) (Colossians 1:23) (1 John 2:28) (1 John 2:6)

June 6

Do you believe in the Son of Man?

Who is he, sir?

The Son reflects God's own glory, and everything about him represents God exactly. ▪ The blessed and only almighty God, the King of kings and Lord of lords. He alone can never die, and he lives in light so brilliant that no human can approach him. No one has ever seen him, nor ever will. To him be honor and power forever. Amen. ▪ "I am the Alpha and the Omega—the beginning and the end," says the Lord God. "I am the one who is, who always was, and who is still to come, the Almighty One."

Yes, Lord, . . . I believe! ▪ I know the one in whom I trust, and I am sure that he is able to guard what I have entrusted to him until the day of his return. ▪ We believe because we have heard him ourselves, not just because of what you told us. He is indeed the Savior of the world.

"I am placing a stone in Jerusalem, a chosen cornerstone, and anyone who believes in him will never be disappointed." Yes, he is very precious to you who believe.

Jesus Christ is the same yesterday, today, and forever.

Alpha and omega are the first and last letters of the Greek alphabet. The Lord God is the beginning and the end. Without him you have nothing that is eternal, nothing that can change your life, nothing that can save you from sin. Is the Lord your Alpha and Omega?

LAB note for Revelation 1:8

(JOHN 9:35) (JOHN 9:36) (HEBREWS 1:3) (1 TIMOTHY 6:15-16) (REVELATION 1:8) (JOHN 9:38) (2 TIMOTHY 1:12) (JOHN 4:42) (1 PETER 2:6-7) (HEBREWS 13:8)

June 7

My dear Martha, you are so upset over all these details!

Look at the ravens. They don't need to plant or harvest or put food in barns because God feeds them. And you are far more valuable to him than any birds! Look at the lilies and how they grow. They don't work or make their clothing. And don't worry about food—what to eat or drink. Don't worry whether God will provide it for you. These things dominate the thoughts of most people, but your Father already knows your needs.

If we have enough food and clothing, let us be content. But people who long to be rich fall into temptation and are trapped by many foolish and harmful desires that plunge them into ruin and destruction. For the love of money is at the root of all kinds of evil. And some people, craving money, have wandered from the faith and pierced themselves with many sorrows.

All too quickly the message is crowded out by the cares of this life, the lure of wealth, and the desire for nice things.

Let us strip off every weight that slows us down, especially the sin that so easily hinders our progress. And let us run with endurance the race that God has set before us.

Jesus commands us not to worry because it's pointless—it can't fill any of our needs. Worry is foolish because the Creator of the universe loves us and knows what we need. He promises to meet all our real needs but not necessarily all our desires. *LAB note for Luke 12:22-34*

(LUKE 10:41) (LUKE 12:24, 27, 29-30) (1 TIMOTHY 6:8-10) (MARK 4:19) (HEBREWS 12:1)

June 8

One day Jesus told his disciples a story to illustrate their need for constant prayer and to show them that they must never give up.

Then, teaching them more about prayer, he used this illustration: "Suppose you went to a friend's house at midnight, wanting to borrow three loaves of bread. You would say to him, 'A friend of mine has just arrived for a visit, and I have nothing for him to eat.' He would call out from his bedroom, 'Don't bother me. The door is locked for the night, and we are all in bed. I can't help you this time.' But I tell you this—though he won't do it as a friend, if you keep knocking long enough, he will get up and give you what you want so his reputation won't be damaged. ■ Pray at all times and on every occasion in the power of the Holy Spirit. Stay alert and be persistent in your prayers for all Christians everywhere.

"I will not let you go unless you bless me." "You have struggled with both God and men and have won." ■ Devote yourselves to prayer with an alert mind and a thankful heart.

Jesus went to a mountain to pray, and he prayed to God all night.

To persist in prayer and not give up does not mean endless repetition or painfully long prayer sessions. Constant prayer means keeping our requests continually before God as we live for him day by day, believing he will answer. As we persist in prayer, we grow in character, faith, and hope.

LAB note for Luke 18:1

(LUKE 18:1) (LUKE 11:5-8) (EPHESIANS 6:18) (GENESIS 32:26, 28) (COLOSSIANS 4:2) (LUKE 6:12)

June 9

Be careful how you live, not as fools but as those who are wise. Make the most of every opportunity for doing good in these evil days.

Be very careful to obey all the commands. . . . Love the LORD your God, walk in all his ways, obey his commands, be faithful to him, and serve him with all your heart and all your soul. ▪ Live wisely among those who are not Christians, and make the most of every opportunity. Let your conversation be gracious and effective so that you will have the right answer for everyone. ▪ Keep away from every kind of evil.

When the bridegroom was delayed, they all lay down and slept. At midnight they were roused by the shout, "Look, the bridegroom is coming! Come out and welcome him!" So stay awake and be prepared, because you do not know the day or hour of my return.

Work hard to prove that you really are among those God has called and chosen. Doing this, you will never stumble or fall away. And God will open wide the gates of heaven for you to enter into the eternal Kingdom of our Lord and Savior Jesus Christ. ▪ There will be special favor for those who are ready and waiting for his return. You must be ready all the time, for the Son of Man will come when least expected.

By referring to these days as evil, the apostle Paul was communicating his sense of urgency, due to evil's pervasiveness. We need the same sense of urgency because our days are also difficult. We must keep our standards high, act wisely, and do good whenever we can.

LAB note for Ephesians 5:15-16

(EPHESIANS 5:15-16) (JOSHUA 22:5) (COLOSSIANS 4:5-6) (1 THESSALONIANS 5:22) (MATTHEW 25:5-6, 13) (2 PETER 1:10-11) (LUKE 12:37, 40)

June 10

All of your works will thank you, LORD, and your faithful followers will bless you.

Praise the LORD, I tell myself; with my whole heart, I will praise his holy name. Praise the LORD, I tell myself, and never forget the good things he does for me. ▪ I will praise the LORD at all times. I will constantly speak his praises. I will boast only in the LORD. ▪ I will praise you, my God and King, and bless your name forever and ever. I will bless you every day, and I will praise you forever. Great is the LORD! He is most worthy of praise! His greatness is beyond discovery! Let each generation tell its children of your mighty acts. I will meditate on your majestic, glorious splendor and your wonderful miracles. Your awe-inspiring deeds will be on every tongue; I will proclaim your greatness.

Your unfailing love is better to me than life itself; how I praise you! I will honor you as long as I live, lifting up my hands to you in prayer. You satisfy me more than the richest of foods. I will praise you with songs of joy.

Oh, how I praise the Lord. How I rejoice in God my Savior!

You are worthy, O Lord our God, to receive glory and honor and power. For you created everything, and it is for your pleasure that they exist and were created.

We have plenty for which to praise God. He forgives our sins, heals our diseases, redeems us from death, crowns us with love and compassion, satisfies our desires, and gives righteousness and justice. No matter how difficult your life's journey, you can always count your blessings—past, present, and future. *LAB note for Psalm 103:1ff.*

(PSALM 145:10) (PSALM 103:1-2) (PSALM 34:1-2) (PSALM 145:1-6) (PSALM 63:3-5) (LUKE 1:46-47) (REVELATION 4:11)

June 11

Seek to live a clean and holy life, for those who are not holy will not see the Lord.

I assure you, unless you are born again, you can never see the Kingdom of God. ▩ Nothing evil will be allowed to enter—no one who practices shameful idolatry and dishonesty.

You must be holy because I, the LORD your God, am holy. ▩ Obey God because you are his children. Don't slip back into your old ways of doing evil; you didn't know any better then. But now you must be holy in everything you do, just as God—who chose you to be his children—is holy. For he himself has said, "You must be holy because I am holy." And remember the heavenly Father to whom you pray has no favorites when he judges. He will judge or reward you according to what you do. So you must live in reverent fear of him during your time as foreigners here on earth. ▩ Throw off your old evil nature and your former way of life, which is rotten through and through, full of lust and deception. Instead, there must be a spiritual renewal of your thoughts and attitudes. You must display a new nature because you are a new person, created in God's likeness—righteous, holy, and true. ▩ Long ago, even before he made the world, God loved us and chose us in Christ to be holy and without fault in his eyes.

Sin always blocks our vision of God; so if we want to see God, we must renounce sin and obey him. Holiness is coupled with living in peace. A right relationship with God leads to right relationships with fellow believers.

LAB note for Hebrews 12:14

(HEBREWS 12:14) (JOHN 3:3) (REVELATION 21:27) (LEVITICUS 19:2) (1 PETER 1:14-17) (EPHESIANS 4:22-24) (EPHESIANS 1:4)

June 12

Gold that has been purified by fire.

I assure you that everyone who has given up house or brothers or sisters or mother or father or children or property, for my sake and for the Good News, will receive now in return, a hundred times over, houses, brothers, sisters, mothers, children, and property—with persecutions. And in the world to come they will have eternal life.

Don't be surprised at the fiery trials you are going through, as if something strange were happening to you. ▪ Be truly glad! There is wonderful joy ahead, even though it is necessary for you to endure many trials for a while. These trials are only to test your faith, to show that it is strong and pure. It is being tested as fire tests and purifies gold—and your faith is far more precious to God than mere gold. So if your faith remains strong after being tried by fiery trials, it will bring you much praise and glory and honor on the day when Jesus Christ is revealed to the whole world.

After you have suffered a little while, he will restore, support, and strengthen you, and he will place you on a firm foundation. ▪ Here on earth you will have many trials and sorrows. But take heart, because I have overcome the world.

Anyone who gives up something valuable for Jesus' sake will be repaid a hundred times over in this life, although not necessarily in the same way. Along with these rewards, however, we experience persecution because the world hates God. Jesus emphasized persecution to make sure that we do not selfishly follow him only for the rewards.

LAB note for Mark 10:29-30

(REVELATION 3:18) (MARK 10:29-30) (1 PETER 4:12) (1 PETER 1:6-7) (1 PETER 5:10) (JOHN 16:33)

June 13

Christ . . . is your example. Follow in his steps.

For even I, the Son of Man, came here not to be served but to serve others, and to give my life as a ransom for many. ▪ Whoever wants to be first must be the slave of all. ▪ Though he was God, [Jesus] . . . took the humble position of a slave and appeared in human form.

Jesus went around doing good. ▪ Share each other's troubles and problems, and in this way obey the law of Christ.

I plead with the gentleness and kindness that Christ himself would use. ▪ Be humble, thinking of others as better than yourself.

Father, forgive these people, because they don't know what they are doing. ▪ Be kind to each other, tenderhearted, forgiving one another, just as God through Christ has forgiven you.

Those who say they live in God should live their lives as Christ did. ▪ We do this by keeping our eyes on Jesus, on whom our faith depends from start to finish. He was willing to die a shameful death on the cross because of the joy he knew would be his afterward. Now he is seated in the place of highest honor beside God's throne in heaven.

Businesses, organizations, and institutions measure greatness by personal achievement. In Christ's Kingdom, however, service is the way to get ahead. The desire to be on top will hinder, not help. Look for ways you can minister to the needs of others. *LAB note for Mark 10:42-45*

(1 Peter 2:21) (Mark 10:45) (Mark 10:44) (Philippians 2:6-7) (Acts 10:38) (Galatians 6:2) (2 Corinthians 10:1) (Philippians 2:3) (Luke 23:34) (Ephesians 4:32) (1 John 2:6) (Hebrews 12:2)

June 14

I searched for him, but I couldn't find him anywhere. I called to him, but there was no reply.

Lord, what am I to say, now that Israel has fled from its enemies? But the LORD said to Joshua, "Get up! Why are you lying on your face like this? Israel has sinned and broken my covenant! They have stolen the things that I commanded to be set apart for me. And they have not only stolen them; they have also lied about it and hidden the things among their belongings. That is why the Israelites are running from their enemies in defeat. For now Israel has been set apart for destruction. I will not remain with you any longer unless you destroy the things among you that were set apart for destruction."

Listen! The LORD is not too weak to save you, and he is not becoming deaf. He can hear you when you call. But there is a problem—your sins have cut you off from God. Because of your sin, he has turned away and will not listen anymore.

Dear friends, if our conscience is clear, we can come to God with bold confidence. And we receive whatever we request when we obey him and do the things that please him.

God is not content with our doing what is right some of the time. He wants us to do what is right all the time. We are under his orders to eliminate any thoughts, practices, or possessions that hinder our devotion to him.

LAB note for Joshua 7:10-12

(SONG OF SONGS 5:6) (JOSHUA 7:8, 10-12) (ISAIAH 59:1-2) (1 JOHN 3:21-22)

June 15

I will ask the Father, and he will give you another Counselor, who will never leave you. He is the Holy Spirit, who leads into all truth.

It is actually best for you that I go away, because if I don't, the Counselor won't come. If I do go away, he will come because I will send him to you.

His Holy Spirit speaks to us deep in our hearts and tells us that we are God's children. ▪ So you should not be like cowering, fearful slaves. You should behave instead like God's very own children, adopted into his family—calling him "Father, dear Father." ▪ The Holy Spirit helps us in our distress. For we don't even know what we should pray for, nor how we should pray. But the Holy Spirit prays for us with groanings that cannot be expressed in words.

I pray that God, who gives you hope, will keep you happy and full of peace as you believe in him. May you overflow with hope through the power of the Holy Spirit. ▪ This expectation will not disappoint us. For we know how dearly God loves us, because he has given us the Holy Spirit to fill our hearts with his love.

The Holy Spirit is the very presence of God within us and all believers, helping us live as God wants and building Christ's church on earth. By faith we can appropriate the Spirit's power each day.

LAB note for John 14:15-16

(JOHN 14:16-17) (JOHN 16:7) (ROMANS 8:16) (ROMANS 8:15) (ROMANS 8:26) (ROMANS 15:13) (ROMANS 5:5)

June 16

Be still in the presence of the LORD, and wait patiently for him to act.

There is a special rest still waiting for the people of God. ▩ My people will live in safety, quietly at home. ▩ They will rest from all their toils and trials.

Jesus has already gone in there for us. He has become our eternal High Priest in the line of Melchizedek.

Come to me, all of you who are weary and carry heavy burdens, and I will give you rest. Take my yoke upon you. Let me teach you, because I am humble and gentle, and you will find rest for your souls. For my yoke fits perfectly, and the burden I give you is light. ▩ Only in returning to me and waiting for me will you be saved. In quietness and confidence is your strength. ▩ Look for the old, godly way, and walk in it. Travel its path, and you will find rest for your souls.

The LORD is my shepherd; I have everything I need. He lets me rest in green meadows; he leads me beside peaceful streams. ▩ Now I can rest again, for the LORD has been so good to me.

As the Lord is the good shepherd, so we are his sheep—not frightened, passive animals but obedient followers, wise enough to follow one who will lead us in the right places and in right ways. When you recognize the good shepherd, follow him! *LAB note for Psalm 23:1*

(PSALM 37:7) (HEBREWS 4:9) (ISAIAH 32:18) (REVELATION 14:13) (HEBREWS 6:20) (MATTHEW 11:28-30) (ISAIAH 30:15) (JEREMIAH 6:16) (PSALM 23:1-2) (PSALM 116:7)

June 17

Don't worry about tomorrow, for tomorrow will bring its own worries. Today's trouble is enough for today.

My future is in your hands. ▪ He subdues the nations before us, putting our enemies beneath our feet. He chose the Promised Land as our inheritance, the proud possession of Jacob's descendants, whom he loves. ▪ Lead me in the right path, O LORD. . . . Tell me clearly what to do, and show me which way to turn.

Commit everything you do to the LORD. Trust him, and he will help you. ▪ Seek his will in all you do, and he will direct your paths. ▪ You will hear a voice say, "This is the way; turn around and walk here."

The LORD is my shepherd; I have everything I need. He lets me rest in green meadows; he leads me beside peaceful streams. ▪ The LORD is like a father to his children, tender and compassionate to those who fear him. For he understands how weak we are; he knows we are only dust. ▪ Don't worry about having enough food or drink or clothing. Why be like the pagans who are so deeply concerned about these things? Your heavenly Father already knows all your needs. ▪ Give all your worries and cares to God, for he cares about what happens to you.

Planning for tomorrow is time well spent; worrying about tomorrow is time wasted. Worriers are consumed by fear and find it difficult to trust God. They let their plans interfere with their relationship with God. Don't let worries about tomorrow affect your relationship with God today.

LAB note for Matthew 6:34

(MATTHEW 6:34) (PSALM 31:15) (PSALM 47:3-4) (PSALM 5:8) (PSALM 37:5) (PROVERBS 3:6) (ISAIAH 30:21) (PSALM 23:1-2) (PSALM 103:13-14) (MATTHEW 6:31-32) (1 PETER 5:7)

June 18

When he comes we will be like him, for we will see him as he really is.

To all who believed him and accepted him, he gave the right to become children of God. ■ And by that same mighty power, he has given us all of his rich and wonderful promises. He has promised . . . that you will share in his divine nature.

For since the world began, no ear has heard, and no eye has seen a God like you, who works for those who wait for him!

Now we see things imperfectly as in a poor mirror, but then we will see everything with perfect clarity. All that I know now is partial and imcomplete, but then I will know everything completely, just as God knows me now. ■ Jesus Christ . . . will take these weak mortal bodies of ours and change them into glorious bodies like his own, using the same mighty power that he will use to conquer everything, everywhere. ■ But because I have done what is right, I will see you. When I awake, I will be fully satisfied, for I will see you face to face.

The Christian life is a process of becoming more and more like Christ. The process will not be complete until we see Christ face to face, but knowing that it is our ultimate destiny should motivate us to stay pure.

LAB note for 1 John 3:2-3

(1 JOHN 3:2) (JOHN 1:12) (2 PETER 1:4) (ISAIAH 64:4) (1 CORINTHIANS 13:12) (PHILIPPIANS 3:20-21) (PSALM 17:15)

June 19

Who will be able to survive?

Who will be able to endure it when he comes? . . . For he will be like a blazing fire that refines metal or like a strong soap that whitens clothes.

I saw a vast crowd, too great to count, from every nation and tribe and people and language, standing in front of the throne and before the Lamb. They were clothed in white and held palm branches in their hands. "These are the ones coming out of the great tribulation. They washed their robes in the blood of the Lamb and made them white. That is why they are standing in front of the throne of God, serving him day and night in his Temple. And he who sits on the throne will live among them and shelter them. They will never again be hungry or thirsty, and they will be fully protected from the scorching noontime heat. For the Lamb who stands in front of the throne will be their Shepherd. He will lead them to the springs of life-giving water. And God will wipe away all their tears."

Now there is no condemnation for those who belong to Christ Jesus. ▪ So Christ has really set us free. Now make sure that you stay free, and don't get tied up again in slavery to the law.

All who have been faithful through the ages will sing before God's throne. Their tribulations and sorrows will be over: no more tears for sin, for all sins are forgiven; no more tears for suffering, for all suffering is over; no more tears for death, for all believers will have been resurrected to die no more. *LAB note for Revelation 7:17*

(Revelation 6:17) (Malachi 3:2) (Revelation 7:9, 14-17) (Romans 8:1) (Galatians 5:1)

June 20

Don't bring your servant to trial! Compared to you, no one is perfect.

"Come now, let us argue this out," says the LORD. "No matter how deep the stain of your sins, I can remove it. I can make you as clean as freshly fallen snow. Even if you are stained as red as crimson, I can make you as white as wool."

He forgave all our sins. He canceled the record that contained the charges against us. He took it and destroyed it by nailing it to Christ's cross.

Since we have been made right in God's sight by faith, we have peace with God because of what Jesus Christ our Lord has done for us. ▪ We have believed in Christ Jesus, that we might be accepted by God because of our faith in Christ. ▪ For no one can ever be made right in God's sight by doing what his law commands. For the more we know God's law, the clearer it becomes that we aren't obeying it.

Everyone who believes in him is freed from all guilt and declared right with God. ▪ How we thank God, who gives us victory over sin and death through Jesus Christ our Lord!

Peace with God means we have been reconciled with him. There is no more hostility between us, no sin blocking our relationship. It is possible only because Jesus paid the price for our sins through his death on the cross. *LAB note for Romans 5:1*

(PSALM 143:2) (ISAIAH 1:18) (COLOSSIANS 2:13-14) (ROMANS 5:1) (GALATIANS 2:16) (ROMANS 3:20) (ACTS 13:39) (1 CORINTHIANS 15:57)

June 21

The Holy Spirit tells us clearly that in the last times some will turn away from what we believe; they will follow lying spirits and teachings that come from demons.

Be sure to pay attention to what you hear. ■ Let the words of Christ, in all their richness, live in your hearts and make you wise. ■ In every battle you will need faith as your shield to stop the fiery arrows aimed at you by Satan.

Those who love your law have great peace and do not stumble. How sweet are your words to my taste; they are sweeter than honey. Your commandments give me understanding; no wonder I hate every false way of life.

Your word is a lamp for my feet and a light for my path. Your commands make me wiser than my enemies, for your commands are my constant guide.

Satan can disguise himself as an angel of light. ■ Let God's curse fall on anyone, including myself, who preaches any other message than the one we told you about. Even if an angel comes from heaven and preaches any other message, let him be forever cursed.

But as for me, how good it is to be near God! I have made the Sovereign LORD my shelter, and I will tell everyone about the wonderful things you do.

It is not enough that a teacher appears to know what he is talking about, is disciplined and moral, or says that he is speaking for God. If his words contradict the Bible, his teaching is false. We must guard against any teaching that causes believers to dilute or reject any aspect of their faith.

LAB note for 1 Timothy 4:1–2

(1 TIMOTHY 4:1) (LUKE 8:18) (COLOSSIANS 3:16) (EPHESIANS 6:16) (PSALM 119:165, 103–104) (PSALM 119:105, 98) (2 CORINTHIANS 11:14) (GALATIANS 1:8) (PSALM 73:28)

June 22

Loving God means keeping his commandments.

It is my Father's will that all who see his Son and believe in him should have eternal life. ▩ We can come to God with bold confidence. And we will receive whatever we request because we obey him and do the things that please him.

Take my yoke upon you. Let me teach you, because I am humble and gentle, and you will find rest for your souls. For my yoke fits perfectly, and the burden I give you is light. ▩ If you love me, obey my commandments. Those who obey my commandments are the ones who love me. And because they love me, my Father will love them, and I will love them. And I will reveal myself to each one of them.

Happy is the person who finds wisdom and gains understanding. [Wisdom] will guide you down delightful paths; all her ways are satisfying. ▩ Those who love your law have great peace and do not stumble. ▩ I love God's law with all my heart.

And this is his commandment: We must believe in the name of his Son, Jesus Christ, and love one another. ▩ Love does no wrong to anyone, so love satisfies all of God's requirements.

Jesus never promised that obeying him would be easy. But the hard work and self-discipline of serving Christ is no burden to those who love him. And if our load starts to feel heavy, we can always trust Christ to help us bear it. *LAB note for 1 John 5:3*

(1 JOHN 5:3) (JOHN 6:40) (1 JOHN 3:21-22) (MATTHEW 11:29-30) (JOHN 14:15, 21) (PROVERBS 3:13, 17) (PSALM 119:165) (ROMANS 7:22) (1 JOHN 3:23) (ROMANS 13:10)

June 23

Forgive the rebellious sins of my youth.

I have swept away your sins like the morning mists. I—yes, I alone—am the one who blots out your sins for my own sake and will never think of them again. "Come now, let us argue this out," says the LORD. "No matter how deep the stain of your sins, I can remove it. I can make you as clean as freshly fallen snow. Even if you are stained as red as crimson, I can make you as white as wool." I will forgive their wickedness and will never again remember their sins. You will trample our sins under your feet and throw them into the depths of the ocean!

Yes, it was good for me to suffer this anguish, for you have rescued me from death and have forgiven all my sins. Where is another God like you, who pardons the sins of the survivors among his people? You cannot stay angry with your people forever, because you delight in showing mercy. All praise to him who loves us and has freed us from our sins by shedding his blood for us. He has made us his kingdom and his priests who serve before God his Father. Give to him everlasting glory! He rules forever and ever! Amen!

How tempting it is to remind someone of a past offense! But when God forgives our sins, he totally forgets them. We never have to fear that he will remind us of them later. Because God forgives our sins, we need to forgive others. *LAB note for Isaiah 43:25*

(PSALM 25:7) (ISAIAH 44:22) (ISAIAH 43:25) (ISAIAH 1:18) (JEREMIAH 31:34) (MICAH 7:19) (ISAIAH 38:17) (MICAH 7:18) (REVELATION 1:5-6)

June 24

I am the one who corrects and disciplines everyone I love.

My child, don't ignore it when the Lord disciplines you, and don't be discouraged when he corrects you. For the Lord disciplines those he loves, and he punishes those he accepts as his children. ▪ The LORD corrects those he loves, just as a father corrects a child in whom he delights. ▪ For though he wounds, he also bandages. ▪ Humble yourselves under the mighty power of God, and in his good time he will honor you. ▪ I have refined you in the furnace of suffering. ▪ I am the LORD your God, who teaches you what is good and leads you along the paths you should follow.

He does not enjoy hurting people or causing them sorrow. ▪ He has not punished us for all our sins, nor does he deal with us as we deserve. For his unfailing love toward those who fear him is as great as the height of the heavens above the earth. He has removed our rebellious acts as far away from us as the east is from the west. The LORD is like a father to his children, tender and compassionate to those who fear him. For he understands how weak we are; he knows we are only dust.

Are you lukewarm in your devotion to God? God may discipline you to help you out of your uncaring attitude, but he uses only loving discipline. Just as the spark of love can be rekindled in marriage, so the Holy Spirit can reignite our zeal for God when we allow him to work in our heart. *LAB note for Revelation 3:19*

(REVELATION 3:19) (HEBREWS 12:5-6) (PROVERBS 3:12) (JOB 5:18) (1 PETER 5:6) (ISAIAH 48:10) (ISAIAH 48:17) (LAMENTATIONS 3:33) (PSALM 103:10-14)

June 25

He is in heaven, and you are only here on earth. So let your words be few.

When you pray, don't babble on and on as people of other religions do. They think their prayers are answered only by repeating their words again and again. Don't be like them, because your Father knows exactly what you need even before you ask him!

They called on the name of Baal all morning, shouting, "O Baal, answer us!"

Two men went to the Temple to pray. One was a Pharisee, and the other was a dishonest tax collector. The proud Pharisee stood by himself and prayed this prayer: "I thank you, God, that I am not a sinner like everyone else, especially like that tax collector over there! For I never cheat, I don't sin, I don't commit adultery." But the tax collector stood at a distance and dared not even lift his eyes to heaven as he prayed. Instead, he beat his chest in sorrow, saying, "O God, be merciful to me, for I am a sinner." I tell you, this sinner, not the Pharisee, returned home justified before God. For the proud will be humbled, but the humble will be honored.

We don't even know what we should pray for, nor how we should pray. ◆ Lord, teach us to pray.

When we enter the house of God, we should have the attitude of being open and ready to listen to God, not to dictate to him what we think he should do. *LAB note for Ecclesiastes 5:1*

(ECCLESIASTES 5:2) (MATTHEW 6:7-8) (1 KINGS 18:26) (LUKE 18:10-11, 13-14) (ROMANS 8:26) (LUKE 11:1)

June 26

Draw close to God, and God will draw close to you.

Enoch . . . enjoyed a close relationship with God. ▪ Can two people walk together without agreeing on the direction? ▪ But as for me, how good it is to be near God! I have made the Sovereign LORD my shelter, and I will tell everyone about the wonderful things you do.

The LORD will stay with you as long as you stay with him! Whenever you seek him, you will find him. But if you abandon him, he will abandon you. Whenever you were in distress and turned to the LORD, the God of Israel, and sought him out, you found him.

"I know the plans I have for you," says the LORD. "They are plans for good and not for disaster, to give you a future and a hope. In those days when you pray, I will listen. If you look for me in earnest, you will find me when you seek me."

We can boldly enter heaven's Most Holy Place because of the blood of Jesus. This is the new, life-giving way that Christ has opened up for us through the sacred curtain, by means of his death for us. And since we have a great High Priest who rules over God's people, let us go right into the presence of God, with true hearts fully trusting him.

According to God's wise plan, we are to have a future and a hope; consequently we can call upon him in confidence. If we seek him wholeheartedly, he will be found. Nothing can break our fellowship with God.

LAB note for Jeremiah 29:13

(JAMES 4:8) (GENESIS 5:24) (AMOS 3:3) (PSALM 73:28) (2 CHRONICLES 15:2, 4) (JEREMIAH 29:11-13) (HEBREWS 10:19-22)

June 27

[Jesus] went back to pray a third time.

While Jesus was here on earth, he offered prayers and pleadings, with a loud cry and tears, to the one who could deliver him out of death.

Oh, that we might know the LORD! Let us press on to know him! Then he will respond to us as surely as the arrival of dawn or the coming of rains in early spring. ▪ Be patient in trouble, and always be prayerful. ▪ Pray at all times and on every occasion in the power of the Holy Spirit. Stay alert and be persistent in your prayers for all Christians everywhere. ▪ Don't worry about anything; instead, pray about everything. Tell God what you need, and thank him for all he has done. If you do this, you will experience God's peace, which is far more wonderful than the human mind can understand. His peace will guard your hearts and minds as you live in Christ Jesus.

I want your will, not mine. ▪ We can be confident that he will listen to us whenever we ask him for anything in line with his will. ▪ Take delight in the LORD, and he will give you your heart's desires. Commit everything you do to the LORD. Trust him, and he will help you.

Have you ever felt that God didn't hear your prayers? Be sure you are praying with reverent submission, willing to do what God wants. God responds to his obedient children. *LAB note for Hebrews 5:7*

(MATTHEW 26:44) (HEBREWS 5:7) (HOSEA 6:3) (ROMANS 12:12) (EPHESIANS 6:18) (PHILIPPIANS 4:6-7) (MATTHEW 26:39) (1 JOHN 5:14) (PSALM 37:4-5)

June 28

Since we are his children, we will share his treasures—for everything God gives to his Son, Christ, is ours, too.

Now that you belong to Christ, you are the true children of Abraham. You are his heirs, and now all the promises God gave to him belong to you.

See how very much our heavenly Father loves us, for he allows us to be called his children, and we really are! ▪ Now you are no longer a slave but God's own child. And since you are his child, everything he has belongs to you. ▪ His unchanging plan has always been to adopt us into his own family by bringing us to himself through Jesus Christ. And this gave him great pleasure.

Father, I want these whom you've given me to be with me, so they can see my glory. You gave me the glory because you loved me even before the world began!

To all who are victorious, who obey me to the very end, I will give authority over all the nations. They will rule the nations with an iron rod and smash them like clay pots. ▪ I will invite everyone who is victorious to sit with me on my throne, just as I was victorious and sat with my Father on his throne.

To live as Jesus did—serving others, giving up one's rights, resisting pressures to conform to the world—always exacts a price. Nothing we suffer, however, can compare to the great price that Jesus paid to save us.

LAB note for Romans 8:17

(ROMANS 8:17) (GALATIANS 3:29) (1 JOHN 3:1) (GALATIANS 4:7) (EPHESIANS 1:5) (JOHN 17:24) (REVELATION 2:26-27) (REVELATION 3:21)

June 29

God chose things despised by the world.

How can this be? . . . These people are all from Galilee, and yet we hear them speaking the languages of the lands where we were born!

Jesus . . . saw two brothers—Simon, also called Peter, and Andrew—fishing with a net, for they were commercial fishermen. Jesus called out to them, "Come, be my disciples, and I will show you how to fish for people!" ※ The members of the council were amazed when they saw the boldness of Peter and John, for they could see that they were ordinary men who had had no special training. They also recognized them as men who had been with Jesus.

My message and my preaching were very plain. I did not use wise and persuasive speeches, but the Holy Spirit was powerful among you.

You didn't choose me. I chose you. I appointed you to go and produce fruit that will last. Those who remain in me, and I in them, will produce much fruit. For apart from me you can do nothing. ※ This precious treasure—this light and power that now shine within us—is held in perishable containers, that is, in our weak bodies. So everyone can see that our glorious power is from God and is not our own.

We all need to fish for souls. If we practice Christ's teachings and share the Good News with others, we will be able to draw those around us to Christ like a fisherman who pulls fish into his boat with nets.

LAB note for Matthew 4:18–20

(1 Corinthians 1:28) (Acts 2:7) (Matthew 4:18–19) (Acts 4:13) (1 Corinthians 2:4) (John 15:16, 5) (2 Corinthians 4:7)

June 30

Don't try to act important, but enjoy the company of ordinary people.

How can you claim that you have faith in our glorious Lord Jesus Christ if you favor some people more than others? Listen to me, dear brothers and sisters. Hasn't God chosen the poor in this world to be rich in faith? Aren't they the ones who will inherit the kingdom God promised to those who love him?

Don't think only of your own good. Think of other Christians and what is best for them. ■ If we have enough food and clothing, let us be content. But people who long to be rich fall into temptation and are trapped by many foolish and harmful desires that plunge them into ruin and destruction.

God deliberately chose things the world considers foolish in order to shame those who are powerful. God chose things despised by the world, things counted as nothing at all, and used them to bring to nothing what the world considers important, so that no one can ever boast in the presence of God.

God alone made it possible for you to be in Christ Jesus.

Are you easily impressed by status, wealth, or fame? Are you partial to the "haves" while ignoring the "have nots"? This attitude is sinful. God views all people as equals, and if he favors anyone, it is the poor and the powerless. We should follow his example.

LAB note for James 2:1-7

(ROMANS 12:16) (JAMES 2:1, 5) (1 CORINTHIANS 10:24) (1 TIMOTHY 6:8-9) (1 CORINTHIANS 1:27-29) (1 CORINTHIANS 1:30)

July

On Freedom's Wings

Courage and integrity, truth and grace
Safe boundaries without divisive barriers
These are the foundation of freedom.

Any government can offer religious freedom, but only God offers spiritual freedom. During this independence season, don't miss out on the far greater treasure that can be found only in God.

July 1

Your love for me is very great. You have rescued me from the depths of death.

Do not be afraid, for I have ransomed you. I have called you by name; you are mine. I am the LORD, and there is no other Savior. I—yes, I alone—am the one who blots out your sins for my sake and will never think of them again. ▩ They trust in their wealth and boast of great riches. Yet they cannot redeem themselves from death by paying a ransom to God. Redemption does not come so easily, for no one can pay enough. ▩ I have found a ransom for his life. ▩ God is so rich in mercy, and he loved us so very much, that even while we were dead because of our sins, he gave us life when he raised Christ from the dead.

There is salvation in no one else! There is no other name in all of heaven for people to call on to save them. ▩ God our Savior . . . wants everyone to be saved and to understand the truth. For there is only one God and one Mediator who can reconcile God and people. He is the man Christ Jesus. He gave his life to purchase freedom for everyone.

Your unfailing love will last forever. Your faithfulness is as enduring as the heavens.

God created the people of Israel, and they were special to him. God redeemed them and called them by name to be those who belong to him. He protected them in times of trouble. We are important to God, too. And if we claim to belong to God, we should never do anything that would bring shame to him. *LAB note for Isaiah 43:1-4*

(PSALM 86:13) (ISAIAH 43:1, 11, 25) (PSALM 49:6-8) (JOB 33:24) (EPHESIANS 2:4-5) (ACTS 4:12) (1 TIMOTHY 2:3-6) (PSALM 89:2)

July 2

If sinners entice you, turn your back on them! They may say, "Come and join us."

The woman was convinced . . . it would make her so wise! So she ate some of the fruit. She also gave some to her husband, who was with her. Then he ate it, too. ▪ Didn't God punish all the people of Israel when Achan, a member of the clan of Zerah, sinned by stealing the things set apart for the LORD?

Do not join a crowd that intends to do evil.

You can enter God's Kingdom only through the narrow gate. The highway to hell is broad, and its gate is wide for the many who choose the easy way.

For we are not our own masters when we live or when we die. ▪ You have been called to live in freedom—not freedom to satisfy your sinful nature, but freedom to serve one another in love. ▪ You must be careful with this freedom of yours. Do not cause a brother or sister with a weaker conscience to stumble. You are sinning against Christ when you sin against other Christians by encouraging them to do something they believe is wrong.

All of us have strayed away like sheep. We have left God's paths to follow our own. Yet the LORD laid on him the guilt and sins of us all.

Sin, even when attractive, is deadly. We must learn to make choices, not on the basis of flashy appeal or short-range pleasure, but in view of the long-range effects. Sometimes this means steering clear of people who want to entice us into activities that we know are wrong.

LAB note for Proverbs 1:10

(PROVERBS 1:10) (GENESIS 3:6) (JOSHUA 22:20) (EXODUS 23:2) (MATTHEW 7:13) (ROMANS 14:7) (GALATIANS 5:13) (1 CORINTHIANS 8:9, 12) (ISAIAH 53:6)

July 3

I am constantly aware of your unfailing love, and I have lived according to your truth.

The LORD is kind and merciful, slow to get angry, full of unfailing love. ▩ Your Father in heaven . . . gives his sunlight to both the evil and the good, and he sends rain on the just and on the unjust, too. ▩ Follow God's example in everything you do, because you are his dear children. Live a life filled with love for others, following the example of Christ, who loved you and gave himself as a sacrifice to take away your sins. And God was pleased, because that sacrifice was like sweet perfume to him. ▩ Be kind to each other, tenderhearted, forgiving one another, just as God through Christ has forgiven you. ▩ Now you can have sincere love for each other as brothers and sisters because you were cleansed from your sins when you accepted the truth of the Good News. So see to it that you really do love each other intensely with all your hearts. ▩ Whatever we do, it is because Christ's love controls us.

Love your enemies! Do good to them! Lend to them! And don't be concerned that they might not repay. Then your reward from heaven will be very great, and you will truly be acting as children of the Most High, for he is kind to the unthankful and to those who are wicked.

"Sincere" love involves selfless giving. God's love and forgiveness free you to take your eyes off yourselves and meet others' needs. By sacrificing his life, Christ showed that he truly loves you. Now you can love others by following his example and giving of yourself sacrificially.

LAB note for 1 Peter 1:22

(PSALM 26:3) (PSALM 145:8) (MATTHEW 5:45) (EPHESIANS 5:1-2) (EPHESIANS 4:32) (1 PETER 1:22) (2 CORINTHIANS 5:14) (LUKE 6:35)

July 4

Jesus was led out into the wilderness by the Holy Spirit to be tempted there by the Devil.

While Jesus was here on earth, he offered prayers and pleadings, with a loud cry and tears, to the one who could deliver him out of death. And God heard his prayers because of his reverence for God. So even though Jesus was God's Son, he learned obedience from the things he suffered. In this way, God qualified him as a perfect High Priest, and he became the source of eternal salvation for all those who obey him. ▪ This High Priest of ours understands our weaknesses, for he faced all of the same temptations we do, yet he did not sin.

The temptations that come into your life are no different from what others experience. And God is faithful. He will keep the temptation from becoming so strong that you can't stand up against it. When you are tempted, he will show you a way out so that you will not give in to it. ▪ My gracious favor is all you need. My power works best in your weakness.

A person has not shown true obedience if he or she has never had an opportunity to disobey. When God led Israel into the wilderness to humble and test them, he wanted to see whether or not they would really obey him. We, too, will be tested—and we should be alert and ready for it!

LAB note for Matthew 4:1

(Matthew 4:1) (Hebrews 5:7-9) (Hebrews 4:15)
(1 Corinthians 10:13) (2 Corinthians 12:9)

July 5

Even I, the Son of Man, came here not to be served but to serve others, and to give my life as a ransom for many.

Under the old system, the blood of goats and bulls and the ashes of a young cow could cleanse people's bodies from ritual defilement. Just think how much more the blood of Christ will purify our hearts from deeds that lead to death so that we can worship the living God. For by the power of the eternal Spirit, Christ offered himself to God as a perfect sacrifice for our sins.

He was led as a lamb to the slaughter. ▪ I lay down my life for the sheep. No one can take my life from me. I lay down my life voluntarily. For I have the right to lay it down when I want to and also the power to take it again.

The life of any creature is in its blood. I have given you the blood so you can make atonement for your sins. It is the blood, representing life, that brings you atonement. ▪ Without the shedding of blood, there is no forgiveness of sins.

God showed his great love for us by sending Christ to die for us while we were still sinners. And since we have been made right in God's sight by the blood of Christ, he will certainly save us from God's judgment.

You cannot work hard to make yourself good enough for God. Rules and rituals have never cleansed people's hearts. Only Jesus' death and what it means for you can heal your conscience and deliver you from the frustration of trying to earn God's favor. *LAB note for Hebrews 9:12-14*

(MATTHEW 20:28) (HEBREWS 9:13-14) (ISAIAH 53:7) (JOHN 10:15, 18) (LEVITICUS 17:11) (HEBREWS 9:22) (ROMANS 5:8-9)

July 6

If we confess our sins to him, he is faithful and just to forgive us and to cleanse us from every wrong.

Have mercy on me, O God, because of your unfailing love. Because of your great compassion, blot out the stain of my sins. Wash me clean from my guilt. Purify me from my sin. For I recognize my shameful deeds—they haunt me day and night. Against you, and you alone, have I sinned.

He returned home to his father. And while he was still a long distance away, his father saw him coming. Filled with love and compassion, he ran to his son, embraced him, and kissed him. ▪ I have swept away your sins like the morning mists. I have scattered your offenses like the clouds. Oh, return to me, for I have paid the price to set you free. ▪ Your sins have been forgiven because of Jesus. ▪ God through Christ has forgiven you.

I will sprinkle clean water on you, and you will be clean. . . . And I will give you a new heart with new and right desires, and I will put a new spirit in you. I will take out your stony heart of sin and give you a new, obedient heart. And I will put my Spirit in you so you will obey my laws and do whatever I command. ▪ They will walk with me in white, for they are worthy.

When we come to Christ, he forgives all the sins we have committed or will ever commit. We don't need to confess the sins of the past all over again, and we don't need to fear that God will reject us if we don't keep our slate perfectly clean. Our relationship with Christ is secure.

LAB note for 1 John 1:9

(1 John 1:9) (Psalm 51:1-4) (Luke 15:20) (Isaiah 44:22) (1 John 2:12) (Ephesians 4:32) (Ezekiel 36:25-27) (Revelation 3:4)

July 7

A student is not greater than the teacher.

You call me "Teacher" and "Lord," and you are right, because it is true.

The student shares the teacher's fate. The servant shares the master's fate. ▪ Since they persecuted me, naturally they will persecute you. And if they had listened to me, they would listen to you! ▪ I have given them your word. And the world hates them because they do not belong to the world, just as I do not.

Think about all he endured when sinful people did such terrible things to him, so that you don't become weary and give up. After all, you have not yet given your lives in your struggle against sin.

Let us run with endurance the race that God has set before us. We do this by keeping our eyes on Jesus, on whom our faith depends from start to finish. He was willing to die a shameful death on the cross because of the joy he knew would be his afterward. Now he is seated in the place of highest honor beside God's throne in heaven. ▪ Since Christ suffered physical pain, you must arm yourselves with the same attitude he had, and be ready to suffer, too.

The world hates Christians because Christians' values differ from the world's. Because Christ's followers don't cooperate with the world by joining in their sin, they are living accusations against the world's immorality. The world follows Satan's agenda. *LAB note for John 17:14*

(MATTHEW 10:24) (JOHN 13:13) (MATTHEW 10:25) (JOHN 15:20) (JOHN 17:14) (HEBREWS 12:3-4) (HEBREWS 12:1-2) (1 PETER 4:1)

July 8

My son, give me your heart.

Oh, that they would always have hearts like this, that they might fear me and obey all my commands! If they did, they and their descendants would prosper forever.

Your heart is not right before God. ▩ The sinful nature is always hostile to God. It never did obey God's laws, and it never will. That's why those who are still under the control of their sinful nature can never please God.

Their first action was to dedicate themselves to the Lord. ▩ Above all else, guard your heart, for it affects everything you do.

Work hard and cheerfully at whatever you do, as though you were working for the Lord rather than for people. ▩ Work hard, but not just to please your masters when they are watching. As slaves of Christ, do the will of God with all your heart. Work with enthusiasm, as though you were working for the Lord rather than for people.

If you will help me, I will run to follow your commands.

There is a difference between doing something because it is required and doing something because we want to. God is not interested in forced religious exercises and rule keeping. He wants our hearts and lives completely dedicated to him. *LAB note for Deuteronomy 5:29*

(Proverbs 23:26) (Deuteronomy 5:29) (Acts 8:21) (Romans 8:7-8) (2 Corinthians 8:5) (Proverbs 4:23) (Colossians 3:23) (Ephesians 6:6-7) (Psalm 119:32)

July 9

I will protect and deliver you.

Who can snatch the plunder of war from the hands of a warrior? Who can demand that a tyrant let his captives go? But the LORD says, "The captives of warriors will be released, and the plunder of tyrants will be retrieved. For I will fight those who fight you, and I will save your children. I will feed your enemies with their own flesh. They will be drunk with rivers of their own blood. All the world will know that I, the LORD, am your Savior and Redeemer, the Mighty One of Israel." ▩ Don't be afraid, for I am with you. Do not be dismayed, for I am your God. I will strengthen you. I will help you. I will uphold you with my victorious right hand.

This High Priest of ours understands our weaknesses, for he faced all of the same temptations we do, yet he did not sin. ▩ Since he himself has gone through suffering and temptation, he is able to help us when we are being tempted. ▩ The steps of the godly are directed by the LORD. He delights in every detail of their lives. Though they stumble, they will not fall, for the LORD holds them by the hand.

God proved to the world that he is God by doing the impossible—causing warriors to set their captives free and even return the plunder they had taken! Never should we doubt that God will fulfill his promises. He will even do the impossible to make them come true.

Isaiah 49:24–25

(JEREMIAH 15:20) (ISAIAH 49:24–26) (ISAIAH 41:10) (HEBREWS 4:15) (HEBREWS 2:18) (PSALM 37:23–24)

July 10

He satisfies the thirsty and fills the hungry with good things.

You have had a taste of the Lord's kindness.

O God, you are my God; I earnestly search for you. My soul thirsts for you; my whole body longs for you in this parched and weary land where there is no water. I have seen you in your sanctuary and gazed upon your power and glory. Your unfailing love is better to me than life itself; how I praise you! I will honor you as long as I live, lifting up my hands to you in prayer. ▪ I long, yes, I faint with longing to enter the courts of the LORD. ▪ I long to go and be with Christ.

When I awake, I will be fully satisfied, for I will see you face to face. ▪ They will never again be hungry or thirsty, and they will be fully protected from the scorching noontime heat. For the Lamb who stands in front of the throne will be their Shepherd. He will lead them to the springs of life-giving water. And God will wipe away all their tears. ▪ You feed them from the abundance of your own house, letting them drink from your river of delight. ▪ "I will satisfy my people with my bounty. I, the LORD, have spoken!"

Those who recognize their own lostness can receive the offer of Jesus to satisfy their needs. Jesus is the way, the bread from heaven, the living water, and the giver of rest. Have you received his life-giving offer?

LAB note for Psalm 107:4-9

(PSALM 107:9) (1 PETER 2:3) (PSALM 63:1-4) (PSALM 84:2) (PHILIPPIANS 1:23) (PSALM 17:15) (REVELATION 7:16-17) (PSALM 36:8) (JEREMIAH 31:14)

July 11

I will personally go with you. . . . I will give you rest—everything will be fine for you.

Be strong and courageous! Do not be afraid of them! The LORD your God will go ahead of you. He will neither fail you nor forsake you. ▩ I command you—be strong and courageous! Do not be afraid or discouraged. For the LORD your God is with you wherever you go. ▩ You will find favor with both God and people, and you will gain a good reputation. Trust in the LORD with all your heart; do not depend on your own understanding. Seek his will in all you do, and he will direct your paths. ▩ Happy is the person who finds wisdom and gains understanding. For the profit of wisdom is better than silver, and her wages are better than gold. Wisdom is more precious than rubies; nothing you desire can compare with her.

God has said, "I will never fail you. I will never forsake you." That is why we can say with confidence, "The Lord is my helper, so I will not be afraid. What can mere mortals do to me?" ▩ Our only power and success come from God.

I know, LORD, that a person's life is not his own. No one is able to plan his own course.

To receive God's guidance we must seek God's will in all we do. This means turning every area of life over to him. Examine your values and priorities. What is important to you? In what areas have you not acknowledged him? *LAB note for Psalm 3:6*

(EXODUS 33:14) (DEUTERONOMY 31:6, 8) (JOSHUA 1:9) (PROVERBS 3:4-6) (PROVERBS 3:13-15) (HEBREWS 13:5-6) (2 CORINTHIANS 3:5) (JEREMIAH 10:23)

July 12

Think of ways to encourage one another to outbursts of love and good deeds.

Timely advice is as lovely as golden apples in a silver basket.

Those who feared the LORD spoke with each other, and the LORD listened to what they said. In his presence, a scroll of remembrance was written to record the names of those who feared him and loved to think about him. ■ If two of you agree down here on earth concerning anything you ask, my Father in heaven will do it for you.

The LORD God said, "It is not good for the man to be alone." ■ Two people can accomplish more than twice as much as one; they get a better return for their labor. If one person falls, the other can reach out and help. But people who are alone when they fall are in real trouble.

Live in such a way that you will not put an obstacle in another Christian's path. If another Christian is distressed by what you eat, you are not acting in love if you eat it. Don't let your eating ruin someone for whom Christ died. Don't tear apart the work of God over what you eat. Remember, there is nothing wrong with these things in themselves. But it is wrong to eat anything if it makes another person stumble. ■ Share each other's troubles and problems, and in this way obey the law of Christ.

God will remember those who remain faithful to him, and who love, fear, honor, and respect him. Is your name written in the scroll of remembrance? *LAB note for Malachi 3:16*

(HEBREWS 10:24) (PROVERBS 25:11) (MALACHI 3:16) (MATTHEW 18:19) (GENESIS 2:18) (ECCLESIASTES 4:9-10) (ROMANS 14:13, 15, 20) (GALATIANS 6:2)

July 13

Search the book of the LORD.

Commit yourselves completely to these words of mine. Tie them to your hands as a reminder, and wear them on your forehead. ▪ Study this Book of the Law continually. Meditate on it day and night so you may be sure to obey all that is written in it. Only then will you succeed.

The godly offer good counsel. ▪ I have followed your commands, which have kept me from going along with cruel and evil people. ▪ I had hidden your word in my heart, that I might not sin against you.

Because [we ourselves heard the voice], we have even greater confidence in the message proclaimed by the prophets. Pay close attention to what they wrote, for their words are like a light shining in a dark place—until the day Christ appears and his brilliant light shines in your hearts. ▪ Such things were written in the Scriptures long ago to teach us. They give us hope and encouragement as we wait patiently for God's promises.

Hiding (keeping) God's Word in our heart is a deterrent to sin. This alone should inspire us to memorize Scripture. But memorization alone will not keep us from sin; we must also put God's Word to work in our life, making it a vital guide for everything we do. *LAB note for Psalm 119:11*

(ISAIAH 34:16) (DEUTERONOMY 11:18) (JOSHUA 1:8) (PSALM 37:30) (PSALM 17:4) (PSALM 119:11) (2 PETER 1:19) (ROMANS 15:4)

July 14

Whatever is in your heart determines what you say.

Let the words of Christ, in all their richness, live in your hearts and make you wise. ▪ A good person produces good words from a good heart.

Those who love to talk will experience the consequences, for the tongue can kill or nourish life. ▪ A good person produces good deeds from a good heart. . . . Whatever is in your heart determines what you say. ▪ The godly offer good counsel; they know what is right from wrong. ▪ Don't use foul or abusive language. Let everything you say be good and helpful, so that your words will be an encouragement to those who hear them.

You must give an account on judgment day of every idle word you speak. The words you say now reflect your fate then; either you will be justified by them or you will be condemned.

If anyone acknowledges me publicly here on earth, I will openly acknowledge that person before my Father in heaven. ▪ Make the most of every opportunity. Let your conversation be gracious and effective so that you will have the right answer for everyone.

Jesus reminds us that our speech and actions reveal our true underlying beliefs, attitudes, and motivations. The good impressions we try to make cannot last if our heart is deceptive. What is in your heart will come out in your speech and behavior. *LAB note for Luke 6:45*

(MATTHEW 12:34) (COLOSSIANS 3:16) (MATTHEW 12:35) (PROVERBS 18:21) (LUKE 6:45) (PSALM 37:30) (EPHESIANS 4:29) (MATTHEW 12:36-37) (MATTHEW 10:32) (COLOSSIANS 4:5-6)

July 15

We prayed to our God and guarded the city day and night to protect ourselves.

Keep alert and pray. Otherwise temptation will overpower you. ▩ Devote yourselves to prayer with an alert mind and a thankful heart. ▩ Give all your worries and cares to God, for he cares about what happens to you. Be careful! Watch out for attacks from the Devil, your great enemy. He prowls around like a roaring lion, looking for some victim to devour. Take a firm stand against him, and be strong in your faith.

Why do you call me "Lord," when you won't obey me? ▩ It is a message to obey, not just to listen to.

Then the LORD said to Moses, "Why are you crying out to me? Tell the people to get moving!"

Don't worry about anything; instead, pray about everything. Tell God what you need, and thank him for all he has done. If you do this, you will experience God's peace, which is far more wonderful than the human mind can understand. His peace will guard your hearts and minds as you live in Christ Jesus.

The way to overcome temptation is to keep alert and pray. Because temptation strikes where we are most vulnerable, we can't resist it alone. Prayer is essential because God's strength can shore up our defenses and defeat Satan's power. *LAB note for Matthew 26:40-41*

(NEHEMIAH 4:9) (MATTHEW 26:41) (COLOSSIANS 4:2) (1 PETER 5:7-9) (LUKE 6:46) (JAMES 1:22) (EXODUS 14:15) (PHILIPPIANS 4:6-7)

July 16

A gracious and compassionate God, slow to get angry and filled with unfailing love.

Please, Lord, prove that your power is as great as you have claimed it to be. For you said, "The LORD is slow to anger and rich in unfailing love, forgiving every kind of sin and rebellion. Even so he does not leave sin unpunished, but he punishes the children for the sins of their parents to the third and fourth generations."

Oh, do not hold us guilty for our former sins! Let your tenderhearted mercies quickly meet our needs, for we are brought low to the dust. Help us, O God of our salvation! Help us for the honor of your name. Oh, save us and forgive our sins. ▪ LORD, our wickedness has caught up with us. We have sinned against you. So please, help us for the sake of your own reputation. LORD, we confess our wickedness and that of our ancestors, too. ▪ Oh, don't be so angry with us, LORD. Please don't remember our sins forever. Look at us, we pray, and see that we are all your people.

LORD, if you kept a record of our sins, who, O Lord, could ever survive? But you offer forgiveness, that we might learn to fear you.

Jonah didn't want the Ninevites forgiven; he wanted them destroyed. He did not understand that the God of Israel was also the God of the whole world. Are you surprised when some unlikely person turns to God? We must not forget that in reality we do not deserve to be forgiven by God. *LAB note for Jonah 4:1–2*

(JONAH 4:2) (NUMBERS 14:17–18) (PSALM 79:8–9) (JEREMIAH 14:7, 20) (ISAIAH 64:9) (PSALM 130:3–4)

July 17

She has done what she could.

This poor widow has given more than all the rest of them. ▪ If anyone gives you even a cup of water because you belong to the Messiah, I assure you, that person will be rewarded. ▪ If you are really eager to give, it isn't important how much you are able to give. God wants you to give what you have, not what you don't have.

Let us stop just saying we love each other; let us really show it by our actions. ▪ Suppose you see a brother or sister who needs food or clothing, and you say, "Well, good-bye and God bless you; stay warm and eat well"—but then you don't give that person any food or clothing. What good does that do? ▪ A farmer who plants only a few seeds will get a small crop. But the one who plants generously will get a generous crop. You must each make up your own mind as to how much you should give. Don't give reluctantly or in response to pressure. For God loves the person who gives cheerfully.

When you obey me you should say, "We are not worthy of praise. We are servants who have simply done our duty."

When we consider ourselves generous in giving a small percentage of our income to the Lord, we resemble those who gave "a tiny part of their surplus." As believers we should consider increasing our giving—whether money, time, or talents—to a point beyond mere convenience.

LAB note for Luke 21:1-4

(MARK 14:8) (LUKE 21:3) (MARK 9:41) (2 CORINTHIANS 8:12) (1 JOHN 3:18) (JAMES 2:15-16) (2 CORINTHIANS 9:6-7) (LUKE 17:10)

July 18

He, the Mighty One, is holy, and he has done great things for me.

Who else among the gods is like you, O LORD? Who is glorious in holiness like you—so awesome in splendor, performing such wonders? ▪ Nowhere among the pagan gods is there a god like you, O Lord. There are no other miracles like yours. ▪ Who will not fear, O Lord, and glorify your name? For you alone are holy. ▪ May your name be honored.

Praise the Lord, the God of Israel, because he has visited his people and redeemed them.

Who is this who comes from Edom, from the city of Bozrah, with his clothing stained red? Who is this in royal robes, marching in the greatness of his strength? "It is I, the LORD, announcing your salvation! It is I, the LORD, who is mighty to save!" ▪ For the LORD your God has arrived to live among you. He is a mighty savior. He will rejoice over you with great gladness.

Now glory be to God! By his mighty power at work within us, he is able to accomplish infinitely more than we would ever dare to ask or hope. May he be given glory in the church and in Christ Jesus forever and ever through endless ages.

The God of the Bible is unique! He is alive and able to do mighty deeds for those who love him. All human-created deities are powerless because they are merely inventions of the mind, not living beings. You need never fear that God is only one among many or that you may be worshiping the wrong God. The Lord alone is God.

LAB note for Psalm 86:8-10

(LUKE 1:49) (EXODUS 15:11) (PSALM 86:8) (REVELATION 15:4) (MATTHEW 6:9) (LUKE 1:68) (ISAIAH 63:1) (ZEPHANIAH 3:17) (EPHESIANS 3:20-21)

July 19

Whatever you do or say, let it be as a representative of the Lord Jesus.

He was despised and rejected—a man of sorrows, acquainted with bitterest grief. ▪ Here on earth you will have many trials and sorrows. But take heart, because I have overcome the world.

He is the kind of high priest we need because he is holy and blameless, unstained by sin. He has now been set apart from sinners, and he has been given the highest place of honor in heaven. ▪ No one can speak a word of blame against you. You are to live clean, innocent lives as children of God in a dark world full of crooked and perverse people.

Jesus of Nazareth . . . went around doing good and healing all who were oppressed by the Devil, for God was with him. ▪ Whenever we have the opportunity, we should do good to everyone, especially to our Christian brothers and sisters.

The one who is the true light, who gives light to everyone, was going to come into the world. ▪ You are the light of the world—like a city on a mountain, glowing in the night for all to see. Let your good deeds shine out for all to see, so that everyone will praise your heavenly Father.

As a Christian, you represent Christ at all times—wherever you go and whatever you say. What impression do people have of Christ when they see or talk with you? What changes would you make in your life in order to honor Christ? *LAB note for Colossians 3:17*

(COLOSSIANS 3:17) (ISAIAH 53:3) (JOHN 16:33) (HEBREWS 7:26) (PHILIPPIANS 2:15) (ACTS 10:38) (GALATIANS 6:10) (JOHN 1:9) (MATTHEW 5:14, 16)

July 20

Live in such a way that God's love can bless you.

Remain in me, and I will remain in you. For a branch cannot produce fruit if it is severed from the vine, and you cannot be fruitful apart from me. Yes, I am the vine; you are the branches. Those who remain in me, and I in them, will produce much fruit. For apart from me you can do nothing.

When the Holy Spirit controls our lives, he will produce . . . love.

My true disciples produce much fruit. This brings great glory to my Father. I have loved you even as the Father has loved me. Remain in my love. When you obey me, you remain in my love, just as I obey my Father and remain in his love. ■ Those who obey God's word really do love him.

I command you to love each other in the same way that I love you. ■ God showed his great love for us by sending Christ to die for us while we were still sinners. ■ We know how much God loves us, and we have put our trust in him. God is love, and all who live in love live in God, and God lives in them.

In order for God's love to bless you, you must live close to God and his people. You must not listen to false teachers—those who would try to pull you away from God. That means you should constantly check what others do and say against the Scriptures. *LAB note for Jude 1:21*

(JUDE 1:21) (JOHN 15:4-5) (GALATIANS 5:22) (JOHN 15:8-10) (1 JOHN 2:5) (JOHN 15:12) (ROMANS 5:8) (1 JOHN 4:16)

July 21

We have passed from death to eternal life.

Those who listen to my message and believe in God who sent me have eternal life. They will never be condemned for their sins, but they have already passed from death into life. ▪ Whoever has God's Son has life; whoever does not have his Son does not have life.

It is God who gives us, along with you, the ability to stand firm for Christ. He has commissioned us, and he has identified us as his own by placing the Holy Spirit in our hearts as the first installment of everything he will give us. ▪ It is by our actions that we know we are living in the truth, so we will be confident when we stand before the Lord. If our conscience is clear, we can come to God with bold confidence. ▪ We know that we are children of God.

Once you were dead, doomed forever because of your many sins. Even while we were dead because of our sins, he gave us life when he raised Christ from the dead. (It is only by God's special favor that you have been saved!) ▪ He has rescued us from the one who rules in the kingdom of darkness, and he has brought us into the Kingdom of his dear Son.

"Eternal life"—living forever with God—begins when you accept Jesus Christ as Savior. At that moment new life begins in you. It is a completed transaction. You still will face physical death, but when Christ returns again, your body will be resurrected to live forever.

LAB note for John 5:24

(1 JOHN 3:14) (JOHN 5:24) (1 JOHN 5:12) (2 CORINTHIANS 1:21-22) (1 JOHN 3:19, 21) (1 JOHN 5:19) (EPHESIANS 2:1, 5) (COLOSSIANS 1:13)

July 22

You will show me the way of life, granting me the joy of your presence.

The LORD says: Take your choice of life or death! ▪ I will continue to teach you what is good and right. ▪ I am the way, the truth, and the life. No one can come to the Father except through me. ▪ Come.

There is a path before each person that seems right, but it ends in death. ▪ You can enter God's Kingdom only through the narrow gate. The highway to hell is broad, and its gate is wide for the many who choose the easy way. But the gateway to life is small, and the road is narrow, and only a few ever find it.

A main road will go through that once deserted land. It will be named the Highway of Holiness. Evil-hearted people will never travel on it. It will be only for those who walk in God's ways; fools will never walk there. ▪ Oh, that we might know the LORD! Let us press on to know him!

There are many rooms in my Father's home, and I am going to prepare a place for you.

As the way, Jesus is our path to the Father. As the truth, he is the reality of all God's promises. As the life, he joins his divine life to ours, both now and eternally. *LAB note for John 14:6*

(PSALM 16:11) (JEREMIAH 21:8) (1 SAMUEL 12:23) (JOHN 14:6) (MATTHEW 4:19) (PROVERBS 14:12) (MATTHEW 7:13-14) (ISAIAH 35:8) (HOSEA 6:3) (JOHN 14:2)

July 23

It was by faith that Abraham obeyed when God called him to leave home and go to another land that God would give him as an inheritance.

He chose the Promised Land as our inheritance, the proud possession of Jacob's descendants, whom he loves. ▪ He found them in a desert land, in an empty, howling wasteland. He surrounded them and watched over them; he guarded them as his most precious possession. Like an eagle that rouses her chicks and hovers over her young, so he spread his wings to take them in and carried them aloft on his pinions. The LORD alone guided them; they lived without any foreign gods. He made them ride over the highlands; he let them feast on the crops of the fields.

I am the LORD your God, who teaches you what is good and leads you along the paths you should follow. ▪ Who is a teacher like him?

We live by believing and not by seeing. ▪ For this world is not our home; we are looking forward to our city in heaven, which is yet to come. ▪ Dear brothers and sisters, you are foreigners and aliens here. So I warn you to keep away from evil desires because they fight against your very souls.

Abraham's life was filled with faith. He obeyed God without question—even when it meant going to another land. Do not be surprised if God asks you to give up secure, familiar surroundings in order to carry out his will. *LAB note for Hebrews 11:8–10*

(HEBREWS 11:8) (PSALM 47:4) (DEUTERONOMY 32:10-13) (ISAIAH 48:17) (JOB 36:22) (2 CORINTHIANS 5:7) (HEBREWS 13:14) (1 PETER 2:11)

July 24

May all who are godly be happy in the LORD and praise his holy name!

Even the heavens cannot be absolutely pure in his sight. How much less pure is a corrupt and sinful person with a thirst for wickedness! ▪ God is so glorious that even the moon and stars scarcely shine compared to him. How much less are mere people, who are but worms in his sight?

Who else among the gods is like you, O LORD? Who is glorious in holiness like you? ▪ Holy, holy, holy is the LORD Almighty!

Now you must be holy in everything you do, just as God—who chose you to be his children—is holy. For he himself has said, "You must be holy because I am holy." ▪ Share in his holiness.

God's temple is holy, and you Christians are that temple. ▪ What holy, godly lives you should be living! Make every effort to live a pure and blameless life. And be at peace with God.

Let everything you say be good and helpful, so that your words will be an encouragement to those who hear them. And do not bring sorrow to God's Holy Spirit by the way you live. Remember, he is the one who has identified you as his own, guaranteeing that you will be saved on the day of redemption.

The God of Israel and of the Christian church is holy—he sets the standard for morality. He is a God of mercy and justice who cares personally for each of his followers. Our holy God expects us to imitate him by following his high moral standards and by being both merciful and just. *LAB note for 1 Peter 1:14-16*

(PSALM 97:12) (JOB 15:15-16) (JOB 25:5-6) (EXODUS 15:11) (ISAIAH 6:3) (1 PETER 1:15-16) (HEBREWS 12:10) (1 CORINTHIANS 3:17) (2 PETER 3:11, 14) (EPHESIANS 4:29-30)

July 25

You have armed me with strength for the battle; you have subdued my enemies under my feet.

When I am weak, then I am strong.

O LORD, no one but you can help the powerless against the mighty! Help us, O LORD our God, for we trust in you alone. It is in your name that we have come against this vast horde. O LORD, you are our God; do not let mere men prevail against you! ▪ Jehoshaphat cried out to the LORD to save him, and God helped him by turning the attack away from him.

It is better to trust the LORD than to put confidence in people. It is better to trust the LORD than to put confidence in princes. ▪ The best-equipped army cannot save a king, nor is great strength enough to save a warrior. Don't count on your warhorse to give you victory—for all its strength, it cannot save you.

For we are not fighting against people made of flesh and blood, but against the evil rulers and authorities of the unseen world, against those mighty powers of darkness who rule this world, and against wicked spirits in the heavenly realms.

We face a powerful army whose goal is to defeat Christ's church. When we believe in Christ, these beings become our enemies, and they try every device to turn us away from him and back to sin. We need supernatural power to defeat Satan, and God has provided this by giving us his Holy Spirit within us and his armor surrounding us.

LAB note for Ephesians 6:12

(PSALM 18:39) (2 CORINTHIANS 12:10) (2 CHRONICLES 14:11) (2 CHRONICLES 18:31) (PSALM 118:8-9) (PSALM 33:16-17) (EPHESIANS 6:12)

July 26

Live a life filled with love.

I am giving you a new commandment: Love each other. Just as I have loved you, you should love each other. ▪ Continue to show deep love for each other, for love covers a multitude of sins. ▪ Love covers all offenses.

When you are praying, first forgive anyone you are holding a grudge against, so that your Father in heaven will forgive your sins, too. ▪ Love your enemies! Do good to them! Lend to them! And don't be concerned that they might not repay. ▪ Do not rejoice when your enemies fall into trouble. Don't be happy when they stumble. ▪ Don't repay evil for evil. Don't retaliate when people say unkind things about you. Instead, pay them back with a blessing. That is what God wants you to do, and he will bless you for it. ▪ Do your part to live in peace with everyone, as much as possible. ▪ Be kind to each other, tenderhearted, forgiving one another, just as God through Christ has forgiven you.

Dear children, let us stop just saying we love each other; let us really show it by our actions. It is by our actions that we know we are living in the truth, so we will be confident when we stand before the Lord.

We are to love others based on Jesus' sacrificial love for us. Such love will not only bring unbelievers to Christ, it will also keep believers strong and united in a world hostile to God. Jesus was a living example of God's love, as we are to be living examples of Jesus' love.

LAB note for John 13:34

(Ephesians 5:2) (John 13:34) (1 Peter 4:8) (Proverbs 10:12) (Mark 11:25) (Luke 6:35) (Proverbs 24:17) (1 Peter 3:9) (Romans 12:18) (Ephesians 4:32) (1 John 3:18-19)

July 27

May . . . the love of God, and the fellowship of the Holy Spirit be with you all.

I will ask the Father, and he will give you another Counselor, who will never leave you. He is the Holy Spirit, who leads into all truth. The world at large cannot receive him, because it isn't looking for him and doesn't recognize him. But you do, because he lives with you now and later will be in you. ▪ He will not be presenting his own ideas; he will be telling you what he has heard. He will bring me glory by revealing to you whatever he receives from me.

We know how dearly God loves us, because he has given us the Holy Spirit to fill our hearts with his love.

The person who is joined to the Lord becomes one spirit with him. Don't you know that your body is the temple of the Holy Spirit, who lives in you and was given to you by God? You do not belong to yourself.

Do not bring sorrow to God's Holy Spirit by the way you live. Remember, he is the one who has identified you as his own, guaranteeing that you will be saved on the day of redemption. ▪ The Holy Spirit helps us in our distress. For we don't even know what we should pray for, nor how we should pray. But the Holy Spirit prays for us with groanings that cannot be expressed in words.

The Holy Spirit has been active among people from the beginning of time, but after Pentecost he came to live in all believers. Many people are unaware of the Holy Spirit's activities, but to those who hear Christ's words and understand the Spirit's power, the Spirit gives a whole new way to look at life. *LAB note for John 14:17ff.*

(2 Corinthians 13:13) (John 14:16-17) (John 16:13-14) (Romans 5:5)
(1 Corinthians 6:17, 19) (Ephesians 4:30) (Romans 8:26)

July 28

The God of peace . . . produce in you, through the power of Jesus Christ, all that is pleasing to him.

Rejoice. Change your ways. Encourage each other. Live in harmony and peace.

God saved you by his special favor when you believed. And you can't take credit for this; it is a gift from God. Salvation is not a reward for the good things we have done, so none of us can boast about it. ▪ Whatever is good and perfect comes to us from God above, who created all heaven's lights. Unlike them, he never changes or casts shifting shadows.

Be even more careful to put into action God's saving work in your lives, obeying God with deep reverence and fear. For God is working in you, giving you the desire to obey him and the power to do what pleases him. ▪ Let God transform you into a new person by changing the way you think. Then you will know what God wants you to do, and you will know how good and pleasing and perfect his will really is. ▪ May you always be filled with the fruit of your salvation—those good things that are produced in your life by Jesus Christ—for this will bring much glory and praise to God.

It is not that we think we can do anything of lasting value by ourselves. Our only power and success come from God.

God works in us to make us the kind of people that would please him, and he equips us to do the kind of work that would please him. Let God change you from within and then use you to help others.

Hebrews 13:20–21

(HEBREWS 13:20–21) (2 CORINTHIANS 13:11) (EPHESIANS 2:8–9) (JAMES 1:17) (PHILIPPIANS 2:12–13) (ROMANS 12:2) (PHILIPPIANS 1:11) (2 CORINTHIANS 3:5)

July 29

The Temple of the LORD must be a magnificent structure, famous and glorious.

Now God is building you, as living stones, into his spiritual temple. ▪ Don't you realize that all of you together are the temple of God and that the Spirit of God lives in you? God will bring ruin upon anyone who ruins this temple. For God's temple is holy, and you Christians are that temple. ▪ Don't you know that your body is the temple of the Holy Spirit, who lives in you and was given to you by God? You do not belong to yourself, for God bought you with a high price. So you must honor God with your body. ▪ What union can there be between God's temple and idols? For we are the temple of the living God. ▪ You are members of God's family. We are his house, built on the foundation of the apostles and the prophets. And the cornerstone is Christ Jesus himself. We who believe are carefully joined together, becoming a holy temple for the Lord. Through him you Gentiles are also joined together as part of this dwelling where God lives by his Spirit.

Just as our bodies are the "temple of the Holy Spirit," the local church or Christian community is God's temple. Just as the Jews' Temple in Jerusalem was not to be destroyed, the church is not to be spoiled and ruined by divisions, controversy, or other sins as members come together to worship God. *LAB note for 1 Corinthians 3:16–17*

(1 CHRONICLES 22:5) (1 PETER 2:5) (1 CORINTHIANS 3:16–17)
(1 CORINTHIANS 6:19–20) (2 CORINTHIANS 6:16) (EPHESIANS 2:19–22)

July 30

God did not abandon us.

Dear friends, don't be surprised at the fiery trials you are going through, as if something strange were happening to you. ▩ As you endure this divine discipline, remember that God is treating you as his own children. Whoever heard of a child who was never disciplined? If God doesn't discipline you as he does all of his children, it means that you are illegitimate and are not really his children after all.

The LORD your God is testing you to see if you love him with all your heart and soul.

The LORD will not abandon his chosen people, for that would dishonor his great name. He made you a special nation for himself. ▩ Can a mother forget her nursing child? Can she feel no love for a child she has borne? But even if that were possible, I would not forget you! ▩ Happy are those who have the God of Israel as their helper, whose hope is in the LORD their God.

Don't you think God will surely give justice to his chosen people who plead with him day and night? Will he keep putting them off? I tell you, he will grant justice to them quickly!

Who loves his child more—the father who allows the child to do what will harm him, or the one who corrects, trains, and even punishes the child to help him learn what is right? It's never pleasant to be corrected and disciplined by God, but his discipline is a sign of his deep love for us.

LAB note for Hebrews 12:5–11

(EZRA 9:9) (1 PETER 4:12) (HEBREWS 12:7–8) (DEUTERONOMY 13:3) (1 SAMUEL 12:22) (ISAIAH 49:15) (PSALM 146:5) (LUKE 18:7–8)

July 31

My Father! If it is possible, let this cup of suffering be taken away from me. Yet I want your will, not mine.

Now my soul is deeply troubled. Should I pray, "Father, save me from what lies ahead"? But that is the very reason why I came!

I have come down from heaven to do the will of God who sent me, not to do what I want. ◾ He obediently humbled himself even further by dying a criminal's death on a cross. ◾ While Jesus was here on earth, he offered prayers and pleadings, with a loud cry and tears, to the one who could deliver him out of death. And God heard his prayers because of his reverence for God. So even though Jesus was God's Son, he learned obedience from the things he suffered.

Don't you realize that I could ask my Father for thousands of angels to protect us, and he would send them instantly? ◾ Yes, it was written long ago that the Messiah must suffer and die and rise again from the dead on the third day. With my authority, take this message of repentance to all the nations, beginning in Jerusalem: "There is forgiveness of sins for all who turn to me."

Jesus was not rebelling against his Father's will when he asked that the cup be taken away. In fact, he reaffirmed his desire to do God's will. Instead, his prayer reveals his terrible suffering. His agony was worse than death because he paid for all our sin by being separated from God.

LAB note for Matthew 26:39

(Matthew 26:39) (John 12:27) (John 6:38) (Philippians 2:8) (Hebrews 5:7-8) (Matthew 26:53) (Luke 24:46-47)

August

Summer's Goodness

Bright sunny days and clear star-filled nights
Nurturing mornings in the garden and
lazy afternoons at the beach
There's nothing quite like a perfect summer day.

Summer is the time to break from the normal rush
of work and busyness. It's the season for refreshment
and relaxation. Make your summer days events to
remember and celebrate the whole year!

August 1

When the Holy Spirit controls our lives, he will produce . . . goodness.

Follow God's example in everything you do, because you are his dear children. ◾ Love your enemies! Pray for those who persecute you! In that way, you will be acting as true children of your Father in heaven. For he gives his sunlight to both the evil and the good, and he sends rain on the just and on the unjust. ◾ You must be compassionate, just as your Father is compassionate.

For this light within you produces only what is good and right and true.

Then God our Savior showed us his kindness and love. He saved us, not because of the good things we did, but because of his mercy. He washed away our sins and gave us a new life through the Holy Spirit. He generously poured out the Spirit upon us because of what Jesus Christ our Savior did. ◾ The LORD is good to everyone. He showers compassion on all his creation. ◾ Since God did not spare even his own Son but gave him up for us all, won't God, who gave us Christ, also give us everything else?

By telling us not to retaliate, Jesus keeps us from taking the law into our own hands. By loving and praying for our enemies, we can overcome evil with good. If you love your enemies and treat them well, you will truly show that Jesus is Lord of your life. *LAB note for Matthew 5:43-44*

(GALATIANS 5:22) (EPHESIANS 5:1) (MATTHEW 5:44-45) (LUKE 6:36) (EPHESIANS 5:9) (TITUS 3:4-6) (PSALM 145:9) (ROMANS 8:32)

August 2

You have given me an inheritance reserved for those who fear your name.

No weapon turned against you will succeed. And everyone who tells lies in court will be brought to justice. These benefits are enjoyed by the servants of the LORD; their vindication will come from me. I, the LORD, have spoken! ▪ The angel of the LORD guards all who fear him, and he rescues them. Taste and see that the LORD is good. Oh, the joys of those who trust in him! Let the LORD's people show him reverence, for those who honor him will have all they need. Even strong young lions sometimes go hungry, but those who trust in the LORD will never lack any good thing. ▪ The land you have given me is a pleasant land. What a wonderful inheritance!

For you who fear my name, the Sun of Righteousness will rise with healing in his wings. And you will go free, leaping with joy like calves let out to pasture. ▪ Since God did not spare even his own Son but gave him up for us all, won't God, who gave us Christ, also give us everything else?

If you feel you don't have everything you need, ask: (1) Is this really a need? (2) Is this good for me? (3) Is this the best time for me to have that desire? Even if you answer yes to all three questions, God may want you to learn that you need him more than you need your immediate desires met.

LAB note for Psalm 34:9-10

(PSALM 61:5) (ISAIAH 54:17) (PSALM 34:7-10) (PSALM 16:6) (MALACHI 4:2) (ROMANS 8:32)

August 3

I will praise you with songs of joy.

How precious are your thoughts about me, O God! They are innumerable! I can't even count them; they outnumber the grains of sand! And when I wake up in the morning, you are still with me! ▪ How sweet are your words to my taste; they are sweeter than honey. ▪ Your love is sweeter than wine.

Your unfailing love, O LORD, is as vast as the heavens; your faithfulness reaches beyond the clouds. Your righteousness is like the mighty mountains, your justice like the ocean depths. You care for people and animals alike, O LORD. How precious is your unfailing love, O God! All humanity finds shelter in the shadow of your wings. You feed them from the abundance of your own house, letting them drink from your rivers of delight. ▪ Whom have I in heaven but you? I desire you more than anything on earth. ▪ You will show me the way of life, granting me the joy of your presence and the pleasures of living with you forever.

Oh, what a wonderful God we have! How great are his riches and wisdom and knowledge! How impossible it is for us to understand his decisions and his methods! For everything comes from him; everything exists by his power and is intended for his glory.

God is faithful, righteous, and just. His love is as vast as the heavens; his faithfulness reaches beyond the clouds; his righteousness is as solid as mighty mountains; his judgments are as full of wisdom as the oceans are with water. We need not fear evil people because we know God loves us, judges evil, and will care for us throughout eternity.

LAB note for Psalm 36:5-8

(PSALM 63:5) (PSALM 139:17-18) (PSALM 119:103) (SONG OF SONGS 1:2) (PSALM 36:5-8) (PSALM 73:25) (PSALM 16:11) (ROMANS 11:33, 36)

August 4

Nicodemus, the leader who had met with Jesus earlier.

Peter was following far behind. ▪ Many people, including some of the Jewish leaders, believed in him. But they wouldn't admit it to anyone because of their fear that the Pharisees would expel them from the synagogue. For they loved human praise more than the praise of God. ▪ Fearing people is a dangerous trap, but to trust the LORD means safety.

Those the Father has given me will come to me, and I will never reject them. ▪ He will not crush those who are weak or quench the smallest hope. ▪ Faith as small as a mustard seed.

God has not given us a spirit of fear and timidity, but of power, love, and self-discipline. So you must never be ashamed to tell others about our Lord. ▪ And now, dear children, continue to live in fellowship with Christ so that when he returns, you will be full of courage and not shrink back from him in shame. ▪ If anyone acknowledges me publicly here on earth, I will openly acknowledge that person before my Father in heaven.

Since most of the Pharisees hated Jesus and wanted to kill him, Nicodemus risked his reputation and high position when he spoke up for Jesus. His statement was bold, and the Pharisees immediately became suspicious. After Jesus' death Nicodemus brought spices for his body.

LAB note for John 7:50-52

(JOHN 7:50) (MATTHEW 26:58) (JOHN 12:42-43) (PROVERBS 29:25) (JOHN 6:37) (ISAIAH 42:3) (MATTHEW 17:20) (2 TIMOTHY 1:7-8) (1 JOHN 2:28) (MATTHEW 10:32)

August 5

Endure suffering along with me, as a good soldier of Christ Jesus.

Jesus, on whom our faith depends from start to finish. He was willing to die a shameful death on the cross. ▪ It was only right that God—who made everything and for whom everything was made—should bring his many children into glory. Through the suffering of Jesus, God made him a perfect leader, one fit to bring them into their salvation. ▪ They must enter into the Kingdom of God through many tribulations.

For we are not fighting against people made of flesh and blood, but against the evil rulers and authorities of the unseen world, against those mighty powers of darkness who rule this world, and against wicked spirits in the heavenly realms. Use every piece of God's armor. ▪ We are human, but we don't wage war with human plans and methods. We use God's mighty weapons, not mere worldly weapons, to knock down the Devil's strongholds.

In his kindness God called you to his eternal glory by means of Jesus Christ. After you have suffered a little while, he will restore, support, and strengthen you, and he will place you on a firm foundation.

Despite suffering, we must keep going because of the thought of victory, the vision of winning, and the hope of harvest. We will see that our suffering is worthwhile when we achieve our goal of glorifying God, winning people to Christ, and one day living eternally with him.

LAB note for 2 Timothy 2:3-7

(2 Timothy 2:3) (Hebrews 12:2) (Hebrews 2:10) (Acts 14:22) (Ephesians 6:12-13) (2 Corinthians 10:3-4) (1 Peter 5:10)

August 6

The Lord . . . is full of tenderness and mercy.

The LORD is like a father to his children, tender and compassionate to those who fear him. ▪ Who can forget the wonders he performs? How gracious and merciful is our LORD! He gives food to those who trust him; he always remembers his covenant.

He will not let you stumble and fall; the one who watches over you will not sleep. Indeed, he who watches over Israel never tires and never sleeps. ▪ Like an eagle that rouses her chicks and hovers over her young, so he spread his wings to take them in and carried them aloft on his pinions.

The unfailing love of the LORD never ends! By his mercies we have been kept from complete destruction. Great is his faithfulness; his mercies begin afresh each day.

A vast crowd was there as he [Jesus] stepped from the boat, and he had compassion on them and healed their sick. ▪ Jesus Christ is the same yesterday, today, and forever.

Not even a sparrow, worth only half a penny, can fall to the ground without your Father knowing it. And the very hairs on your head are all numbered. So don't be afraid; you are more valuable to him than a whole flock of sparrows.

Perhaps there is some sin in your life that you think God will not forgive. But God willingly responds with help when we ask. His steadfast love and mercy are greater than any sin, and he promises forgiveness.

LAB note for Lamentations 3:21–23

(James 5:11) (Psalm 103:13) (Psalm 111:4–5) (Psalm 121:3–4) (Deuteronomy 32:11) (Lamentations 3:22–23) (Matthew 14:14) (Hebrews 13:8) (Matthew 10:29–31)

August 7

I have trodden the winepress alone.

Who else among the gods is like you, O LORD? Who is glorious in holiness like you—so awesome in splendor, performing such wonders? ▪ He was amazed to see that no one intervened to help the oppressed. So he himself stepped in to save them with his mighty power and justice. ▪ He personally carried away our sins in his own body on the cross so we can be dead to sin and live for what is right. You have been healed by his wounds!

Sing a new song to the LORD, for he has done wonderful deeds. He has won a mighty victory by his power and holiness. ▪ God disarmed the evil rulers and authorities. He shamed them publicly by his victory over them on the cross of Christ. ▪ When he sees all that is accomplished by his anguish, he will be satisfied. And because of what he has experienced, my righteous servant will make it possible for many to be counted righteous, for he will bear all their sins.

March on, my soul, with courage! ▪ Overwhelming victory is ours through Christ, who loved us.

Because redemption is an impossible task for any human, God himself, as the Messiah, personally stepped in to help. Whether we sin once or many times, out of rebellion or out of ignorance, our sin separates us from God and will continue to separate us until God forgives us and removes it. *LAB note for Isaiah 59:16-17*

(ISAIAH 63:3) (EXODUS 15:11) (ISAIAH 59:16) (1 PETER 2:24) (PSALM 98:1) (COLOSSIANS 2:15) (ISAIAH 53:11) (JUDGES 5:21) (ROMANS 8:37)

August 8

For the LORD corrects those he loves, just as a father corrects a child in whom he delights.

There is no god other than me! I am the one who kills and gives life; I am the one who wounds and heals; no one delivers from my power! ▪ "For I know the plans I have for you," says the LORD. "They are plans for good and not for disaster, to give you a future and a hope." ▪ "My thoughts are completely different from yours," says the LORD. "And my ways are far beyond anything you could imagine."

But then I will win her back once again. I will lead her out into the desert and speak tenderly to her there. ▪ So you should realize that just as a parent disciplines a child, the LORD your God disciplines you to help you. ▪ For the Lord disciplines those he loves, and he punishes those he accepts as his children. ▪ No discipline is enjoyable while it is happening—it is painful! But afterward there will be a quiet harvest of right living for those who are trained in this way. ▪ Humble yourselves under the mighty power of God, and in his good time he will honor you.

I know, O LORD, that your decisions are fair; you disciplined me because I needed it.

God doesn't punish us because he enjoys inflicting pain but because he is deeply concerned about our development. He knows that in order to become morally strong and good, we must learn the difference between right and wrong. His loving discipline enables us to do that.

LAB note for Proverbs 3:11-12

(PROVERBS 3:12) (DEUTERONOMY 32:39) (JEREMIAH 29:11) (ISAIAH 55:8) (HOSEA 2:14) (DEUTERONOMY 8:5) (HEBREWS 12:6) (HEBREWS 12:11) (1 PETER 5:6) (PSALM 119:75)

August 9

The earth is the LORD's, and everything in it. The world and all its people belong to him.

She doesn't realize that it was I who gave her everything she has—the grain, the wine, the olive oil. Even the gold and silver she used in worshiping the god Baal were gifts from me! But now I will take back the wine and ripened grain I generously provided each harvest season. I will take away the linen and wool clothing I gave her to cover her nakedness.

Everything we have has come from you, and we give you only what you have already given us! We are here for only a moment, visitors and strangers in the land as our ancestors were before us. Our days on earth are like a shadow, gone so soon without a trace. O LORD our God, even these materials that we have gathered . . . come from you! It all belongs to you! ▪ For everything comes from him; everything exists by his power and is intended for his glory. To him be glory evermore. Amen.

[Our] trust should be in the living God, who richly gives us all we need for our enjoyment.

This same God who takes care of me will supply all your needs from his glorious riches, which have been given to us in Christ Jesus.

Because "the earth is the LORD's," all of us are stewards, or caretakers. We should be committed to the proper management of this world and its resources, but we are not to become devoted to anything created or act as sole proprietors, because this world will pass away.

LAB note for Psalm 24:1

(PSALM 24:1) (HOSEA 2:8-9) (1 CHRONICLES 29:14-16) (ROMANS 11:36) (1 TIMOTHY 6:17) (PHILIPPIANS 4:19)

August 10

Cracked cisterns that can hold no water at all!

They began to talk about construction projects. "Let's build a great city with a tower that reaches to the skies—a monument to our greatness!" The LORD scattered them all over the earth; and that ended the building of the city. ▪ I worked hard to distinguish wisdom from foolishness. But now I realize that even this was like chasing the wind. For the greater my wisdom, the greater my grief. To increase knowledge only increases sorrow. ▪ I also tried to find meaning by building huge homes for myself and by planting beautiful vineyards. I made gardens and parks, filling them with all kinds of fruit trees. I built reservoirs to collect the water to irrigate my many flourishing groves. I collected great sums of silver and gold, the treasure of many kings and provinces. But as I looked at everything I had worked so hard to accomplish, it was all so meaningless. It was like chasing the wind. There was nothing really worthwhile anywhere.

If you are thirsty, come to me! ▪ For he satisfies the thirsty and fills the hungry with good things.

Let heaven fill your thoughts. Do not think only about things down here on earth.

Who would set aside a fountain of living water for a cracked cistern, a pit that collected rainwater but could not hold it? Why should we cling to the broken promises of unstable "cisterns" (money, power, religious systems, or whatever transitory thing we are putting in place of God) when God promises to constantly refresh us with living water?

LAB note for Jeremiah 2:13

(JEREMIAH 2:13) (GENESIS 11:3-4, 8) (ECCLESIASTES 1:17-18) (ECCLESIASTES 2:4-6, 8, 11) (JOHN 7:37) (PSALM 107:9) (COLOSSIANS 3:2)

August 11

I'm not asking you to take them out of the world, but to keep them safe from the evil one.

Live clean, innocent lives as children of God in a dark world full of crooked and perverse people. Let your lives shine brightly before them. ▪ You are the salt of the earth. . . . You are the light of the world. Let your good deeds shine out for all to see, so that everyone will praise your heavenly Father.

I kept you from sinning against me. ▪ The temptations that come into your life are no different from what others experience. And God is faithful. He will keep the temptation from becoming so strong that you can't stand up against it. When you are tempted, he will show you a way out so that you will not give in to it.

The Lord is faithful; he will make you strong and guard you from the evil one. ▪ He died for our sins, just as God our Father planned, in order to rescue us from this evil world in which we live. ▪ And now, all glory to God, who is able to keep you from stumbling, and who will bring you into his glorious presence innocent of sin and with great joy. All glory to him, who alone is God our Savior, through Jesus Christ our Lord. Yes, glory, majesty, power, and authority belong to him, in the beginning, now, and forevermore. Amen.

Belief in Christ should unite those who trust him. If your church has some members who are always complaining and arguing, it lacks the unifying power of Jesus Christ. If we stop arguing with other Christians or complaining about people and conditions within the church, the world will see Christ.

LAB note for Philippians 2:14-16

(John 17:15) (Philippians 2:15) (Matthew 5:13-14, 16) (Genesis 20:6) (1 Corinthians 10:13) (2 Thessalonians 3:3) (Galatians 1:4) (Jude 1:24-25)

August 12

To trust the LORD means safety.

The LORD is very great and lives in heaven. ■ The LORD is high above the nations; his glory is far greater than the heavens. Far below him are the heavens and the earth. He stoops to look, and he lifts the poor from the dirt and the needy from the garbage dump. He sets them among princes.

But God is so rich in mercy, and he loved us so very much, that even while we were dead because of our sins, he gave us life when he raised Christ from the dead. (It is only by God's special favor that you have been saved!) For he raised us from the dead along with Christ, and we are seated with him in the heavenly realms—all because we are one with Christ Jesus.

Since God did not spare even his own Son but gave him up for us all, won't God, who gave us Christ, also give us everything else? And I am convinced that nothing can ever separate us from his love. Death can't, and life can't. The angels can't, and the demons can't. Our fears for today, our worries about tomorrow, and even the powers of hell can't keep God's love away. Whether we are high above the sky or in the deepest ocean, nothing in all creation will ever be able to separate us from the love of God that is revealed in Christ Jesus our Lord.

Fear of people can hamper everything you try to do. By contrast, fear of God—respect, reverence, and trust—is liberating. Why fear people who can do no eternal harm? Instead, trust God who can turn the harm intended by others into good for those who trust him.

LAB note from Proverbs 29:25

(PROVERBS 29:25) (ISAIAH 33:5) (PSALM 113:4, 6-8)
(EPHESIANS 2:4-6) (ROMANS 8:32, 38-39)

August 13

God deliberately chose things the world considers foolish in order to shame those who think they are wise.

When Israel cried out to the LORD for help, the LORD raised up a man to rescue them. His name was Ehud son of Gera, of the tribe of Benjamin, who was left-handed. After Ehud, Shamgar son of Anath rescued Israel. He killed six hundred Philistines with an ox goad.

Then the LORD turned to him [Gideon] and said, "Go with the strength you have and rescue Israel from the Midianites. I am sending you!" "But Lord," Gideon replied, "how can I rescue Israel? My clan is the weakest in the whole tribe of Manasseh, and I am the least in my entire family!"

The LORD said to Gideon, "You have too many warriors with you. If I let all of you fight the Midianites, the Israelites will boast to me that they saved themselves by their own strength."

"It is not by force nor by strength, but by my Spirit," says the LORD Almighty. Be strong with the Lord's mighty power.

Is Christianity against rational thinking? Christians clearly do believe in using their minds to weigh the evidence and make wise choices. But no amount of human knowledge can replace or bypass Christ's work on the cross. *LAB note for 1 Corinthians 1:27*

(1 CORINTHIANS 1:27) (JUDGES 3:15, 31) (JUDGES 6:14-15) (JUDGES 7:2) (ZECHARIAH 4:6) (EPHESIANS 6:10)

August 14

The joy of the LORD is your strength.

Sing for joy, O heavens! Rejoice, O earth! Burst into song, O mountains! For the LORD has comforted his people and will have compassion on them in their sorrow. ■ God has come to save me. I will trust in him and not be afraid. The LORD God is my strength and my song; he has become my salvation. ■ The LORD is my strength, my shield from every danger. I trust in him with all my heart. He helps me, and my heart is filled with joy. I burst out in songs of thanksgiving.

Now we can rejoice in our wonderful new relationship with God—all because of what our Lord Jesus Christ has done for us in making us friends of God. ■ Even though the fig trees have no blossoms, and there are no grapes on the vine; even though the olive crop fails, and the fields lie empty and barren; even though the flocks die in the fields, and the cattle barns are empty, yet I will rejoice in the LORD! I will be joyful in the God of my salvation. The Sovereign LORD is my strength! He will make me as surefooted as a deer and bring me safely over the mountains.

Celebration is not to be self-centered (just when we feel like it). Often when we celebrate and give to others (even when we don't feel like it), we are strengthened spiritually and filled with joy. Enter into celebrations that honor God, and allow him to fill you with his joy!

LAB note for Nehemiah 8:9-10

(NEHEMIAH 8:10) (ISAIAH 49:13) (ISAIAH 12:2) (PSALM 28:7) (ROMANS 5:11) (HABAKKUK 3:17-19)

August 15

He existed before everything else began.

The faithful and true witness, the ruler of God's creation. ▩ Christ is the Head of the church, which is his body. He is the first of all who will rise from the dead, so he is first in everything.

The LORD formed me from the beginning, before he created anything else. I was appointed in ages past, at the very first, before the earth began. I was there when he established the heavens, when he drew the horizon on the oceans. I was there when he set the clouds above, when he established the deep fountains of the earth. I was there when he set the limits of the seas, so they would not spread beyond their boundaries. And when he marked off the earth's foundations, I was the architect at his side. I was his constant delight, rejoicing always in his presence. ▩ From eternity to eternity I am God.

Jesus, on whom our faith depends from start to finish. He was willing to die a shameful death on the cross because of the joy he knew would be his afterward. Now he is seated in the place of highest honor beside God's throne in heaven.

God is not only the creator of the world but also its sustainer. Because Christ is the sustainer of all life, none of us is independent from him. We are all his servants who must daily trust him to protect us, care for us, and sustain us. *LAB note for Colossians 1:17*

(COLOSSIANS 1:17) (REVELATION 3:14) (COLOSSIANS 1:18)
(PROVERBS 8:22-23, 27-30) (ISAIAH 43:13) (HEBREWS 12:2)

August 16

Is there any god in heaven or on earth who can perform such great deeds as yours?

Who in all of heaven can compare with the LORD? What mightiest angel is anything like the LORD? O LORD God Almighty! Where is there anyone as mighty as you, LORD? Faithfulness is your very character. ▪ Nowhere among the pagan gods is there a god like you, O Lord. There are no other miracles like yours. ▪ All heaven will praise your miracles, LORD; myriads of angels will praise you for your faithfulness. ▪ For the sake of your promise and according to your will, you have done all these great things and have shown them to me. How great you are, O Sovereign LORD! . . . We have never even heard of another god like you!

"No eye has seen, no ear has heard, and no mind has imagined what God has prepared for those who love him." But we know these things because God has revealed them to us by his Spirit, and his Spirit searches out everything and shows us even God's deep secrets.

Have you never heard or understood? Don't you know that the LORD is the everlasting God, the Creator of all the earth? He never grows faint or weary.

In the courts of heaven, a host of angels praise the Lord. The scene is one of such majesty and grandeur to show that our God is beyond compare. His power and purity place him high above nature and angels.

LAB note for Psalm 89:5

(DEUTERONOMY 3:24) (PSALM 89:6, 8) (PSALM 86:8) (PSALM 89:5) (2 SAMUEL 7:21-22) (1 CORINTHIANS 2:9-10) (ISAIAH 40:28)

August 17

The person who wishes to boast should boast only of what the Lord has done.

Let not the wise man gloat in his wisdom, or the mighty man in his might, or the rich man in his riches. Let them boast in this alone: that they truly know me and understand that I am the LORD.

Everything else is worthless when compared with the priceless gain of knowing Christ Jesus my Lord. I have discarded everything else, counting it all as garbage, so that I may have Christ. ▪ His unchanging plan has always been to adopt us into his own family by bringing us to himself through Jesus Christ. ▪ I am not ashamed of this Good News about Christ. It is the power of God at work, saving everyone who believes—Jews first and also Gentiles.

Whom have I in heaven but you? I desire you more than anything on earth. ▪ My heart rejoices in the LORD!

Not to us, O LORD, but to you goes all the glory for your unfailing love and faithfulness. ▪ He must become greater and greater, and I must become less and less.

People tend to admire three things about others: wisdom, power (might), and riches. But God puts a higher priority on knowing him personally and living a life that reflects his justice and righteousness. What do you want people to admire most about you? *LAB note for Jeremiah 9:23-24*

(1 CORINTHIANS 1:31) (JEREMIAH 9:23-24) (PHILIPPIANS 3:8) (EPHESIANS 1:5) (ROMANS 1:16) (PSALM 73:25) (1 SAMUEL 2:1) (PSALM 115:1) (JOHN 3:30)

August 18

LORD, you are mine!

Everything belongs to you . . . and you belong to Christ, and Christ belongs to God. ▪ Jesus Christ . . . gave his life to free us from every kind of sin, to cleanse us, and to make us his very own people, totally committed to doing what is right. ▪ God has put all things under the authority of Christ, and he gave him this authority for the benefit of the church. ▪ Christ . . . gave up his life for her [the church]. He did this to present her to himself as a glorious church without a spot or wrinkle or any other blemish. Instead, she will be holy and without fault.

I will boast only in the LORD. ▪ I am overwhelmed with joy in the LORD my God! For he has dressed me with the clothing of salvation and draped me in a robe of righteousness.

Whom have I in heaven but you? I desire you more than anything on earth. My health may fail, and my spirit may grow weak, but God remains the strength of my heart; he is mine forever. ▪ I said to the LORD, "You are my Master! All the good things I have are from you." LORD, you alone are my inheritance, my cup of blessing. You guard all that is mine. The land you have given me is a pleasant land. What a wonderful inheritance!

As Christians we can be confident that God has won the final victory and is in control of everything. We need not fear any dictator or nation or even death or Satan himself. The contract has been signed and sealed; we are waiting just a short while for delivery.

LAB note for Ephesians 1:20-22

(PSALM 119:57) (1 CORINTHIANS 3:21, 23) (TITUS 2:13-14) (EPHESIANS 1:22) (EPHESIANS 5:25, 27) (PSALM 34:2) (ISAIAH 61:10) (PSALM 73:25-26) (PSALM 16:2, 5-6)

August 19

There is a path before each person that seems right, but it ends in death.

Trusting oneself is foolish, but those who walk in wisdom are safe.

Your word is a lamp for my feet and a light for my path. ■ I have followed your commands, which have kept me from going along with cruel and evil people.

Suppose there are prophets among you, or those who have dreams about the future, and they promise you signs or miracles, and the predicted signs or miracles take place. If the prophets then say, "Come, let us worship the gods of foreign nations," do not listen to them. The LORD your God is testing you to see if you love him with all your heart and soul. Serve only the LORD your God and fear him alone. Obey his commands, listen to his voice, and cling to him.

The LORD says, "I will guide you along the best pathway for your life. I will advise you and watch over you. Do not be like a senseless horse or mule that needs a bit and bridle to keep it under control." Many sorrows come to the wicked, but unfailing love surrounds those who trust the LORD. So rejoice in the LORD and be glad, all you who obey him! Shout for joy, all you whose hearts are pure!

The "path . . . that seems right" may offer many options and require few sacrifices. But easy choices merit a second look. Is this solution attractive because it allows you to be lazy or not change your lifestyle? because it requires no moral restraints? The right choice often requires hard work and self-sacrifice. *LAB note for Proverbs 14:12*

(PROVERBS 14:12) (PROVERBS 28:26) (PSALM 119:105) (PSALM 17:4) (DEUTERONOMY 13:1-4) (PSALM 32:8-11)

August 20

God gave Solomon great wisdom and understanding.

Now someone greater than Solomon is here. ▪ Prince of Peace.

No one is likely to die for a good person, though someone might be willing to die for a person who is especially good. But God showed his great love for us in sending Christ to die for us while we were still sinners. ▪ Though [Jesus] was God, he did not demand and cling to his rights as God. He made himself nothing; he took the humble position of a slave and appeared in human form. And in human form he obediently humbled himself even further by dying a criminal's death on a cross. ▪ May you experience the love of Christ, though it is so great you will never fully understand it.

Christ is the mighty power of God and the wonderful wisdom of God. ▪ In him lie hidden all the treasures of wisdom and knowledge. ▪ The endless treasures available . . . in Christ. ▪ God alone made it possible for you to be in Christ Jesus. For our benefit God made Christ to be wisdom itself. He is the one who made us acceptable to God. He made us pure and holy, and he gave himself to purchase our freedom.

Even the queen of Sheba recognized the truth about God when it was presented to her—unlike Israel's religious leaders, who ignored the truth even though it stared them in the face. How have you responded to the evidence and truth that you have? *LAB note for Matthew 12:41-42*

(1 Kings 4:29) (Matthew 12:42) (Isaiah 9:6) (Romans 5:7-8) (Philippians 2:5-8) (Ephesians 3:19) (1 Corinthians 1:24) (Colossians 2:3) (Ephesians 3:8) (1 Corinthians 1:30)

August 21

I made you, and I will care for you.

But now, O Israel, the LORD who created you says: "Do not be afraid, for I have ransomed you. I have called you by name; you are mine. When you go through deep waters and great trouble, I will be with you. When you go through rivers of difficulty, you will not drown! When you walk through the fire of oppression, you will not be burned up; the flames will not consume you." ▪ I will be your God throughout your lifetime—until your hair is white with age.

Like an eagle that rouses her chicks and hovers over her young, so he spread his wings to take them in and carried them aloft on his pinions. The LORD alone guided them. ▪ In his love and mercy he redeemed them. He lifted them up and carried them through all the years.

Jesus Christ is the same yesterday, today, and forever. ▪ I am convinced that nothing can ever separate us from . . . the love of God that is revealed in Christ Jesus our Lord.

Can a mother forget her nursing child? Can she feel no love for a child she has borne? But even if that were possible, I would not forget you!

Our great God created us and cares for us. His love is so enduring that he will care for us throughout our lifetime and even through death. Then, if you have accepted Christ as your Savior, you will go to heaven to spend eternity with him! *LAB note for Isaiah 46:1-4*

(ISAIAH 46:4) (ISAIAH 43:1-2) (ISAIAH 46:4) (DEUTERONOMY 32:11-12) (ISAIAH 63:9) (HEBREWS 13:8) (ROMANS 8:38-39) (ISAIAH 49:15)

August 22

Consider the quarry from which you were mined, the rock from which you were cut!

I was born a sinner—yes, from the moment my mother conceived me. ▩ No one had the slightest interest in you; no one pitied you or cared for you. On the day you were born, you were dumped in a field and left to die, unwanted. But I came by and saw you there, helplessly kicking about in your own blood. As you lay there, I said, "Live!" And I helped you to thrive like a plant in the field.

He lifted me out of the pit of despair, out of the mud and the mire. He set my feet on solid ground and steadied me as I walked along. He has given me a new song to sing, a hymn of praise to our God.

When we were utterly helpless, Christ came at just the right time and died for us sinners. Now, no one is likely to die for a good person, though someone might be willing to die for a person who is especially good. But God showed his great love for us by sending Christ to die for us while we were still sinners. ▩ God is so rich in mercy, and he loved us so very much, that even while we were dead because of our sins, he gave us life when he raised Christ from the dead.

The faithful remnant may have felt alone because they were few. But God reminded them of their spiritual heritage: Abraham was only one person, but much came from his faithfulness. If we Christians, even a faithful few, remain faithful, think what God can do through us!

LAB note for Isaiah 51:1–2

(Isaiah 51:1) (Psalm 51:5) (Ezekiel 16:5–6) (Psalm 40:2–3) (Romans 5:6–8) (Ephesians 2:4–5)

August 23

I am overwhelmed with joy in the LORD my God!

I will praise the LORD at all times. I will constantly speak his praises. I will boast only in the LORD; let all who are discouraged take heart. Come, let us tell of the LORD's greatness; let us exalt his name together. ▩ The LORD our God is our light and protector. He gives us grace and glory. No good thing will the LORD withhold from those who do what is right. O LORD Almighty, happy are those who trust in you. ▩ With my whole heart, I will praise his holy name.

Those who have reason to be thankful should continually sing praises to the Lord. ▩ Let the Holy Spirit fill and control you. Then you will sing psalms and hymns and spiritual songs among yourselves, making music to the Lord in your hearts. And you will always give thanks for everything to God the Father in the name of our Lord Jesus Christ. ▩ Sing psalms and hymns and spiritual songs to God with thankful hearts.

Around midnight, Paul and Silas were praying and singing hymns to God. ▩ Always be full of joy in the Lord. I say it again—rejoice!

God promises great blessings to his people, but many of them require our active participation: We must seek him, cry out to him, trust him, fear him, reverence him, refrain from lying, turn from evil, do good, seek peace, be brokenhearted, and serve him. *LAB note for Psalm 34:1ff.*

(ISAIAH 61:10) (PSALM 34:1-3) (PSALM 84:11-12) (PSALM 103:1) (JAMES 5:13) (EPHESIANS 5:18-20) (COLOSSIANS 3:16) (ACTS 16:25) (PHILIPPIANS 4:4)

August 24

My cup overflows with blessings!

Taste and see that the LORD is good. Oh, the joys of those who trust in him! Let the LORD's people show him reverence, for those who honor him will have all they need. Even strong young lions sometimes go hungry, but those who trust in the LORD will never lack any good thing. ▩ The unfailing love of the LORD never ends! . . . Great is his faithfulness; his mercies begin afresh each day.

LORD, you alone are my inheritance, my cup of blessing. You guard all that is mine. The land you have given me is a pleasant land. What a wonderful inheritance! ▩ The whole world and life and death; the present and the future. Everything belongs to you. ▩ How we praise God, the Father of our Lord Jesus Christ, who has blessed us with every spiritual blessing in the heavenly realms because we belong to Christ.

I have learned how to get along happily whether I have much or little. ▩ True religion with contentment is great wealth. ▩ God . . . will supply all your needs from his glorious riches, which have been given to us in Christ Jesus.

You say you belong to the Lord, but do you show reverence to him? To revere the Lord means to show deep respect and honor to him. We demonstrate true reverence by our humble attitude and genuine worship. *LAB note for Psalm 34:9*

(PSALM 23:5) (PSALM 34:8-10) (LAMENTATIONS 3:22-23) (PSALM 16:5-6) (1 CORINTHIANS 3:22) (EPHESIANS 1:3) (PHILIPPIANS 4:11) (1 TIMOTHY 6:6) (PHILIPPIANS 4:19)

August 25

Your word is a lamp for my feet and a light for my path.

Wherever you walk, their counsel can lead you. When you sleep, they will protect you. When you wake up in the morning, they will advise you. For these commands and this teaching are a lamp to light the way ahead of you. The correction of discipline is the way to life. ▪ You will hear a voice say, "This is the way; turn around and walk here."

I am the light of the world. If you follow me, you won't be stumbling through the darkness, because you will have the light that leads to life. ▪ We have . . . confidence in the message proclaimed by the prophets. Pay close attention to what they wrote, for their words are like a light shining in a dark place—until the day Christ appears and his brilliant light shines in your hearts. ▪ Now we see things imperfectly as in a poor mirror, but then we will see everything with perfect clarity. All that I know now is partial and incomplete, but then I will know everything completely, just as God knows me now.

In this life we walk through a dark forest of evil. But the Bible can be our light to show us the way ahead so we won't stumble as we walk. It reveals the entangling roots of false values and philosophies. Study the Bible so you will be able to see your way clear enough to stay on the right path.

LAB note for Psalm 119:105

(PSALM 119:105) (PROVERBS 6:22-23) (ISAIAH 30:21)
(JOHN 8:12) (2 PETER 1:19) (1 CORINTHIANS 13:12)

August 26

Those who trust the LORD will be happy.

Abraham never wavered in believing God's promise. In fact, his faith grew stronger, and in this he brought glory to God. He was absolutely convinced that God was able to do anything he promised. ▪ Judah defeated Israel because they trusted in the LORD, the God of their ancestors.

God is our refuge and strength, always ready to help in times of trouble. So we will not fear, even if earthquakes come and the mountains crumble into the sea. ▪ It is better to trust the LORD than to put confidence in people. It is better to trust the LORD than to put confidence in princes. ▪ The steps of the godly are directed by the LORD. He delights in every detail of their lives. Though they stumble, they will not fall, for the LORD holds them by the hand.

Taste and see that the LORD is good. Oh, the joys of those who trust in him! Let the LORD's people show him reverence, for those who honor him will have all they need.

"Taste and see" does not mean "check out God's credentials." Instead, it is a warm invitation: "Try this: I know you'll like it." When we take that first step of obedience in following God, we cannot help discovering that he is good and kind. *LAB note for Psalm 34:8*

(PROVERBS 16:20) (ROMANS 4:20-21) (2 CHRONICLES 13:18) (PSALM 46:1-2) (PSALM 118:8-9) (PSALM 37:23-24) (PSALM 34:8-9)

August 27

I will lie down in peace and sleep, for you alone, O LORD, will keep me safe.

Do not be afraid of the terrors of the night, nor fear the dangers of the day, nor dread the plague that stalks in darkness, nor the disaster that strikes at midday. He will shield you with his wings. He will shelter you with his feathers. His faithful promises are your armor and protection. ▪ He will not let you stumble and fall; the one who watches over you will not sleep. Indeed, he who watches over Israel never tires and never sleeps. The LORD himself watches over you! The LORD stands beside you as your protective shade. The sun will not hurt you by day, nor the moon at night. The LORD keeps you from all evil and preserves your life. The LORD keeps watch over you as you come and go, both now and forever.

Let me live forever in your sanctuary, safe beneath the shelter of your wings! ▪ Even in darkness I cannot hide from you. To you the night shines as bright as day. Darkness and light are both alike to you.

Since God did not spare even his own Son but gave him up for us all, won't God, who gave us Christ, also give us everything else? ▪ You belong to Christ, and Christ belongs to God. ▪ I will trust in him and not be afraid.

Do you ever think that because you aren't good enough for God, he will not save you? Because Christ gave his life for you, God isn't going to hold back the gift of salvation! He will not condemn you. And he will not withhold anything you need to live for him. *LAB note for Romans 8:31–34*

(PSALM 4:8) (PSALM 91:5–6, 4) (PSALM 121:3–8) (PSALM 61:4) (PSALM 139:12) (ROMANS 8:32) (1 CORINTHIANS 3:23) (ISAIAH 12:2)

August 28

If any of you wants to be my follower, you must put aside your selfish ambition, shoulder your cross daily, and follow me.

We serve God whether people honor us or despise us, whether they slander us or praise us. ▪ Everyone who wants to live a godly life in Christ Jesus will suffer persecution. ▪ The fact that I am still being persecuted proves that I am still preaching salvation through the cross of Christ alone.

Be happy if you are insulted for being a Christian, for then the glorious Spirit of God will come upon you. If you suffer, however, it must not be for murder, stealing, making trouble, or prying into other people's affairs. But it is no shame to suffer for being a Christian. Praise God for the privilege of being called by his wonderful name! So if you are suffering according to God's will, keep on doing what is right, and trust yourself to the God who made you.

For you have been given not only the privilege of trusting in Christ but also the privilege of suffering for him. ▪ If we endure hardship, we will reign with him.

Christians follow their Lord by imitating his life and obeying his commands. We must deny our selfish desires to use our time and money our own way and choose our own direction. Following Christ in this life may be costly, but in the long run, it is well worth the pain and effort.

LAB note for Luke 9:23

(LUKE 9:23) (2 CORINTHIANS 6:8) (2 TIMOTHY 3:12) (GALATIANS 5:11) (1 PETER 4:14-16, 19) (PHILIPPIANS 1:29) (2 TIMOTHY 2:12)

August 29

Wait patiently for the LORD. Be brave and courageous. Yes, wait patiently for the LORD.

Have you never heard or understood? Don't you know that the LORD is the everlasting God, the Creator of all the earth? He never grows faint or weary. . . . He gives power to those who are tired and worn out; he offers strength to the weak. ▩ Don't be afraid, for I am with you. Do not be dismayed, for I am your God. I will strengthen you. I will help you. I will uphold you with my victorious right hand. ▩ To the poor, O LORD, you are a refuge from the storm. To the needy in distress, you are a shelter from the rain and the heat. For the oppressive acts of ruthless people are like a storm beating against a wall.

When your faith is tested, your endurance has a chance to grow. So let it grow, for when your endurance is fully developed, you will be strong in character and ready for anything. ▩ Do not throw away this confident trust in the Lord, no matter what happens. Remember the great reward it brings you! Patient endurance is what you need now, so you will continue to do God's will. Then you will receive all that he has promised. "For in just a little while, the Coming One will come and not delay."

Waiting for God is not easy. Often it seems he isn't answering our prayers or doesn't understand the urgency of our situation. But that kind of thinking implies God is not in control or not fair. God is worth waiting for—and he often uses our times of waiting to refresh, renew, and teach us.

LAB note for Psalm 27:14

(PSALM 27:14) (ISAIAH 40:28-29) (ISAIAH 41:10) (ISAIAH 25:4) (JAMES 1:3-4) (HEBREWS 10:35-37)

*A*ugust 30

You don't understand now why I am doing it; someday you will.

Remember how the LORD your God led you through the wilderness for forty years, humbling you and testing you to prove your character, and to find out whether or not you would really obey his commands.

I made a covenant with you, says the Sovereign LORD, and you became mine. ▪ The Lord disciplines those he loves.

Dear friends, don't be surprised at the fiery trials you are going through, as if something strange were happening to you. Instead, be very glad—because these trials will make you partners with Christ in his suffering, and afterward you will have the wonderful joy of sharing his glory when it is displayed to all the world. ▪ Our present troubles are quite small and won't last very long. Yet they produce for us an immeasurably great glory that will last forever! So we don't look at the troubles we can see right now; rather, we look forward to what we have not yet seen. For the troubles we see will soon be over, but the joys to come will last forever.

Imagine being Peter and watching Jesus wash the others' feet, all the while moving closer to you. Seeing his Master behave like a slave must have confused Peter. He still did not understand Jesus' teaching that to be a leader, a person must be a servant. How do you treat those who work under you?

LAB note for John 13:6-7

(JOHN 13:7) (DEUTERONOMY 8:2) (EZEKIEL 16:8) (HEBREWS 12:6) (1 PETER 4:12-13) (2 CORINTHIANS 4:17-18)

August 31

Let us lift our hearts and hands to God in heaven.

Who can be compared with the LORD our God, who is enthroned on high? Far below him are the heavens and the earth. He stoops to look, and he lifts the poor from the dirt and the needy from the garbage dump. He sets them among princes. ▩ To you, O LORD, I lift up my soul. ▩ I reach out for you. I thirst for you as parched land thirsts for rain. Come quickly, LORD, and answer me, for my depression deepens. Don't turn away from me, or I will die. Let me hear of your unfailing love to me in the morning, for I am trusting you. Show me where to walk, for I have come to you in prayer.

Your unfailing love is better to me than life itself; how I praise you! I will honor you as long as I live, lifting up my hands to you in prayer. ▩ Give me happiness, O Lord, for my life depends on you. O Lord, you are so good, so ready to forgive, so full of unfailing love for all who ask your aid. Listen closely to my prayer, O LORD; hear my urgent cry. I will call to you whenever trouble strikes, and you will answer me.

If our conscience is clear, we can come to God with bold confidence. And we will receive whatever we request because we obey him and do the things that please him.

Sometimes our trouble or pain is so great that all we can do is cry out to God for protection. And often when there is no relief in sight, all we can do is acknowledge the greatness of God and wait for better days. The conviction that God answers prayer will sustain us in such difficult times. *LAB note for Psalm 86:7*

(LAMENTATIONS 3:41) (PSALM 113:5-8) (PSALM 25:1) (PSALM 143:6-8) (PSALM 63:3-4) (PSALM 86:4-7) (1 JOHN 3:21-22)

September

Teachable Moments

Playpens and classrooms

Offices and family rooms

Learning can happen anywhere.

Although September is the traditional month for school to begin each year, learning is a year-round activity and a lifelong endeavor. If learning ceases, growth ends. What has life been teaching you lately?

September 1

I will give them one heart and mind to worship me forever, for their own good and for the good of all their descendants.

I will give you a new heart with new and right desires, and I will put a new spirit in you. I will take out your stony heart of sin and give you a new, obedient heart. ▪ The LORD is good and does what is right; he shows the proper path to those who go astray. He leads the humble in what is right, teaching them his way. The LORD leads with unfailing love and faithfulness all those who keep his covenant and obey his decrees.

That they will be one, just as you and I are one, Father—that just as you are in me and I am in you, so they will be in us, and the world will believe you sent me.

Lead a life worthy of your calling, for you have been called by God. Be humble and gentle. Be patient with each other, making allowance for each other's faults because of your love. Always keep yourselves united in the Holy Spirit, and bind yourselves together with peace. We are all one body, we have the same Spirit, and we have all been called to the same glorious future. There is only one Lord, one faith, one baptism, and there is only one God and Father, who is over us all and in us all and living through us all.

God uses his power to accomplish his purposes through his people. God doesn't give you power to be all you want to be, but the power to be all he wants you to be. We must develop "one heart" toward him, loving God above everything else. *LAB note for Jeremiah 32:36-42*

(JEREMIAH 32:39) (EZEKIEL 36:26) (PSALM 25:8-10)
(JOHN 17:21) (EPHESIANS 4:1-6)

September 2

Watchman . . . when will the night be over?

Time is running out. Wake up, for the coming of our salvation is nearer now than when we first believed. The night is almost gone; the day of salvation will soon be here. So don't live in darkness. Get rid of your evil deeds. Shed them like dirty clothes. Clothe yourselves with the armor of right living, as those who live in the light.

Now learn a lesson from the fig tree. When its buds become tender and its leaves begin to sprout, you know without being told that summer is near. Just so, when you see the events I've described beginning to happen, you can know his return is very near, right at the door. Heaven and earth will disappear, but my words will remain forever.

I am counting on the LORD; yes, I am counting on him. I have put my hope in his word. I long for the Lord more than sentries long for the dawn, yes, more than sentries long for the dawn.

He who is the faithful witness to all these things says, "Yes, I am coming soon!" Amen! Come, Lord Jesus!

So stay awake and be prepared, because you do not know the day or hour of my return.

We don't know the day or the hour, but Jesus is coming soon and unexpectedly. This is good news to those who trust him but a terrible message for those who have rejected him. Soon means "at any moment," and we must be ready for him. *LAB note for Revelation 22:20*

(ISAIAH 21:11) (ROMANS 13:11-12) (MATTHEW 24:32-33, 35) (PSALM 130:5-6) (REVELATION 22:20) (MATTHEW 25:13)

September 3

Don't copy the behavior and customs of this world, but let God transform you into a new person by changing the way you think.

Don't you realize that friendship with this world makes you an enemy of God? I say it again, that if your aim is to enjoy this world, you can't be a friend of God.

Don't team up with those who are unbelievers. How can goodness be a partner with wickedness? How can light live with darkness? What harmony can there be between Christ and the Devil? How can a believer be a partner with an unbeliever? ▪ Stop loving this evil world and all that it offers you, for when you love the world, you show that you do not have the love of the Father in you. This world is fading away, along with everything it craves. But if you do the will of God, you will live forever.

You used to live just like the rest of the world, full of sin, obeying Satan, the mighty prince of the power of the air. ▪ That isn't what you were taught when you learned about Christ. Since you have heard all about him and have learned the truth that is in Jesus, throw off your old evil nature.

God has good, pleasing, and perfect plans for his children. He wants us to be transformed people with renewed minds, living to honor and obey him. Because he wants only what is best for us and gave his Son to make our new life possible, we should joyfully give ourselves as living sacrifices for his service. *LAB note for Romans 12:1-2*

(ROMANS 12:2) (JAMES 4:4) (2 CORINTHIANS 6:14-15) (1 JOHN 2:15, 17) (EPHESIANS 2:2) (EPHESIANS 4:20-22)

September 4

The Lord is thinking about me right now.

"For I know the plans I have for you," says the LORD. "They are plans for good and not for disaster, to give you a future and a hope." ▪ "My thoughts are completely different from yours," says the LORD. "And my ways are far beyond anything you could imagine. For just as the heavens are higher than the earth, so are my ways higher than your ways and my thoughts higher than your thoughts."

How precious are your thoughts about me, O God! They are innumerable! I can't even count them; they outnumber the grains of sand! And when I wake up in the morning, you are still with me! ▪ O LORD, what great miracles you do! And how deep are your thoughts. ▪ O LORD my God, you have done many miracles for us. Your plans for us are too numerous to list.

Few of you were wise in the world's eyes, or powerful, or wealthy when God called you. ▪ Hasn't God chosen the poor in this world to be rich in faith? Aren't they the ones who will inherit the kingdom God promised to those who love him? ▪ Our hearts ache, but we always have joy. ▪ The endless treasures available . . . in Christ.

God knows the future, and his plans for us are good and full of hope. As long as God, who knows the future, provides our agenda, and goes with us as we fulfill his mission, we can have boundless hope—even in times of pain, suffering, or hardship. *LAB note for Jeremiah 29:11*

(PSALM 40:17) (JEREMIAH 29:11) (ISAIAH 55:8-9) (PSALM 139:17-18) (PSALM 92:5) (PSALM 40:5) (1 CORINTHIANS 1:26) (JAMES 2:5) (2 CORINTHIANS 6:10) (EPHESIANS 3:8)

September 5

My feet were slipping, and I was almost gone.

I cried out, "I'm slipping!" and your unfailing love, O LORD, supported me. ▩ Simon, Simon, Satan has asked to have all of you, to sift you like wheat. But I have pleaded in prayer for you, Simon, that your faith should not fail.

They may trip seven times, but each time they will rise again. ▩ Though they stumble, they will not fall, for the LORD holds them by the hand.

Do not gloat over me, my enemies! For though I fall, I will rise again. Though I sit in darkness, the LORD himself will be my light.

He will rescue you again and again so that no evil can touch you.

If you do sin, there is someone to plead for you before the Father. He is Jesus Christ, the one who pleases God completely. ▩ He is able, once and forever, to save everyone who comes to God through him. He lives forever to plead with God on their behalf.

Satan wanted to crush Simon Peter and the other disciples like grains of wheat. He hoped to find only chaff and blow it away. But Jesus assured Peter that his faith, although it would falter, would not be destroyed. It would be renewed, and Peter would become a powerful leader.

LAB note for Luke 22:31–32

(PSALM 73:2) (PSALM 94:18) (LUKE 22:31–32) (PROVERBS 24:16) (PSALM 37:24) (MICAH 7:8) (JOB 5:19) (1 JOHN 2:1) (HEBREWS 7:25)

September 6

When the Holy Spirit controls our lives, he will produce . . . faithfulness.

God saved you by his special favor when you believed. And you can't take credit for this; it is a gift from God. ▪ It is impossible to please God without faith. Anyone who wants to come to him must believe that there is a God and that he rewards those who sincerely seek him. ▪ There is no judgment awaiting those who trust him. But those who do not trust him have already been judged for not believing in the only Son of God. ▪ I do believe, but help me not to doubt!

Those who obey God's word really do love him. That is the way to know whether or not we live in him.

That is why we live by believing and not by seeing. ▪ I have been crucified with Christ. I myself no longer live, but Christ lives in me. So I live my life in this earthly body by trusting in the Son of God, who loved me and gave himself for me. ▪ You love him even though you have never seen him. Though you do not see him, you trust him; and even now you are happy with a glorious, inexpressible joy.

When someone gives you a gift, do you say, "That's very nice—now how much do I owe you?" No, the appropriate response is "Thank you." Yet how often Christians feel obligated to try to work their way to God. Instead, we should respond with gratitude, praise, and joy.

LAB note for Ephesians 2:8-9

(Galatians 5:22) (Ephesians 2:8) (Hebrews 11:6) (John 3:18) (Mark 9:24) (1 John 2:5) (2 Corinthians 5:7) (Galatians 2:19-20) (1 Peter 1:8)

September 7

Those who wait on the LORD will find new strength.

When I am weak, then I am strong. ▩ My God has given me strength. ▩ "My gracious favor is all you need. My power works best in your weakness." So now I am glad to boast about my weaknesses, so that the power of Christ may work through me. ▩ Trust in the LORD always, for the LORD God is the eternal Rock.

Give your burdens to the LORD, and he will take care of you. He will not permit the godly to slip and fall. ▩ His arms were strengthened by the Mighty One of Jacob, the Shepherd, the Rock of Israel.

You come to me with sword, spear, and javelin, but I come to you in the name of the LORD Almighty—the God of the armies of Israel, whom you have defied. ▩ I will rejoice in the LORD. I will be glad because he rescues me. I will praise him from the bottom of my heart: "LORD, who can compare with you? Who else rescues the weak and helpless from the strong?"

Waiting on the Lord is the patient expectation that God will fulfill his promises in his Word and strengthen us to rise above life's difficulties. It means to completely trust in God. *LAB note for Isaiah 40*

(ISAIAH 40:31) (2 CORINTHIANS 12:10) (ISAIAH 49:5) (2 CORINTHIANS 12:9) (ISAIAH 26:4) (PSALM 55:22) (GENESIS 49:24) (1 SAMUEL 17:45) (PSALM 35:9-10)

September 8

Be glad for all God is planning for you.

You are looking forward to the joys of heaven. ▪ If we have hope in Christ only for this life, we are the most miserable people in the world. ▪ They must enter into the Kingdom of God through many tribulations. ▪ You cannot be my disciple if you do not carry your own cross and follow me. ▪ You know that such troubles are going to happen to us Christians.

Always be full of joy in the Lord. I say it again—rejoice! ▪ I pray that God, who gives you hope, will keep you happy and full of peace as you believe in him. ▪ All honor to the God and Father of our Lord Jesus Christ, for it is by his boundless mercy that God has given us the privilege of being born again. Now we live with a wonderful expectation because Jesus Christ rose again from the dead. ▪ You love him even though you have never seen him. Though you do not see him, you trust him; and even now you are happy with a glorious, inexpressible joy. ▪ Because of our faith, Christ has brought us into this place of highest privilege where we now stand, and we confidently and joyfully look forward to sharing God's glory.

When Paul says that we look forward to the joys of heaven, he is emphasizing the security of the believer. Because we know our future destination and salvation are sure, we are free to live for Christ and love others. *LAB note for Colossians 1:5*

(Romans 12:12) (Colossians 1:5) (1 Corinthians 15:19) (Acts 14:22) (Luke 14:27) (1 Thessalonians 3:3) (Philippians 4:4) (Romans 15:13) (1 Peter 1:3) (1 Peter 1:8) (Romans 5:2)

September 9

The LORD is for me; he will help me.

In times of trouble, may the LORD respond to your cry. May the God of Israel keep you safe from all harm. May he send you help from his sanctuary and strengthen you from Jerusalem. May we shout for joy when we hear of your victory, flying banners to honor our God. May the LORD answer all your prayers. Some nations boast of their armies and weapons, but we boast in the LORD our God. Those nations will fall down and collapse, but we will rise up and stand firm.

He will come like a flood tide driven by the breath of the LORD. ▪ Remember that the temptations that come into your life are no different from what others experience. And God is faithful. He will keep the temptation from becoming so strong that you can't stand up against it. When you are tempted, he will show you a way out so that you will not give in to it.

If God is for us, who can ever be against us? ▪ The LORD is for me, so I will not be afraid. What can mere mortals do to me?

The God whom we serve is able to save us. He will rescue us from your power.

As long as there have been armies and weapons, nations have boasted of their power, but such power does not last. True might is in God's power. Because God alone can preserve a nation or an individual, be sure your confidence is in God, who gives eternal victory.

LAB note for Psalm 20:6–8

(PSALM 118:7) (PSALM 20:1–2, 5, 7–8) (ISAIAH 59:19) (1 CORINTHIANS 10:13) (ROMANS 8:31) (PSALM 118:6) (DANIEL 3:17)

September 10

You are the salt of the earth.

You should be known for the beauty that comes from within, the unfading beauty of a gentle and quiet spirit, which is so precious to God. ▩ For you have been born again. Your new life did not come from your earthly parents because the life they gave you will end in death. But this new life will last forever because it comes from the eternal, living word of God. Those who believe in me, even though they die like everyone else, will live again. ▩ They are children of God raised up to new life. ▩ The glorious, ever-living God.

(Those who do not have the Spirit of Christ living in them are not Christians at all.) Since Christ lives within you, even though your body will die because of sin, your spirit is alive because you have been made right with God. The Spirit of God, who raised Jesus from the dead, lives in you. And just as he raised Christ from the dead, he will give life to your mortal body by this same Spirit living within you. ▩ Our earthly bodies, which die and decay, will be different when they are resurrected, for they will never die.

Salt is good for seasoning. But if it loses its flavor, how do you make it salty again? You must have the qualities of salt among yourselves and live in peace with each other.

If a seasoning has no flavor, it has no value. If Christians make no effort to affect the world around them, they are of little value to God. If we are too much like the world, we are worthless. Instead, we should affect others positively, just as seasoning brings out the best flavor in food.

LAB note for Matthew 5:13

(Matthew 5:13) (1 Peter 3:4) (1 Peter 1:23) (John 11:25) (Luke 20:36) (Romans 1:23) (Romans 8:9-11) (1 Corinthians 15:42) (Mark 9:50)

September 11

I, even I, am the one who comforts you.

All praise to the God and Father of our Lord Jesus Christ. He is the source of every mercy and the God who comforts us. He comforts us in all our troubles so that we can comfort others. When others are troubled, we will be able to give them the same comfort God has given us. ▪ The LORD is like a father to his children, tender and compassionate to those who fear him. For he knows how weak we are; he knows we are only dust. ▪ I will comfort you there as a child is comforted by its mother. ▪ Give all your worries and cares to God, for he cares about what happens to you.

But you, O Lord, are a merciful and gracious God, slow to get angry, full of unfailing love and truth.

He will give you another Counselor . . . the Holy Spirit, who leads into all truth. ▪ The Holy Spirit helps us in our distress.

He will remove all of their sorrows, and there will be no more death or sorrow or crying or pain. For the old world and its evils are gone forever.

Many think that when God comforts us, our troubles should go away. But being "comforted" can also mean receiving strength, encouragement, and hope to deal with our troubles. The more we suffer, the more comfort God gives us. If you are feeling overwhelmed, allow God to comfort you. *LAB note for 2 Corinthians 1:3-5*

(Isaiah 51:12) (2 Corinthians 1:3-4) (Psalm 103:13-14) (Isaiah 66:13) (1 Peter 5:7) (Psalm 86:15) (John 14:16-17) (Romans 8:26) (Revelation 21:4)

September 12

A doubtful mind is as unsettled as a wave of the sea that is driven and tossed by the wind.

Anyone who puts a hand to the plow and then looks back is not fit for the Kingdom of God.

It is impossible to please God without faith. Anyone who wants to come to him must believe that there is a God and that he rewards those who sincerely seek him. ▪ When you ask him, be sure that you really expect him to answer, for a doubtful mind is as unsettled as a wave of the sea that is driven and tossed by the wind. People like that should not expect to receive anything from the Lord. ▪ You can pray for anything, and if you believe, you will have it.

Then we will no longer be like children, forever changing our minds about what we believe because someone has told us something different or because someone has cleverly lied to us and made the lie sound like the truth. Instead, we will hold to the truth in love, becoming more and more in every way like Christ, who is the head of his body, the church.

Remain in me. ▪ Be strong and steady, always enthusiastic about the Lord's work, for you know that nothing you do for the Lord is ever useless.

Doubt leaves a person as unsettled as restless waves. If you want to stop being tossed about, rely on God to show you what is best for you. Ask him for wisdom, and trust that he will give it to you. Then your decisions will be sure and solid. *LAB note for James 1:6–8*

(James 1:6) (Luke 9:62) (Hebrews 11:6) (James 1:6–7) (Mark 11:24) (Ephesians 4:14–15) (John 15:4) (1 Corinthians 15:58)

September 13

Weeping may go on all night, but joy comes with the morning.

Such troubles are going to happen to us Christians. Even while we were with you, we warned you that troubles would soon come—and they did, as you well know. ▩ I have told you all this so that you may have peace in me. Here on earth you will have many trials and sorrows. But take heart, because I have overcome the world.

When I awake, I will be fully satisfied, for I will see you face to face. ▩ The night is almost gone; the day of salvation will soon be here.

He is like the light of the morning, like the sunrise bursting forth in a cloudless sky, like the refreshing rains that bring tender grass from the earth.

He will swallow up death forever! The Sovereign LORD will wipe away all tears. ▩ He will remove all of their sorrows, and there will be no more death or sorrow or crying or pain. For the old world and its evils are gone forever. ▩ We who are still alive and remain on the earth will be caught up in the clouds to meet the Lord in the air and remain with him forever. So comfort and encourage each other with these words.

Some think that troubles are always caused by sin or a lack of faith. Trials may be a part of God's plan for believers, building character, perseverance, and sensitivity toward others who also face trouble. Your troubles may be a sign of effective Christian living.

LAB note for 1 Thessalonians 3:1–3

(PSALM 30:5) (1 THESSALONIANS 3:3–4) (JOHN 16:33) (PSALM 17:15) (ROMANS 13:12) (2 SAMUEL 23:4) (ISAIAH 25:8) (REVELATION 21:4) (1 THESSALONIANS 4:17–18)

September 14

He will not crush those who are weak.

The sacrifice you want is a broken spirit. A broken and repentant heart, O God, you will not despise. ▪ He heals the brokenhearted, binding up their wounds. ▪ The high and lofty one who inhabits eternity, the Holy One, says this: "I live in that high and holy place with those whose spirits are contrite and humble. I refresh the humble and give new courage to those with repentant hearts. For I will not fight against you forever; I will not always show my anger. If I did, all people would pass away—all the souls I have made."

I will search for my lost ones who strayed away, and I will bring them safely home again. I will bind up the injured and strengthen the weak. ▪ When they walk through the Valley of Weeping, it will become a place of refreshing springs, where pools of blessing collect after the rains! ▪ So take a new grip with your tired hands and stand firm on your shaky legs. Mark out a straight path for your feet. Then those who follow you, though they are weak and lame, will not stumble and fall but will become strong. ▪ Your God . . . is coming to save you.

God wants a broken spirit and a broken and repentant heart. You can never please God by outward actions—no matter how good—if your heart attitude is not right. Are you sorry for your sin? Do you genuinely intend to stop? God is pleased by this kind of repentance.

LAB note for Psalm 51:17

(MATTHEW 12:20) (PSALM 51:17) (PSALM 147:3) (ISAIAH 57:15-16) (EZEKIEL 34:16) (PSALM 84:6) (HEBREWS 12:12-13) (ISAIAH 35:4)

September 15

Open my eyes to see the wonderful truths in your law.

He opened their minds to understand these many Scriptures. ▩ Then he explained to them, "You have been permitted to understand the secrets of the Kingdom of Heaven, but others have not. ▩ Then Jesus prayed this prayer: "O Father, Lord of heaven and earth, thank you for hiding the truth from those who think themselves so wise and clever, and for revealing it to the childlike. Yes, Father, it pleased you to do it this way! ▩ And God has actually given us his Spirit (not the world's spirit) so we can know the wonderful things God has freely given us. ▩ How precious are your thoughts about me, O God! They are innumerable! I can't even count them; they outnumber the grains of sand! And when I wake up in the morning, you are still with me! ▩ Oh, what a wonderful God we have! How great are his riches and wisdom and knowledge! How impossible it is for us to understand his decisions and his methods! For who can know what the Lord is thinking? Who knows enough to be his counselor? For everything comes from him; everything exists by his power and is intended for his glory. To him be glory evermore. Amen.

Have you ever wondered how to understand a difficult Bible passage? Besides reading surrounding passages, asking other people, and consulting reference works, pray that the Holy Spirit will open your mind to understand, giving you the needed insight to put God's Word into action in your life. *LAB note for Luke 24:45*

(PSALM 119:18) (LUKE 24:45) (MATTHEW 13:11) (MATTHEW 11:25-26) (1 CORINTHIANS 2:12) (PSALM 139:17-18) (ROMANS 11:33-34, 36)

September 16

"The Spring of the One Who Cried Out."

If you only knew the gift God has for you and who I am, you would ask me, and I would give you living water. ▩ "If you are thirsty, come to me!" (When he said "living water," he was speaking of the Spirit, who would be given to everyone believing in him.)

"Bring all the tithes into the storehouse so there will be enough food in my Temple. If you do," says the LORD Almighty, "I will open the windows of heaven for you. I will pour out a blessing so great that you won't have enough room to take it in. Try it! Let me prove it to you!" ▩ If you sinful people know how to give good gifts to your children, how much more will your heavenly Father give the Holy Spirit to those who ask him. ▩ Keep on asking, and you will be given what you ask for. Keep on looking, and you will find.

Because you Gentiles have become his children, God has sent the Spirit of his Son into your hearts, and now you can call God your dear Father. ▩ So you should not be like cowering, fearful slaves. You should behave instead like God's very own children, adopted into his family—calling him "Father, dear Father."

What did Jesus mean by "living water"? God is called the fountain of living water. In saying he would bring living water that could forever quench a person's thirst for God, Jesus was claiming to be the Messiah. Only the Messiah could give this gift that satisfies the soul's desire.

LAB note for John 4:10

(JUDGES 15:19) (JOHN 4:10) (JOHN 7:37, 39) (MALACHI 3:10) (LUKE 11:13) (LUKE 11:9) (GALATIANS 4:6) (ROMANS 8:15)

September 17

In his kindness God called you to his eternal glory by means of Jesus Christ.

I will make all my goodness pass before you, and I will call out my name, "the LORD," to you. I will show kindness to anyone I choose, and I will show mercy to anyone I choose. ▪ God will be gracious and say, "Set him free. Do not make him die, for I have found a ransom for his life." ▪ Yet now God in his gracious kindness declares us not guilty. He has done this through Christ Jesus, who has freed us by taking away our sins. For God sent Jesus to take the punishment for our sins and to satisfy God's anger against us. We are made right with God when we believe that Jesus shed his blood, sacrificing his life for us. God was being entirely fair and just when he did not punish those who sinned in former times. And he is entirely fair and just in this present time when he declares sinners to be right in his sight because they believe in Jesus. ▪ God's unfailing love and faithfulness came through Jesus Christ.

God saved you by his special favor when you believed. And you can't take credit for this; it is a gift from God. ▪ May God our Father and Christ Jesus our Lord give you grace, mercy, and peace. ▪ God has given gifts to each of you from his great variety of spiritual gifts. Manage them well so that God's generosity can flow through you. ▪ He gives us more and more strength.

When a judge in a court of law declares the defendant not guilty, all the charges are removed from his record. Legally, it is as if the person had never been accused. When God forgives our sins, our record is wiped clean. From his perspective, it is as though we had never sinned.

LAB note for Romans 3:24

(1 PETER 5:10) (EXODUS 33:19) (JOB 33:24) (ROMANS 3:24-26) (JOHN 1:17) (EPHESIANS 2:8) (1 TIMOTHY 1:2) (1 PETER 4:10) (JAMES 4:6)

September 18

I look up to the mountains—does my help come from there? My help comes from the LORD, who made the heavens and the earth!

Just as the mountains surround and protect Jerusalem, so the LORD surrounds and protects his people. ▪ The sun will not hurt you by day, nor the moon at night. The LORD keeps you from all evil and preserves your life. The LORD keeps watch over you as you come and go, both now and forever.

I lift my eyes to you, O God, enthroned in heaven. We look to the LORD our God for his mercy, just as servants keep their eyes on their master, as a slave girl watches her mistress for the slightest signal. ▪ I think how much you have helped me; I sing for joy in the shadow of your protecting wings.

O our God, won't you stop them? We are powerless against this mighty army that is about to attack us. We do not know what to do, but we are looking to you for help. ▪ Help us, O LORD our God, for we trust in you alone. It is in your name that we have come against this vast horde. ▪ My eyes are always looking to the LORD for help, for he alone can rescue me from the traps of my enemies. ▪ Our help is from the LORD, who made the heavens and the earth.

If you are facing battles you feel you can't possibly win, don't give up. The secret of victory is first to admit the futility of unaided human effort and then trust God to save. His power works best through those who recognize their limitations. *LAB note for 2 Chronicles 14:11*

(PSALM 121:1-2) (PSALM 125:2) (PSALM 121:6-8) (PSALM 123:1-2) (PSALM 63:7) (2 CHRONICLES 20:12) (2 CHRONICLES 14:11) (PSALM 25:15) (PSALM 124:8)

September 19

But as for me, how good it is to be near God!

I love your sanctuary, LORD, the place where your glory shines. ▩ A single day in your courts is better than a thousand anywhere else! I would rather be a gatekeeper in the house of my God than live the good life in the homes of the wicked. ▩ What joy for those you choose to bring near, those who live in your holy courts. What joy awaits us inside your holy Temple.

The LORD is wonderfully good to those who wait for him and seek him. ▩ The LORD still waits for you to come to him so he can show you his love and compassion. For the LORD is a faithful God. Blessed are those who wait for him to help them.

And so, dear brothers and sisters, we can boldly enter heaven's Most Holy Place because of the blood of Jesus. This is the new, life-giving way that Christ has opened up for us through the sacred curtain, by means of his death for us. Let us go right into the presence of God, with true hearts fully trusting him. For our evil consciences have been sprinkled with Christ's blood to make us clean, and our bodies have been washed with pure water.

Access to God, the joy of living in the Temple courts, was a great honor. God had chosen a special group of Israelites from the tribe of Levi to serve as priests, and they were the only ones who could enter the sacred rooms where God's presence resided. Because of Jesus' death on the cross, believers today have access to God's presence in every place and at any time.

LAB note for Psalm 65:4

(PSALM 73:28) (PSALM 26:8) (PSALM 84:10) (PSALM 65:4) (LAMENTATIONS 3:25) (ISAIAH 30:18) (HEBREWS 10:19-20, 22)

September 20

Let it grow, for when your endurance is fully developed, you will be strong in character and ready for anything.

There is wonderful joy ahead, even though it is necessary for you to endure many trials for a while. These trials are only to test your faith, to show that it is strong and pure. It is being tested as fire tests and purifies gold—and your faith is far more precious to God than mere gold. So if your faith remains strong after being tried by fiery trials, it will bring you much praise and glory and honor on the day when Jesus Christ is revealed to the whole world. ▪ We can rejoice, too, when we run into problems and trials, for we know that they are good for us—they help us learn to endure. And endurance develops strength of character in us, and character strengthens our confident expectation of salvation.

It is good to wait quietly for salvation from the LORD. ▪ When all you owned was taken from you, you accepted it with joy. You knew you had better things waiting for you in eternity. Do not throw away this confident trust in the Lord, no matter what happens. Remember the great reward it brings you! Patient endurance is what you need now, so you will continue to do God's will. Then you will receive all that he has promised.

Instead of complaining about our struggles, we should see them as opportunities for growth. Thank God for promising to be with you in rough times. Ask him to help you solve your problems or to give you the strength to endure them. Then be patient. God will stay close and help you grow.

LAB note for James 1:2-4

(JAMES 1:4) (1 PETER 1:6-7) (ROMANS 5:3-4) (LAMENTATIONS 3:26) (HEBREWS 10:34-36)

September 21

Humble yourselves under the mighty power of God, and in his good time he will honor you.

The LORD despises pride; be assured that the proud will be punished.

And yet, LORD, you are our Father. We are the clay, and you are the potter. We are all formed by your hand. Oh, don't be so angry with us, LORD. Please don't remember our sins forever. Look at us, we pray, and see that we are all your people. ▪ You disciplined me severely, but I deserved it. I was like a calf that needed to be trained for the yoke and plow. Turn me again to you and restore me, for you alone are the Lord my God. I turned away from God, but then I was sorry. I kicked myself for my stupidity! I was thoroughly ashamed of all I did in my younger days. ▪ It is good for the young to submit to the yoke of his discipline. Let them sit alone in silence beneath the LORD's demands. Let them lie face down in the dust; then at last there is hope for them.

Evil does not spring from the soil, and trouble does not sprout from the earth. People are born for trouble as predictably as sparks fly upward from a fire. ▪ Though he brings grief, he also shows compassion according to the greatness of his unfailing love. For he does not enjoy hurting people or causing them sorrow.

We often worry about our position and status, hoping to get proper recognition for what we do. But God's recognition counts more than human praise. God is able and willing to bless us according to his timing. Humbly obey God regardless of present circumstances, and in his good time—either in this life or in the next—he will honor you.

LAB note for 1 Peter 5:6

(1 PETER 5:6) (PROVERBS 16:5) (ISAIAH 64:8-9) (JEREMIAH 31:18-19) (LAMENTATIONS 3:27-29) (JOB 5:6-7) (LAMENTATIONS 3:32-33)

September 22

The heavens tell of the glory of God. The skies display his marvelous craftsmanship.

From the time the world was created, people have seen the earth and sky and all that God made. They can clearly see his invisible qualities—his eternal power and divine nature. ■ He never left himself without a witness. ■ Day after day they continue to speak; night after night they make him known. They speak without a sound or a word; their voice is silent in the skies.

When I look at the night sky and see the work of your fingers—the moon and the stars you have set in place—what are mortals that you should think of us, mere humans that you should care for us?

The sun has one kind of glory, while the moon and stars each have another kind. And even the stars differ from each other in their beauty and brightness. It is the same way for the resurrection of the dead. Our earthly bodies, which die and decay, will be different when they are resurrected, for they will never die. ■ Those who are wise will shine as bright as the sky, and those who turn many to righteousness will shine like stars forever.

To say that the universe happened by chance is absurd. Its design, intricacy, and orderliness point to a personally involved Creator. As you look at God's handiwork in nature and the heavens, thank him for such magnificent beauty and the truth it reveals about the Creator.

LAB note for Psalm 19:1-6

(PSALM 19:1) (ROMANS 1:20) (ACTS 14:17) (PSALM 19:2-3) (PSALM 8:3-4) (1 CORINTHIANS 15:41-42) (DANIEL 12:3)

September 23

The Son can do nothing by himself. He does only what he sees the Father doing. Whatever the Father does, the Son also does.

The LORD grants wisdom! From his mouth come knowledge and understanding. He grants a treasure of good sense to the godly. He is their shield, protecting those who walk with integrity. He guards the paths of justice and protects those who are faithful to him. ▪ I will give you the right words and such wisdom that none of your opponents will be able to reply!

Wait patiently for the LORD. Be brave and courageous. Yes, wait patiently for the LORD. ▪ My gracious favor is all you need. My power works best in your weakness.

Called to live in the love of God the Father and the care of Jesus Christ. ▪ Jesus and the ones he makes holy have the same Father. That is why Jesus is not ashamed to call them his brothers and sisters.

Am I not everywhere in all the heavens and earth? ▪ And the church is his body; it is filled by Christ, who fills everything everywhere with his presence.

I am the LORD, and there is no other Savior. ▪ He is indeed the Savior of the world.

May God the Father and Christ Jesus our Savior give you grace and peace.

Because of his unity with God, Jesus lived as God wanted him to live. Because of our identification with Jesus, we must honor him and live as he wants us to live. The questions "What would Jesus do?" and "What would Jesus have me do?" may help us make the right choices.

LAB note for John 5:19–23

(JOHN 5:19) (PROVERBS 2:6–8) (LUKE 21:15) (PSALM 27:14) (2 CORINTHIANS 12:9) (JUDE 1:1) (HEBREWS 2:11) (JEREMIAH 23:24) (EPHESIANS 1:23) (ISAIAH 43:11) (JOHN 4:42) (TITUS 1:4)

September 24

Show me the path where I should walk, O LORD; point out the right road for me to follow.

Moses said to the LORD, ". . . You call me by name and tell me I have found favor with you. Please, if this is really so, show me your intentions so I will understand you more fully and do exactly what you want me to do. . . ." And the LORD replied, "I will personally go with you, Moses. I will give you rest—everything will be fine for you." ▪ He revealed his character to Moses and his deeds to the people of Israel.

He leads the humble in what is right, teaching them his way. Who are those who fear the LORD? He will show them the path they should choose. ▪ Trust in the LORD with all your heart; do not depend on your own understanding. Seek his will in all you do, and he will direct your paths.

You will show me the way of life, granting me the joy of your presence and the pleasures of living with you forever. ▪ The LORD says, "I will guide you along the best pathway for your life. I will advise you and watch over you." ▪ The way of the righteous is like the first gleam of dawn, which shines ever brighter until the full light of day.

How do we receive God's guidance? The first step is to want to be guided and to realize that God's primary guidance system is in his Word, the Bible. By reading it and constantly learning from it, we will gain the wisdom to perceive God's direction for our lives. *LAB note for Psalm 25:4*

(PSALM 25:4) (EXODUS 33:12-14) (PSALM 103:7) (PSALM 25:9, 12) (PROVERBS 3:5-6) (PSALM 16:11) (PSALM 32:8) (PROVERBS 4:18)

September 25

What makes you better than anyone else? What do you have that God hasn't given you? And if all you have is from God, why boast as though you have accomplished something on your own?

Whatever I am now, it is all because God poured out his special favor on me—and not without results. ▪ In his goodness he chose to make us his own children by giving us his true word. ▪ Receiving God's promise is not up to us. We can't get it by choosing it or working hard for it. God will show mercy to anyone he chooses! ▪ Can we boast, then, that we have done anything to be accepted by God? No. ▪ God alone made it possible for you to be in Christ Jesus. For our benefit God made Christ to be wisdom itself. . . . "The person who wishes to boast should boast only of what the Lord has done."

Once you were dead, doomed forever because of your many sins. You used to live just like the rest of the world, full of sin, obeying Satan, the mighty prince of the power of the air. He is the spirit at work in the hearts of those who refuse to obey God. All of us used to live that way, following the passions and desires of our evil nature. We were born with an evil nature, and we were under God's anger just like everyone else. ▪ Now your sins have been washed away, and you have been set apart for God. You have been made right with God because of what the Lord Jesus Christ and the Spirit of our God have done for you.

Don't let your loyalty to church leaders cause strife, slander, or broken relationships. Make sure that your deepest loyalties are to Christ and not to his human agents. Those who spend more time in debating church leadership than in declaring Christ's message don't have the mind of Christ.

LAB note for 1 Corinthians 4:6-7

(1 Corinthians 4:7) (1 Corinthians 15:10) (James 1:18) (Romans 9:16) (Romans 3:27) (1 Corinthians 1:30-31) (Ephesians 2:1-3) (1 Corinthians 6:11)

September 26

All praise to him who loves us and has freed us from our sins by shedding his blood for us.

Many waters cannot quench love, neither can rivers drown it. Love is as strong as death. ▪ The greatest love is shown when people lay down their lives for their friends.

He personally carried away our sins in his own body on the cross so we can be dead to sin and live for what is right. You have been healed by his wounds! ▪ He is so rich in kindness that he purchased our freedom through the blood of his Son, and our sins are forgiven.

Your sins have been washed away, and you have been set apart for God. You have been made right with God because of what the Lord Jesus Christ and the Spirit of our God have done for you. ▪ You are a chosen people. You are a kingdom of priests, God's holy nation, his very own possession. This is so you can show others the goodness of God, for he called you out of the darkness into his wonderful light. ▪ I plead with you to give your bodies to God. Let them be a living and holy sacrifice—the kind he will accept. When you think of what he has done for you, is this too much to ask?

We are to love each other as Jesus loved us, and he loved us enough to give his life for us. We may not have to die for someone, but there are other ways to practice sacrificial love: listening, helping, encouraging, giving. Think of someone in particular who needs this kind of love today—and give it! *LAB note for John 15:12-13*

(REVELATION 1:5) (SONG OF SONGS 8:7, 6) (JOHN 15:13) (1 PETER 2:24) (EPHESIANS 1:7) (1 CORINTHIANS 6:11) (1 PETER 2:9) (ROMANS 12:1)

September 27

There are different kinds of service in the church, but it is the same Lord we are serving.

Azmaveth son of Adiel was in charge of the palace treasuries. Jonathan son of Uzziah was in charge of the regional treasuries throughout the towns, villages, and fortresses of Israel. Ezri son of Kelub was in charge of the field workers who farmed the king's lands. Shimei from Ramah was in charge of the king's vineyards. Zabdi from Shepham was responsible for the grapes and the supplies of wine. All these officials were overseers of King David's property.

Here is a list of some of the members that God has placed in the body of Christ: first are apostles, second are prophets, third are teachers, then those who do miracles, those who have the gift of healing, those who can help others, those who can get others to work together, those who speak in unknown languages.

God has given gifts to each of you from his great variety of spiritual gifts. Manage them well so that God's generosity can flow through you. Are you called to be a speaker? Then speak as though God himself were speaking through you. Are you called to help others? Do it with all the strength and energy that God supplies. Then God will be given glory in everything through Jesus Christ. All glory and power belong to him forever and ever. Amen.

Some people, well aware of their abilities, believe that they have the right to use their abilities as they please. Others feel they have no special talents at all. But everyone has some gifts; find yours and use them. All our abilities should be used in serving others; none are for our own exclusive enjoyment. *LAB note for 1 Peter 4:10–11*

(1 CORINTHIANS 12:5) (1 CHRONICLES 27:25–27, 31)
(1 CORINTHIANS 12:28) (1 PETER 4:10–11)

September 28

When Moses came down the mountain carrying the stone tablets inscribed with the terms of the covenant, he wasn't aware that his face glowed because he had spoken to the LORD face to face.

To you goes all the glory for your unfailing love and faithfulness. ▪ Lord, when did we ever see you hungry and feed you? Or thirsty and give you something to drink? ▪ When you did it to one of the least of these my brothers and sisters, you were doing it to me! ▪ Be humble, thinking of others as better than yourself. ▪ Serve each other in humility.

Jesus' appearance changed so that his face shone like the sun, and his clothing became dazzling white. ▪ Everyone in the council stared at Stephen because his face became as bright as an angel's. ▪ Glorify your Son so he can give glory back to you. ▪ All of us have had that veil removed so that we can be mirrors that brightly reflect the glory of the Lord. And as the Spirit of the Lord works within us, we become more and more like him and reflect his glory even more.

You are the light of the world—like a city on a mountain, glowing in the night for all to see. Don't hide your light under a basket! ▪ Let your lives shine brightly before them. Hold tightly to the word of life.

Moses' face glowed after he spent time with God. The people could clearly see God's presence in him. How often do you spend time alone with God? Although your face may not light up a room, time spent in prayer, reading the Bible, and meditating should have such an effect on your life that people will know you have been with God.

LAB note for Exodus 34:28-35

(Exodus 34:29) (Psalm 115:1) (Matthew 25:37) (Matthew 25:40) (Philippians 2:3) (1 Peter 5:5) (Matthew 17:2) (Acts 6:15) (John 17:22) (2 Corinthians 3:18) (Matthew 5:14-15) (Philippians 2:15-16)

September 29

There are different ways God works in our lives, but it is the same God who does the work through all of us.

Some men from Manasseh defected from the Israelite army and joined David. They were all brave and able warriors who became commanders in his army. ▪ A spiritual gift is given to each of us as a means of helping the entire church.

From the tribe of Issachar, there were 200 leaders of the tribe with their relatives. All these men understood the temper of the times and knew the best course for Israel to take. ▪ To one person the Spirit gives the ability to give wise advice; to another he gives the gift of special knowledge.

From the tribe of Zebulun, there were 50,000 skilled warriors. They were fully armed and prepared for battle and completely loyal to David. ▪ I take joy in doing your will, my God, for your law is written on my heart.

God made our bodies with many parts, and he has put each part just where he wants it. If one part suffers, all the parts suffer with it, and if one part is honored, all the parts are glad.

One Lord, one faith, one baptism.

People are often drawn to a great cause and the brave determined people who support it. As believers, we have the greatest cause—the salvation of people. If we are brave, determined, and faithful, others will be drawn to work with us. *LAB note for 1 Chronicles 12:22*

(1 Corinthians 12:6) (1 Chronicles 12:19, 21) (1 Corinthians 12:7) (1 Chronicles 12:32) (1 Corinthians 12:8) (1 Chronicles 12:33) (Psalm 40:8) (1 Corinthians 12:18, 26) (Ephesians 4:5)

September 30

The Coming One will come and not delay.

Write my answer in large, clear letters on a tablet, so that a runner can read it and tell everyone else. But these things I plan won't happen right away. Slowly, steadily, surely, the time approaches when the vision will be fulfilled. If it seems slow, wait patiently, for it will surely take place. It will not be delayed.

You must not forget, dear friends, that a day is like a thousand years to the Lord, and a thousand years is like a day. The Lord isn't really being slow about his promise to return, as some people think. No, he is being patient for your sake. He does not want anyone to perish, so he is giving more time for everyone to repent. ▪ You, O Lord, are a merciful and gracious God, slow to get angry, full of unfailing love and truth. ▪ Oh, that you would burst from the heavens and come down! How the mountains would quake in your presence! For since the world began, no ear has heard, and no eye has seen a God like you, who works for those who wait for him!

It isn't easy to be patient when evil and injustice seem to have the upper hand in the world. But it helps to remember that God hates sin even more than we do. Punishment of sin will certainly come. We must wait patiently, trusting God even when we don't understand why events occur as they do. *LAB note for Habakkuk 2:3*

(Hebrews 10:37) (Habakkuk 2:2-3) (2 Peter 3:8-9)
(Psalm 86:15) (Isaiah 64:1, 4)

October

Autumn's Abundance

Apple picking and pumpkin pie
Crackling leaves and hayrides
Autumn brings a harvest of blessing.

As the crisp winds of autumn chase away summer's greenery, take time to notice the fiery display of new colors. What a creative God he is to make such a beautiful world for us!

October 1

You will always reap what you sow!

Experience shows that those who plant trouble and cultivate evil will harvest the same. ▪ They have planted the wind and will harvest the whirlwind. ▪ Those who live only to satisfy their own sinful desires will harvest the consequences of decay and death.

The reward of the godly will last. ▪ Those who live to please the Spirit will harvest everlasting life from the Spirit. So don't get tired of doing what is good. Don't get discouraged and give up, for we will reap a harvest of blessing at the appropriate time. Whenever we have the opportunity, we should do good to everyone, especially to our Christian brothers and sisters.

It is possible to give freely and become more wealthy, but those who are stingy will lose everything. The generous prosper and are satisfied; those who refresh others will themselves be refreshed. ▪ Remember this—a farmer who plants only a few seeds will get a small crop. But the one who plants generously will get a generous crop.

It would certainly be a surprise if you planted corn and pumpkins came up. It's a natural law to reap what we sow. If you plant to please your own desires, you'll reap a crop of sorrow and evil. If you plant to please God, you'll reap joy and everlasting life. What kinds of seeds are you sowing?

LAB note for Galatians 6:7–8

(GALATIANS 6:7) (JOB 4:8) (HOSEA 8:7) (GALATIANS 6:8) (PROVERBS 11:18) (GALATIANS 6:8–10) (PROVERBS 11:24–25) (2 CORINTHIANS 9:6)

October 2

Never be lazy in your work, but serve the Lord enthusiastically.

Whatever you do, do well. For when you go to the grave, there will be no work or planning or knowledge or wisdom. ▪ Work hard and cheerfully at whatever you do, as though you were working for the Lord rather than for people. Remember that the Lord will give you an inheritance as your reward, and the Master you are serving is Christ. ▪ Remember that the Lord will reward each one of us for the good we do.

All of us must quickly carry out the tasks assigned us by the one who sent me, because there is little time left before the night falls and all work comes to an end.

So, dear brothers and sisters, work hard to prove that you really are among those God has called and chosen. Doing this, you will never stumble or fall away. ▪ Our great desire is that you will keep right on loving others as long as life lasts, in order to make certain that what you hope for will come true. Then you will not become spiritually dull and indifferent. Instead, you will follow the example of those who are going to inherit God's promises because of their faith and patience. ▪ Run in such a way that you will win.

Considering the uncertainties of the future and the certainty of death, Solomon recommends enjoying life as God's gift. He may have been criticizing those who put off all present pleasures in order to accumulate wealth, much like those who get caught up in today's rat race. Enjoy God's gifts while you are able! *LAB note for Ecclesiastes 9:7-10*

(ROMANS 12:11) (ECCLESIASTES 9:10) (COLOSSIANS 3:23-24) (EPHESIANS 6:8) (JOHN 9:4) (2 PETER 1:10) (HEBREWS 6:11-12) (1 CORINTHIANS 9:24)

October 3

It is good to wait quietly for salvation from the LORD.

Has God forgotten to be kind? Has he slammed the door on his compassion? ▪ In sudden fear I had cried out, "I have been cut off from the LORD!" But you heard my cry for mercy and answered my call for help. Love the LORD, all you faithful ones! For the LORD protects those who are loyal to him, but he harshly punishes all who are arrogant. So be strong and take courage, all you who put your hope in the LORD!

Don't you think God will surely give justice to his chosen people who plead with him day and night? Will he keep putting them off? I tell you, he will grant justice to them quickly! ▪ Wait for the LORD to handle the matter. ▪ Be still in the presence of the LORD, and wait patiently for him to act. Don't worry about evil people who prosper.

You will not even need to fight. Take your positions; then stand still and watch the LORD's victory.

Don't get tired of doing what is good. Don't get discouraged and give up, for we will reap a harvest of blessing at the appropriate time. ▪ Be patient as you wait for the Lord's return. Consider the farmers who eagerly look for the rains in the fall and in the spring. They patiently wait for the precious harvest to ripen.

Asaph cried out to God for courage during a time of deep distress. But as he expressed his requests and doubts to God, his focus changed from thinking of himself to worshiping God. Only after he put aside his doubts about God's holiness and care for him did he eliminate his distress.

LAB note for Psalm 77:1-12

(LAMENTATIONS 3:26) (PSALM 77:9) (PSALM 31:22-24) (LUKE 18:7-8) (PROVERBS 20:22) (PSALM 37:7) (2 CHRONICLES 20:17) (GALATIANS 6:9) (JAMES 5:7)

October 4

The LORD's promises are pure, like silver refined in a furnace, purified seven times over.

Your promises have been thoroughly tested; that is why I love them so much. ▪ The law of the LORD is perfect, reviving the soul. The commandments of the LORD are right, bringing joy to the heart. The commands of the LORD are clear, giving insight to life. ▪ Every word of God proves true. He defends all who come to him for protection. Do not add to his words, or he may rebuke you, and you will be found a liar.

I have hidden your word in my heart, that I might not sin against you. I will study your commandments and reflect on your ways. ▪ The laws of the LORD are true; each one is fair. They are more desirable than gold, even the finest gold. They are sweeter than honey, even honey dripping from the comb. ▪ Fix your thoughts on what is true and honorable and right. Think about things that are pure and lovely and admirable. Think about things that are excellent and worthy of praise. ▪ You must crave pure spiritual milk so that you can grow into the fullness of your salvation. Cry out for this nourishment as a baby cries for milk.

As for God, his way is perfect. All the LORD's promises prove true. He is a shield for all who look to him for protection. For who is God except the LORD? Who but our God is a solid rock?

Sincerity and truth are extremely valuable because they are so rare. When we feel as though sincerity and truth have nearly gone out of existence, we have one hope—the word of God. God's words are as flawless as refined silver. So listen carefully when he speaks. *LAB note for Psalm 12:6*

(PSALM 12:6) (PSALM 119:140) (PSALM 19:7-8) (PROVERBS 30:5-6) (PSALM 119:11, 15) (PSALM 19:9-10) (PHILIPPIANS 4:8) (1 PETER 2:2) (PSALM 18:30-31)

October 5

You, O God, are my place of safety.

The LORD is my rock, my fortress, and my savior; my God is my rock, in whom I find protection. He is my shield, the strength of my salvation, and my stronghold, my high tower. ▪ The LORD is my strength, my shield from every danger. I trust in him with all my heart. He helps me, and my heart is filled with joy. I burst out in songs of thanksgiving.

They will respect and glorify the name of the LORD throughout the world. For he will come like a flood tide driven by the breath of the LORD. ▪ That is why we can say with confidence, "The Lord is my helper, so I will not be afraid. What can mere mortals do to me?"

The LORD is my light and my salvation—so why should I be afraid? The LORD protects me from danger—so why should I tremble? ▪ Though I sit in darkness, the LORD himself will be my light.

Just as the mountains surround and protect Jerusalem, so the LORD surrounds and protects his people, both now and forever. ▪ I think how much you have helped me; I sing for joy in the shadow of your protecting wings.

For the honor of your name, lead me out of this peril. ▪ Be our strength each day and our salvation in times of trouble.

We become content when we realize God's sufficiency for our needs. Christians who become materialistic are saying by their actions that God can't take care of them—or at least that he won't take care of them the way they want. The only antidote to this insecurity is to trust God to meet all our needs. *LAB note for Hebrews 13:5-6*

(PSALM 59:9) (2 SAMUEL 22:2-3) (PSALM 28:7) (ISAIAH 59:19) (HEBREWS 13:6) (PSALM 27:1) (MICAH 7:8) (PSALM 125:2) (PSALM 63:7) (PSALM 31:3) (ISAIAH 33:2)

October 6

He leads the humble in what is right, teaching them his way.

God blesses those who are gentle and lowly.

I have observed something else in this world of ours. The fastest runner doesn't always win the race, and the strongest warrior doesn't always win the battle. The wise are often poor, and the skillful are not necessarily wealthy. ▪ We can make our plans, but the LORD determines our steps.

I lift my eyes to you, O God, enthroned in heaven. We look to the LORD our God for his mercy, just as servants keep their eyes on their master, as a slave girl watches her mistress for the slightest signal. ▪ Show me where to walk, for I have come to you in prayer.

O our God, won't you stop them? We are powerless against this mighty army that is about to attack us. We do not know what to do, but we are looking to you for help.

If you need wisdom—if you want to know what God wants you to do—ask him, and he will gladly tell you. He will not resent your asking.

When the Spirit of truth comes, he will guide you into all truth.

In the Kingdom of Heaven, wealth and power and authority are unimportant. Kingdom people seek different blessings and benefits, and they have different attitudes. Are your attitudes a carbon copy of the world's selfishness, pride, and lust for power, or do they reflect the humility and self-sacrifice of Jesus, your king? *LAB note for Matthew 5:3-12*

(PSALM 25:9) (MATTHEW 5:5) (ECCLESIASTES 9:11) (PROVERBS 16:9) (PSALM 123:1-2) (PSALM 143:8) (2 CHRONICLES 20:12) (JAMES 1:5) (JOHN 16:13)

October 7

Do not stay so far from me, for trouble is near.

O LORD, how long will you forget me? Forever? How long will you look the other way? How long must I struggle with anguish in my soul, with sorrow in my heart every day? ▪ Do not hide yourself from me. Do not reject your servant in anger. You have always been my helper. Don't leave me now; don't abandon me, O God of my salvation!

When they call on me, I will answer; I will be with them in trouble. I will rescue them and honor them. ▪ The LORD is close to all who call on him, yes, to all who call on him sincerely. He fulfills the desires of those who fear him; he hears their cries for help and rescues them.

I will not abandon you as orphans—I will come to you. ▪ I am with you always, even to the end of the age.

God is our refuge and strength, always ready to help in times of trouble. ▪ I wait quietly before God, for my hope is in him. He alone is my rock and my salvation, my fortress where I will not be shaken.

God's loving concern does not begin on the day we are born and conclude on the day we die. It reaches back to those days before we were born and reaches ahead along the unending path of eternity. Our only sure help comes from a God whose concern for us reaches beyond our earthly existence.

LAB note for Psalm 22:9–11

(PSALM 22:11) (PSALM 13:1–2) (PSALM 27:9) (PSALM 91:15) (PSALM 145:18–19) (JOHN 14:18) (MATTHEW 28:20) (PSALM 46:1) (PSALM 62:5–6)

October 8

I am the Alpha and the Omega—the beginning and the end.

The LORD is king! He is robed in majesty. Indeed, the LORD is robed in majesty and armed with strength. The world is firmly established; it cannot be shaken. Your throne, O LORD, has been established from time immemorial. You yourself are from the everlasting past.

He displays his power. ▪ If God is for us, who can ever be against us? ▪ The God whom we serve is able to save us. He will rescue us from your power. ▪ My Father has given them to me, and he is more powerful than anyone else. So no one can take them from me. ▪ You belong to God, my dear children. You have already won your fight with these false prophets, because the Spirit who lives in you is greater than the spirit who lives in the world.

Not to us, O LORD, but to you goes all the glory. ▪ Yours, O LORD, is the greatness, the power, the glory, the victory, and the majesty. Everything in the heavens and on earth is yours, O LORD, and this is your kingdom. We adore you as the one who is over all things. O, our God, we thank you and praise your glorious name! But who am I, and who are my people, that we could give anything to you? Everything we have has come from you, and we give you only what you have already given us!

Just as a shepherd protects his sheep, Jesus protects his people from eternal harm. While believers can expect to suffer on earth, Satan cannot harm their souls or take away their eternal life with God. If you choose to follow Jesus, he will give you everlasting safety.

LAB note for John 10:28-29

(REVELATION 1:8) (PSALM 93:1-2) (NAHUM 1:3) (ROMANS 8:31) (DANIEL 3:17) (JOHN 10:29) (1 JOHN 4:4) (PSALM 115:1) (1 CHRONICLES 29:11, 13-14)

October 9

The LORD is your security.

Human opposition only enhances your glory, for you use it as a sword of judgment. ▪ The king's heart is like a stream of water directed by the LORD; he turns it wherever he pleases. ▪ When the ways of people please the LORD, he makes even their enemies live at peace with them.

I am counting on the LORD; yes, I am counting on him. I have put my hope in his word. I long for the Lord more than sentries long for the dawn. ▪ I prayed to the LORD, and he answered me, freeing me from all my fears.

The eternal God is your refuge, and his everlasting arms are under you. He thrusts out the enemy before you; it is he who cries, "Destroy them!" ▪ Blessed are those who trust in the LORD and have made the LORD their hope and confidence. They are like trees planted along a riverbank, with roots that reach deep into the water. Such trees are not bothered by the heat or worried by long months of drought. Their leaves stay green, and they go right on producing delicious fruit.

What can we say about such wonderful things as these? If God is for us, who can ever be against us?

How can wrath bring praise to God? Hostility to God and his people gives God the opportunity to do great deeds. God turns the tables of evildoers and brings glory to himself from the foolishness of those who deny him or revolt against him. *LAB note for Psalm 76:10*

(PROVERBS 3:26) (PSALM 76:10) (PROVERBS 21:1) (PROVERBS 16:7) (PSALM 130:5-6) (PSALM 34:4) (DEUTERONOMY 33:27) (JEREMIAH 17:7-8) (ROMANS 8:31)

October 10

A servant is not greater than the master. Nor are messengers more important than the one who sends them. You know these things—now do them! That is the path of blessing.

They began to argue among themselves as to who would be the greatest in the coming Kingdom. Jesus told them, "In this world the kings and great men order their people around, and yet they are called 'friends of the people.' But among you, those who are the greatest should take the lowest rank, and the leader should be a servant. Normally the master sits at the table and is served by his servants. But not here! For I am your servant." ▪ Whoever is the least among you is the greatest. ▪ Whoever wants to be a leader among you must be your servant, and whoever wants to be first must become your slave. For even I, the Son of Man, came here not to be served but to serve others, and to give my life as a ransom for many.

He [Jesus] got up from the table, took off his robe, wrapped a towel around his waist, and poured water into a basin. Then he began to wash the disciples' feet and to wipe them with the towel he had around him.

Lead them by your good example.

Jesus did not wash his disciples' feet just to get them to be nice to each other. His far greater goal was to extend his mission on earth after he was gone. These men were to move into the world serving God, serving each other, and serving all people to whom they took the message of salvation. *LAB note for John 13:12ff.*

(JOHN 13:16-17) (LUKE 22:24-27) (LUKE 9:48) (MATTHEW 20:26-28)
(JOHN 13:4-5) (1 PETER 5:3)

October 11

My heart is confident in you, O God; no wonder I can sing your praises!

The LORD is my light and my salvation—so why should I be afraid?

You will keep in perfect peace all who trust in you, whose thoughts are fixed on you! For those who are righteous, the path is not steep and rough. You are a God of justice, and you smooth out the road ahead of them. ▪ They do not fear bad news; they confidently trust the LORD to care for them. They are confident and fearless and can face their foes triumphantly.

But when I am afraid, I put my trust in you. ▪ He will conceal me there when troubles come; he will hide me in his sanctuary. He will place me out of reach on a high rock. . . . At his Tabernacle I will offer sacrifices with shouts of joy, singing and praising the LORD with music.

After you have suffered a little while, he will restore, support, and strengthen you, and he will place you on a firm foundation. All power is his forever and ever. Amen.

At times the "path" of the righteous doesn't seem smooth, and it isn't easy to do God's will, but we are never alone when we face tough times. God is there to help us, to comfort us, and to lead us. He gives us wisdom to make decisions and faith to trust him. *LAB note for Isaiah 26:7–8*

(PSALM 108:1) (PSALM 27:1) (ISAIAH 26:3, 7) (PSALM 112:7–8) (PSALM 56:3) (PSALM 27:5–6) (1 PETER 5:10–11)

October 12

Real life is not measured by how much we own.

It is better to be godly and have little than to be evil and possess much. ■ It is better to have little with fear for the LORD than to have great treasure with turmoil. ■ True religion with contentment is great wealth. So if we have enough food and clothing, let us be content. ■ Give me neither poverty nor riches! Give me just enough to satisfy my needs. For if I grow rich, I may deny you and say, "Who is the LORD?" And if I am too poor, I may steal and thus insult God's holy name. ■ Give us our food for today.

Don't worry about everyday life—whether you have enough food, drink, and clothes. Doesn't life consistent of more than food and clothing? ■ "When I sent you out to preach the Good News and you did not have money, a traveler's bag, or extra clothing, did you lack anything?" "No," they replied. ■ Stay away from the love of money; be satisfied with what you have. For God has said, "I will never fail you. I will never forsake you."

How do you respond to the constant pressure to buy? Jesus says that the good life has nothing to do with being wealthy, so be on guard against greed. Learn to tune out expensive enticements and concentrate instead on the truly fulfilled life—living in a relationship with God and doing his work.

LAB note for Luke 12:15

(LUKE 12:15) (PSALM 37:16) (PROVERBS 15:16) (1 TIMOTHY 6:6, 8) (PROVERBS 30:8-9) (MATTHEW 6:11) (MATTHEW 6:25) (LUKE 22:35) (HEBREWS 13:5)

October 13

It is the Spirit who gives eternal life.

The Scriptures tell us, "The first man, Adam, became a living person." But the last Adam—that is, Christ—is a life-giving Spirit. ▩ Humans can reproduce only human life, but the Holy Spirit gives new life from heaven. ▩ He saved us, not because of the good things we did, but because of his mercy. He washed away our sins and gave us a new life through the Holy Spirit.

You are controlled by the Spirit if you have the Spirit of God living in you. . . . Since Christ lives within you, even though your body will die because of sin, your spirit is alive because you have been made right with God. The Spirit of God, who raised Jesus from the dead, lives in you. And just as he raised Christ from the dead, he will give life to your mortal body by this same Spirit living within you.

I have been crucified with Christ. I myself no longer live, but Christ lives in me. So I live my life in this earthly body by trusting in the Son of God, who loved me and gave himself for me. ▩ So you should consider yourselves dead to sin and able to live for the glory of God through Christ Jesus.

The Holy Spirit gives spiritual life; without the work of the Holy Spirit, we cannot even see our need for new life. All spiritual renewal begins and ends with God. He reveals truth to us, lives within us, and then enables us to respond to that truth. *LAB note for John 6:63-65*

(JOHN 6:63) (1 CORINTHIANS 15:45) (JOHN 3:6) (TITUS 3:5) (ROMANS 8:9-11) (GALATIANS 2:19-20) (ROMANS 6:11)

October 14

The end of the world is coming soon.

I saw a great white throne, and I saw the one who was sitting on it. The earth and sky fled from his presence, but they found no place to hide. ▪ God has commanded that the heavens and the earth will be consumed by fire on the day of judgment, when ungodly people will perish.

God is our refuge and strength, always ready to help in times of trouble. So we will not fear, even if earthquakes come and the mountains crumble into the sea. Let the oceans roar and foam. Let the mountains tremble as the waters surge! ▪ Wars will break out near and far, but don't panic. Yes, these things must come, but the end won't follow immediately.

We will have a home in heaven, an eternal body made for us by God himself and not by human hands. ▪ We are looking forward to the new heavens and new earth he has promised, a world where everyone is right with God. And so, dear friends, while you are waiting for these things to happen, make every effort to live a pure and blameless life. And be at peace with God.

When the disciples asked Jesus when he would come in power and what they could expect then, Jesus pointed out that they should be less concerned with knowing the exact date and more concerned with being prepared. They should live God's way consistently so that no matter when Jesus came, they would be ready. *LAB note for Matthew 24:3ff.*

(1 PETER 4:7) (REVELATION 20:11) (2 PETER 3:7) (PSALM 46:1-3) (MATTHEW 24:6) (2 CORINTHIANS 5:1) (2 PETER 3:13-14)

October 15

The LORD is king!

Do you have no respect for me? Why do you not tremble in my presence? I, the LORD, am the one who defines the ocean's sandy shoreline, an everlasting boundary that the waters cannot cross. The waves may toss and roar, but they can never pass the bounds I set. ▪ For no one on earth—from east or west, or even from the wilderness —can raise another person up. It is God alone who judges; he decides who will rise and who will fall.

He determines the course of world events; he removes kings and sets others on the throne. He gives wisdom to the wise and knowledge to the scholars. ▪ Wars will break out near and far, but don't panic. Yes, these things must come, but the end won't follow immediately.

If God is for us, who can ever be against us? ▪ Not even a sparrow, worth only half a penny, can fall to the ground without your Father knowing it. And the very hairs on your head are all numbered. So don't be afraid; you are more valuable to him than a whole flock of sparrows.

When we see evil leaders who live long and good leaders who die young, we may wonder if God is still in control. But God governs the world according to his purposes. You may be dismayed when you see evil people prosper, but God is in control. Let this knowledge give you confidence and peace no matter what happens. *LAB note for Daniel 2:21*

(PSALM 99:1) (JEREMIAH 5:22) (PSALM 75:6-7) (DANIEL 2:21) (MATTHEW 24:6) (ROMANS 8:31) (MATTHEW 10:29-31)

October 16

The enemy.

Be careful! Watch out for attacks from the Devil, your great enemy. He prowls around like a roaring lion, looking for some victim to devour. ▩ Resist the Devil, and he will flee from you.

Put on all of God's armor so that you will be able to stand firm against all strategies and tricks of the Devil. For we are not fighting against people made of flesh and blood, but against the evil rulers and authorities of the unseen world, against those mighty powers of darkness who rule this world, and against wicked spirits in the heavenly realms. Use every piece of God's armor to resist the enemy in the time of evil, so that after the battle you will still be standing firm. Stand your ground, putting on the sturdy belt of truth and the body armor of God's righteousness. For shoes, put on the peace that comes from the Good News, so that you will be fully prepared. In every battle you will need faith as your shield to stop the fiery arrows aimed at you by Satan.

Do not gloat over me, my enemies! For though I fall, I will rise again.

When you feel alone, weak, helpless, and cut off from other believers, you can become so focused on your troubles that you forget to watch for danger. That is when you are especially vulnerable to Satan's attacks. During suffering, seek other Christians for support, keep your eyes on Christ, and resist the Devil—he will flee from you!

LAB note for 1 Peter 5:8–9

(LUKE 10:19) (1 PETER 5:8) (JAMES 4:7) (EPHESIANS 6:11–16) (MICAH 7:8)

October 17

David found strength in the LORD his God.

Lord, to whom would we go? You alone have the words that give eternal life. ▪ I know the one in whom I trust, and I am sure that he is able to guard what I have entrusted to him until the day of his return.

In my distress I cried out to the LORD; yes, I prayed to my God for help. He heard me from his sanctuary; my cry reached his ears. They attacked me at a moment when I was weakest, but the LORD upheld me. He led me to a place of safety; he rescued me because he delights in me. He reached down from heaven and rescued me; he drew me out of deep waters. He delivered me from my powerful enemies, from those who hated me and were too strong for me.

I will praise the LORD at all times. I will constantly speak his praises. I will boast only in the LORD; let all who are discouraged take heart. Come, let us tell of the LORD's greatness; let us exalt his name together. I prayed to the LORD, and he answered me, freeing me from all my fears. Taste and see that the LORD is good. Oh, the joys of those who trust in him!

Faced with the tragedy of losing their families, David's soldiers began to turn against him. But David found his strength in God and began looking for a solution instead of a scapegoat. When facing problems, remember that it is useless to look for someone to blame or criticize. Instead, consider how you can help find a solution. *LAB note for 1 Samuel 30:6*

(1 SAMUEL 30:6) (JOHN 6:68) (2 TIMOTHY 1:12) (PSALM 18:6, 18-19, 16-17) (PSALM 34:1-4, 8)

October 18

He set my feet on solid ground and steadied me as I walked along.

All drank from the miraculous rock that traveled with them, and that rock was Christ. ▩ Simon Peter answered, "You are the Messiah, the Son of the living God." Upon this rock I will build my church, and all the powers of hell will not conquer it. ▩ There is salvation in no one else! There is no other name in all of heaven for people to call on to save them.

Fully trusting him . . . without wavering. ▩ A doubtful mind is as unsettled as a wave of the sea that is driven and tossed by the wind.

Can anything ever separate us from Christ's love? Does it mean he no longer loves us if we have trouble or calamity, or are persecuted, or are hungry or cold or in danger or threatened with death? No, despite all these things, overwhelming victory is ours through Christ, who loved us. And I am convinced that nothing can ever separate us from . . . the love of God that is revealed in Christ Jesus our Lord.

Waiting for God to help us is not easy, but David received four benefits from waiting: God (1) lifted him out of his despair, (2) set his feet on solid ground, (3) steadied him as he walked, and (4) put a new song of praise in his mouth. Often blessings cannot be received unless we go through the trial of waiting. *LAB note for Psalm 40:1-3*

(Psalm 40:2) (1 Corinthians 10:4) (Matthew 16:16, 18) (Acts 4:12) (Hebrews 10:22-23) (James 1:6) (Romans 8:35, 37-39)

October 19

May the words of my mouth and the thoughts of my heart be pleasing to you, O LORD, my rock and my redeemer.

How can I know all the sins lurking in my heart? Cleanse me from these hidden faults. ■ Look after each other so that none of you will miss out on the special favor of God. Watch out that no bitter root of unbelief rises up among you, for whenever it springs up, many are corrupted by its poison.

I am sure that God, who began the good work within you, will continue his work until it is finally finished on that day when Christ Jesus comes back again. You must live in a manner worthy of the Good News about Christ. ■ So also, the tongue is a small thing, but what enormous damage it can do. A tiny spark can set a great forest on fire. And the tongue is a flame of fire. It is full of wickedness that can ruin your whole life. It can turn the entire course of your life into a blazing flame of destruction, for it is set on fire by hell itself. No one can tame the tongue. It is an uncontrollable evil, full of deadly poison. ■ Let your conversation be gracious and effective.

Many Christians are plagued by guilt. Guilt can play an important role in bringing us to Christ and in keeping us behaving properly, but it should not cripple us or make us fearful. God fully and completely forgives us—even for those sins we do unknowingly.

LAB note for Psalm 19:12-13

(PSALM 19:14) (PSALM 19:12) (HEBREWS 12:15) (PHILIPPIANS 1:6, 27) (JAMES 3:5-6, 8) (COLOSSIANS 4:6)

October 20

Not by force nor by strength, but by my Spirit, says the LORD Almighty.

Who is able to advise the Spirit of the LORD? Who knows enough to be his teacher or counselor?

God deliberately chose things the world considers foolish in order to shame those who think they are wise. And he chose those who are powerless to shame those who are powerful. God chose things despised by the world, things counted as nothing at all, and used them to bring to nothing what the world considers important, so that no one can ever boast in the presence of God.

Just as you can hear the wind but can't tell where it comes from or where it is going, so you can't explain how people are born of the Spirit. ▪ Reborn! This is not a physical birth resulting from human passion or plan—this rebirth comes from God.

My Spirit remains among you, just as I promised. . . . So do not be afraid. ▪ The battle is not yours, but God's.

The LORD does not need weapons to rescue his people. It is his battle, not ours.

Many people believe that to survive in this world a person must be tough, strong, unbending, and harsh. But it is only through God's Spirit that anything of lasting value is accomplished. As you live for God, determine not to trust in your own strength or abilities. Instead, depend on God and work in the power of his Spirit! *LAB note for Zechariah 4:6*

(ZECHARIAH 4:6) (ISAIAH 40:13) (1 CORINTHIANS 1:27-29) (JOHN 3:8) (JOHN 1:13) (HAGGAI 2:5) (2 CHRONICLES 20:15) (1 SAMUEL 17:47)

October 21

Always try to do good.

This suffering is all part of what God has called you to. Christ, who suffered for you, is your example. Follow in his steps. He never sinned, and he never deceived anyone. He did not retaliate when he was insulted. When he suffered, he did not threaten to get even. He left his case in the hands of God, who always judges fairly. ▪ Think about all he endured when sinful people did such terrible things to him, so that you don't become weary and give up.

Let us strip off every weight that slows us down, especially the sin that so easily hinders our progress. And let us run with endurance the race that God has set before us. We do this by keeping our eyes on Jesus, on whom our faith depends from start to finish. He was willing to die a shameful death on the cross because of the joy he knew would be his afterward. Now he is seated in the place of highest honor beside God's throne in heaven.

Let me say one more thing as I close this letter. Fix your thoughts on what is true and honorable and right. Think about things that are pure and lovely and admirable. Think about things that are excellent and worthy of praise.

Christ never sinned, and yet he suffered so that we could be set free. When we follow Christ's example and live for others, we, too, may suffer. Our goal should be to face suffering as he did—with patience, calmness, and confidence that God is in control of the future.

LAB note for 1 Peter 2:21–22

(1 THESSALONIANS 5:15) (1 PETER 2:21–23) (HEBREWS 12:3)
(HEBREWS 12:1–2) (PHILIPPIANS 4:8)

October 22

The paths of the LORD are true and right, and righteous people live by walking in them. But sinners stumble and fall along the way.

He is very precious to you who believe. But for those who reject him . . . "He is the stone that makes people stumble, the rock that will make them fall." They stumble because they do not listen to God's word or obey it, and so they meet the fate that has been planned for them. ▪ The LORD protects the upright but destroys the wicked.

Anyone who is willing to hear should listen and understand! ▪ Those who are wise will take all this to heart; they will see in our history the faithful love of the LORD. ▪ A pure eye lets sunshine into your soul. ▪ Anyone who wants to do the will of God will know whether my teaching is from God or is merely my own. ▪ To those who are open to my teaching, more understanding will be given, and they will have an abundance of knowledge.

Anyone whose Father is God listens gladly to the words of God. Since you don't, it proves you aren't God's children. ▪ You refuse to come to me so that I can give you this eternal life. ▪ My sheep recognize my voice; I know them, and they follow me.

The book of Hosea closes with an appeal to listen, learn, and benefit from God's word. All readers have a choice: to listen to the message and follow God's ways or refuse to walk along the Lord's path. If you are lost, you can find the way by turning from your sin and following God.

LAB note for Hosea 14:9

(HOSEA 14:9) (1 PETER 2:7-8) (PROVERBS 10:29) (MATTHEW 11:15) (PSALM 107:43) (MATTHEW 6:22) (JOHN 7:17) (MATTHEW 13:12) (JOHN 8:47) (JOHN 5:40) (JOHN 10:27)

October 23

There is wonderful joy ahead, even though it is necessary for you to endure many trials for a while.

Dear friends, don't be surprised at the fiery trials you are going through, as if something strange were happening to you. Instead, be very glad—because these trials will make you partners with Christ in his suffering, and afterward you will have the wonderful joy of sharing his glory. ▪ Have you entirely forgotten the encouraging words God spoke to you, his children? He said, "My child, don't ignore it when the Lord disciplines you, and don't be discouraged when he corrects you." ▪ No discipline is enjoyable while it is happening—it is painful! But afterward there will be a quiet harvest of right living for those who are trained in this way.

This High Priest of ours understands our weaknesses, for he faced all of the same temptations we do, yet he did not sin. ▪ Since he himself has gone through suffering and temptation, he is able to help us when we are being tempted. ▪ Remember that the temptations that come into your life are no different from what others experience. And God is faithful. He will keep the temptation from becoming so strong that you can't stand up against it. When you are tempted, he will show you a way out so that you will not give in to it.

All believers face trials when they let their light shine into the darkness. We must accept trials as part of the refining process that burns away impurities and prepares us to meet Christ. Trials teach us patience and help us grow to be the kind of people God wants.

LAB note for 1 Peter 1:6-7

(1 Peter 1:6) (1 Peter 4:12-13) (Hebrews 12:5) (Hebrews 12:11) (Hebrews 4:15) (Hebrews 2:18) (1 Corinthians 10:13)

October 24

Praise the LORD for his great love and for all his wonderful deeds.

Taste and see that the LORD is good. Oh, the joys of those who trust in him! ▩ Your goodness is so great! You have stored up great blessings for those who honor you. You have done so much for those who come to you for protection, blessing them before the watching world.

His unchanging plan has always been to adopt us into his own family by bringing us to himself through Jesus Christ. And this gave him great pleasure. So we praise God for the wonderful kindness he has poured out on us because we belong to his dearly loved Son.

How wonderful and beautiful they will be! The young men and women will thrive on the abundance of grain and new wine. ▩ The LORD is good to everyone. He showers compassion on all his creation. All of your works will thank you, LORD, and your faithful followers will bless you. They will talk together about the glory of your kingdom; they will celebrate examples of your power. They will tell about your mighty deeds and about the majesty and glory of your reign.

God's "unchanging plan" is another way of saying that salvation is God's work and not our own doing. In his infinite love, God has adopted us as his own children. Through Jesus' sacrifice he has brought us into his family and made us heirs along with Jesus. *LAB note for Ephesians 1:5*

(PSALM 107:8) (PSALM 34:8) (PSALM 31:19) (EPHESIANS 1:5-6) (ZECHARIAH 9:17) (PSALM 145:9-12)

October 25

Lead me by your truth and teach me.

When the Spirit of truth comes, he will guide you into all truth. He will not be presenting his own ideas; he will be telling you what he has heard. ▪ The Holy Spirit has come upon you, and all of you know the truth.

"Check their predictions against my testimony," says the LORD. "If their predictions are different from mine, it is because there is no light or truth in them." ▪ All Scripture is inspired by God and is useful to teach us what is true and to make us realize what is wrong in our lives. It straightens us out and teaches us to do what is right. It is God's way of preparing us in every way, fully equipped for every good thing God wants us to do.

The LORD says, "I will guide you along the best pathway for your life. I will advise you and watch over you." ▪ A pure eye lets sunshine into your soul. ▪ Anyone who wants to do the will of God will know whether my teaching is from God or is merely my own. ▪ It will be only for those who walk in God's ways; fools will never walk there.

Jesus said the Holy Spirit would tell them "about the future"—the nature of their mission, the opposition they would face, and the final outcome of their efforts. They didn't fully understand these promises until the Holy Spirit came after Jesus' death and resurrection.

LAB note for John 16:13

(PSALM 25:5) (JOHN 16:13) (1 JOHN 2:20) (ISAIAH 8:20) (2 TIMOTHY 3:16-17) (PSALM 32:8) (MATTHEW 6:22) (JOHN 7:17) (ISAIAH 35:8)

October 26

We give great honor to those who endure under suffering.

We can rejoice, too, when we run into problems and trials, for we know that they are good for us—they help us learn to endure. And endurance develops strength of character in us, and character strengthens our confident expectation of salvation. And this expectation will not disappoint us. For we know how dearly God loves us, because he has given us the Holy Spirit to fill our hearts with his love.

No discipline is enjoyable while it is happening—it is painful! But afterward there will be a quiet harvest of right living for those who are trained in this way. Let it grow, for when your endurance is fully developed, you will be strong in character and ready for anything.

I am glad to boast about my weaknesses, so that the power of Christ may work through me. Since I know it is all for Christ's good, I am quite content with my weaknesses and with insults, hardships, persecutions, and calamities. For when I am weak, then I am strong.

We will experience difficulties that help us grow. We can rejoice in suffering, not because we like pain or deny its tragedy, but because we know God is using life's difficulties and Satan's attacks to build our character. Thank God for these opportunities to grow!

LAB note for Romans 5:3-4

(JAMES 5:11) (ROMANS 5:3-5) (HEBREWS 12:11) (JAMES 1:4)
(2 CORINTHIANS 12:9-10)

October 27

The way you live will always honor and please the Lord, and you will continually do good, kind things for others. All the while, you will learn to know God better and better.

Dear brothers and sisters, I plead with you to give your bodies to God. Let them be a living and holy sacrifice—the kind he will accept. When you think of what he has done for you, is this too much to ask? Don't copy the behavior and customs of this world, but let God transform you into a new person by changing the way you think. Then you will know what God wants you to do, and you will know how good and pleasing and perfect his will really is. ▪ Before, you let yourselves be slaves of impurity and lawlessness. Now you must choose to be slaves of righteousness so that you will become holy. ▪ What counts is whether we really have been changed into new and different people. May God's mercy and peace be upon all those who live by this principle. They are the new people of God.

My true disciples produce much fruit. This brings great glory to my Father. ▪ You didn't choose me. I chose you. I appointed you to go and produce fruit that will last, so that the Father will give you whatever you ask for, using my name. I command you to love each other.

Knowledge is not merely to be accumulated; it should give us direction for living. It is not a secret that only a few can discover; it is open to everyone. God wants us to learn more about him and put belief into practice by helping others. *LAB note for Colossians 1:9–14*

(COLOSSIANS 1:10) (ROMANS 12:1-2) (ROMANS 6:19) (GALATIANS 6:15-16) (JOHN 15:8) (JOHN 15:16)

October 28

I will get up now and roam the city, searching for him.

Return, O Israel, to the LORD your God, for your sins have brought you down. Bring your petitions, and return to the LORD. Say to him, "Forgive all our sins and graciously receive us, so that we may offer you the sacrifice of praise."

Remember, no one who wants to do wrong should ever say, "God is tempting me." God is never tempted to do wrong, and he never tempts anyone else either. Temptation comes from the lure of our own evil desires. These evil desires lead to evil actions, and evil actions lead to death. So don't be misled, my dear brothers and sisters. Whatever is good and perfect comes to us from God above, who created all heaven's lights. Unlike them, he never changes or casts shifting shadows.

Wait patiently for the LORD. Be brave and courageous. Yes, wait patiently for the LORD. ■ It is good to wait quietly for salvation from the LORD. ■ Don't you think God will surely give justice to his chosen people who plead with him day and night?

I wait quietly before God, for my salvation comes from him.

When you love someone, you will do all you can to care for his or her needs, even at a cost to your personal comfort. This is demonstrated most often in small actions—getting your spouse a glass of water, leaving work early to attend some function your child is involved in, or sacrificing time to tend to a friend's needs. *LAB note for Song of Songs 3:1-4*

(SONG OF SONGS 3:2) (HOSEA 14:1-2) (JAMES 1:13-17) (PSALM 27:14) (LAMENTATIONS 3:26) (LUKE 18:7) (PSALM 62:1)

October 29

God can use sorrow in our lives to help us turn away from sin and seek salvation.

Jesus' words flashed through Peter's mind: "Before the rooster crows, you will deny me three times." And he went away, crying bitterly. ▪ If we confess our sins to him, he is faithful and just to forgive us and to cleanse us from every wrong. ▪ The blood of Jesus, his Son, cleanses us from every sin.

Troubles surround me—too many to count! They pile up so high I can't see my way out. They are more numerous than the hairs on my head. I have lost all my courage. Please, LORD, rescue me! Come quickly, LORD, and help me.

Your sins have brought you down. ▪ Come back to your God! Act on the principles of love and justice, and always live in confident dependence on your God. ▪ Be still in the presence of the LORD, and wait patiently for him to act.

The sacrifice you want is a broken spirit. A broken and repentant heart, O God, you will not despise. ▪ He heals the brokenhearted, binding up their wounds. ▪ The LORD has already told you what is good, and this is what he requires: to do what is right, to love mercy, and to walk humbly with your God.

Sorrow for our sins can result in changed behavior. Many people are sorry only for the effects of their sins or for being caught. Compare Peter's remorse and repentance with Judas's bitterness and suicide. Both denied Christ. One repented and was restored to faith and service; the other took his own life. *LAB note for 2 Corinthians 7:10*

(2 CORINTHIANS 7:10) (MATTHEW 26:75) (1 JOHN 1:9) (1 JOHN 1:7) (PSALM 40:12-13) (HOSEA 14:1) (HOSEA 12:6) (PSALM 37:7) (PSALM 51:17) (PSALM 147:3) (MICAH 6:8)

October 30

These trials are only to test your faith, to show that it is strong and pure.

We are well known, but we are treated as unknown. We live close to death, but here we are, still alive. We have been beaten within an inch of our lives. Our hearts ache, but we always have joy. We are poor, but we give spiritual riches to others. We own nothing, and yet we have everything.

We are pressed on every side by troubles, but we are not crushed and broken. We are perplexed, but we don't give up and quit. We are hunted down, but God never abandons us. We get knocked down, but we get up again and keep going.

Though our bodies are dying, our spirits are being renewed every day. For our present troubles are quite small and won't last very long. Yet they produce for us an immeasurably great glory that will last forever!

So we don't look at the troubles we can see right now; rather, we look forward to what we have not yet seen. For the troubles we see will soon be over, but the joys to come will last forever.

As gold is heated, impurities float to the top and can be skimmed off. Steel is tempered or strengthened by heating it in fire. Likewise, our trials, struggles, and persecutions refine and strengthen our faith, making us useful to God. *LAB note for 1 Peter 1:7*

(1 PETER 1:7) (2 CORINTHIANS 6:9-10) (2 CORINTHIANS 4:8-9)
(2 CORINTHIANS 4:16-17) (2 CORINTHIANS 4:18)

October 31

Love each other in the same way that I love you.

Live a life filled with love for others, following the example of Christ, who loved you and gave himself as a sacrifice to take away your sins. And God was pleased, because that sacrifice was like sweet perfume to him. ▪ This is the message we have heard from the beginning: We should love one another. ▪ Our lives are a fragrance presented by Christ to God.

You have been born again. Your new life did not come from your earthly parents because the life they gave you will end in death. But this new life will last forever because it comes from the eternal, living word of God. ▪ Make them pure and holy by teaching them your words of truth. ▪ No one can enter the Kingdom of God without being born of water and the Spirit. ▪ He saved us, not because of the good things we did, but because of his mercy. He washed away our sins and gave us a new life through the Holy Spirit. ▪ Your promise revives me.

May God, who gives this patience and encouragement, help you live in complete harmony with each other—each with the attitude of Christ Jesus toward the other.

When Christians preach the Good News, it is good news to some and repulsive news to others. Believers recognize the life-giving fragrance of the message. To unbelievers, however, it smells foul, like death—their own.

LAB note for 2 Corinthians 2:14–16

(John 15:12) (Ephesians 5:2) (1 John 3:11) (2 Corinthians 2:15) (1 Peter 1:23) (John 17:17) (John 3:5) (Titus 3:5) (Psalm 119:50) (Romans 15:5)

November

We Give Thanks

Daily necessities and moment-by-moment protection;
Loving guidance and heartwarming friendship;
God's generous character flows into
every area of our lives.

It's the annual season for giving thanks.
As the year nears its end, spend a few moments
appreciating the countless blessings that
are often overlooked in daily life.

November 1

With all my heart I will praise you, O Lord my God.

Giving thanks is a sacrifice that truly honors me. ▪ It is good to give thanks to the LORD, to sing praises to the Most High. It is good to proclaim your unfailing love in the morning, your faithfulness in the evening.

Let everything that lives sing praises to the LORD!

Dear brothers and sisters, I plead with you to give your bodies to God. Let them be a living and holy sacrifice—the kind he will accept. When you think of what he has done for you, is this too much to ask? ▪ As a sacrifice for sin . . . Jesus suffered and died outside the city gates in order to make his people holy by shedding his own blood. With Jesus' help, let us continually offer our sacrifice of praise to God by proclaiming the glory of his name. ▪ Always give thanks for everything to God the Father in the name of our Lord Jesus Christ.

The Lamb is worthy—the Lamb who was killed. He is worthy to receive power and riches and wisdom and strength and honor and glory and blessing.

Thanks should be on our lips every day. When thanksgiving becomes an integral part of your life, you will find that your attitude toward life will change. You will become more positive, gracious, loving, and humble.

LAB note for Psalm 92:1-2

(PSALM 86:12) (PSALM 50:23) (PSALM 92:1-2) (PSALM 150:6) (ROMANS 12:1) (HEBREWS 13:11-12, 15) (EPHESIANS 5:20) (REVELATION 5:12)

November 2

If you need wisdom—if you want to know what God wants you to do—ask him, and he will gladly tell you.

Jesus . . . said to her, "Where are your accusers? Didn't even one of them condemn you?" "No, Lord," she said. And Jesus said, "Neither do I. Go and sin no more."

What a difference between our sin and God's generous gift of forgiveness. For this one man, Adam, brought death to many through his sin. But this other man, Jesus Christ, brought forgiveness to many through God's bountiful gift. And the result of God's gracious gift is very different from the result of that one man's sin. For Adam's sin led to condemnation, but we have the free gift of being accepted by God, even though we are guilty of many sins.

God is so rich in mercy, and he loved us so very much, that even while we were dead because of our sins, he gave us life when he raised Christ from the dead. (It is only by God's special favor that you have been saved!) For he raised us from the dead along with Christ, and we are seated with him in the heavenly realms—all because we are one with Christ Jesus. And so God can always point to us as examples of the incredible wealth of his favor and kindness toward us, as shown in all he has done for us through Christ Jesus.

Since God did not spare even his own Son but gave him up for us all, won't God, who gave us Christ, also give us everything else?

Christ offers us the opportunity to be born into his spiritual family—the family line that begins with forgiveness and leads to eternal life. If we do nothing, we receive death through Adam; but if we come to God by faith, we receive life through Christ. To which family line do you now belong?

LAB note for Romans 5:15-19

(JAMES 1:5) (JOHN 8:10-11) (ROMANS 5:15-16)
(EPHESIANS 2:4-7) (ROMANS 8:32)

November 3

Make them pure and holy by teaching them your words of truth.

You have already been pruned for greater fruitfulness by the message I have given you. ▪ Let the words of Christ, in all their richness, live in your hearts and make you wise.

How can a young person stay pure? By obeying your word and following its rules. I have tried my best to find you—don't let me wander from your commands.

For wisdom will enter your heart, and knowledge will fill you with joy. Wise planning will watch over you. Understanding will keep you safe.

I have stayed in God's paths; I have followed his ways and not turned aside. I have not departed from his commands but have treasured his word in my heart. ▪ Even perfection has its limits, but your commands have no limit. Oh, how I love your law! I think about it all day long. Your commands make me wiser than my enemies, for your commands are my constant guide. Yes, I have more insight than my teachers, for I am always thinking of your decrees. ▪ You are truly my disciples if you keep obeying my teachings. And you will know the truth, and the truth will set you free.

A follower of Christ becomes pure and holy through believing and obeying the Word of God. He or she has already accepted forgiveness through Christ's sacrificial death. But daily application of God's Word has a purifying effect on our minds and hearts. *LAB note for John 17:17*

(JOHN 17:17) (JOHN 15:3) (COLOSSIANS 3:16) (PSALM 119:9-10)
(PROVERBS 2:10-11) (JOB 23:11-12) (PSALM 119:96-99) (JOHN 8:31-32)

November 4

How deep are your thoughts.

We have continued praying for you ever since we first heard about you. We ask God to give you a complete understanding of what he wants to do in your lives, and we ask him to make you wise with spiritual wisdom. ❖ I pray that Christ will be more and more at home in your hearts as you trust in him. May your roots go down deep into the soil of God's marvelous love. And may you have the power to understand, as all God's people should, how wide, how long, how high, and how deep his love really is. May you experience the love of Christ, though it is so great you will never fully understand it. Then you will be filled with the fullness of life and power that comes from God.

Oh, what a wonderful God we have! How great are his riches and wisdom and knowledge! How impossible it is for us to understand his decisions and his methods! ❖ "My thoughts are completely different from yours," says the LORD. "And my ways are far beyond anything you could imagine. For just as the heavens are higher than the earth, so are my ways higher than your ways and my thoughts higher than your thoughts." ❖ O LORD my God, you have done many miracles for us. Your plans for us are too numerous to list. If I tried to recite all your wonderful deeds, I would never come to the end of them.

God is ultimately wise. Although his methods and means are beyond our comprehension, God himself is not arbitrary. He governs the universe and our life in perfect wisdom, justice, and love.

LAB note for Romans 11:33

(PSALM 92:5) (COLOSSIANS 1:9) (EPHESIANS 3:17-19)
(ROMANS 11:33) (ISAIAH 55:8-9) (PSALM 40:5)

November 5

When the Holy Spirit controls our lives, he will produce . . . gentleness.

The humble will be filled with fresh joy from the LORD. Those who are poor will rejoice in the Holy One of Israel.

Unless you turn from your sins and become as little children, you will never get into the Kingdom of Heaven. Therefore, anyone who becomes as humble as this little child is the greatest in the Kingdom of Heaven. ▪ You should be known for the beauty that comes from within, the unfading beauty of a gentle and quiet spirit, which is so precious to God. ▪ Love is patient and kind. Love is not jealous or boastful or proud.

Pursue a godly life, along with faith, love, perseverance, and gentleness. ▪ Take my yoke upon you. Let me teach you, because I am humble and gentle. ▪ He was oppressed and treated harshly, yet he never said a word. He was led as a lamb to the slaughter. And as a sheep is silent before the shearers, he did not open his mouth.

This suffering is all part of what God has called you to. Christ, who suffered for you, is your example. Follow in his steps. He never sinned, and he never deceived anyone. He did not retaliate when he was insulted. When he suffered, he did not threaten to get even. He left his case in the hands of God, who always judges fairly.

Jesus used a child to help his self-centered disciples get the point. We are not to be childish (like the disciples, arguing over petty issues) but childlike, with humble and sincere hearts. Are you being childlike or childish?

LAB note for Matthew 18:1-4

(GALATIANS 5:22-23) (ISAIAH 29:19) (MATTHEW 18:3-4) (1 PETER 3:4) (1 CORINTHIANS 13:4) (1 TIMOTHY 6:11) (MATTHEW 11:29) (ISAIAH 53:7) (1 PETER 2:21-23)

November 6

He has punished Israel only a little. He has exiled her from her land as though blown away in a storm from the east.

Let us fall into the hands of the LORD, for his mercy is great. Do not let me fall into human hands. ❖ I am with you and will save you, says the LORD. . . . I will not destroy you. But I must discipline you; I cannot let you go unpunished. ❖ He will not constantly accuse us, nor remain angry forever. He has not punished us for all our sins, nor does he deal with us as we deserve. He knows we are only dust. ❖ I will spare them as a father spares an obedient and dutiful child.

Remember that the temptations that come into your life are no different from what others experience. And God is faithful. He will keep the temptation from becoming so strong that you can't stand up against it. When you are tempted, he will show you a way out so that you will not give in to it. ❖ Satan has asked to have all of you, to sift you like wheat. But I have pleaded in prayer for you . . . that your faith should not fail.

To the poor, O LORD, you are a refuge from the storm. To the needy in distress, you are a shelter from the rain and the heat. For the oppressive acts of ruthless people are like a storm beating against a wall.

David wisely chose the form of punishment that came most directly from God. He knew how brutal and harsh men in war could be, and he also knew God's great mercy. When you sin greatly, turn back to God. To be punished by him is far better than to take your chances without him. *LAB note for 2 Samuel 24:12-14*

(ISAIAH 27:8) (2 SAMUEL 24:14) (JEREMIAH 30:11) (PSALM 103:9-10, 14) (MALACHI 3:17) (1 CORINTHIANS 10:13) (LUKE 22:31-32) (ISAIAH 25:4)

November 7

Though I sit in darkness, the LORD himself will be my light.

When you go through deep waters and great trouble, I will be with you. When you go through rivers of difficulty, you will not drown! When you walk through the fire of oppression, you will not be burned up; the flames will not consume you. For I am the LORD, your God, the Holy One of Israel, your Savior. ▪ I will lead blind Israel down a new path, guiding them along an unfamiliar way. I will make the darkness bright before them and smooth out the road ahead of them. ▪ Who among you fears the LORD and obeys his servant? If you are walking in darkness, without a ray of light, trust in the LORD and rely on your God.

Even when I walk through the dark valley of death, I will not be afraid, for you are close beside me. Your rod and your staff protect and comfort me. ▪ When I am afraid, I put my trust in you. O God, I praise your word. I trust in God, so why should I be afraid? What can mere mortals do to me? ▪ The LORD is my light and my salvation—so why should I be afraid?

Micah showed great faith in God as he waited on God to bring his people through tough times. We, too, can have a relationship with God that can allow us to have confidence like Micah's. It doesn't take unusual talent; it simply takes faith in God and a willingness to act on that faith.

LAB note for Micah 7:7-10

(MICAH 7:8) (ISAIAH 43:2-3) (ISAIAH 42:16) (ISAIAH 50:10) (PSALM 23:4) (PSALM 56:3-4) (PSALM 27:1)

November 8

Pray as you are directed by the Holy Spirit.

God is Spirit, so those who worship him must worship in spirit and in truth. ▪ All of us, both Jews and Gentiles, may come to the Father through the same Holy Spirit because of what Christ has done for us.

My Father! If it is possible, let this cup of suffering be taken away from me. Yet I want your will, not mine.

The Holy Spirit helps us in our distress. For we don't even know what we should pray for, nor how we should pray. But the Holy Spirit prays for us with groanings that cannot be expressed in words. And the Father who knows all hearts knows what the Spirit is saying, for the Spirit pleads for us believers in harmony with God's own will. ▪ And we can be confident that he will listen to us whenever we ask him for anything in line with his will. ▪ When the Spirit of truth comes, he will guide you into all truth.

Pray at all times and on every occasion in the power of the Holy Spirit. Stay alert and be persistent in your prayers for all Christians everywhere.

To pray as we are "directed by the Holy Spirit" means to pray in the power and strength of the Holy Spirit. He prays for us, opens our mind to Jesus, and teaches us about him. *LAB note for Jude 1:20*

(JUDE 1:20) (JOHN 4:24) (EPHESIANS 2:18) (MATTHEW 26:39) (ROMANS 8:26-27) (1 JOHN 5:14) (JOHN 16:13) (EPHESIANS 6:18)

November 9

If a tree is cut down, there is hope that it will sprout again and grow new branches.

He will not crush those who are weak. ▪ He renews my strength.

God can use sorrow in our lives to help us turn away from sin and seek salvation. We will never regret that kind of sorrow. But sorrow without repentance is the kind that results in death. ▪ No discipline is enjoyable while it is happening—it is painful! But afterward there will be a quiet harvest of right living for those who are trained in this way.

I used to wander off until you disciplined me; but now I closely follow your word.

Do not gloat over me, my enemies! For though I fall, I will rise again. Though I sit in darkness, the LORD himself will be my light. I will be patient as the LORD punishes me, for I have sinned against him. But after that, he will take up my case and punish my enemies for all the evil they have done to me. The LORD will bring me out of my darkness into the light, and I will see his righteousness.

Job's pessimism about death is understandable, since Jesus had not yet conquered death. What is remarkable is his budding hope: If only he could die and live again! When we must endure suffering, we have an advantage over Job. We know that the dead will rise—because Christ rose!

LAB note for Job 14:7-22

(JOB 14:7) (ISAIAH 42:3) (PSALM 23:3) (2 CORINTHIANS 7:10) (HEBREWS 12:11) (PSALM 119:67) (MICAH 7:8-9)

*N*ovember 10

My Kingdom is not of this world.

Our High Priest offered himself to God as one sacrifice for sins, good for all time. Then he sat down at the place of highest honor at God's right hand. ▪ In the future you will see me, the Son of Man, sitting at God's right hand in the place of power and coming back on the clouds of heaven.

Christ must reign until he humbles all his enemies beneath his feet.

How we thank God, who gives us victory over sin and death through Jesus Christ our Lord! ▪ This is the same mighty power that raised Christ from the dead and seated him in the place of honor at God's right hand in the heavenly realms. Now he is far above any ruler or authority or power or leader or anything else in this world or in the world to come. And God has put all things under the authority of Christ, and he gave him this authority for the benefit of the church. And the church is his body; it is filled by Christ, who fills everything everywhere with his presence. ▪ For at the right time Christ will be revealed from heaven by the blessed and only almighty God, the King of kings and Lord of lords.

Jesus declared his royalty in no uncertain terms. In saying he was the Son of Man, Jesus was claiming to be the Messiah, as his listeners well knew. He knew this declaration would be his undoing, but he did not panic. He was calm, courageous, and determined. *LAB note for Matthew 26:64*

(JOHN 18:36) (HEBREWS 10:12–13) (MATTHEW 26:64) (1 CORINTHIANS 15:25) (1 CORINTHIANS 15:57) (EPHESIANS 1:19–23) (1 TIMOTHY 6:15)

*N*ovember 11

What are you doing here, Elijah?

He knows where I am going. ▪ O LORD, you have examined my heart and know everything about me. You know when I sit down or stand up. You know my every thought when far away. You chart the path ahead of me and tell me where to stop and rest. I can never escape from your spirit! I can never get away from your presence! If I ride the wings of the morning, if I dwell by the farthest oceans, even there your hand will guide me, and your strength will support me.

Elijah was as human as we are. ▪ Fearing people is a dangerous trap, but to trust the LORD means safety. ▪ Though they stumble, they will not fall, for the LORD holds them by the hand. ▪ They may trip seven times, but each time they will rise again.

Don't get tired of doing what is good. Don't get discouraged and give up, for we will reap a harvest of blessing at the appropriate time. ▪ Though the spirit is willing enough, the body is weak! ▪ The LORD is like a father to his children, tender and compassionate to those who fear him. For he understands how weak we are; he knows we are only dust.

God is omnipresent—he is present everywhere. Because this is so, you can never escape from his Spirit. This is good news to those who know and love God, because no matter what we do or where we go, we can never be far from God's comforting presence. *LAB note for Psalm 139:7*

(1 KINGS 19:9) (JOB 23:10) (PSALM 139:1-3, 7, 9-10) (JAMES 5:17) (PROVERBS 29:25) (PSALM 37:24) (PROVERBS 24:16) (GALATIANS 6:9) (MATTHEW 26:41) (PSALM 103:13-14)

November 12

Now you are free from sin, your old master, and you have become slaves to your new master, righteousness.

No one can serve two masters. . . . You cannot serve both God and money. ▩ When you were slaves of sin, you weren't concerned with doing what was right. And what was the result? It was not good, since now you are ashamed of the things you used to do, things that end in eternal doom. But now you are free from the power of sin and have become slaves of God. Now you do those things that lead to holiness and result in eternal life.

Christ has accomplished the whole purpose of the law. All who believe in him are made right with God.

All those who want to be my disciples must come and follow me, because my servants must be where I am. And if they follow me, the Father will honor them. ▩ Take my yoke upon you. Let me teach you, because I am humble and gentle, and you will find rest for your souls. For my yoke fits perfectly, and the burden I give you is light.

O LORD our God, others have ruled us, but we worship you alone. ▩ If you will help me, I will run to follow your commands.

All people have a master and pattern themselves after him. Without Jesus we would have no choice but to be enslaved to sin. But thanks to him, we can now choose God as our Master. Following him we can enjoy new life and learn how to work for him.

LAB note for Romans 6:16–18

(ROMANS 6:18) (MATTHEW 6:24) (ROMANS 6:20–22) (ROMANS 10:4) (JOHN 12:26) (MATTHEW 11:29–30) (ISAIAH 26:13) (PSALM 119:32)

November 13

Anyone who calls on the name of the Lord will be saved.

Manasseh . . . rebuilt the pagan shrines his father, Hezekiah, had destroyed. He constructed altars for Baal and set up an Asherah pole, just as King Ahab of Israel had done. He even built pagan altars in the Temple of the LORD, the place where the LORD had said his name should be honored. He built these altars for all the forces of heaven in both courtyards of the LORD's Temple. Manasseh even sacrificed his own son in the fire. He practiced sorcery and divination, and he consulted with mediums and psychics. He did much that was evil in the LORD's sight, arousing his anger. ▪ While in deep distress, Manasseh sought the LORD his God and cried out humbly to the God of his ancestors. And when he prayed, the LORD listened to him and was moved by his request for help. So the LORD let Manasseh return to Jerusalem and to his kingdom. Manasseh had finally realized that the LORD alone is God!

"Come now, let us argue this out," says the LORD. "No matter how deep the stain of your sins, I can remove it. I can make you as clean as freshly fallen snow. Even if you are stained as red as crimson, I can make you as white as wool." ▪ He does not want anyone to perish.

Today, many books, television shows, and games emphasize fortune-telling, séances, and other occult practices. Don't let desire to know the future or the belief that superstition is harmless lead you into condoning occult practices. They are counterfeits of God's power and have as their root a system of beliefs totally opposed to God.

LAB note for 2 Kings 21:6

(ACTS 2:21) (2 KINGS 21:1, 3-6) (2 CHRONICLES 33:12-13) (ISAIAH 1:18) (2 PETER 3:9)

November 14

When the Holy Spirit controls our lives, he will produce . . . patience, kindness.

I am the LORD, I am the LORD, the merciful and gracious God. I am slow to anger and rich in unfailing love and faithfulness.

Lead a life worthy of your calling, for you have been called by God. Be humble and gentle. Be patient with each other, making allowance for each other's faults because of your love. ▪ Be kind to each other, tenderhearted, forgiving one another, just as God through Christ has forgiven you. ▪ The wisdom that comes from heaven is first of all pure. It is also peace loving, gentle at all times, and willing to yield to others. It is full of mercy and good deeds. It shows no partiality and is always sincere. ▪ Love is patient and kind.

Don't get tired of doing what is good. Don't get discouraged and give up, for we will reap a harvest of blessing at the appropriate time. ▪ Dear brothers and sisters, you must be patient as you wait for the Lord's return. Consider the farmers who eagerly look for the rains in the fall and in the spring. They patiently wait for the precious harvest to ripen. You, too, must be patient. And take courage, for the coming of the Lord is near.

No one is ever going to be perfect here on earth, so we must accept, love, and be patient with other Christians in spite of their faults. Rather than dwelling on a person's weaknesses or looking for faults, pray for him or her. *LAB note for Ephesians 4:2*

(GALATIANS 5:22) (EXODUS 34:6) (EPHESIANS 4:1-2) (EPHESIANS 4:32) (JAMES 3:17) (1 CORINTHIANS 13:4) (GALATIANS 6:9) (JAMES 5:7-8)

November 15

Just as the body is dead without a spirit, so also faith is dead without good deeds.

Not all people who sound religious are really godly. They may refer to me as "Lord," but they still won't enter the Kingdom of Heaven. The decisive issue is whether they obey my Father in heaven.

Seek to live a clean and holy life, for those who are not holy will not see the Lord. ✥ Make every effort to apply the benefits of these promises to your life. Then your faith will produce a life of moral excellence. A life of moral excellence leads to knowing God better. Knowing God leads to self-control. Self-control leads to patient endurance, and patient endurance leads to godliness. Godliness leads to love for other Christians, and finally you will grow to have genuine love for everyone. The more you grow like this, the more you will become productive and useful in your knowledge of our Lord Jesus Christ. But those who fail to develop these virtues are blind or, at least, very shortsighted. They have already forgotten that God has cleansed them from their old life of sin. So, dear brothers and sisters, work hard to prove that you really are among those God has called and chosen. Doing this, you will never stumble or fall away.

Salvation is not a reward for the good things we have done, so none of us can boast about it.

Jesus is more concerned about our walk than our talk. He wants us to do right, not just say the right words. You can only withstand the storms of life if you do what is right instead of just talking about it. What you do cannot be separated from what you believe. *LAB note for Matthew 7:21*

(JAMES 2:26) (MATTHEW 7:21) (HEBREWS 12:14)
(2 PETER 1:5-10) (EPHESIANS 2:9)

November 16

Do you . . . believe?

What's the use of saying you have faith if you don't prove it by your actions? That kind of faith can't save anyone. It isn't enough just to have faith. Faith that doesn't show itself by good deeds is no faith at all—it is dead and useless.

It was by faith that Abraham offered Isaac as a sacrifice when God was testing him. Abraham, who had received God's promises, was ready to sacrifice his only son, Isaac, though God had promised him, "Isaac is the son through whom your descendants will be counted." Abraham assumed that if Isaac died, God was able to bring him back to life again. ■ Don't you remember that our ancestor Abraham was declared right with God because of what he did when he offered his son Isaac on the altar? So you see, we are made right with God by what we do, not by faith alone.

The way to identify a tree or a person is by the kind of fruit that is produced. Not all people who sound religious are really godly. They may refer to me as "Lord," but they still won't enter the Kingdom of Heaven. The decisive issue is whether they obey my Father in heaven. ■ You know these things—now do them! That is the path of blessing.

When someone claims to have faith, what he or she may have is intellectual assent—agreement with a set of Christian teachings—and as such it would be incomplete faith. True faith transforms our conduct as well as our thoughts. If our life remains unchanged, we don't truly believe the truths we claim to hold. *LAB note for James 2:14*

(JOHN 16:31) (JAMES 2:14, 17) (HEBREWS 11:17-19) (JAMES 2:21, 24) (MATTHEW 7:20-21) (JOHN 13:17)

November 17

May the Lord of peace himself always give you his peace no matter what happens. The Lord be with you all.

Grace and peace from the one who is, who always was, and who is still to come. ■ You will experience God's peace, which is far more wonderful than the human mind can understand. His peace will guard your hearts and minds as you live in Christ Jesus.

Jesus himself was suddenly standing there among them. He said, "Peace be with you." ■ I am leaving you with a gift—peace of mind and heart. And the peace I give isn't like the peace the world gives. So don't be troubled or afraid.

The Counselor—the Spirit of truth. ■ When the Holy Spirit controls our lives, he will produce this kind of fruit in us: love, joy, peace. ■ His Holy Spirit speaks to us deep in our hearts and tells us that we are God's children.

"I will personally go with you, Moses. I will give you rest—everything will be fine for you." Then Moses said, "If you don't go with us personally, don't let us move a step from this place. If you don't go with us, how will anyone ever know that your people and I have found favor with you?"

God's peace is different from the world's peace. True peace is not found in positive thinking, in absence of conflict, or in good feelings. It comes from knowing that God is in control. Our citizenship in Christ's Kingdom is sure, our destiny is set, and we can have victory over anxiety.

LAB note for Philippians 4:7

(2 Thessalonians 3:16) (Revelation 1:4) (Philippians 4:7) (Luke 24:36) (John 14:27) (John 15:26) (Galatians 5:22) (Romans 8:16) (Exodus 33:14-16)

November 18

We can rejoice, too, when we run into problems and trials, for we know that they are good for us.

If we have hope in Christ only for this life, we are the most miserable people in the world.

Dear friends, don't be surprised at the fiery trials you are going through, as if something strange were happening to you. Instead, be very glad—because these trials will make you partners with Christ in his suffering, and afterward you will have the wonderful joy of sharing his glory when it is displayed to all the world. ▪ Our hearts ache, but we always have joy.

Always be full of joy in the Lord. I say it again—rejoice! ▪ The apostles left the high council rejoicing that God had counted them worthy to suffer dishonor for the name of Jesus.

I pray that God, who gives you hope, will keep you happy and full of peace as you believe in him.

Even though the fig trees have no blossoms, and there are no grapes on the vine; even though the olive crop fails, and the fields lie empty and barren; even though the flocks die in the fields, and the cattle barns are empty, yet I will rejoice in the LORD! I will be joyful in the God of my salvation.

What a difference it makes to know Jesus! He cares for us in spite of what the world thinks. Don't let circumstances or people's expectations control you. Be firm as you stand true to God, and refuse to compromise his standards for living. *LAB note for 2 Corinthians 6:8–10*

(ROMANS 5:3) (1 CORINTHIANS 15:19) (1 PETER 4:12–13) (2 CORINTHIANS 6:10) (PHILIPPIANS 4:4) (ACTS 5:41) (ROMANS 15:13) (HABAKKUK 3:17–18)

*N*ovember 19

My eyes are always looking to the LORD for help.

Is anything too hard for the LORD? ▪ Commit everything you do to the LORD. Trust him, and he will help you. ▪ Don't worry about anything; instead, pray about everything. Tell God what you need, and thank him for all he has done. ▪ Give all your worries and cares to God, for he cares about what happens to you. ▪ Take delight in the LORD, and he will give you your heart's desires.

Moses and Aaron were among his priests; Samuel also called on his name. They cried to the LORD for help, and he answered them. He spoke to them from the pillar of cloud, and they followed the decrees and principles he gave them.

I will answer them before they even call to me. While they are still talking to me about their needs, I will go ahead and answer their prayers! ▪ The earnest prayer of a righteous person has great power and wonderful results.

I love the LORD because he hears and answers my prayers. Because he bends down and listens, I will pray as long as I have breath!

"Is anything too hard for the LORD?" The obvious answer is, "Of course not!" Make it a habit to insert your specific needs into the question. "Is the communication problem I'm having too hard for him?" Asking the question this way reminds you that God is personally involved in your life.

LAB note for Genesis 18:14

(PSALM 25:15) (GENESIS 18:14) (PSALM 37:5) (PHILIPPIANS 4:6) (1 PETER 5:7) (PSALM 37:4) (PSALM 99:6–7) (ISAIAH 65:24) (JAMES 5:16) (PSALM 116:1–2)

November 20

Do people know where to find wisdom?

If you need wisdom—if you want to know what God wants you to do—ask him, and he will gladly tell you. He will not resent your asking. But when you ask him, be sure that you really expect him to answer, for a doubtful mind is as unsettled as a wave of the sea that is driven and tossed by the wind. ▪ Trust in the LORD with all your heart; do not depend on your own understanding. Seek his will in all you do, and he will direct your paths. ▪ He is the eternal King, the unseen one who never dies; he alone is God. ▪ Don't be impressed with your own wisdom.

"O Sovereign LORD," I said, "I can't speak for you! I'm too young!" "Don't say that," the LORD replied, "for you must go wherever I send you and say whatever I tell you. And don't be afraid of the people, for I will be with you and take care of you. I, the LORD, have spoken!"

Go directly to the Father and ask him, and he will grant your request because you use my name. You haven't done this before. Ask, using my name, and you will receive, and you will have abundant joy. ▪ If you believe, you will receive whatever you ask for in prayer.

Wisdom is not only knowledge, but the ability to make wise decisions in difficult circumstances. Whenever we need wisdom, we can pray to God, and he will generously supply what we need to guide our choices.

LAB note for James 1:5

(JOB 28:12) (JAMES 1:5-6) (PROVERBS 3:5-6) (1 TIMOTHY 1:17) (PROVERBS 3:7) (JEREMIAH 1:6-8) (JOHN 16:23-24) (MATTHEW 21:22)

November 21

The suffering you sent was good for me, for it taught me to pay attention to your principles.

Even though Jesus was God's Son, he learned obedience from the things he suffered. ▩ If we are to share his glory, we must also share his suffering. Yet what we suffer now is nothing compared to the glory he will give us later. ▩ Whenever trouble comes your way, let it be an opportunity for joy. For when your faith is tested, your endurance has a chance to grow. So let it grow, for when your endurance is fully developed, you will be strong in character and ready for anything.

He knows where I am going. And when he has tested me like gold in a fire, he will pronounce me innocent. For I have stayed in God's paths; I have followed his ways and not turned aside.

Remember how the LORD your God led you through the wilderness for forty years, humbling you and testing you to prove your character, and to find out whether or not you would really obey his commands. So you should realize that just as a parent disciplines a child, the LORD your God disciplines you to help you. So obey the commands of the LORD your God by walking in his ways and fearing him.

Jesus' human life was not a script that he passively followed. It was a life that he chose freely—and a continuous process of making the will of God the Father his own. Because Jesus obeyed perfectly, even under great trial, he can help us obey, no matter how difficult obedience seems to be.

LAB note for Hebrews 5:8

(PSALM 119:71) (HEBREWS 5:8) (ROMANS 8:17-18) (JAMES 1:2-4) (JOB 23:10-11) (DEUTERONOMY 8:2, 5-6)

November 22

No one will succeed by strength alone.

David shouted in reply, "You come to me with sword, spear, and javelin, but I come to you in the name of the LORD Almighty—the God of the armies of Israel, whom you have defied." Reaching into his shepherd's bag and taking out a stone, he hurled it from his sling and hit the Philistine in the forehead. The stone sank in, and Goliath stumbled and fell face downward to the ground. So David triumphed over the Philistine giant with only a stone and sling.

The best-equipped army cannot save a king, nor is great strength enough to save a warrior. But the LORD watches over those who fear him, those who rely on his unfailing love. ※ Riches and honor come from you alone, for you rule over everything. Power and might are in your hand, and it is at your discretion that people are made great and given strength.

I am glad to boast about my weaknesses, so that the power of Christ may work through me. Since I know it is all for Christ's good, I am quite content with my weaknesses and with insults, hardships, persecutions, and calamities. For when I am weak, then I am strong.

We should be confident of God's ultimate control over the events in our lives, and we should be thankful for the ways God has blessed us. By praising God for all good gifts, we acknowledge his ultimate control over all the affairs of life. *LAB note for 1 Samuel 2:1-10*

(1 SAMUEL 2:9) (1 SAMUEL 17:45, 49-50) (PSALM 33:16, 18)
(1 CHRONICLES 29:12) (2 CORINTHIANS 12:9-10)

November 23

Though the spirit is willing enough, the body is weak!

LORD, we love to obey your laws; our heart's desire is to glorify your name. All night long I search for you; earnestly I seek for God.

I know I am rotten through and through so far as my old sinful nature is concerned. No matter which way I turn, I can't make myself do right. I want to, but I can't. I love God's law with all my heart. But there is another law at work within me that is at war with my mind. This law wins the fight and makes me a slave to the sin that is still within me. ▪ The old sinful nature loves to do evil, which is just opposite from what the Holy Spirit wants. And the Spirit gives us desires that are opposite from what the sinful nature desires. These two forces are constantly fighting each other, and your choices are never free from the conflict.

I can do everything with the help of Christ who gives me the strength I need. ▪ Our only power and success come from God. ▪ My gracious favor is all you need.

We must never use the power of sin or Satan as an excuse, because they are defeated enemies. But without Christ's help, sin is stronger than we are. That is why we should never stand up to it all alone. Jesus Christ, who has conquered sin once and for all, promises to fight by our side.

LAB note for Romans 7:17-20

(MATTHEW 26:41) (ISAIAH 26:8-9) (ROMANS 7:18, 22-23) (GALATIANS 5:17) (PHILIPPIANS 4:13) (2 CORINTHIANS 3:5) (2 CORINTHIANS 12:9)

November 24

God made Christ, who never sinned, to be the offering for our sin, so that we could be made right with God through Christ.

The LORD laid on him the guilt and sins of us all. ▪ He personally carried away our sins in his own body on the cross so we can be dead to sin and live for what is right. You have been healed by his wounds! ▪ Because one person disobeyed God, many people became sinners. But because one other person obeyed God, many people will be made right in God's sight.

God our Savior showed us his kindness and love. He saved us, not because of the good things we did, but because of his mercy. He washed away our sins and gave us a new life through the Holy Spirit. He generously poured out the Spirit upon us because of what Jesus Christ our Savior did. He declared us not guilty because of his great kindness. And now we know that we will inherit eternal life. ▪ So now there is no condemnation for those who belong to Christ Jesus.

The LORD Is Our Righteousness.

When we trust in Christ, we make an exchange: He takes our sin and makes us right with God. In the world, bartering works only when two people exchange goods of relatively equal value. But God offers to trade his righteousness for our sin—something of immeasurable worth for something completely worthless. *LAB note for 2 Corinthians 5:21*

(2 CORINTHIANS 5:21) (ISAIAH 53:6) (1 PETER 2:24) (ROMANS 5:19) (TITUS 3:4-7) (ROMANS 8:1) (JEREMIAH 23:6)

*N*ovember 25

The dust will return to the earth.

Our earthly bodies, which die and decay . . . now disappoint us. . . . They are weak . . . natural human bodies. ▪ Adam, the first man, was made from the dust of the earth.

You were made from dust, and to the dust you will return. ▪ One person dies in prosperity and security, the very picture of good health. Another person dies in bitter poverty, never having tasted the good life. Both alike are buried in the same dust, both eaten by the same worms.

No wonder my heart is filled with joy, and my mouth shouts his praises! My body rests in safety. ▪ After my body has decayed, yet in my body I will see God! ▪ The Lord Jesus Christ . . . will take these weak mortal bodies of ours and change them into glorious bodies like his own, using the same mighty power that he will use to conquer everything, everywhere.

LORD, remind me how brief my time on earth will be. Remind me that my days are numbered, and that my life is fleeing away. ▪ Teach us to make the most of our time, so that we may grow in wisdom.

Stripped of the life-giving spirit breathed into us by God, our bodies return to dust. Stripped of God's purpose, our work is in vain. Stripped of God's love, our service is futile. We must put God first over all we do and in all we do because without him we have nothing.

LAB note for Ecclesiastes 12:7–8

(ECCLESIASTES 12:7) (1 CORINTHIANS 15:42–44) (1 CORINTHIANS 15:47) (GENESIS 3:19) (JOB 21:23–26) (PSALM 16:9) (JOB 19:26) (PHILIPPIANS 3:20–21) (PSALM 39:4) (PSALM 90:12)

November 26

The LORD is more pleased when we do what is just and right than when we give him sacrifices.

The LORD has told you what is good, and this is what he requires: to do what is right, to love mercy, and to walk humbly with your God. ■ What is more pleasing to the LORD; your burnt offerings and sacrifices or your obedience to his voice? Obedience is far better than sacrifice. Listening to him is much better than offering the fat of rams. ■ I know it is important to love him with all my heart and all my understanding and all my strength, and to love my neighbor as myself. This is more important than to offer all of the burnt offerings and sacrifices required in the law.

Come back to your God! Act on the principles of love and justice, and always live in confident dependence on your God. ■ Mary . . . sat at the Lord's feet, listening to what he taught. "There is really only one thing worth being concerned about. Mary has discovered it—and I won't take it away from her."

God is working in you, giving you the desire to obey him and the power to do what pleases him. ■ May he produce in you, through the power of Jesus Christ, all that is pleasing to him. . . . To him be glory forever and ever. Amen.

Sacrifices are not bribes to make God overlook our character faults. If our personal and business dealings are not characterized by justice, no amount of generosity when the offering plate is passed will make up for it. *LAB note for Proverbs 21:3*

(PROVERBS 21:3) (MICAH 6:8) (1 SAMUEL 15:22) (MARK 12:33) (HOSEA 12:6) (LUKE 10:39, 42) (PHILIPPIANS 2:13) (HEBREWS 13:21)

November 27

The spirit will return to God who gave it.

The LORD God formed a man's body from the dust of the ground and breathed into it the breath of life. And the man became a living person. ▪ It is God's Spirit within people, the breath of the Almighty within them, that makes them intelligent. But sometimes the elders are not wise. Sometimes the aged do not understand justice.

We are always confident, even though we know that as long as we live in these bodies we are not at home with the Lord. ▪ I long to go and be with Christ. That would be far better for me. ▪ And now, brothers and sisters, I want you to know what will happen to the Christians who have died so you will not be full of sorrow like people who have no hope. For since we believe that Jesus died and was raised to life again, we also believe that when Jesus comes, God will bring back with Jesus all the Christians who have died.

There are many rooms in my Father's home, and I am going to prepare a place for you. If this were not so, I would tell you plainly. When everything is ready, I will come and get you, so that you will always be with me where I am.

It is not enough to recognize a great truth; it must be lived out each day. Elihu [Job's "friend"] recognized the truth that God was the only source of real wisdom, but he did not use God's wisdom to help Job. Becoming wise is an ongoing, lifelong pursuit. Don't be content just to know about wisdom; make it part of your life. *LAB note for Job 32:7-9*

(ECCLESIASTES 12:7) (GENESIS 2:7) (JOB 32:8-9) (2 CORINTHIANS 5:6) (PHILIPPIANS 1:23) (1 THESSALONIANS 4:13-14) (JOHN 14:2-3)

November 28

No one can take them from me.

I know the one in whom I trust, and I am sure that he is able to guard what I have entrusted to him until the day of his return. ▪ The Lord will deliver me from every evil attack and will bring me safely to his heavenly Kingdom. ▪ Overwhelming victory is ours through Christ, who loved us. And I am convinced that nothing can ever separate us from his love. Death can't, and life can't. The angels can't, and the demons can't. Our fears for today, our worries about tomorrow, and even the powers of hell can't keep God's love away. Whether we are high above the sky or in the deepest ocean, nothing in all creation will ever be able to separate us from the love of God that is revealed in Christ Jesus our Lord. ▪ Your real life is hidden with Christ in God.

Hasn't God chosen the poor in this world to be rich in faith? Aren't they the ones who will inherit the kingdom God promised to those who love him?

May our Lord Jesus Christ and God our Father, who loved us and in his special favor gave us everlasting comfort and hope, comfort your hearts and give you strength in every good thing you do and say.

Paul was in prison, but that did not stop his ministry. He trusted God to use him regardless of his circumstances. If your situation looks bleak, give your concerns to Christ. He will guard your faith and safely keep all you have entrusted to him until the day of his return.

LAB note for 2 Timothy 1:12

(John 10:29) (2 Timothy 1:12) (2 Timothy 4:18) (Romans 8:37-39) (Colossians 3:3) (James 2:5) (2 Thessalonians 2:16-17)

November 29

You will not be condemned for doing something you know is all right.

Keep away from every kind of evil. ▪ We are careful to be honorable before the Lord, but we also want everyone else to know we are honorable. ▪ It is God's will that your good lives should silence those who make foolish accusations against you.

If you suffer, however, it must not be for murder, stealing, making trouble, or prying into other people's affairs. But it is no shame to suffer for being a Christian. Praise God for the privilege of being called by his wonderful name!

For you have been called to live in freedom—not freedom to satisfy your sinful nature, but freedom to serve one another in love. ▪ The Kingdom of God is not a matter of what we eat or drink, but of living a life of goodness and peace and joy in the Holy Spirit. ▪ You must be careful with this freedom of yours. Do not cause a brother or sister with a weaker conscience to stumble. ▪ If anyone causes one of these little ones who trusts in me to lose faith, it would be better for that person to be thrown into the sea with a large millstone tied around the neck. ▪ When you refused to help the least of these my brothers and sisters, you were refusing to help me.

As Christians, we cannot avoid every kind of evil because we live in a sinful world. We can, however, make sure that we don't give evil a foothold by avoiding tempting situations and concentrating on obeying God.

LAB note for 1 Thessalonians 5:22–24

(ROMANS 14:16) (1 THESSALONIANS 5:22) (2 CORINTHIANS 8:21) (1 PETER 2:15) (1 PETER 4:15–16) (GALATIANS 5:13) (ROMANS 14:17) (1 CORINTHIANS 8:9) (MATTHEW 18:6) (MATTHEW 25:45)

November 30

Awake, O sleeper, rise up from the dead, and Christ will give you light.

Wake up, for the coming of our salvation is nearer now than when we first believed. ▪ So be on your guard, not asleep like the others. Stay alert and be sober. Night is the time for sleep and the time when people get drunk. But let us who live in the light think clearly, protected by the body armor of faith and love, and wearing as our helmet the confidence of our salvation.

Let your light shine for all the nations to see! For the glory of the LORD is shining upon you. Darkness as black as night will cover all the nations of the earth, but the glory of the LORD will shine over you.

Think clearly and exercise self-control. Look forward to the special blessings that will come to you at the return of Jesus Christ. ▪ Be dressed for service and well prepared, as though you were waiting for your master to return from the wedding feast. Then you will be ready to open the door and let him in the moment he arrives and knocks. ▪ If you do these things, your salvation will come like the dawn. Yes, your healing will come quickly. Your godliness will lead you forward, and the glory of the LORD will protect you from behind.

The imminent return of Christ should motivate us to live for him. This means being mentally alert ("think clearly"), disciplined ("exercise self-control"), and focused ("look forward"). Are you ready to meet Christ?

LAB note for 1 Peter 1:13

(EPHESIANS 5:14) (ROMANS 13:11) (1 THESSALONIANS 5:6-8) (ISAIAH 60:1-2) (1 PETER 1:13) (LUKE 12:35-36) (ISAIAH 58:8)

December

The Giver of Life

Creator and Provider

Comforter and Friend

Eternal, infinite, awesome God

In this special season of giving, take a minute to reflect on God's generosity to you. He truly is the giver of all good things. How is your life changed by God's greatest gift on that first Christmas?

December 1

His royal titles: Wonderful Counselor, Mighty God.

The Word became human and lived here on earth among us. He was full of unfailing love and faithfulness. And we have seen his glory, the glory of the only Son of the Father. ▪ Your promises are backed by all the honor of your name.

He will be called Immanuel (meaning, God is with us). ▪ Jesus, for he will save his people from their sins.

Everyone will honor the Son, just as they honor the Father. ▪ God raised him up to the heights of heaven and gave him a name that is above every other name. ▪ He is far above any ruler or authority or power or leader or anything else in this world or in the world to come. And God has put all things under the authority of Christ. ▪ A name was written on him, and only he knew what it meant . . . King of kings and Lord of lords.

We cannot imagine the power of the Almighty. ▪ What is his name—and his son's name? Tell me if you know!

In a time of great darkness, God promised to send a light who would shine on everyone living in the shadow of death. He is both "Wonderful Counselor" and "Mighty God." This message of hope was fulfilled in the birth of Christ and the establishment of his eternal Kingdom.

LAB note for Isaiah 9:2-6

(Isaiah 9:6) (John 1:14) (Psalm 138:2) (Matthew 1:23) (Matthew 1:21) (John 5:23) (Philippians 2:9) (Ephesians 1:21-22) (Revelation 19:12, 16) (Job 37:23) (Proverbs 30:4)

December 2

You judge all people according to what they have done.

No one can lay any other foundation than the one we already have—Jesus Christ. If the work survives the fire, that builder will receive a reward. But if the work is burned up, the builder will suffer great loss. The builders themselves will be saved, but like someone escaping through a wall of flames. ▩ For we must all stand before Christ to be judged. We will each receive whatever we deserve for the good or evil we have done in our bodies.

When you give to someone, don't tell your left hand what your right hand is doing. Give your gifts in secret, and your Father, who knows all secrets, will reward you. ▩ There will be glory and honor and peace from God for all who do good.

It is not that we think we can do anything of lasting value by ourselves. Our only power and success come from God. ▩ LORD, you will grant us peace, for all we have accomplished is really from you.

It is tempting to use honor, power, wealth, or prestige to measure people. We may even think that such people are really getting ahead in life. But God weighs us by different scales. Only the faithful work we do for him has eternal value. *LAB note for Psalm 62:9-12*

(PSALM 62:12) (1 CORINTHIANS 3:11, 14-15) (2 CORINTHIANS 5:10) (MATTHEW 6:3-4) (ROMANS 2:10) (2 CORINTHIANS 3:5) (ISAIAH 26:12)

December 3

Make every effort to live a pure and blameless life. And be at peace with God.

Now you are no longer a slave but God's own child. And since you are his child, everything he has belongs to you.

You should consider yourselves dead to sin and able to live for the glory of God through Christ Jesus. Do not let sin control the way you live; do not give in to its lustful desires. Do not let any part of your body become a tool of wickedness, to be used for sinning. Instead, give yourselves completely to God since you have been given new life. And use your whole body as a tool to do what is right for the glory of God. ■ Obey God because you are his children. Don't slip back into your old ways of doing evil; you didn't know any better then. But now you must be holy in everything you do, just as God—who chose you to be his children—is holy. ■ If you keep yourself pure, you will be a utensil God can use for his purpose. Your life will be clean, and you will be ready for the Master to use you for every good work.

So, my dear brothers and sisters, be strong and steady, always enthusiastic about the Lord's work, for you know that nothing you do for the Lord is ever useless.

We should not become lazy and complacent because Christ has not yet returned. Instead, we should live in eager expectation of his coming. What would you like to be doing when Christ returns? That is how you should be living each day. *LAB note for 2 Peter 3:14*

(2 PETER 3:14) (GALATIANS 4:7) (ROMANS 6:11-13) (1 PETER 1:14-15) (2 TIMOTHY 2:21) (1 CORINTHIANS 15:58)

December 4

God's deep secrets.

I no longer call you servants, because a master doesn't confide in his servants. Now you are my friends, since I have told you everything the Father told me.

And God has actually given us his Spirit (not the world's spirit) so we can know the wonderful things God has freely given us.

When I think of the wisdom and scope of God's plan, I fall to my knees and pray to the Father, the Creator of everything in heaven and on earth. I pray that from his glorious, unlimited resources he will give you mighty inner strength through his Holy Spirit. And I pray that Christ will be more and more at home in your hearts as you trust in him. May your roots go down deep into the soil of God's marvelous love. And may you have the power to understand, as all God's people should, how wide, how long, how high, and how deep his love really is. May you experience the love of Christ, though it is so great you will never fully understand it. Then you will be filled with the fullness of life and power that comes from God.

"God's deep secrets" refers to God's unfathomable nature and his wonderful plan—Jesus' death and resurrection—and to the promise of salvation, revealed only to those who believe that what God says is true. Those who believe in Christ's death and resurrection and put their faith in him will know all they need to know to be saved. *LAB note for 1 Corinthians 2:10*

(1 Corinthians 2:10) (John 15:15) (1 Corinthians 2:12) (Ephesians 3:14-19)

December 5

Revive us so we can call on your name once more.

It is the Spirit who gives eternal life. ▪ And the Holy Spirit helps us in our distress. For we don't even know what we should pray for, nor how we should pray. But the Holy Spirit prays for us with groanings that cannot be expressed in words. And the Father who knows all hearts knows what the Spirit is saying, for the Spirit pleads for us believers in harmony with God's own will. ▪ Pray at all times and on every occasion in the power of the Holy Spirit. Stay alert and be persistent in your prayers for all Christians everywhere.

I will never forget your commandments, for you have used them to restore my joy and health. ▪ The old way ends in death; in the new way, the Holy Spirit gives life. ▪ If you stay joined to me and my words remain in you, you may ask any request you like, and it will be granted! ▪ We can be confident that he will listen to us whenever we ask him for anything in line with his will.

How can anyone pray at all times? One way is to make quick, brief prayers your habitual response to every situation you meet throughout the day. Another way is to order your life around God's desires and teachings so that your very life becomes a prayer. *LAB note for Ephesians 6:18*

(PSALM 80:18) (JOHN 6:63) (ROMANS 8:26-27) (EPHESIANS 6:18)
(PSALM 119:93) (2 CORINTHIANS 3:6) (JOHN 15:7) (1 JOHN 5:14)

December 6

Let us come boldly to the throne of our gracious God. There we will receive his mercy, and we will find grace to help us when we need it.

Don't worry about anything; instead, pray about everything. Tell God what you need, and thank him for all he has done. If you do this, you will experience God's peace, which is far more wonderful than the human mind can understand. His peace will guard your hearts and minds as you live in Christ Jesus. ■ So you should not be like cowering, fearful slaves. You should behave instead like God's very own children, adopted into his family—calling him "Father, dear Father."

Yes, ask anything in my name, and I will do it! ■ So, dear brothers and sisters, we can boldly enter heaven's Most Holy Place because of the blood of Jesus. Let us go right into the presence of God, with true hearts fully trusting him. For our evil consciences have been sprinkled with Christ's blood to make us clean, and our bodies have been washed with pure water. ■ "The Lord is my helper, so I will not be afraid. What can mere mortals do to me?"

Prayer is our approach to God, and we are to come "boldly." Some Christians approach God meekly with heads hung low, afraid to ask him to meet their needs. Others pray flippantly, giving little thought to what they say. Come with reverence because he is your King. But also come with bold assurance because he is your Friend and Counselor.

LAB note for Hebrews 4:16

(Hebrews 4:16) (Philippians 4:6–7) (Romans 8:15) (John 14:14) (Hebrews 10:19, 22) (Hebrews 13:6)

December 7

When darkness overtakes the godly, light will come bursting in.

Who among you fears the LORD and obeys his servant? If you are walking in darkness, without a ray of light, trust in the LORD and rely on your God. ▪ Though they stumble, they will not fall, for the LORD holds them by the hand. ▪ These commands and this teaching are a lamp to light the way ahead of you. The correction of discipline is the way to life.

Do not gloat over me, my enemies! For though I fall, I will rise again. Though I sit in darkness, the LORD himself will be my light. I will be patient as the LORD punishes me, for I have sinned against him. But after that, he will take up my case and punish my enemies for all the evil they have done to me. The LORD will bring me out of my darkness into the light, and I will see his righteousness.

A pure eye lets sunshine into your soul. But an evil eye shuts out the light and plunges you into darkness. If the light you think you have is really darkness, how deep that darkness will be!

If we walk by our own light and reject God's, we become self-sufficient, and the result of self-sufficiency is torment. When we place confidence in our own intelligence, appearance, or accomplishments instead of in God, we risk torment later when these strengths fade.

LAB note for Isaiah 50:10-11

(PSALM 112:4) (ISAIAH 50:10) (PSALM 37:24) (PROVERBS 6:23) (MICAH 7:8-9) (MATTHEW 6:22-23)

December 8

That couldn't happen even if the LORD opened the windows of heaven!

Have faith in God. ▪ It is impossible to please God without faith. ▪ With God everything is possible.

Was I too weak to save you? Is that why the house is silent and empty when I come home? Is it because I have no power to rescue?

"My thoughts are completely different from yours," says the LORD. "And my ways are far beyond anything you could imagine. For just as the heavens are higher than the earth, so are my ways higher than your ways and my thoughts higher than your thoughts." ▪ I will open the windows of heaven for you. I will pour out a blessing so great you won't have enough room to take it in!

The LORD is not too weak to save you, and he is not becoming deaf. He can hear you when you call. ▪ O LORD, no one but you can help the powerless against the mighty! Help us, O LORD our God, for we trust in you alone. It is in your name that we have come against this vast horde. O LORD, you are our God; do not let mere men prevail against you.

We expected to die. But as a result, we learned not to rely on ourselves, but on God who can raise the dead.

Sometimes we become preoccupied with problems when we should be looking for opportunities. Instead of focusing on the negatives, develop an attitude of expectancy. To say that God cannot rescue someone or that a situation is impossible demonstrates a lack of faith.

LAB note for 2 Kings 7:2

(2 KINGS 7:2) (MARK 11:22) (HEBREWS 11:6) (MATTHEW 19:26) (ISAIAH 50:2) (ISAIAH 55:8-9) (MALACHI 3:10) (ISAIAH 59:1) (2 CHRONICLES 14:11) (2 CORINTHIANS 1:9)

December 9

Your days of mourning will come to an end.

Here on earth you will have many trials and sorrows. ▪ For we know that all creation has been groaning as in the pains of childbirth right up to the present time. And even we Christians, although we have the Holy Spirit within us as a foretaste of future glory, also groan to be released from pain and suffering. We, too, wait anxiously for that day when God will give us our full rights as his children, including the new bodies he has promised us. ▪ Our dying bodies make us groan and sigh.

These are the ones coming out of the great tribulation. They washed their robes in the blood of the Lamb and made them white. That is why they are standing in front of the throne of God, serving him day and night in his Temple. And he who sits on the throne will live among them and shelter them. They will never again be hungry or thirsty, and they will be fully protected from the scorching noontime heat. For the Lamb who stands in front of the throne will be their Shepherd. He will lead them to the springs of life-giving water. And God will wipe away all their tears.

As Christians we should expect continuing tension with an unbelieving world that is "out of sync" with Christ, his Good News, and his people. At the same time we can expect our relationship with Christ to produce peace and comfort because we are "in sync" with him.

LAB note for John 16:31–33

(Isaiah 60:20) (John 16:33) (Romans 8:22–23) (2 Corinthians 5:4) (Revelation 7:14–17)

December 10

Teacher, don't you even care that we are going to drown?

The LORD is good to everyone. He showers compassion on all his creation.

All the wild animals, large and small, and all the birds and fish will be afraid of you. I have placed them in your power. I have given them to you for food, just as I have given you grain and vegetables. ▪ As long as the earth remains, there will be springtime and harvest, cold and heat, winter and summer, day and night.

The LORD is good. When trouble comes, he is a strong refuge. And he knows everyone who trusts in him. ▪ Then God heard the boy's cries, and the angel of God called to Hagar from the sky, "Hagar, what's wrong? Do not be afraid! God has heard the boy's cries from the place where you laid him." Then God opened Hagar's eyes, and she saw a well. She immediately filled her water container and gave the boy a drink.

Don't worry about having enough food or drink or clothing. Why be like the pagans who are so deeply concerned about these things? Your heavenly Father already knows all your needs. ▪ Trust . . . in the living God, who richly gives us all we need for our enjoyment.

Think about the storms in your life—the situations that cause you great anxiety. Whatever your difficulty, you have two options: You can worry and assume that Jesus no longer cares, or you can resist fear, putting your trust in him. When you feel like panicking, confess your need for God and then trust him to care for you. *LAB note for Mark 4:38-40*

(MARK 4:38) (PSALM 145:9) (GENESIS 9:2-3) (GENESIS 8:22) (NAHUM 1:7) (GENESIS 21:17, 19) (MATTHEW 6:31-32) (1 TIMOTHY 6:17)

December 11

Your faithful work.

This is what God wants you to do: Believe in the one he has sent.

Faith that doesn't show itself by good deeds is no faith at all—it is dead and useless. ▩What is important is faith expressing itself in love. ▩ Those who live only to satisfy their own sinful desires will harvest the consequences of decay and death. But those who live to please the Spirit will harvest everlasting life from the Spirit. ▩ We are God's masterpiece. He has created us anew in Christ Jesus, so that we can do the good things he planned for us long ago. ▩ He gave his life to free us from every kind of sin, to cleanse us, and to make us his very own people, totally committed to doing what is right.

We keep on praying for you, that our God will make you worthy of the life to which he called you. And we pray that God, by his power, will fulfill all your good intentions and faithful deeds. ▩ God is working in you, giving you the desire to obey him and the power to do what pleases him.

The Thessalonians had stood firm when they were persecuted. Paul commended these young Christians for their faithful work, loving deeds, and anticipation of the Lord's return. These characteristics are the marks of effective Christians in any age. *LAB note for 1 Thessalonians 1:3*

(1 THESSALONIANS 1:3) (JOHN 6:29) (JAMES 2:17) (GALATIANS 5:6) (GALATIANS 6:8) (EPHESIANS 2:10) (TITUS 2:14) (2 THESSALONIANS 1:11) (PHILIPPIANS 2:13)

December 12

This is what God has testified: He has given us eternal life, and this life is in his Son.

The Father has life in himself, and he has granted his Son to have life in himself. He will even raise from the dead anyone he wants to, just as the Father does.

I am the resurrection and the life. Those who believe in me, even though they die like everyone else, will live again. They are given eternal life for believing in me and will never perish. ▪ I am the good shepherd. The good shepherd lays down his life for the sheep. The Father loves me because I lay down my life that I may have it back again. No one can take my life from me. I lay down my life voluntarily. For I have the right to lay it down when I want to and also the power to take it again. For the Father has given me this command. ▪ I am the way, the truth, and the life. No one can come to the Father except through me. ▪ So whoever has God's Son has life; whoever does not have his Son does not have life. ▪ For you died when Christ died, and your real life is hidden with Christ in God. And when Christ, who is your real life, is revealed to the whole world, you will share in all his glory.

Jesus has power over life and death as well as power to forgive sins. This is because he is the Creator of life. He who is life can surely restore life. When we realize his power and how wonderful his offer to us really is, how can we not commit our lives to him? *LAB note for John 11:25-26*

(1 JOHN 5:11) (JOHN 5:26, 21) (JOHN 11:25-26) (JOHN 10:11, 17-18) (JOHN 14:6) (1 JOHN 5:12) (COLOSSIANS 3:3-4)

December 13

Then the LORD did exactly what he had promised. Sarah became pregnant, and she gave a son to Abraham in his old age.

Trust in him at all times. Pour out your heart to him, for God is our refuge. ▪ David found strength in the LORD his God. ▪ God will surely come for you, to lead you out of this land of Egypt. He will bring you back to the land he vowed to give to the descendants of Abraham, Isaac, and Jacob. ▪ I have seen the misery of my people in Egypt. I have heard their cries. So I have come to rescue them. Now go, for I will send you to Egypt. And by means of many miraculous signs and wonders, he led them out of Egypt, through the Red Sea, and back and forth through the wilderness for forty years. ▪ All of the good promises that the LORD had given Israel came true.

God can be trusted to keep his promise. ▪ God is not a man, that he should lie. He is not a human, that he should change his mind. Has he ever spoken and failed to act? Has he ever promised and not carried it through? ▪ God also bound himself with an oath, so that those who received the promise could be perfectly sure that he would never change his mind. ▪ Heaven and earth will disappear, but my words will remain forever. ▪ The grass withers, and the flowers fade, but the word of our God stands forever.

Who could believe that Abraham would have a son at one hundred years of age—and live to raise him to adulthood? But doing the impossible is everyday business for God. Our big problems won't seem so impossible if we let God handle them. *LAB note for Genesis 21:1-7*

(GENESIS 21:1-2) (PSALM 62:8) (1 SAMUEL 30:6) (GENESIS 50:24) (ACTS 7:34, 36) (JOSHUA 21:45) (HEBREWS 10:23) (NUMBERS 23:19) (HEBREWS 6:17) (MATTHEW 24:35) (ISAIAH 40:8)

December 14

He will save his people from their sins.

You know that Jesus came to take away our sins, for there is no sin in him. ▪ He personally carried away our sins in his own body on the cross so we can be dead to sin and live for what is right. ▪ He is able, once and forever, to save everyone who comes to God through him.

He was wounded and crushed for our sins. He was beaten that we might have peace. He was whipped, and we were healed! All of us have strayed away like sheep. We have left God's paths to follow our own. Yet the LORD laid on him the guilt and sins of us all. He was oppressed and treated harshly, yet he never said a word. He was led as a lamb to the slaughter. And as a sheep is silent before the shearers, he did not open his mouth. From prison and trial they led him away to his death. ▪ It was written long ago that the Messiah must suffer and die and rise again from the dead on the third day. . . . Take this message of repentance to all the nations, beginning in Jerusalem: "There is forgiveness of sins for all who turn to me." ▪ He came . . . to remove the power of sin forever by his sacrificial death for us.

Then God put him in the place of honor at his right hand as Prince and Savior. ▪ In this man Jesus there is forgiveness of your sins. Everyone who believes in him is freed from all guilt and declared right with God—something the Jewish law could never do. ▪ Your sins have been forgiven because of Jesus.

Jesus came to earth to save us because we can't save ourselves from sin and its consequences. No matter how good we are, we can't eliminate the sinful nature present in all of us. Only Jesus can do that. Thank Christ for his death on the cross for your sin, and then ask him to take control of your life. *LAB note for Matthew 1:21*

(MATTHEW 1:21) (1 JOHN 3:5) (1 PETER 2:24) (HEBREWS 7:25) (ISAIAH 53:5-8) (LUKE 24:46-47) (HEBREWS 9:26) (ACTS 5:31) (ACTS 13:38-39) (1 JOHN 2:12)

December 15

The Philistine commanders demanded, "What are these Hebrews doing here?"

Be happy if you are insulted for being a Christian, for then the glorious Spirit of God will come upon you.

You will not be condemned for doing something you know is all right. ▧ Be careful how you live among your unbelieving neighbors. Even if they accuse you of doing wrong, they will see your honorable behavior, and they will believe and give honor to God when he comes to judge the world.

Don't team up with those who are unbelievers. How can goodness be a partner with wickedness? How can light live with darkness? And what union can there be between God's temple and idols? For we are the temple of the living God. As God said: "I will live in them and walk among them. I will be their God, and they will be my people."

You are a chosen people . . . so you can show others the goodness of God, for he called you out of the darkness into his wonderful light.

Christ will send his Spirit to strengthen those who are persecuted for their faith, but not all suffering is the result of good Christian conduct. It may take careful thought or wise counsel to determine the real cause of our suffering. We can be assured, however, that whenever we suffer because of our loyalty to Christ, he will be with us all the way.

LAB note for 1 Peter 4:16

(1 SAMUEL 29:3) (1 PETER 4:14) (ROMANS 14:16) (1 PETER 2:12) (2 CORINTHIANS 6:14, 16) (1 PETER 2:9)

December 16

He calls his own sheep by name and leads them out.

God's truth stands firm like a foundation stone with this inscription: "The Lord knows those who are his." ▩ On judgment day many will tell me, "Lord, Lord, we prophesied in your name and cast out demons in your name and performed many miracles in your name." But I will reply, "I never knew you. Go away; the things you did were unauthorized." ▩ For the LORD watches over the path of the godly, but the path of the wicked leads to destruction.

I have written your name on my hand. ▩ Place me like a seal over your heart, or like a seal on your arm. For love is as strong as death, and its jealousy is as enduring as the grave. ▩ The LORD is good. When trouble comes, he is a strong refuge. And he knows everyone who trusts in him.

There are many rooms in my Father's home, and I am going to prepare a place for you. If this were not so, I would tell you plainly. When everything is ready, I will come and get you, so that you will always be with me where I am.

Jesus exposed those who sounded religious but had no personal relationship with him. Many people think that if they are "good" people and say religious things they will be rewarded with eternal life. In reality, faith in Christ is what will count at the judgment.

LAB note for Matthew 7:21–23

(JOHN 10:3) (2 TIMOTHY 2:19) (MATTHEW 7:22–23) (PSALM 1:6) (ISAIAH 49:16) (SONG OF SONGS 8:6) (NAHUM 1:7) (JOHN 14:2–3)

December 17

He will keep you free from all blame on the great day when our Lord Jesus Christ returns.

You who were once so far away from God . . . were his enemies, separated from him by your evil thoughts and actions, yet now he has brought you back as his friends. He has done this through his death on the cross in his own human body. As a result, he has brought you into the very presence of God, and you are holy and blameless as you stand in it firmly. Don't drift away from the assurance you received when you heard the Good News. ❖ Live clean, innocent lives as children of God in a dark world full of crooked and perverse people. Let your lives shine brightly before them.

And now, all glory to God, who is able to keep you from stumbling, and who will bring you into his glorious presence innocent of sin and with great joy. All glory to him, who alone is God our Savior, through Jesus Christ our Lord. Yes, glory, majesty, power, and authority belong to him, in the beginning, now, and forevermore. Amen.

The guarantee to be "free from all blame" is not because of our great gifts or our shining performance but because of what Jesus Christ accomplished for us through his death and resurrection. All who have received the Lord Jesus as their Savior will be considered blameless when he returns.

LAB note for 1 Corinthians 1:7-9

(1 CORINTHIANS 1:8) (COLOSSIANS 1:21-23) (PHILIPPIANS 2:15) (JUDE 1:24-25)

December 18

He will protect his godly ones.

We are lying if we say we have fellowship with God but go on living in spiritual darkness. We are not living in the truth. But if we are living in the light of God's presence, just as Christ is, then we have fellowship with each other, and the blood of Jesus, his Son, cleanses us from every sin. ❖ Let us strip off every weight that slows us down, especially the sin that so easily hinders our progress.

I will teach you wisdom's ways and lead you in straight paths. If you live a life guided by wisdom, you won't limp or stumble as you run. Do not do as the wicked do, or follow the path of evildoers. Avoid their haunts. Turn away and go somewhere else. Look straight ahead, and fix your eyes on what lies before you. Mark out a straight path for your feet; then stick to the path and stay safe. Don't get sidetracked; keep your feet from following evil.

The Lord will deliver me from every evil attack and will bring me safely to his heavenly Kingdom. To God be the glory forever and ever. Amen.

How does Jesus' blood cleanse us from every sin? Jesus died for the sins of the world. When we commit our life to Christ and thus identify ourselves with him, his death becomes ours. He has paid the penalty for our sins, and his blood has purified us. *LAB note for 1 John 1:7*

(1 SAMUEL 2:9) (1 JOHN 1:6-7) (HEBREWS 12:1)
(PROVERBS 4:11-12, 14-15, 25-27) (2 TIMOTHY 4:18)

December 19

Try to understand what the Lord wants you to do.

God wants you to be holy. ▪ Stop quarreling with God! If you agree with him, you will have peace at last, and things will go well with you. ▪ This is the way to have eternal life—to know you, the only true God, and Jesus Christ, the one you sent to earth. ▪ We know that the Son of God has come, and he has given us understanding so that we can know the true God. And now we are in God because we are in his Son, Jesus Christ. He is the only true God, and he is eternal life.

We have continued praying for you ever since we first heard about you. We ask God to give you a complete understanding of what he wants to do in your lives, and we ask him to make you wise with spiritual wisdom. ▪ God, the glorious Father of our Lord Jesus Christ, . . . give you spiritual wisdom and understanding, so that you might grow in your knowledge of God. I pray that your hearts will be flooded with light so that you can understand the wonderful future he has promised to those he called. I want you to realize what a rich and glorious inheritance he has given to his people. I pray that you will begin to understand the incredible greatness of his power for us who believe him.

Being made holy is the process of living the Christian life. The Holy Spirit works in us, conforming us to the image of Christ. Do you seek for holiness in your daily life, with the Holy Spirit's help?

LAB note for 1 Thessalonians 4:3

(Ephesians 5:17) (1 Thessalonians 4:3) (Job 22:21) (John 17:3) (1 John 5:20) (Colossians 1:9) (Ephesians 1:17-19)

December 20

Be strong with the special favor God gives you in Christ Jesus.

You will be strengthened by his glorious power so that you will have all the patience and endurance you need. May you be filled with joy. ▪ Just as you accepted Christ as your Lord, you must continue to live in obedience to him. Let your roots grow down into him and draw up nourishment from him, so you will grow in faith, strong and vigorous in the truth you were taught. Let your lives overflow with thanksgiving for all he has done. ▪ The LORD has planted them like strong and graceful oaks for his own glory. ▪ We are his house, built on the foundation of the apostles and the prophets. And the cornerstone is Christ Jesus himself.

And now I entrust you to God and the word of his grace—his message that is able to build you up and give you an inheritance with all those he has set apart for himself. ▪ May you always be filled with the fruit of your salvation—those good things that are produced in your life by Jesus Christ—for this will bring much glory and praise to God.

Fight the good fight for what we believe. ▪ Don't be intimidated by your enemies.

Just as we are saved by God's special, undeserved favor, we should live by it. This means trusting completely in Christ and his power and not trying to live for Christ in our strength alone. Receive and utilize Christ's power. He will give you the strength to do his work. *LAB note for 2 Timothy 2:1*

(2 TIMOTHY 2:1) (COLOSSIANS 1:11) (COLOSSIANS 2:6-7) (ISAIAH 61:3) (EPHESIANS 2:20) (ACTS 20:32) (PHILIPPIANS 1:11) (1 TIMOTHY 6:12) (PHILIPPIANS 1:28)

December 21

Wonderful Counselor.

And the Spirit of the LORD will rest on him—the Spirit of wisdom and understanding, the Spirit of counsel and might, the Spirit of knowledge and the fear of the LORD. He will delight in obeying the LORD.

Listen as wisdom calls out! Hear as understanding raises her voice! She stands on the hilltop and at the crossroads. At the entrance to the city, at the city gates, she cries aloud, "I call to you, to all of you! I am raising my voice to all people. How naive you are! Let me give you common sense. O foolish ones, let me give you understanding. Listen to me! For I have excellent things to tell you. Everything I say is right, for I speak the truth and hate every kind of deception. Good advice and success belong to me. Insight and strength are mine."

The LORD Almighty is a wonderful teacher, and he gives the farmer great wisdom. ▪ If you need wisdom—if you want to know what God wants you to do—ask him, and he will gladly tell you. He will not resent your asking. ▪ Trust in the LORD with all your heart; do not depend on your own understanding. Seek his will in all you do, and he will direct your paths.

God takes all our individual circumstances and weaknesses into account, much as the farmer uses special tools to plant and harvest the fragile plants. God deals with each of us sensitively. We should follow his example when we deal with others. Different people require different treatment.

LAB note for Isaiah 28:23-29

(ISAIAH 9:6) (ISAIAH 11:2-3) (PROVERBS 8:1-7, 14) (ISAIAH 28:29) (JAMES 1:5) (PROVERBS 3:5-6)

December 22

Mighty God.

You are the most handsome of all. Gracious words stream from your lips. God himself has blessed you forever. Put on your sword, O mighty warrior! You are so glorious, so majestic! In your majesty, ride out to victory, defending truth, humility, and justice. Go forth to perform awe-inspiring deeds! Your throne, O God, endures forever and ever. Your royal power is expressed in justice. ▪ Who is this . . . with his clothing stained red? Who is this in royal robes, marching in the greatness of his strength? "It is I, the LORD, announcing your salvation! It is I, the LORD, who is mighty to save!"

See, God has come to save me. I will trust in him and not be afraid. The LORD God is my strength and my song; he has become my salvation. ▪ But thanks be to God, who made us his captives and leads us along in Christ's triumphal procession.

The Son reflects God's own glory, and everything about him represents God exactly. He sustains the universe by the mighty power of his command. After he died to cleanse us from the stain of sin, he sat down in the place of honor at the right hand of the majestic God of heaven. ▪ Glory to God, who is able to keep you from stumbling, and who will bring you into his glorious presence innocent of sin and with great joy. . . . Amen.

What a glorious day it will be when Jesus Christ comes to reign over the earth! Even now we need to express our gratitude to God, thanking him, praising him, and telling others about him. From the depths of our gratitude, we must praise him. And we should share the Good News with others. *LAb note for Isaiah 12:1ff.*

(ISAIAH 9:6) (PSALM 45:2-4, 6) (ISAIAH 63:1) (ISAIAH 12:2) (2 CORINTHIANS 2:14) (HEBREWS 1:3) (JUDE 1:24-25)

December 23

Everlasting Father.

Hear, O Israel! The LORD is our God, the LORD alone.

The Father and I are one. The Father is in me, and I am in the Father. ▩ Since you don't know who I am, you don't know who my Father is. If you knew me, then you would know my Father, too. ▩ Philip said, "Lord, show us the Father and we will be satisfied." Jesus replied, "Philip, don't you even yet know who I am, even after all the time I have been with you? Anyone who has seen me has seen the Father! So why are you asking to see him?" ▩ Here I am—together with the children God has given me. ▩ When he sees all that is accomplished by his anguish, he will be satisfied. ▩ "I am the Alpha and the Omega—the beginning and the end," says the Lord God. "I am the one who is, who always was, and who is still to come, the Almighty One." ▩ I existed before Abraham was ever born! ▩ I AM THE ONE WHO ALWAYS IS. . . . I AM has sent me.

To his Son he says, "Your throne, O God, endures forever and ever." ▩ He existed before everything else began, and he holds all creation together. ▩ In Christ the fullness of God lives in a human body.

Monotheism—belief in only one God—was a distinctive feature of Hebrew religion. Many ancient religions believed in many gods. Then and today there are people who prefer to place their trust in many different "gods." But the day is coming when God will be recognized as the only one. He will be the king over the whole earth. *LAB note for Deuteronomy 6:4*

(ISAIAH 9:6) (DEUTERONOMY 6:4) (JOHN 10:30, 38) (JOHN 8:19) (JOHN 14:8–9) (HEBREWS 2:13) (ISAIAH 53:11) (REVELATION 1:8) (JOHN 8:58) (EXODUS 3:14) (HEBREWS 1:8) (COLOSSIANS 1:17) (COLOSSIANS 2:9)

December 24

Prince of Peace.

Help him judge your people in the right way; let the poor always be treated fairly. May the mountains yield prosperity for all, and may the hills be fruitful, because the king does what is right. Help him to defend the poor, to rescue the children of the needy, and to crush their oppressors. May he live as long as the sun shines, as long as the moon continues in the skies. Yes, forever! ▪ Glory to God . . . and peace on earth to all whom God favors.

Because of God's tender mercy, the light from heaven is about to break upon us, to give light to those who sit in darkness and in the shadow of death, and to guide us to the path of peace. ▪ There is peace with God through Jesus Christ, who is Lord of all.

I have told you all this so that you may have peace in me. Here on earth you will have many trials and sorrows. But take heart, because I have overcome the world. ▪ I am leaving you with a gift—peace of mind and heart. And the peace I give isn't like the peace the world gives. So don't be troubled or afraid. ▪ God's peace . . . is far more wonderful than the human mind can understand. His peace will guard your hearts and minds as you live in Christ Jesus.

What qualities do we want most in our leaders? God desires all who rule under him to be just and righteous. Think how the world would change if world leaders would commit themselves to these two qualities. Let us pray that they will! *LAB note for Psalm 72:1-2*

(Isaiah 9:6) (Psalm 72:2-5) (Luke 2:14) (Luke 1:78-79) (Acts 10:36) (John 16:33) (John 14:27) (Philippians 4:7)

December 25

Thank God for his Son—a gift too wonderful for words!

Shout with joy to the LORD, O earth! Worship the LORD with gladness. Come before him, singing with joy. Enter his gates with thanksgiving; go into his courts with praise. Give thanks to him and bless his name. ▪ For a child is born to us, a son is given to us. And the government will rest on his shoulders. These will be his royal titles: Wonderful Counselor, Mighty God, Everlasting Father, Prince of Peace.

For God so loved the world that he gave his only Son. ▪ Since God did not spare even his own Son but gave him up for us all, won't God, who gave us Christ, also give us everything else? ▪ There was only one left—his son whom he loved dearly. The owner finally sent him. ▪ Everyone who believes in him will not perish but have eternal life. ▪ The whole world and life and death; the present and the future. Everything belongs to you, and you belong to Christ, and Christ belongs to God.

Let them praise the LORD for his great love and for all his wonderful deeds to them. ▪ Praise the LORD, I tell myself; with my whole heart, I will praise his holy name.

Oh, how I praise the Lord. How I rejoice in God my Savior!

God's love is not static or self-centered; it reaches out and draws others in. Here God sets the pattern of true love, the basis for all love relationships—when you love someone dearly, you are willing to give freely to the point of self-sacrifice. *LAB note for John 3:16*

(2 CORINTHIANS 9:15) (PSALM 100:1-2, 4) (ISAIAH 9:6) (JOHN 3:16) (ROMANS 8:32) (MARK 12:6) (JOHN 3:16) (1 CORINTHIANS 3:22-23) (PSALM 107:21) (PSALM 103:1) (LUKE 1:46-47)

December 26

Be strong and steady, always enthusiastic about the Lord's work.

You know that nothing you do for the Lord is ever useless. ◼ Just as you accepted Christ Jesus as your Lord, you must continue to live in obedience to him. Let your roots grow down into him and draw up nourishment from him, so you will grow in faith, strong and vigorous in the truth you were taught. Let your lives overflow with thanksgiving for all he has done. ◼ Those who endure to the end will be saved.

Stand firm in your faith.

All of us must quickly carry out the tasks assigned us by the one who sent me, because there is little time left before the night falls and all work comes to an end.

Those who live only to satisfy their own sinful desires will harvest the consequences of decay and death. But those who live to please the Spirit will harvest everlasting life from the Spirit. So don't get tired of doing what is good. Don't get discouraged and give up, for we will reap a harvest of blessing at the appropriate time.

Because of the Resurrection, nothing we do is useless. Knowing that Christ has won the ultimate victory should affect the way we live right now. Don't let discouragement over an apparent lack of results keep you from doing the work of the Lord enthusiastically as you have opportunity.

LAB note for 1 Corinthians 15:58

(1 Corinthians 15:58) (1 Corinthians 15:58) (Colossians 2:6-7) (Matthew 24:13) (2 Corinthians 1:24) (John 9:4) (Galatians 6:8-9)

December 27

He is able, once and forever, to save everyone who comes to God through him.

I am the way, the truth, and the life. No one can come to the Father except through me. ▪ There is salvation in no one else! There is no other name in all of heaven for people to call on to save them.

My sheep recognize my voice; I know them, and they follow me. I give them eternal life, and they will never perish. No one will snatch them away from me ▪ God, who began the good work within you, will continue his work until it is finally finished on that day when Christ Jesus comes back again. ▪ Is anything too hard for the LORD?

And now—all glory to God, who is able to keep you from stumbling, and who will bring you into his glorious presence innocent of sin and with great joy. All glory to him, who alone is God our Savior, through Jesus Christ our Lord. Yes, glory, majesty, power, and authority belong to him, in the beginning, now, and forevermore. Amen.

No one can add to what Jesus did to save us; our past, present, and future sins are all forgiven, and Jesus is with the Father as a sign that our sins are forgiven. If you are a Christian, remember that Christ has paid the price for your sins once and for all. *LAB note for Hebrews 7:25*

(HEBREWS 7:25) (JOHN 14:6) (ACTS 4:12) (JOHN 10:27-28) (PHILIPPIANS 1:6) (GENESIS 18:14) (JUDE 1:24-25)

December 28

For Christ himself has made peace between us.

For God was in Christ, reconciling the world to himself, no longer counting people's sins against them. This is the wonderful message he has given us to tell others. For God made Christ, who never sinned, to be the offering for our sin, so that we could be made right with God through Christ. ❧ By him God reconciled everything to himself. He made peace with everything in heaven and on earth by means of his blood on the cross. As a result, he has brought you into the very presence of God, and you are holy and blameless as you stand before him without a single fault. ❧ He forgave all our sins. He canceled the record that contained the charges against us. He took it and destroyed it by nailing it to Christ's cross.

I am leaving you with a gift—peace of mind and heart. And the peace I give isn't like the peace the world gives. So don't be troubled or afraid.

There are many barriers that can divide us from other Christians: age, appearance, intelligence, political persuasion, economic status, race, theological perspective. Fortunately, Christ has knocked down the barriers and unified all believers into one family. His cross should be the focus of our unity.

LAB note for Ephesians 2:14-22

(EPHESIANS 2:14) (2 CORINTHIANS 5:19, 21) (COLOSSIANS 1:20, 22) (COLOSSIANS 2:13-14) (JOHN 14:27)

December 29

Your sins are forgiven.

I will forgive their wickedness and will never again remember their sins. ▪ Who but God can forgive sins!

I—yes, I alone—am the one who blots out your sins for my own sake and will never think of them again. ▪ Oh, what joy for those whose rebellion is forgiven, whose sin is put out of sight! Yes, what joy for those whose record the LORD has cleared of sin, whose lives are lived in complete honesty! ▪ Where is another God like you, who pardons the sins of the survivors among his people?

God through Christ has forgiven you. ▪ The blood of Jesus, his Son, cleanses us from every sin. If we say we have no sin, we are only fooling ourselves and refusing to accept the truth. But if we confess our sins to him, he is faithful and just to forgive us and to cleanse us from every wrong.

He has removed our rebellious acts as far away from us as the east is from the west. ▪ Sin is no longer your master, for you are no longer subject to the law, which enslaves you to sin. Instead, you are free by God's grace.

God wants to forgive sinners. Forgiveness has always been part of his loving nature. He announced it to Moses; he revealed it to David; and he dramatically showed it to the world through Jesus Christ. He forgives rebellion, puts sin out of sight, and clears our record of sin.

LAB note for Psalm 32:1-2

(MARK 2:5) (JEREMIAH 31:34) (MARK 2:7) (ISAIAH 43:25) (PSALM 32:1-2) (MICAH 7:18) (EPHESIANS 4:32) (1 JOHN 1:7-9) (PSALM 103:12) (ROMANS 6:14)

December 30

You saw how the LORD your God cared for you again and again here in the wilderness, just as a father cares for his child.

I brought you to myself and carried you on eagle's wings. ▪ In his love and mercy he redeemed them. He lifted them up and carried them through all the years. ▪ Like an eagle that rouses her chicks and hovers over her young, so he spread his wings to take them in and carried them aloft on his pinions. The LORD alone guided them.

I will be your God throughout your lifetime—until your hair is white with age. I made you, and I will care for you. I will carry you along and save you. ▪ For that is what God is like. He is our God forever and ever, and he will be our guide until we die. ▪ The steps of the godly are directed by the LORD. He delights in every detail of their lives. Though they stumble, they will not fall, for the LORD holds them by the hand.

Give your burdens to the LORD, and he will take care of you. He will not permit the godly to slip and fall. ▪ Don't worry about everyday life—whether you have enough food, drink, and clothes. Your heavenly Father already knows all your needs.

God wants us to give our burdens to him, but often we continue to bear them ourselves even when we say we are trusting in him. Trust the same strength that sustains you to carry your cares also.

LAB note for Psalm 55:22

(DEUTERONOMY 1:31) (EXODUS 19:4) (ISAIAH 63:9) (DEUTERONOMY 32:11-12) (ISAIAH 46:4) (PSALM 48:14) (PSALM 37:23-24) (PSALM 55:22) (MATTHEW 6:25, 32)

December 31

Much land remains to be conquered.

I don't mean to say that I have already achieved these things or that I have already reached perfection! But I keep working toward that day when I will finally be all that Christ Jesus saved me for and wants me to be.

You are to be perfect, even as your Father in heaven is perfect. ❖ Make every effort to apply the benefits of these promises to your life. Then your faith will produce a life of moral excellence. A life of moral excellence leads to knowing God better. Knowing God leads to self-control. Self-control leads to patient endurance, and patient endurance leads to godliness. Godliness leads to love for other Christians and finally you will grow to have genuine love for everyone.

I pray that your love for each other will overflow more and more, and that you will keep on growing in your knowledge and understanding.

No eye has seen, no ear has heard, and no mind has imagined what God has prepared for those who love him.

There is a special rest still waiting for the people of God. ❖ Your eyes will see the king in all his splendor, and you will see a land that stretches into the distance.

Our culture often glorifies the young and strong and sets aside those who are older. Yet older people are filled with the wisdom that comes from experience. They are very capable of serving if given the chance and should be encouraged to do so. Believers are never allowed to retire from God's service. *LAB note for Joshua 13:1*

(JOSHUA 13:1) (PHILIPPIANS 3:12) (MATTHEW 5:48) (2 PETER 1:5-7) (PHILIPPIANS 1:9) (1 CORINTHIANS 2:9) (HEBREWS 4:9) (ISAIAH 33:17)